CIMA

Paper F1

Financial Reporting and Taxation

Study Text

Published by: Kaplan Publishing UK

Unit 2 The Business Centre, Molly Millars Lane, Wokingham, Berkshire RG41 2QZ

Acknowledgements

We are grateful to the CIMA for permission to reproduce past examination questions. The answers to CIMA Exams have been prepared by Kaplan Publishing, except in the case of the CIMA November 2010 and subsequent CIMA Exam answers where the official CIMA answers have been reproduced.

Notice

British Library Cataloguing in Publication Data

A catalogue record for this book is available from the British Library.

ISBN: 978-1-78415-302-1

Printed and bound in Great Britain.

Chartered Institute of
Management Accountants

This book comes with free EN-gage online resources so that you can study anytime, anywhere. This free online resource is not sold separately and is included in the price of the book.

How to access your on-line resources

You can access additional online resources associated with this CIMA Official book via the EN-gage website at: www.EN-gage.co.uk.

Existing users

If you are an existing EN-gage user, simply log-in to your account, click on the 'add a book' link at the top of your homepage and enter the ISBN of this book and the unique pass key number contained above.

New users

If you are a new EN-gage user then you first need to register at: www.EN-gage.co.uk. Once registered, Kaplan Publishing will send you an email containing a link to activate your account - please check your junk mail if you do not receive this or contact us using the phone number or email address printed on the back cover of this book. Click on the link to activate your account. To unlock your additional resources, click on the 'add a book' link at the top of your home page. You will then need to enter the ISBN of this book (found on page ii) and the unique pass key number contained in the scratch panel below:

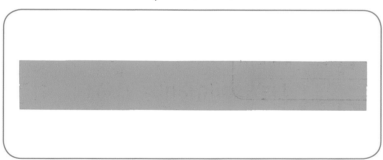

Then click 'finished' or 'add another book'.
Please allow 24 hours from the time you submit your book details for the content to appear in the My Learning and Testing area of your account.

Your code and information

This code can only be used once for the registration of one book online. This registration will expire when this edition of the book is no longer current - please see the back cover of this book for the expiry date.

Existing users

If you are an existing EN-gage user, simply log-in to your account, click on the 'add a book' link at the top of your homepage and enter the ISBN of this book and the unique pass key number contained above.

Contents

chapter

Intro

Introduction

How to use the materials

These official CIMA learning materials have been carefully designed to make your learning experience as easy as possible and to give you the best chances of success in your Objective Test Examination.

The product range contains a number of features to help you in the study process. They include:

- a detailed explanation of all syllabus areas;
- extensive 'practical' materials;
- generous question practice, together with full solutions.

This Study Text has been designed with the needs of home study and distance learning candidates in mind. Such students require very full coverage of the syllabus topics, and also the facility to undertake extensive question practice. However, the Study Text is also ideal for fully taught courses.

The main body of the text is divided into a number of chapters, each of which is organised on the following pattern:

- **Detailed learning outcomes.** These describe the knowledge expected after your studies of the chapter are complete. You should assimilate these before beginning detailed work on the chapter, so that you can appreciate where your studies are leading.
- **Step-by-step topic coverage.** This is the heart of each chapter, containing detailed explanatory text supported where appropriate by worked examples and exercises. You should work carefully through this section, ensuring that you understand the material being explained and can tackle the examples and exercises successfully. Remember that in many cases knowledge is cumulative: if you fail to digest earlier material thoroughly, you may struggle to understand later chapters.
- **Activities.** Some chapters are illustrated by more practical elements, such as comments and questions designed to stimulate discussion.

- **Question practice.** The text contains three styles of question:
  - Exam-style objective test questions (OTQs)
  - 'Integration' questions – these test your ability to understand topics within a wider context. This is particularly important with calculations where OTQs may focus on just one element but an integration question tackles the full calculation, just as you would be expected to do in the workplace.
  - 'Case' style questions – these test your ability to analyse and discuss issues in greater depth, particularly focusing on scenarios that are less clear cut than in the Objective Test Examination, and thus provide excellent practice for developing the skills needed for success in the Operational Level Case Study Examination.
- **Solutions.** Avoid the temptation merely to 'audit' the solutions provided. It is an illusion to think that this provides the same benefits as you would gain from a serious attempt of your own. However, if you are struggling to get started on a question you should read the introductory guidance provided at the beginning of the solution, where provided, and then make your own attempt before referring back to the full solution.

If you work conscientiously through this Official CIMA Study Text according to the guidelines above you will be giving yourself an excellent chance of success in your Objective Test Examination. Good luck with your studies!

Quality and accuracy are of the utmost importance to us so if you spot an error in any of our products, please send an email to mykaplanreporting@kaplan.com with full details, or follow the link to the feedback form in MyKaplan.

Our Quality Co-ordinator will work with our technical team to verify the error and take action to ensure it is corrected in future editions.

Icon Explanations

Definition – These sections explain important areas of knowledge which must be understood and reproduced in an assessment environment.

Key point – Identifies topics which are key to success and are often examined.

Supplementary reading – These sections will help to provide a deeper understanding of core areas. The supplementary reading is **NOT** optional reading. It is vital to provide you with the breadth of knowledge you will need to address the wide range of topics within your syllabus that could feature in an assessment question. **Reference to this text is vital when self studying**.

Test your understanding – Following key points and definitions are exercises which give the opportunity to assess the understanding of these core areas.

Illustration – To help develop an understanding of particular topics. The illustrative examples are useful in preparing for the Test your understanding exercises.

Exclamation mark – This symbol signifies a topic which can be more difficult to understand. When reviewing these areas, care should be taken.

Study technique

Passing exams is partly a matter of intellectual ability, but however accomplished you are in that respect you can improve your chances significantly by the use of appropriate study and revision techniques. In this section we briefly outline some tips for effective study during the earlier stages of your approach to the Objective Test Examination. We also mention some techniques that you will find useful at the revision stage.

Planning

To begin with, formal planning is essential to get the best return from the time you spend studying. Estimate how much time in total you are going to need for each subject you are studying. Remember that you need to allow time for revision as well as for initial study of the material.

With your study material before you, decide which chapters you are going to study in each week, and which weeks you will devote to revision and final question practice.

Prepare a written schedule summarising the above and stick to it!

It is essential to know your syllabus. As your studies progress you will become more familiar with how long it takes to cover topics in sufficient depth. Your timetable may need to be adapted to allocate enough time for the whole syllabus.

Students are advised to refer to the notice of examinable legislation published regularly in CIMA's magazine (Financial Management), the students e-newsletter (Velocity) and on the CIMA website, to ensure they are up-to-date.

The amount of space allocated to a topic in the Study Text is not a very good guide as to how long it will take you. The syllabus weighting is the better guide as to how long you should spend on a syllabus topic.

Tips for effective studying

(1) Aim to find a quiet and undisturbed location for your study, and plan as far as possible to use the same period of time each day. Getting into a routine helps to avoid wasting time. Make sure that you have all the materials you need before you begin so as to minimise interruptions.

(2) Store all your materials in one place, so that you do not waste time searching for items every time you want to begin studying. If you have to pack everything away after each study period, keep your study materials in a box, or even a suitcase, which will not be disturbed until the next time.

(3) Limit distractions. To make the most effective use of your study periods you should be able to apply total concentration, so turn off all entertainment equipment, set your phones to message mode, and put up your 'do not disturb' sign.

(4) Your timetable will tell you which topic to study. However, before diving in and becoming engrossed in the finer points, make sure you have an overall picture of all the areas that need to be covered by the end of that session. After an hour, allow yourself a short break and move away from your Study Text. With experience, you will learn to assess the pace you need to work at. Each study session should focus on component learning outcomes – the basis for all questions.

(5) Work carefully through a chapter, making notes as you go. When you have covered a suitable amount of material, vary the pattern by attempting a practice question. When you have finished your attempt, make notes of any mistakes you made, or any areas that you failed to cover or covered more briefly. Be aware that all component learning outcomes will be tested in each examination.

(6) Make notes as you study, and discover the techniques that work best for you. Your notes may be in the form of lists, bullet points, diagrams, summaries, 'mind maps', or the written word, but remember that you will need to refer back to them at a later date, so they must be intelligible. If you are on a taught course, make sure you highlight any issues you would like to follow up with your lecturer.

(7) Organise your notes. Make sure that all your notes, calculations etc. can be effectively filed and easily retrieved later.

Objective Test

Objective Test questions require you to choose or provide a response to a question whose correct answer is predetermined.

The most common types of Objective Test question you will see are:

- Multiple choice, where you have to choose the correct answer(s) from a list of possible answers. This could either be numbers or text.
- Multiple choice with more choices and answers, for example, choosing two correct answers from a list of eight possible answers. This could either be numbers or text.
- Single numeric entry, where you give your numeric answer, for example, profit is $10,000.
- Multiple entry, where you give several numeric answers.
- True/false questions, where you state whether a statement is true or false.
- Matching pairs of text, for example, matching a technical term with the correct definition.
- Other types could be matching text with graphs and labelling graphs/diagrams.

In every chapter of this Study Text we have introduced these types of questions, but obviously we have had to label answers A, B, C etc rather than using click boxes. For convenience we have retained quite a few questions where an initial scenario leads to a number of sub-questions. There will be questions of this type in the Objective Test Examination but they will rarely have more than three sub-questions.

Guidance re CIMA on-screen calculator

As part of the CIMA Objective Test software, candidates are now provided with a calculator. This calculator is on-screen and is available for the duration of the assessment. The calculator is available in each of the Objective Test Examinations and is accessed by clicking the calculator button in the top left hand corner of the screen at any time during the assessment.

All candidates must complete a 15-minute tutorial before the assessment begins and will have the opportunity to familiarise themselves with the calculator and practise using it.

Candidates may practise using the calculator by downloading and installing the practice exam at http://www.vue.com/athena/. The calculator can be accessed from the fourth sample question (of 12).

Please note that the practice exam and tutorial provided by Pearson VUE at http://www.vue.com/athena/ is not specific to CIMA and includes the full range of question types the Pearson VUE software supports, some of which CIMA does not currently use.

Fundamentals of Objective Tests

The Objective Tests are 90-minute assessments comprising 60 compulsory questions, with one or more parts. There will be no choice and all questions should be attempted.

Structure of subjects and learning outcomes

Each subject within the syllabus is divided into a number of broad syllabus topics. The topics contain one or more lead learning outcomes, related component learning outcomes and indicative knowledge content.

A learning outcome has two main purposes:

(a) To define the skill or ability that a well prepared candidate should be able to exhibit in the examination.

(b) To demonstrate the approach likely to be taken in examination questions.

The learning outcomes are part of a hierarchy of learning objectives. The verbs used at the beginning of each learning outcome relate to a specific learning objective, e.g.

Calculate the break-even point, profit target, margin of safety and profit/volume ratio for a single product or service.

The verb '**calculate**' indicates a level three learning objective. The following tables list the verbs that appear in the syllabus learning outcomes and examination questions.

CIMA VERB HIERARCHY

CIMA place great importance on the definition of verbs in structuring Objective Test Examinations. It is therefore crucial that you understand the verbs in order to appreciate the depth and breadth of a topic and the level of skill required. The Objective Tests will focus on levels one, two and three of the CIMA hierarchy of verbs. However they will also test levels four and five, especially at the management and strategic levels. You can therefore expect to be tested on knowledge, comprehension, application, analysis and evaluation in these examinations.

Level 1: KNOWLEDGE

What you are expected to know.

VERBS USED	DEFINITION
List	Make a list of.
State	Express, fully or clearly, the details of/facts of.
Define	Give the exact meaning of.

For example you could be asked to make a list of the advantages of a particular information system by selecting all options that apply from a given set of possibilities. Or you could be required to define relationship marketing by selecting the most appropriate option from a list.

Level 2: COMPREHENSION

What you are expected to understand.

VERBS USED	DEFINITION
Describe	Communicate the key features of.
Distinguish	Highlight the differences between.
Explain	Make clear or intelligible/state the meaning or purpose of.
Identify	Recognise, establish or select after consideration.
Illustrate	Use an example to describe or explain something.

For example you may be asked to distinguish between different aspects of the global business environment by dragging external factors and dropping into a PEST analysis.

Level 3: APPLICATION

How you are expected to apply your knowledge.

VERBS USED	DEFINITION
Apply	Put to practical use.
Calculate	Ascertain or reckon mathematically.
Demonstrate	Prove with certainty or exhibit by practical means.
Prepare	Make or get ready for use.
Reconcile	Make or prove consistent/compatible.
Solve	Find an answer to.
Tabulate	Arrange in a table.

For example you may need to calculate the projected revenue or costs for a given set of circumstances.

Level 4: ANALYSIS

How you are expected to analyse the detail of what you have learned.

VERBS USED	DEFINITION
Analyse	Examine in detail the structure of.
Categorise	Place into a defined class or division.
Compare/ contrast	Show the similarities and/or differences between.
Construct	Build up or compile.
Discuss	Examine in detail by argument.
Interpret	Translate into intelligible or familiar terms.
Prioritise	Place in order of priority or sequence for action.
Produce	Create or bring into existence.

For example you may be required to interpret an inventory ratio by selecting the most appropriate statement for a given set of circumstances and data.

Level 5: EVALUATION

How you are expected to use your learning to evaluate, make decisions or recommendations.

VERBS USED	DEFINITION
Advise	Counsel, inform or notify.
Evaluate	Appraise or assess the value of.
Recommend	Propose a course of action.

For example you may be asked to recommend and select an appropriate course of action based on a short scenario.

PRESENT VALUE TABLE

Present value of 1.00 unit of currency, that is $(1+r)^{-n}$ where r = interest rate; n = number of periods until payment or receipt.

Periods	Interest rates (r)									
(n)	1%	2%	3%	4%	5%	6%	7%	8%	9%	10%
1	0.990	0.980	0.971	0.962	0.952	0.943	0.935	0.926	0.917	0.909
2	0.980	0.961	0.943	0.925	0.907	0.890	0.873	0.857	0.842	0.826
3	0.971	0.942	0.915	0.889	0.864	0.840	0.816	0.794	0.772	0.751
4	0.961	0.924	0.888	0.855	0.823	0.792	0.763	0.735	0.708	0.683
5	0.951	0.906	0.863	0.822	0.784	0.747	0.713	0.681	0.650	0.621
6	0.942	0.888	0.837	0.790	0.746	0.705	0.666	0.630	0.596	0.564
7	0.933	0.871	0.813	0.760	0.711	0.665	0.623	0.583	0.547	0.513
8	0.923	0.853	0.789	0.731	0.677	0.627	0.582	0.540	0.502	0.467
9	0.914	0.837	0.766	0.703	0.645	0.592	0.544	0.500	0.460	0.424
10	0.905	0.820	0.744	0.676	0.614	0.558	0.508	0.463	0.422	0.386
11	0.896	0.804	0.722	0.650	0.585	0.527	0.475	0.429	0.388	0.350
12	0.887	0.788	0.701	0.625	0.557	0.497	0.444	0.397	0.356	0.319
13	0.879	0.773	0.681	0.601	0.530	0.469	0.415	0.368	0.326	0.290
14	0.870	0.758	0.661	0.577	0.505	0.442	0.388	0.340	0.299	0.263
15	0.861	0.743	0.642	0.555	0.481	0.417	0.362	0.315	0.275	0.239
16	0.853	0.728	0.623	0.534	0.458	0.394	0.339	0.292	0.252	0.218
17	0.844	0.714	0.605	0.513	0.436	0.371	0.317	0.270	0.231	0.198
18	0.836	0.700	0.587	0.494	0.416	0.350	0.296	0.250	0.212	0.180
19	0.828	0.686	0.570	0.475	0.396	0.331	0.277	0.232	0.194	0.164
20	0.820	0.673	0.554	0.456	0.377	0.312	0.258	0.215	0.178	0.149

Periods	Interest rates (r)									
(n)	11%	12%	13%	14%	15%	16%	17%	18%	19%	20%
1	0.901	0.893	0.885	0.877	0.870	0.862	0.855	0.847	0.840	0.833
2	0.812	0.797	0.783	0.769	0.756	0.743	0.731	0.718	0.706	0.694
3	0.731	0.712	0.693	0.675	0.658	0.641	0.624	0.609	0.593	0.579
4	0.659	0.636	0.613	0.592	0.572	0.552	0.534	0.516	0.499	0.482
5	0.593	0.567	0.543	0.519	0.497	0.476	0.456	0.437	0.419	0.402
6	0.535	0.507	0.480	0.456	0.432	0.410	0.390	0.370	0.352	0.335
7	0.482	0.452	0.425	0.400	0.376	0.354	0.333	0.314	0.296	0.279
8	0.434	0.404	0.376	0.351	0.327	0.305	0.285	0.266	0.249	0.233
9	0.391	0.361	0.333	0.308	0.284	0.263	0.243	0.225	0.209	0.194
10	0.352	0.322	0.295	0.270	0.247	0.227	0.208	0.191	0.176	0.162
11	0.317	0.287	0.261	0.237	0.215	0.195	0.178	0.162	0.148	0.135
12	0.286	0.257	0.231	0.208	0.187	0.168	0.152	0.137	0.124	0.112
13	0.258	0.229	0.204	0.182	0.163	0.145	0.130	0.116	0.104	0.093
14	0.232	0.205	0.181	0.160	0.141	0.125	0.111	0.099	0.088	0.078
15	0.209	0.183	0.160	0.140	0.123	0.108	0.095	0.084	0.079	0.065
16	0.188	0.163	0.141	0.123	0.107	0.093	0.081	0.071	0.062	0.054
17	0.170	0.146	0.125	0.108	0.093	0.080	0.069	0.060	0.052	0.045
18	0.153	0.130	0.111	0.095	0.081	0.069	0.059	0.051	0.044	0.038
19	0.138	0.116	0.098	0.083	0.070	0.060	0.051	0.043	0.037	0.031
20	0.124	0.104	0.087	0.073	0.061	0.051	0.043	0.037	0.031	0.026

Please check the CIMA website for the latest version of the maths tables and formulae sheets in advance of sitting your live assessment.

Cumulative present value of 1.00 unit of currency per annum, Receivable or Payable at the end of each year for *n* years $\frac{1-(1+r)^{-n}}{r}$

Periods	Interest rates (*r*)									
(*n*)	1%	2%	3%	4%	5%	6%	7%	8%	9%	10%
1	0.990	0.980	0.971	0.962	0.952	0.943	0.935	0.926	0.917	0.909
2	1.970	1.942	1.913	1.886	1.859	1.833	1.808	1.783	1.759	1.736
3	2.941	2.884	2.829	2.775	2.723	2.673	2.624	2.577	2.531	2.487
4	3.902	3.808	3.717	3.630	3.546	3.465	3.387	3.312	3.240	3.170
5	4.853	4.713	4.580	4.452	4.329	4.212	4.100	3.993	3.890	3.791
6	5.795	5.601	5.417	5.242	5.076	4.917	4.767	4.623	4.486	4.355
7	6.728	6.472	6.230	6.002	5.786	5.582	5.389	5.206	5.033	4.868
8	7.652	7.325	7.020	6.733	6.463	6.210	5.971	5.747	5.535	5.335
9	8.566	8.162	7.786	7.435	7.108	6.802	6.515	6.247	5.995	5.759
10	9.471	8.983	8.530	8.111	7.722	7.360	7.024	6.710	6.418	6.145
11	10.368	9.787	9.253	8.760	8.306	7.887	7.499	7.139	6.805	6.495
12	11.255	10.575	9.954	9.385	8.863	8.384	7.943	7.536	7.161	6.814
13	12.134	11.348	10.635	9.986	9.394	8.853	8.358	7.904	7.487	7.103
14	13.004	12.106	11.296	10.563	9.899	9.295	8.745	8.244	7.786	7.367
15	13.865	12.849	11.938	11.118	10.380	9.712	9.108	8.559	8.061	7.606
16	14.718	13.578	12.561	11.652	10.838	10.106	9.447	8.851	8.313	7.824
17	15.562	14.292	13.166	12.166	11.274	10.477	9.763	9.122	8.544	8.022
18	16.398	14.992	13.754	12.659	11.690	10.828	10.059	9.372	8.756	8.201
19	17.226	15.679	14.324	13.134	12.085	11.158	10.336	9.604	8.950	8.365
20	18.046	16.351	14.878	13.590	12.462	11.470	10.594	9.818	9.129	8.514

Periods	Interest rates (*r*)									
(*n*)	11%	12%	13%	14%	15%	16%	17%	18%	19%	20%
1	0.901	0.893	0.885	0.877	0.870	0.862	0.855	0.847	0.840	0.833
2	1.713	1.690	1.668	1.647	1.626	1.605	1.585	1.566	1.547	1.528
3	2.444	2.402	2.361	2.322	2.283	2.246	2.210	2.174	2.140	2.106
4	3.102	3.037	2.974	2.914	2.855	2.798	2.743	2.690	2.639	2.589
5	3.696	3.605	3.517	3.433	3.352	3.274	3.199	3.127	3.058	2.991
6	4.231	4.111	3.998	3.889	3.784	3.685	3.589	3.498	3.410	3.326
7	4.712	4.564	4.423	4.288	4.160	4.039	3.922	3.812	3.706	3.605
8	5.146	4.968	4.799	4.639	4.487	4.344	4.207	4.078	3.954	3.837
9	5.537	5.328	5.132	4.946	4.772	4.607	4.451	4.303	4.163	4.031
10	5.889	5.650	5.426	5.216	5.019	4.833	4.659	4.494	4.339	4.192
11	6.207	5.938	5.687	5.453	5.234	5.029	4.836	4.656	4.486	4.327
12	6.492	6.194	5.918	5.660	5.421	5.197	4.988	4.793	4.611	4.439
13	6.750	6.424	6.122	5.842	5.583	5.342	5.118	4.910	4.715	4.533
14	6.982	6.628	6.302	6.002	5.724	5.468	5.229	5.008	4.802	4.611
15	7.191	6.811	6.462	6.142	5.847	5.575	5.324	5.092	4.876	4.675
16	7.379	6.974	6.604	6.265	5.954	5.668	5.405	5.162	4.938	4.730
17	7.549	7.120	6.729	6.373	6.047	5.749	5.475	5.222	4.990	4.775
18	7.702	7.250	6.840	6.467	6.128	5.818	5.534	5.273	5.033	4.812
19	7.839	7.366	6.938	6.550	6.198	5.877	5.584	5.316	5.070	4.843
20	7.963	7.469	7.025	6.623	6.259	5.929	5.628	5.353	5.101	4.870

F1
FINANCIAL REPORTING AND TAXATION

Syllabus overview

F1 covers the regulation and preparation of financial statements and how the information contained in them can be used. It provides the competencies required to produce financial statements for both individual entities and groups using appropriate international financial reporting standards. It also gives insight into how to effectively source and manage cash and working capital, which are essential for both the survival and success of organisations. The final part focuses on the basic principles and application of business taxation. The competencies gained from F1 form the basis for developing further insights into producing and analysing complex group accounts (covered in F2) and formulating and implementing financial strategy (covered in F3).

Summary of syllabus

Weight	Syllabus topic
10%	**A.** Regulatory environment for financial reporting and corporate governance
45%	**B.** Financial accounting and reporting
20%	**C.** Management of working capital, cash and sources of short-term finance
25%	**D.** Fundamentals of business taxation

F1 – A. REGULATORY ENVIRONMENT FOR FINANCIAL REPORTING AND CORPORATE GOVERNANCE (10%)

Learning outcomes On completion of their studies, students should be able to:		**Indicative syllabus content**
Lead	**Component**	
1 explain the need for and the process of regulating the financial reporting information of incorporated entities.	(a) explain the need for the regulation of the financial reporting information of incorporated entities and the key elements of an ethical regulatory environment for such information	• The need for the regulation of financial reporting information. • Key elements of the regulatory environment for financial reporting including local corporate law, local and international conceptual frameworks, local and international financial reporting standards and other regulatory bodies. • Sources of professional codes of ethics. • Provisions of the CIMA Code of Ethics for Professional Accountants of particular relevance to the preparation of financial reporting information. • Rules-based versus principles-based approaches to accounting regulation.
	(b) explain the roles and structures of the key bodies involved in the regulation of financial reporting information	• Role and structure of: – The IFRS Foundation. – The International Accounting Standards Board (IASB). – IFRS Advisory Council. – IFRS Interpretations Committee. – International Organisation of Securities Commissions (IOSCO).
	(c) explain the scope of IFRS and how they are developed	• Interaction of local GAAP bodies with the IASB. • Scope of specific standards in specialised circumstances – IAS 26 *Accounting and Reporting by Retirement Benefit Plans*, IAS 41 *Agriculture*, IFRS 4 *Insurance Contracts*, IFRS 6 *Exploration for and Evaluation of Mineral Resources* and IFRS for SMEs (specific knowledge of these standards will not be tested). • The standard setting process for IFRS.

Learning outcomes On completion of their studies, students should be able to:		**Indicative syllabus content**
Lead	**Component**	
	(d) describe the role of the external auditor in the context of the financial reporting information of incorporated entities and the content and significance of the audit report.	• Powers and duties of external auditors. • Content of the audit report. • Types of audit report. • Significance of the audit report.
2 discuss the need for and key principles of corporate governance regulation.	(a) discuss the need for and scope of corporate governance regulation	• The need for corporate governance regulation. • Scope of corporate governance regulation.
	(b) compare and contrast the approach to corporate governance in different markets.	• Approach to corporate governance regulations in primary markets around the world, in particular the US and UK. • Key differences in approach across these markets.

F1 – B. FINANCIAL ACCOUNTING AND REPORTING (45%)

Learning outcomes On completion of their studies, students should be able to:		**Indicative syllabus content**
Lead	**Component**	
1 explain the main elements of and key principles underpinning financial statements prepared in accordance with international financial reporting standards.	(a) describe the main elements of financial statements prepared in accordance with IFRS	• Content of financial statements as specified in: – preface to IFRS – IAS 1 *Presentation of Financial Reporting* – IAS 8 *Accounting Policies, Changes in Accounting Estimates and Errors* – IAS 34 *Interim Financial Reporting* – IFRS 8 *Operating Segments*.
	(b) explain the key principles contained within the IASB's Conceptual Framework for Financial Reporting.	• Key principles of the Conceptual Framework for Financial Reporting. • Broad principles of accounting for fair values (contained in IFRS 13 *Fair Value Measurement*).
2 produce the primary financial statements of an individual entity incorporating accounting transactions and adjustments, in accordance with relevant international financial reporting standards, in an ethical manner.	(a) produce the primary financial statements from trial balance for an individual entity in accordance with IFRS	• Production of the: – statement of financial position – statement of comprehensive income – statement of changes in equity – statement of cash flows – for a single incorporated entity in accordance with IAS 1 *Presentation of Financial Reporting* and IAS 7 *Statement of Cash Flows*.
	(b) apply the rules contained in IFRS to generate appropriate accounting entries in respect of reporting performance, accounting for taxation, employee benefits, non-current assets, accounting for government grants, impairment, inventories and events after the reporting period	• Reporting performance – IFRS 5 *Non-current Assets Held for Sale and Discontinued Operations* and IAS 21 *The Effects of Changes in Foreign Exchange Rates* (individual transactions only). • Accounting for taxation – IAS 12 *Income Taxes* (not deferred tax). • Employee benefits – IAS 19 *Employee Benefits*. • Non-current assets – IAS 16 *Property, Plant and Equipment*, IAS 23 *Borrowing Costs*, IAS 38 *Intangible Assets*, IAS 40 *Investment Property*, and IFRS 5 *Non-current Assets Held for Sales and Discontinued Operations*.

Learning outcomes On completion of their studies, students should be able to:		**Indicative syllabus content**
Lead	**Component**	
		• Accounting for government grants – IAS 20 *Accounting for Government Grants and Disclosure of Government Assistance*. • Impairment – IAS 36 *Impairment of Assets*. • Inventories – IAS 2 *Inventories*. • Events after the reporting period – IAS 10 *Events after the Reporting Period*.
	(c) discuss the ethical selection and adoption of relevant accounting policies and accounting estimates.	• Ethics in financial reporting in respect of selection and adoption of accounting policies and estimates.
3 produce the consolidated statement of financial position and consolidated statement of comprehensive income in accordance with relevant international financial reporting standards, in an ethical manner.	(a) explain whether an investment in another entity constitutes a subsidiary or an associate relationship in accordance with relevant international financial reporting standards	• Provisions of IFRS 10 *Consolidated Financial Statements* and IAS 28 *Investments in Associates* in respect of power to control and significant influence.
	(b) explain situations where a parent entity is exempt from preparing consolidated financial statements	• Exemptions from preparing consolidated financial statements, in accordance with IFRS 10 *Consolidated Financial Statements* and the requirements of IAS 27 *Separate Financial Statements*.
	(c) produce the consolidated statement of financial position and statement of comprehensive income in accordance with relevant IFRS for a group comprising of one or more subsidiaries (being either wholly or partially directly owned) or associates, including interests acquired part way through an accounting period.	• Principles of full consolidation and equity accounting in accordance with IFRS 3 *Business Combinations* and IAS 28 *Investments in Associates*. • Production of: – consolidated statement of financial position – consolidated statement of comprehensive income.

Learning outcomes On completion of their studies, students should be able to:		**Indicative syllabus content**
Lead	**Component**	
		• Including the adoption of both full consolidation and the principles of equity accounting, in accordance with the provisions of IAS 1 *Presentation of Financial Statements*, IAS 28 *Investments in Associates*, IFRS 3 *Business Combinations* and IFRS 10 *Consolidated Financial Statements*. **Note:** Fair value adjustments in respect of assets and liabilities at acquisition will not be tested, however non-controlling interests at either fair value or share of net assets will be tested.

F1 – C. MANAGEMENT OF WORKING CAPITAL, CASH AND SOURCES OF SHORT-TERM FINANCE (20%)

Learning outcomes On completion of their studies, students should be able to:		**Indicative syllabus content**
Lead	**Component**	
1 **describe the sources of short-term finance and cash investment.**	(a) describe the sources of short-term finance and methods of short-term cash investment available to an entity.	• Types of short-term finance including trade payables, overdrafts, short-term loans and debt factoring. • Types of cash investment including interest-bearing deposits, short-term treasury bills and other securities.
2 **evaluate the working capital position of an entity.**	(a) analyse trade receivables, trade payables and inventory ratios	• Calculation of trade receivable, trade payable and inventory days. • Interpretation of the ratios either in comparison to prior periods, competitors or to the industry as a whole, taking into account the nature of the industry.
	(b) discuss policies for the management of the total level of investment in working capital and for the individual elements of working capital	• Working capital cycle. • Policies for the management of the total level of investment in working capital – aggressive, moderate and conservative. • Methods of trade receivables management, including credit control procedures. • Methods of trade payables management and significance of trade payables as a source of finance and how this affects the relationship with suppliers. • Methods of inventory management, including calculations of the economic order quantity (EOQ).
	(c) evaluate working capital policies	• Financial impact of changing working capital policies. • Impact and risks of overtrading. • Identification of areas for improvement.
	(d) discuss approaches to the financing of working capital investment levels.	• Approaches to the financing of the investment in working capital – aggressive, moderate and conservative.

Learning outcomes On completion of their studies, students should be able to:		**Indicative syllabus content**
Lead	**Component**	
3 **analyse the short-term cash position of an entity.**	(a) discuss measures to manage the short-term cash position of an entity.	• Preparation of short-term cash flow forecasts. • Identification of surpluses or deficits from cash flow forecasts. • Selection of appropriate short-term solutions. • Principles of investing short term including maturity, return, security and liquidity.

F1 – D. FUNDAMENTALS OF BUSINESS TAXATION (25%)

Learning outcomes On completion of their studies, students should be able to:		**Indicative syllabus content**
Lead	**Component**	
1 **discuss the types of taxation that typically apply to an incorporated entity and the regulatory environment for taxation.**	(a) discuss the features of the types of indirect and direct taxation that typically apply to an incorporated entity	• Definitions of direct taxation, indirect taxation, taxable person, incidence and competent jurisdiction. • Types of taxation – progressive, proportional and regressive. • Features of the following types of indirect taxation: – unit taxes – ad valorem taxes – excise duties – property and wealth taxes – consumption taxes – mechanism of value added tax in the context of an incorporated entity. • Features of the following types of direct taxation: – tax on trading income – capital taxes. • Impact of employee taxation.
	(b) discuss the regulatory environment for taxation, including the distinction between tax evasion and tax avoidance.	• Sources of taxation rules such as domestic legislation, court rulings, domestic interpretations and guidelines, EU guidelines and taxation agreements between different countries. • Administration of taxation including the principles of record keeping, deadlines and penalties. • Powers of taxation authorities. • Distinction between tax evasion and tax avoidance and the ethical considerations faced by an entity in respect of tax avoidance.

Learning outcomes On completion of their studies, students should be able to:		**Indicative syllabus content**
Lead	**Component**	
2 explain the taxation issues that may apply to an incorporated entity that operates internationally.	(a) explain the taxation issues that may apply to an incorporated entity that operates internationally.	• International taxation issues: – the concept of corporate residence and the key bases of determining residence – types of overseas operations: subsidiary or branch and the implications of each on taxation – issue of double taxation and the methods of gaining relief – types of foreign taxation and the distinction between withholding tax and underlying tax (calculations will not be tested) – transfer pricing and related, ethical and taxation issues.
3 produce computations for corporate income tax and capital tax.	(a) produce corporate income tax computations from a given set of rules	• Distinction between accounting profit and taxable profit and the reconciliation between them. This will include (based upon a set of rules given in the examination): – identification and treatment of exempt income or income taxed under different rules – identification and treatment of disallowable expenditure – replacement of accounting depreciation with tax depreciation – calculation of tax depreciation allowances – calculation of corporate income tax liability – relief for trading losses.
	(b) produce capital tax computations from a given set of rules.	• Principle of a capital tax computation on the sale of an asset. • Allowable costs. • Methods of relieving capital losses. • Concept of rollover relief.

chapter

1

Fundamentals of Business Taxation

Chapter learning objectives

On completion of their studies students should be able to:

- Discuss the features of the types of indirect and direct taxation that typically apply to an incorporated entity.
- Discuss the regulatory environment for taxation, including the sources of taxation rules, record keeping, powers of tax authorities and the distinction between taxation evasion and avoidance.
- Explain the taxation issues that may apply to an incorporated entity that operates internationally such as the concept of corporate residence, the types of overseas operations, the principles of double taxation relief and the types of foreign taxation.
- Prepare corporate income tax calculations based on a given set of rules.
- Prepare capital tax computations from a given set of rules.

1 Session content

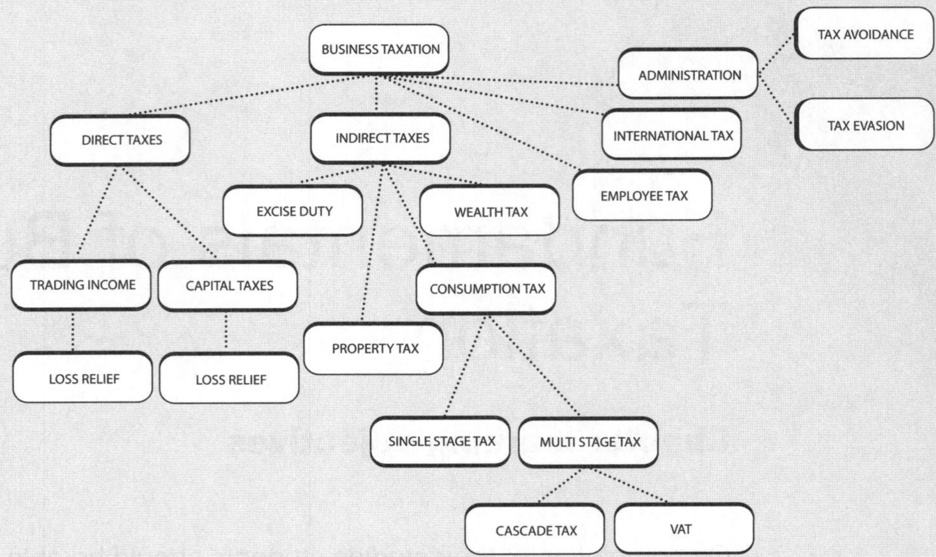

2 Introduction

The Government needs tax revenues to finance expenditure such as the Health Service, Retirement Pensions, Social Benefits and to finance Government borrowing. The Government will use tax to stimulate one sector of the economy and control another. For example, allowances on capital expenditure may develop the manufacturing sector, while high taxes on tobacco and alcohol may discourage sales.

In **Wealth of Nations**, Adam Smith proposed that a good tax should have the following characteristics:

- fair (reflect person's ability to pay)
- absolute (certain not arbitrary)
- convenient (easy to pay)
- efficient (low collection costs)

The 3 major principles of good tax policy are as follows:

- equity – A good tax should be fairly levied between one taxpayer and another.
- efficiency – A good tax should be cheap and easy to collect, i.e. UK tax system uses the PAYE (pay-as-you-earn) to collect tax at source on salaries and wages.
- economic effects – A good tax should consider the way in which a tax should be collected.

What is a good tax?

The American Institution of Certified Public Accountants lists the following principles that a good tax policy should have:

- equity and fairness
- transparency and visibility
- certainty
- economy in collection
- convenience of payment
- simplicity
- appropriate government revenues (determining the amount of tax revenues and date of collection)
- minimum tax gap (the difference between actual collection and amount due)
- neutrality
- economic growth and efficiency

It is not always possible to incorporate all ten into a tax system.

Definition of terms

A tax is either a direct or indirect tax.

Direct taxes

These are imposed directly on the person or enterprise required to pay the tax, i.e. tax on personal income such as salaries, tax on business profits or tax on disposals of chargeable assets. The person or enterprise must pay the tax directly to the tax authorities on their income. Examples in the UK of direct taxes would be income tax, capital gains tax or corporation tax.

Indirect taxes

This tax is imposed on one part of the economy with the intention that the tax burden is passed on to another. The tax is imposed on the final consumer of the goods or services. The more the consumer consumes the greater the tax paid. An example would be sales tax such as VAT in the UK.

Incidence

The incidence of a tax is the distribution of the tax burden, i.e. who is paying the tax.

What is incidence?

Incidence

This can be split into two elements:

(1) **Formal incidence:** this is the person who has direct contact with the tax authorities, i.e. who is legally obliged to pay the tax.

(2) **Actual Incidence:** this is the person who actually ends up bearing the cost of the tax, i.e. who actually bears the burden of the tax.

If we consider VAT – the formal incidence would be the entity making the sale because they will be responsible for making the payment to the relevant tax authorities. The actual incidence would be the consumer who bears the cost of the tax when they make a purchase from the entity.

Taxable person

The person accountable for the tax payment, e.g. individual or entity.

Competent jurisdiction

A taxable person normally pays tax in the country of origin. Competent jurisdiction is the tax authority that has the legal power to assess and collect the taxes. This is usually the combined responsibility of the central government and local authorities within a country. The tax law is enforceable by sanction (fines or imprisonment).

Hypothecation

This means that certain taxes are devoted entirely to certain types of expenditure, e.g. road tax is used entirely on maintaining roads, London congestion charge is used to pay for transport for the area.

Tax gap

This is the gap between the tax theoretically collectable and the amount actually collected. The tax authorities will aim to minimise this gap.

Tax rate structure

There are three types of taxes:

(1) **Progressive taxes:** These take an increasing proportion of income as income rises. (E.g. UK Income tax – 20%, 40%, 50%).

(2) **Proportional taxes:** These take the same proportion of income as income rises.

(3) **Regressive taxes:** These take a decreasing proportion of income as income rises. (E.g. UK National Insurance contributions – 11% then 1%).

Tax rate structure

Progressive tax means the proportion of tax increases as income increases, i.e. salary $10,000 pays tax of $1,000 = 10% but a salary of $20,000 pays tax of $3,000 = 15%.

Proportionate tax means the proportion of tax remains the same, regardless of the level of income, i.e. salary $10,000 pays tax of $1,000 = 10% and a salary of $20,000 pays tax of $2,000 = 10%.

Regressive tax means the proportion of tax reduces as income increases, i.e. salary $10,000 pays tax of $1,000 = 10% but a salary of $20,000 pays tax of $1,800 = 9%.

Source of tax rules

The sources of tax rules are as follows:

- Legislation produced by a national government of the country, e.g. Finance Acts in the UK.
- Precedents based on previous legislation. Tax authorities also issue interpretations, e.g. Tax bulletins in the UK.
- Directives from international bodies such as European Union guidelines on VAT.
- Agreements between different countries such as double tax treaties, e.g. UK/US Double tax treaties.

Income can be taxed twice

Foreign income is often taxed twice, once in the country of origin and once in the country of residency. In order to avoid this "double taxation", countries enter into tax treaties, see later in the chapter for types of double taxation relief.

Tax base

Taxes are classified according to their tax base (what is being taxed).

- Income or profits – e.g. Income and Corporation tax in the UK
- Assets – e.g. Capital gains tax in the UK
- Consumption – e.g. Sales tax in the UK

Most countries separate different types of income into categories and have a set of rules to determine how that income will be taxed.

3 Direct taxes

There are two types of direct tax you need to consider:

Tax on trading income

Trading income relates to income from the main business activity.

The tax base should be profits.

The accounting profit needs to be adjusted for tax purposes as in many countries there are differences between what the accounting standards allow you to show as an income/expense and what the tax system deems to be the income/expense. These adjusted profits will enable you to calculate the taxable profit.

The standard proforma is as follows:

	$
Accounting profit	X
Less: income exempt from tax or taxed under other rules	(X)
Add: disallowable expenses	X
Add: accounting depreciation	X
Less: tax depreciation	(X)
Taxable profit	X

The taxable profit will then be charged at the appropriate tax rate for that accounting period.

The rules for allowed and disallowed items will vary according to the tax regime of the country in question. This will always be given in the assessment question.

Calculation of the trading profit

The **accounting profit** is the profit shown in financial statements before taxation.

Income exempt from tax or taxed under other rules is any income included in the accounting profit which does **not** relate to the main trading activity, i.e. rental income, dividend income, interest receivable, etc, that maybe taxed under other rules or income exempt from taxation under that particular countries rules.

Disallowable expenses are expenses that have been deducted from the accounting profit, i.e. they are allowable under the accounting standards, but for tax purposes can't be claimed. These expenses will differ from country to country and the examiner will always tell you the rules for that particular country in the question. Examples of disallowable expenses in the UK are entertaining customers, gift aid payments, political donations.

Depreciation is added back because it is an accounting entry that is not allowed for tax purposes because it is too subjective (i.e. you can choose the way to depreciate your assets). It is replaced with tax depreciation.

Tax depreciation may be called capital allowances in the exam. The rules will be given in the exam to tell you what can be claimed. It is a replacement for depreciation. They are often given on a reducing balance basis. Allowances are given if the asset is owned at the accounting date, i.e. no time apportionment for mid-year acquisitions.

Test your understanding 1 – Trading income

In year ending 31/03/20X2, an entity George made an accounting profit of $80,000. Profit included $5,500 of entertaining costs which are disallowable for tax purposes and $8,000 of income exempt from taxation.

George has no capital items.

Tax is charged at 25%.

Calculate the tax payable for the year ended 31/03/X2.

Illustration 1 – Trading income

In year ending 31/12/20X1 an entity Zippy made an accounting profit of $50,000. Profit included $3,500 of entertaining expenses which are disallowable for tax purposes and $5,000 of income exempt from taxation.

Zippy has $70,000 of non-current assets which were acquired on 01/01/20X0 and are depreciated at 10% on cost. Tax depreciation rates are 20% reducing balance.

Calculate the accounting depreciation for the year ended 31/12/X1.

Solution

The accounting depreciation is $70,000 × 10% = $7,000

Illustration 2 – Trading income

Using the information from illustration 1 calculate the tax depreciation for the year ended 31/12/X1.

Solution

Tax depreciation

WDV at start of year	$56,000	($70,000 × 80%)
Tax depreciation at 20%	$11,200	

The asset had been purchased in the previous accounting period, therefore tax depreciation has already been claimed for Ye. 31/12/X0. This year's tax depreciation must be calculated on the tax WDV at the beginning of the year, i.e. $56,000.

WDV means written down value. This represents the cost of the asset less accumulated tax depreciation.

Illustration 3 – Trading income

Using the information from illustrations 1 and 2 calculate the taxable profit for the year ended 31/12/X1.

Solution

	$
Accounting profit	50,000
Less: exempt income	(5,000)
Add back: disallowable expenses	3,500
Add back: depreciation (illustration 1)	7,000
Less: tax depreciation (illustration 2)	(11,200)
Taxable profit	**44,300**

Illustration 4 – Trading income

Using the information from illustrations 1 to 3 calculate the tax payable for the year ended 31/12/X1. You should assume a tax rate of 30%.

Solution

	$
Accounting profit	50,000
Less: exempt income	(5,000)
Add back: disallowable expenses	3,500
Add back: depreciation (illustration 1)	7,000
Less: tax depreciation (illustration 2)	(11,200)
Taxable profit	44,300
Tax at 30%	**13,290**

Test your understanding 2 – Trading income

In year ending 31/03/20X2, an entity Bungle made an accounting profit of $60,000. Profit included $4,500 of political donations which are disallowable for tax purposes and $4,000 of income exempt from taxation.

Bungle has $10,000 of plant and machinery which was acquired on 01/04/20X0 and purchased a new machine costing $5,000 on 01/04/20X1. This new machine is entitled to FYAs (first year allowances) of 100% instead of the usual tax depreciation. All plant and machinery is depreciated in the accounts at 10% on cost. Tax depreciation rates on plant and machinery are 20% reducing balance.

Bungle also has a building that cost $100,000 on 01/04/20X0 and is depreciated in the accounts at 4% on a straight line basis. Tax depreciation is calculated at 3% on a straight line basis.

Calculate the total accounting depreciation for the year ended 31/03/X2.

Test your understanding 3 – Trading income

Using the information from TYU 2 calculate the total tax depreciation for the year ended 31/03/X2.

Test your understanding 4 – Trading income

Using the information from TYU's 2 and 3 calculate the taxable profit for the year ended 31/03/X2.

Test your understanding 5 – Trading income

Using the information from TYU's 2 to 4 calculate the tax payable for the year ended 31/03/X2. You should assume a tax rate of 30%.

In the previous illustrations and TYUs we have used a constant rate of tax to calculate the tax payable, e.g. 30%. However, sometimes the tax rate may change during the year and therefore taxable profits will need to be pro-rated. For tax purposes profits are assumed to be accrued evenly.

Illustration 5 – Trading income

Using the illustrations 1 to 4, recalculate the tax if the rates were as follows:

01/04/X0 – 31//03/X1 = 28%

01/04/X1 – 31/03/X2 = 30%

Solution

The taxable profit for Zippy was $44,300 for accounting period to 31/12/X1.

Tax would be:

($44,300 × 3/12 × 28%) + ($44,300 × 9/12 × 30%) = $13,068.50

The taxable profit is pro-rated based on the amount of months that fall into each of the tax rate periods, i.e.

01/01/X1 – 31/03/X1 = 3 months at the rate of 28%
01/04/X1 – 31/12/X1 = 9 months at the rate of 30%

Test your understanding 6 – Trading income

An entity has an accounting period ending 30/06/X1 and a taxable profit of $800,000.

The rates of tax were as follows:

01/04/X0 – 31/03/X1 = 26%

01/04/X1 – 31/03/X2 = 28%

Calculate the tax liability for the period ending 30/06/X1.

When an asset is sold any accounting profit or loss must be disallowed for tax purposes and replaced with the tax equivalent known as a balancing allowance or charge.

A balancing allowance (BA) = a tax loss on disposal

A balancing charge (BC) = a tax profit on disposal

The tax proforma could then be expanded to include the effect of the asset disposal as follows:

	$
Accounting profit	X
Less: income exempt from tax or taxed under other rules	(X)
Add: disallowable expenses	X
Add: accounting depreciation	X
Add: accounting loss on disposal of an asset	X
Less: accounting profit on disposal of an asset	(X)
Less: tax depreciation	(X)
Add: tax profit on disposal of an asset (BC)	X
Less: tax loss on disposal of an asset (BA)	(X)
Taxable profit	X

The taxable profit will then be charged at the appropriate tax rate for that accounting period.

Always remember the tax amount should replace the accounting amount, i.e. reverse the accounting entry and pay tax on the tax profit or receive relief on the tax loss.

Balancing allowances and charges

When an asset is disposed of, we will calculate, for accounting purposes, the accounting profit or loss on disposal. This will be calculated by:

	$
Proceeds	X
Less: Carrying amount (SOFP)	(X)
Accounting profit/(loss)	X

If the proceeds are greater than the carrying amount = profit
If the proceeds are less than the carrying amount = loss

An accounting profit or loss will be treated as disallowable for tax purposes. A profit will be deducted from the accounting profit (similar to non-trade income) and a loss will be added to the accounting profit (similar to depreciation).

This will then be replaced by either a balancing charge or allowance for tax purposes.

These are calculated in the same way as the accounting profit or loss on disposal:

	$
Proceeds	X
Less: tax written down value (TWDV)	(X)
Balancing charge/(allowance)	X

If the proceeds are greater than the TWDV = balancing charge
If the proceeds are less than the TWDV = balancing allowance

A balancing charge will be added back to the accounting profit and a balancing allowance will be deducted from the accounting profit, when computing the taxable profit.

Capital allowances (tax depreciation) are not normally given in the year of disposal of the asset – these are replaced by balancing allowances or charges.

Test your understanding 7 – Balancing allowances/charges

Bungle has $10,000 of plant and machinery which was acquired on 01/04/20X0 .

All plant and machinery is depreciated in the accounts at 10% on cost.

Tax depreciation rates on plant and machinery are 20% reducing balance.

All plant and machinery was sold for $6,000 on 01/04/X2.

Calculate the accounting profit or loss on disposal for the year ended 31/03/X3.

Test your understanding 8 – Balancing allowances/charges

Using the information from TYU 7 calculate the tax balancing allowance or charge on disposal for the year ended 31/03/X3.

Test your understanding 9 – Balancing allowances/charges

Using the information from TYU's 7 and 8 calculate the tax payable for the year ended 31/03/X3 assuming the accounting profit is $50,000 and there are no other tax adjustments. Tax is payable at a rate of 25%.

Test your understanding 10 – Balancing allowances/charges

Re-calculate your answer to TYU 9 if the asset was sold for $9,000 instead of $6,000.

Trading losses

When an entity makes a trading loss the assessment for that tax year will be nil.

The entity must now claim loss relief based on the rules of the country's tax regime. The assessment will tell you the rules of the country in the question.

Possible ways of relieving a loss are:

- Carry losses forwards against future profits of the **same** trade.
- Carry losses backwards against previous periods.
- Offset losses against group company profits.
- Offset losses against capital gains in the same period.

It is important to read the rules of the tax regime for the country. All countries are different as some allow losses to be carried backwards and forwards, others only allow losses to be carried forwards. Many countries do not allow trading losses to be offset against capital gains in any period.

Illustration 6 – Trading losses

In country X, trading losses in any year can be carried back and set off against trading profits in the previous year, and any unrelieved losses can be carried forward to set against the first available trade profits in future years.

Hall and Co had the following taxable profits and losses in year 1 to 4.

Year	Trading profit/(loss)
1	25,000
2	(45,000)
3	15,000
4	35,000

What are Hall and Co's taxable profits in each year?

Solution

Year	Trading profit/(loss)	Workings
1	–	25,000 – 25,000
2	–	
3	–	15,000 – 15,000
4	30,000	35,000 – 5,000 (balance of the loss)

The trading loss is carried back first against the trading profit in year 1, this must be done to the maximum extent, i.e. you can't use part of the profit for relief if all of it is needed. The balance of the loss must then be carried forward against the **first available trading profit** in year 3, again to the maximum extent required until it has been relieved in full. There is no limit on how many years you are able to carry forward a trading loss.

Test your understanding 11 – Trading losses

In country A, trading losses in any year can be carried back and set off against profits in the previous year, and any unrelieved losses can be carried forward to set against profits in future years.

Looser had the following taxable profits and losses in year 1 to 4.

Year	Trading profit/(loss)
1	20,000
2	(45,000)
3	19,000
4	25,000

What are Looser's taxable profits in each year?

Cessation of business

If an enterprise ceases to trade, most countries allow the entity to carry back the loss against profits of previous years to generate a tax refund. In the UK, this is called Terminal Loss Relief and enables the loss to be carried back three years. The assessment will tell you the terminal loss rules of that country.

Test your understanding 12 – Cessation losses

In 20X3, Dunbadly closed its business having made a trading loss of $60,000. In Dunbadly's country of residence, trading losses may be carried back two years on a LIFO basis.

	20X1	20X2	20X3
	$	$	$
Trading profits/losses	100,000	50,000	(60,000)

What is the impact on taxable profits for each year?

Capital taxes

Capital tax gains are gains made on the disposal of investments and other non-current assets. The most common assets taxed are listed stocks and shares.

The tax base should be assets, i.e. what is being taxed.

At a simple level, the gain is calculated as proceeds from sale less cost of the asset.

In most countries, the computation is based on cost but in a few countries an allowance is made for inflation. In the UK, the cost can be indexed, in certain cases, using the Retail Price Index. Indexation will be calculated on all allowable costs from the date of purchase to the disposal date of the asset. This indexation allowance will **reduce** the gain.

The standard proforma is as follows:

	$
Proceeds	X
Less: costs to sell	(X)
Net proceeds	X
Less: cost of original asset	(X)
Less: costs to buy	(X)
Less: enhancement costs	(X)
Less: indexation allowance	(X)
Chargeable gain	X

The chargeable gain will then be charged at the appropriate tax rate for that accounting period.

Allowable costs for deduction

Costs that can be deducted from proceeds are:

- original cost of purchasing the asset
- costs to buy the assets, i.e. legal fees, estate agent fees
- costs to sell the assets, i.e. legal fees, estate agent fees
- enhancement/improvement costs, i.e. extensions to an existing asset
- indexation allowance – if this exists in the country of residency of the asset being disposed of

Illustration 7 – Capital taxes

An entity bought an asset for $20,000 on 01/02/X0. The asset was sold for $50,000 on 21/11/X9.

Capital gains are taxed at 30%.

What is the capital tax to be paid on the disposal?

Solution

	$
Sale proceeds	50,000
Less: Cost	(20,000)
Chargeable gain	30,000

Capital tax = $30,000 × 30% = $9,000

Illustration 8 – Capital taxes

An entity bought an asset for $20,000 on 01/02/X0. The asset was sold for $50,000 on 21/11/X9.

Indexation allowance can be claimed at 30% from February 20X0 to November 20X9.

Capital gains are taxed at 30%.

What is the indexation allowance the entity can claim on disposal of the asset?

Solution

The indexation allowance can be claimed on the cost of the asset = $20,000 × 30% = $6,000

Illustration 9 – Capital taxes

Using the information from illustration 8 calculate the capital tax to be paid on the disposal?

Solution

	$
Sale proceeds	50,000
Less: Cost	(20,000)
	30,000
Less: Indexation allowance 20,000 × 30% (illustration 8)	(6,000)
Chargeable gain	24,000

Capital tax = $24,000 × 30% = $7,200

Test your understanding 13 – Capital taxes

An entity bought a building for $50,000 on 01/02/X0. They incurred costs at the date of purchase of $1,500 for legal fees.

The building was extended on 01/04/X2 at a cost of $12,000 and repairs to the roof were undertaken on 01/06/X3 after a violent storm, costing $5,000.

The building was sold for $150,000 on 21/11/Y1 and costs to sell were incurred of $2,000.

Calculate the chargeable gain on the disposal?

Test your understanding 14 – Capital taxes

Using the information from TYU 13 calculate the indexation allowance for the asset assuming the following indexation factors were given:

February 20X0 to November 20Y1 was 30%

April 20X2 to November 20Y1 was 20%

June 20X3 to November 20Y1 was 10%

Test your understanding 15 – Capital taxes

Using the information from TYU's 13 and 14 calculate the capital tax assuming a rate of 30%.

Items exempt from Capital Gains Tax

Usually, certain types of assets are exempt from Capital Gains Tax. In the UK, exempt assets include:

- Qualifying Corporate Bonds
- private motor vehicles
- chattels sold for less than £6,000 (tangible movable property)
- wasting chattels, e.g. boats and animals

Certain disposals are exempt from Capital Gains Tax and include:

- gifts to charities or certain assets such as works of art
- gifts to museums or government institutions

You will not be expected to remember these; the examiner will state in the question if any items are exempt.

Capital losses

Most countries keep capital losses separate from trading activities.

Possible ways of relieving capital losses are:

- Carry forwards against future capital gains.
- Carry back against previous capital gains.
- Offset against trading income in the current period.

Most countries only allow capital losses to be carried forwards against future capital gains but the examiner will explain the rules of the country in the question.

Illustration 10 – Capital losses

In country X, capital losses can be set off against capital gains in the same tax year, but unrelieved capital losses cannot be carried back. Unrelieved capital losses may be carried forward and set against capital gains in future years.

Hall and Co had the following capital gains and losses in year 1 to 4.

Year	Capital gain/(loss)
1	3,000
2	(4,000)
3	2,500
4	3,000

What are Hall and Co's taxable gains in each year?

Solution

Year	Capital gain/(loss)	Workings
1	3,000	
2	–	
3	–	2,500 – 2,500
4	1,500	3,000 – 1,500 (balance of the loss)

The capital loss **can't** be carried back against year 1, only carried forward against the **first available** capital gain. There is no limit to how many years it can be carried forward for.

Test your understanding 16 – Loss relief

In country Y, capital losses can be set off against capital gains in the same tax year, but unrelieved capital losses cannot be carried back. Unrelieved capital losses may be carried forward and set against capital gains in future years.

Trading losses in any year can be carried back and set off against profits in the previous year, and any unrelieved losses can be carried forward to set against profits in future years. They cannot be relieved against capital gains.

Robbie and Co had the following trading profits/losses and capital gains/losses in year 1 to 3.

Calculate the taxable gains and profits for all years.

Year	Capital gain/(loss)	Trading profit/(loss)
1	4,000	27,000
2	(6,000)	(30,000)
3	9,000	16,000

Rollover relief

In some countries, gains may be postponed using rollover relief. Rollover relief enables an entity to postpone paying tax on a gain if it reinvests the same proceeds in a replacement asset. The gain is effectively postponed until the replacement asset is sold at some time in the future. For example, an entity sells an asset for $100,000, creating a gain of $10,000. If the entity decides to re-invest the $100,000 proceeds into a replacement asset the $10,000 gain can be deferred in full until the replacement asset is sold.

Some countries may also have rules allowing partial deferral of the gain for partial re-investment. For example the entity sells an asset for $100,000, creating a gain of $10,000. If the entity decides to re-invest $95,000 of the proceeds into a replacement asset the country may have a rule stating the lower of the gain or the proceeds not re-invested should be chargeable immediately and the remainder of the gain to be deferred until the replacement asset is sold. In this scenario the entity has not re-invested $5,000 of the proceeds and has created a gain from the first sale of $10,000. This would mean the entity must pay tax immediately on the $5,000 not re-invested and therefore the remainder of the gain ($10,000 – $5,000) would be deferred until the replacement asset is sold.

Countries which operate this system of relief will have strict rules on the types of assets which will qualify for this type of relief and the time scales in which the replacement asset must be purchased. However, for examination purposes you should assume the gain can be deferred as long a replacement asset is acquired, as detailed rules are not examinable.

Group issues

When an entity is part of a group we must consider two issues for tax purposes:

(1) Group loss relief and

(2) appropriations of profit.

Group loss relief

Tax consolidation enables a tax group to be recognised, allowing trading losses to be surrendered between different entities. Some countries enable losses to be surrendered only between resident companies, while others allow overseas entities to be included based on profits within that country. Generally, tax groups are different from groups for accounting purposes. There are various restrictions on the transfer such as in the UK where only losses of the current accounting period can be surrendered.

It is important to appreciate, each entity will still produce their own individual accounts and will be taxed individually. However, if they are part of a group for tax purposes it may enable them to transfer losses between group members to save tax for the group as a whole.

Capital losses cannot usually be surrendered between group entities. In the UK, group entities can transfer ownership of an asset to a group entity at nil gain/nil loss. A capital gain or loss only arises when an asset is sold outside the group to a third party. In this way, the entire capital loss group is effectively treated as one entity by the authorities for capital gains tax.

Group relief may be used to:

- Save tax (the surrendering entity may pay tax at a lower rate that the group entity receiving the loss).
- Enable relief to be gained earlier (the surrendering entity may only be able to carry losses forwards which result in the entity waiting for loss relief).

Appropriations of profit

Appropriations of profit such as dividends cannot be deducted in arriving at an entity's taxable profits and are therefore taxable in the hands of the entity, i.e. tax relief is not given for the dividend.

The dividend is then distributed to the shareholders who may be taxed on the income as part of their personal tax.

As a result, the dividend is often taxed twice. There are four main systems to deal with this situation:

- Classical system
- Imputation system
- Partial imputation system
- Split rate system

Corporate tax system V the personal tax system

Classical system

The shareholder is treated as independent from the entity. The dividend is taxed twice, firstly as part of the entity's taxable earnings and secondly when received by the shareholder as part of shareholder's personal income.

Imputation system

The shareholder receives a tax credit equal to the underlying corporate income tax paid by the entity. In this way, the entity is taxed on the taxable earnings which are used to pay the dividend, while the shareholder receives a full credit and hence pays no tax on the dividend income.

Partial imputation system

A tax credit is offered to the shareholder but only for part of the underlying corporate income tax paid by the entity on its taxable earnings used to pay the dividend.

Split rate system

These systems distinguish between distributed profits and retained profits and charge a lower rate of corporate income tax on distributed profits to avoid the double taxation of dividends.

Re-characterising debt

As a general rule interest is tax deductible and dividends are not. It is therefore advantageous from a tax perspective for group entities to transfer funds from one entity to another in the form of interest on inter-company loans rather than dividends.

Many countries have addressed this issue by limiting the amount of interest that is tax deductible. Interest in excess of this value will be classified as a dividend. The rules which govern the amount of interest that is eligible for tax relief in this situation are knows as thin capitalisation rules.

The following illustration is shown for illustrative purposes only and the student will not be required to answer this type of question in their assessment.

Illustration 11 – The classical and imputation system

Taxable profits are $100,000 and the entity decides to distribute a dividend of $42,500 (net). Profits are taxed at 15% and shareholders are subject to income tax of 20% on all dividends received.

Calculate the total tax paid by the entity and the shareholders under the classical system, the imputation system, and the partial imputation system where a tax credit of 10% is allowed.

Solution

Classical System

Tax on profits for the entity	$100,000 × 15%	$15,000
Tax on dividends for the shareholders	$42,500 × 20%	$8,500
		———
Total tax paid		$23,500

Full Imputation System

Tax on profits for the entity	$100,000 × 15%	$15,000
Tax on dividends for the shareholders:		
Dividend received	$42,500	
Tax credit (42,500/85 × 15)	$ 7,500	
	———	
Gross dividend	$50,000	
Tax at 20%	$10,000	
Less: tax credit	$ (7,500)	$2,500
	———	———
Total tax paid		$17,500

Partial Imputation System

Tax on profits for the entity	$100,000 × 15%	$15,000
Tax on dividends for the shareholders:		
Dividend received	$42,500	
Tax credit (42,500/90 × 10)	$ 4,722	
	———	
Gross dividend	$47,222	
Tax at 20%	$ 9,444	
Less: tax credit	$ (4,722)	$4,722
	———	———
Total tax paid		$19,722

4 Indirect taxes

Types of indirect taxes

Unit taxes

This is a tax based on the number or weight of items, e.g. excise duties.

Ad valorem taxes

This is a tax based on the value of items, e.g. sales tax.

Excise duties

This is a type of unit tax and it is on certain products such as alcoholic drinks, tobacco, mineral oils and motor vehicles. It is based on the weight or size of the tax base. These duties are imposed to:

- discourage over consumption of harmful products;
- to pay for extra costs, such as increased healthcare or road infrastructure;
- to tax luxuries (in the USA, this would include fishing equipment, firearms and air tickets).

The characteristics of commodities that make them most suitable for excise duties are:

- few large producers
- inelastic demand with no close substitutes
- large sales volumes
- easy to define products covered by the duty

Property taxes

Many countries impose tax on property based on either the capital value or the annual rental value. Most countries tax land and buildings although in the USA, certain states also impose a tax on cars, livestock and boats.

Wealth taxes

Some countries also impose a wealth tax on an individual's or enterprise's total wealth. The wealth can include pension funds, insurance policies and works of art.

Consumption taxes

These are taxes imposed on the consumption of goods and added to the purchase price. There are two types of consumption tax.

- **Single stage taxes**

  Single stage taxes apply to one level of production only, for example at either the manufacturing, wholesale or retail level. The USA is a country which uses a retail sales tax although the tax rate is determined at the local state government level instead of at the central government or federal level.

- **Multi-stage sales tax**

  This is a tax charged each time a component or product is sold. There are two types of multi-stage sales tax:

  Cascade tax, and

  Valued added tax (VAT).

Cascade tax

This is where tax is taken at each stage of production and is a business cost because no refunds are provided by local government.

The following illustration is shown for illustrative purposes only and the student will not be required to answer this type of question in their examination.

Illustration 12 – Multi-stage sales tax

A shoe manufacturer sells shoes to a wholesaler who then sells it to a retailer. Finally the retailer sells it to a final consumer.

M sells it to W for $ 50

W sells it to R for $80

R sells it to C for $150

The rate of tax is 10%.

Calculate the total sales tax due.

Solution

Each time a sale is made, sales tax due by each enterprise is computed as follows:

M's sale to W	$50 × 10% = $5
W's sale to R	$80 × 10% = $8
R's sale to C	$150 × 10% = $15
Total Tax Due	**$28**

Each business has to charge tax and pay it to the tax authorities. Total tax paid is $28 and is not recoverable.

Value added tax (VAT)

VAT is charged each time a component or product is sold but the government allows businesses to claim back all the tax they have paid (input tax). The entire tax burden is passed to the final consumer. The VAT system is used by almost all countries in the world.

Vat payable = output tax – input tax

Output tax – VAT charged on sales to customers

Input tax – VAT paid on purchases

VAT aims to tax most business transactions which are referred to as taxable supplies.

Therefore, supplies could be:

Standard Rated	–	Taxed at the standard rate of VAT
Higher Rated	–	Taxed at a higher rate
Zero Rated	–	Taxed at a rate of 0% (Basic food, e.g. bread)
Exempt	–	Not subject to VAT

In the UK, supplies such as food, children's clothing and exports are zero rated for the purpose of VAT. Businesses who sell zero rated sales are allowed to claim back input VAT on purchases.

Alternatively, in the UK, supplies such as finance and insurance are exempt for the purpose of VAT. Businesses who make exempt sales cannot claim back input VAT on purchases.

You will not be required to know the types of goods and services that are zero rated or exempt for the exam; the examiner will make this clear in the question.

It is important to identify the type of supply in order to claim back input tax. Input tax can only be claimed back on taxable supplies, i.e. zero and standard rated goods and services. Exempt supplies are outside the VAT system and VAT cannot be charged to customers but neither can the input tax on purchases be claimed back.

Taxable supplies, therefore, have a selling price exclusive of VAT (net price) and a selling price inclusive of VAT (gross price).

If the exclusive price is given, VAT is calculated by:
exclusive price × tax rate

If the inclusive price is given VAT is calculated by:

$$\frac{\textbf{inclusive price}}{\textbf{100 + tax rate}} \times \textbf{tax rate}$$

VAT registration

VAT registration is required by a taxable person making a taxable supply.

A taxable person can be an individual or a company.

A taxable supply is zero or standard rated sales.

They will be required to register for VAT once their taxable turnover (zero and standard rated sales) reach a certain limit (this will vary from tax year to tax year).

Once registered they must:

- Issue VAT invoices
- Keep appropriate VAT records
- Charge VAT on taxable supplies to customers
- Be able to claim back VAT from purchases that are used for taxable supplies
- Complete a quarterly VAT return and make payments

For example, in the UK VAT **cannot** be recovered on:

- Cars (unless for resale, i.e. by a car dealer)
- Entertaining (unless for staff entertaining)

The following illustration is shown for illustrative purposes only and the student will not be required to answer this type of question in their assessment.

Illustration 13 – VAT

A shoe manufacturer sells shoes to a wholesaler who then sells it to a retailer. Finally the retailer sells it to a final consumer.

M sells it to W for $ 50.

W sells it to R for $80.

R sells it to C for $150.

The rate of value added tax is 10% and all figures are exclusive of VAT.

Calculate the amount of VAT that will be payable by each party.

Solution

Enterprise	Output Tax $	Input Tax $	VAT collected and payable to local government $
M			
– Sale to W = 50 × 10%	5		5 paid by M
W			
– Sale to R = 80 × 10%	8		
– Purchase from M = 50 × 10%		5	3 paid by W
R			
– Sale to C = 150 × 10%	15		
– Purchase from W = 80 × 10%		8	7 paid by R
Total suffered by C = 150 × 10%			15

The total tax on the sale of $15 is suffered by C as unable to claim back the input tax.

Test your understanding 17 – VAT

Country Ozz operates a VAT system where VAT is charged on goods and services and registered traders are able to reclaim input VAT on purchases.

VAT is charged at the following rates:

Standard rate	15%
Luxury rate	20%
Zero rate	0%

During the last VAT period Troyster purchased materials to produce a product called Paws, costing $90,000, excluding VAT and materials to produce a product called Claws, costing $60,000, excluding VAT. All materials were charged at standard rate VAT.

Sales were made of the "Paws" during the year totalling $120,000. These were zero rated supplies.

Sales were made of the "Claws" during the year totalling $240,000, inclusive of VAT. These were luxury rated supplies.

Calculate the amount of VAT to be paid to the tax authorities and the accounting profit Troyster would make during the year.

5 Employee taxation

Employees are taxed on their earnings under income tax. Earnings can include salaries, bonuses, commissions and benefits in kind.

Benefits in kind are non-cash benefits in lieu of further cash payments such as:

- company cars
- living accommodation
- loans
- private medical insurance

The basis of assessment is based on the individual country:

- France – amount earned in previous year
- Switzerland – average of previous two years' earnings
- UK – amount actually received in the current tax year

Employees can deduct certain expenses which are **wholly, exclusively and necessary** for employment, such as business travel, contributions to pension plans, donations to charity through a payroll deduction scheme and professional subscriptions.

Both employees and companies have to pay social security taxes based on salaries paid to employees. This tax is used to fund benefits such as the Public Health Service and Retirement Benefits. In the UK, this is called national insurance.

Most governments expect enterprises to withhold tax on employees' salaries and report earnings to the tax authorities. In the UK, this tax system is referred to as Pay-As-You-Earn (PAYE).

The benefits of having a PAYE system are:

- Tax is collected at source, hence taxpayers are less likely to default payment.
- Tax authorities receive regular payments from employers – helps to budget cash flows for the government.

- The tax authority only has to deal with the employer, rather than a number of individuals.
- Most of the administration costs are borne by the employer, instead of the government.

Certain countries, such as the USA, require banks to collect property taxes with the mortgage payments. In addition to this, in the USA there is a separate Unemployment Compensation Tax.

You will not be assessed on the calculation of employment taxation but you should have a general appreciation of how an entity deals with taxation with regard to employees.

The standard proforma for calculating employee tax would be as follows:

	$
Salary	X
Plus: bonus, commission, benefits	X
Less: subscriptions	(X)
Less: pension contributions	(X)
Less: charity donations	(X)
Less: personal allowances	(X)
Taxable income	X

The taxable income will then be charged at the appropriate tax rate for the tax year.

This will normally be done by the entity using the PAYE system.

The following illustration is shown for illustrative purposes only and the student will not be required to answer this type of question in their assessment.

Illustration 14 – Employee taxation

An entity employs Barry, a 25-year-old accountant who earns $23,000 per annum.

During the tax year, Barry also earned a 5% bonus and has a taxable benefit of medical insurance worth $500.

As a qualified accountant, Barry must pay a membership subscription of $400 each year.

Required:

Calculate the amount of employment tax that Barry would need to pay in the year through the PAYE system assuming the following:

(a) the personal allowance for the year is $6,500 and

(b) the tax rates are as follows based on taxable earnings:

- 10% on the first $1,900
- 22% after that

Solution

	$
Income	23,000
Bonus (23,000 × 5%)	1,150
Benefit in kind – insurance	500
Less subscription	(400)
Less personal allowance	(6,500)
Taxable earnings	**17,750**
Tax	
$1,900 × 10%	190
($17,750 – 1,900) × 22%	3,487
Total	**3,677**

The administrative duties of the entity regarding the PAYE system can be seen later in this chapter under the general heading of administration.

6 International taxation

Corporate residence

Entities normally pay taxation on their worldwide income in the country they are deemed to be resident in.

An enterprise is deemed to be resident for tax purposes either in the place of incorporation or place of control/central management.

Generally an entity will be treated as being resident in the country of control, i.e. place where the head office is located or board meetings held.

Double taxation

An entity may end up being taxed in more than one country, this is called double taxation.

For example, an entity may earn income in country X, despite being located in country Y.

Double taxation may arise if that income is taxed in the country where it was earned (X) as well as the country where the entity is resident (Y). Double taxation relief is often available in this situation.

Double taxation relief

There are three main methods of giving double taxation relief:

(1) Exemption – Two countries agree on certain types of income which will be exempt or partially exempt in one country or the other.

(2) Tax credit – Tax paid in one country may be allowed as a tax credit in another country. Relief is normally restricted to the lower of the foreign or country of residency tax.

(3) Deduction – Tax relief is gained by deducting the foreign tax from the foreign income so that only the "net" amount will be subject to tax in the country of residency.

Types of overseas operations

An overseas operation can be run as a branch or a subsidiary. This section focusses upon tax-related issues only. Issues relating to identification and accounting for a subsidiary are dealt with in chapter 2 of this publication.

Overseas subsidiary

The features of operating as a foreign subsidiary are:

- The overseas subsidiary is a separate entity for tax purposes. The parent entity (or holding company) will only pay tax on any dividends received from the subsidiary. Depending upon the tax regime of a particular country, dividends received from a foreign subsidiary may be treated as exempt, assuming that the recipient holding company has control of the subsidiary.
- Loss relief is not available for the group because the overseas subsidiary will be paying tax under a different tax regime. Under certain circumstances the loss can be surrendered to the parent entity if there are no alternative reliefs available in the overseas country.

- The overseas subsidiary cannot claim the same tax depreciation as the parent entity on any assets, although it may receive an alternative type of tax depreciation or the equivalent in the overseas country. Assets transferred from the parent may also result in capital gains tax.

Overseas Branch

The features of operating as a foreign branch are:

- The branch is treated as an extension of the domestic activity and usually all profits from it will be subject to domestic taxation. Double taxation relief is then given when an overseas branch has profits which have also been taxed overseas. Relief is restricted to the amount of domestic tax paid on the overseas branch's profits. If an overseas branch makes a trading loss, then the loss can, in some circumstances, be relieved against the parent entity's profits.
- Loss relief is available to the parent entity from the branch in most circumstances. It should be noted that, in some countries, that there is the option to elect for branch exemption. If this exemption was claimed, there would be no loss relief available.
- Assets can be transferred between the branch and parent at no gain/no loss.
- The parent can claim tax depreciation on all assets, including the branch assets.

Types of foreign tax

Withholding tax

Some countries will deduct tax at source on items such as interest, royalties, rent, dividends and capital gains. The net income (gross payment less tax) is then received by the beneficiary in the foreign country.

Underlying tax

When an entity pays out a dividend, it is done so out of post tax profits. Therefore, the amount of profit distributed as a dividend will have already suffered tax on profits.

If an entity receives a dividend from an overseas subsidiary, the dividend will have been taxed once in the overseas country as part of normal tax on profits, and then again in the country of receipt, as income on dividends. This tax is known as underlying tax.

This is calculated as follows:

$$\frac{\text{Tax on profits}}{\text{Profit after tax}} \times \text{Gross dividend}$$

Both withholding and underlying tax may be reduced by various methods of double tax relief. Methods of double tax relief include exemption, tax credits for foreign tax suffered, and deduction of foreign tax from tax due in the home country.

You will not be assessed on the calculation of foreign taxation but you should have a general appreciation what it represents.

The following illustrations are shown for illustrative purposes only and the student will not be required to answer this type of question in their assessment.

Illustration 15 – International taxation

Homely is a UK entity and owns 100% of the shares in a foreign entity called Faraway.

During the year Faraway earned the following income:

Profit before tax	$200,000
Income tax	$(40,000)
Profit after tax	$160,000

Faraway pays a dividend of $80,000 out of profit after tax to Homely. This dividend is subject to 15% withholding tax.

What is the total foreign tax suffered on the dividend?

Solution

	$
Withholding tax	
$80,000 × 15%	12,000
Underlying tax	
($40,000/$160,000) × $80,000	20,000
Total foreign tax	**32,000**

This means:

The dividend distributed by Faraway was $80,000.

The foreign country deducted withholding tax of $12,000 and, therefore, the shareholder would only receive $68,000 in cash.

The profits in Faraway were taxed before the $80,000 was distributed. Therefore, the underlying tax is the amount of tax the dividend has already suffered prior to distribution when it was taxed as a profit.

Illustration 16 – Double tax relief

Use the information from the previous illustration:

A tax treaty exists between the two countries using the tax credit method, calculate the tax payable in the UK (Homely's country of residence) assuming a tax rate of 40%.

Solution

	$
Net dividend received	68,000
Add back WHT	12,000
	80,000
Add back UT	20,000
Gross dividend	100,000
Total foreign tax ($100,000 – $68,000)	**32,000**
Tax in UK	
Tax at 40%	40,000
Less DTR (lower of foreign and UK tax)	(32,000)
Tax paid in UK	8,000

Test your understanding 18 – International taxation

Britas is a UK entity and owns 80% of the shares in a foreign entity called Cheers.

During the year, Cheers earned the following income:

Profit before tax	\$372,000
Income tax	\$(62,000)
Profit after tax	\$310,000

Cheers pays a total dividend of \$100,000 out of profit after tax to its shareholders. This dividend is subject to 5% withholding tax.

Calculate the total foreign tax suffered on the dividend and show how double tax relief would apply in the UK using the tax credit method, assuming a rate of 40% tax is charge.

OECD model tax convention

The OECD model addresses the issues of double residency.

This model states that business profits of an enterprise will only be taxable in a state if an enterprise has a permanent establishment in that country. A permanent establishment could include the following:

(1) A factory

(2) A workshop

(3) An office

(4) A branch

(5) A place of management

(6) A mine, an oil or gas well, or a place of extraction of natural resources

(7) A construction project or building site if it lasts more than 12 months

If an entity has a permanent establishment in a country, it can be taxed in that country, causing a possible problem of double taxation.

Where an entity is deemed to have residency in several countries, the OECD model suggests that the entity is resident in the country of its effective management.

Corporation tax and transfer pricing

There is potential for entities with overeaseas subsidiaries or associates to manipulate transfer pricing in order to benefit from a lower tax rate.

Transfer pricing applies to group situations when either goods are sold inter-company or a loans take place at a favourable price. Therefore, this results in transactions not taking place at "arms length" and profits being effected by the group members. This could be done when an overseas entity moves profits to another country at a lower tax rate.

There are measures in place to counter-act this from happening and the OECD are currently working on the measurement of base profits and charging between connected international entities.

This could also be perceived by the public as a method of tax avoidance and entities may be criticised for not paying their fair share of tax.

The correct rules regarding taxation for transfer pricing are as follows:

(1) Goods and services – An adjustment will be made in the corporate tax computation for the entity gaining the tax advantage to reflect profit that would have been achieved if the transaction had been arms length.

(2) Provision of loan finance – The rules apply to the amount of the loan and interest charged on the loan. Thin capitalisation refers to the situation where the amount of loan finance provided to a connected company exceeds the amount a third party would be willing to provide. This results in the Interest charged on the amount of the loan that exceeds the amount a third party would lend is not allowable for tax purposes and will therefore be disallowed.

Test your understanding 19 – Transfer pricing

Aston sells to Marvin, a group entity, 5,000 units at $1.50 each. The market value was $3 per each.

Explain the effect of the transfer pricing legislation on this transaction.

7 Administration

Record-keeping

Enterprises need to keep records to satisfy tax requirements for the following taxes.

Corporate income tax

All records required to support their financial statements and also the additional documents required to support the adjustments made to those statements when completing their tax returns.

Sales tax

Adequate records should be maintained of all the sales and purchases records such as:

- Orders and delivery notes
- Purchase and sales invoices
- Credit and debit notes
- Purchase and Sales Books
- Import and Export Documents
- Bank Statements
- Cashbooks and receipts
- VAT account

Overseas subsidiaries

Tax authorities would require documentation about the transfer pricing policy between the subsidiary and the parent. These are the prices charged for goods or services provided from one to the other. Most tax authorities require the price to be the same as it would be if charged to a third party.

Employee tax

Employers have to keep detailed records of employee tax and social security contributions. They will also be required to prepare a number of year end returns to show the total deductions they have made from employees wages, the employer's contributions and an analysis of any other amounts deducted. The employer is also required to provide details to the employee.

Tax authorities set deadlines for the payment of tax and the submission of the tax return. The enterprise will either be required to pay tax following an assessment from the tax authorities or will pay tax via self-assessment. In the UK and the USA, tax is paid via self-assessment. The tax authorities will then check the tax return to confirm if the correct tax has been paid.

Minimum retention of records

There will be a minimum length of time for the retention of records; in the UK this is six years for all records relating to earnings and capital gains. The purpose of this is to enable the tax authorities to question or challenge records up to several years later.

Payment of tax

This will depend on the rules of the tax authority and will depend on the type of tax that is due. The tax is not always paid when the return is filed, it may happen earlier or later. Interest will be charged on late payments of tax.

Powers of tax authorities

The revenue authorities have various powers to impose penalties and interest on late payment of tax. In addition, they have the power to:

- Review and query filed returns.
- Request special reports if they believe inaccurate information has been submitted.
- Examine records of previous years (in the US, tax authorities can go back 20 years).
- Enter and search the entity's premises and seize documents.
- Pass on information to foreign tax authorities.

Tax avoidance and tax evasion

Tax avoidance is tax planning to arrange affairs, within the scope of the law, to minimise tax liabilities. This could include setting up a subsidiary overseas in a low-tax economy. More common examples of tax avoidance include claiming tax reliefs by paying amounts into pension schemes or by making your spouse a salaried employee of your own business.

There have been a number of large entities which have been accused of tax avoidance in recent years. The public perception is that these entities are not paying their fair share of tax and they have been criticised in the press for organising their tax affairs so that they pay very little tax. Consequently, these entities have suffered from negative publicity which has had an adverse effect on business reputation and profitability.

Some high profile examples of entities accused of tax avoidance are global organisations such as Starbucks, Google and Amazon. These large organisations have come under public scrutiny for avoiding tax on their British sales. All three organisations have reported significant UK sales revenue but paid very little, if any, UK corporation tax. What these entities are doing is legal, but the tide of negative public opinion has turned against them, with the belief that such avoidance is unethical. This perception has led to customer boycotts, bad publicity and loss of reputation. The increase in awareness of tax avoidance and the ethical and moral implication of doing so is particularly prevalent to members of the public during times of austerity, when governments are under pressure to cut public expenditure.

Tax evasion is the illegal manipulation of the tax system to not pay tax. Evasion is the intentional disregard of the law to escape tax and can include claiming a tax deduction for expenses that are not tax deductible, under-declaring income or overstating expenses. Those caught evading taxes are generally subject to criminal charges and substantial criminal penalties.

Examples of how tax evasion can take place in a practical sense would be an entity intentionally not declaring income, overstating expenses incurred, or reporting the payment of charitable donations when the payments have not been made. All of these examples would reduce taxable profits and therefore reduce the entity's tax expense. One approach to tax evasion becoming more common is for an entity to use offshore bank accounts in an attempt to hide money and evade any tax liability due on that account.

One example of tax evasion, which led to criminal conviction is the case of Arlette Ricci, the heir to the Nina Ricci perfume dynasty. Arlette Ricci was sentenced to three years in prison, two of them suspended, after being convicted of hiding money from the French tax authorities with the help of HSBC using Swiss bank accounts to hide inheritance money left to her from her father. This led to the Swiss branch of HSBC, Britains' biggest bank, officially being put under investigation.

Prevention of tax avoidance and tax evasion

The tax authorities use various methods to prevent both tax avoidance and tax evasion:

(1) Reducing opportunity, e.g. by deduction of tax at source and the use of third party reporting.

(2) Simplifying tax structure by minimising reliefs, allowances and exemptions available.

(3) Increasing the perceived risk of being caught by auditing tax returns and payments.

(4) Developing good communication between tax authorities and enterprises.

(5) Changing social attitudes towards evasion and avoidance by maintaining an honest and customer friendly tax system. The government should create a fair tax system and should encourage an increasing commitment.

(6) Reducing lost revenue by reviewing the penalty structure.

(7) Concise drafting of tax legislation to minimise the opportunity for taxpayers to exploit 'loopholes' in the legislation.

Test your understanding 20 – Practice questions

(1) Most governments require detailed records to be kept for certain taxes. **List three taxes for which records should be maintained.**

(2) As a management accountant it is necessary to understand the difference between tax evasion and tax avoidance. **In no more than 45 words, define both tax evasion and tax avoidance.**

(3) **List five possible powers that a tax authority may have to ensure that enterprises comply with the tax legislation.**

(4) Many countries impose duties on petrol and diesel to compensate for the damage caused to the environment.

This duty is a:

A Direct tax

B Excise duties

C Single stage tax

D Cascade tax

(5) Enterprises reward employees with a remuneration package consisting of a salary and benefits in kind.

Define 'benefits in kind' in less than 30 words.

(6) Many countries impose duties on alcoholic drinks and cigarettes to discourage excessive consumption.

This duty is a:

A Excise duty

B Ad valorem tax

C Direct tax

D Cascade tax

(7) In the UK, the Pay-As-You-Earn system requires enterprises to withhold tax on employees' salaries.

What are the advantages for the government and employees?

(8) A South American country has a VAT system which allows enterprises to reclaim input tax paid. VAT is at 20% of selling price.

A manufactures mobile phones and sells them to B, a wholesaler. B resells them to C a retailer. C eventually sells them to D for $140 (excluding VAT). The prices at which transactions take place (excluding VAT) are as follows:

– A sells to B for $60;

– B sells to C for $90.

Calculate the VAT due from A, B and C.

(9) An enterprise imports goods from an overseas enterprise at a cost of $40. The goods are subject to excise duties of $10 per item and VAT at 15%. **If the enterprise imports 100 items, what is the TOTAL tax payable?**

A $1000

B $750

C $1,750

D $1,500

(10) An enterprise purchases raw materials for $2000 and pays VAT at standard rate on them. The materials are used to produce two products R and S. The enterprise sells 400 units of product R at $20 each and 800 units of product S at $30 each. Product R is zero rated for VAT purposes and product S is standard rated.

Assume that there are no other transactions affecting the VAT payments and that the standard rate of VAT is 17.5%. All figures are exclusive of VAT.

At the end of the accounting period how much VAT is due to the tax authorities?

A $4,200

B $350

C $3,850

D $2,550

(11) **If a product is zero rated for VAT purposes, it means that an enterprise:**

A Can charge VAT on sales at standard rate and cannot reclaim input tax on purchases

B Cannot charge VAT on sales and can reclaim input taxes paid on purchases

C Cannot charge VAT on sales and cannot reclaim input taxes paid on purchases

D Can charge VAT on sales and can reclaim input taxes paid on purchases

(12) **Which of the following could NOT be used to indicate an enterprise is resident in a country?**

A Country in which directors' meetings are held

B Country of incorporation

C Country in which control and management is exercised

D Country in which goods are sold.

(13) **In no more than 30 words, define the meaning of a overseas subsidiary.**

(14) **Which of the following would not be subject to a withholding tax?**

A Profits of the enterprise

B Rental profits

C Equity dividends

D Interest received from finance companies

(15) A double taxation treaty between two countries usually allows relief of foreign tax through a number of methods.

Which one of the following is not a method of relieving foreign tax?

A Deduction based on lower tax

B Exemption from corporate tax in one country

C Tax Credits (deduction from tax liability)

D Loss relief

(16) **Permanent establishment is defined under the OECD model in several ways.**

Which of the following would not be classed as a 'permanent establishment'?

A An office

B An agent with authority to enter into contracts

C A workshop

D A warehouse used for storage

(17) **Define 'Incidence of Tax' using a maximum of 15 words.**

(18) **Which of the following is not one of Adam Smith's characteristics of a Good Tax?**

A Fair

B Absolute

C Convenient

D Simple

(19) **An indirect tax is a tax which is:**

A Paid by one person with the intention of passing on

B Imposed directly on a person

C Paid indirectly to tax authorities

D Based on a person's income

(20) **Define 'hypothecation' using no more than 30 words.**

Test your understanding 21 – Practice questions

(1) **Which of the following is not usually a source of tax rules in a country:**

A Local legislation

B Double tax treaties

C Statements of practice of tax authorities

D International law

(2) **What does 'competent jurisdiction' mean in the context of an enterprise being subject to a tax liability?**

A Country where enterprise has an office

B Country who has enforcement laws that apply to an enterprise

C Country where enterprise has business operations

D Country where enterprise has employees

(3) **List the three main tax bases used in developed countries.**

(4) BM has a taxable profit of $30,000 and receives a tax assessment of $3,000.

BV has a taxable profit of $60,000 and receives a tax assessment of $7,500.

BM and BV are resident in the same tax jurisdiction. **This tax could be said to be:**

A a progressive tax

B a regressive tax

C a direct tax

D a proportional tax

(5) **Accounting depreciation is replaced by tax depreciation:**

A To reduce the amount of depreciation allowed for tax

B To increase the amount of depreciation allowed for tax

C To ensure that standard rates of depreciation are used by all organisations for tax purposes

D So that government can more easily manipulate the amount of tax organisations pay

(6) **Rollover relief allows:**

A Deferral of the payment of corporate income tax on gains arising from the disposal of a business asset

B Stock values to be rolled over, replacing cost of purchases with current values

C Trading losses to be carried forward or rolled over to future periods

D Capital losses to be carried forwards or rolled over to future periods

(7) **An imputation system of corporate income tax means:**

A All the underlying corporate income tax on the dividend distribution is passed as a credit to the shareholders

B The organisation pays corporate income tax on its profits and the shareholder pays income tax on the dividend received

C Withholding tax paid on dividends is passed as a credit to shareholders

D A percentage of the underlying tax is passed as credit to shareholders

(8) Country IDT has a duty that is levied on all drinks of an alcoholic nature where the alcohol is above 20% by volume. This levy is $2 per 1 litre bottle. This duty could be said to be:

A Ad valorem tax

B Unit tax

C Direct tax

D VAT

(9) **Which ONE of the following powers is a tax authority least likely to have granted to them?**

A Power of arrest

B Power to examine records

C Power of entry and search

D Power to give information to other countries' tax authorities

(10) **List THREE possible reasons why governments set deadlines for filing returns and/or paying taxes.**

(11) **In no more than 15 works define the meaning of a "branch".**

(12) EB has an investment of 25% of the equity shares of XY, an entity resident in a foreign country. EB receives a dividend of $90,000 from XY, the amount being after the deduction of withholding tax of 10%. XY had profits before tax for the year of $1,200,000 and paid corporate tax of $200,000. **How much underlying tax can EB claim for double taxation relief?**

(13) The following details relate to EA:

- Incorporated in Country A
- Carries out its main business activities in Country B
- Its senior management operate from Country C and effective control is exercised from Country C
- Assume countries A, B and C have all signed double tax treaties with each other, based on the OECD model tax convention.

Which country will EA be deemed to be resident in for tax purposes?

A Country A

B Country B

C Country C

D Both countries B and C

(14) **Explain the meaning of withholding and underlying tax.**

(15) **Explain the meaning of indexation allowance.**

(16) An entity has an accounting profit of $100,000 and includes entertaining costs of $10,000 and accounting depreciation of $15,000. The entity operates in a country where these expense are disallowed for tax purposes but tax depreciation of $9,000 is allowable. **Calculate the taxable profit for the entity.**

(17) An entity disposes of an asset for $40,000 which cost $15,000 to purchase plus purchase costs of $2,000. The entity operates in a country where indexation allowance can be claimed amounting to $5,000. **Calculate the chargeable gain on disposal.**

(18) **Explain the meaning of chargeable gains and capital taxes.**

(19) **Balancing charges increase taxable profits, true or false?**

8 Summary diagram

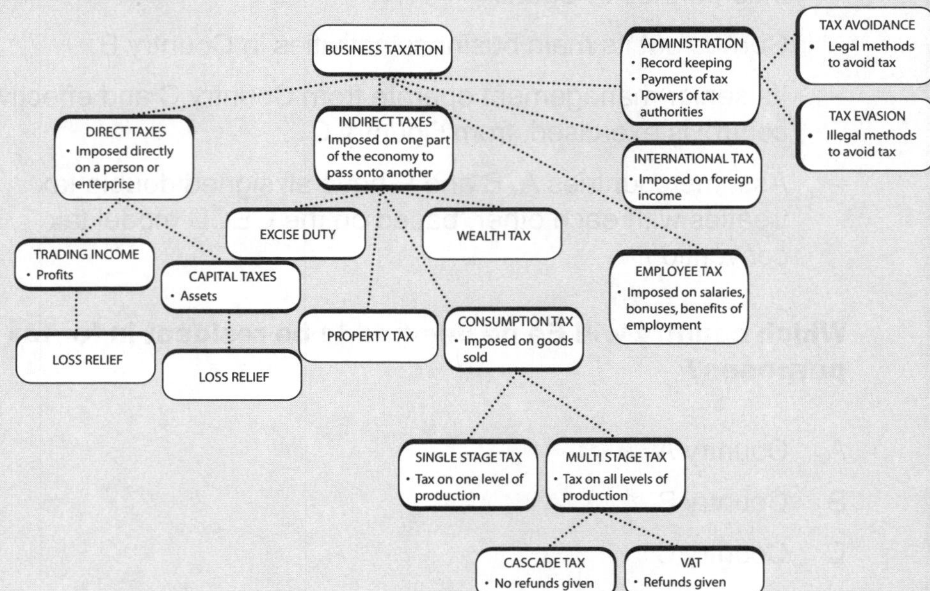

Test your understanding answers

Test your understanding 1 – Trading income

	$
Accounting profit	80,000
Less: exempt income	(8,000)
Add back: disallowable expenses	5,500
Taxable profit	77,500
Tax at 25%	**19,375**

Test your understanding 2 – Trading income

Plant and machinery

Accounting depreciation $1,500 ($10,000 + $5,000 × 10%)

Building

Accounting depreciation $4,000 ($100,000 × 4%)

Total accounting depreciation = ($1,500 + $4,000) = $5,500

Test your understanding 3 – Trading income

Plant and machinery

Tax depreciation

TWDV at start of year	$8,000	($10,000 × 80%)
Tax depreciation at 20%	$1,600	

The asset had been purchased in the previous accounting period, therefore tax depreciation has already been claimed for Ye. 31/03/X1. This year's tax depreciation must be calculated on the tax written down value at the beginning of the year, i.e. $8,000.

The new plant and machinery is given 100% FYA which means relief in given on the total cost in the year of purchase of $5,000.

The building tax depreciation of 3% is based on cost of $100,000 = $3,000

Total tax depreciation = ($1,600 + $5,000 + $3,000) = $9,600

Test your understanding 4 – Trading income

	$	
Accounting profit	60,000	
Less exempt income	(4,000)	
Add back disallowable expenses	4,500	
Add accounting depreciation	5,500	(TYU 2)
Less tax depreciation	(9,600)	(TYU 3)
Taxable profit	**56,400**	

Test your understanding 5 – Trading income

	$	
Accounting profit	60,000	
Less exempt income	(4,000)	
Add back disallowable expenses	4,500	
Add accounting depreciation	5,500	(TYU 2)
Less tax depreciation	(9,600)	(TYU 3)
Taxable profit	56,400	
Tax at 30%	**16,920**	

Test your understanding 6 – Trading income

Tax payable is:

(\$800,000 × 9/12 × 26%) + (\$800,000 × 3/12 × 28%) = \$212,000

The accounting period runs from 01/07/X0 to 30/06/X1.

9 months of the accounting period profit (01/07/X0 – 31/03/X1) is charged at 26% and 3 months of the accounting period profit (01/04/X1 – 30/06/X1) is charged at 28%.

Test your understanding 7 – Balancing allowances/charges

Carrying amount at the date of sale = $10,000 – $2,000 = $8,000

Accounting depreciation ($10,000 × 10% × 2 years) = $2,000

Total accounting loss = (proceeds $6,000 – CA $8,000) = $2,000

Test your understanding 8 – Balancing allowances/charges

Plant and machinery

Tax depreciation in year 1	$2,000	($10,000 × 20%)
TWDV at start of year 2	$8,000	($10,000 × 80%)
Tax depreciation at 20%	$1,600	

The total tax depreciation = $2,000 + $1,600 = $3,600.

Tax written down value at the date of sale = $10,000 – $3,600 = $6,400

Total tax loss = (proceeds $6,000 – TWDV $6,400) = $400

This $400 would be classed as a balancing allowance

Test your understanding 9 – Balancing allowances/charges

	$	
Accounting profit	50,000	
Add accounting loss	2,000	(TYU 7)
Less tax loss (BA)	(400)	(TYU 8)
Taxable profit	51,600	
Tax at 25%	**12,900**	

Test your understanding 10 – Balancing allowances/charges

	$	
Accounting profit	50,000	
Less accounting profit	(1,000)	(W1)
Less tax loss (BA)	2,600	(W2)
Taxable profit	51,600	
Tax at 25%	**12,900**	

(W1)

Carrying amount at the date of sale = $10,000 – $2,000 = $8,000

Accounting depreciation ($10,000 × 10% × 2 years) = $2,000

Total accounting profit = (proceeds $9,000 – CA $8,000) = $1,000

(W2)

Tax depreciation in year 1	$2,000	($10,000 × 20%)
TWDV at start of year 2	$8,000	($10,000 × 80%)
Tax depreciation at 20%	$1,600	

The total tax depreciation = $2,000 + $1,600 = $3,600.

Tax written down value at the date of sale = $10,000 – $3,600 = $6,400

Total tax profit = (proceeds $9,000 – TWDV $6,400) = $2,600

This $2,600 would be classed as a balancing charge

Test your understanding 11 – Trading losses

Year	Trading profit/(loss)	Workings
1	–	20,000 – 20,000
2	–	
3	–	19,000 – 19,000
4	19,000	25,000 – 6,000 (balance of the loss)

The trading loss is carried back first against the trading profit in year 1, this must be done to the maximum extent, i.e. you cannot use part of the profit for relief if all of it is needed. The balance of the loss must then be carried forward against the **first available trading profit** in year 3, again to the maximum extent and this means year 4 will be reduced by the remainder of the loss $6,000, i.e. ($45,000 – $20,000 – $19,000). Year 4 will therefore have trading profits of $19,000 ($25,000 – $6,000).

Test your understanding 12 – Cessation losses

	20X1	20X2	20X3
	$	$	$
Trading profits	100,000	50,000	–
Loss relief	(10,000)	(50,000)	–
Revised trading profits	90,000	–	–

On cessation, trading losses must be carried back on a LIFO basis, i.e. most recent trading profits are used first. When you carry back make sure you relieve the loss against the profit to the maximum possible extent in the year, you can't use part of it.

If the loss has been carried back as far as possible, (years dependent on the rule for that country), and still not fully relieved, then the remainder of the loss would be wasted.

Test your understanding 13 – Capital taxes

		$
Sale proceeds		150,000
Less: cost to sell		(2,000)
Net proceeds		148,000
Cost to purchase	50,000	
Cost to buy	1,500	
Enhancements	12,000	(63,500)
Chargeable gain		**84,500**

NB: Roof repairs are not an allowable cost for deduction, i.e. they are not a "new" capital cost or a cost to buy/sell. They are a cost to replace an existing structure.

Test your understanding 14 – Capital taxes

The indexation allowance would be as follows:

($50,000 + $1,500) × 30% = $15,450
12,000 × 20% = $2,400
Total allowance = $15,450 + $2,400 = $17,850

The allowance is given based on the movement in the RPI between the purchase date to the disposal date to give relief for inflation.

Test your understanding 15 – Capital taxes

		$
Sale proceeds		150,000
Less: cost to sell		(2,000)
Net proceeds		148,000
Cost to purchase	50,000	
Cost to buy	1,500	
Enhancements	12,000	(63,500)
		84,500
Less: Indexation allowance		
($50,000 + $1,500) × 30%	(15,450)	
12,000 × 20%	(2,400)	(17,850)
Chargeable gain		66,650

Capital tax = $66,650 × 30% =$19,995

Test your understanding 16 – Loss relief

Year	Capital gain/(loss)	Trading profit/(loss)
1	4,000	–
2	–	–
3	3,000	13,000

The capital loss **cannot** be carried back against year 1, only carried forward against the **first available** capital gain. It will be used against the gain in year 3 to reduce it to $3,000 ($9,000 – $6,000).

The trading loss is carried back first against year 1 to reduce the profit to nil. The remainder of the loss of $3,000 ($30,000 – $27,000) is carried forward against year 3 to reduce the profit to $13,000 ($16,000 – $3,000).

Test your understanding 17 – VAT

Output VAT		**VAT**
		$
Sales of Paws – $120,000 × 0%		–
Sales of Claws – $240,000 × 20/120		40,000
		40,000
Input VAT		
Purchases $90,000 × 15%	13,500	
Purchases $60,000 × 15%	9,000	
		(22,500)
Total VAT payable		**17,500**

Profit is based on **net sales and purchases.**

	$
Sales of Paws	120,000
Sales of Claws (240,000 – 40,000)	200,000
	320,000
Purchases (90,000 + 60,000)	(150,000)
Profit	**170,000**

Test your understanding 18 – International taxation

	$
Net dividend received	76,000
WHT 5%	4,000
($100,000 × 80%)	80,000
UT – $80,000 × (62/310)	16,000
Gross dividend	96,000
Total foreign tax ($96,000 – $76,000)	**20,000**
Tax in UK	
Tax at 40% on gross dividend $96,000	38,400
Less DTR (lower of foreign and UK tax)	(20,000)
Tax paid in UK	18,400

Test your understanding 19 – Transfer pricing

Aston must increase its taxable profits by $7,500 ($1.50 × 5,000 units).

The taxable profits must reflect the sale at market value, i.e. arms length price.

Test your understanding 20 – Practice questions

(1) (a) VAT

(b) Employee tax deducted from salaries

(c) Corporate income tax (corporation tax)

(2) Tax evasion is the illegal manipulation of the tax system to avoid paying tax.

Tax avoidance is tax planning to arrange the affairs of the enterprise within the scope of the law to minimise the income tax liability.

(3) Tax authorities may have the following powers:

- Power to review and query filed returns.
- Power to request special reports if inadequate information has been submitted.
- Power to examine records of previous periods.
- Powers of entry and search.
- Power to pass on information to foreign tax authorities.

(4) B – Excise duties

(5) Benefits in kind are non-cash benefits given by the employer to an employee, often in place of cash payments.

(6) A – Excise duty

(7) The advantages for the government are:

- The tax is collected earlier than the usual self-assessment systems which collect tax after the tax year which gives a cash flow benefit.
- The costs of tax collection and administration are passed on to the employer who acts as a tax collector.

The advantage for the employee is:

- The tax is collected gradually over the year thus is easier to bear than a single lump sum payment.

(8)

Enterprise	Input tax $	Output tax $	VAT paid $
A Sale to B		12	12 paid by A
B Purchase from B Sale to C	12	 18	 6 paid by B
C Purchase from B Sale to D	18	 28	 10 paid by C
Total suffered by D			28

(9) C – You need to add the excise duty of $1,000 (100 items × $10) and compute VAT on the inclusive price of $5,000 (100 items × $40 plus excise duty of $1,000). The VAT is 15% of $5,000 which results in 750. Total tax payable is $1,000 excise duty and $750 VAT = $1,750.

(10) It is necessary to compute the VAT on sales (output VAT) and the VAT on purchases (input VAT):

Output VAT charged on standard rated sales (800 × $30) × 17.5% =	$4,200
Input VAT paid (2,000 × 17.5%)	($350)
VAT paid to tax authorities	$3,850

The VAT can be claimed back on standard-rated and zero-rated supplies. The correct answer is C.

(11) B

(12) D – The correct answer is country in which goods are sold.

(13) An overseas subsidiary is an enterprise resident for tax purposes in a foreign country whose share capital is owned by an entity resident in another country.

(14) A – Profits of the enterprise.

(15) D – Loss relief.

(16) D – A warehouse used for storage.

(17) Incidence of Tax is the distribution of the tax burden – who actually pays the tax.

(18) D

(19) A – Paid by one person with the intention of passing it on.

(20) Hypothecation is the extent to which a certain type of tax is entirely allocated to a certain type of expenditure.

Test your understanding 21 – Practice questions

(1) D – International Law.

(2) B – Country that has enforceable laws that apply to an enterprise.

(3) The three main tax bases are: assets (capital), Income and consumption.

(4) A – $3,000 tax on $30,000 = 10% and $7,500 tax on $60,000 = 12.5%. The tax rates increase as the income rises, hence a progressive tax.

(5) C – To ensure that standard rates of depreciation are used by all organisations for tax purposes.

(6) A – Deferral of the payment of corporate income tax on gains arising from the disposal of a business asset.

(7) A – All the underlying corporate income tax on the dividend distribution is passed as a credit to the shareholders.

(8) B – Unit tax. This is a tax based on the number or weight of items, e.g. excise duties.

(9) A – Power of arrest.

(10) Answers could be:

- So that entities know when payment is required;
- It enables the tax authorities to forecast their cash flows more accurately;
- Provides a reference for late payment – useful for applying penalties for not paying;
- To prevent entities spending tax money deducted from employees. If tax is deducted from employees at source and not paid to the tax authorities fairly quickly, there is more chance of an entity spending the amount deducted, instead of paying it to the tax authorities.

(11) A branch of the entity is merely an extension of the entity's business.

(12) Gross dividend = $90,000/90 × 100 = $100,000
Underlying tax = (Tax on profits/profits after tax) × gross dividend
Underlying tax = (200,000/1,000) × 100,000 = $20,000

(13) C – Country C. An entity is considered to be resident in the country of effective management.

(14) Withholding tax is a tax deducted at source from a payment before it is made to the recipient. Underlying tax is the tax on the profits out of which a dividend is paid.

(15) Indexation allowance is a relief given on the disposal of capital assets. The relief is based on the movement of RPIs between the date costs were incurred on the asset and the disposal date and represents relief for inflation. The indexation allowance will reduce the amount of gain charged for tax purposes.

(16) Taxable profit = $100,000 + $10,000 + $15,000 – $9,000 = $116,000

(17) Chargeable gain = $40,000 – $15,000 – $2,000 – $5,000 = $18,000

(18) Chargeable gains are created when assets are sold at a profit. They are calculated based on the difference between proceeds and allowable costs. Capital taxes represent the tax charged on the chargeable gains.

(19) True. Balancing charges represent the tax profit on disposal of an asset for corporate tax purposes. They are calculated on the difference between proceeds and tax written down value. The balance charge will increase the taxable profits.

chapter

2

Accounting for Investments in Subsidiaries and Associates

Chapter learning objectives

On completion of their studies students should be able to:

- Explain the relationships between investors and investees and the meaning of control and significant influence.
- Identify the circumstances in which a subsidiary is excluded from consolidation.

1 Introduction

This chapter introduces the appropriate accounting for investments in other entities. The extent of the investment will often determine the appropriate accounting treatment, and this chapter examines the investments that will be accounted for as:

- Basic investments
- Investments in associates
- Investments in subsidiaries

2 Accounting for investments

Entities will often invest in the equity of other businesses. The extent of the equity shareholding will determine how the investment should be accounted for. The accounting treatment applied for investments is intended to reflect the importance of the investment in the financial statements of the investing entity and how the future performance and financial position might be affected by these investments. It follows then that the greater the level of investment, the more detailed the financial information will be. A significant investment in another entity may require additional financial statements to be produced.

When an entity buys shares in another entity by making a cash payment, the investing entity will normally account for the investment as follows:

Dr Investment
Cr Cash.

This investment will be included in the non-current asset section of the parent's statement of financial position (see later in chapter 3).

If the investment has not been acquired for cash, it may be acquired as a result of a share exchange, which would be accounted for as follows:

Dr Investment (fair value of the cost of the investment

Cr Issued share capital (nominal value of shares issued)

Cr Share premium (difference between the fair value of the cost of the investment and the nominal value of shares issued).

Investment in associates

An investor who has significant influence over another entity would treat that investment as an associate and would account for it in accordance with IAS 28 Investments in Associates and Joint Ventures. IAS 28 states that there is a presumption that the investor has significant influence over the entity where it holds, directly or indirectly, between twenty per cent and fifty per cent of the voting rights, unless it can be clearly demonstrated that this is not the case.

The key concept in the definition is 'significant influence'. IAS 28 explains that significant influence is the power to participate in the financial and operating policy decisions of the entity but is not control over those policies. The existence of significant influence by an investor is usually evidenced in one or more of the following ways:

- representation on the board of directors
- participation in policy-making processes
- material transactions between the investor and the entity
- interchange of managerial personnel
- provision of essential technical information

The impact of this level of investment on the investing entity is likely to be greater than that of a simple investment. There is greater exposure to the results of the associate and a decline in its value will have a greater negative impact on the statement of financial position of the investing entity. The information provided therefore is a step further than that provided for simple investments.

The investment in the associate is equity accounted, (see later in chapter 5 for more detail on equity accounting), and the investment shown in the statement of financial position will include the investing entity's share of the gains of the associate from the date the investment was made. The investing entity will show the share of realised and recognised gains it is entitled to by virtue of this investment rather than just the dividend received.

Investment in subsidiaries

It is often the case that businesses conduct part of their operations by making investments in other business entities. For example, a business that aims to expand its market share could opt to purchase one or more of its competitors, rather than taking the slower route of building market share by gradual growth. Another example is where a business purchases an investment in one or more of its suppliers of key goods and services in order to integrate and secure its supply chain.

In order to fulfil the needs of investors and other users, additional information is likely to be required, and therefore the IASB has in issue several accounting standards setting out the principles and practices that must be followed where an investment comprises a significant proportion (usually a majority) of the total equity of the investee entity.

3 The principle of control

This chapter will start to examine the accounting requirements of IFRS relating to investments in subsidiaries. The accounting standard that sets out the requirements for recognition of an entity as a subsidiary is IFRS 10 Consolidated Financial Statements. This standard was issued in May 2011, but its basic principles have been part of IFRS for many years.

First, some relevant definitions taken from the standard:

A **parent** is an entity that has one or more subsidiaries.

A **subsidiary** is an entity, including an unincorporated entity such as a partnership, which is controlled by another entity (known as the parent).

The key concept in determining whether or not an investment constitutes a subsidiary is that of **control.**

IFRS 10 Consolidated Financial Statements sets out a new definition of control and gives guidance on how to determine whether or not a control relationship exists between two entities.

An investor (the parent) controls an investee (the subsidiary) when the investor is exposed, or has rights, to variable returns from its involvement with the investee and has the ability to affect those returns through its power over the investee.

Power is defined as existing rights that give the investor the ability to direct the relevant activities.

In accordance with IFRS 10, an investor controls an investee if and only if the investor has all of the following elements:

- power over the investee (see definition of power above)
- exposure, or rights, to variable returns from its involvement with the investee and
- the ability to use its power over the investee to affect the amount of the investor's returns.

Consolidated financial statements should be prepared when the parent has control over the subsidiary (for assessment purposes control is usually established based on ownership of more than 50% of the voting rights).

There may be situations when an investor has 50% or less of the voting rights of the investee, and may still have control of that entity. Consider the situation if the largest investor P held 47% of the issued share capital and voting rights of another entity S. Normally, this would not be regarded as sufficient to demonstrate a control relationship between the two entities. However, if all of the other shareholders in S were independent of each other and no individual shareholder held more than 1% of the voting rights, then it may be that P is able to comply with the three elements required to demonstrate control of S. Consequently, P would then account for S as a subsidiary and prepare group accounts.

Note that this accounting treatment decision involves the exercise of judgement. It is not necessarily a simple 'yes' or 'no' answer to determine whether one entity has control of another. Note also that an entity should consider at each reporting date whether it still retains control of the other entity, or whether control has been lost, so that the accounting treatment in the group accounts fairly reflects the current commercial reality of the relationship.

4 The requirements to prepare consolidated financial statements

IFRS 10 Consolidated Financial Statements

Where a parent/subsidiary relationship exists, IFRS 10 requires that the parent should prepare consolidated financial statements. It is important to realise from the outset that this is an additional set of financial statements. The parent and subsidiary continue to prepare their own financial statements. Therefore in a group comprising one parent and one subsidiary, a total of three sets of financial statements are required. Where a group comprises, say, the parent and four subsidiaries, a total of six sets of financial statements are required: one for the parent, one for each of the four subsidiaries and one set of consolidated financial statements.

Exclusion from preparing consolidated accounts

A full set of financial statements in addition to those already prepared is, of course, quite an onerous requirement. Therefore, IFRS 10 includes some exemptions as follows:

A parent need not present consolidated financial statements if and only if all four of the following conditions are satisfied:

(a) The parent is itself a wholly owned subsidiary, or is a partially-owned subsidiary of another entity and its other owners, including those not otherwise entitled to vote, have been informed about, and do not object to, the parent not presenting consolidated financial statements.

(b) The parent's debt or equity instruments are not traded in a public market (a domestic or foreign stock exchange or an over-the-counter market, including local and regional markets).

(c) The parent did not file, nor is it in the process of filing, its financial statements with a securities commission or other regulatory organisation for the purpose of issuing any class of instruments in a public market.

(d) The ultimate or any intermediate parent of the parent produces consolidated financial statements available for public use that comply with IFRS and are available for public use.

IAS 27 Separate Financial Statements

IAS 27 was amended in May 2011 to deal only with single entity financial statements of the parent entity. The group accounting or consolidated accounts provisions are now contained in IFRS 10.

Goodwill

When a controlling investment is made the parent is investing in the net assets of the subsidiary. The value of the assets presented on the statement of financial position is unlikely to be what is paid by the investing entity.

Usually, the owners of a profitable business will expect to receive more in exchange for the investment than its net asset value. This additional amount arises for various reasons. It is quite likely that the assets recognised in the statement of financial position do not represent all the assets of the entity acquired and intangibles such as good reputation and customer loyalty may be worth something to the purchaser. The difference between the cost of investment and the fair value of the net assets acquired is known as goodwill on acquisition, and accounting standard IFRS 3 Business Combinations requires its recognition in consolidated financial statements.

IFRS 3 Business Combinations

IFRS 3 was originally issued in March 2004 replacing an earlier standard. However, it was just the first stage in a longer term IASB project on accounting for business combinations. The next stage culminated in the issue, in January 2008, of a revised edition of IFRS 3.

IFRS 3 requires that entities should account for business combinations by applying the acquisition method of accounting. The following two chapters will concentrate on the acquisition method of accounting and the production of consolidated financial statements.

chapter

3

Consolidated Statement of Financial Position

Chapter learning objectives

On completion of their studies students should be able to:

- Prepare the consolidated statement of financial position for a group of companies.
- Explain the treatment in the consolidated statement of financial position for pre and post-acquisition reserves, goodwill (including its impairment), unrealised profit and intra-group transactions.
- Prepare non-controlling interests and goodwill calculations using both the proportion of net assets method and fair value method.
- Adjust for mid-year acquisitions.

1 Session content

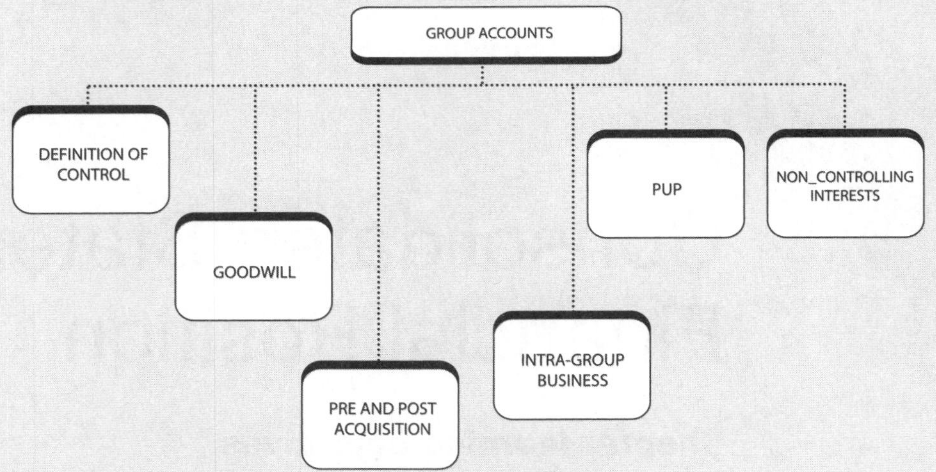

2 What is a Group?

IFRS 10 Consolidated Financial Statements

A group will exist where one entity **controls** another entity.

Control is the power to govern the financial and operating policies so as to obtain benefits from its activities.

Control is normally achieved by the parent company owning more than 50% of the voting rights of the subsidiary.

Non-controlling interest (NCI) shareholders own the shares in the subsidiary not owned by the parent entity.

NCI shareholders are considered to be shareholders of the group and thus their shareholding is reflected with the equity of the group.

Legally, the parent and subsidiary are separate entities and separate financial statements must be prepared.

However, in substance, the parent and subsidiary can be viewed as a single entity, known as the group.

Group financial statements are prepared to reflect the substance of the situation. They are referred to as consolidated financial statements and are prepared in addition to single entity financial statements.

Further details on the definition of a group

Although from a legal point of view every entity is a separate entity, from an economic point of view several entities can come together to form a group.

In particular, when one entity owns enough shares in another entity to have a majority of votes at that entity's annual general meeting (AGM), the first entity may appoint all the directors of, and decide what dividends should be paid by, the second entity.

This degree of control enables the first entity to manage the trading activities and future plans of the second entity as if it were merely a department of the first entity.

The first entity referred to above is called the parent, and the second is called a subsidiary. For the moment, it is sufficient to note that the essential feature of a group is that one entity controls all the others.

International Financial Reporting Standards recognise that this state of affairs often arises, and require a parent entity to produce consolidated financial statements showing the position and results of the whole group.

3 Acquisition accounting

IFRS 3 requires acquisition accounting (the purchase method) to be used to prepare consolidated financial statements.

This requires the following rules to be followed:

- Add 100% of the parent's and subsidiary's assets, liabilities, income and expenses.
- The investment in the parent's books is not included in the consolidated statement of financial position because it is effectively eliminated as a result of including the subsidiary's net assets and calculating goodwill.
- Goodwill is calculated at acquisition as the difference between the sum of the fair value of the investment in the subsidiary plus a value for non-controlling interest and the fair value of the net assets acquired.
- The balance for non-controlling interest will need to be calculated and included in the consolidated financial statements. Rationale for this being that although the parent controls 100% of the subsidiary's net assets, it may not own 100% of the subsidiary's net assets. The non-controlling interest adjustment reflects ownership.
- The share capital of the group is always only the share capital of the parent.

- Adjustments are made to record the subsidiary's net assets at fair value.
- Uniform accounting policies must be used.
- Intra-group balances and transactions must be eliminated in full.
- Profits/losses on intra-group transactions that are recognised in assets should be eliminated in full (the provision for unrealised profit adjustment – PUP adjustment).

A standard approach to preparing consolidated financial statements is adopted within the manual in order to aid the learning process. However, assessment on this will be largely in the form of OTQ's which will only test one or two principles at a time. You will not be expected to prepare consolidated financial statements in totality. It is therefore important you understand the accounting entries behind the workings and adjustments.

Standard consolidated statement of financial position (CSFP) workings

(W1) **Group structure**

Parent
|
% |
|
Subsidiary

(W2) **Net assets of subsidiary**

	Acquisition Date	**Reporting Date**
Share capital	X	X
Retained earnings	X	X
Other reserves	X	X
	X	X

(W3) **Goodwill**

Fair value of parent's investment	X
Value of NCI at acquisition	X
Fair value of sub's net assets (NAs) acquired (W2)	(X)
Goodwill at acquisition	X
Impairment	(X)
Goodwill at reporting date	X

Fair value adjustments are not assessed until students study F2. Therefore students should always assume the value of the subsidiaries net assets acquired are already at fair value

(W4) **Non-controlling interests (NCI)**

Value of NCI at acquisition (as per W3)	X
NCI % × post-acquisition reserves (W2)	X
NCI % × impairment (W3) (fair value method only)	(X)
NCI at reporting date	X

(W5) **Retained earnings**

Parent	X
Sub (% × post-acq reserves)	X
Impairment of goodwill	(X)
	X

Illustration 1 – Simple groups

Statements of financial position at 31 December 20X0

	P	S
	$000	$000
Non-current assets		
Property, plant and equipment	1,000	600
Investment in S	900	–
Current assets	200	200
	2,100	800
Equity		
Share capital	1,000	500
Retained earnings	800	200
Current liabilities	300	100
	2,100	800

P acquires 100% of S on 31 December 20X0.

Required:

Prepare a consolidated statement of financial position (CSFP) at 31 December 20X0.

Solution

Firstly, draw up the group structure to understand what the relationship is between the entities. This is a good habit to form as it will be very useful when the group becomes more complex.

(W1) **Group structure**

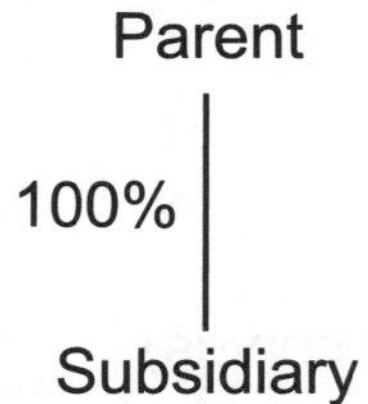

The next task is to add across the parent and subsidiary's assets and liabilities in the consolidated statement of financial position.

The share capital and share premium of the group is only ever the share capital and premium of the parent.

The parent's investment in the subsidiary is ignored in the consolidated statement of financial position because the investment in the subsidiary is cancelled against the share of net assets acquired and the excess is calculated as goodwill.

This is a 100% subsidiary and therefore there is no NCI. However, NCI is included below at a value of nil to show you it's position writhing the CSFP.

Consolidated statement of financial position as at 31 December 20X0

		$000
Non-current assets		
Goodwill	(W3)	
Property, plant and equipment	(1,000 + 600)	1,600
Current assets	(200 + 200)	400
Equity		
Share capital		1,000
Retained earnings	(W5)	
Non-controlling interest	(W4)	0
Current liabilities	(300 + 100)	400

Then we can continue with the standard workings (W2) to (W5) to complete the remainder within the CSFP.

(W2) **Net assets of subsidiary**

	Acquisition date	Reporting date
	$000	$000
Share capital	500	500
Retained earnings	200	200
	700	700

The purpose of W2 is to establish the net assets of the subsidiary at acquisition in order to calculate the goodwill amount in W3 and to identify the post-acquisition profit that belongs to the group in W5.

In this case the acquisition date was 31 December 20X0 which was the same as the reporting date so the columns include the same figures. The share capital and retained earnings are taken from the subsidiary's individual statement of financial position (SFP).

The accounting equation states that net assets = share capital + reserves.

The totals from the two columns are then used in subsequent workings.

(W3) **Goodwill**

	$000
Fair value of the investment	900
Fair value of net assets (NAs) acquired (100% × 700) (W2)	(700)
Goodwill at reporting date	200

The fair value of the investment is taken directly from the parent's statement of financial position in this case. The amount paid by the parent may alternatively be given to you as a separate figure.

(W4) **Non-controlling interests**

Not applicable because the parent owns 100% of the subsidiary's shares.

(W5) **Retained earnings**

	$000
Parent	800
Subsidiary (100% × post acq profits)	–
Impairment	–
	800

Working 5 includes the parent's share of the subsidiary's post acquisition profits. Because S was acquired on the reporting date there are no post acquisition profits to include.

Now we can take the figures for goodwill and group retained earnings onto the CSFP to complete the requirement.

Consolidated statement of financial position as at 31 December 20X0

		$000
Non-current assets		
Goodwill	(W3)	200
Property, plant and equipment	(1,000 + 600)	1,600
Current assets	(200 + 200)	400
		2,200
Equity		
Share capital		1,000
Retained earnings	(W5)	800
Non-controlling interest	(W4)	0
Current liabilities	(300 + 100)	400
		2,200

4 Goodwill

As mentioned in the previous section, goodwill is treated in accordance with IFRS 3 (revised) Business Combinations.

The parent may pay more than the value of the entity's net assets because of:

- the entity's positive reputation
- a loyal customer base or
- staff expertise, etc.

This excess is called goodwill and is capitalised on the consolidated statement of financial position (CSFP). It is subject to an annual impairment review to ensure its value has not fallen below the carrying value.

Occasionally the parent company may pay less than the value of the subsidiary's net assets. This may occur because a quick purchase is necessary. In this rare situation the "negative goodwill", or discount on acquisition, is credited to group retained earnings (to increase group profits).

IFRS 3 allows two methods to be used to calculate the value of NCI's holding at the date of acquisition:

- Fair value
- Proportion of net assets

IFRS 3 permits groups to choose how to value NCI on an acquisition by acquisition basis. In other words, it is possible for a group to apply the fair value method for some subsidiaries and the proportion of net assets method for other subsidiaries. An OT question will state which method is to be used.

Fair value method

The fair value of the NCI's interests may be calculated using the market value of the subsidiary's shares at the date of acquisition or other valuation techniques if the subsidiary's shares are not traded in an active market. You will be given the fair value of the NCI in the assessment if you are asked to use this method.

Proportion of net assets method

Under this method, the NCI's holding is measured by calculating their share of the fair value of the subsidiary's net assets at acquisition (W2).

Illustration 2 – Simple groups 2

Statements of financial position at 31 March 20X1

	P	S
	$000	$000
Non-current assets		
Property, plant and equipment	1,650	750
Investment in S	1,100	–
Current assets	250	650
	3,000	1,400
Equity		
Share capital	1,500	500
Retained earnings	900	400
Current liabilities	600	500
	3,000	1,400

P acquires 80% of S on 31 March 20X1.

NCI should be valued using proportion of net assets method.

Required:

Prepare a consolidated statement of financial position (CSFP) at 31 March 20X1.

Solution

Consolidated statement of financial position as at 31 March 20X1

		$000
Non-current assets		
Goodwill	(W3)	380
Property, plant and equipment	(1,650 + 750)	2,400
Current assets	(250 + 650)	900
		3,680
Equity		
Share capital		1,500
Retained earnings	(W5)	900
Non-controlling interest	(W4)	180
Current liabilities	(600 + 500)	1,100
		3,680

Workings

(W1) **Group structure**

The parent owns 80% of the issued shares of the subsidiary

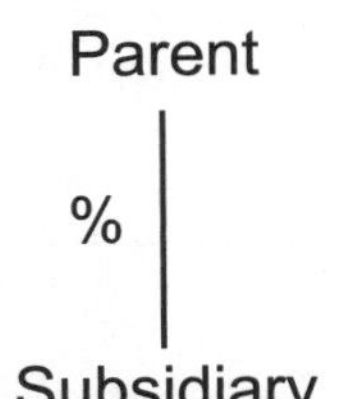

(W2) **Net assets of subsidiary**

	Acquisition date	**Reporting date**
	$000	$000
Share capital	500	500
Retained earnings	400	400
	900	900

In this case the acquisition date was 31 March 20X1 which was the same as the reporting date so the columns include the same figures. Therefore, there are no post-acquisition profits.

(W3) **Goodwill**

	$000
Fair value of investment	1,100
Value of NCI at acquisition (20% × 900) (W2)	180
Fair value of net assets (NAs) acquired (100% × 900) (W2)	(900)
Goodwill at reporting date	380

The fair value of the net assets acquired will always be 100% because this is being compared against the fair value of the investment and the NCI value at acquisition.

(W4) **Non-controlling interests**

	$000
Value of NCI at acquisition (as per W3)	180
NCI × post-acquisition reserves (W2)	–
NCI × impairment (W3) (fair value method only)	–
NCI at reporting date	180

(W5) **Retained earnings**

	$000
Parent	900
Subsidiary (80% × post acq profits)	–
Impairment	–
	900

Illustration 3 – Simple groups 3

Using the information from the previous question show how the answer would change if the fair value method was used for valuation of NCI at acquisition.

You should assume NCI was valued at fair value at acquisition at $200,000.

Solution

Consolidated statement of financial position as at 31 March 20X1

		$000
Non-current assets		
Goodwill	(W3)	400
Property, plant and equipment	(1,650 + 750)	2,400
Current assets	(250 + 650)	900
		3,700
Equity		
Share capital		1,500
Retained earnings	(W5)	900
Non-controlling interest	(W4)	200
Current liabilities	(600 + 500)	1,100
		3,700

Workings

(W1) **Group structure**

The parent owns 80% of the issued shares of the subsidiary.

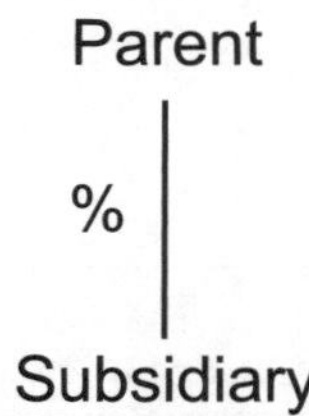

(W2) **Net assets of subsidiary**

	Acquisition date	**Reporting date**
	$000	$000
Share capital	500	500
Retained earnings	400	400
	900	900

In this case the acquisition date was 31 March 20X1 which was the same as the reporting date so the columns include the same figures. Therefore, there are no post-acquisition profits.

(W3) **Goodwill**

	$000
Fair value of investment	1,100
Value of NCI at acquisition (given in the question)	200
Fair value of net assets (NAs) acquired (100% × 900) (W2)	(900)
Goodwill at reporting date	400

(W4) **Non-controlling interests**

	$000
Value of NCI at acquisition (as per question)	200
NCI × post-acquisition reserves (W2)	–
NCI × impairment (W3) (fair value method only)	–
NCI at reporting date	200

(W5) **Retained earnings**

	$000
Parent	900
Subsidiary (80% × post acq profits)	–
Impairment	–
	900

5 Pre and post-acquisition

In illustrations 1 to 3 the parent acquired its shares in the subsidiary on the reporting date. In the case where the parent made the purchase some months or years prior to the reporting date, the subsidiary's reserves must be split out into pre and post-acquisition reserves.

The parent has influenced any change in reserves since the acquisition date only, e.g. the parent can only share in the change in asset value after acquisition. Any changes before this date would have been due to the influence of the previous parent.

e.g

Illustration 4 – Pre and post-acquisition reserves

Statements of financial position at 31 December 20X0

	P	S
	$000	$000
Non-current assets		
Property, plant and equipment	3,330	550
Investment in S	1,540	–
Current assets	1,030	660
	5,900	1,210
Equity		
Ordinary share capital	2,500	525
Retained earnings	3,000	585
Current liabilities	400	100
	5,900	1,210

P acquired 80% of S one year ago on 1 January 20X0 when the balance on the retained earnings of S stood at $505,000.

NCI should be calculated using the proportion of net assets method.

Required:

Prepare the consolidated statement of financial position (CSFP) at 31 December 20X0.

Solution

Firstly, draw up the group structure to understand what the relationship is between the entities.

(W1) **Group structure**

The parent owns 80% of the issued shares of the subsidiary.

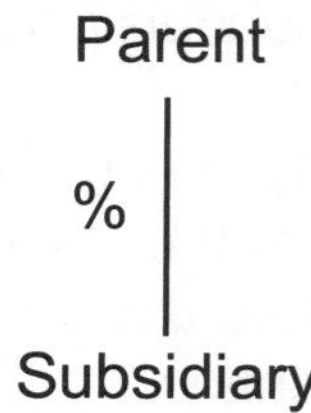

The next task is to add across the parent's and subsidiary's assets and liabilities in the consolidated statement of financial position. The share capital of the group is always only the share capital of the parent.

Note: Use the statement of financial position in the question as a starting point but insert a row below non-current assets for goodwill and ignore the parent's investment in the subsidiary.

The parent's investment in the subsidiary is ignored in the CSFP because the investment in the subsidiary is cancelled against the share of net assets acquired and the excess is calculated as goodwill.

Consolidated statement of financial position as at 31 December 20X0		$000
Non-current assets		
Goodwill	(W3)	
Property, plant and equipment	(3,330 + 550)	3,880
Current assets	(1,030 + 660)	1,690

Equity		
Share capital		2,500
Retained earnings	(W5)	
Non-controlling interest	(W4)	
Current liabilities	(400 + 100)	500
		——
		——

Then we can continue with the standard workings (W2) to (W5) to complete the remainder of the CSFP.

(W2) **Net assets of subsidiary**

	Acquisition date	**Reporting date**
	$000	$000
Share capital	525	525
Retained earnings	505	585
	——	——
	1,030	1,110
	——	——

The subsidiary's retained earnings at the acquisition date will be given to you in the question.

Share capital of the subsidiary will not change from acquisition to reporting date so you can copy the share capital from the subsidiary's SFP to W2 in both columns.

The totals from the two columns are then used in subsequent workings.

(W3) **Goodwill**

	$000
Fair value of investment	1,540
Value of NCI at acquisition (20% × 1030) (W2)	206
Fair value of net assets (NAs) acquired (100% × 1,030) (W2)	(1,030)
	——
Goodwill at acquisition	716
	——

The fair value of the investment is taken from the parent's SFP. The fair value of net assets acquired must be taken from the **acquisition date** column of (W2).

(W4) **Non-controlling interests**

	$000
Value of NCI at acquisition (as per W3)	206
NCI × post-acquisition reserves 20% × (1,110 – 1,030) (W2)	16
NCI × impairment (W3) (fair value method only)	–
NCI at reporting date	222

(W5) **Retained earnings**

	$000
Parent	3,000
Subsidiary (% × post acquisition profits)	
80% × (1,110 – 1,030) (W2)	64
Impairment (W3)	–
	3,064

The parent is responsible for its share of the subsidiary's post acquisition profits only. The parent's percentage holding is multiplied by the **change** in net assets from (W2), i.e. the difference between the totals in each column.

Now we can take the figures for goodwill, NCI and group retained earnings onto the CSFP to complete the requirement.

Consolidated statement of financial position as at 31 December 20X0

		$000
Non-current assets		
Goodwill	(W3)	716
Property, plant and equipment	(3,330 + 550)	3,880
Current assets	(1,030 + 660)	1,690
		6,286

Equity		
Share capital		2,500
Retained earnings	(W5)	3,064
Non-controlling interest	(W4)	222
Current liabilities	(400 + 100)	500
		6,286

6 Impairment

IFRS 3 requires that goodwill is tested at each reporting date for impairment. This means that goodwill is reviewed to ensure that its value is not overstated in the consolidated statement of financial position.

In the exam you will either be told the amount of the impairment loss or you will be told to calculate it as a percentage of the goodwill. You will not be required to calculate the impairment loss by carrying out an impairment review.

If an impairment loss exists, goodwill is written down and the loss is charged against profits in the consolidated statement of profit or loss (see next chapter for more detail).

The charge against profits will result in a reduction in the equity section of the CSFP. How the impairment loss is charged against equity in the CSFP will depend on the method adopted by the entity for valuing NCI, or in other words, the method used to calculate goodwill.

Fair value method

When valuing NCI at the fair value method we should record the impairment loss by:

- Reduce goodwill (W3) by the full impairment loss (Cr goodwill)
- Reduce NCI (W4) by the NCI % of the impairment loss (Dr NCI)
- Reduced retained earnings for the group (W5) by the parent's % of the impairment loss (Dr RE)

Proportion of net assets method

When valuing NCI at the proportion of net assets method we should record the impairment loss by:

- Reduce goodwill (W3) by the full impairment loss (Cr goodwill)
- Reduced retained earnings for the group (W5) by the full impairment loss (Dr RE)

Illustration 5 – Impairment

Using the information from illustration 4, now assume impairment of $120,000 at the year end.

Required:

(a) Prepare (W3) to (W5) using the proportion of net assets method.

(b) Prepare (W3) to (W5) using the fair value method assuming NCI was valued at fair value of $220,000 at acquisition.

Solution

(a) **Proportion of net assets method**

(W3) **Goodwill**

	$000
Fair value of investment	1,540
Value of NCI at acquisition (20% × 1030) (W2)	206
Fair value of net assets (NAs) acquired (100% × 1,030) (W2)	(1,030)
Impairment	(120)
Goodwill at acquisition	596

(W4) **Non-controlling interests**

	$000
Value of NCI at acquisition (as per W3)	206
NCI × post-acquisition reserves 20% × (1,110 – 1,030) (W2)	16
NCI × impairment (W3) (fair value method only)	–
NCI at reporting date	222

(W5) **Retained earnings**

	$000
Parent	3,000
Subsidiary (% × post acquisition profits) 80% × (1,110 – 1,030) (W2)	64
Impairment (W3)	(120)
	2944

(b) **Fair value method**

(W3) **Goodwill**

	$000
Fair value of investment	1,540
Value of NCI at acquisition (given in question)	220
Fair value of net assets (NAs) acquired (100% × 1,030) (W2)	(1,030)
Impairment	(120)
Goodwill at acquisition	610

(W4) **Non-controlling interests**

	$000
Value of NCI at acquisition (as per W3)	220
NCI × post-acquisition reserves 20% × (1,110 – 1,030) (W2)	16
NCI × impairment (W3) (20% × 120)	(24)
NCI at reporting date	212

(W5) **Retained earnings**

	$000
Parent	3,000
Subsidiary (% × post acquisition profits)	
80% × (1,110 – 1,030) (W2)	64
Impairment (W3) (80% × 120)	(96)
	2,968

Note: When using the fair value method of calculating NCI the impairment of goodwill must be **pro-rated** between the NCI and group retained earnings based on ownership, whereas the proportion of net asset methods takes the **whole** impairment loss to group retained earnings.

Test your understanding 1 – Pre and post-acquisition reserves

Statements of financial position at 31 May 20X3

	P	S
	$000	$000
Non-current assets		
Property, plant and equipment	2,300	400
Investment in S	1,000	
Current assets	900	500
	4,200	900
Equity		
Share capital	1,000	475
Retained earnings	2,750	275
Current liabilities	450	150
	4,200	900

P acquired 75% of S two years ago on 1 June 20X1 when the balance on the retained earnings of S stood at $125,000. Goodwill should be written down to 75% of its original value to allow for impairment and NCI to be valued using the fair value method. The fair value of NCI at acquisition is $180,000.

Required:

Prepare the consolidated statement of financial position (CSFP) at 31 May 20X3.

Test your understanding 2 – Pre and post-acquisition reserves

The following summarised statements of financial position are provided for Kemp and Solent as at 31 December 20X9

	Kemp	**Solent**
	$000	$000
Non-current assets		
Property, plant and equipment	2,000	500
Investment in Solent	1,900	
Current assets	200	800
	4,100	1,300
Equity		
Share capital ($1 ordinary)	3,000	300
Retained earnings	1,000	900
Current liabilities	100	100
	4,100	1,300

Kemp purchased 225,000 shares in Solent on 1 January 20X8 for $1.9m when Solent's retained earnings were $750,000. Goodwill should be impaired by $193,000 at 31 December 20X9.

NCI should be valued using the proportion of net assets method.

Required:

Prepare the consolidated statement of financial position (CSFP) at 31 December 20X9.

7 Intra-group balances

Intra-group balances must be eliminated in full. The group is viewed as a single entity, cannot owe or be owed balances to itself, e.g. the parent may have a receivable due from the subsidiary and the subsidiary may have a payable owed to the parent. This is fine in the individual accounts but must be eliminated on consolidation.

Intra-group balances may arise in the following situations:

- P and S trading with each other, resulting in current account balances, i.e. receivables and payables
- Intra-group loans, resulting in an investment and loan balance

These are amounts owing within the group rather than outside the group and, therefore, must not appear in the consolidated statement of financial position.

They are, therefore, cancelled off against each other on consolidation:

- Reduce receivables/investment
- Reduce payables/loan

Current account balances may disagree. This is most likely to be due to cash in transit or goods in transit between the parent and the subsidiary.

Cash in transit

Cash has been sent by one group entity, but has not been received and so is not recorded in the books of the other group entity. The following journal entry will be required in order to record the cash in transit:

Dr Bank

Cr Receivables current account

You may find it easier to remember the following:

Increase Bank (cash in transit)

Reduce Receivables (amount in the seller's books)

Goods in transit

Goods have been sent by one entity, but have not been received and so are not recorded in the books of the other group entity.

The following journal entry will be required in order to record the goods in transit:

Dr	Inventory
Cr	Payables current account
Increase	Inventory (goods in transit)
Increase	Payables (amount in the buyer's books)

These adjustments are for the purpose of consolidation only.

Once these adjustments have been made, the current account balances should agree and can be removed from both the receivables and payables in the consolidated statement of financial position.

e.g

Illustration 6 – Intra-group balances

The following extracts are provided from the statements of financial position of P and S at the year-end:

	P	S
	$000	$000
Current assets		
Inventory	100	50
Receivables	270	80
Cash and cash equivalents	120	40
Current liabilities		
Payables	160	90

P's statement of financial position includes a receivable of $40,000 being due from S. S has a payables balance of $30,000 due to P.

Shortly before the year-end, S sent a cheque for $4,000 to P. P did not receive this cheque until after the year-end. Also, P had dispatched goods to S with a value of $6,000 but S had not received them by the year-end.

Required:

What balances will be shown in the consolidated statement of financial position (CSFP) of the P group for the above items?

Solution

Consolidated statement of financial position (extract)

		$000
Current assets		
Inventory	(100 + 50 + 6)	156
Receivables	(270 + 80 – 4 – 36)	310
Cash and cash equivalents	(120 + 40 + 4)	164
Current liabilities		
Payables	(160 + 90 + 6 – 36)	220

Start by adding across P and S's assets and liabilities for the consolidated statement of financial position.

For the cash in transit, neither entity is recording the cash so this needs to be amended, i.e. add $4,000 to cash and reduce receivables by $4,000.

			$000
Dr	Bank	↑	4
Cr	Receivables	↓	4

The goods in transit have also not been recorded in the receiving entity's books. The $6,000 must be added to both inventory and payables to record the transaction.

			$000
Dr	Inventory	↑	6
Cr	Payables	↑	6

The inter-company balance will now agree at $36,000. The original receivables balance of $40,000 has been reduced by $4,000 in the journal entry above to a new balance of $36,000 and the original payables balance of $30,000 has been increased by $6,000 in the journal entry above to a new balance of $36,000.

Test your understanding 3 – Intra-group balances

The following statements of financial position exist at the 31 December 20X0.

	P	S
	$000	$000
Non-current assets		
Property, plant and equipment	5,400	2,000
Investment in S	3,700	
Current assets		
Inventory	750	140
Receivables	650	95
Cash and cash equivalents	400	85
	10,900	2,320
Equity		
Share capital	7,000	1,400
Share premium	1,950	280
Retained earnings	1,050	440
Current liabilities	900	200
	10,900	2,320

P acquired 60% of S five years ago when the balance on the retained earnings of S was $300,000. Any goodwill arising is now thought to be worth 2/3 of its original value. The share premium in S arose on the issue of its ordinary shares many years ago.

P and S traded with each other and at the reporting date P owed S an amount of $25,000. On 30 December 20X0 P sent a cheque for $5,000 to S which S had not received by year end.

NCI should be valued using the proportion of net assets method.

Required:

Prepare a consolidated statement of financial position (CSFP) as at 31 December 20X0.

8 Provisions for Unrealised Profits (PUPs)

P and S may sell goods to each other, resulting in a profit being recorded in the selling entity's financial statements. If these goods are still held by the purchasing entity at the year-end, the goods have not been sold outside of the group. The profit is therefore unrealised from the group's perspective and should be removed.

The adjustment is also required to ensure that inventory is stated at the cost to the group.

The following journal entry will be required in order to record the unrealised profit if the **parent sells** (profit in the books of the parent, hence no impact on NCI):

Dr Retained earnings of the parent within the group retained earnings

Cr Inventory

You may find it easier to remember the following:

Reduce (W5)

Reduce Inventory on the face of the CSFP

The following journal entry will be required in order to record the unrealised profit if the **subsidiary sells** (profit in the books of the subsidiary, hence will impact on NCI):

Dr Post acquisition reserves of the subsidiary within the group retained earnings (this should be the groups share of the PUP)

Dr Post acquisition reserves of the subsidiary within the NCI (this should be the NCI share of the PUP)

Cr Inventory

You may find it easier to remember the following:

Reduce (W2) at the reporting date which leads into (W4) and (W5)

Reduce Inventory on the face of the CSFP

Illustration 7 – PUPs

Parent sells to subsidiary

P sells goods to S for $400 at cost plus 25%. All goods remain in the inventory of S at the end of the year. P owns 80% of S.

Profit made on the sale $\frac{25}{125} \times 400 = 80.$

Individual FS

P records profit	80
S records inventory	400

Group financial statements should show the cost to the group

Profit	0
Inventory	320

PUP adjustment

Dr Group profit reserves (W5)	↓	80
Cr Group inventory (CSFP)	↓	80

The group profit figure for the parent will be reduced as it is the parent that recorded the profit in this case.

It is important to note that the adjustment takes place in the group accounts only. The individual accounts are correct as they stand and will not be adjusted as a result.

Subsidiary sells to parent

Individual FS

S records profit	80
P records inventory	400

PUP adjustment

Dr Group profit reserves (80% × 80) (W5)	↓ 64
Dr NCI (20% × 80) (W4)	↓ 16
Cr Group inventory (CSFP)	↓ 80

The subsidiary's profit will be reduced as it is the subsidiary that recorded the profit in this case. It is important that the adjustment is made in W2 as the amended figures then flow through to the remaining standard workings.

The distinction between making the adjustment in W2 or W5 is important for when the parent does not own 100% of the subsidiary.

Cost structures

The cost structure of the intra-group sale may be given to you in one of two ways.

Mark up on cost

The mark up on cost gives the profit as a percentage of cost. If, for example, goods are sold for $440 and there is a 25% mark up on cost, you need to calculate the profit included within the $440.

	%	$	
Revenue	125	440	
Cost of sales	100		
Gross profit	25	88	= 440 × 25/125

The PUP is $88.

Gross profit margin

The gross profit margin gives the profit as a percentage of revenue. Using the same figures as above but with a gross profit margin of 25%.

	%	$	
Revenue	100	440	
Cost of sales	75		
Gross profit	25	110	= 440 × 25/100

The PUP is $110.

Test your understanding 4 – PUPs

P sells goods to S for $522 at a mark-up of 20%. 40% of these goods were sold on by S to external parties by the year end. P owns 75% of S.

Required:

What is the PUP adjustment in the consolidated financial statements?

Test your understanding 5 – PUPs

S sells goods to P at a margin of 20%. The selling price is $360. All goods remained unsold at the year end. P owns 75% of S.

Required:

What is the PUP adjustment in the consolidated financial statements?

Illustration 8 – PUPs

The following statements of financial position exist at 30 June 20X1:

	P	S
	$000	$000
Non-current assets		
Property, plant and equipment	4,000	2,000
Investment in S	3,400	
Current assets		
Inventory	500	100
Other current assets	100	300
	8,000	2,400
Equity		
Share capital	6,000	1,500
Retained earnings	1,600	700
Current liabilities	400	200
	8,000	2,400

P acquired 80% of S when the balance on S's retained earnings stood at $250,000.

During the year, P sold goods to S for $120,000 at a mark-up of 20%. Half of these goods remain in inventory at the year end.

NCI should be valued using the fair value method. NCI was valued at acquisition at $330,000.

Required:

Prepare the consolidated statement of financial position (CSFP) of the P group as at 30 June 20X1.

Solution

Consolidated statement of financial position as at 30 June 20X1

		$000
Non-current assets		
Goodwill	(W3)	1,980
Property, plant and equipment	(4,000 + 2,000)	6,000
Current assets		
Inventory	(500 + 100 − 10) (W6)	590
Other current assets	(100 + 300)	400
		8,970
Equity		
Share capital		6,000
Retained earnings	(W5)	1,950
Non-controlling interest	(W4)	420
Current liabilities	(400 + 200)	600
		8,970

Workings

(W1) **Group structure**

P owns 80% of the issued share capital of S.

Parent

%

Subsidiary

(W2) **Net assets of subsidiary**

	Acquisition date	Reporting date
	$000	$000
Share capital	1,500	1,500
Retained earnings	250	700
	1,750	2,200

P sells the goods to S so no adjustment is required in (W2).

(W3) **Goodwill**

	$000
Fair value of investment	3,400
Value of NCI at acquisition (given in the question)	330
NAs acquired	
100% × 1,750 (W2)	(1,750)
Goodwill at reporting date	1,980

(W4) **Non-controlling interests**

	$000
Value of NCI at acquisition (given in the question)	330
NCI × post-acquisition reserves 20% × (2,200 − 1,750) (W2)	90
NCI × impairment (W3) (fair value method only)	–
NCI at reporting date	420

(W5) **Retained earnings**

	$000
Parent	1,600
Subsidiary (80% × (2,200 − 1,750)) (W2)	360
PUP (W6)	(10)
	1,950

(W6) **PUP**

Profit on sale   20/120 × 120 = 20

Profit in inventory = PUP = ½ × 20 = 10

Since P sold to S, adjust W5 and inventory on CSFP.

When answering a question such as this you would be well advised to follow these steps:

(1) Draw up the group structure including all group companies and when the shares were purchased.

(2) Draw up an outline consolidated statement of financial position (CSFP) and add across assets and liabilities and insert the parent's share capital figure.

(3) Start on (W2) net assets of the subsidiary working. Ensure you read all the information in the question before proceeding in case an item will effect (W2).

(4) If calculations are required, e.g. for a PUP, add an extra working and call it (W6).

(5) Then proceed to (W3) through to (W5).

(6) Complete the CSFP with goodwill and retained earnings figures.

Test your understanding 6 – PUPs

The following statements of financial position exist at 30 June 20X1

	P	S
	$000	$000
Non-current assets		
Property, plant and equipment	4,000	2,000
Investment in S	3,400	
Current assets		
Inventory	500	100
Other current assets	100	300
	8,000	2,400
Equity		
Ordinary share capital	6,000	1,500
Retained earnings	1,600	700
Current liabilities	400	200
	8,000	2,400

P acquired 80% of S when the balance on S's retained earnings stood at $250,000.

During the year, S sold goods to P for $120,000 at a mark-up of 20%. Half of these goods remain in inventory at the year end.

NCI should be valued using the proportion of net assets method.

Required:

Prepare the consolidated statement of financial position (CSFP) of the P group as at 30 June 20X1.

Note: This TYU uses the same figures as Illustration 8 in the expandable text above but in Illustration 8, P sells the goods to S.

9 Non-current assets PUPs

P and S may sell non-current assets to each other, resulting in a profit being recorded in the selling entity's financial statements. If these non-current assets are still held by the purchasing entity at the year-end, the profit is unrealised from the group's perspective and should be removed.

The profit on disposal should be removed from the seller's books.

In addition to the profit based on the excess of the transfer price over the carrying value in the selling entity's books, there is depreciation to deal with.

Prior to the transfer, the asset is depreciated based on the original cost. After the transfer depreciation is calculated on the transfer price, i.e. a higher value. Therefore depreciation charged is higher after the transfer and this extra cost must be eliminated in the consolidated accounts, i.e. profits increased.

The extra depreciation should be removed from the purchaser's books. This is an adjustment purely for consolidation purposes.

The following journal entry will be required in order to record the unrealised profit if the **parent sells** (profit in the books of the parent, hence no impact on NCI):

Dr	Retained earnings of the parent within the group retained earnings by the difference in CA
Cr	PPE by the difference in CA
Dr	PPE by the difference in depreciation
Cr	Retained earnings of the parent within the group retained earnings by the difference in depreciation

You may find it easier to remember the following:

Reduce (W5) by the difference in CA

Reduce PPE on the face of the CSFP by the difference in CA

Increase (W5) by the difference in depreciation

Increase PPE on the face of the CSFP by the difference in depreciation

The following journal entry will be required in order to record the unrealised profit if the **subsidiary sells** (profit in the books of the subsidiary, hence will impact on NCI):

Dr Post-acquisition reserves of the subsidiary within the group retained earnings by the difference in CA (this should be the groups share of the CA)

Dr Post-acquisition reserves of the subsidiary within the NCI by the difference in CA (this should be the NCI share of the CA)

Cr PPE by the difference in CA

Dr PPE by the difference in depreciation

Cr Post-acquisition reserves of the subsidiary within the group retained earnings by the difference in depreciation (this should be the groups share of the depreciation

Cr Post-acquisition reserves of the subsidiary within the NCI by the difference in depreciation(this should be the NCI share of the depreciation)

You may find it easier to remember the following:

Reduce (W2) at the reporting date which leads into (W4) and (W5) by the difference in CA

Reduce PPE on the face of the CSFP by the difference in CA

Increase PPE on the face of the CSFP by the difference in depreciation

Increase (W2) at the reporting date which leads into (W4) and (W5) by the difference in depreciation

Illustration 9 – Non-current assets PUPs

If P transfers a non-current asset to its subsidiary

P acquired 80% of the share capital of S some years ago. P's reporting date is 31 August. P transfers an asset on 1 March 20X8 for $75,000 when its carrying value is $60,000. The remaining useful life at the date of sale is 2.5 years. The group depreciation policy is the straight line basis with a proportionate charge in the years of acquisition and disposal.

What adjustment is required in the consolidated financial statements of P for the year ended 31 August 20X9?

CA at transfer date with transfer	75,000
CA at transfer date without transfer	60,000
Adjustment required	15,000

Adjustment (parent sells – no impact on NCI)

Dr	Group retained earnings (W5)	↓	15,000
Cr	PPE (CSFP)	↓	15,000

We must now consider the effect on depreciation. The extra depreciation charged since transfer = (75,000 – 60,000) × 1.5/2.5 = 9,000 (we transferred the asset one and half years ago before the reporting date). This extra depreciation charge must be removed from the books.

Adjustment (parent sells – no impact on NCI)

Dr	PPE (CSFP)	↑	9,000
Cr	Group retained earnings (W5)	↑	9,000

If S transfers a non-current asset to its parent

Adjustment (sub sells – impact on NCI)

Dr	Post acquisition reserves of sub within group retained earnings (80% × $15,000) (W5)	↓	12,000
Dr	Post acquisition reserves of sub within NCI (20% × $15,000)	↓	3,000
Cr	PPE (CSFP)	↓	15,000

Adjustment (sub sells - impact on NCI)

Dr	PPE (CSFP)	↑	9,000
Cr	Post acquisition reserves of sub within group retained earnings (80% × $9,000) (W5)	↑	7,200
Cr	Post acquisition reserves of sub within NCI (20% × $9,000)	↑	1,800

An easier way to calculate the adjustment required is to compare the carrying amount (CA) of the asset now with the carrying amount that it would have been held at had the transfer never occurred:

CA at reporting date with transfer	X
CA at reporting date without transfer	(X)
Adjustment required	X

The following journal entry will be required in order to record the unrealised profit if the **parent sells** (profit in the books of the parent, hence no impact on NCI):

Dr	Retained earnings of the parent within the group retained earnings
Cr	PPE

You may find it easier to remember the following:

Reduce (W5)

Reduce PPE on the face of the CSFP

The following journal entry will be required in order to record the unrealised profit if the **subsidiary sells** (profit in the books of the subsidiary, hence will impact on NCI):

Dr	Post acquisition reserves of the subsidiary within the group retained earnings (this should be the groups share of the PUP)
Dr	Post acquisition reserves of the subsidiary within the NCI (this should be the NCI share of the PUP)
Cr	PPE

You may find it easier to remember the following:

Reduce (W2) at the reporting date which leads into (W4) and (W5)

Reduce PPE on the face of the CSFP

Illustration 10 – Non-current assets PUPs

Alternative method

Using the previous illustration we could have accounted for this by just looking at the net change in the carrying amount at the reporting date as follows:

	CA before transfer	CA after transfer	Difference
Carrying amount	60,000	75,000	
Additional depreciation (1.5/2.5)	36,000	45,000	
Carrying amount	24,000	30,000	6,000

Adjustment (parent sells – no impact on NCI)

Dr	Group retained earnings (W5)	↓	6,000
Cr	PPE (CSFP)	↓	6,000

Adjustment (sub sells – impact on NCI)

Dr	Post acquisition reserves of sub within group retained earnings (80% × $6,000) (W5)	↓	4,800
Dr	Post acquisition reserves of sub within group retained earnings (80% × $6,000) (W5)	↓	1,200
Cr	PPE (CSFP)	↓	6,000

Alternative approach

The approach we have taken is the most common way of dealing with non-current asset PUP's. However, there is an alternative view that states the profit on the transfer should be adjusted from the sellers books and additional depreciation expense should be adjusted from the buyers books. This would result in the following adjustments:

If the parent transfers a non-current asset to the subsidiary

If the parent sells:

- Difference in non-current asset CA at acquisition reduces W5
- Difference in depreciation charge increases W2

If we applied this view in the previous illustration it would give us the following results:

Adjustment (parent sells)

Dr	Group retained earnings (W5)	↓	15,000
Cr	Net assets of subsidiary at reporting date (W2)	↑	9,000
Cr	PPE(CSFP)	↓	6,000

If the subsidiary transfers a non-current asset to the parent

If the subsidiary sells:

- Difference in non-current asset CA at acquisition reduces W2
- Difference in depreciation charge increases W5

Using the same example as above, but S has sold the asset to P.

Adjustment (sub sells)

Dr	Net assets of subsidiary at reporting date (W2)	↓	15,000
Cr	Group retained earnings (W5)	↑	9,000
Cr	PPE (CSFP)	↓	6,000

Test your understanding 7 – Non-current assets PUPs

Rio purchased 90% of Salvador on 1 January 20X8. On 30 June 20X9 Salvador sold a lorry to Rio for $25,000. Its carrying value in Salvador's books was $20,000 and the remaining useful economic life at the date of transfer was 3 years.

Required:

What adjustment is required to the financial statements of the Rio group for the year ended 31 December 20X9?

Test your understanding 8 – Practice question

Aston and Martin

Aston acquired 90% of the share capital of Martin for $40,000 on 1 January 20X6 when the balance on the retained earnings of Martin stood at $9,000. The statements of financial position of the two companies are as follows at the 31 December 20X9:

		Aston		**Martin**
		$000		$000
Non-current assets				
Property, plant and equipment		88		39
Investment in Martin		40		
		128		39
Current assets				
Inventory	80		26	
Receivables	24		32	
Cash and cash equivalents			15	
		104		73
		232		112

Equity				
Share capital		100		24
Retained earnings		46		48
Current liabilities				
Overdraft	14		10	
Payables	72		30	
		86		40
		232		112

Aston's payables balance includes $6,000 payable to Martin, and Martin's receivables balance includes $20,000 owing from Aston. At the year end, it was established that Martin had despatched goods to Aston with a selling price of $9,000 and that Aston did not receive delivery of these items until after the year end. At the same time, Aston had put a cheque in the post to Martin for $5,000 which also did not arrive until after the year end.

In addition to the goods in transit of $9,000, there were also some items included in Aston's inventory which had been purchased by Aston at the price of $21,000 from Martin. Martin had priced these goods at a mark-up of 20%.

The group policy toward goodwill arising on consolidation is to subject it to an annual impairment review. It was felt that the goodwill should be carried at 80% of its original value.

NCI should be calculated using the fair value method assuming a value at acquisition of $3,000.

Required:

Prepare a consolidated statement of financial position (CSFP) as at 31 December 20X9 for the Aston Group.

10 Mid year acquisitions

Mid year acquisitions are only relevant to the statement of financial position when completing (W2) Net assets of the subsidiary. Reserves at acquisition are required and this figure may not be readily available if the acquisition took place part way through an accounting period at which point financial statements of the subsidiary are not prepared.

It is assumed that profits accrue evenly over the year and therefore profits for the year can be time apportioned and added to the reserves brought forward at the beginning of the year to calculate pre acquisition reserves.

For example, an entity is acquired on 1 March 20X0, its profits for the year ended 31 December 20X0 are $12,000 and retained earnings carried forward on 31 December 20X0 are $55,000. Retained earnings at acquisition will be 55,000 – (10/12 × $12,000) = $45,000.

Test your understanding 9 – Practice questions

Use the following information to answer questions 1 to 5 below.

On 1 June 20X9 K bought 80% of S paying $140,000 cash.

The summarised statements of financial position for the two companies as at 30 November 20X9 are:

		K		S
		$		$
Non-current assets				
Property, plant and equipment		138,000		115,000
Investments		162,000		
		300,000		115,000
Current assets				
Inventory	15,000		17,000	
Receivables	19,000		20,000	
Cash and cash equivalents	2,000		–	
		36,000		37,000
		336,000		152,000
Equity				
Share capital		114,000		40,000
Retained earnings		189,000		69,000
		303,000		109,000
Non-current liabilities				
8% Loan		–		20,000
Current liabilities				
Payables		33,000		23,000
		336,000		152,000

The following information is relevant:

(1) The inventory of S includes $8,000 of goods purchased from K at cost plus 25%.

(2) Goodwill is impaired by $5,100 to date.

(3) S earned a profit after tax of $5,250 in the year ended 30 November 20X9 and did not pay any dividends during the year.

(4) The loan in S's books represents monies borrowed from K on 1 June 20X9. All of the loan interest has been accounted for.

(5) Included in K's receivables is $4,000 relating to inventory sold to S since acquisition. S raised a cheque for $2,500 and sent it to K on 29 November 20X9. K did not receive this cheque until 4 December 20X9.

(6) NCI should be valued using the proportion of net assets method.

Test your understanding questions

(1) **What is the correct figure for goodwill?**

A $49,800

B $33,625

C $54,900

D $28,525

(2) **What is the correct figure for inventory?**

A $32,000

B $24,000

C $30,000

D $30,400

(3) **What is the correct figure for retained earnings?**

A $186,000

B $189,000

C $184,925

D $184,400

(4) **What is the correct figure for NCI?**

A $20,780

B $20,255

C $21,800

D $21,275

(5) **What is the correct figure for receivables?**

A $39,000

B $35,000

C $43,000

D $36,500

Test your understanding 10 – Practice questions

(1) LPD buys goods from its 80% owned subsidiary QPR. QPR earns a mark-up of 25% on such transactions. At the group's year end, 30 June 20X1 LPD had not yet taken delivery of goods, at a sales value of $100,000, which were despatched by QPR on 29 June 20X1.

Calculate the unrealised profit in inventory at the year-end?

(2) **Using the information from question 1, what amount would the goods in transit appear in the consolidated statement of financial position of the LPD group at 30 June 20X1?**

A $60,000

B $75,000

C $80,000

D $100,000

(3) STV owns 90% of the ordinary share capital of its subsidiary TUW. At the group's year end, 28 February 20X1, STV's payables include $3,600 in respect of inventories sold by TUW.

TUW's receivables include $6,700 in respect of inventories sold to STV. Two days before the year end STV sent a payment of $3,100 to TUW that was not recorded by the latter until two days after the year end.

The in-transit item should be dealt with as follows in the consolidated statement of financial position at 28 February 20X1:

A $2,325 to be included as cash in transit

B $3,100 to be added to consolidated payables

C $3,100 to be included as inventories in transit

D $3,100 to be included as cash in transit

(4) **Where the purchase price of an acquisition is less than the aggregate fair value of the net assets acquired, which ONE of the following accounting treatments of the difference is required by IFRS 3 Business Combinations?**

A Deduction from goodwill in the consolidated statement of financial position.

B Immediate recognition as a gain in the statement of changes in equity.

C Recognition in the statement of comprehensive income over its useful life

D Immediate recognition as a gain in profit or loss.

(5) On 30 September 20X1 GHI purchased 60% of the ordinary share capital of JKL for $1.80 million. NCI should be valued using the proportion of net assets method. The net assets of JKL at the date of acquisition were $1,350,000.

Calculate goodwill on acquisition in accordance with IFRS 3 Business Combinations.

(6) **It can be presumed that one entity controls another when it acquires which of the following?**

A More than 50% of the ordinary share capital.

B More than 50% of the preference share capital.

C Both of the above.

D Either of the above.

(7) Pop acquired 60% of Star on 1st May 20X5 when Star's retained earnings were $65,000. At 30th April 20X6 retained earnings of the two entities were as follows:

Pop $254,950
Star $135,000

What will be the balance for consolidated retained earnings as at 30th April 20X6?

A $335,950

B $296,950

C $324,950

D $389,950

(8) A purchases 80% of B and 10% of C on the last day of its financial year. At this date the current assets in each entity are as follows:

A $595,000

B $115,000

C $50,000

What figure will be the group current assets be in the consolidated statement of financial position?

A $595,000

B $687,000

C $760,000

D $710,000

(9) Boutaina controls another entity, Cansick owning 60% of that entity's ordinary share capital. At the group's year end, 31 December 20X8, Cansick included $18,000 in its receivables in respect of goods supplied to Boutaina. However, the payables of Boutaina included only $12,000 in respect of amounts due to Cansick. The difference arose because, on 31 December 20X8, Boutaina sent a cheque for $6,000 to Cansick, which was not received by Cansick until 3 January 20X9.

Which of the following sets of consolidation adjustments to current assets and current liabilities is correct?

A Deduct $18,000 from both consolidated receivables and consolidated payables.

B Deduct $12,000 from both consolidated receivables and consolidated payables.

C Deduct $18,000 from consolidated receivables and $12,000 from consolidated payables, and include cash in transit of $6,000.

D Deduct $18,000 from consolidated receivable and $12,000 from consolidated payables, and include inventories in transit of $6,000.

(10) Grand acquire 80% of National for $25million. At the acquisition date the fair value of the net assets were $21million and the fair value of the 20% shareholding not acquired was $5million.

Calculate the goodwill acquired on the basis the non-controlling interest is measured at fair value.

A $8,200,000

B $7,400,000

C $4,000,000

D $9,000,000

11 Summary diagram

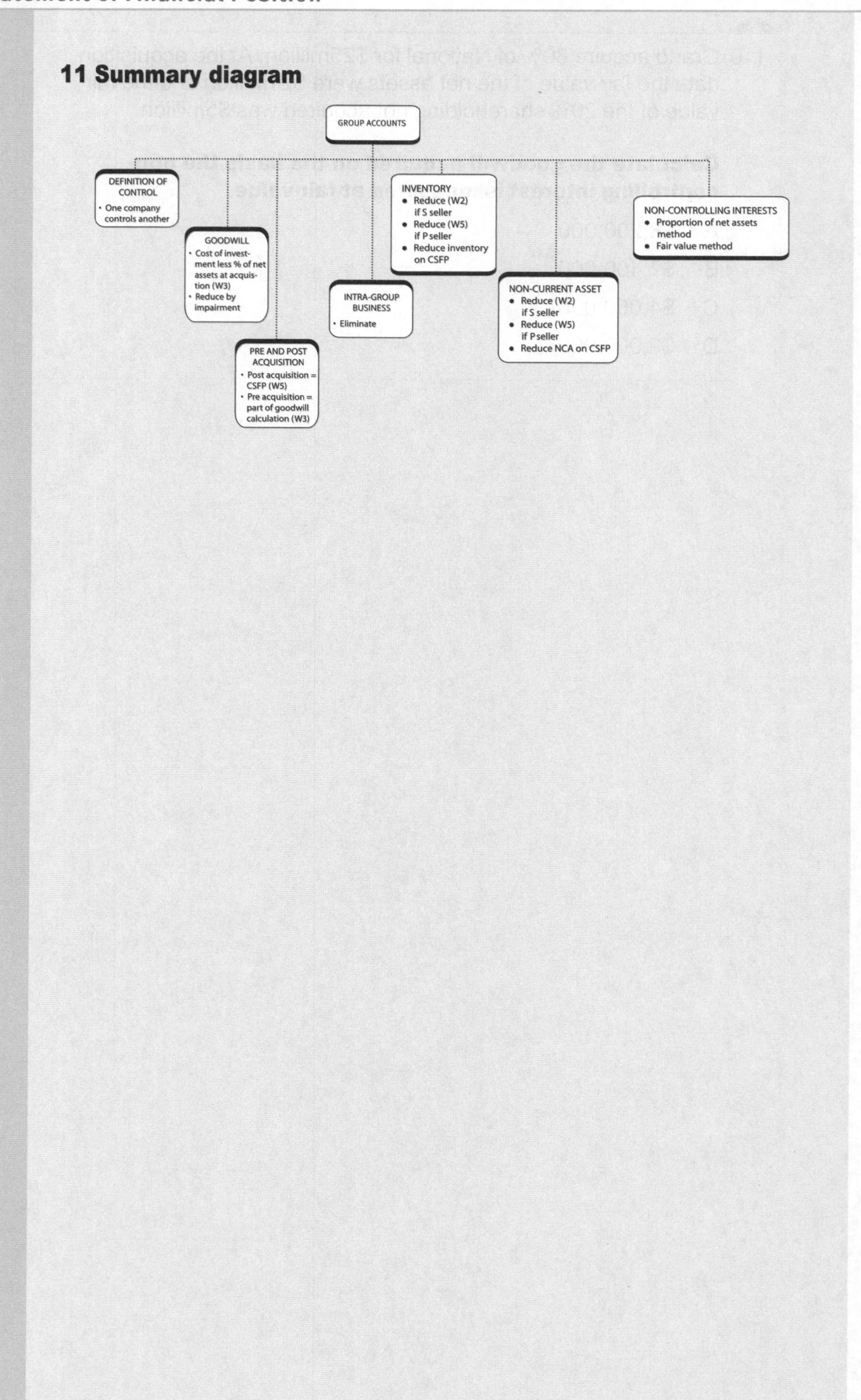

GROUP ACCOUNTS
DEFINITION OF CONTROL
• One company controls another
GOODWILL
• Cost of investment less % of net assets at acquisition (W3)
• Reduce by impairment
PRE AND POST ACQUISITION
• Post acquisition = CSFP (W5)
• Pre acquisition = part of goodwill calculation (W3)
INTRA-GROUP BUSINESS
• Eliminate
INVENTORY
• Reduce (W2) if S seller
• Reduce (W5) if P seller
• Reduce inventory on CSFP
NON-CURRENT ASSET
• Reduce (W2) if S seller
• Reduce (W5) if P seller
• Reduce NCA on CSFP
NON-CONTROLLING INTERESTS
• Proportion of net assets method
• Fair value method

Test your understanding answers

Test your understanding 1 – Pre and post-acquisition reserves

Consolidated statement of financial position as at 31 May 20X3

		$000
Non-current assets		
Goodwill	(W3)	435
Property, plant and equipment	(2,300 + 400)	2,700
Current assets	(900 + 500)	1,400
		4,535
Equity		
Share capital		1,000
Retained earnings	(W5)	2,754
Non-controlling interest	(W4)	181
Current liabilities	(450 + 150)	600
		4,535

Workings

(W1) **Group structure**

The parent owns 75% of the issued shares of the subsidiary.

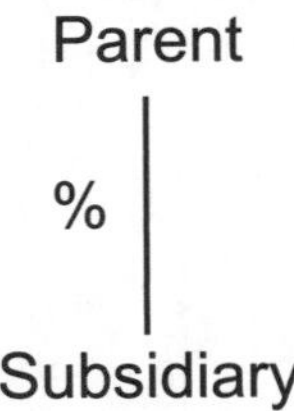

(W2) **Net assets of subsidiary**

	Acquisition date	**Reporting date**
	$000	$000
Share capital	475	475
Retained earnings	125	275
	600	750

(W3) **Goodwill**

	$000
Fair value of investment	1,000
Value of NCI at acquisition (given in question)	180
Fair value of net assets (NAs) acquired (100% × 600) (W2)	(600)
Goodwill at acquisition	580
Impairment (25% × 580)	(145)
Goodwill at reporting date	435

(W4) **Non-controlling interests**

	$000
Value of NCI at acquisition (given in question)	180
NCI × post-acquisition reserves 25% × (750 – 600) (W2)	37
NCI × impairment (W3) (25% × 145)	(36)
NCI at reporting date	181

(W5) **Retained earnings**

	$000
Parent	2,750
Subsidiary (100% × post acq profits)	
75% × (750 – 600) (W2)	113
Impairment (75% × 145) (W3)	(109)
	2,754

Test your understanding 2 – Pre and post-acquisition reserves

Kemp Group consolidated statement of financial position as at 31 December 20X9

		$000
Non-current assets		
Goodwill	(W3)	920
Property, plant and equipment	(2000 + 500)	2,500
Current assets	(200 + 800)	1,000
		4,420
Equity		
Share capital		3,000
Retained earnings	(W5)	920
Non-controlling interest	(W4)	300
Current liabilities	(100 + 100)	200
		4,420

Workings

(W1) **Group structure**

We own 75% of Solent = 225,000/300,000

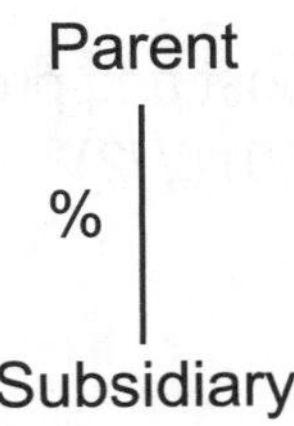

(W2) **Net assets of subsidiary**

	Acquisition Date	Reporting Date
	$000	$000
Share capital	300	300
Retained earnings	750	900
	1,050	1,200

(W3) **Goodwill**

	$000
Fair value of investment	1,900
Value of NCI at acquisition (25% × 1,050) (W2)	263
Fair value of net assets (NAs) acquired (100% × 1,050) (W2)	(1,050)
Goodwill at acquisition	1,113
Impairment 20%	(193)
Goodwill at reporting date	920

(W4) **Non-controlling interests**

	$000
Value of NCI at acquisition (W3)	263
NCI × post-acquisition reserves 25% × (1,200 – 1,050) (W2)	37
NCI × impairment (W3) (fair value method only)	–
NCI at reporting date	300

(W5) **Retained earnings**

	$000
Parent	1,000
Subsidiary (75% × post acq profits)	
75% × (1,200 – 1,050) (W2)	113
Impairment (W3)	(193)
	920

Test your understanding 3 – Intra-group balances

Consolidated statement of financial position as at 31 December 20X0

		$000
Non-current assets		
Goodwill	(W3)	1,675
Property, plant and equipment	(5,400 + 2,000)	7,400
Current assets		
Inventory	(750 + 140)	890
Receivables	(650 + 95 – 30)	715
Cash and cash equivalents	(400 + 85 + 5)	490
		11,170
Equity		
Share capital		7,000
Share premium		1,950
Retained earnings	(W5)	297
Non-controlling interest	(W4)	848
Current liabilities	(900 + 200 – 25)	1,075
		11,170

Workings

(W1) **Group structure**

The parent owns 60% of the issued shares of the subsidiary.

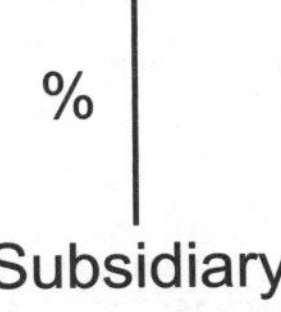

(W2) **Net assets of subsidiary**

	Acquisition date	Reporting date
	$000	$000
Share capital	1,400	1,400
Share premium	280	280
Retained earnings	300	440
	1,980	2,120

(W3) **Goodwill**

	$000
Fair value of investment	3,700
Value of NCI at acquisition (40% × 1,980) (W2)	792
Net assets acquired (100% × 1,980)	(1,980)
Goodwill on acquisition	2,512
Impairment (1/3 × 2,512)	(837)
Goodwill at reporting date	1,675

(W4) **Non-controlling interests**

	$000
Value of NCI at acquisition (W3)	792
NCI × post-acquisition reserves 40% × (2,120 – 1,980) (W2)	56
NCI × impairment (W3) (fair value method only)	–
NCI at reporting date	848

(W5) **Retained earnings**

	$000
Parent retained earnings	1,050
Subsidiary (60% × (2,120 – 1,980)) (W2)	84
Impairment	(837)
	297

(W6) **Intra-group balances**

Cash (increase)	$5,000
Receivables (decrease)	$30,000
Payables (decrease)	$25,000

Test your understanding 4 – PUPs

The PUP will be:

$$(522 \times \frac{20}{120}) \times 60\% \qquad = 52.2$$

The value of the goods sold intra-group is $522 and included within the selling price is the profit mark up of 20% on cost. Multiply 522 by 20/120 to extract the unrealised profit.

40% of the goods were sold on to external parties so only 60% is still unrealised.

PUP = 52.2

Reduce W5 and inventory on the CSFP. P is the seller and overstating their profit will have only have an impact on both the parents retained earnings.

This will result in the following journal entry:

Dr	Retained earnings of the parent within the group retained earnings	$52.2
Cr	Inventory	$52.2

Test your understanding 5 – PUPs

The PUP will be: $360 × 20% = $72

Reduce W2 and inventory on the CSFP. Remember S is the seller and overstating their profit will have an impact on both the parent and NCI.

This will result in the following journal entry:

Dr	Post acquisition reserves of the subsidiary within the group retained earnings (this should be the groups share of the PUP) (75% × $72)	$54
Dr	Post acquisition reserves of the subsidiary within the NCI (this should be the NCI share of the PUP) (25% × $72)	$18
Cr	Inventory	$72

Test your understanding 6 – PUPs

P Group consolidated statement of financial position as at 30 June 20X1

		$000
Non-current assets		
Goodwill	(W3)	2,000
Property, plant and equipment	(4,000 + 2,000)	6,000
Current assets		
Inventory	(500 + 100 − 10) (W6)	590
Other current assets	(100 + 300)	400
		8,990
Equity		
Share capital		6,000
Retained earnings	(W5)	1,952
Non-controlling interest	(W4)	438
Current liabilities	(400 + 200)	600
		8,990

Workings

(W1) **Group structure**

P owns 80% of the issued share capital of S.

Parent
%
Subsidiary

(W2) **Net assets of subsidiary**

	Acquisition date	Reporting date
	$000	$000
Share capital	1,500	1,500
Retained earnings	250	700
PUP (W6)	–	(10)
	1,750	2,190

(W3) **Goodwill**

	$000
Fair value of investment	3,400
Value of NCI at acquisition (20% × 1,750) (W2)	350
NAs acquired (100% × 1,750) (W2)	(1,750)
Goodwill at reporting date	2,000

(W4) **Non-controlling interests**

	$000
Value of NCI at acquisition (W3)	350
NCI × post-acquisition reserves 20% × (2,190 – 1,750) (W2)	88
NCI × impairment (W3) (fair value method only)	–
NCI at reporting date	438

(W5) **Retained earnings**

	$000
Parent	1,600
Subsidiary (80% × (2,190 – 1,750)) (W2)	352
	1,952

(W6) **PUP**

Profit on sale = 20/120 × 120 = 20

Profit in inventory = PUP = ½ × 20 = 10

Since S sold to P, adjust W2 and inventory on CSFP.

Test your understanding 7 – Non-current assets PUPs

The most common approach would be:

CA at transfer date with transfer	25,000
CA at transfer date without transfer	20,000
Adjustment required	5,000

Adjustment (sub sells)

Dr	Post acquisition reserves of sub within group retained earnings (90% × $5,000) (W5)	↓	4,500
Dr	Post acquisition reserves of sub within NCI (10% × $5,000)	↓	500
Cr	PPE (CSFP)	↓	5,000

We must now consider the effect on depreciation. The extra depreciation charged since transfer = (25,000 – 20,000) × 0.5/3 = 833 (we transferred the asset half a year ago before the reporting date). This extra depreciation charge must be removed from the books.

Adjustment (sub sells)

Dr	PPE (CSFP)	↑	833
Cr	Post acquisition reserves of sub within NCI (10% × $833)	↑	83
Cr	Post acquisition reserves of sub within group retained earnings (90% × $833) (W5)	↑	750

We could have accounted for this by just looking at the net change in the carrying amount as follows:

	CA before transfer	**CA after transfer**	**Difference**
Carrying amount	20,000	25,000	
Additional depreciation (0.5/3)	3,333	4,167	
Carrying amount	16,667	20,833	4,167

Adjustment (sub sells)

Dr	Post acquisition reserves of sub within group retained earnings (90% × $4,167) (W5)	↓	3,750
Dr	Post acquisition reserves of sub within NCI (10% × $4,167)	↓	417
Cr	PPE (CSFP)	↓	4,167

The alternative approach could have been:

Adjustment (sub sells)

Dr	Net assets of subsidiary at reporting date (W2)	↓	5,000
Cr	Group retained earnings (W5)	↑	833
Cr	NCA (CSFP)	↓	4,167

Notice how the full amount of the PUP is adjusted for, i.e. we do not make any adjustments for the 90% ownership. This is because we consolidate **all** of the subsidiary and therefore need to adjust for **all** of the PUP in our workings. The NCI adjustment would be calculated as normal in W4.

Test your understanding 8 – Practice question

Consolidated statement of financial position – Aston Group as at 31 December 20X9

		$000
Non-current assets		
Goodwill	(W3)	8.0
Property, plant and equipment	(88 + 39)	127.0
Current assets		
Inventory	(80 + 26 + 9 goods in transit – 5 pup)	110.0
Receivables	(24 + 32 – 20 intercompany)	36.0
Bank & cash	(15 + 5 cash in transit)	20.0
		301.0
Equity		
Share capital		100.0
Retained earnings	(W5)	74.8
Non-controlling interest	(W4)	6.2
Current liabilities		
Overdraft	(14 + 10)	24.0
Payables	(72 + 30 – 6 intercompany)	96.0
		301.0

Workings

(W1) **Group structure**

The parent acquired a 90% interest in the subsidiary.

Parent

%

Subsidiary

(W2) **Net assets of subsidiary**

	Acquisition date	**Reporting date**
	$000	$000
Share capital	24	24
Retained earnings	9	48
PUP (W6)	–	(5)
	33	67

(W3) **Goodwill**

	$000
Fair value of investment	40
Value of NCI at acquisition (given in the question)	3
FV of NAs acquired (100% × 33) (W2)	(33)
Goodwill at acquisition	10
Impairment (20%)	(2)
Goodwill at reporting date	8

(W4) **Non-controlling interests**

	$000
Value of NCI at acquisition (given in question)	3.0
NCI × post-acquisition reserves 10% × (67 – 33) (W2)	3.4
NCI × impairment (W3) (10% × 2)	(0.2)
NCI at reporting date	6.2

(W5) Retained earnings

	$000
Aston	46.0
Martin (90% × (67 – 33)) (W2)	30.6
Impairment (W3) (90% × 2)	(1.8)
	74.8

(W6) PUP

Goods in Aston inventory	21
Goods in transit	9
	30

PUP = 20/120 × 30 = 5

Martin (sub) sold the goods – adjust W2 and inventory on CSFP.

(W7) Intra-group balances

Cash (increase)	$5,000
Inventory (increase)	$9,000
Receivables (decrease)	$20,000
Payables (decrease)	$6,000

Test your understanding 9 – Practice questions

(1) A

(2) D

(3) D

(4) C

(5) B

Consolidated statement of financial position – K Group as at 30 November 20X9

		$
Non-current assets		
Goodwill	(W3)	49,800
Property, plant and equipment	(138,000 + 115,000)	253,000
Investments	(162,000 – 140,000 – 20,000)	2,000
		304,800
Current Assets		
Inventory	(15,000 + 17,000 – 1,600 (W6))	30,400
Receivables	(19,000 + 20,000 – 4,000 inter co)	35,000
Bank & cash	(2,000 + 0 + 2,500 cash in transit)	4,500
		374,700
Equity		
Share capital		114,000
Retained earnings	(W5)	184,400
Non-controlling interest	(W4)	21,800
Non-current liabilities		
8% Loan	(0 + 20,000 – 20,000)	–
Current liabilities		
Payables	(33,000 + 23,000 – 1,500 inter co)	54,500
		374,700

Workings

(W1) **Group structure**

We acquired an 80% interest in the subsidiary 6 months ago

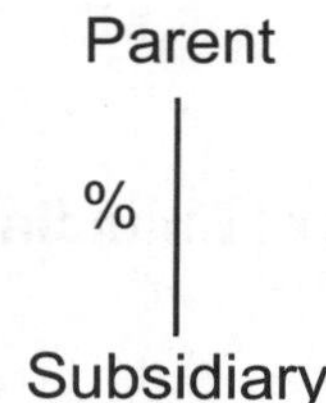

(W2) **Net assets of subsidiary**

	Acquisition date	**Reporting date**
	$	$
Share capital	40,000	40,000
Retained earnings (69,000 – (6/12 × 5,250)	66,375	69,000
	106,375	109,000

(W3) **Goodwill**

	$
Fair value of investment	140,000
Value of NCI at acquisition (20% × 106,375) (W2)	21,275
Fair value of net assets acquired (100% × 106,375)	(106,375)
Goodwill @ acquisition	54,900
Impairment	(5,100)
Goodwill @ reporting date	49,800

(W4) **Non-controlling interests**

	$
Value of NCI at acquisition (W3)	21,275
NCI × post-acquisition reserves 20% × (109,000 – 106,375) (W2)	525
NCI × impairment (W3) (fair value method only)	–
NCI at reporting date	21,800

(W5) **Retained earnings**

	$
K	189,000
PUP (W6)	(1,600)
S (80% × (109,000 – 106,375)) (W2)	2,100
Impairment (W3)	(5,100)
	184,400

(W6) **PUP**

25/125 × 8,000 = 1,600

K sold the goods and so adjust W5 and inventory on the CSFP.

Note: All investments have not been eliminated in this question because the investments are not just from subsidiary and associate investments.

Don't forget we can have investments with entities outside of the group. In this case we had a total investment by the parent of $162,000 but only $140,000 and $20,000 related to the group. Hence, investments will not be eliminated in full and a balance of £2,000 will remain in the consolidated accounts.

Test your understanding 10 – Practice questions

(1) PUP is calculated as $100,000/125 × 25 = $20,000.
No adjustment is made to the PUP for the ownership of 80% as all of the subsidiary will be consolidated.

(2) C – Inventory in transit is valued at $100,000 but we must remove PUP.
The value of goods in transit to the group is $80,000.
Hence we increase inventory by $100,000 but remove the PUP of $20,000.

(3) D – $3,100 to be included in cash in transit.

(4) D

(5) Goodwill:

Fair value of investment	1,800,000
Value of NCI at acquisition (40% × 1,350,000)	540,000
Fair value of net assets acquired (100% × 1,350,000)	(1,350,000)
Goodwill @ acquisition	990,000

(6) A – Preference shares do not give voting rights, hence no control.

(7) B.
The consolidated statement of financial position includes P's reserves plus P's share of S's post acquisition reserves as these reserves have been generated under P's control.
In this case, $254,950 + 60% ($135,000 – $65,000) = $296,950

(8) D.
The statement of financial position is a snap-shot in time. Therefore the date of acquisition is irrelevant so long as it is on or before the reporting date.

Only A and B's assets will be consolidated as the parent does not control entity C. We consolidate the 100% of entity B, although we do not own 100%.

$595,000 + $115,000 = $710,000.

(9) C

(10) D
Goodwill = FV of investment $25m – $21m + $5m = $9m

chapter

4

Consolidated Statement of Profit or Loss and other comprehensive income

Chapter learning objectives

On completion of their studies students should be able to:

- Prepare a consolidated statement of profit or loss for a group of companies.
- Explain the treatment in consolidated financial statements of pre and post-acquisition reserves, goodwill (including its impairment), unrealised profit, intra-group transactions and dividends.
- Calculate non-controlling interests.
- Adjust for mid-year acquisitions.

1 Session content

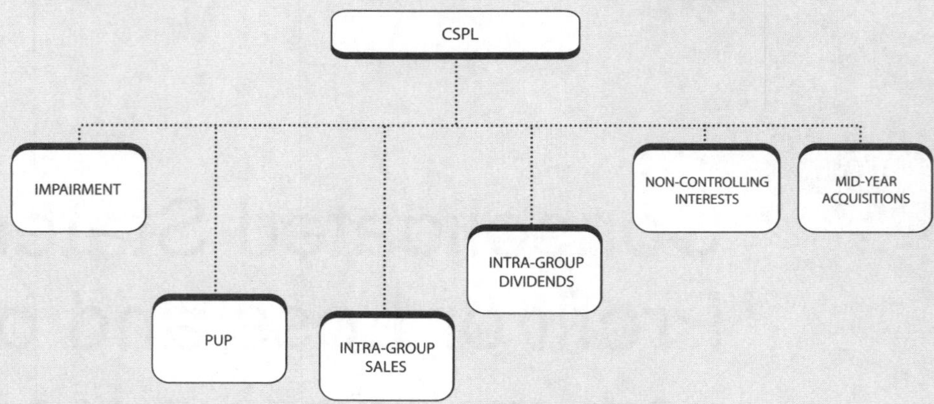

2 Consolidated statement of Profit or Loss and other comprehensive income

The principles of consolidation are continued to the statement of profit or loss (CSPL).

A statement of profit and loss reflects the income and expenses generated by the net assets reflected on the statement of financial position.

Since the group controls the net assets of the subsidiary, the income and expenses of the subsidiary should be fully included in the consolidated statement of profit and loss, i.e. add across 100% parent plus 100% subsidiary.

To reflect that the parent may not own 100% of the subsidiary, the profit for the year will be split between the amount attributable to the parent shareholders and the non-controlling interest shareholders (NCI).

It is important to remember you should only consolidate the subsidiary **since** acquisition when completing the subsidiary column of the proforma.

A standard approach to preparing consolidated financial statements is adopted within the manual in order to aid the learning process. However, assessment on this will be largely in the form of OTQ's which will only test one or two principles at a time. You will not be expected to prepare consolidated financial statements in totality. It is therefore important you understand the accounting entries behind the workings and adjustments.

The basic proforma for preparing a consolidated statement of profit or loss and other comprehensive income can be seen as follows:

	Parent	**Subsid -iary**	**Adjust- ments**	**Consoli- dated**
	$	$	$	$
Revenue	X	X		X
– Intra-group trading			(X)	
Cost of sales	(X)	(X)		
– Intra-group trading			X	
– Inventory adjustment		(X)		
– PUP (if P selling)	(X)			
– PUP (if S selling)		(X)		(X)
Gross profit				X
Distribution costs	(X)	(X)		(X)
Administrative expenses	(X)	(X)		
– Impairment (if NCI proportionate method)	(X)			
– Impairment (if NCI FV method)		(X)		(X)
Operating profit				X
Investment income	X			–
– Intra-group dividend	(X)			
– Intra-group interest			(X)	X
Finance cost	(X)	(X)		
– Intra-group interest			X	(X)
Profit before tax				X
Tax	(X)	(X)		(X)
Profit for the year		X		X
Other comprehensive income (e.g. property revaluation)	X	X		X
Total comprehensive income		X		X
Attributable to:				
Non-controlling interests (profit for the year from the sub × NCI %)				X
Parent shareholders (balance of total profit for the year)				X
				X

The adjustment column should only be used when you have an adjustment which effects two items on the statement of profit or loss such as:

- intra-group sales
- intra-group interest
- management fees
- redeemable preference share dividends

All other adjustments to the statement should be made in either the parent or subsidiaries column accordingly. Always consider which entities profit is being effected by the adjustment and adjust their column accordingly. Remember, any adjustments you make to the subsidiaries profit will ultimately effect the calculation of the NCI.

3 Consolidated statement of profit or loss adjustments

Adjustments will be necessary to the parent and subsidiary's own accounts to reflect that the group is one economic unit.

The consolidated figures will be calculated as:

Parent + subsidiary +/– adjustments

Consolidation adjustments should be dealt with as follows:

Impairments

Impairments of goodwill relating to the current year will be charged as an expense in the consolidated statement of profit or loss. If the proportion of net assets method for valuing NCI is used, the adjustment should be made in the parent column against administrative expenses because the group in effect bears all of this cost. Alternatively, use the subsidiary column if the fair value method is used because in this instance the impairment charge will affect both the group and the NCI.

Intra-group transactions – sales and interest

The group as a single economic entity cannot generate profit with itself and so intra-group transactions will need eliminating, e.g. sales between group entities and interest paid by one company and received in another. Intra-group sales will reduce both revenue and cost of sales and intra-group interest will reduce both investment income and finance costs. These adjustments must be shown in the adjustments column of the statement because in effect there is no overall impact on group profit or loss – only an impact on individual lines with the profit or loss statement.

Intra-group transactions – dividend

Dividends from subsidiary to parent must be eliminated for the same reason as sales and interest. However, the adjustment should be shown in the parents column by reducing the investment income line.

Provision for unrealised profit (PUP)

An adjustment is required to increase the cost of sales of the selling entity to remove the unrealised profit included in inventories at the reporting date, which will be the parent or the subsidiary depending on which entity made the profit.

Mid-year acquisitions

Time apportion the income and expenses of the subsidiary to reflect the period of ownership, i.e. if a subsidiary is acquired on 1 September and the reporting date is 31 December, 4/12 of the subsidiary's income and expenses should be consolidated.

It is important to remember that the statement of profit or loss will only deal with **current year** adjustments, whereas the statement of financial position will deal with **cumulative** adjustments.

Further explanation of adjustments

Impairments

Once the impairment of goodwill is calculated for the **current year**, it will be charged as an expense in the consolidated statement of profit or loss. Goodwill is reflected in the consolidated financial statements only and so any impairment in the goodwill must be recorded as a consolidation adjustment as it will not be reflected in the individual entity's financial statements.

The entry required to adjust for the impairment is as follows:

Dr Profits	↓
Cr Goodwill on CSFP	↓

Impairments are most commonly charged as an increase to administrative expenses (reduction in profits) and they do not adjust the subsidiary's profit attributable to non-controlling interest unless the assessment has asked you to use the fair value method of valuing NCI, i.e. adjust in the parent's column when using the proportion of net assets method and the subsidiary's column when using the fair value method.

However, read the assessment instructions as you may be asked to treat them as a cost of sales expense.

Intra-group transactions and PUPs

In the case of intra-group trading between the parent and subsidiary, there are two effects to bear in mind when preparing the consolidated statement of profit or loss.

- The intra-group trading must be eliminated from revenue and cost of sales. It is irrelevant who sold the goods; the revenue of one entity is the cost to the other. Therefore, adjust both revenue and cost of sales by the same amount; the amount of the sale.
- If the goods are still held by the buying entity at the reporting date, there needs to be a provision for unrealised profits (PUP).

Chapter 3 looked at PUPs with respect to the CSFP and stated that the adjustment required is:

Dr Profits of selling entity ↓
Cr Inventory of CSFP ↓

When this adjustment is applied to the CSPL, it is necessary to identify where the reduction to profits will take place. The PUP is adjusted for as an increase to cost of sales (a reduction in profits) in the column of the selling entity. So if the subsidiary sold the goods, adjust the cost of sales in the subsidiary's column and if the parent sold the goods, adjust the cost of sales in the parent's column.

Dividends that are paid by the subsidiary will be received in part or in full by the parent, depending on the percentage of shares held. These intra-group dividends are eliminated on consolidation, i.e. deduct the dividend received from the subsidiary, from the parent's investment income.

Any other intra-group transactions, for example interest paid by one entity in the group and received by another, are cancelled out against each other as a consolidation adjustment in the adjustment column. The amount is deducted from investment income and deducted from finance cost.

Mid-year acquisitions

The parent controls the subsidiary's assets and liabilities from the acquisition date and so should include only the subsidiary's income and expenses from the acquisition date.

Time apportion the subsidiary's results on a line by line basis when including them in the statement.

Illustration 1 – Consolidated statement of profit & loss

On 1 January 20X0 Zebedee acquired all of the ordinary shares of Xavier.

The following statements of profit or loss and other comprehensive income have been produced by Zebedee and Xavier for the year ended 31 December 20X0.

	Zebedee	Xavier
	$000	$000
Revenue	1,260	520
Cost of sales	(420)	(210)
Gross profit	840	310
Distribution costs	(180)	(60)
Administrative expenses	(120)	(90)
Profit from operations	540	160
Investment income from Xavier	36	–
Profit before taxation	576	160
Taxation	(130)	(26)
Profit for the year	446	134
Other comprehensive income	–	–
Total comprehensive income	446	134

During the year ended 31 December 20X0, Zebedee had sold $84,000 worth of goods to Xavier. These goods were sold at a mark up of 50% on cost. On 31 December 20X0 Xavier still had $36,000 worth of these goods in inventories.

Required:

Prepare the consolidated statement of profit or loss and other comprehensive income for the Zebedee group for the year ended 31 December 20X0.

Solution

For the purpose of teaching we will follow these steps to answer a CSPL question:

(1) Prepare the CSPL proforma with a column for the parent, each subsidiary, adjustments and a final column for the consolidated figures.

(2) Prepare W1 Group structure to determine the subsidiary status of each entity and add dates to highlight any mid-year acquisitions and the number of months since control was acquired.

(3) Complete the proforma with the parent and subsidiary's figures from the question. Take care to note any mid-year acquisitions from W1 and to time apportion the subsidiary's income and expenses.

(4) Review the extra information in the question to determine any adjustments required. Calculate the adjustment needed in a separate working to ensure your workings are clear.

(5) Look out for dividend income from the subsidiary in the parent's books as this must be eliminated.

Zebedee consolidated statement of profit or loss and other comprehensive income for the year ended 31 December 20X0

	Zebedee	**Xavier**	**Adjust-ments**	**Consoli-dated**
	$000	$000	$000	$000
Revenue	1,260	520	(84)	1,696
Cost of sales	(420)	(210)	84	(558)
– PUP (W2)	(12)			
Gross profit				1,138
Distribution costs	(180)	(60)		(240)
Administrative expenses	(120)	(90)		(210)
Profit from operations				688
Investment income	36			–
– intra-group dividend	(36)			
Taxation	(130)	(26)		(156)
Profit for the year				532
Other comprehensive income	–	–		–
Total comprehensive income				532

Amount attributable to:	
Non-controlling interests (N/A)	–
Parent shareholders	532
	532

Workings

(W1) **Group structure**

Zebedee
100% | 1 January 20X0
Xavier i.e. 1 year

(W2) **PUP**

The goods were sold at a mark up of 50% on cost so the unrealised profit is stripped out by multiplying by 50/150. The profit is unrealised on only the inventory remaining in Xavier at the reporting date.

$36,000 × 50/150 = $12,000

Zebedee sold the goods so the adjustment should be made in Zebedee's column, i.e. the column of the seller.

(W3) **COS**

Cost of sales = parent $420 + sub $210 – intra-group sale $84 + PUP $12 = $558

Illustration 2 – Consolidated statement of profit & loss

Kew bought 75% of Richmond on 1 April 20X7. The following are the statements of profit or loss and other comprehensive income for Kew and Richmond for the year ended 31 March 20X9:

	Kew	Richmond
	$	$
Revenue	44,500	15,900
Cost of sales	(32,300)	(10,500)
Gross profit	12,200	5,400
Operating expenses	(8,000)	(2,300)
Profit from operations	4,200	3,100
Investment income	1,100	–
Profit before tax	5,300	3,100
Tax	(1,600)	(1,000)
Profit for the year	3,700	2,100
Other comprehensive income		
Revaluation gain	600	–
Total comprehensive income	4,300	2,100

The following are the statements of changes in equity for Kew and Richmond for the year ended 31 March 20X9:

	Kew	Richmond
	$	$
Equity b/f	20,300	11,000
Comprehensive income	4,300	2,100
Dividends paid	(2,000)	(1,100)
Equity c/f	22,600	12,000

The following information is available:

(1) During the year Richmond sold goods to Kew for $2,200. Of this amount, $500 was included in the inventory of Kew at the year-end. Richmond earns a 20% profit margin on its sales.

(2) NCI was valued using the proportion of net assets method.

Required:

Prepare the consolidated statement of profit or loss and other comprehensive income for the year ended 31 March 20X9.

Solution

Kew Group consolidated statement of profit or loss and other comprehensive income for the year ended 31 March 20X9

	Kew	Rich-mond	Adjust-ment	Consoli-dated
	$	$	$	$
Revenue	44,500	15,900	(2,200)	58,200
Cost of sales	(32,300)	(10,500)	2,200	(40,700)
– PUP (W3)		(100)		
Gross profit				17,500
Operating expenses	(8,000)	(2,300)		(10,300)
Profit from operations				7,200
Investment income	1,100	–		275
– 75% × 1,100	(825)			
Profit before tax				7,475
Tax	(1,600)	(1,000)		(2,600)
Profit for the year				4,875
Other comprehensive income				
Revaluation gain	600	–		600
Total comprehensive income		2,000		5,475

Profit for the year attributable to:	
Non-controlling interests (25% × 2,000)	500
Parent shareholders (balance)	4,375
	4,875
Total comprehensive income for the year attributable to:	
Non-controlling interests (25% × 2,000)	500
Parent shareholders (balance)	4,975
	5,475

Workings

(W1) **Group structure**

Kew
75% | 1 April 20X7
Richmond i.e. 2 years

(W2) **PUP**

Inventory remaining at reporting date = \$500

Unrealised profit within inventory = \$500 × 20% = \$100

The subsidiary sells to the parent so we must increase the COS of the subsidiary column.

(W3) **COS**

COS = parent \$32,300 + sub \$10,500 – intra-group sale \$2,200 + PUP \$100 = \$40,700

(W4) **NCI**

Subs profit after tax in individual statements \$2,100 – PUP (sub sells) \$100 = \$2,000 × 25% = \$500

Test your understanding 1 – Simple CSPL

Given below are the statements of profit or loss and other comprehensive income for Paris and its subsidiary London for the year ended 31 December 20X9.

	Paris	London
	$000	$000
Revenue	3,200	2,560
Cost of sales	(2,200)	(1,480)
Gross profit	1,000	1,080
Distribution costs	(160)	(120)
Administrative expenses	(400)	(80)
	440	880
Investment income	160	–
	600	880
Taxation	(400)	(480)
Profit for the year	200	400

Additional information:

- Paris acquired 80% of London's share capital on 31 December 20X5.
- Goodwill was calculated valuing NCI using the fair value method. A goodwill impairment of $38,000 was found to be necessary at the year end. Impairments are included within administrative expenses.
- Paris made sales to London, at a selling price of $600,000 during the year. Not all of the goods had been sold externally by the year end. The profit element included in London's closing inventory was $30,000.
- The figure for investment income in Paris's statement of profit or loss represents the dividend received from London for the year.

Required:

Prepare a consolidated statement of profit or loss and other comprehensive income for the year ended 31 December 20X9 for the Paris group.

Test your understanding 2 – CSPL

On 1 July 20X0 Tudor purchased 80% of the shares in Windsor. The summarised draft statement of profit or loss and other comprehensive income for each entity for the year ended 31 March 20X1 were as follows:

	Tudor	Windsor
	$000	$000
Revenue	60,000	24,000
Cost of sales	(42,000)	(20,000)
Gross profit	18,000	4,000
Distribution costs	(2,500)	(50)
Administrative expenses	(3,500)	(150)
Profit from operations	12,000	3,800
Investment income	75	–
Finance cost	–	(200)
Profit before tax	12,075	3,600
Tax	(3,000)	(600)
Profit for the year	9,075	3,000
Other comprehensive income	–	–
Total comprehensive income	9,075	3,000

The following information is relevant:

(1) During the post-acquisition period Tudor sold Windsor some goods for $12 million. The goods had originally cost $9 million. During the remaining months of the year Windsor sold $10 million (at cost to Windsor) of these goods to third parties for $13 million.

(2) Tudor purchased 1,000,000 of Windsor's 15% $1 loan notes on 1 October 20X0.

(4) Revenues and expenses should be deemed to accrue evenly throughout the year.

(5) At 31 March 20X1 it was determined that impairment losses of $300,000 had arisen for the current year. The NCI holding in Windor was valued using the fair value method.

Required:

Prepare a consolidated statement of profit or loss and other comprehensive income for the Tudor group for the year to 31 March 20X1.

Test your understanding 3 – CSPL

P acquired 80% of S on 1 April 20X6 when S's retained earnings were $5,000. The following are the statements of profit or loss and other comprehensive income of P and S for the year ended 31 March 20X9:

	P	S
	$	$
Revenue	31,200	10,400
Cost of sales	(17,800)	(5,600)
Gross profit	13,400	4,800
Operating expenses	(8,500)	(1,200)
Profit from operations	4,900	3,600
Investment income	2,000	–
Profit before tax	6,900	3,600
Tax	(2,100)	(500)
Profit for the year	4,800	3,100
Other comprehensive income	–	–
Total comprehensive income	4,800	3,100

The following are the statements of changes in equity for P and S for the year ended 31 March 20X9:

	P	S
	$	$
Equity b/f	50,600	22,670
Comprehensive income	4,800	3,100
Dividends paid	(2,500)	(500)
Equity c/f	52,900	25,270

The following information is available:

(1) During the year S sold goods to P for $4,400. Of this amount, $500 was included in the inventory of P at the year-end. S earns a 35% margin on its sales.

(2) Goodwill amounting to $800 arose on the acquisition of S. Goodwill was impaired by 10% in the year ended 31 March 20X8 and is to be impaired by another 10% on the book value at 31 March 20X8 for the current year. Impairment losses should be charged to operating expenses.

(3) It is P's group policy to value NCI at fair value at acquisition.

Required:

Prepare the consolidated statement of profit or loss and other comprehensive income for the year ended 31 March 20X9.

Test your understanding 4 – Practice questions

Use the following information to answer questions 1 to 5 below.

Wolf acquired a 75% holding of the ordinary share capital of Hawk on 1 January 20X8. The share capital of Wolf and Hawk is $350,000 and $200,000 respectively. The retained earnings at that date for Hawk were $10,000. The goodwill impairment charges for this year are $6,000 ($2,000 last year) and NCI is valued using the proportion of net assets method.

During the year, Wolf sold goods to Hawk at an invoice value of $20,000. Wolf has a pricing policy based upon a mark-up of 25%. A quarter of these goods remain in inventory at the year end.

The individual statements of profit or loss and other comprehensive income for the year ended 31 December 20X9 are as follows:

	Wolf	Hawk
	$000	$000
Revenue	1,000	2,000
Cost of sales	(600)	(1,200)
Gross profit	400	800
Distribution costs	(300)	(50)
Administrative expenses	(18)	(500)
Profit from operations	82	250
Investment income	8	
Profits before tax	90	250
Tax	(40)	(100)
Profit for the year	50	150
Other comprehensive income	–	–
Total comprehensive income	50	150

The individual statement of changes in equity for the year ended 31 December 20X9 is as follows:

	Wolf	Hawk
	$000	$000
Equity b/f	450	310
Comprehensive income	50	150
Dividends paid	(15)	(8)
Equity c/f	485	452

(1) **What is the correct figure for PUP?**

A $5,000

B $1,000

C $1,250

D $4,000

(2) **What is the correct figure for NCI in the CSPL?**

A $37,500

B $36,000

C $34,500

D $nil

(3) **What is the correct figure for COS?**

A $1,800,000

B $1,781,000

C $1,780,000

D $1,779,000

(4) **What is the correct figure for revenue?**

A $2,980,000

B $3,000,000

C $2,500,000

D $2,480,000

(5) **What is the correct figure for investment income?**

A $nil

B $8,000

C $6,000

D $2,000

Test your understanding 5 – Practice questions

(1) GPT regularly sells goods to its subsidiary in which it owns 100% of the ordinary share capital. During the group's financial year ended 31 August 20X1, GPT sold goods to its subsidiary valued at $100,000 (selling price) upon which it makes a margin of 20%. By the group's year end all of the goods had been sold to parties outside the group.

What is the correct consolidation adjustment in respect of these sales for the year ended 31 August 20X1?

A No adjustment required.

B DR Revenue $60,000; CR Cost of sales $60,000

C DR Revenue $80,000; CR Cost of sales $80,000.

D DR Revenue $100,000; CR Cost of sales $100,000.

The following information should be used to answer Questions 2 to 5:

The individual statements of profit or loss and other comprehensive income of Hope and Despair for the year ended 30 June 20X9 are as follows:

	Hope	Despair
	$	$
Revenue	159,800	108,400
Cost of sales	(79,200)	(61,600)
Gross profit	80,600	46,800
Administrative expenses	(27,000)	(16,000)
Profit from operations	53,600	30,800
Investment income	10,000	1,500
Finance cost	(6,000)	(4,000)
Profits before tax	57,600	28,300
Tax	(29,400)	(14,800)
Profit for the year	28,200	13,500
Other comprehensive income	–	–
Total comprehensive income	28,200	13,500

The following information is available:

- Hope acquired 90% of Despair on 30 June 20X5 A dividend was paid by Despair during the year amounting to $9,000.
- During the year Hope sold good to Despair at a selling price of $19,000. The goods yielded a profit margin of 20%. $8,000 of these goods were still held in inventory at the end of the year by Despair.

(2) **What would be the revenue figure to be included on the group consolidated statement of profit or loss and other comprehensive income ?**

A $268,200
B $249,200
C $260,200
D $253,000

(3) **What would be the unrealised profit figure to be adjusted for in the group consolidated statement of profit or loss and other comprehensive income ?**

A $1,600
B $1,333
C $3,800
D $3,167

(4) **What would be the cost of sales figure to be included on the group consolidated statement of profit or loss and other comprehensive income?**

A $140,800
B $121,800
C $123,400
D $134,640

(5) **What would be the attributable profit for the period for the parent ?**

A $30,810
B $32,000
C $30,650
D $29,500

4 Summary diagram

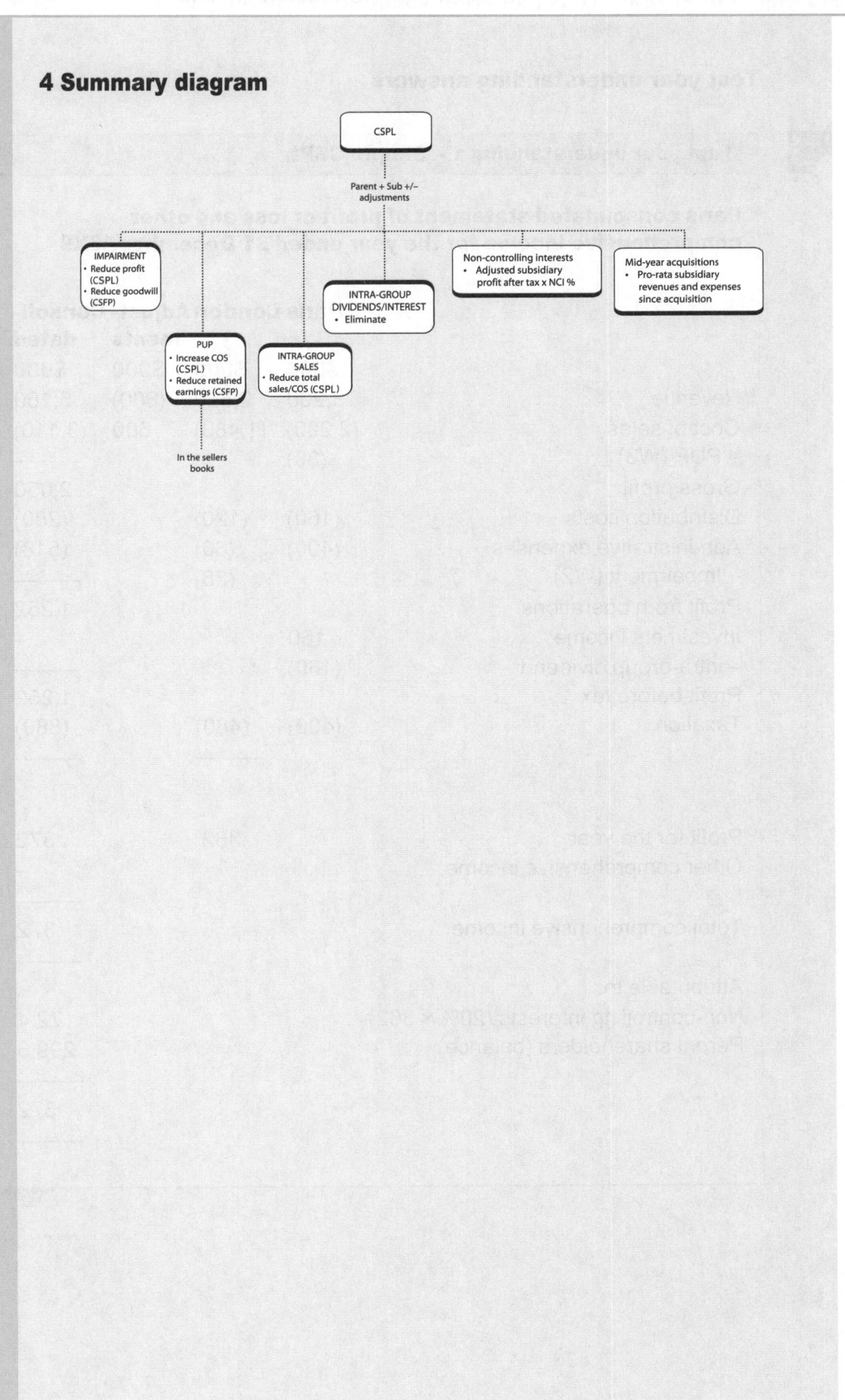

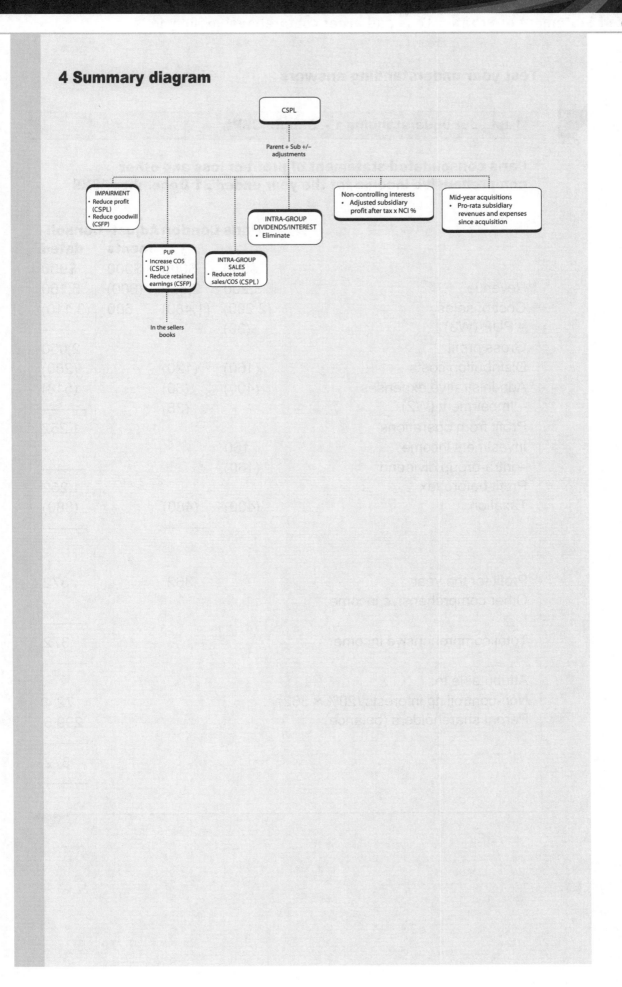

Test your understanding answers

Test your understanding 1 – Simple CSPL

Paris consolidated statement of profit or loss and other comprehensive income for the year ended 31 December 20X9

	Paris	London	Adjust-ments	Consoli-dated
	$000	$000	$000	$000
Revenue	3,200	2,560	(600)	5,160
Cost of sales	(2,200)	(1,480)	600	(3,110)
– PUP (W3)	(30)			
Gross profit				2,050
Distribution costs	(160)	(120)		(280)
Administrative expenses	(400)	(80)		(518)
– Impairment (W2)		(38)		
Profit from operations				1,252
Investment income	160			–
– intra-group dividend	(160)			
Profit before tax				1,252
Taxation	(400)	(480)		(880)
Profit for the year		362		372
Other comprehensive income				–
Total comprehensive income				372
Attributable to:				
Non-controlling interests (20% × 362)				72.4
Parent shareholders (balance)				299.6
				372

Workings

(W1) **Group structure**

Paris
80% | 31 December 20X5
London i.e. 4 years

(W2) **Impairment**

Impairment will increase the administrative expenses of the subsidiary column because the group are using the fair value method to value NCI and therefore impairment is deemed to affect the subsidiary's profit.

(W3) **PUP**

The parent sold the goods so the adjustment should be made in Parent's column, i.e. the column of the seller, to reflect the adjustment to the parents profit.

(W4) **COS**

COS = parent \$2,200 + sub \$1,480 – intra-group sale \$600 + PUP \$30 = \$3,110

(W5) **NCI**

Subs profit after tax in individual statements \$400 – impairment \$38 (FV method of valuing NCI) = \$362 × 20% = \$72.4

Test your understanding 2 – CSPL

Consolidated statement of profit or loss and other comprehensive income for period ended 31 March 20X1

	Tudor	Windsor 9/12	Adjust-ments	Consoli-dated
	$000	$000	$000	$000
Revenue	60,000	18,000		66,000
– Intra-group trading			(12,000)	
Cost of sales	(42,000)	(15,000)		(45,500)
– Intra-group trading			12,000	
– PUP (W3)	(500)			
Gross profit				20,500
Distribution costs	(2,500)	(37.5)		(2,537.5)
Administrative expenses	(3,500)	(112.5)		(3,912.5)
– Impairment (W4)		(300)		
Profit from operations				14,050
Investment income	75	–		–
– Intra-group interest (W3)			(75)	
Finance cost	–	(150)		(75)
– Intra-group interest (W3)			75	
Profit before tax				13,975
Tax	(3,000)	(450)		(3,450)
Profit for the year		1,950		10,525
Other comprehensive income				–
Total comprehensive income				10,525
Attributable to:				
Non-controlling interests (20% × 1,950)				390
Parent shareholders (Balance)				10,135
				10,525

Workings

(W1) **Group structure**

Tudor
80% | 1 July 20X0
Windsor i.e. 9 months

(W2) **PUP**

	$000	**Gross profit margin cost structure**	**Mark up cost structure**
Selling price	12,000	100%	133 ⅓%
Cost of sales	(9,000)	75%	100%
Gross profit	3,000	25%	33 ⅓ %

The goods were sold at a gross profit margin of 25% or a mark-up of one third.

Of the inventory sold to Windsor for $2,000,000 and remaining at the reporting date, there is unrealised profit to be eliminated of:

- $2,000,000 × 25% = $500,000; or
- $2,000,000 × 33 ⅓/133 ⅓ = $500,000

The parent sold the goods so the adjustment should be made in Parent's column, i.e. the column of the seller.

(W3) **Loan interest**

Interest = 15% × 1,000,000 = 150,000 × 6/12 = 75,000

The loan was taken out on 1 October, hence 6 months interest would be due at the reporting date of 31 March.

(W4) **Impairment**

Impairment will increase the administration expenses of the subsidiary column because the group are using the fair value method to value NCI .

(W5) **COS**

COS = parent $42,000 + sub $15,000 – intra-group sale $12,000 + PUP $500 = $45,500

(W6) **NCI**

Subs profit after tax in individual statements ($3,000 × 9/12) – impairment $300 (FV method of valuing NCI) = $1,950 × 20% = $390

Test your understanding 3 – CSPL

Consolidated statement of profit or loss and other comprehensive income for the year ended 31 March 20X9

	P	S	Adjust-ments	Consoli-dated
	$	$	$	$
Revenue	31,200	10,400	(4,400)	37,200
Cost of sales	(17,800)	(5,600)	4,400	(19,175)
– PUP (W2)		(175)		
Gross profit				18,025
Operating expenses	(8,500)	(1,200)		(9,772)
– Impairment (W3)		(72)		
Profit from operations				8,253
Investment income	2,000			1,600
– 80% × 500	(400)			
Profit before tax				9,853
Tax	(2,100)	(500)		(2,600)
Profit for the year				7,253
Other comprehensive income	–	–		–
Total comprehensive income		2,853		7,253
Attributable to:				
Non-controlling interests (20% × 2,853)				570.6
Parent shareholders (balance)				6,682.4
				7,253

Workings

(W1) **Group Structure**

P
80% | 1 April 20X6
S i.e. 3 years

(W2) **Intra-group sales and PUP**

Intra-group sales of $4,400 need eliminating from revenue and cost of sales.

PUP in inventory = 35% × $500 = $175

The PUP will increase cost of sales in the subsidiary's column as the subsidiary is the seller.

(W3) **Impairment**

		$
Goodwill on acquisition		800
Impairment year ended 31 March 20X8	(10% × 800)	(80)
Goodwill at 31 March 20X8		720
Impairment year ended 31 March 20X9	(10% × 720)	(72)
Goodwill at 31 March 20X9		648

Impairment will increase the operating costs of the subsidiary column because the group are using the fair value method to value NCI .

(W4) **COS**

COS = parent $17,800 + sub $5,600 – intra-group sale $4,400 + PUP $175 = $19,175

(W5) **NCI**

Subs profit after tax in individual statements $3,100 – impairment $72 (FV method of valuing NCI) – PUP (sub sells) $175 = $2,853 × 20% = $570.6

Test your understanding 4 – Practice questions

(1) B – see (W2) below

(2) A – Sub profit after tax × NCI 25%

(3) B – Parent $600 + Sub $1,200 – intra-group sale $20 + PUP $1 = $1,781

(4) A – Parent $1,000 + Sub $2,000 – intra-group sale $20 = $2,980

(5) D – Parent $8 – intra-group dividend $6 = $2

Consolidated statement of profit or loss and other comprehensive income for the year ended 31 December 20X9

	Wolf	**Hawk**	**Adj**	**Total**
	$000	$000	$000	$000
Revenue	1,000	2,000	(20)	2,980
Cost of sales	(600)	(1,200)	20	
– PUP (W2)	(1)			(1,781)
Gross profit				1,199
Distribution costs		(300)	(50)	(350)
Administrative expenses		(18)	(500)	
– Impairment (W3)		(6)		
				(524)
Operating profit				325
Investment income		8		2
– 75% × 8		(6)		
Profit before tax				327
Tax		(40)	(100)	(140)
Profit for the year			150	187
Other comprehensive income				–
Total comprehensive income				187
Attributable to:				
Non-controlling interests (25% × 150)				37.5
Parent shareholders (balance)				149.5
				187

Workings

(W1)

	Wolf	
75%	|	1 January 20X8
	Hawk	i.e. 2 years

(W2) **PUP**

Inventory remaining = 20 × 1/4 = 5

Unrealised profit in inventory = 5 × 25/125 = 1

The PUP will increase cost of sales in the parent's column as the parent is the seller.

(W3) **Impairment**

Impairment will increase the administration expenses of the parent's column because the group are using the proportion of net assets method to value NCI .

Test your understanding 5 – Practice questions

(1) D – The sales of $100,000 must be removed from the revenue and cost of sales for the group.

(2) B

(3) A

(4) C

(5) C

The consolidated statement of profit or loss and other comprehensive income would be as follows:

	$
Revenue (159,800 + 108,400 - 19,000)	249,200
Cost of sales (79,200 + 61,600 – 19,000 + 1,600 (W1))	(123,400)
Gross profit	125,800
Administrative expenses (27,000 + 16,000)	(43,000)
Profit from operations	82,800
Investment income (10,000 + 1,500 – 8,100 (W2))	3,400
Finance cost (6,000 + 4,000)	(10,000)
	76,200
Taxation (29,400 + 14,800)	(44,200)
Profit for the year	32,000
Other comprehensive income	–
Total comprehensive income	32,000
Attributable to:	
Non-controlling interests (10% × 13,500)	1,350
Parent shareholders (balance)	30,650
	32,000

(W1) **Inter-company dividend**

$9,000 × 90% = $8,100

(W2) **PUP**

8,000 × 20% = $1,600

chapter

5

Associates

Chapter learning objectives

On completion of their studies students should be able to:

- Explain the conditions required for an entity to be a subsidiary or an associate of another entity.
- Explain and apply the accounting treatment of associates (IAS 28).

1 Session content

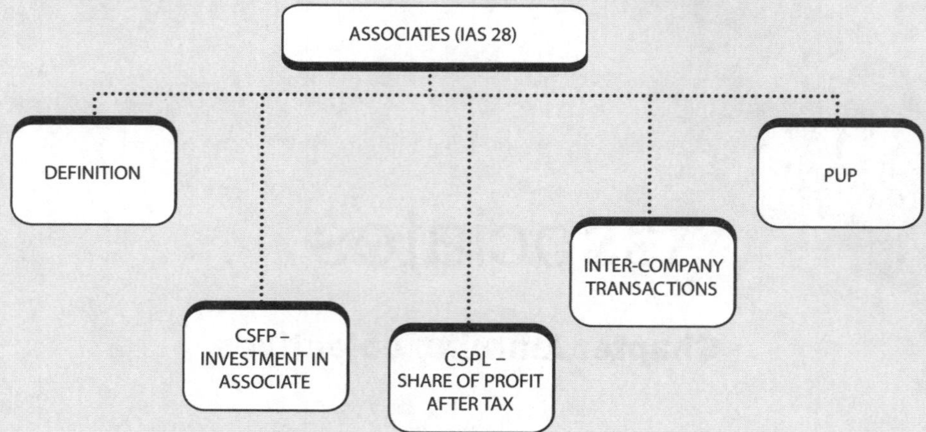

2 Associates (IAS 28)

Definition:

- An **associate** is an entity over which the investor has **significant influence** and which is neither a subsidiary nor a joint venture of the investor.

Joint ventures are not examined at F1.

- **Significant influence** is the power to participate in, but not control, the financial and operating policy decisions of an entity. A holding of 20% or more of the voting power is presumed to give significant influence unless it can be clearly demonstrated that this is not the case. At the same time a holding of less than 20% is assumed not to give significant influence unless such influence can be clearly demonstrated.

IAS 28 explains that an investor probably has significant influence if:

- It is represented on the board of directors.
- It participates in policy-making processes, including decisions about dividends or other distributions.
- There are material transactions between the investor and investee.
- There is interchange of managerial personnel.
- There is provision of essential technical information.

In situations where one entity, X, is able to exercise significant influence over another entity, A, this usually implies the absence of another entity also having control of entity A. Why is that the case? Normally, control is 'all or nothing' and allows the parent or controlling entity to make decisions regarding its subsidiary without consideration of the other shareholders. In effect, it can always outvote other shareholders at shareholders' meetings to appoint or remove directors as it considers appropriate.

Consider the situation of entity A controlling 75%, and entity B owning 25% of the voting rights of entity C. Normally, we would regard entity A as the parent and entity C as its subsidiary. What about the 25% interest owned by entity B? Depending upon the relationship between entities A and B, entity B may (or may not) be able to exercise significant influence in entity C., even though it is controlled by entity A. This will be a subjective assessment and, depending upon the outcome of that assessment, entity B will have an associate if it is able to exercise significant influence, or it will have a simple trade investment in entity C if entity A exercises control without any regard to other shareholders.

In an examination, the wording of any question will make it clear whether one entity is able to exercise significant influence over another and therefore whether it is an associate.

3 Accounting for associates

Associates are not consolidated in the way that subsidiaries are because the parent does not have control. Instead they are **equity accounted** within the consolidated financial statements.

Consolidated statement of financial position

The CSFP will continue to consolidate 100% of the assets and liabilities of the parent and subsidiary on a line by line basis.

Where there is also an associate in the group, there will be a line within non-current assets representing the associate called 'Investment in associate'.

This is calculated as follows:

Investment in associate

	$000
Cost of investment	X
Add: share of increase in net assets, i.e. share of post acquisition reserves	X
Less: impairment losses of the associate	(X)
Less: PUP (where P is selling – see later)	(X)
	X

The increase in net assets, (which is the same as the post-acquisition reserves), of the associate can be found from doing a W2 for the associate in exactly the same way that you would do such a working for a subsidiary.

As well as showing the investment in associate within the CSFP the associate will have an impact of group reserves where the group's share of the associates post acquisition profits will be included in W5. You will therefore need to include in W5 (group retained earnings) the **group's share of A's post acquisition profits** less any impairments in both the subsidiary and the associate.

Consolidated statement of profit and loss and other comprehensive income

Where there is also an associate in the group the CSPL will continue to consolidate 100% of the income and expenses of the parent and subsidiary on a line by line basis.

There will also be a line before profit before tax representing the group's share of the associate's profit after tax less any impairment losses less any PUP (where A is the seller), called **"share of profit of associate".**

Dividends received by the parent from the associate are excluded from the statement and replaced with the share of associate's profit calculated above.

Note: Non-controlling interests are not applicable for associates as the group only reflects its share in the associate's net assets and profit for the year.

4 Trading with the associate

Inter-company transactions

Remember that you do **not** eliminate inter-company sales and purchases, receivables or payables between the group and the associate as the associate is outside the group. The only exception to this is any unrealised profit on transactions, of which the **group's share** must be eliminated.

Provisions for unrealised profit (PUP)

IAS 28 requires that only the group share of unrealised profit is removed:

PUP = **A%** × unrealised profit in inventory

Parent sells to associate

In the CSFP, the following adjustment is necessary for the group share of the PUP:

- Reduce W5 retained earnings (group reserves)
- Reduce investment in associate (CSFP)

When the parent sells to the associate the profit must be eliminated from the investment in the associate because the inventory is in the books of the associate. The associates inventory is not consolidated so we cannot remove the profit from the inventory line on the CSFP. Therefore, the adjustment is made to reduce the investment in associate.

In the CSPL, the reduction in profit for the current year is adjusted for as follows:

- Increase the cost of sales of the parent company by the parent's share of the PUP.

The journal entries would therefore be:

Dr	COS (which has an impact on Group retained earnings in W5)
Cr	Investment in associate

Illustration 1 – Parent sells to associate

The parent (P) has an associate (A). P owns 40% of A.

P has sold $200,000 of goods to A at a price which represents cost plus 25%.

At the reporting date 60% of these items remain in inventory.

There is no intra-group trading to be eliminated between a group and associate as the associate is not a group member. The only adjustment will be for the PUP on closing inventory.

Profit on sale	200,000 × 25/125 = 40,000
Profit in inventory	60% × 40,000 = 24,000
PUP (group share of profit)	40% × 24,000 = 9,600

CSFP treatment

Dr Retained earnings (W5)	↓	9,600
Cr Investment in associate	↓	9,600

CSPL treatment

The $9,600 represents the fall in the parent's gross profit.

This is achieved by recording the following double entry:

Dr Cost of sales	↑	9,600
And so Gross profit	↓	9,600

Associate sells to the parent

In the CSFP, the following adjustment is necessary for the group share of the PUP:

- Reduce retained earnings (W5)
- Reduce inventory (CSFP)

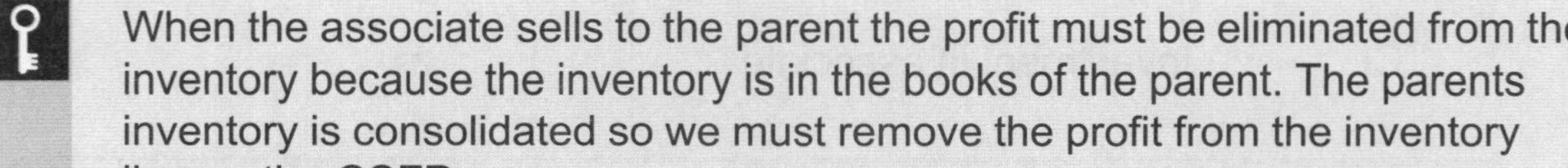

When the associate sells to the parent the profit must be eliminated from the inventory because the inventory is in the books of the parent. The parents inventory is consolidated so we must remove the profit from the inventory line on the CSFP.

In the CSPL, the reduction in profit for the current year is adjusted for as follows:

- Reduce share of associate's profits

The journal entries would therefore be:

Dr	Share of associates profit (which has an impact on Group retained earnings in W5)
Cr	Inventory

Illustration 2 – Associate sells to parent

Using the same scenario as illustration 1 above, the parent's share of the PUP is $9,600.

CSFP treatment

Dr Retained earnings	↓	9,600 (W5)
Cr Inventory	↓	9,600 (CSFP)

The reduction in retained earnings is achieved by reducing the share of associates post acquisition profit.

CSPL treatment

Dr Share of associates profits	↓	9,600

No adjustment is required to sales and cost of sales.

Test your understanding 1 – PUP

A parent company owns 25% of its associate. The parent made sales to the associate during the year amount to $450,000. The sales have been made at cost plus 20%. At the reporting date, 30% of these items remain in inventory.

Required:

Identify the relevant adjustments required to be made to the group accounts in the statement of financial position and the statement of profit or loss and other comprehensive income.

Illustration 3 – CSFP

Below are the statements of financial position of three companies as at 31 December 20X0.

	Tom	James	Emily
	$000	$000	$000
Non-current assets			
Property, plant & equipment	959	980	840
Investments			
630,000 shares in James	805	–	–
168,000 shares in Emily	224	–	–
	1,988	980	840
Current assets			
Inventory	380	640	190
Receivables	190	310	100
Cash and cash equivalents	35	58	46
	605	1,008	336
	2,593	1,988	1,176
Equity			
Share Capital $1	1,120	840	560
Retained earnings	1,232	602	448
	2,352	1,442	1,008

Current liabilities			
Trade payables	150	480	136
Taxation	91	66	32
	241	546	168
	2,593	1,988	1,176

You are also given the following information:

(1) Tom acquired its shares in James on 1 January 20X0 when James had a debit balance in retained earnings of $56,000.

(2) Tom acquired its shares in Emily on 1 January 20X0 when Emily had retained earnings of $140,000.

(3) An impairment test at the year end shows the goodwill for James remains unimpaired but the investment arising on the acquisition of Emily has impaired by $2,800.

(4) NCI should be calculated using the proportion of net assets method.

Required:

Prepare the consolidated statement of financial position for the year ended 31 December 20X0.

Solution

Tom consolidated statement of financial position as at 31 December 20X0

	$000	$000
Non-current assets		
Goodwill (W3)		217.0
Property, plant & equipment (959 + 980)		1,939.0
Investment in associate (W6)		313.6
		2,469.6

Current assets		
Inventory (380 + 640)	1,020.0	
Receivables (190 + 310)	500.0	
Cash and cash equivalents(35 + 58)	93.0	
		1,613.0
		4,082.6
Equity		
Share capital		1,120.0
Retained earnings (W5)		1,815.1
		2,935.1
Non-controlling interest (W4)		360.5
Current liabilities		
Trade payables (150 + 480)	630.0	
Taxation (91 + 66)	157.0	
		787.0
		4,082.6

Workings

(W1) **Group structure**

Tom

630/840 = 75% | 1 January 20X0

James i.e. 1 year

Tom

168/560 = 30% | 1 January 20X0

Emily i.e. 1 year

(W2) **Net assets – James**

	Acquisition date	Reporting date
	$000	$000
Share capital	840.0	840.0
Retained earnings	(56.0)	602.0
	784.0	1,442.0

Note that James has a debit balance in retained earnings at the date of acquisition rather than the more usual retained earnings credit balance.

(W2) **Net assets – Emily**

	Acquisition date	Reporting date
	$000	$000
Share capital	560.0	560. 0
Retained earnings	140.0	448.0
	700.0	1,008.0

(W3) **Goodwill – James**

	$000
Fair value of investment	805.0
NCI at acquisition 25% × 784 (W2)	196
Fair value of net assets acquired	
100% × 784 (W2)	(784.0)
Goodwill	217.0

Note that goodwill is only ever calculated for the subsidiary and never the associate. Goodwill will only arise when the parent controls an entity.

(W4) **Non-controlling interests**

	$000
Value of NCI at acquisition (W3)	196.0
NCI × post-acquisition reserves 25% × (1,442 – 784) (W2)	164.5
NCI × impairment (W3) (fair value method only)	–
NCI at reporting date	360.5

(W5) **Retained earnings (group reserves)**

	$000
Tom	1,232.0
James – share of post-acquisition reserves (75% × (1,442 – 784)) (W2)	493.5
Emily – share of post-acquisition reserves (30% × (1,008 – 700)) (W2)	92.4
Less: impairments to date	(2.8)
	1,815.1

(W6) **Investment in associate**

	$000
Fair value of investment	224.0
Share of post-acquisition profits (W5)	92.4
Less: impairment	(2.8)
	313.6

Test your understanding 2 – CSFP

P acquired 75% of S on 1 December 20X6 paying $2,675,000. At this date the balance on S's retained earnings was $870,000. On 1 December 20X8 P acquired 30% of A's ordinary shares paying $500,000.

The statements of financial position of the three companies as at 30 November 20X9 are as follows:

	P	**S**	**A**
	$000	$000	$000
Non-current assets			
Property	890	850	900
Plant and equipment	450	210	150
Investments	3,175	–	–
Current assets			
Inventory	270	230	200
Receivables	100	340	400
Cash and cash equivalents	160	50	140
	5,045	1,680	1,790

Equity			
Share capital $1	1,900	500	250
Share premium	650	80	–
Retained earnings	1,145	400	1,200
	3,695	980	1,450
Non-current liabilities			
10% Loan notes	500	300	–
Current liabilities			
Trade payables	520	330	250
Income tax	330	70	90
	5,045	1,680	1,790

The following information is relevant:

- During the year, S sold goods to P for $400,000 at a mark-up of 25%. P had a quarter of these goods still in inventory at the year-end.
- In September A sold goods to P for $150,000. These goods had cost A $100,000. P had $90,000 (at cost to P) in inventory at the year-end.
- As a result of the above inter-company sales, P's books showed $50,000 and $20,000 as owing to S and A respectively at the year-end. These balances agreed with the amounts recorded in S's and A's books.
- Goodwill in the subsidiary is to be impaired by 40% at the reporting date. An impairment review found the investment in the associate was to be impaired by $15,000 at the year-end.
- A's profit after tax for the year is $450,000.
- The group policy is the value NCI at fair value at acquisition. The fair value of the NCI holding in S at acquisition was $400,000.

Required:

Prepare a consolidation statement of financial position for the P group as at 30 November 20X9.

Test your understanding 3 – CSPL

Below are the statements of profit or loss and other comprehensive income the Barbie group and its associated companies, as at 31 December 20X0.

	Barbie	**Ken**	**Shelly**
	$000	$000	$000
Revenue	385	100	60
Cost of sales	(185)	(60)	(20)
Gross profit	200	40	40
Operating expenses	(50)	(15)	(10)
Profit before tax	150	25	30
Tax	(50)	(12)	(10)
Profit for the year	100	13	20
Other comprehensive income	–	–	–
Total comprehensive income	100	13	20

You are also given the following information:

(1) Barbie acquired 60,000 ordinary shares in Shelly for $80,000 when that entity had a credit balance on its retained earnings of $50,000 a number of years ago. Shelly has 200,000 $1 ordinary shares.

(2) Barbie acquired 75% of the ordinary shares in Ken, a number of years ago, for $70,000 when retained earnings were $20,000.

(3) During the year Shelly sold goods to Barbie for $28,000. Barbie still holds some of these goods in inventory at the year end. The profit element included in these remaining goods is $2,000.

(4) Goodwill and the investment in the associate were impaired for the first time during the year as follows:

Shelly $2,000
Ken $3,000

Impairment of the subsidiary's goodwill should be charged to operating expenses.

(5) The group values NCI using the proportion of net assets method.

Required:

Prepare the consolidated statement of profit or loss and other comprehensive income for Barbie for the year ended 31 December 20X0.

Test your understanding 4 – Practice questions

Use the following information to questions TYU's 1 to 5 below.

The following are the summarised accounts of H, S, and A for the year ended 30 June 20X9.

Statements of financial position as at 30 June 20X9

	H	S	A
	$	$	$
Non-current assets			
Property, plant and equipment	87,000	88,000	62,000
Investments			
S (80%)	115,000		
A (30%)	15,000		
Current assets	74,000	40,000	9,000
	291,000	128,000	71,000
Share capital ($1 shares)	200,000	75,000	35,000
Retained earnings	89,000	51,000	34,000
Liabilities	2,000	2,000	2,000
	291,000	128,000	71,000

Statements of profit or loss and other comprehensive income for the year ended 30 June 20X9

	H	S	A
	$	$	$
Revenue	500,000	200,000	100,000
Operating costs	(400,000)	(140,000)	(60,000)
Profit from operations	100,000	60,000	40,000
Tax	(23,000)	(21,000)	(14,000)
Profit after tax	77,000	39,000	26,000
Other comprehensive income	–	–	–
Total comprehensive income	77,000	39,000	26,000

The shares in S and A were acquired on 1 July 20X6 when the retained profits of S were $15,000 and the retained profits of A were $10,000.

During the year S sold goods to H for $10,000 at a margin of 50%. At the year-end H had sold 80% of the goods.

At 30 June 20X9 the goodwill in respect of S had been impaired by 30% of its original amount, of which the current year loss was $1,200. At 30 June 2009 the investment in A had been impaired by $450, of which the current year loss was $150.

NCI is valued by the group using the proportion of net assets method.

(1) **What is the correct figure for revenue?**

A $700,000

B $710,000

C $690,000

D $790,000

(2) **What is the correct figure for investment in associate?**

A $22,200

B $21,750

C $14,550

D $15,000

(3) **What is the correct figure for retained earnings?**

A $110,850

B $124,200

C $224,000

D $117,250

(4) **What is the correct figure for NCI in equity?**

A $25,000

B $18,000

C $7,000

D $7,600

(5) **What is the correct figure for profit in associate?**

A $7,800

B $7,650

C $7,350

D $7,950

5 Summary diagram

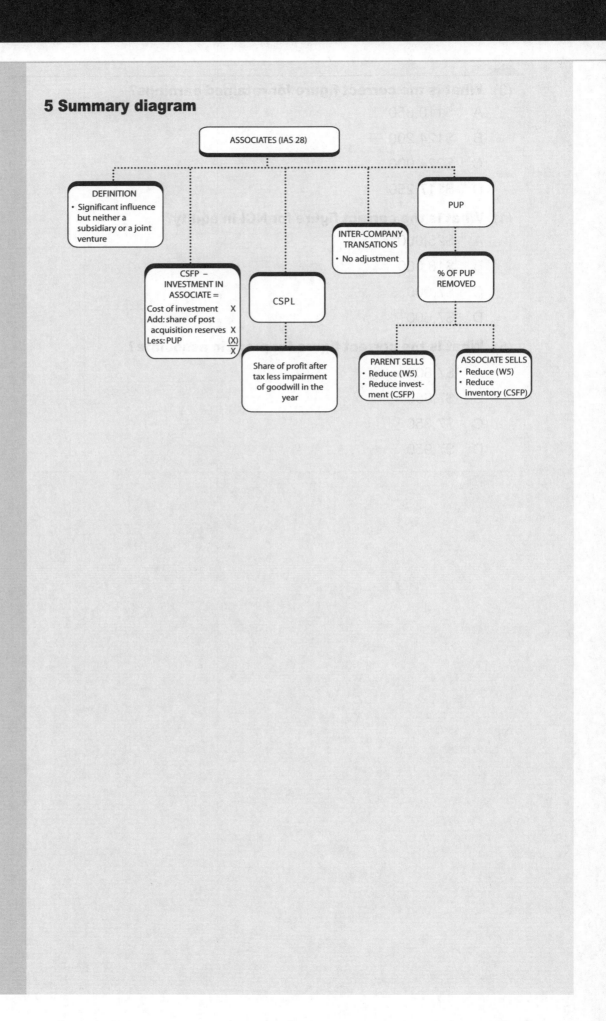

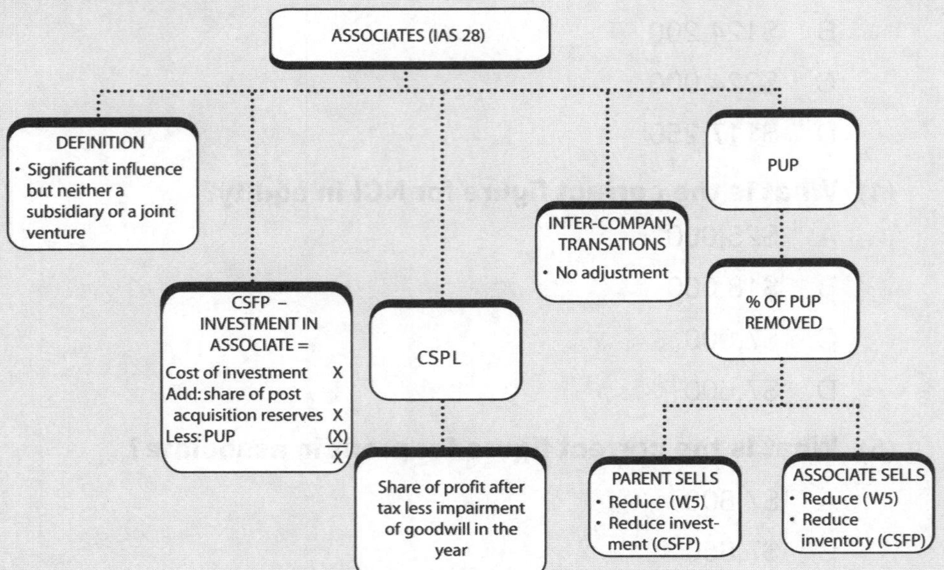

Test your understanding answers

Test your understanding 1 – PUP

Inventory remaining at reporting date = 450,000 × 30% = 135,000

Profit within closing inventory = 135,000 × 20/120 = 22,500

Parent's share of PUP = 22,500 × 25% = 5,625

Adjustments required to group financial statements

Dr Retained earnings (W5)	5,625
Cr Investment in associate (CSFP)	5,625

In the statement of profit or loss, the sales and cost of sales of the group must be adjusted to allow for an overall reduction in profits of $5,625.

Increase cost of sales by 5,625

Test your understanding 2 – CSFP

(1) C

(2) B

(3) A

P Group consolidated statement of financial position as at 30 November 20X9

	$000
Non-current assets	
Goodwill (W3)	975
Property (890 + 850)	1,740
Plant & equipment (450 + 210)	660
Investment in associate (W6)	620
Current assets	
Inventory (270 + 230 – 20 (W7) – 9 (W8))	471
Receivables (100 + 340 – 50)	390
Cash and cash equivalents(160 + 50)	210
	5,066
Equity	
Share capital	1,900
Share premium	650
Retained earnings (W5)	401
	2,951
Non-controlling interests (W4)	115
Non-current liabilities	
10% Loan notes (500 + 300)	800
Current liabilities	
Trade payables (520 + 330 – 50)	800
Tax (330 + 70)	400
	5,066

Workings

(W1) **Group structure**

```
        P
75%  |  1 December 20X6
        S  i.e. 3 years

        P
     |  1 December 20X8
30%  |
        A  i.e. 1 year
```

(W2) **Net assets of subsidiary**

	Acquisition date	Reporting date
	$000	$000
Share capital	500	500
Share premium	80	80
Retained earnings	870	400
PUP (W7)	–	(20)
	1,450	960

Net assets of associate

	Acquisition date	Reporting date
	$000	$000
Share capital	250	250
Retained earnings (see below)	750	1,200
	1,000	1,450

Retained earnings at acquisition (balance)	750
Post acquisition profit	450
Retained earnings at reporting date	1,200

(W3) **Goodwill**

	$000
Fair value of investment	2,675
Value of NCI at acquisition (as per question)	400
Fair value of net assets acquired (100% × 1,450) (W2)	(1,450)
Goodwill on acquisition	1,625
Impairment (40% × 1,625)	(650)
Goodwill at reporting date	975

(W4) **NCI**

	$000
Value of NCI at acquisition (as per question)	400
NCI × post-acquisition reserves 25% × (960 – 1,450) (W2)	(122.5)
NCI × impairment (W3) (fair value method only) 25% × 650	(162.5)
NCI at reporting date	115.0

(W5) **Group retained earnings**

	$000
Parent	1,145
PUP (W8)	(9)
Subsidiary (75% × (960 – 1,450))	(367.5)
Associate (30% × (1,450 – 1,000))	135
Impairment (15 + (75% × 650) (W3)	(502.5)
	401.0

(W6) **Investment in associate**

	$000
Cost of investment	500
Share of post-acquisition profits (30% × (1,450 – 1,000)) (W2)	135
Less: impairment	(15)
	620

(W7) **PUP – Subsidiary**

Profit on sale (25/125 × 400)	80
Profit in inventory (1/4 × 80)	20

The sub sells so reduce the subs profit via W2 and also reduce inventory

(W8) **PUP – Associate**

Profit on sale (150 – 100)	50
Profit in inventory (90/150 × 50)	30
Group share (30% × 30)	9

The associate sells so reduce (W5) and inventory

Test your understanding 3 – CSPL

Barbie consolidated statement of profit or loss and other comprehensive income for the year ended 31 December 20X0

	Barbie	Ken	Adjust-ments	Consoli-dated
	$000	$000	$000	$000
Revenue	385	100		485.0
Cost of sales	(185)	(60)		(245.0)
Gross profit				240.0
Operating expenses	(50)	(15)		(68.0)
Impairment in subsidiary (W3)	(3)			
Profit from operations				172.0
Share of profits of associate company (W2)				3.4
Profit before tax				175.4
Taxation	(50)	(12)		(62.0)
Profit for the year		13		113.4
Other comprehensive income				–
Total comprehensive income				113.4
Amount attributable to:				
Non-controlling interests (25% × 13)				3.25
Parent shareholders (balance)				110.15
				113.40

Workings

(W1) **Group structure**

	Barbie
75% given	|
	Ken
	Barbie
60/200 = 30%	|
	Shelly

(W2) **Share of profit of associate**

Share of associate profit for the year (30% × $20)	6
Less:	
PUP (30% × $2)	(0.6)
Impairment	(2)
	3.4

(W3) **Impairment**

NCI is valued using the proportion of net assets method so impairment will increase the operating expenses of the parent column.

Test your understanding 4 – Practice questions

(1) C

(2) B

(3) A

(4) A

(5) B

H Group statement of profit or loss and other comprehensive income for the year ended 30 June 20X9

	H	S	Adjust-ments	Consoli-dated
	$	$	$	$
Revenue	500,000	200,000	(10,000)	690,000
Operating costs	(400,000)	(140,000)	10,000	(532,200)
Impairment in S (W4)	(1,200)			
PUP (W7)		(1,000)		
Profit from operations				157,800
Share of profit of associate (W9)				7,650
Profit before tax				165,450
Tax	(23,000)	(21,000)		(44,000)
Profit for the period		38,000		121,450
Other comprehensive income				–
Total comprehensive income				121,450
Attributable to:				
Non-controlling interests (20% × 38,000)				7,600
Parent shareholders (balance)				113,850
				121,450

Consolidated statement of financial position as at 30 June 20X9

	$
Non-current assets	
Goodwill (W3)	30,100
Investment in associate (W6)	21,750
Property, plant and equipment (87,000 + 88,000)	175,000
Current assets (74,000 + 40,000 – 1,000 PUP (W7))	113,000
	339,850
Equity	
Share capital	200,000
Retained earnings (W5)	110,850
Non-controlling interest (W4)	25,000
Liabilities (2,000 + 2,000)	4,000
	339,850

Workings

(W1) **Group structure**

H
80%/30% | 1 July 20X6
S and A i.e. 3 years

(W2) **Net assets**

	S		A	
	Acq Date	**Rep Date**	**Acq Date**	**Rep Date**
	$	$	$	$
Share capital	75,000	75,000	35,000	35,000
Retained earnings	15,000	51,000	10,000	34,000
PUP		(1,000)		
	90,000	125,000	45,000	69,000

(W3) **Goodwill**

	$
	$
Fair value of investment	115,000
Value of NCI at acquisition (20% × 90,000) (W2)	18,000
Fair value of net assets at acquisition (100% 90,000)	(90,000)
	43,000
Less: impairment loss (30% × 43,000)	(12,900)
	30,100

(W4) **NCI**

	$
Value of NCI at acquisition (W3)	18,000
NCI × post-acquisition reserves 20% × (125,000 – 90,000) (W2)	7,000
NCI × impairment (W3) (fair value method only)	–
NCI at reporting date	25,000

(W5) **Retained earnings**

	$
Parent	89,000
Less: Impairments (12,900 (W3) + 450)	(13,350)
Share of post acquisition profits	
(S: 80% × (125,000 – 90,000)) (W2)	28,000
(A: 30% × (69,000 – 45,000)) (W2)	7,200
	110,850

(W6) **Investment in associate**

	$
Cost	15,000
Share of increase in net assets (30% × (69,000 – 45,000)) (W2)	7,200
	22,200
Less: impairment	(450)
	21,750

(W7) **PUP**

$10,000 × 20% × 50% = $1,000
Subsidiary sells so increase COS of sub column in the CSPL and reduce (W2) and inventory in CSFP

(W8) **Impairment**

NCI is valued using the proportion of net assets method so impairment will increase the operating expenses of the parent column.

(W9) **Share of associate profit**

(30% × $26,000) – current year impairment $150 = $7,650

chapter

6

The Regulatory Environment

Chapter learning objectives

On completion of their studies students should be able to:

- Explain the need for regulation of financial reporting information.
- Explain key elements of the regulatory environment for financial reporting.
- Explain the difference between a rules based approach and a principles based approach to financial reporting regulation.
- Explain the roles and structures of key regulatory bodies.
- Explain the scope of IFRS and how they are developed.

1 Session content

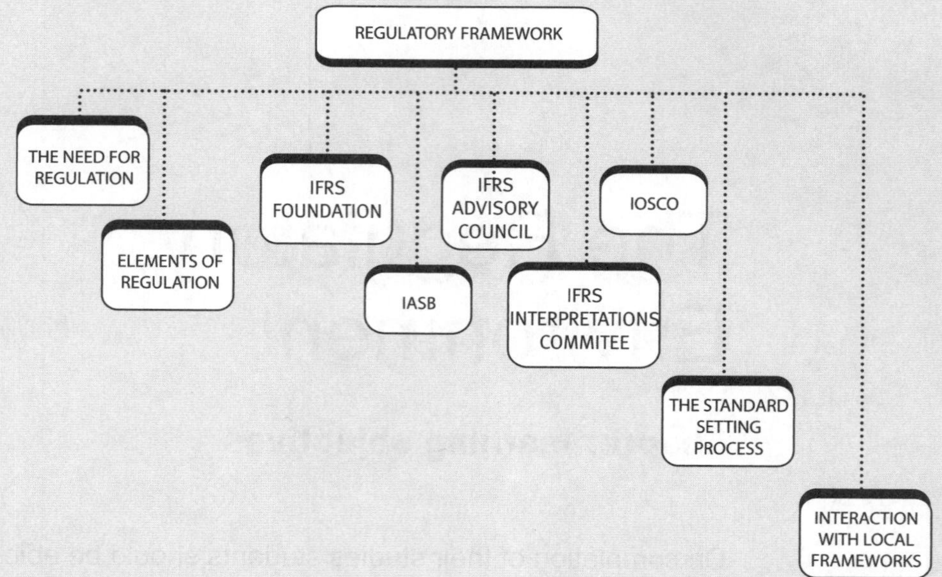

2 The regulatory environment

Need for regulation

Financial statements will be used by shareholders and many other types of users to make decisions. In order that they can be relied upon by users, published financial statements should be subject to regulation.

Regulation can also promote consistency and so helps users when interpreting financial statements.

Different countries will be subject to a variety of economic, social and political factors. As a result, the way in which published financial statements are regulated will vary from country to country.

The need for regulation

Financial statements and reports for shareholders and other users are prepared using principles and rules that can be interpreted in different ways. To provide guidance and try and ensure that they are interpreted in the same way each time, some form of regulation is required.

We have identified that taxable profits are based on accounting profit and that the number and type of adjustments required to compute taxable profits varies from country to country. Part of this variation was due to the differences in the tax regulations, but a part of it was due to the different approaches to the calculation of accounting profit. We have identified that in some countries taxable income is closely linked to the accounting profit and that accounting rules are largely driven by taxation laws. These countries are usually known as code law countries, countries where the legal system originated in Roman law. These countries tend to have detailed laws relating to trading entities and accounting standards are usually embodied within the law. Accounting regulation in these countries is usually in the hands of the government and financial reporting is a matter of complying with a set of legal rules.

In other countries the common law system is used, common law is based on case law and tends to have less detailed regulations. In countries with common law systems, the accounting regulation within the legal system is usually kept to a minimum, with detailed accounting regulations produced by professional organisations or other private sector accounting standard-setting bodies.

Whichever system is adopted, there is a need for every country to have a system for regulating the preparation of financial statements and reports.

3 Elements of a regulatory environment

A regulatory environment may consist of any of the following elements:

- local law;
- local accounting standards;
- international accounting standards;
- conceptual frameworks e.g. Statement of Principles in the UK;
- requirements of international bodies e.g. EU, IOSCO.

GAAP (Generally accepted accounting practice) encompasses the conventions, the rules and procedures necessary to define accepted accounting practice at a particular time. It includes not only broad guidelines of general application but also detailed practices and procedures. It includes local legislation requirements, accounting standards and any other local regulations. This will therefore vary from country to country as different countries have different regulations, i.e. UK GAAP, US GAAP, etc.

The regulatory environment

The regulatory environment for accounting in individual countries will be affected by a number of legislative and quasi-legislative influences:

- national company law
- EU directives or other trading body directives
- security exchange rules.

Why is regulation necessary

Regulation of accounting information is aimed at ensuring that users of financial statements receive a minimum amount of information that will enable them to make meaningful decisions regarding their interest in a reporting entity. A regulation is required to ensure that relevant and reliable financial reporting is achieved to meet the needs of shareholders and other users.

Accounting standards on their own would not provide complete regulation. In order to fully regulate the preparation of financial statements and the obligations of companies and directors, legal and market regulations are also required.

Principles-based and rules-based approaches for accounting standards

Principles-based approach:

- based upon a conceptual framework such as the IASB's Framework
- accounting standards are set on the basis of the conceptual framework.

Rules-based approach:

- 'Cookbook' approach
- accounting standards are a set of rules which companies must follow.

In the UK there is a principles-based approach in terms of the Statement of Principles and accounting standards and a rules-based approach in terms of the Companies Acts, EU directives and stock exchange rulings.

Variation from country to country

Accounting and information disclosure practices around the world are influenced by a variety of economic, social and political factors. In addition to the legal system and tax legislation, a range of other factors that contribute to variations between the accounting regulations of countries are discussed below. The wide range of factors influencing the development of accounting regulations have resulted in a wide range of different systems, this has made it difficult and time consuming to try and harmonise accounting practices around the world. With the growth in international investing, there is a growing need for harmonisation of financial statements between countries.

Sources of finance and capital markets

There is more demand for financial information and disclosure where a higher proportion of capital is raised from external shareholders, rather than from banks or family members. Stock markets rely on published financial information by entities. Banks and family members are usually in a position to demand information directly from the entity, whereas shareholders have to rely on publicly available information.

The political system

The nature of regulation and control exerted on accounting will reflect political philosophies and objectives of the ruling party, for example, environmental concerns.

Entity ownership

The need for public accountability and disclosure will be greater where there is a broad ownership of shares as opposed to family ownership or government ownership.

Cultural differences

The culture within a country can influence societal and national values which can influence accounting regulations.

Harmonisation versus standardisation

Harmonisation tends to mean the process of increasing the compatibility of accounting practices by setting bounds to their degree of variation.

Standardisation tends to imply the imposition of a rigid and narrower set of rules. Standardisation also implies that one technically correct method can be identified for every aspect of accounting and then this can be imposed on all preparers of accounts.

Due to the variations between countries discussed above, full standardisation of accounting practices is unlikely. Harmonisation is more likely, as the agreement of a common conceptual framework of accounting may enable a closer harmonisation of accounting practices.

The need for harmonisation of accounting standards

Each country has its own accounting regulation, financial statements and reports prepared for shareholders and other uses are based on principles and rules that can vary widely from country to country. Multinational entities may have to prepare reports on activities on several bases for use in different countries, and this can cause unnecessary financial costs. Furthermore, preparation of financial statements based on different principles makes it difficult for investors and analysts to interpret financial information. This lack of comparability in financial reporting can affect the credibility of the entity's reporting and the analysts' reports and can have a detrimental effect on financial investment.

The increasing levels of cross-border financing transactions, securities trading and direct foreign investment has resulted in the need for a single set of rules by which assets, liabilities and income are recognised and measured.

The number of foreign listings on major exchanges around the world is continually increasing and many worldwide entities may find that they are preparing accounts using a number of different rules and regulations in order to be listed on various markets.

4 International financial reporting standards

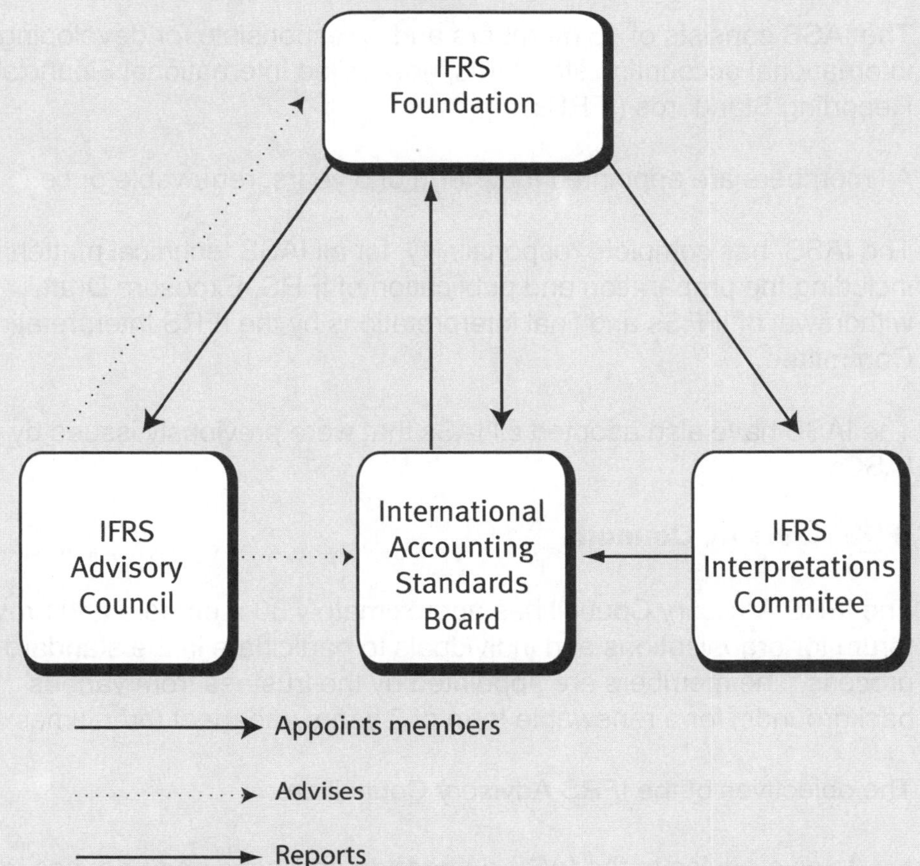

IFRS Foundation

In 1997 it was decided to restructure the IASC into two main bodies – the Trustees and the International Accounting Standards Board (IASB). As a result the IFRS Foundation was established in March 2001 as a non-profit making corporation with 22 Trustees. The trustees are responsible for:

- appointing the members of the IASB, the International Financial Reporting Interpretations Committee and IFRS Advisory Council;
- reviewing annually the strategy of the IASB and its effectiveness;
- approving annually the budget and determining the funding of the IASB;
- reviewing broad strategic issues affecting accounting standards;
- promoting the IASB and its work and the rigorous application of IASs;
- establishing and amending operating procedures for the IASB, IFRS Interpretations Committee and IFRS Advisory Council.

International Accounting Standards Board (IASB)

The IASB consists of 15 members and is responsible for developing international accounting standards, now called International Financial Reporting Standards (IFRSs).

All members are appointed for a term of 5 years, renewable once.

The IASB has complete responsibility for all IASB technical matters, including the preparation and publication of IFRS, Exposure Draft, withdrawal of IFRSs and final interpretations by the IFRS Interpretations Committee.

The IASB have also adopted all IASs that were previously issued by the IASC.

IFRS Advisory Council

The IFRS Advisory Council has approximately 30 members and provides a forum for organisations and individuals to participate in the standard setting process. The members are appointed by the trustees from various backgrounds, for a renewable term of 3 years and meet three times a year.

The objectives of the IFRS Advisory Council are:

- to give advice to the IASB on agenda decisions and priorities in its work;
- to inform the IASB of the views of organisations and individuals on the Council on major standard setting projects;
- to give other advice to the Board or to the Trustees.

IFRS Interpretations Committee

The IFRS Interpretations Committee (formally known as IFRIC), assists the IASB by reviewing accounting issues that are likely to receive divergent or unacceptable treatment in the absence of authoritative guidance, with a view to reaching an appropriate accounting treatment. It was established in 2002 by the IFRS Foundation to replace the Standing Interpretations Committee (SIC). Previously SIC Interpretations were issued, now IFRS Interpretation Committee Interpretations are issued.

The IFRS Interpretations Committee has two main responsibilities:

- Review, on a timely basis, new financial reporting issues not specifically addressed in IFRSs.
- Clarify issues where unsatisfactory or conflicting interpretations have developed, with a view to reaching a consensus on the most appropriate treatment.

International Organisation of Securities Commissions (IOSCO)

IOSCO is the representative body of the world's securities markets regulators.

Financial information is vital to the operation of markets and differences in the financial information from entities in different countries can reduce the efficiency of markets.

IOSCO has been working with the IASB since 1987 in promoting the improvement of International Standards. Since the mid-1990s IOSCO and IASB have been working on a programme of 'core standards' which could be used by listed companies who offer securities abroad. This project was completed in 1999.

In May 2000, IOSCO issued a report to its members recommending that they use International Financial Reporting Standards when preparing their financial statements.

IOSCO representatives also sit as observers on the IFRS Interpretations Committee.

5 Standard-setting process

There is no strict procedure for the development of a Standard. However, the process may involve the following steps:

- Establishment of an advisory committee to give advice on the issues arising on the project. The IASB will consult with this committee and IFRS Advisory Committee throughout the process.
- On major projects, the IASB develops and publishes a Discussion Paper for public comment. This will give an overview of the issue, possible approaches to address the issue, views of the authors or the IASB and an invitation to comment.

- Following the receipt and review of comments, an Exposure Draft is produced for public comment. The Exposure Draft is based upon the earlier Discussion Paper, together with the IASB review of feedback received from the public – i.e. mainly firms of accountants and companies who are likely to be affected by the introduction of a new or changed reporting standard.

  The Exposure Draft is then the draft standard made available for final review, which can still be amended before final approval as a reporting standard.
- Following the receipt and review of comments, the final Standard will be issued.

The role of national standard setters

- The harmonisation process has gathered pace in the last few years. From 2005 all European listed entities were required to adopt IFRS in their group financial statements. Many other countries including Australia, Canada and New Zealand decided to follow a similar process. National standard setters are committed to a framework of accounting standards based on IFRS.
- Additionally, the US are committed to harmonise with IFRS and the FASB and the IASB are aiming for convergence over the next few years.
- The overall impact of the above is that the trend towards closer international harmonisation of accounting practices is now set. It will become increasingly difficult for domestic standard setters to justify domestic standards at odds with IFRSs.

The role of accounting standard setters and the IASB

- In February 2005, the IASB issued a memorandum setting out the responsibilities of the IASB and national standard setters. It is most relevant to those who have adopted or converged with IFRSs'. It deals with the responsibilities of national standard setters to facilitate adoption or convergence with IFRS.
- It includes the responsibilities of the IASB to ensure that it makes information available on a timely basis so that national standard setters can be informed of the IASB's plans. Sufficient time should be allowed in relation to consultative documents so that national standard setters have sufficient time to prepare the information in their own context and to receive comments from their own users.

- The national standard setters should deal with domestic barriers to adopting or converging with IFRS. They should avoid amending an IFRS when adopting it in their own jurisdiction, so that the issue of noncompliance with the IFRS does not arise. They should encourage their own constituents to communicate their technical views to the IASB and they themselves should respond with comments on a timely basis. They should also make known any differences of opinion that they have with a project as early as possible in the process.

6 Interaction with local frameworks

The IASB invites comments from national standard-setters on exposure drafts and in the past have worked together with both the FASB (Financial Accounting Standards Board – US) and IASB (International Accounting Standards Board) to develop accounting standards.

The IFRS advisory council also consults national standard-setters and co-ordinate the agendas and priorities of the IASB and national standard-setters.

Some countries will adopt International Financial Reporting Standards as their local accounting standards, or will be heavily influenced by IFRSs when preparing local standards. This may particularly be the case in countries without a strong accountancy profession.

A country choosing to adopt international standards can apply them in a number of ways:

- Adoption of international standards as local GAAP – This is usually countries where the accounting profession isn't well developed and they adopt the international standards with little or no amendments. This is quick to implement but does not take into account any specific requirements of that country.
- International standards used as a model to create local GAAP – This involves countries taking the international standards and then amending them to reflect the countries needs.
- International standards used as persuasive influence in preparing local GAAP – This is where a country already has their own standards but they may differ to the international ones. They will use the international standards to update their local ones to ensure that they comply with IFRSs in all material aspects.

Alternatively a country may choose to prepare local GAAP with no reference to international standards!

Special circumstances

There are specific standards that exist in special circumstances such as:

- IAS 26 – Accounting and Reporting by Retirement Benefit Plans - applies to the preparation of financial reports by retirement benefit plans. It is mainly a presentation and disclosure standard.
- IAS 41 – Agriculture – governs the initial and subsequent measurement of biological assets and also the measurement of agricultural produce at the point of harvest.
- IFRS 4 – Insurance Contracts – deals with the measurement of the liability where one party, the insurer, agrees to compensate the other party, the policyholder, if it is adversely affected by an uncertain future event.
- IFRS6 – Exploration for and Evaluation of Mineral Resources - deals with expenditure on the exploration and evaluation of such mineral resources as: gold, copper, oil and gas.
- IFRS for SME – IFRS for small and medium-sized entities has been issued for use by entities that have no public accountability. It simplifies or omits many of the requirements of full IFRS and therefore reduces the burden of producing information that is not likely to be of interest to the stakeholders of a small or medium entity.

Test your understanding 1 – Setting standards

Yozz is a small developing country which currently has no accounting standards and recently a new professional accounting body was created.

Yozz's government has asked the new professional accounting body to prepare a report setting out the country's options for developing and implementing a set of high quality standards.

Required:

As an advisor to the professional accounting body, outline THREE options open to Yozz for the development of accounting standards. Identify any advantages or disadvantages for each option.

Test your understanding 2 – Roles

The existing procedures for setting international accounting standards are now well established.

Required:

Explain the roles of the following in relation to International Accounting Standards:

- The IFRS Foundation;
- The International Accounting Standards Board (IASB);
- The IFRS Interpretations Committee.

Test your understanding 3 – The development of a standard

Explain how the standard-setting authority approaches the task of producing a standard, with particular reference to the ways in which comment or feedback from interested parties is obtained.

Test your understanding 4 – Practice questions

(1) **Under the current structure of regulatory bodies, which of the bodies listed below acts as the overall supervisory body?**

A IFRS Interpretations Committee

B International Accounting Standards Board

C IFRS Advisory Council

D IFRS Foundation

(2) **Which of the bodies listed below is responsible for reviewing International Accounting Standards and issuing guidance on their application?**

A IFRS Interpretations Committee

B International Accounting Standards Board

C IFRS Advisory Council

D IFRS Foundation

(3) **Which of the bodies listed below is responsible for issuing International Financial Reporting Standards?**

A IFRS Interpretations Committee

B International Accounting Standards Board

C IFRS Advisory Council

D IFRS Foundation

(4) **Which of the bodies listed below is responsible for the approval of IFRS Interpretations?**

A IFRS Interpretations Committee

B International Accounting Standards Board

C IFRS Advisory Council

D IFRS Foundation

(5) **Which of the following best describes the role of the IFRS Advisory Council?**

A To prepare interpretations of International Accounting Standards

B To provide the IASB with the views of its' members on standard setting projects

C To promote the use of International Accounting Standards amongst its members

D To select the members of the IASB

7 Summary diagram

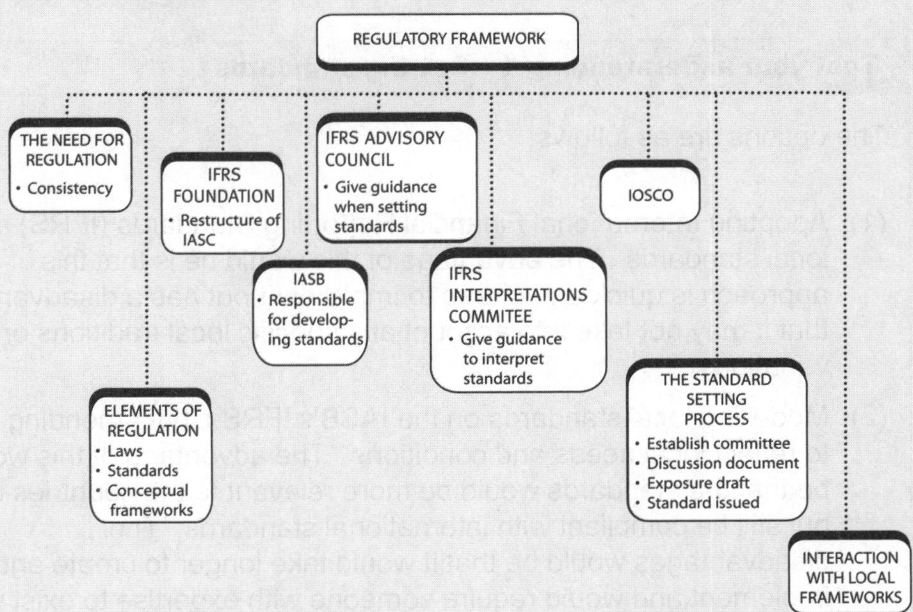

Test your understanding answers

Test your understanding 1 – Setting standards

The options are as follows:

(1) Adopting International Financial Reporting Standards (IFRS) as its local standards. The advantage of this would be is that this approach is quick and cheap to implement but has a disadvantage that it may not take into account any specific local traditions or variations.

(2) Modelling local standards on the IASB's IFRSs, but amending them to reflect local needs and conditions. The advantage of this would be that the standards would be more relevant to the countries needs but still be compliant with international standards. The disadvantages would be that it would take longer to create and implement and would require someone with expertise to exist within the local country to help create these standards.

(3) Yozz could develop its own accounting standards with little or no reference to IFRSs. The advantage would be that the standards would be specific to the needs of the country but have the disadvantage that they could be lengthy and costly to create. The standards may not be compliant with international standards and also require a person in Yozz with the appropriate expertise to help create these standards.

Test your understanding 2 – Roles

The IFRS Foundation

The IFRS Foundation is an independent organisation made up of 22 Trustees. The Trustees hold the responsibility for governance and fundraising and will publish an annual report on IASB's activities, including audited financial statements and priorities for the coming year. They will review annually the strategy of the IASB and its effectiveness and approve the annual budget and determine the basis of funding.

The Trustees also appoint the members of the IASB, the IFRS Advisory Council and the IFRS Interpretations Committee. Although the Trustees will decide on the operating procedures of the committees in the IASB family, they will be excluded from involvement in technical matters relating to accounting standards.

The IASB

The Board has complete responsibility for all IASB technical matters, including the preparation and issuing of International Financial Reporting Standards and Exposure Drafts, and final approval of Interpretations by the International Financial Reporting Interpretations Committee. Some of the full-time members of staff are responsible for liaising with national standard-setters in order to promote the convergence of accounting standards.

IASB publishes its standards in a series of pronouncements called International Financial Reporting Standards (IFRSs). It has also adopted the standards issued by the board of the International Accounting Standards Committee.

The Board may form advisory committees or other specialist technical groups to advise on major projects and outsource detailed research or other work to national standard-setters.

IFRS Interpretations Committee

The IFRS Interpretations Committee provides timely guidance on the application and interpretation of IFRSs, normally dealing with complex accounting issues that could, in the absence of guidance, produce wide-ranging or unacceptable accounting treatments.

Test your understanding 3 – The development of a standard

The process for the development of a standard involves the following steps:

- During the early stages of a project, the IASB may establish an Advisory Committee to advise on the issues arising in the project. Consultation with this committee and the IFRS Advisory Council occurs throughout the project.
- The IASB may develop and publish Discussion Papers for public comment.
- Following receipt and review of comments, the IASB develops and publishes an Exposure Draft for public comment.
- Following the receipt and review of comments, the IASB issues a final International Financial Reporting Standard.

When the IASB publishes a standard, it also publishes a Basis of Conclusions to explain publicly how it reached its conclusions and to provide background information that may help users apply the standard in practice.

Each IASB member has one vote on technical matters and the publication of a Standard, Exposure Draft, or final IFRS Interpretation requires approval by eight of the Board's 15 members. Other decisions including agenda decisions and the issue of a Discussion Paper, require a simple majority of the Board members present at a meeting, provided that the meeting is attended by at least 50 per cent of the members.

Meetings of the IASB, IFRS Advisory Council and IFRS Interpretations Committee are open to public observation. Where the IASB issues Exposure Drafts, Discussion Papers and other documents for public comment, the usual comment period is 90 days. Draft IFRS Interpretations Committee Interpretations are exposed for a 60-day comment period.

Test your understanding 4 – Practice questions

(1) D

(2) A

(3) B

(4) A

(5) B

chapter

7

The Conceptual Framework

Chapter learning objectives

On completion of their studies students should be able to:

- Explain the key principles of The Conceptual Framework for Financial Reporting, issued by the IASB. Specifically
  - Explain the purpose and status of the framework.
  - Identify what the framework covers.
  - Explain the objectives of financial statements.
  - Identify and explain the underlying assumption.
  - Define the fundamental qualitative characteristics.
  - Define and describe the qualities that enhance the fundamental characteristics.
  - Identify and define the elements of financial statements.
  - Explain how elements are recognised in financial statements.
  - Identify and explain the different ways of measuring the elements.
  - Identify and define the two concepts of capital maintenance.
  - Understand the framework and the standard-setting process.

1 Session content

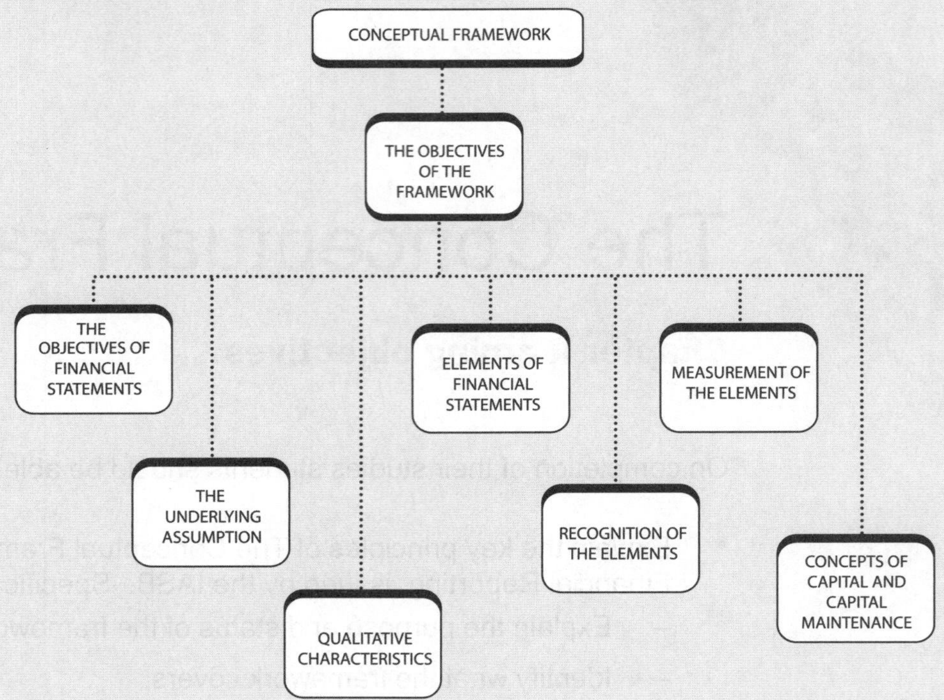

2 Introduction

Over time, transactions that entities enter into have become increasingly complex. Although the detail of the transactions may vary from situation to situation the basic accounting issues are often the same. As a result, the IASB have developed a conceptual framework, which lays out the broad principles that should be applied when developing accounting standards and when determining an appropriate accounting treatment. This conceptual framework is called the 'The Conceptual Framework for Financial Reporting' (the Framework).

3 Purpose and status of the framework

According to the Framework, its purpose is to:

- assist the IASB in the development of future IFRSs and in its review of existing IFRSs;
- assist the IASB in promoting harmonisation of regulations, accounting standards and procedures by reducing the number of alternative treatments permitted by IFRSs;
- assist national standard-setting bodies in developing national standards;
- assist preparers of financial statements in applying IFRSs and in dealing with topics that are not subject to an IFRS;

- assist auditors in forming an opinion as to whether financial statements comply with IFRSs;
- assist users of financial statements in interpreting the information contained in a set of financial statements;
- provide those who are interested in the work of the IASB information about its approach to the formulation of IFRSs.

The Framework is not an accounting standard and does not override the requirements of any IFRS.

4 What does the framework cover?

However, the framework covers the following topics:

- The objectives of financial statements;
- The underlying assumption of financial statements;
- Qualitative characteristics of financial statements;
- Definition of the elements of financial statements;
- Recognition of the elements of financial statements;
- Measurement of the elements of financial statements;
- Concepts of capital and capital maintenance.

The Conceptual Framework

The Conceptual Framework is currently in the process of development.

The Framework currently consists of 4 chapters as follows:

- Chapter 1 – The objective of general purpose financial reporting – covers the objectives.
- Chapter 2 – The reporting entity – not yet released.
- Chapter 3 – Qualitative characteristics of useful financial information – covers the qualitative characteristics.
- Chapter 4 – The Framework (1989): the remaining text – covers the underlying assumption, elements, recognition of the elements of financial statements, measurement of the elements of financial statements and the concepts of capital and capital maintenance.

5 Objectives of financial statements

The objective of financial reporting is to provide information about the reporting entity that is useful to a wide range of users in making economic decisions.

Objectives of financial statements

Information about the financial position of an entity is primarily found in the Statement of Financial Position (SOFP). The financial position is affected by the resources that it controls, its financial structure, its liquidity and its solvency.

Information about the financial performance of an entity is primarily found in the Statement of Profit or loss (SPL). The financial performance of an entity reflects its profitability. To make decisions about an entities ability to generate future cash flows investors need this information.

Information about the changes in financial positions is primarily found in the Statement of Cash Flow.

6 Underlying assumption

The Framework states that the underlying assumption for the preparation of financial statements is

- Going concern.

The going concern concept means the financial statements are prepared on the basis that the enterprise will continue trading for the foreseeable future. It is assumed that the enterprise neither has an intention nor the need to liquidate or significantly reduce the scale of its operations. If this was to be the case the financial statements would be prepared on a different basis, e.g. valuation of assets on the statement of financial position.

Although the accruals concept is no longer considered to be an underlying assumption it is still covered by the Conceptual Framework as an important concept of financial accounting. The accruals concept states events should be dealt with in the accounting period they occur, rather than the period they are paid.

7 Qualitative characteristics of financial statements

For information to be useful to make economic decisions it must have qualitative characteristics.

The Framework splits qualitative characteristics into two categories:

(i) Fundamental qualitative characteristics – must have characteristics.

- Relevance;
- Faithful representation

(ii) Enhancing qualitative characteristics – would like to have characteristics.

- Comparability;
- Verifiability;
- Timeliness;
- Understandability.

Fundamental qualitative characteristics

(i) **Relevance –** Information is relevant when it influences the economic decisions of users by helping them evaluate past, present or future events or confirming or correcting their past evaluations.

The relevance of information can be affected by its nature and materiality. Some items may be relevant to users simply because of their nature whereas some items may only become relevant once they are material. Hence, materiality is a threshold quality of information rather than a primary characteristic.

According to the Framework, information is material if its omission or misstatement could influence the decisions of users.

Materiality

Materiality is an entity specific aspect of relevance and depends on the size of the item or error judged in the particular circumstances of its omission or misstatement.

A threshold quality is:

- one that needs to be studied before considering the other qualities of that information
- a cut-off-point – if any information does not pass the test of the threshold quality, it is not material and does not need to be considered further.

(ii) **Faithful representation** – If information is to represent faithfully the transactions and other events that it purports to represent, they must be accounted for and presented in accordance with their substance and economic reality and not merely their legal form.

To be a perfectly faithful representation, financial information would possess the following characteristics:

Completeness

To be understandable information must contain all the necessary descriptions and explanations.

Neutrality

Information must be neutral, i.e. free from bias. Financial statements are not neutral if, by the selection or presentation of information, they influence the making of a decision or judgement in order to achieve a predetermined result or outcome.

Free from error

Information must be free from error within the bounds of materiality. A material error or an omission can cause the financial statements to be false or misleading and thus unreliable and deficient in terms of their relevance.

Free from error does not mean perfectly accurate in all respects. For example, where an estimate has been used the amount must be described clearly and accurately as being an estimate.

Enhancing qualitative characteristics

Comparability

Users must be able to compare financial statements over a period of time in order to identify trends in financial position and performance. Users must also be able to compare financial statements of different entities to be able to assess their relative financial position and performance.

In order to achieve comparability, similar items should be treated in a consistent manner from one period to the next and from one entity to another. However, it is not appropriate for an entity to continue accounting for transactions in a certain manner if alternative treatments exist that would be more relevant and reliable.

Disclosure of accounting policies should also be made so that users can identify any changes in these policies or differences between the policies of different entities.

Verifiability

Verification can be direct or indirect. Direct verification means verifying an amount or other representation through direct observation i.e. counting cash. Indirect verification means checking the inputs to a model, formula or other technique and recalculating the outputs using the same methodology i.e. recalculating inventory amounts using the same cost flow assumption such as first-in, first-out method.

Timeliness

Timeliness means having information available to decision makers in time to be capable of influencing their decisions. Generally, the older the information is the less useful it becomes.

Understandability

Information needs to be readily understandable by users. Information that may be relevant to decision making should not be excluded on the grounds that it may be too difficult for certain users to understand.

Understandability depends on:

- the way in which information is presented; and
- the capabilities of users.

It is assumed that users:

- have a reasonable knowledge of business and economic activities; and
- are willing to study the information provided with reasonable diligence.

For information to be understandable users need to be able to perceive its significance.

8 The elements of financial statements

Financial statements show the effect of financial transactions by grouping them into broad classes, i.e. the elements of financial statements. The elements of financial statements are:

- Assets;
- Liabilities;
- Equity;
- Income;
- Expenses.

Assets

An asset is a resource controlled by the entity as a result of a past event and from which future economic benefits are expected to flow to the entity.

Liabilities

A liability is a present obligation arising from past events, the settlement of which is expected to result in an outflow of resources from the entity.

Equity

Equity is the residual interest in the assets of the entity after deducting all its liabilities.

Income

Income is increases in economic benefits during the accounting period in the form of inflows or enhancements of assets or decreases of liabilities that result in increases in equity, other than those relating to contributions from equity participants.

The definition of income includes revenue and gains.

Revenue is income that arises in the course of ordinary activities, i.e. sales.

Gains represent other items that meet the definition of income, e.g. gains on disposal of non-current assets and unrealised gains.

Expenses

Expenses are decreases in economic benefits during the accounting period in the form of outflows or depletions of assets or incurrence's of liabilities that result in decreases in equity, other than those relating to distributions to equity participants.

The definition of expenses includes losses as well as expenses that arise in the course of ordinary activities.

Expenses that arise in the ordinary course of activities are items such as wages, purchases and depreciation.

Losses include items such as losses on disposal of non-current assets and unrealised losses, e.g. losses on revaluation.

Assets, liabilities and equity interest

Assets

An asset is a resource controlled by the entity as a result of past events and from which future economic benefits are expected to flow to the entity.

To explain further the parts of the definition of an asset:

- Controlled by the entity – control is the ability to obtain the economic benefits and to restrict the access to others (e.g. by an entity being the sole user of its plant and machinery, or by selling surplus plant and machinery). An asset does not have to be legally owned, the key factor is whether the entity has control over the future economic benefits that the item will provide. A leased vehicle could therefore be an asset.
- Past events – the event must be past before an asset can arise, e.g. equipment will only become an asset when there is a right to demand delivery or access to the asset. Dependant on the terms of a contract this could be on acceptance of an order or on delivery.
- Future economic benefits – these are evidenced by the prospective receipt of cash. This could be the cash itself, a debt receivable or any item which may be sold, e.g. a factory may not be sold if it houses the materials for manufacturing. When the goods are sold the economic benefit resulting from the use of the factory will be realised in cash.

Liabilities

A liability is a present obligation arising from past events, the settlement of which is expected to result in an outflow of resources from the entity.

To explain further the parts of the definition of a liability:

- Obligations – these may be legal or constructive. A constructive obligation is an obligation which is the result of expected practice rather than required by law or legal contract.
- Transfer of economic benefits – this could be a transfer of cash, or other property, the provision of a service, or the refraining from activities which would otherwise be profitable.
- Past transactions or events – the event must be past before a liability can arise, e.g. a loan will only become a liability when there is a right to demand repayment of the balance, i.e. a formal agreement has been made and the cash has been recognised in the entity bank account.

Equity

Equity is the residual amount after deducting all liabilities of the entity from all of the entity's assets.

Equity may be sub-classified in the financial statements into share capital, retained earnings and other reserves.

9 Recognition of the elements of financial statements

In order to recognise items in the statement of financial position or statement of profit or loss, the following criteria should be satisfied:

- It meets the definition of an element of financial statements.
- It is probable that any future economic benefit associated with the item will flow to or from the entity.
- The item has a cost or value that can be measured with reliability.

Recognition of assets, liabilities, income and expenses

An asset is recognised if:

- it gives rights or other access to future economic benefits controlled by an entity as a result of past events;
- it can be measured with reliability.

A liability is recognised if:

- there is an obligation to transfer economic benefits as a result of past transactions or events;
- it can be measured with reliability.

Income is recognised if:

- an increase in future economic benefits arises from an increase in an asset (or a reduction in a liability); and
- the increase can be measured reliably.

Expenses are recognised if:

- a decrease in future economic benefit arises from a decrease in an asset (or an increase in a liability); and
- the decrease can be measured reliably.

10 Measurement of the elements of financial statements

Measurement is the process of determining the monetary amounts at which the elements of financial statements are to be recognised and carried in the statement of financial position and statement of profit or loss.

There are a number of different ways of measuring the elements including:

Historical cost

Assets are recorded at the amount of cash paid or the fair value of the consideration given to acquire them at the time of their acquisition. Liabilities are recorded at the amount of proceeds received in exchange for the obligation or at the amounts of cash expected to be paid to satisfy the liabilities.

Current cost

Assets are carried at the amount of cash that would have to be paid if the same or an equivalent asset was acquired currently. Liabilities are carried at the amount of cash that would be required to settle the obligation currently.

Realisable (settlement) value

Assets are carried at the amount of cash that could currently be obtained by selling the asset in an orderly disposal. Liabilities are carried at their settlement values, i.e. the undiscounted amount of cash expected to be paid to satisfy the liabilities.

Present value

Assets are carried at the present discounted value of the future net cash inflows that the item is expected to generate. Liabilities are carried at the present discounted value of the future net cash outflows that are expected to be required to settle the liabilities.

The Framework does not state which measurement basis should be used by entities but highlights that the historical cost basis is the most commonly used, often combined with other bases, e.g. inventories being valued at the lower of cost and net realisable value.

Historical cost

Traditionally, accounts have been presented using the historical cost convention:

- assets are stated in the statement of financial position at their cost,
- less any amounts written off (e.g. depreciation in the case of property, plant and equipment).

The objective of financial statements is to provide information about the reporting entity's financial performance and position that is useful to a wide range of users for assessing the stewardship of management and for making economic decisions.

Whilst being both easy to ascertain and objective, the historical cost basis of measurement fails to relate directly to any of the three decisions that might reasonably be made about an asset:

- Another, similar asset might be purchased. Management need to know the current replacement cost which might have changed substantially since the present asset was purchased at its historical cost.
- The asset might be sold. Management need to know the amount which would be realised from sale, less any costs involved in disposal, i.e. the net realisable value. Again, this may bear no relationship to historical cost.
- The asset might be used in the business. Management need to estimate the future cash flows arising from the asset and discount these to their present value, i.e. their 'economic value'. Clearly, there is no direct link with historical cost in this case.

Historical cost accounting

The traditional approach to accounting has the following features:

- Accounting transactions are recorded at their original historical monetary cost.
- Items or events for which no monetary transaction has occurred are usually ignored altogether.
- Income for each period is normally taken into account only when revenue is realised in the form of cash or in some form which will soon be converted into cash.

- Profit for the period is found by matching income against the cost of items consumed in generating the revenue for the period (such items include non-current assets which depreciate through use, obsolescence or the passage of time).

These features of accounting have served users well over many years in accounting for the stewardship of the directors.

Advantages of historical cost accounting

- Easy to understand
- Straightforward to produce
- Historical cost accounts are objective and free from bias
- Historical cost values are reliable and original values can be confirmed based on original invoices/accompanying documents
- Historical cost accounts do not record gains until they are realised

Disadvantages of historical cost accounts

In periods in which prices change significantly, historical cost accounts have grave deficiencies:

- Carrying value (CV) of non-current assets is often substantially below current value;
- Inventory in the statement of financial position reflects prices at the date of purchase or manufacture rather than those current at the year end;
- Statement of profit or loss expenses do not reflect the current value of assets consumed so profit in real terms is exaggerated;
- If profit were distributed in full, the level of operations would have to be curtailed;
- No account is taken of the effect of increasing prices on monetary items (items designated or settled in cash); and
- The overstatement of profits and the understatement of assets prevent a meaningful calculation of return on capital employed (ROCE).

As a result of the above, users of accounts find it extremely difficult to assess an entity's progress from year to year or to compare the results of different operations.

Example of the deficiencies of historical cost accounts

Entity A acquires a new machine in 20X4. This machine costs $50,000 and has an estimated useful life of ten years.

Entity B acquires an identical one-year old machine in 20X5. The cost of the machine is $48,000 and it has an estimated useful life of nine years.

Depreciation charges (straight-line basis) in 20X5 are as follows.

Entity A	$50,000/10	= $5,000
Entity B	$48,000/9	= $5,333

CVs at the end of 20X5 are:

Entity A $50,000 – (2 × $5,000)	= $40,000
Entity B $48,000 – $5,333	= $42,667

Both entities are using identical machines during 20X5, but the statements of profit or loss will show quite different profit figures because of adherence to historical cost.

Other asset values

Current cost is the cost to the business of replacing the asset. For example, the cost of replacing inventory. However, in a non-current asset situation you will need to determine the assets net replacement cost. Net replacement cost is the replacement cost of an asset minus an appropriate amount of depreciation i.e. the provision for depreciation to reflect the life already used.

Realisable value is the estimated sales proceeds less any costs involved in selling the asset.

Present value is the present value of the future cash flows from an asset.

Example of other asset values

An entity owns a machine which it purchased four years ago for $100,000. The accumulated depreciation on the machine to date is $40,000. The machine could be sold to another manufacturer for $50,000 but there would be dismantling costs of $5,000. To replace the machine with a new version would cost $110,000. The cash flows from the existing machine are estimated to be $25,000 for the next two years followed by $20,000 per year for the remaining four years of the machine's life.

The relevant discount rate for this entity is 10% and the discount factors are:

Year 1	0.909
Year 2	0.826
Years 3-6 inclusive	2.619 (annuity rate)

Calculate the following values for the machine:

(a) Historical cost

(b) Realisable value

(c) Current cost

(d) Present value

Solution

(a) Historical cost

	$
Cost	100,000
Less: depreciation	(40,000)
	60,000

(b) Realisable value

	$
Selling price	50,000
Less: costs to sell	(5,000)
	45,000

(c) Current cost

	$
Replacement cost for new asset	110,000
Less: 4 years' depreciation (4 × 10% × $110,000)	(44,000)
	66,000

(d) Present value

	$
$25,000 × 0.909	22,725
$25,000 × 0.826	20,650
$20,000 × 2.619	52,380
	95,755

11 Concepts of capital and capital maintenance

There are two concepts of capital:

- **A financial concept of capital**. With this method capital = net assets or equity of the entity. This concept should be used if the main concern of the user of the financial statements is the maintenance of the nominal value invested capital. This is used by most entities to prepare financial statements.
- **A physical concept of capital.** With this method capital = productive capacity of the entity (measured as units of output per day). This method should be used if the main concern of the user of the financial statements is the operating capacity of the entity.

Capital maintenance means preserving the value of the capital of the entity, and reporting profit only if the capital of the entity has been increased by activities and events in the accounting period.

Capital maintenance

Capital maintenance is a theoretical concept which tries to ensure that excessive dividends are not paid in times of changing prices.

Capital maintenance concepts can be classified as follows:

- Physical capital maintenance (PCM), alternatively known as operating capital maintenance (OCM).
- Financial capital maintenance (FCM).

Physical capital maintenance (PCM)

PCM sets aside profits in order to allow the business to continue to operate at current levels of activity. In practice, this tends to mean adjusting opening capital by **specific** price changes

Example:

An entity starts trading on 1 January X1 with contribution of $2,000 from owners. This is used to purchase 200 units at $10 each, which are sold for $2,200 cash. Opening capital is $2,000 and closing is $2,200 so profit is usually measured as $200.

However, over the year, the price of the units has increased to $10.75 (a specific price change hitting the business, rather than general). This is a price increase of 7.5% (10.75 – 10.00/10.00).

Therefore increase opening capital by 7.5% to $2,150 (1.075 × 2,000)

Profit is therefore $2,200 – $2,150 = $50

Even if the profit is paid out, the entity is left with cash of $2,150. This is enough to buy 200 more units at $10.75 each. In other words, the productive capacity of the business has been maintained.

Financial capital maintenance (FCM)

FCM sets aside profits in order to preserve the value of shareholders' funds in 'real terms', i.e. after inflation.

Can measure the increase in monetary terms or in terms of constant purchasing power:

- Monetary terms

  An entity starts trading on 1 January X1 with contribution of $2,000 from owners. This is used to purchase 200 units at $10 each, which are sold for $2,200 cash.

  Opening capital is $2,000 and closing is $2,200 so profit is usually measured as $200.

- Constant purchasing power

  Inflation over time makes comparisons difficult so constant purchasing power adjusts for general indices of inflation – e.g. retail prices index.

  If increase in RPI is 5%

  Increase opening capital by 5% to $2,100 (1.05 × 2,000

  So profit is only $2,200 – $2,100 = $100.

12 The Framework and the standard-setting process

The Conceptual Framework provides a point of reference to the IASB when developing individual standards. Since the standards will then be developed with reference to a common set of concepts the standards themselves will become more consistent.

The IFRS Interpretations Committee issues guidance where issues have arisen which are not specifically covered by a standard. The IFRS Interpretations Committee can therefore ensure its guidance is consistent with agreed underlying principles by referring to the Framework.

Currently many IASs allow alternative treatments. The development of the Framework is expected to result in these alternatives being removed and the preferred treatment will be the one that is consistent with the Framework.

Current developments

In May 2015, the IASB issued an Exposure Draft (ED) Conceptual Framework to update and improve the existing Framework. Many of the proposed amendments will help the standard-setting process by providing enhanced guidance and clarification as to what should be included in the financial statements and how it should be measured.

In summary, the proposed changes comprise:

- refinement to the definition of an asset and a liability, with consequent amendment of the definition of income and expenses
- the inclusion of guidance on how items included in the financial statements should be measured, together with factors to consider when deciding which measurement basis to adopt
- updated criteria to determine when assets and liabilities should be recognised and derecognised in the financial statements. The updated criteria will be grounded in the qualitative characteristics of useful financial information to ensure that it is relevant and faithfully represented
- improvement of presentation and disclosure of financial information, including how to present financial performance. This includes guidance on whether items should be included in profit or loss or included as items of other comprehensive income, and
- clarification of what constitutes the reporting entity. This will normally be based upon a reporting entity having control of other entities and required to produce group accounts.

Test your understanding 1 – Qualitative characteristics

The International Accounting Standards Board's (IASB's) The Conceptual Framework for Financial Reporting identifies fundamental and enhancing qualitative characteristics of financial information.

Required:

Identify and explain the TWO fundamental qualitative characteristics of financial information listed in the IASB's Framework.

Test your understanding 2 – IASB objectives

The Conceptual Framework for Financial Reporting has a number of purposes, including:

- assisting the Board in the development of future IFRSs and in its review of existing IFRSs;
- assisting the Board in promoting harmonisation of regulations, accounting standards and procedures relating to the presentation of financial statements by providing a basis for reducing the number of alternative treatments permitted by IFRSs;
- assisting preparers of financial statements in applying IFRSs and in dealing with topics that are yet to be covered in an IFRS.

Required:

Discuss how the Conceptual Framework can help the IASB achieve these objectives.

Test your understanding 3 – Purpose of the framework

The Conceptual Framework for Financial Reporting was first published in 1989 and updated in 2010.

Required:

Explain the purposes of the Framework.

Test your understanding 4 – Practice questions

(1) **Under The Conceptual Framework for Financial Reporting, which of the following is the 'threshold quality' of useful information?**

A Relevance

B Reliability

C Materiality

D Understandability

(2) **According to The Conceptual Framework for Financial Reporting, which of the following is the underlying assumption of a set of financial statements?**

A Prudence

B Going Concern

C Accruals

D Comparability

(3) **Which of the following best defines relevant financial information to the users of financial statements?**

A Information that is free from material error, bias and is a faithful representation

B Information that has been prudently prepared

C Information that is comparable from one period to the next

D Information that influences the decisions of users

(4) **Which of the following criteria need to be satisfied in order for an item to be recognised in the financial statements?**

(i) It meets the definition of an element of the financial statements

(ii) It is probable that future economic benefits will flow to or from the entity

(iii) It is certain that future economic benefits will flow to or from the entity

(iv) The item has a cost or value

(v) The item has a cost or value that can be reliably measured

A i, ii and v

B i, iii and v

C i, ii and iv

D i, iii and iv

(5) **Which of the following measurement bases should be used by an entity according to The Conceptual Framework for Financial Reporting?**

A Historical cost

B Current cost

C Present value

D Any of the above

(6) The IASB's Framework identifies qualitative characteristics.

(i) Relevance

(ii) Comparability

(iii) Verifiability

(iv) Understandability

(v) Faithful representation.

Which of the above are not listed as an enhancing characteristics?

A (i), (iv) and (v)

B (ii), (iii) and (iv)

C (ii) and (iii)

D (i) and (v)

(7) The Conceptual Framework for Financial Reporting provides definitions of the elements of financial statement. One of the elements defined by the framework is 'expenses'.

In no more than 35 words, give the IASB Framework's definition of expenses.

(8) The International Accounting Standards Board's (IASB) Conceptual Framework for Financial Reporting sets out two fundamental qualitative characteristics of financial information, relevance and faithful representation.

Which characteristics would you expect information to possess if it is to have faithful representation?

(9) **According to the International Accounting Standards Board's Conceptual Framework for Financial Reporting, what is the objective of financial statements?**

(10) The Conceptual Framework for Financial Reporting lists the qualitative characteristics of financial statements.

(i) Comparability,

(ii) Verifiability,

(iii) Timeliness,

(iv) Understandability,

(v) Relevance,

(vi) Faithful representation.

Which TWO of the above are NOT included in the enhancing qualitative characteristics listed by the Framework?

A (i) and (vii)

B (ii) and (v)

C (iv) and (v)

D (v) and (vi)

13 Summary diagram

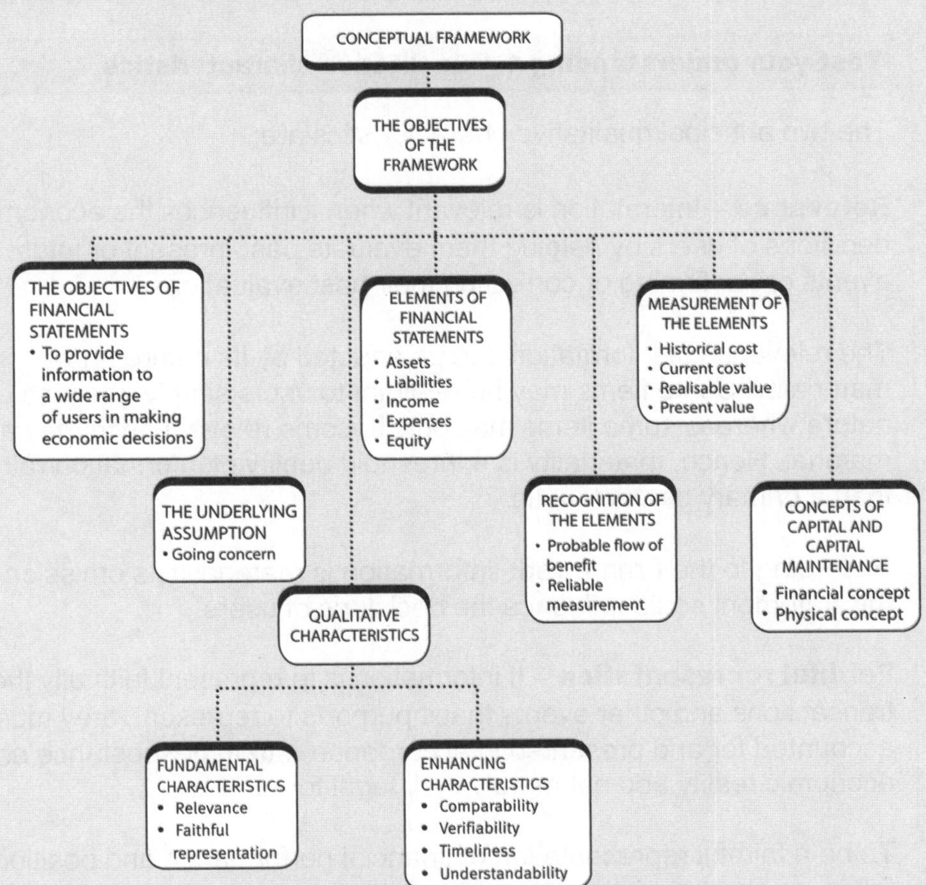

Test your understanding answers

Test your understanding 1 – Qualitative characteristics

The two principal qualitative characteristics are:

Relevance – Information is relevant when it influences the economic decisions of users by helping them evaluate past, present or future events or confirming or correcting their past evaluations.

The relevance of information can be affected by its nature and materiality. Some items may be relevant to users simply because of their nature whereas some items may only become relevant once they are material. Hence, materiality is a threshold quality of information rather than a primary characteristic.

According to the Framework, information is material if its omission or misstatement could influence the decisions of users.

Faithful representation – If information is to represent faithfully the transactions and other events that it purports to represent, they must be accounted for and presented in accordance with their substance and economic reality and not merely their legal form.

To be a faithful representation of financial performance and position, the following characteristics should be evident:

Completeness – To be understandable information must contain all the necessary descriptions and explanations.

Neutrality – Information must be neutral, i.e. free from bias. Financial statements are not neutral if, by the selection or presentation of information, they influence the making of a decision or judgement in order to achieve a predetermined result or outcome.

Free from error – Information must be free from error within the bounds of materiality. A material error or an omission can cause the financial statements to be false or misleading and thus unreliable and deficient in terms of their relevance.

Free from error does not mean perfectly accurate in all respects. For example, where an estimate has been used the amount must be described clearly and accurately as being an estimate.

Test your understanding 2 – IASB objectives

A conceptual Framework provides guidance on the broad principles of financial reporting. It highlights how items should be recorded, on how they should be measured and presented. The setting of broad principles could assist in the development of accounting standards, ensuring that the principles are followed consistently as standards and rules are developed.

A conceptual Framework can provide guidance on how similar items are treated. By providing definitions and criteria that can be used in deciding the recognition and measurement of items, conceptual Frameworks can act as a point of reference for those setting standards, those preparing and those using financial information.

The existence of a conceptual Framework can remove the need to address the underlying issues over and over again. Where underlying principles have been established and the accounting standards are based on these principles, there is no need to deal with them fully in each of the standards. This will save the standard-setters time in developing standards and will again ensure consistent treatment of items.

Where a technical issue is raised but is not specifically addressed in an accounting standard, a conceptual Framework can help provide guidance on how such items should be treated. Where a short-term technical solution is provided by the standard-setters, the existence of a conceptual Framework will ensure that the treatment is consistent with the broad set of agreed principles

Test your understanding 3 – Purpose of the framework

According to the Framework, its purposes are to:

- assist the Board in the development of future IFRSs and in its review of existing IFRSs;
- assist the Board in promoting harmonisation of regulations, accounting standards and procedures relating to the presentation of financial statements by providing a basis for reducing the number of alternative treatments permitted by IFRSs;
- assist national standard-setting bodies in developing national standards;
- assist preparers of financial statements in applying IFRSs and in dealing with topics that have yet to be covered in an IFRS;
- assist auditors in forming an opinion as to whether financial statements conform with IFRSs;
- assist users of financial statements that are prepared using IFRSs;
- provide information about how the IASB has formulated its approach to the development of IFRSs.

Test your understanding 4 – Practice questions

(1) C

(2) B

(3) D

(4) A

(5) D

(6) D

(7) Expenses are decreases in economic benefits during the accounting period in the form of outflows or depletions of assets that result in decreases in equity, other than those relating to distributions to equity participants.

(8) Completeness, neutrality and free from error.

(9) The objective of financial statements is to provide information about the reporting entity that is useful to a wide range of users in making economic decisions.

(10) D

chapter

8

External Audit

Chapter learning objectives

On completion of their studies students should be able to:

- Describe the objective of an external audit and the role of the external auditor.
- Describe the duties of the directors and auditors.
- Describe the rights of auditors.
- Identify the benefits and disadvantages of an external audit and the process of the external audit.
- Describe the contents of the audit report and its significance.
- Identify the different types of audit report.

1 Session content

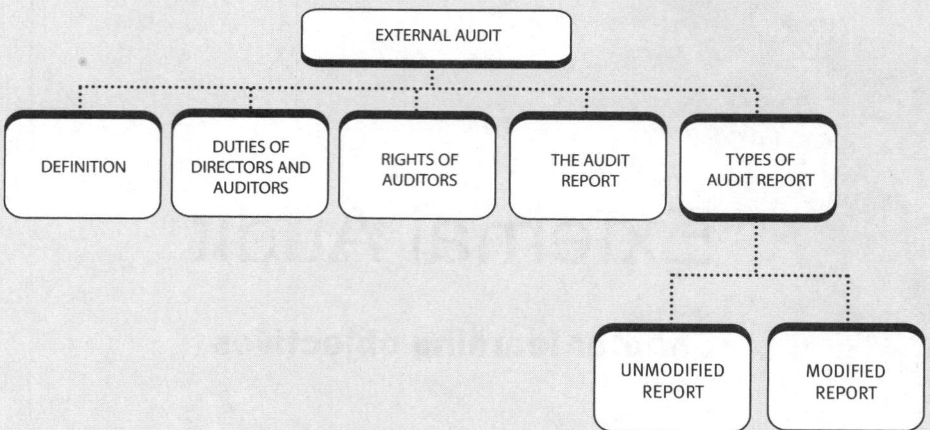

2 External audit

An external audit is when an independent expert examines and checks the financial statements. The auditor will then prepare a report to present to the shareholders.

The objective of an audit is for the auditor to express an opinion as to whether the financial statements are fairly presented, i.e that they

- show a true (accurate) and fair (unbiased) view;
- have been prepared in accordance with 'specific legislation' (this will vary internationally).

(This implies that either accounting standards have been complied with or that non-compliance with the accounting standards was necessary in order to show a true and fair view.)

The purpose of an audit is to give users confidence in the financial statements. This is not 100% guarantee, but reasonable assurance.

Duties of directors

Duties of directors can vary from country to country. Typically the legal duties of the directors will include a requirement to:

- safeguard the entity's assets and to prevent fraud and errors in the entity;
- ensure that the entity keeps proper accounting records;
- prepare annual financial statements showing the financial position, financial performance and changes in the financial position during the reporting period;

- deliver to the relevant national regulatory authority a copy of the entity's audited financial statements within a defined time limit;
- set up an internal control system in the entity to ensure that all of the above requirements are met.

Duties of auditors

The primary duty of the auditor is to report to the shareholders of the entity on whether or not the financial statements show a true and fair view and have been prepared in accordance with the applicable reporting framework.

Auditors also have a duty to report by exception, which means they have a duty to report any problems to shareholders. Again, their duties will vary from country to country but typically they would report on any of the following matters which have not been achieved:

R returns from branches have been received

A accounts are in agreement with underlying accounting records

P proper accounting records have been kept

I information and explanations has been received

D Directors report is consistent with the financial statements, e.g. director's emoluments, related party transactions. The Directors' Report is a document produced by the board of directors under the requirements of UK company law, which details the state of the entity and its compliance with a set of financial, accounting and corporate social responsibility standards.

Rights of auditors

In order to carry out their duties, auditors are given certain rights:

- access to accounting records;
- access to information and explanations as necessary;
- to receive notice of, attend and speak at general meetings of shareholders;
- rights relating to their removal, resignation and retirement.

Benefits and disadvantages of an external audit

Benefits

- Disputes between management may be more easily settled as there is an external third party involved.
- Applications to third parties for finance may be enhanced due to the reliability that the audit report brings.

- The external audit should give an independent opinion on the truth and fairness of the accounts and therefore the shareholders should have comfort that there is no material error or misrepresentation of the financial position of the entity in the statements presented (assuming the opinion is not modified).
- Auditor may be able to give constructive advice to management on improvements needed for controls
- It acts as a fraud deterrent.
- Audits may not be an option for some entities and are required by law. Local legislation relating to entities may require an annual independent audit to be carried out and local stock exchange regulations will usually require an annual audit.

Disadvantages

- Cost – the audit fee.
- Disruption caused – time management must devote to consulting with the auditors.
- In a small entity the shareholders may also be the directors, hence no real benefit from the audit.

The audit process

You will not be required to explain in detail the process of an audit but you should be aware of the main steps an auditor will take in order to form an audit opinion.

- Step 1 – The auditor is usually appointed by the shareholders at the annual general meeting (AGM).
- Step 2 – The auditor will agree terms with the client, identify the client's business and external factors and identify the risks of material misstatements in the financial statements.
- Step 3 – The auditor will plan the audit, i.e. decide upon their sample sizes and who is to perform the various tests.
- Step 4 – The auditor will begin to gather evidence to support an opinion about the financial statements. This will involve checking the bookkeeping entries to ensure a sample of transactions have been recorded correctly and then a review of the accounting policies adopted by the entity.
- Step 5 – The auditor and senior management will review all work files.
- Step 6 – An audit opinion will be formed.
- Step 7 – An audit report is published.
- Step 8 – The auditor will attend the AGM and report their opinion to the shareholders.

3 The audit report

The auditors' work culminates in the audit report. The audit report is usually the only channel of communication between the auditor and the shareholders of the entity.

The contents of the audit report are:

- Title and addressee – 'Independent' audit report – This should specify that the auditors are independent, that the report is for the shareholders of the entity and the name of the entity.
- Introductory paragraph:
  - identifies the name of the entity audited, the year end and the statements that have been audited (alternatively, the pages of the financial statements that have been audited);
  - identifies the responsibilities of directors to prepare financial statements, auditors to express opinion on financial statements.
- Scope paragraph – audit carried out in accordance with International standards of auditing, reasonable assurance that financial statements are free from material misstatement.
- Opinion – Basis of opinion and the auditor's opinion of the financial statements. The name and address of the auditors and the date of the audit report should be shown.
- Signature of the auditor or in the name of the audit firm.

A closer look at the audit report

A typical report is analysed in the following sections, to show what the various elements of it mean and why they are required:

Title

The auditor's report should have an appropriate title. It may be appropriate to use the term 'independent auditor' in the title to distinguish the auditor's report from reports that might be issued by others, such as by officers of the entity, the board of directors, or from the reports of other auditors who may not have to abide by the same ethical requirements as the independent auditor.

Addressee

The auditor's report should be appropriately addressed as required by the circumstances of the engagement and local regulations. The report is ordinarily addressed either to the shareholders or the board of directors of the entity whose financial statements are being audited.

Opening or introductory paragraph

The auditor's report should identify the entity whose financial statements have been audited and state that the financial statements have been audited. It should identify the title of each of the financial statements that comprise the complete set of financial statements. It should specify the date of and period covered by the financial statements.

Management's responsibility for the financial statements

The auditor's report should state that management is responsible for the preparation and the fair presentation of financial statements in accordance with the applicable financial reporting framework and that this responsibility includes:

(a) Designing, implementing and maintaining internal control relevant to the preparation and fair presentation of financial statements that are free from material misstatement, whether due to fraud or error;

(b) Selecting and applying appropriate accounting policies; and

(c) Making accounting estimates that are reasonable in the circumstances.

The preparation of such statements requires management to make significant accounting estimates and judgements, as well as to determine the appropriate accounting principles and methods used in preparation of the financial statements. In contrast, the auditor's responsibility is to audit these financial statements in order to express an opinion thereon.

Auditor's responsibility

The auditor's report should state that the responsibility of the auditor is to express an opinion on the financial statements based on the audit.

The auditor's report should state that the audit was conducted in accordance with International Standards on Auditing (these are standards that give guidance to the auditor to enable them to prepare the audit report but are not specifically examinable in F1). The auditor's report should also explain that those standards require that the auditor comply with ethical requirements and that the auditor plan and perform the audit to obtain reasonable assurance whether the financial statements are free from material misstatement.

The auditor's report should describe an audit by stating that:

(a) An audit involves performing procedures to obtain audit evidence about the amounts and disclosures in the financial statements;

(b) The procedures selected depend on the auditor's judgement, including the assessment of the risks of material misstatement of the financial statements, whether due to fraud or error. In making those risk assessments, the auditor considers internal control relevant to the entity's preparation and fair presentation of the financial statements in order to design audit procedures that are appropriate in the circumstances, but not for the purpose of expressing an opinion on the effectiveness of the entity's internal control. In circumstances when the auditor also has a responsibility to express an opinion on the effectiveness of internal control in conjunction with the audit of the financial statements, the auditor should omit the phrase that the auditor's consideration of internal control is not for the purpose of expressing an opinion on the effectiveness of internal control; and

(c) An audit also includes evaluating the appropriateness of the accounting policies used, the reasonableness of accounting estimates made by management, as well as the overall presentation of the financial statements.

The auditor's report should state that the auditor believes that the audit evidence the auditor has obtained is sufficient and appropriate to provide a basis for the auditor's opinion.

Auditor's opinion

An unmodified opinion should be expressed when the auditor concludes that the financial statements give a true and fair view and are presented fairly, in all material respects, in accordance with the applicable financial reporting framework. When expressing an unmodified opinion, the auditor's report should state the auditor's opinion that the financial statements give a true and fair view or present fairly, in all material respects, in accordance with the applicable financial reporting framework (unless the auditor is required by law or regulation to use different wording for the opinion, in which case the prescribed wording should be used).

The terms used to express the auditor's opinion are 'give a true and fair view' or 'present fairly, in all material respects,' and are equivalent. Both terms indicate, among other things, that the auditor considers only those matters that are material to the financial statements.

Date of report

The auditor should date the report as of the completion date of the audit. This informs the reader that the auditor has considered the effect on the financial statements and on the report of events and transactions of which the auditor became aware and that occurred up to that date.

Since the auditor's responsibility is to report on the financial statements as prepared and presented by management, the auditor should not date the report earlier than the date on which the financial statements are signed or approved by management.

Auditor's address

The report should name a specific location, which is ordinarily the city where the auditor maintains the office that has responsibility for the audit.

Auditor's signature

The report should be signed in the name of the audit firm, the personal name of the auditor, or both, as appropriate. The auditor's report is ordinarily signed in the name of the firm because the firm assumes responsibility for the audit.

4 Types of audit report

An audit report will result in one of the following:

Unmodified opinion

When an auditor is able to conclude that the financial statements are free from material misstatement they express an unmodified opinion. To express this they typically use one of the following phrases:

- "The financial statements present fairly, in all material respects.........."; or
- "The financial statements give a true and fair view of..............".

Modified opinion

There are two circumstances when the auditor may choose to not issue an unmodified opinion:

- When the financial statements are not free from material misstatement; or
- When they have been unable to gather sufficient appropriate evidence.

In these circumstances the auditor has to issue a modified version of their opinion. There are three types of modification. Their use depends upon the nature and severity of the matter under consideration.

They are:

- The **qualified** opinion is an "except for" opinion and will be given when there are material misstatements that are not pervasive or where there is insufficient evidence where there might be an undetected misstatement which is material but not pervasive.
- The **adverse** opinion is given when there is material and pervasive misstatement or misstatements.
- The **disclaimer** of opinion is given when there is material and pervasive inability to obtain sufficient, appropriate evidence and hence the auditor is unable to form an opinion.

Their usage has been summarised in the table below:

	Auditor's Judgement about the Pervasiveness of the Matter	
Nature of the Matter	**Material but NOT Pervasive**	**Material AND Pervasive**
Financial statements are materially misstated	Qualified opinion ("...except for...")	Adverse opinion ("...do not present fairly...")
Unable to obtain sufficient appropriate audit evidence	Qualified opinion ("...except for...")	Disclaimer of opinion ("...we do not express an opinion...")

Pervasiveness is a matter of professional judgement regarding whether the matter is isolated to specific components of the financial statements or whether the matter pervades many elements of the financial statements, rendering them unreliable as a whole.

To summarise, if the auditor believes that the financial statements may be relied upon in some part for decision making then the matter is material and not pervasive. If, however, they believe the financial statements should not be relied upon at all for making decisions then the matter is pervasive.

Emphasis of Matter (EOM)

Emphasis of matter and modified opinions are totally separate matters and must not be considered as related. The purpose of an EOM paragraph is to draw the users attention to a matter already disclosed in the financial statements because the auditor believes it is fundamental to their understanding. It is a way of saying to the users; "you know that note in the financial statements, the one about the uncertainty surrounding the legal dispute? Well the auditors think it's really important, so make sure you've read it!"

There are three circumstances when the usage of EOM is appropriate:

- When there is uncertainty about exceptional future events;
- Early adoption of new accounting standards; and
- When a major catastrophe has had a major effect on the financial position.

Of course, in all of these examples the auditor can only refer back to disclosures already made in the financial statements. If the directors haven't disclosed these matters then the auditor may perceive that the financial statements are materially misstated and modify the opinion instead.

5 Summary of audit reports

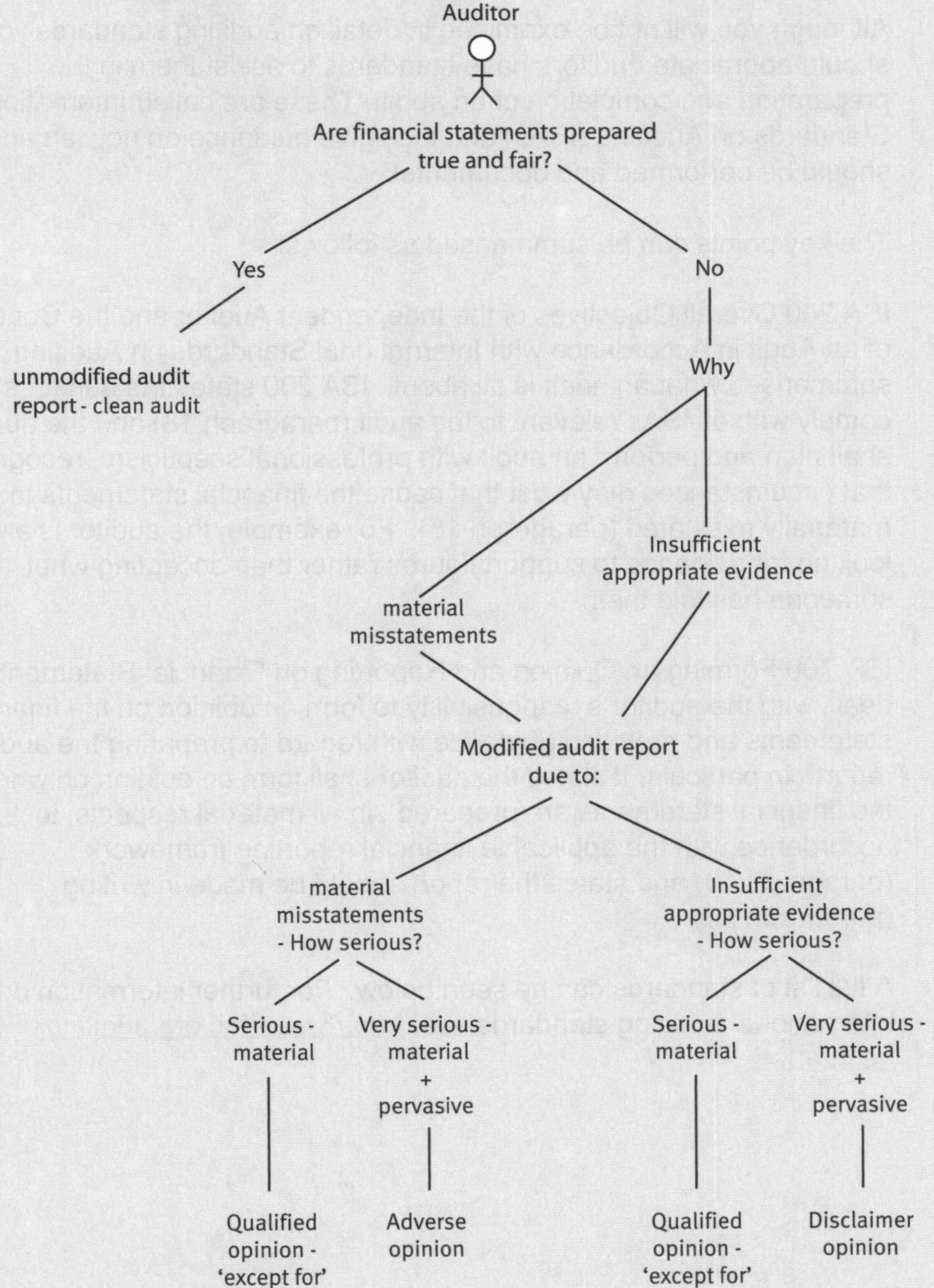

Auditor
Are financial statements prepared true and fair?
Yes
No
unmodified audit report - clean audit
Why
Insufficient appropriate evidence
material misstatements
Modified audit report due to:
material misstatements - How serious?
Insufficient appropriate evidence - How serious?
Serious - material
Very serious - material + pervasive
Serious - material
Very serious - material + pervasive
Qualified opinion - 'except for'
Adverse opinion
Qualified opinion - 'except for'
Disclaimer opinion

International Standard on Auditing

Although you will not be examined in detail on auditing standards you should appreciate auditors have standards to assist them in the preparation and completion of an audit. These are called International Standards on Auditing (ISAs) and they give guidance on how an audit should be performed and documented.

The key points can be summarised as follows:

ISA 200 Overall Objectives of the Independent Auditor and the Conduct of an Audit in Accordance with International Standards on Auditing summarises what an audit is all about. ISA 200 states the auditor shall comply with all ISAs relevant to the audit (paragraph 18) and the auditor shall plan and perform an audit with professional scepticism, recognizing that circumstances may exist that cause the financial statements to be materially misstated (paragraph 15). For example, the auditor is always looking for evidence to support figures rather than accepting what someone has told them.

ISA 700 Forming an Opinion and Reporting on Financial Statements deals with the auditor's responsibility to form an opinion on the financial statements and provides guidance with regard to preparing the auditor's report. In particular it states the auditor shall form an opinion on whether the financial statements are prepared , in all material respects, in accordance with the applicable financial reporting framework (paragraph 10) and states the report should be made in writing (paragraph 20).

A full list of standards can be seen below. For further information on international auditing standards see: http://www.ifac.org/auditing-assurance

Illustration 1 – Audit reports

(a) An entity Aragon made a very poor attempt to conduct its inventory count. You attended, however there was insufficient evidence that the inventory valuation at $4 million is accurate. Sales revenue was $50 million and profit for the year was $15 million.

(b) An entity Boleyn did not provide for a bad debt of $50,000 despite the fact that the customer went bankrupt just after the year end. Profit for the year was $500,000 and trade receivables $200,000.

(c) An entity Seymour is being sued by a competitor entity for the theft of intellectual property for $500,000. The lawyers believe that the case could go either way. However, this is not mentioned anywhere in the financial statements.

(d) An entity Howard is a cash retailer. There is no system to confirm the accuracy of cash sales.

(e) An entity Cleves has neglected to include a statement of profit or loss in its financial statements.

(f) An entity Parr is undergoing a major court case that would bankrupt the entity if lost. The directors assess and disclose the case as a contingent liability in the accounts. The auditors agree with the treatment and disclosure.

Required:

For each of the above situations state what type of audit report should be issued and explain your choice.

Solution

(a) There is "insufficient appropriate evidence" since there is a lack of evidence available to determine whether inventory valuation is correct.

The inventory value is a material amount since it is 8% of sales revenue and 27% of profit.

A modified report with a "qualified opinion" over inventory will be issued.

(b) There is a "material misstatement" as the event after the reporting date is an adjusting event in accordance with IAS 10 and therefore the debt should be written off.

The debt of $50,000 is material since it is 10% of profit and 25% of the total receivables.

A modified report with a "qualified" opinion over receivables will be issued.

(c) There is a "material misstatement" since this is a contingent liability in accordance with IAS 37 and so should be disclosed by note.

The matter is material.

A modified report with a "qualified" opinion will be issued.

(d) There is "insufficient appropriate evidence" since if there is no method available to confirm cash sales.

It can be considered "so material and pervasive" since if cash sales cannot be confirmed, other figures in the financial statements may also be incorrect.

A modified report with a "disclaimer opinion" will be issued.

(e) There is a "material misstatement" since legislation requires companies to publish statement of profit or loss.

This can be considered "so material and pervasive".

A modified report with an "adverse opinion" will be issued.

(f) An unqualified opinion since the auditors agree with the treatment and disclosure of the contingent liability.

However, there is a material inherent uncertainty (the outcome of the court case will be determined in the future).

An unmodified report with a 'fundamental uncertainty' emphasis of matter paragraph.

Test your understanding 1 – Practice questions

(1) **What is the purpose of an audit?**

A To prepare the financial statements and ensure that they provide a true and fair view

B To detect fraud

C To issue an opinion as to whether the financial statements provide a true and fair view

D To detect any misstatements in the financial statements

(2) An external audit of an entity's financial statements has discovered that a material amount of depreciation has not been recorded.

What type of audit report should be issued in this situation?

A An unmodified report with a qualified opinion

B A modified report, based on an insufficient appropriate evidence, with a qualified opinion

C A modified report, based on material misstatements, with a qualified opinion

D A modified report, based on material misstatements, with an adverse opinion

(3) At its year-end an entity is being sued for breaching health and safety legislation. If found liable, it is likely that the entity will be forced into liquidation. However, the situation will not be resolved until after the financial statements have been approved. The external audit has discovered that this matter has been adequately disclosed in the financial statements.

What type of audit report will be issued in this situation?

A An unmodified report with an emphasis of matter paragraph

B A modified report with an emphasis of matter paragraph

C An unmodified report

D A modified report, based on material misstatements, with an 'adverse' opinion

(4) At its year-end an entity is being sued for breaching health and safety legislation. If found liable, it is likely that the entity will be forced into liquidation. However, the situation will not be resolved until after the financial statements have been approved. The external audit has discovered that this matter has not been adequately disclosed in the financial statements.

What type of audit report will be issued in this situation?

A An unmodified report with an emphasis of matter paragraph

B A modified report with an emphasis of matter paragraph

C A modified report, based on material misstatements, with an 'adverse' opinion

D An unmodified report

(5) **Which of the following statements are true?**

(i) External audits are carried out by employees of the entity

(ii) External auditors are appointed by the shareholders of the entity

(iii) External auditors report to the directors of the entity

(iv) The audit report gives assurance that the financial statements are free from all errors

A ii only

B i, iii and iv

C ii and iv

D i and iii

6 Summary diagram

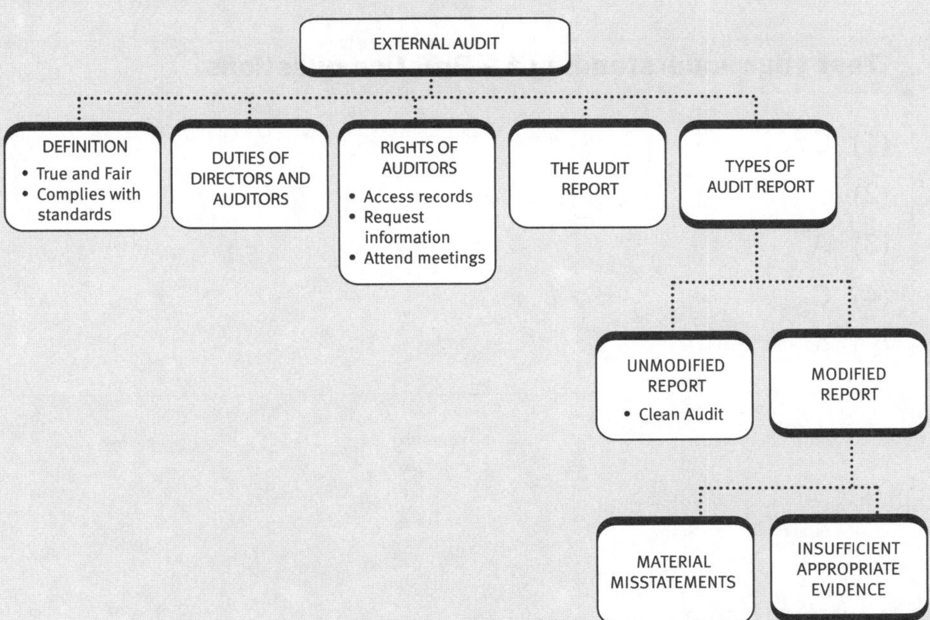

Test your understanding answers

Test your understanding 1 – Practice questions

(1) C

(2) C

(3) A

(4) C

(5) A

chapter

9

Code of Ethics

Chapter learning objectives

On completion of their studies students should be able to:

- Describe the importance of the exercise of ethical principles in reporting and assessing information.
- Describe the sources of ethical codes for those involved in the reporting or taxation affairs of an organisation, including the external auditors.
- Apply the provisions of the CIMA Code of Ethics for Professional Accountants of particular relevance to the information reporting, assurance and tax related activities of the accountant.

1 Session content

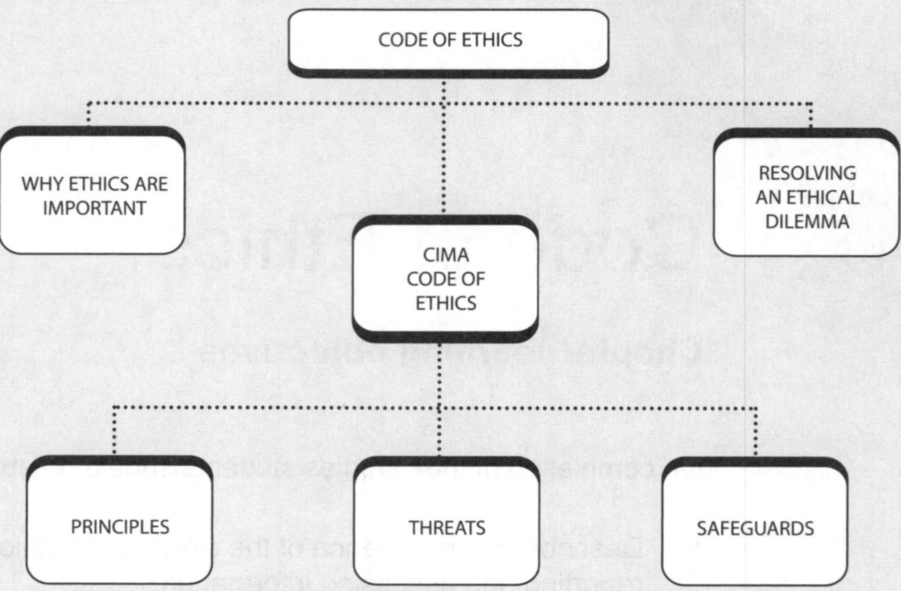

2 Introduction

Chartered Management Accountants (and registered students) have a duty to observe the highest standards of conduct and integrity and, to uphold the good standing and reputation of the profession. They must also refrain from any conduct which might discredit the profession. Members and registered students must have regard for these guidelines irrespective of their field of activity, of their contract of employment, or of any other professional memberships they may hold.

CIMA upholds the aims and principles of equal opportunities and fundamental human rights worldwide, including the handling of personal information. CIMA promotes the highest ethical and business standards, and encourages members to be responsible professionals.

Good ethical behaviour may be above that required by the law. In a highly competitive, complex business world, it is essential that CIMA members sustain their integrity and remember the trust and confidence which is placed in them by whoever relies on their objectivity and professionalism. Members must avoid actions or situations which are inconsistent with their professional obligations. They should also be guided not merely by the terms but by the spirit of this code.

CIMA members should conduct themselves with courtesy and consideration towards all with whom they have professional dealings and should not behave in a manner which could be considered offensive or discriminatory.

To ensure that CIMA members protect the good standing and reputation of the profession, members must inform the institute if they are convicted or disqualified from acting as an officer of an entity, or if they are subject to any sanction resulting from disciplinary action taken by another professional body.

CIMA has adopted the following code of ethics. This code is based on the IFAC (International Federation of Accountants) code of ethics. It was developed with input from CIMA and the global accountancy profession. If a member cannot resolve an ethical issue by following this code or by consulting the ethics support information on CIMA's website, he or she should seek legal advice as to both his or her legal rights and any obligations he or she may have. The CIMA charter, bylaws and regulations should also be referred to for definitive rules on many matters. For further information see www.cimaglobal.com/ethics

NB: All references to 'professional accountants' in this code should be taken to refer, as appropriate, to CIMA members or registered students.

3 Why are ethics important?

Ethics relate to fairness, honesty and responsibility. Ethics are a set of moral principles to guide behaviour.

They are important because:

- Accountants should perform their work properly. Ethics describe "how" an entity does its business not what it does. If an accountant carried out work in bad faith this can affect the accountant (who may be disciplined by CIMA), it may have an effect on the business, e.g. financial viability, and in the public sector tax payers money could be wasted.

4 CIMA's code at a glance

Principles

Whether you are employed in business or the public sector or work in practice, CIMA's code of ethics can help you to identify and deal with situations where your professional integrity may be at risk. The code describes the high ethical standards every CIMA member and student must demonstrate, and gives guidance on how to uphold these.

Five fundamental principles form the basis of the code: integrity, objectivity, professional competence and due care and professional behaviour. These are summarised below, but a full explanation, along with guidance on applying the principles, is available in the complete code of ethics.

- **Objectivity** means not allowing bias, conflict of interest, or the influence of other people to override your professional judgement. To protect your objectivity, you should avoid relationships that could bias or overly influence your professional opinion.
- **Professional competence and due care** is an ongoing commitment to maintain your level of professional knowledge and skill so that your client or employer receives a competent professional service. This should be based on current developments in practice, legislation and techniques, and you must also make sure that those working under your authority have the appropriate training and supervision. Work should be completed carefully, thoroughly and diligently, in accordance with relevant technical and professional standards, e.g. accountants will use judgement and estimation when preparing financial statements such as identifying accruals/prepayments, making provisions, counting and valuing inventory, and choosing depreciation methods.
- **Professional behaviour** requires you to comply with relevant laws and regulations. You must also avoid any action that could negatively affect the reputation of the profession.
- **Integrity** means being straightforward, honest and truthful in all professional and business relationships. You should not be associated with any information that you believe contains a materially false or misleading statement, or which is misleading because it omits or obscures the facts.
- **Confidentiality** means respecting the confidential nature of information you acquire through professional relationships such as past or current employment. You should not disclose such information unless you have specific permission or a legal or professional duty to do so. You should also never use confidential information for your or another person's advantage.

The code itself contains further explanation of these principles, and examples of how they can be applied for both Professional Accountants in Business (Part B) and Professional Accountants in Practice (Part C). It is impossible to define every situation that could create a threat to the principles, and it is equally impossible to set out specific safeguards for each case, so instead the code sets out common examples of when these principles might be threatened and guidance as to what action should be taken to reduce or remove the threats.

A principles-based code such as CIMA's is widely considered to be more effective than a set of rules. Whereas there can be a tendency to try and circumvent rules, principles are more flexible and can be applied in a wider variety of situations. Principles also encourage users to think about the underlying intent of the code rather than simply adopting a check-box approach to compliance with rules.

Threats

To apply the fundamental principles of the code (integrity, objectivity, professional competence and due care, confidentiality, and professional behaviour), you first need to be able to identify and evaluate existing or potential threats to them. If a threat exists that is anything other than trivial, you will need to take action to remove the threat or reduce it to an acceptable level.

Although it is impossible to define all the situations that could create a threat to the fundamental principles, the code does identify five categories of common threat:

- **Self-interest threats** can occur as a result of your own or your close family's interests – financial or otherwise. These threats often result in what is commonly called a 'conflict of interest' situation. Working in business, a self-interest threat could result from concern over job security, or from incentive remuneration arrangements. For those in practice it might be the possibility of losing a client or holding a financial interest in a client.
- **Self-review threats** occur when you are required to re-evaluate your own previous judgement, for example if you have been asked to review and justify a business decision you made, or if you are reporting on the operation of financial systems that you were involved in designing or implementing.
- **Familiarity threats** can be present when you become so sympathetic to the interests of others as a result of a close relationship that your professional judgement becomes compromised. Sometimes this can result from long association with business contacts who influence business decisions, long association with colleagues, or from accepting gifts or preferential treatment from a client.
- **Intimidation threats** occur when you are deterred from acting objectively by actual or perceived threats. It could be the threat of dismissal over a disagreement about applying an accounting principle or reporting financial information, or it could be a dominant personality attempting to influence the decision making process.
- **Advocacy threats** can be a problem when you are promoting a position or opinion to the point that your subsequent objectivity is compromised. It could include acting as an advocate on behalf of an assurance client in litigation or disputes with third parties. In general, promoting the legitimate goals of your employer does not create an advocacy threat, provided that any statements you make are not misleading.

Although it is important to be able to explain the ethical principles and threats, you must also be able to apply them to a scenario in an OT question or in the case study, i.e. you are likely to be given a scenario where you will need to identify the principles and/or threats that may result in the code not being adhered to. It is important that students are able to apply their knowledge to a given situation and not just define the principles or threats.

Safeguards

So what should you do if there is a threat (or potential threat), to the principles of the code?

CIMA's code of ethics has a 'threats and safeguards' approach to resolving ethical issues. This means that if you are in a situation where there might be a threat to any of the code's fundamental principles you should first assess whether the threat is significant. If it is, you should to take action to remove or mitigate it.

Safeguards can be found in employing organisations, such as whistle blowing or grievance procedures, or can be embedded within the profession in the form of standards or legislation. Safeguards are also the actions that a professional accountant takes to resolve an ethical conflict or dilemma.

If a colleague, employer or client has done something that you think is unethical, if you are under pressure to do something you think goes against the principles of the code of ethics or if you are facing a conflict of interest, then you will need to think about what safeguards or actions to take to resolve it. These safeguards could take a number of forms. The code does not describe all the safeguards that could be implemented, but instead gives general guidance for handling ethical issues, both for accountants working in business and for those in practice.

5 Resolving an ethical dilemma?

What should you do if you think you might be facing an ethical dilemma? How can you decide whether to take action?

All CIMA students should be able to identify, explain, resolve or address ethical problems.

If you think something might be unethical, you will need to think about the relevant facts, the ethical issues involved, the fundamental principles of CIMA's code of ethics that apply and internal company procedures. You can then identify and weigh up alternative courses of action, thinking about the consequences for those affected. What would be the outcome of going down a particular route? How would this compare with the alternatives?

An ethical dilemma exists when one or more principles of the code are threatened. You may have discovered something unethical, illegal or fraudulent going on where you work, or perhaps you feel that you have been asked to do something that compromises your professional integrity. Maybe someone is putting pressure on you to mislead, or to report in a way that is inconsistent, or goes against accepted accounting standards.

Conflicts of interest and confidentiality issues are also ethical problems. In general, ethical issues should be dealt with by taking actions (called safeguards) to reduce them to a level where they are no longer significant or of any consequence.

If you are not sure whether something is significant, it can help to think about what a reasonable third party might think if they had the facts of the situation. How would you feel if someone you know discovered how you had acted? Would you feel proud or embarrassed by your actions?

Whether you work in business, the public sector, or in practice, the following is a process for addressing situations where you have discovered possible fraud or malpractice or where you feel your professional integrity is at risk. If, having read this guidance, you are still unsure what to do or would like to talk the matter through, contact CIMA's ethics helpline for more help.

(1) Start by gathering all the relevant information so you can be sure of the facts and decide whether there really is an ethical problem.

(2) Raise your concern internally. Your manager could be an appropriate person to approach, or you could speak to a trusted colleague. If these are not options, consider escalating the issue, such as to your manager's boss, to the Board, or perhaps to a non-executive director. There might also be an internal grievance or whistle blowing procedure you can follow. If you are in practice, you could raise your concern with the client, unless you suspect money laundering.

(3) If you have raised the issue within the entity, your concerns have not been addressed, and you feel that it is a significant or persistent problem, you should think about reporting it externally. You could speak to your entity 's auditors (if you have them) or contact the relevant trade, industry or regulatory authority. Remember that confidentiality still applies, and get legal advice to be sure of your obligations and rights.

(4) Finally, if you have exhausted these avenues and you are still unable to resolve the ethical conflict, you should consider how you could remove yourself from the situation. Sometimes it might be enough to stop working with a particular team or client or to refuse to be associated with a misleading report. In the most extreme cases of significant unethical behaviour, however, where this is likely to continue despite your best efforts to resolve it, you may need to consider resigning. Again, legal advice will help to clarify your rights and obligations and should be sought before you take the step of resigning.

Throughout the process, document the steps you take to resolve the issue. For example, raise your concern in writing and keep copies of relevant correspondence. This will allow you to demonstrate how you dealt with the problem should you ever need to do so.

Examples of ethical issues

Managers face ethical issues all of the time. Examples include:

- dealing with direct and indirect demands for bribes and attempts at extortion;
- dealing with attempts at unfair competition;
- expectations of social responsibility in relation to society and the environment;
- demand for safety and compliance with legislative standards in relation to products and production;
- honesty in advertising jobs and products;
- management of closures and redundancies;
- non-exploitation of countries and people;
- effects on customer of consuming products;
- dealing with oppressive governments;
- fairness in settling pay and work conditions.

Illustration 1 – Ethical dilemma

You work for a large entity as the assistant financial controller. One of your duties is to reconcile the sales ledger each month. Every month it does not agree and you feel sure it is associated with irrecoverable debts being written off in the individual customer accounts but not included in the nominal ledger. You consider the differences to be material and have bought this to the attention of the financial controller but he seems unwilling to act.

Required:

What action would you take in this situation?

Solution

The main ethical issue is integrity. It would not be appropriate for an accountant to assist someone with a potentially fraudulent act, or to allow misleading information to be presented to others.

There is also a potential issue of objectivity if you are placed under pressure by the financial controller, as this would mean you have a conflict of interest between your personal prospects and the requirement to behave with integrity.

The possible actions could be:

- informing the financial controller of your concern and also formally asking the financial controller to address it;
- informing the financial controller that you are going to bring the matter to the attention of the financial director or the audit committee;

It would not be advisable to report externally until legal advice has been taken. Hopefully, this situation can be resolved with one of the above actions.

Test your understanding 1 – Ethical dilemma

You manage a number of trainee accountants whom the entity sponsors through training at their first attempt at each paper. In June 20X1 you employed a final level student who told you during her interview that she did not sit her final exams in May 20X1 but was going to sit them for the first time in November of that year. She had actually sat them in May 20X1 but worried that she would fail, tarnishing her record with the entity, and also she would not get financial support for her re-sit. She passed her exams in May 20X1.

Required:

What action would you take in this matter?

Test your understanding 2 – Practice questions

(1) **Which of the following would be unacceptable in an entity's code of conduct for employees?**

A Maximum number of days off for sickness each year

B No smoking of cigarettes inside the building

C Employees who meet the public must be smartly dressed

D No personal use of entity photocopying machines without prior permission from a manager

(2) **Which of the following conditions would be unacceptable in a job advertisement for an accountant?**

A Must be a qualified accountant

B Must be a non-smoker

C Must be at least 5' 6" tall

D Must be punctual and self-motivated

(3) **Which of the following is not a fundamental ethical principle identified by CIMA?**

A Integrity

B Objectivity

C Confidentiality

D Independence

(4) **CIMA's code of ethics requires members to comply with five fundamental principles. Which of the following contains three of these principles?**

A Integrity, objectivity, honesty

B Professional competence and due care, professional behaviour, confidentiality

C Social responsibility, independence, scepticism

D Courtesy, reliability, responsibility

(5) **In which of the following situations would the entity be viewed as having behaved unethically?**

A Delaying payments to its suppliers despite repeated requests to pay

B Printing warning signs on its potentially dangerous plastic packaging

C Informing investors that the profit forecast may not materialise

D Stating that it will aim to recruit more people from ethnic minority groups

(6) **Mumta thinks it is acceptable to take a "sickie" when she wants a day off. Which of the fundamental principles is she flouting?**

A Integrity

B Professional competence and due care

C Objectivity

D Confidentiality

(7) **You have an ethical dilemma. What should you do first?**

A Inform the auditors

B Inform senior management

C Inform the appropriate professional body

D Speak to your immediate supervisor

(8) **Monica receives confidential information that could negatively affect the stock price of her employer. What should she do?**

A Talk to her manager and get some advice.

B Sell her shares immediately before she makes a loss.

C Do nothing.

D Report her findings to the newspaper.

(9) **Rajesh is being pressured by his employer to change figures in his report as it will affect his managers bonus. What threat is Rajesh facing?**

A Self-review

B Intimidation

C Advocacy

D Self-interest

(10) **Which of the following is not a reason to disclose confidential information?**

A Disclosure permitted by law

B Disclosure for professional duties regarding a loan application by the entity to a bank

C Disclosure to help a friend

D Disclosure for professional duties regarding a legal case the entity is dealing with

6 Summary diagram

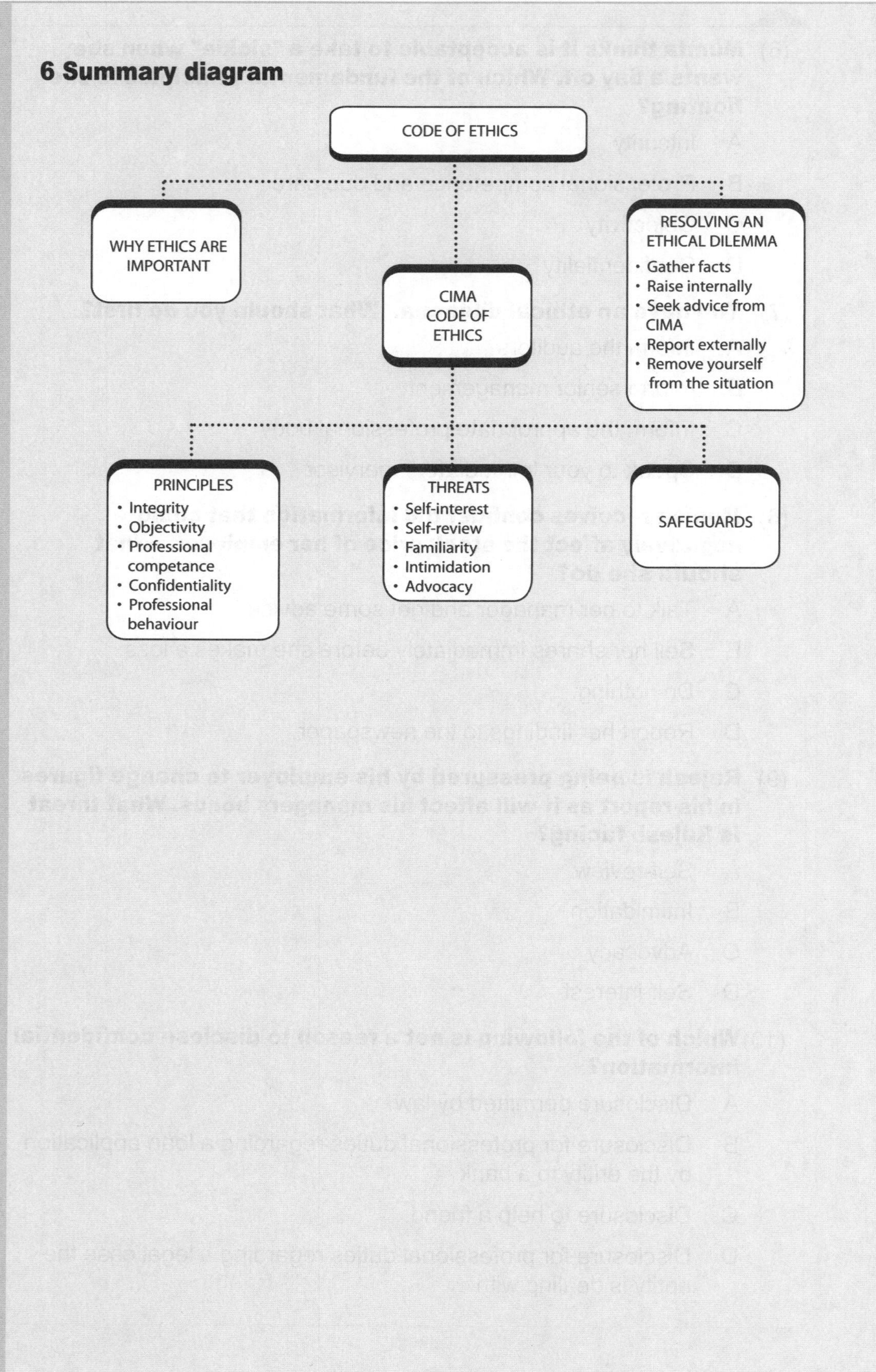
CODE OF ETHICS
WHY ETHICS ARE IMPORTANT
CIMA CODE OF ETHICS
RESOLVING AN ETHICAL DILEMMA
• Gather facts
• Raise internally
• Seek advice from CIMA
• Report externally
• Remove yourself from the situation
PRINCIPLES
• Integrity
• Objectivity
• Professional competance
• Confidentiality
• Professional behaviour
THREATS
• Self-interest
• Self-review
• Familiarity
• Intimidation
• Advocacy
SAFEGUARDS

Test your understanding answers

Test your understanding 1 – Ethical dilemma

The main ethical issue is integrity.

The new employee has not behaved with integrity by lying, and doing so with the deliberate attempt to further her career, and to defraud the entity of her examination and tuition fees. This must be taken seriously as it could suggest that she may not behave with integrity in other situations.

Possible actions could be:

- the employee should be disciplined through the formal corporate disciplinary channels, such as a formal written warning;
- depending on how serious this is viewed, the entity could consider dismissal and possible reporting to CIMA.

Test your understanding 2 – Practice questions

(1) A – It would be unacceptable to state a fixed number of days for sickness for employees. As long as the employee has a doctors certificate to prove their sickness is genuine.

(2) C – As men are generally taller than women, this would be considered discriminatory.

(3) D

(4) B

(5) A – In situations B and C it is rectifying the results of previous doubtful actions. Option D is an example of an entity's ethical aspirations.

(6) A – Mumta is not being honest and truthful

(7) D – your first step should be to report internally to your immediate supervisor. If they do not act on your information you would take further steps to report higher internally and then externally to the auditors/professional body.

(8) A – Monica should report her findings to her manager.

(9) B

(10) C

chapter

10

Corporate governance

Chapter learning objectives

On completion of their studies students should be able to:

- Discuss the objective, relevance and importance of corporate governance.
- Identify the different approaches to corporate governance in primary markets across the world.
- Discuss the key differences in approaches to corporate governance across the markets.

1 Session Content

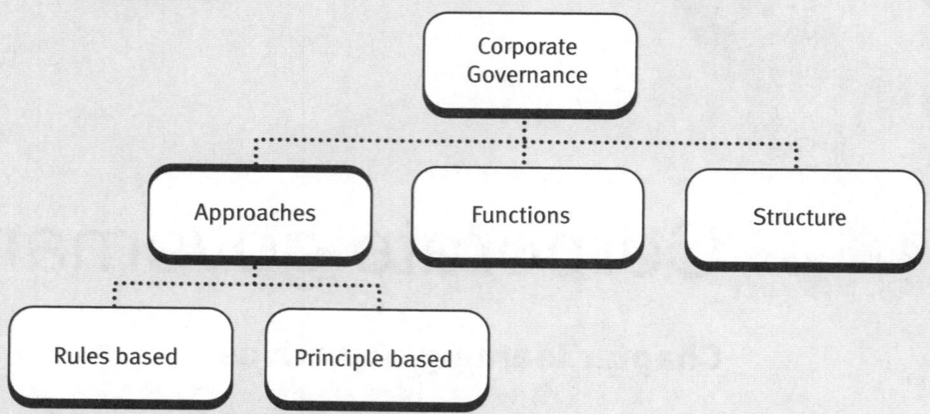

2 Introduction

Corporate governance has been around for many years, however in response to major accounting scandals (e.g. Enron), regulators sought to change the rules surrounding the governance of entities, particularly publically owned ones.

The purpose was to protect shareholders by giving them more information about the entity.

The US were effected more so by the "Enron" scandal and therefore decided to use a legal approach, whilst other countries, like the UK, decided to use a principle based approach.

In the US the Sarbanes Oxley Act (2002) introduced a set of rigorous corporate governance laws and at the same time the UK Corporate Governance Code (previously the Combined Code) introduced a set of best practice corporate governance initiatives into the UK.

What is corporate governance?

Corporate governance is the means by which a company is **operated** and **controlled**.

The aim of corporate governance initiatives is to ensure that entities are run well in the interests of their shareholders and the wider community. It concerns such matters as:

- the responsibilities of directors
- the appropriate composition of the board of directors
- the necessity for good internal control
- the necessity for an audit committee
- relationships with the external auditors

It is particularly important for publicly traded entities because large amounts of money are invested in them, either by 'small' shareholders, or from pension schemes and other financial institutions. The wealth of these entities significantly affects the health of the economies where their shares are traded.

Enron

In the year 2000, Enron, a US based energy company, employed 22,000 people and reported revenues of $101 billion. In late 2001 they filed for bankruptcy protection. After a lengthy investigation it was revealed that Enron's financial statements were sustained substantially by systematic, and creatively planned, accounting fraud.

In the wake of the fraud case the shares of Enron fell from over $90 each to just a few cents each, a number of directors were prosecuted and jailed and their auditors, Arthur Andersen, were accused of obstruction of justice and forced to stop auditing public companies. This ruling against Arthur Andersen was overturned at a later date but the damage was done and the firm ceased trading soon after.

This was just one of a number of high profile frauds to occur at the turn of the millennium.

The Enron scandal is an example of the abuse of the trust placed in the management of publicly traded companies by investors. This abuse of trust usually takes one of two forms:

- the direct extraction from the company of excessive benefits by management, e.g. large salaries, pension entitlements, share options, use of company assets (jets, apartments etc.)
- manipulation of the share price by misrepresenting the company's profitability, usually so that shares in the company can be sold or options 'cashed in'.

In response regulators sought to change the rules surrounding the governance of companies, particularly publically owned ones. In the US the Sarbanes Oxley Act (2002) introduced a set of rigorous corporate governance laws and at the same time the Combined Code introduced a set of best practice corporate governance initiatives into the UK.

3 Approaches to corporate governance

There are different approaches to corporate governance.

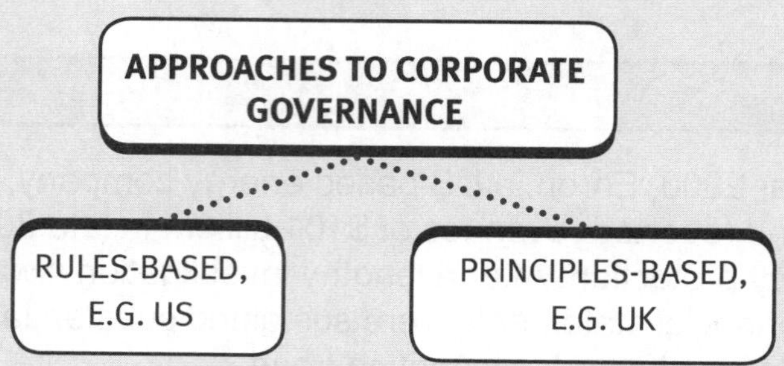

- A rules-based approach instils the code into law with appropriate penalties for transgression.
- A principles-based approach requires the entity to adhere to the spirit rather than the letter of the code. The entity must either comply with the code or explain why it has not through reports to the appropriate body and its shareholders.

The UK model is a principles-based one, although since adherence is part of stock exchange listing requirements it cannot be considered to be voluntary for large entities.

The US model is enshrined into law by virtue of Sarbanes Oxley Act (SOX). It is, therefore, a rules-based approach.

Choice of governance regime

The decision as to which approach to use for a country can be governed by many factors:

- dominant ownership structure (bank, family or multiple shareholder)
- legal system and its power/ability
- government structure and policies
- state of the economy
- culture and history
- levels of capital inflow or investment coming into the country
- global economic and political climate.

Comply or explain

A principles-based code requires the entity to state that it has complied with the requirements of the code or to explain why it could not do so in its annual report. This will leave shareholders to draw their own conclusions regarding the governance of the entity.

Arguments in favour of a rules-based approach (and against a principles-based approach)

Organisation's perspective:

- Clarity in terms of what the entity must do – the rules are a legal requirement, clarity should exist and hence no interpretation is required.
- Standardisation for all companies – there is no choice as to complying or explaining and this creates a standardised and possibly fairer approach for all businesses.
- Binding requirements – the criminal nature makes it very clear that the rules must be complied with.

Wider stakeholder perspective:

- Standardisation across all companies – a level playing field is created.
- Sanction – the sanction is criminal and therefore a greater deterrent to transgression.
- Greater confidence in regulatory compliance.

Arguments against a rules-based approach (and in favour of a principles-based approach)

Organisation's perspective:

- Exploitation of loopholes – the exacting nature of the law lends itself to the seeking of loopholes.
- Underlying belief – the belief is that you must only play by the rules set. There is no suggestion that you should **want** to play by the rules (i.e. no 'buy-in' is required).
- Flexibility is lost – there is no choice in compliance to reflect the nature of the organisation, its size or stage of development.
- Checklist approach – this can arise as companies seek to comply with all aspects of the rules and start 'box-ticking'.

Wider stakeholder perspective:

- 'Regulation overload' – the volume of rules and amount of legislation may give rise to increasing costs for businesses and for the regulators.
- Legal costs – to enact new legislation to close loopholes.
- Limits – there is no room to improve, or go beyond the minimum level set.
- 'Box-ticking' rather than compliance – this does not lead to well governed organisations.

Sarbanes-Oxley (SOX)

In 2002, following a number of corporate governance scandals such as Enron and WorldCom, tough new corporate governance regulations were introduced in the US by SOX.

- SOX is a rules-based approach to governance.
- SOX is extremely detailed and carries the full force of the law.
- SOX includes requirements for the Securities and Exchange Commission (SEC) to issue certain rules on corporate governance.
- It is relevant to US companies, directors of subsidiaries of US-listed businesses and auditors who are working on US-listed businesses.

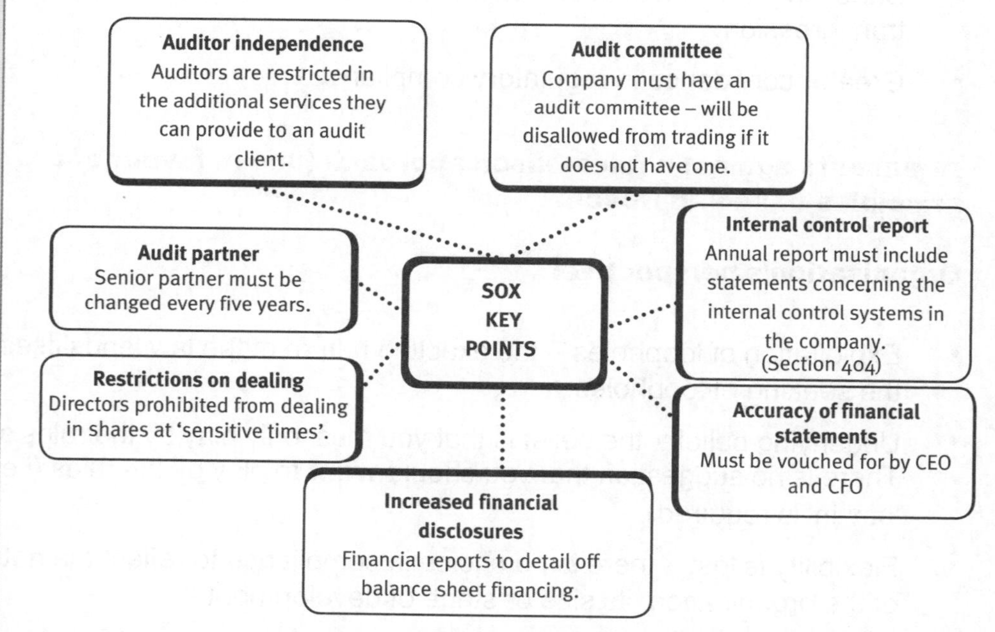

4 Best practice – policies and procedure

The UK uses a principle based approach to corporate governance which is required for listed entities but guidance for other entities. Entities should either comply or explain why they haven't applied the code

Obviously, best practice is intricately tied up with the size and resources of the entity in question. For listed entities, the most important issues of best practice are contained in the UK Corporate Governance Code. This was first issued in 1998 and has been updated at regular intervals since then, most recently in 2014.

The UK Corporate Governance Code can be seen in full on the FRC website at:

https://www.frc.org.uk/Our-Work/Codes-Standards/Corporate-governance/UK-Corporate-Governance-Code.aspx

The Code is not a rigid (or enforced) set of rules. Instead it consists of principles (main and supporting) and provisions. In the UK all entities quoted on the stock exchange have to comply with the FSA listing rules and these include a requirement that all entities include in their annual report:

- a statement of how the entity has applied the main principles set out in the Code and
- a statement as to whether the entity has complied with all relevant provisions set out in the Code.

The main provisions of the Code are:

Leadership

- Every entity should be headed by an effective board with collective responsibility.
- There should be a clear division of responsibilities between the Chairman and the Chief Executive.
- No one individual should have unfettered powers of decision.
- Non-executive directors should constructively challenge and help develop proposals on strategy.

Effectiveness

- The board should have the appropriate balance of skills, experience, independence and knowledge.
- There should be a formal, rigorous and transparent procedure for the appointment of new directors.
- All directors should receive induction and should regularly update and refresh their skills and knowledge.
- The board should be supplied with quality and timely information to enable it to discharge its duties.
- The board and individuals should be subject to a formal and rigorous annual evaluation of performance.
- All directors should be submitted for re-election at regular intervals.

Accountability

- The board should present a fair, balanced and understandable assessment of the entity's position and prospects.
- The board is responsible for determining the nature and extent of the significant risks it is willing to take in achieving its strategic objectives.
- The board should maintain sound risk management and internal control systems.
- The board should establish formal and transparent arrangements for corporate reporting and risk management and internal control principles and for maintaining an appropriate relationship with the entity's auditor.

Remuneration

- This should be sufficient to attract, retain and motivate directors of the quality required to run the entity successfully, but should not be excessive.
- This should be structured so as to link a significant proportion of the rewards to corporate and individual performance.
- There should be a formal and transparent procedure for developing policy on executive remuneration.
- No director should be involved in deciding his or her own remuneration.

Relations with Shareholders

- There should be a dialogue with shareholders based on the mutual understanding of objectives.
- The board as a whole has responsibility for ensuring that a satisfactory dialogue with shareholders takes place.
- The board should use the AGM to communicate with investors and to encourage their participation.

Update of Code in 2014

This update to the Code focused upon the provision of information by entities relating to the risks they face and how those risks may affect long-term viability. Consequently, entities will need to present information that gives a clearer and broader view of solvency, liquidity, risk management and viability.

In addition, in relation to directors' remuneration, the performance-related components should be transparent, challenging and rigorously applied. The Code has also been clarified to include provisions relating to withholding or recovery of performance-related remuneration and when this may be appropriate.

The OECD Principles of Corporate Governance

The OECD consists of 34 countries who want a free market economy with one set of rules for corporate governance.

Although there have always been well run entities as well as those where scandals have occurred, the fact that scandals do occur has led to the development of codes of practice for good corporate governance.

Often this is due to pressures exerted by stock exchanges. In 1999 the Organisation for Economic Co-operation and Development, OECD, assisted with the development of their 'Principles of Corporate Governance.' These were intended to:

- assist member and non-member governments in their efforts to evaluate and improve the legal, institutional and regulatory framework for corporate governance in their countries.
- provide guidance and suggestions for stock exchanges, investors, corporations, and other parties that have a role in the process of developing good corporate governance.

The OECD principles were first published in 1999 and were revised in 2004. Their focus is on publicly traded entities. However, to the extent they are deemed applicable, they are a useful tool to improve corporate governance in non-traded entities.

There are six principles, each backed up by a number of sub principles. The principles, and those sub-principles relevant to the auditor, are reproduced on the following page.

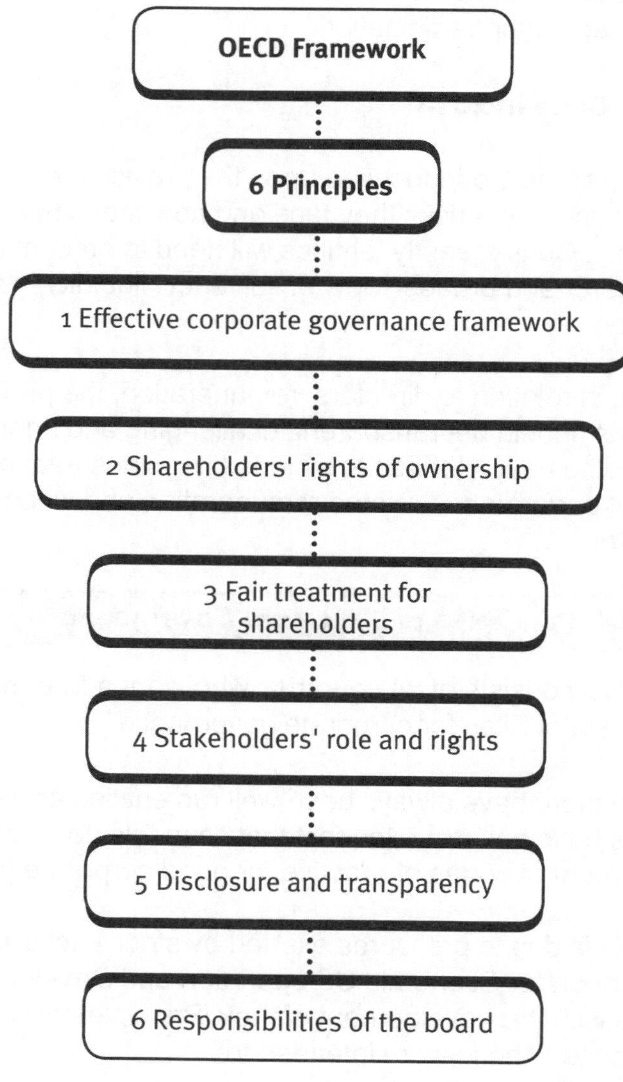

The principles in detail

Structure of the Principles

The six Principles:

(i) **Ensuring the basis for an effective corporate governance framework**

The corporate governance framework should promote transparent and efficient markets, be consistent with the rule of law and clearly articulate the division of responsibilities among different supervisory, regulatory and enforcement authorities. In other words, making sure everyone involved is aware of their individual responsibilities so no party is in doubt as to what they are accountable for.

(ii) **The rights of shareholders and key ownership functions**

The corporate governance framework should protect and facilitate the exercise of shareholders' rights. The directors are the stewards of the entity and should be acting in the best interests of the shareholders. However, the existence of the corporate collapses mentioned above proves that this isn't always the case and shareholders need protecting from such people.

(iii) **The equitable treatment of shareholders**

The corporate governance framework should ensure the equitable treatment of all shareholders, including minority and foreign shareholders. All shareholders should have the opportunity to obtain effective redress for violation of their rights.

(iv) **The role of stakeholders in corporate governance**

The corporate governance framework should recognise the rights of stakeholders established by law or through mutual agreements and encourage active co-operation between corporations and stakeholders in creating wealth, jobs, and the sustainability of financially sound enterprise.

(v) **Disclosure and transparency**

The corporate governance framework should ensure that timely and accurate disclosure is made on all material matters regarding the corporation, including the financial situation, performance, ownership and governance of the entity. Therefore, the annual financial statements should be produced on a timely basis and include all matters of interest to the shareholders. For any matters of significance arising during the year, these should be communicated to the shareholders as appropriate.

(vi) **The responsibilities of the board**

The corporate governance framework should ensure the strategic guidance of the entity, the effective monitoring of management by the board, and the board's accountability to the entity and the shareholders. The introduction of audit committees and non executive directors on the board is the usual way for monitoring management. Non executive directors are not involved in the day to day running of the entity and are therefore more independent. They can evaluate the effectiveness of the executive board on its merits and make sure they are carrying out their duties properly.

The status of the OECD principles

- The Principles represent a common basis that OECD Member countries consider essential for the development of good governance practice.
- They are intended to be concise, understandable and accessible to the international community.
- They are not intended to be a substitute for government or private sector initiatives to develop more detailed 'best practice' in governance.

The history of corporate governance

The United States

The collapses of Enron and WorldCom in the United States gave renewed impetus to governments to take action in order to restore public confidence in the corporate sector.

Enron's problems came about because of unsustainable growth which had to be financed through increased borrowing. Following an investigation by the Securities and Exchange Commission, it became clear that in order to hide its excessive borrowing and thus maintain confidence in its stock, Enron effectively created a number of subsidiaries, each a legal entity in its own right, for the purpose of keeping Enron's borrowing off its balance sheet and thus maintaining its creditworthiness. In December 2001, Enron filed for protection under Chapter 11 of the United States Bankruptcy Code with debts of approximately $3 billion. The investigation also revealed that the persons primarily responsible for Enron's fraud and subsequent collapse were the directors, chief executives and the company's auditors. To date there have been guilty pleas in relation to fraud, money laundering and insider dealing by Enron executives and a plea of guilty to obstructing justice by destroying Enron-related documents by Arthur Andersen, Enron's lead auditor. As may be imagined, the collapse of such a large corporation as Enron and the criminal activities revealed led to attention being given to the effectiveness of corporate governance measures.

The Sarbanes-Oxley Act was passed in July 2002 seeking to protect investors by improving the accuracy of corporate disclosure and reporting procedures and increasing corporate openness.

In addition, it had become clear that in many cases the relationship between corporations and their auditors was far too close. Auditors are required to carry out their work independently of the interests of the company's board or senior executives and to provide a check for the benefit of the shareholders. However, the auditors of Enron had conspired with the company in attempts to remove excessive debt from the Enron accounts. In practice, the independence of the auditors was compromised by the fact that they also received fees from the company for acting as financial consultants. As a result, the Sarbanes-Oxley Act created the Public Company Accounting Oversight Board which is charged with the task of policing the auditing of public companies in the United States. All auditors of public companies must be registered with the board which is required to set up quality assurance procedures, ethics and independent standards to which auditors are required to adhere. The Act also prohibits auditors from providing certain non-audit services to the companies for which they act. In addition, the Act requires the separate disclosure of the fees received by auditors for audit and all other fees. It follows that the independence of the scrutineers is now also subject to scrutiny!

The United Kingdom

In the United Kingdom, there were a number of scandals involving the likes of Guinness and Robert Maxwell and these highlighted the continuing ability of directors to involve public entities in mismanagement. These scandals and high-profile entity frauds made it clear that effective control of the directors of public companies was not being carried out by the shareholders, with the result that governments and regulators have had to look to other means for effective control mechanisms.

Corporate governance of public listed entities was the subject of numerous reports prepared in the 1990s, including Cadbury and Greenbury, which culminated in the issue of the Combined Code. This was later developed into the first draft of the UK Corporate Governance Code in 1998.

Europe

In 2003, the European Commission announced that it did not believe it necessary to formulate a separate code of European corporate governance. Rather such matters could safely be left to individual member states. However, it did see the need for a common approach to be taken in regard to fundamental governance issues throughout the European Union. These are to be developed over time through the issue of Directives. Thus such matters as the greater involvement in management of independent non-executive directors, more information regarding directors' remuneration and greater disclosure of and access to other financial information should form the basis of the corporate governance of all EU member states.

5 Corporate governance in action

Corporate governance can either be rules based, i.e. legal or principle based, i.e. guidance.

Corporate guidance generally incorporates the following:

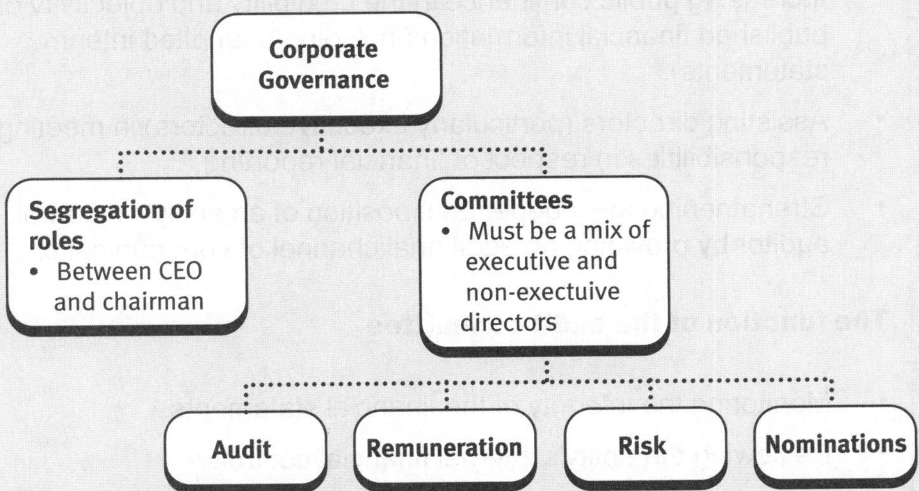

Segregation of Roles

Best practice recommends that the roles of Chairman and Chief Executive Officer should be held be different people to reduce the power of prominent board members.

Committees

The committees act as a control mechanism by having specialists to co-ordinate internal and external auditors, deal with remuneration, risk and nominations.

Internal audit

Internal audit is the control of all controls.

Further detail

Audit Committees

An audit committee is a committee consisting of non-executive directors which is able to view an entity's affairs in a detached and independent way and liaise effectively between the main board of directors and the external auditors.

Best practice for listed entities:

- The entity should have an audit committee of at least three non-executive directors (or, in the case of smaller entities, two).
- At least one member of the audit committee should have recent and relevant financial experience.

The objectives of the audit committee

- Increasing public confidence in the credibility and objectivity of published financial information (including unaudited interim statements).
- Assisting directors (particularly executive directors) in meeting their responsibilities in respect of financial reporting.
- Strengthening the independent position of an entity's external auditor by providing an additional channel of communication.

The function of the audit committee

- Monitoring the integrity of the financial statements.
- Reviewing the entity's internal financial controls.
- Monitoring and reviewing the effectiveness of the internal audit function.
- Making recommendations in relation to the appointment and removal of the external auditor and their remuneration.
- Reviewing and monitoring the external auditor's independence and objectivity and the effectiveness of the audit process.
- Developing and implementing policy on the engagement of the external auditor to supply non-audit services.
- Reviewing arrangements for confidential reporting by employees and investigation of possible improprieties ('whistleblowing').

Benefits:

- Improved credibility of the financial statements, through an impartial review of the financial statements, and discussion of significant issues with the external auditors.
- Increased public confidence in the audit opinion, as the audit committee will monitor the independence of the external auditors.
- Stronger control environment, as the audit committee help to create a culture of compliance and control.

- The internal audit function will report to the audit committee increasing their independence and adding weight to their recommendations.
- The skills, knowledge and experience (and independence) of the audit committee members can be an invaluable resource for a business.
- It may be easier and cheaper to arrange finance, as the presence of an audit committee can give a perception of good corporate governance.
- It would be less burdensome to meet listing requirements if an audit committee (which is usually a listing requirement) is already established.

Problems:

- Difficulties recruiting the right non-executive directors who have relevant skills, experience and sufficient time to become effective members of the committee.
- The cost. Non-executive directors are normally remunerated, and their fees can be quite expensive.

Internal controls and risk management

One way of minimising risk is to incorporate internal controls into an entity's systems and procedures.

It is the director's responsibility to implement internal controls and monitor their application and effectiveness.

Auditors are not responsible for the design and implementation of their clients' control systems. Auditors have to assess the effectiveness of controls for reducing the risk of material misstatement of the financial statements. They incorporate this into their overall risk assessment, which allows them to design their further audit procedures.

UK Stewardship Code

The UK Stewardship Code was published in 2012 and comprises seven principles to which institutional investors should adhere as follows:

(1) publicly disclose their policy on how they will discharge their stewardship responsibilities

(2) have a robust policy on managing conflicts of interest in relation to stewardship which should be publicly disclosed

(3) monitor their investee companies

(4) establish clear guidelines on when and how they will escalate their stewardship activities

(5) be willing to act collectively with the other investors where appropriate

(6) have a clear policy on voting and disclosure of voting activity. and

(7) report periodically on their stewardship and voting activities.

Each institutional investor is required to disclose on its own website how it has applied each of the even principles of the code, or explain any element of non-compliance.

Test your understanding 1 – Practice questions

(1) **An entity using a rules based approach to corporate governance means .....**

A the entity must legally apply the rules.

B the entity does not have to legally apply the rules but must disclose if not applied.

C the entity does not have to legally apply the rules and need not disclose if not applied.

D the entity can ignore the rules.

(2) **An entity using a principle based approach to corporate governance means .....**

A the entity must legally apply the rules.

B the entity does not have to legally apply the rules but must disclose if not applied.

C the entity does not have to legally apply the rules and need not disclose if not applied.

D the entity can ignore the rules.

(3) **Corporate governance rules were strengthened to**

A protect shareholders.

B protect directors.

C protect auditors.

D protect employees.

(4) A principle of corporate governance is segregation of duties. **This is in place so**

A the roles of the chairman and CEO are held by different people to reduce the power of prominent board members.

B the roles of employees are segregated to prevent fraud.

C the auditors are independent to employees.

D only non-executive directors can be on the audit committee.

(5) Corporate governance rules suggests committees should be used within an entity. **Which of the following is NOT a corporate governance driven committee?**

A Nominations

B Audit

C Remuneration

D Leadership

6 Chapter summary

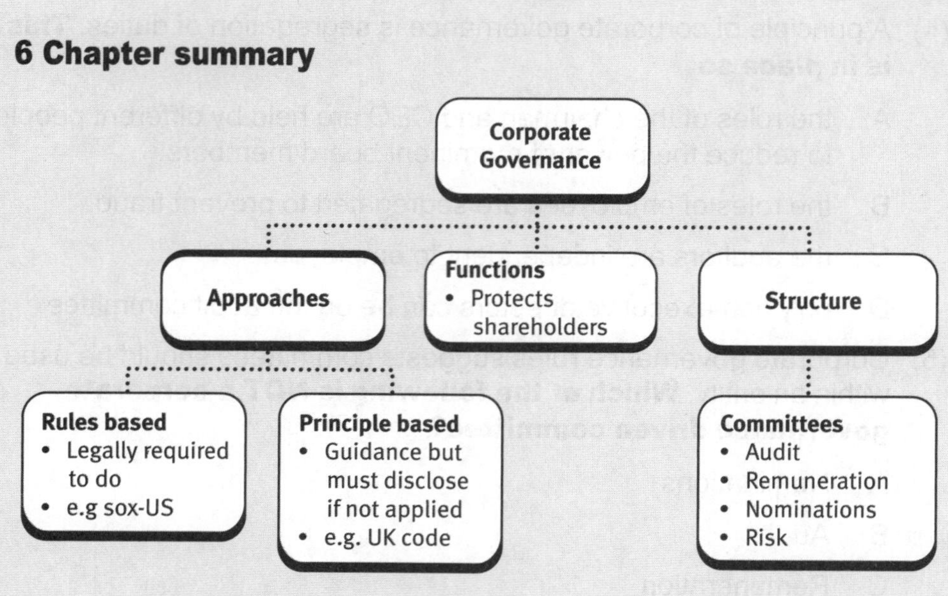
Corporate Governance
Approaches
Functions
• Protects shareholders
Structure
Rules based
• Legally required to do
• e.g sox-US
Principle based
• Guidance but must disclose if not applied
• e.g. UK code
Committees
• Audit
• Remuneration
• Nominations
• Risk

Test your understanding answers

Test your understanding 1 – Practice questions

(1) A

(2) B

(3) A

(4) A

(5) D

chapter

11

Introduction to Single Entity Accounts

Chapter learning objectives

On completion of their studies students should be able to:

- Produce financial statements in a form suitable for publication from trial balance.
- Identify the concepts affecting financial statements.
- Produce the statement of financial position in accordance with IAS 1.
- Produce the statement of changes in equity in accordance with IAS 1.
- Produce the statement of profit or loss and other comprehensive income in accordance with IAS 1.

1 Session content

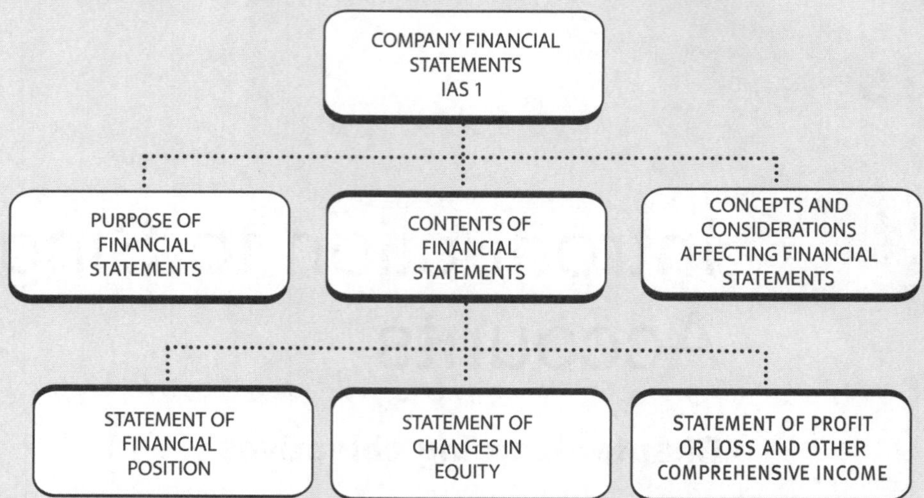

2 IAS 1 Presentation of Financial Statements

All entities preparing their financial statements in accordance with International Accounting Standards should follow the requirements of IAS 1, Presentation of Financial Statements which was amended most recently in 2014. IAS 1 prescribes what a set of financial statements should contain and how they should be presented.

Purpose of financial statements

IAS 1 states that the objective of financial statements is to provide information about the financial position, performance and cash flows of an enterprise that is useful in making economic decisions. The financial statements will also show how effectively management have looked after the resources of the entity, i.e. it will help users assess the stewardship of management.

Contents of financial statements

A complete set of financial statements includes:

- a statement of financial position
- either:
  - a statement of profit or loss and other comprehensive income, or
  - a statement of profit or loss plus a statement showing other comprehensive income
- a statement of changes in equity
- a statement of cash flows
- accounting policies note and other explanatory notes

IAS 1 does not require the above titles to be used by entities. It is likely that many entities in practice will continue to use the previous terms of balance sheet rather than statement of financial position and cash flow statement rather than statement of cash flows.

Entities are also encouraged to present a financial review by management which describes and explains the main features of the entities financial performance and financial position.

This chapter looks at the formats of the statement of profit or loss and other comprehensive income, statement of financial position and statement of changes in equity. The statement of cash flow is considered in a later chapter. Notes to the financial statements are considered with their relevant standards, where appropriate.

Responsibility for financial statements

The board of directors (and/or other governing body) of an entity is responsible for the preparation and presentation of its financial statements.

3 Concepts and other considerations affecting financial statements

Fair presentation

IAS 1 states that 'Financial statements shall present fairly the financial position, financial performance and cash flows of an entity'. Entities that comply with all relevant IAS's will virtually always achieve this objective.

A fair presentation requires that entities:

- show a faithful representation of the effects of transactions
- select definitions and recognition criteria set down in the in accordance with the conceptual framework and apply accounting policies in accordance with IAS 8 (see later)
- present information in a manner which provides relevant, reliable, comparable and understandable information;
- provide additional disclosures if the requirements of an IFRS or IAS are insufficient to enable users to understand the impact of the transaction on the financial position and performance

If, however, an entity feels that compliance with an IFRS would be misleading and that it is necessary to depart from the requirements of an IFRS in order to show a fair presentation, the entity should make the following disclosures:

- that management have concluded that the financial statements do present fairly the financial position, financial performance and cash flows
- that the entity has complied with IFRSs except that it has departed from an IFRS in order to show a fair presentation
- the IFRS that has been departed from, the nature of the departure i.e. the treatment that the IFRS would require and the reason why such treatment would be misleading and the treatment adopted instead
- the financial impact of the departure on net profit/loss, assets, liabilities, equity and cash flows

However, departing from the provisions of the standards in the interests of fair presentation, would be very rare.

Going concern

IAS 1 states that financial statements should be prepared on the going concern basis unless management intend to liquidate the business or to cease trading.

Preparing financial statements on the going concern basis means preparing them on the assumption that the entity will continue to trade for the foreseeable future.

Accruals basis

IAS 1 requires entities to prepare their financial statements (except for cash flow information) using the accruals basis of accounting.

This means that transactions should be recorded in the accounting period to which they relate regardless of whether or not cash has been received or paid.

This concept also means that expenses should be recognised in the statement of profit or loss and other comprehensive income so as to match against directly related income.

Consistency

Presentation and classification of items should be consistent from one period to the next.

Changes are allowed, if required by an IFRS or if it is deemed more appropriate to change the presentation of information.

Materiality and aggregation

Each material class of similar items should be presented separately in the financial statements. Immaterial amounts should be aggregated with amounts of a similar nature and need not be disclosed separately.

Omissions or misstatements of items are material if they could influence the economic decisions of users. Materiality depends on the size and nature of the omission or misstatement.

Off-setting

Assets and liabilities, and income and expenses, should not be offset except when offsetting is required or allowed by an IFRS.

Comparative information

Comparative information should be disclosed in respect of the previous period for all amounts reported in the financial statements unless an IFRS requires or allows otherwise.

Other requirements

Financial statements should be presented at least annually and should be issued on a timely basis (within 6 months of the end of the reporting period for public entities and 9 months for private entities) to be useful to users.

IAS 1 does not specify the format of financial statements, but it does provide an appendix which sets out illustrative formats for the statements to be included in financial statements. In addition, it provides guidance on the items that should be disclosed in these statements and those that can be relegated to the notes that accompany the statements (see below suggested formats).

The statement of financial position

The suggested format for the statement of financial position (SOFP) is as follows:

XYZ Statement of Financial Position as at 31 December 20X0

	$000	$000
Assets		
Non-current assets		
Property, plant and equipment	X	
Investment property	X	
Goodwill	X	
Other Intangible assets	X	
Investments in associates	X	
Available-for-sale financial assets	X	
	—	
		X
Current assets		
Inventories	X	
Trade and other receivables (e.g. prepayments)	X	
Cash and cash equivalents	X	
	—	
		X
Non-current assets held for sale		X
		—
Total assets		X
		—
Equity and liabilities		
Capital and reserves		
Issued share capital	X	
Share premium	X	
Revaluation reserve	X	
Retained earnings	X	
	—	
		X
Non-controlling interests		X
		—
Total equity		X

Non-current liabilities		
Long-term borrowings	X	
Provisions	X	
	—	
		X
Current liabilities		
Trade and other payables	X	
Short-term borrowings	X	
Current tax payable	X	
	—	
		X
		—
Total equity and liabilities		X
		—

The format requires comparative figures for the previous year, these have been omitted as you will not need to prepare comparatives in questions.

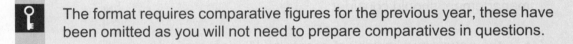

Information to be presented in the SOFP

IAS 1 requires that, as a minimum, the following line items appear in the statement of financial position (where there are amounts to be classified within these categories):

(a) property, plant and equipment

(b) investment property

(c) intangible assets

(d) financial assets (excluding amounts shown under (e), (h) and (i))

(e) investments accounted for using the equity method

(f) biological assets

(g) inventories

(h) trade and other receivables

(i) cash and cash equivalents

(j) the total of assets classified as held for sale in accordance with IFRS 5 Non-current Assets Held for Sale and Discontinued Operations

(k) trade and other payables

(l) provisions

(m) financial liabilities (excluding amounts shown under (k) or (l))

(n) liabilities and assets for current tax as defined in IAS 12 Income Taxes

(o) deferred tax liabilities and deferred tax assets, as defined in IAS 12 Income Taxes

(p) liabilities included in disposal groups classified as held for sale in accordance with IFRS 5

(q) non-controlling interest, presented within equity

(r) issued capital and reserves attributable to owners of the parent

The above list includes items that the IASB believes are so different in nature or function that they should be separately disclosed, but does not require them to appear in a fixed order or format.

Additional line items, headings and subtotals should be shown in the statement of financial position if another IFRS requires it or where it is necessary to show a fair presentation of the financial position. In deciding whether additional items should be separately presented, management should consider:

- the nature and liquidity of assets and their materiality (e.g. the separate disclosure of monetary and non-monetary amounts and current and non-current assets)
- their function within the entity (e.g. the separate disclosure of operating assets and financial assets, inventories and cash) and
- the amounts, nature and timing of liabilities (e.g. the separate disclosure of interest-bearing and non-interest-bearing liabilities and provisions and current and non-current liabilities).

Assets and liabilities that have a different nature or function within an entity are sometimes subject to different measurement bases, for example, plant and equipment may be carried at cost or held at a revalued amount (in accordance with IAS 16). The use of these different measurement bases for different classes of items suggests separate presentation is necessary for users to fully understand the accounts.

Information to be presented in either the SOFP/notes

Further subclassifications of the line items should be presented either in the statement of financial position or in the notes. The size, nature and function of the amounts involved, or the requirements of another IFRS will normally determine whether the disclosure is in the statement of financial position or in the notes.

The disclosures will vary for each item, but IAS 1 gives the following examples:

(a) tangible assets are analysed (IAS 16) by class e.g. property, plant and equipment, land and buildings, etc

(b) receivables are analysed between:

– amounts receivable from trade customers

– receivables from related parties

– prepayments

– other amounts

(c) inventories are classified (IAS 2) into merchandise, production supplies, materials, work in progress and finished goods

(d) provisions are analysed showing provisions for employee benefits separate from any other provisions

(e) equity capital and reserves are analysed showing separately the various classes of paid-in capital, share premium and reserves

Share capital and reserves disclosures

IAS 1 also requires that the following information on share capital and reserves be made either in the statement of financial position or in the notes:

(a) for each class of share capital:

– the number of shares authorised

– the number of shares issued and fully paid, and issued but not fully paid

– par value per share, or that the shares have no par value

– a reconciliation of the number of shares outstanding at the beginning and at the end of the year, the rights, preferences and restrictions attaching to that class, including restrictions on the distribution of dividends and the repayment of capital,

– shares in the entity held by the entity itself or by subsidiaries or associates of the entity, and

– shares reserved for issuance under options and sales contracts, including the terms and amounts

(b) a description of the nature and purpose of each reserve within owners' equity;

IAS 1 requires the following to be disclosed in the notes:

- the amount of dividends that were proposed or declared after the reporting period but before the financial statements were authorised for issue
- the amount of any cumulative preference dividends not recognised.

Note: IAS 1 and IAS 10 do not allow proposed dividends to be included as a liability in the statement of financial position, unless the dividend was declared before the end of the reporting period.

Current/Non-current distinction

An entity shall present current and non-current assets and current and non-current liabilities as separate classifications in the statement of financial position except when a presentation based on liquidity provides information that is reliable and more relevant.

Where an entity chooses not to classify by current and non-current, assets and liabilities should be presented broadly in order of their liquidity.

Whichever method of presentation is adopted, an entity should disclose, for each asset and liability, the amount that is expected to be recovered or settled after more than 12 months.

Most entities will show both current and non-current liabilities in the statement of financial position. However, say, for example, an entity does not normally have non-current trade liabilities but as a result of one particular transaction has a payable due 20 months from the end of the reporting period. The entity may, in this case, classify the entire amount as a trade payable under current liabilities and then show separately a one-off amount that is due in 20 months' time (i.e. in more than 12 months from the end of the reporting period).

In judging the most suitable presentation, management should consider the usefulness of the information they are providing. Information about the financial position of an entity is often used to predict the expected future cash flows and the timing of those cash flows. Information about the expected date of recovery and settlement of items is likely to be useful and therefore worth disclosing.

Current assets

An asset should be classified as a current asset when it is any of the following:

- is expected to be realised in, or is intended for sale or consumption in the entity's normal operating cycle
- is held primarily for trading purposes
- is expected to be realised within 12 months of the end of the reporting period or
- is cash or cash equivalent

All other assets should be classified as non-current assets.

Current liabilities

A liability should be classified as a current liability when it:

- is expected to be settled in the entity's normal operating cycle
- is due to be settled within 12 months of the end of the reporting period
- is held primarily for the purpose of being traded or
- the entity does not have an unconditional right to defer settlement of the liability for at least 12 months after the end of the reporting period

All other liabilities should be classified as non-current liabilities.

4 Statement of changes in equity

The statement of changes in equity (SOCIE) provides a summary of all changes in equity arising from transactions with owners in their capacity of owners.

This includes the effect of share issues and dividends.

This statement is useful since the total change in equity reflects the increase or decreases in the net assets of the enterprise in the period and so reflects the change in the wealth of the enterprise in the period.

XYZ Statement of changes in equity for the year ended 31 December 20X0

	Share capital	Share premium	Revaluation reserve	Retained earnings	Total
	$000	$000	$000	$000	$000
Balance at 31 December 20W9	X	X	X	X	X
Change in accounting policy				X/(X)	X/(X)
	—	—	—	—	—
Restated balance				X	X
Revaluation gain/loss			X(X)		X/(X)
Transfer to retained earnings			(X)	X	–
Total comprehensive income for the period			X	X	X
Dividends				(X)	(X)
Issue of share capital	X	X			X
	—	—	—	—	—
Balance at 31 December 20X0	X	X	X	X/(X)	X
	—	—	—	—	—

Dividends and shares

Share capital in the SOFP may include both ordinary and preference shares.

Ordinary shares

- Ordinary shareholders own a percentage of the entities net assets.
- Voting rights are attached to the shares.
- A year-end dividend may be paid to shareholders based on the performance of the entity.
- The dividend is paid as an amount per share.
- A dividend will first be proposed by directors, then declared (confirmed) and then paid.
- Ordinary dividends should only be accounted for when declared.
- Dividends may be interim, i.e. paid part way through the year and final, i.e declared and/or paid at year-end.

Ordinary shares will be accounted for as follows:

Debit	Cash/Bank
Credit	Share capital (nominal value)
Credit	Share premium (excess of proceeds above nominal value)

Ordinary dividends will be accounted for as follows:

Debit	Retained earnings (shown in SOCIE)
Credit	Cash/Bank

Preference shares

- Preference shareholders own a percentage of the entities share capital.
- Voting rights are not attached to the shares.
- A year-end dividend will be paid to shareholders based on a percentage of the investment.
- Preference dividends should be accounted for on an accruals basis.

Preference dividends will be accounted for as follows:

Debit	Finance Cost (SPL)
Credit	Accruals (SOFP)

Test your understanding 1 – SOCIE

An entity Apple has the following balances at 1 January 20X1:

	$
Share capital ($1 nominal value)	100,000
Share premium	50,000
Retained earnings	200,000

During the year Apple issued 50,000 shares at $1.20 and paid all shareholders a dividend of $0.10 per share.

Profit after tax amounted to $120,000.

Required:

Prepare the statement of changes in equity for the year ended 31 December 20X1 for Apple.

Assessment on this will be largely in the form of OTQ's which will only test one or two principles at a time. You will not be expected to prepare a set of financial statements in totality. However, it is important you practice these types of questions as you do not know which element will be tested in your assessment. Therefore, as part of the learning and understanding process, you may be asked to calculate individual amounts or values for inclusion in a set of financial statements, rather than the full financial statement.

Illustration 1 – SOFP and SOCIE

Bernie is an entity with authorised share capital of $500,000, consisting of ordinary shares of $1 each. The entity prepares its accounts as on 31 March each year and the trial balance before adjustments, extracted on 31 March 20X1 is as follows:

	Dr	**Cr**
	$	$
Ordinary share capital		400,000
Share premium		15,000
Retained earnings at 1 April 20X0		122,000
6% Loan		100,000
Leasehold factory		
Cost at 1 April 20X0	400,000	
Accumulated depreciation at 1 April 20X0		152,000
Plant and machinery		
Cost at 1 April 20X0	150,000	
Additions in year	20,000	
Accumulated depreciation at 1 April 20X0		60,000
Trade payables		280,000
Accrued expenses		60,000
Inventory as at 31 March 20X1	320,000	
Trade receivables	200,000	
Prepayments	160,000	
Cash and cash equivalents	180,000	
Profit for year (subject to items in the following notes)		222,000
Interim dividend paid	5,000	
Sale proceeds of plant		24,000
	1,435,000	1,435,000

You ascertain that:

(1) The loan is repayable at par by five equal annual instalments starting on 31 December 20X1.

(2) The plant disposed of originally cost $32,000 and depreciation of $6,400 had been charged by the date of disposal.

(3) Annual depreciation is calculated at the year end as:
   - leasehold factory 2% on cost and
   - plant and machinery 20% reducing balance.

(4) A final dividend of 20 cents per share is declared on 5 April 20X1.

(5) Tax for the year is estimated to be $20,000.

(6) During the year 100,000 shares had been issued at $1.10 each. This share issue has been accounted for.

Required:

Prepare, in a form suitable for publication, the statement of financial position and statement of changes in equity as at 31 March 20X1.

Solution

Bernie Statement of financial position as at 31 March 20X1

	$	$
Non-current assets		
Property, plant and equipment (W1)		307,520
Current assets		
Inventories	320,000	
Trade receivables	200,000	
Prepayments	160,000	
Cash and cash equivalents	180,000	
		860,000
Total assets		1,167,520

Equity and liabilities		
Capital and reserves		
Share capital	400,000	
Share premium	15,000	
Retained earnings	292,520	
		707,520
Non-current liabilities		
6% Loan (W5)		80,000
Current liabilities		
6% Loan (W5)	20,000	
Trade payables	280,000	
Accrued expenses	60,000	
Income tax	20,000	
		380,000
		1,167,520

Bernie Statement of changes in equity for the year ended 31 March 20X1

	Share capital	Share premium	Retained earnings	Total
	$	$	$	$
Balance at 1 April 20X0	300,000	5,000	122,000	427,000
Profit for the year (W2)	–	–	175,520	175,520
Dividends paid (trial balance figure)	–	–	(5,000)	(5,000)
Issue of share capital (W7)	100,000	10,000	–	110,000
Balance at 31 March 20X1	400,000	15,000	292,520	707,520

Workings

(W1) **Property, plant and equipment**

	Leasehold factory	Plant and machinery	Total
	$	$	$
Cost			
At 1 April 20X0	400,000	150,000	550,000
Additions	–	20,000	20,000
Disposals	–	(32,000)	(32,000)
At 31 March 20X1	400,000	138,000	538,000
Acc dep'n			
At 1 April 20X0	152,000	60,000	212,000
Disposals	–	(6,400)	(6,400)
Charge for year (W4)	8,000	16,880	24,880
At 31 March 20X1	160,000	70,480	230,480
Carrying amount at 31 March 20X1	240,000	67,520	307,520
Carrying amount at 1 April 20X0	248,000	90,000	338,000

(W2) **Profit for the year**

	$
Per TB	222,000
Loss on disposal (W3)	(1,600)
Depreciation – factory (W4)	(8,000)
Depreciation – P&M (W4)	(16,880)
Income tax expense	(20,000)
	175,520

(W3) **Loss on disposal**

	$
Proceeds (TB)	24,000
Carrying value (32,000 – 6,400)	25,600
Loss on disposal	1,600

(W4) **Depreciation**

Factory 2% × $400,000 = $8,000

P & M 20% × (cost $138,000 – depn ($60,000 – $6,400)) = 20% × $84,400 = $16,880

(W5) **Loan**

This is repaid in 5 equal instalments. The first payment is due within 12 months of the reporting date and therefore must be shown as a current liability. Total liability = $100,000 split $20,000 current (1/5) and $80,000 non-current (4/5).

(W6) **Dividends**

No adjustments are made for the final dividend as they were declared after the reporting date.

(W7) **Share issue**

Total proceeds = 100,000 × $1.10 = $110,000

Nominal value = 100,000 × $1 = $100,000 (share capital account)

Premium = 100,000 × $0.10 = $10,000 (share premium account)

5 Statement of Profit or Loss and other Comprehensive Income

IAS 1 allows a choice of two presentations of comprehensive income:

- A single statement of profit or loss and other comprehensive income; or
- A statement of profit or loss showing the profit or loss for the period PLUS a separate statement of other comprehensive income, which will also include a total for total comprehensive income

Total comprehensive income is the profit or loss for the period, plus other comprehensive income.

Other comprehensive income (OCI) is income and expenses that are not recognised in profit or loss (i.e. they are recorded in reserves rather than as an element of the profit for the period). For the purpose of F1, other comprehensive income mainly includes any change in the revaluation reserve and actuarial gains and losses on defined benefit plans (see later in chapter 19) . Further detail on other comprehensive income items can be found later on in this chapter in expandable text.

The most common format would be to use the function method.

This would be presented as one statement as follows:

XYZ Statement of profit or loss and other comprehensive Income for the year ended 31 December 20X0

	$000
Revenue	X
Cost of sales	(X)
Gross profit/(loss)	X/(X)
Distribution costs	(X)
Administrative expenses	(X)
Profit/(loss) from operations	X/(X)
Income from investments	X
Finance cost	(X)
Profit/(loss) before tax	X/(X)
Income tax expense	(X)
Profit/(loss) for the period	X/(X)
Other comprehensive income	
Items that will not be reclassified to profit or loss in future accounting periods:	
e.g. Gain (or loss) on revaluation	X/(X)
Total comprehensive income for the year	X

This analysis of expenses is based on the function method. This presentation method is the format most likely to appear in the OTQ's and case study. The alternative method for presentation of expenses is called the nature of expenses and can be seen in expandable text later on in this chapter.

Material items

- When items of income and expenses are material, their nature and amount shall be disclosed separately before operating profit.
- This may either be done on the face of the statement of profit or loss and other comprehensive income or in the notes.
- Examples:
  - inventory write-offs
  - impairment losses (see later in chapter 13)
  - restructuring costs
  - disposals of property, plant and equipment
  - litigation settlements

The statement of profit or loss used to be called the income statement. The current revised IAS 1 states either title can be used. For assessment purposes always use the current title of statement of profit or loss, however, on occasions the assessment may refer to the income statement in questions.

Other comprehensive income

IAS 1 requires other comprehensive income to be split between two headings:

- items that will not be reclassified to profit or loss and
- items that may be reclassified subsequently to profit or loss

For the purposes of F1 students will mainly deal with revaluation gains or losses in other comprehensive income and these should be shown as "items that will not be reclassified to profit or loss". Other items that may appear in this category could be the remeasurement component gains or losses on defined benefit pension plans (see chapter 19), share of other comprehensive income of associates or income tax relating to any items not reclassified.

Items that may be reclassified subsequently to profit or loss could be exchange differences on translating foreign operations (see chapter 18), available-for-sale financial assets, cash flow hedges and income tax relating to any items reclassified (covered in the F2 syllabus).

Alternative presentation

An entity may present two statements instead of one: a separate statement of profit or loss and a statement of other comprehensive income.

Statement of profit or loss plus statement of other comprehensive income – function method

A recommended format for the statement of profit or loss would be as follows:

XYZ Statement of profit or loss for the year ended 31 December 20X0

	$000
Revenue	X
Cost of sales	(X)
Gross profit/(loss)	X/(X)
Distribution costs	(X)
Administrative expenses	(X)
Profit/(loss) from operations	X/(X)
Income from investments	X
Finance cost	(X)
Profit/(loss) before tax	X/(X)
Income tax expense	(X)
Profit/(loss) for the period	X/(X)

A recommended format for the presentation of other comprehensive income would be:

XYZ Other comprehensive income for the year ended 31 December 20X0

Profit/(loss) for the period	X/(X)
Other comprehensive income	
e.g. Gain/loss on revaluation	X/(X)
Total comprehensive income for the year	X

Information to be presented in the SPL

IAS 1 requires that certain information (as a minimum) is presented in the statement of profit or loss, including:

(a) revenue

(b) finance costs

(c) share of profits and losses of associates (examined) and joint ventures (beyond the scope of this syllabus), accounted for using the equity method

(d) tax expense

(e) a single amount for the total of discontinued operations (see chapter 14 later for more detail)

Additional line items, headings and subtotals should be shown in the statement of profit or loss if another IFRS requires it or where it is necessary to show a fair presentation of the financial position.

Materiality, the nature and function of the item are likely to be the main considerations when deciding whether to include an additional line item in the statement of profit or loss.

Nature of expenses method

In this method expenses are presented according to their nature rather than their function as follows:

XYZ Statement of profit or loss and other comprehensive Income for the year ended 31 December 20X0

	$000
Revenue	X
Other operating income	X
Changes in inventory of WIP and finished goods	(X)
Work performed by the entity and capitalised	X
Raw material and consumables used	(X)
Employee benefits expense	(X)
Depreciation and amortisation expense	(X)
Impairment of property, plant and equipment	(X)
Other expenses	(X)
Finance costs	(X)
Profit/(loss) before tax	X/(X)
Income tax expense	(X)
Profit/(loss) for the period	X/(X)
Other comprehensive income	
Gain/loss on revaluation	X
Total comprehensive income for the year	X

Illustration 2 – Statement of profit or loss

The following is an extract from the trial balance of an entity Lafford, at 30 September 20X1.

	Dr	Cr
	$000	$000
Revenue		41,600
Purchases	22,600	
Inventory at 1 October 20X0	13,000	
Distribution costs	6,000	
Administrative expenses	5,000	
Irrecoverable debts written off	600	
Hire of machinery	500	
Production wages	400	
Loan interest paid 1 April 20X1 (loan repayable 20X9)	525	
Dividends received		900
Warehouse machinery:		
Cost	3,000	
Accumulated depreciation at 1 October 20X0		1,700
Motor vehicles:		
Cost	1,000	
Accumulated depreciation at 1 October 20X0		500

The following information should also be taken into account:

(1) Closing inventory at 30 September 20X1 was $15.6 million.

(2) Irrecoverable debts written off are to be included in administrative expenses.

(3) Depreciation is to be provided for on the straight line basis as follows:

– Warehouse machinery 10 per cent

– Motor vehicles 25 per cent

(4) Depreciation of motor vehicles is to be divided equally between distribution costs and administrative expenses, and depreciation of warehouse machinery is to be charged wholly to cost of sales.

(5) The estimated income tax expense for the year ended 30 September 20X1 is $3 million.

(6) Loan interest is paid in arrears every six months on 1 April and 1 October annually.

Required:

Using individual workings for each item, produce extracts from Lafford's statement of profit or loss and other comprehensive income for the year ended 30 September 20X1 in a form suitable for publication as follows:

(a) finance costs

(b) administrative expenses

(c) distribution costs

(d) gross profit

(e) based upon the information in the question, together with your answers to parts (a) - (d), prepare the statement of profit or loss of Lafford for the year ended 30 September 20X1.

Solution

(a) Finance costs

	$000
Per trial balance	525
Add: accrual 6 months interest to 1 October 20X1	525
	1,050

(b) Administrative expenses

	$000
Per trial balance	5,000
Add: irrecoverable debt written off	600
Add: motor dep'n (25% × $1,000 × 50%)	125
	5,725

(c) Distribution costs

	$000
Per trial balance	6,000
Add: motor dep'n (25% × $1,000 × 50%)	125
	6,125

(d) Gross profit

	$000	$000
Revenue - per trial balance		41,600
Cost of sales:		
Opening inventory - per trial balance	13,000	
Purchases - per trial balance	22,600	
Hire of machinery - per trial balance	500	
Production wages - per trial balance	400	
Closing inventory - per notes to question	(15,600)	
Add: warehouse machinery dep'n (10% × $3,000)	300	
		(21,200)
		20,400

(e) The statement of profit or loss and other comprehensive income

Lafford Statement of profit or loss and other comprehensive income for the year ended 30 September 20X1

	$000
Revenue	41,600
Cost of sales	(21,200)
Gross profit (part (d))	20,400
Distribution costs (part (c))	(6,125)
Administrative expenses (part (b))	(5,725)
Profit from operations	8,550
Income from investments	900
Finance cost (part (a))	(1,050)
Profit before tax	8,400
Income tax expense	(3,000)
Profit for the period	5,400
Other comprehensive income:	–
Total comprehensive income for the year	5,400

Notes to financial statements

Notes to the financial statements normally include narrative descriptions or more detailed analysis of items in the financial statements, as well as additional information such as contingent liabilities and commitments.

IAS 1 also provides guidance on the structure of the accompanying notes to financial statements, the accounting policies and other required disclosures.

The notes to the financial statements of an entity should:

(a) present information about the basis of preparation of the financial statements and the specific accounting policies adopted for significant transactions

(b) disclose the information required by other IFRSs that is not presented elsewhere in the financial statements

(c) provide additional information which is not presented elsewhere in financial statements but is relevant to an understanding of any of them

Notes to the financial statements should be presented in a systematic manner and any item in the financial statements should be cross-referenced to any related information in the notes.

Notes are normally provided in the following order, which assists users in understanding the financial statements and comparing them with those of other entities:

(a) statement of compliance with IFRSs

(b) summary of the significant accounting policies applied

(c) supporting information for items presented in each financial statement in the order in which each line item and each financial statement is presented

(d) other disclosures, including:

- contingent liabilities, commitments and unrecognised contractual commitments other financial disclosures
- non-financial disclosures

Accounting policies

The summary of significant accounting policies in the notes to the financial statements should describe the following:

- the measurement basis (or bases) used in preparing the financial statements and
- each specific accounting policy that is necessary for a proper understanding of the financial statements

Test your understanding 2 – P (part 1)

The following information has been extracted from the accounting reports of an entity P:

P – trial balance as at 31 March 20X1

	Dr	Cr
	$000	$000
Revenue		5,300
Purchases	1,564	
Inventory at 1 April 20X0	164	
Dividends received		210
Administrative expenses	490	
Distribution costs	370	
Interest paid 1 October 20X0	54	
Prepayments	25	
Dividends paid	390	
Property, plant and equipment	4,250	
Short-term investments	2,700	
Trade receivables	418	
Cash and cash equivalents	12	
Trade payables		136
Long-term loans - 9% (repayable 20X9)		1,200
Share capital		1,500
Share premium		800
Retained earnings at 31 March 20X0		1,291
	10,437	10,437

The following information should also be taken into account:

(1) During the year, P paid a final dividend of $240,000 in respect of the year ended 31 March 20X0. This was in addition to the interim dividend paid on 1 September 2010 in respect of the year ended 31 March 20X1.

(2) The tax charge for the year has been estimated at $470,000.

(3) The directors declared a final dividend of $270,000 on 3 April 20X1.

(4) The inventory valuation at 31 March 20X1 was $150,000,

(5) Interest is paid on the long-term loan on 1 April and 1 October annually.

Required:

Produce ther following extracts of the financial statements of P for the year ended 31 March 20X1:

(a) Cost of sales

(b) Profit from operations

(c) Interest payable

(d) Profit before tax

(e) Total comprehensive income for the year

(f) A summary of retained earnings for the year to include in the statement of changes in equity

Test your understanding 3 - P (part 2)

The following information has been extracted from the accounting reports of an entity P:

P – trial balance as at 31 March 20X1

	Dr	**Cr**
	$000	$000
Revenue		5,300
Purchases	1,564	
Inventory at 1 April 20X0	164	
Dividends received		210
Administrative expenses	490	
Distribution costs	370	
Interest paid 1 October 20X0	54	
Prepayments	25	
Dividends paid	390	
Property, plant and equipment	4,250	
Short-term investments	2,700	
Trade receivables	418	
Cash and cash equivalents	12	
Trade payables		136
Long-term loans - 9% (repayable 20X9)		1,200
Share capital		1,500
Share premium		800
Retained earnings at 31 March 20X0		1,291
	10,437	10,437

The following information should also be taken into account:

(1) During the year, P paid a final dividend of $240,000 in respect of the year ended 31 March 20X0. This was in addition to the interim dividend paid on 1 September 2010 in respect of the year ended 31 March 20X1.

(2) The tax charge for the year has been estimated at $470,000.

(3) The directors declared a final dividend of $270,000 on 3 April 20X1.

(4) The inventory valuation at 31 March 20X1 was $150,000,

(5) Interest is paid on the long-term loan on 1 April and 1 October annually.

(6) Profit after tax for the year was $2,494,000.

Required:

Produce ther following extracts of the financial statements of P as at 31 March 20X1:

(a) Current assets

(b) Retained earnings

(c) Current liabilities

(d) The statement of changes in equity for the year ended 31 March 20X1

Test your understanding 4 – Picklette (part 1)

The following information has been extracted from the books of an entity Picklette for the year ended 31 March 20X1:

	Dr	Cr
	$000	$000
Administrative expenses	170	
Interest paid	5	
Distribution costs	240	
Share capital (ordinary $1 shares)		200
Dividends paid	6	
Cash and cash equivalents	9	
Land and Buildings		
Cost at 1 April 20X0 (land $110, buildings $100)	210	
Accumulated depreciation at 1 April 20X0		48
Plant and machinery		
Cost at 1 April 20X0	125	
Accumulated depreciation at 1 April 20X0		75
Accruals		90
Retained earnings at 1 April 20X0		270
Trade receivables and payables	738	60
Inventory as at 1 April 20X0	150	
Purchases	470	
10% Loan		80
Revenue		1,300
	2,123	2,123

Additional information:

(1) Inventory at 31 March 20X1 was valued at $250,000.

(2) Buildings and plant and machinery are depreciated on a straight-line basis (assuming no residual value) at the following rate:

On cost:	Buildings	5%
	Plant and machinery	20%

(3) There were no purchases or sales of non-current assets for the year to 31 March 20X1.

(4) The depreciation charges for the year to 31 March 20X1 are to be apportioned as follows:

Cost of sales	60%
Distribution costs	20%
Administrative expenses	20%

(5) Income tax for the year to 31 March 20X1 is estimated at $135,000.

(6) The loan is repayable in five years and the balance has been outstanding for the whole year.

Required:

Produce a statement of profit or loss and other comprehensive income for the year ended 31 March 20X1 for Picklette. Show all workings clearly.

Test your understanding 5 - Picklette (part 2)

The following information has been extracted from the books of an entity Picklette for the year ended 31 March 20X1:

	Dr	Cr
	$000	$000
Administrative expenses	170	
Interest paid	5	
Distribution costs	240	
Share capital (ordinary $1 shares)		200
Dividends paid	6	
Cash and cash equivalents	9	
Land and Buildings		
Cost at 1 April 20X0 (land $110, buildings $100)	210	
Accumulated depreciation at 1 April 20X0		48
Plant and machinery		
Cost at 1 April 20X0	125	
Accumulated depreciation at 1 April 20X0		75
Accruals		90
Retained earnings at 1 April 20X0		270
Trade receivables and payables	738	60
Inventory as at 1 April 20X0	150	
Purchases	470	
10% Loan		80
Revenue		1,300
	2,123	2,123

Additional information:

(1) Inventory at 31 March 20X1 was valued at $250,000.

(2) Buildings and plant and machinery are depreciated on a straight-line basis (assuming no residual value) at the following rate:

On cost:	Buildings	5%
	Plant and machinery	20%

(3) There were no purchases or sales of non-current assets for the year to 31 March 20X1.

(4) Profit after tax for the year ended 31 March 20X1 was $347,000.

(5) Income tax for the year to 31 March 20X1 is estimated at $135,000.

(6) The loan is repayable in five years and the balance has been outstanding for the whole year.

Required:

Produce a statement of financial position as at 31 March 20X1 for Picklette. Show all workings clearly.

Test your understanding 6 - Picklette (part 3)

The following information has been extracted from the books of an entity Picklette for the year ended 31 March 20X1:

	Dr	Cr
	$000	$000
Administrative expenses	170	
Interest paid	5	
Distribution costs	240	
Share capital (ordinary $1 shares)		200
Dividends paid	6	
Cash and cash equivalents	9	
Land and Buildings		
Cost at 1 April 20X0 (land $110, buildings $100)	210	
Accumulated depreciation at 1 April 20X0		48
Plant and machinery		
Cost at 1 April 20X0	125	
Accumulated depreciation at 1 April 20X0		75
Accruals		90
Retained earnings at 1 April 20X0		270
Trade receivables and payables	738	60
Inventory as at 1 April 20X0	150	
Purchases	470	
10% Loan		80
Revenue		1,300
	2,123	2,123

Additional information:

(1) Total comprehensive income for the year ended 31 March 20X1 was $347,000.

(2) On 1 January 20X1, there was a share issue of $30,000 at par value.

Required:

Produce a statement of changes in equity for the year to 31 March 20X1 for Picklette. Show all workings clearly.

Test your understanding 7 – Thistle

Thistle is an entity with authorised share capital of 2,000,000 50c ordinary shares. At the year-end the entity has in issue 1,600,000 ordinary shares, all of which are fully paid.

The entity prepares its accounts annually to 30 June and its trial balance for the year ended 30 June 20X1, before final adjustments, is as follows:

	Dr	**Cr**
	$	$
Ordinary share capital		800,000
Share premium		100,000
Retained earnings at 1 July 20X0		540,000
10% Loan		80,000
Land and Buildings		
Cost at 1 July 20X0	1,400,000	
Accumulated depreciation at 1 July 20X0		58,000
Motor Vehicles		
Cost at 1 July 20X0	67,500	
Accumulated depreciation at 1 July 20X0		30,250
Fixtures & Fittings		
Cost at 1 July 20X0	19,800	
Accumulated depreciation at 1 July 20X0		8,400
Trade receivables and payables	71,500	60,820
Prepayments and accruals	970	1,360
Inventory as at 30 June 20X1		
Raw materials	32,500	
Finished goods	29,700	
Cash and cash equivalents	217,360	
Profit for year (subject to items in the following notes)		160,500
	1,839,330	1,839,330

The following information should also be taken into account:

(1) Land is included in the trial balance at its original cost of $800,000 and the following transactions have happened during the year in relation to non-current assets, **neither** of which have yet been recorded in the books:

- A building was purchased which cost $100,000.
- Motor vehicles which had originally cost $24,000 were sold during the year for $12,000. Accumulated depreciation of $14,000 had been charged on these motor vehicles at 1 July 20X0.

(2) Depreciation for the year is to be provided using the following policies:

Land	nil depreciation
Buildings	2% per annum, straight line
Motor vehicles	20% per annum, reducing balance
Fixtures & fittings	10% per annum, straight line

A full year's charge is made in the year of acquisition and none in the year of disposal.

(3) The directors have estimated that the entity's tax liability for the year will be $18,500.

(4) The directors would like to declare a final ordinary dividend of 7 cents per share.

(5) Interest on the loan is paid annually in arrears on 1 July. The loan is repayable in 20X9.

(6) During the year 100,000 ordinary shares were issued at a premium of 40 cents per share. This share issue is reflected in the trial balance.

Required:

Produce, in a form suitable for publication, the statement of financial position and statement of changes in equity for the year ended 30 June 20X1.

Test your understanding 8 – Practice questions

(1) **Which of the following best describes the purpose of financial statements according to IAS 1 Presentation of Financial Statements?**

A To provide information that enables users to assess the stewardship of management

B To provide information about the financial position, financial performance and cash flows of an enterprise

C To provide a summary of all financial transactions entered into in the accounting period

D To provide an statement of profit or loss and other comprehensive income and a statement of financial position

(2) **Which of the following are concepts that should be applied when preparing financial statements according to IAS 1 Presentation of Financial Statements?**

(i) Going concern

(ii) Accruals

(iii) Consistency

(iv) Off-setting

A i and ii

B i and iii

C i, ii and iv

D All of them

(3) **Which of the following items must be shown on the face of the statement of profit or loss and other comprehensive income according to IAS 1 Presentation of Financial Statements?**

(i) Revenue

(ii) Cost of sales

(iii) Gross profit

(iv) Finance costs

(v) Income tax expense

A All of them

B i, ii, iii and iv

C i, iv and v

D i, ii and iii

(4) **Which of the following items would be shown in the statement of changes in equity?**

(i) Profit for period

(ii) Dividends paid

(iii) Dividends proposed after the reporting period

(iv) Issue of shares

(v) Revaluation surplus

A i, ii, iv and v

B i, ii, iii and iv

C i, iii, iv and v

D All of them

(5) **Which of the following items would be shown as other comprehensive income on the statement of profit or loss and other comprehensive income?**

(i) Profit for period

(ii) Dividends paid

(iii) Dividends proposed

(iv) Issue of shares

(v) Revaluation surplus

A i, ii, iv and v

B i, ii, and iv

C v

D All of them

Data for Questions 6 and 7:

Trade receivables as at 31 December 20X0 were $18,000.

The irrecoverable debt allowance as at 1 January 20X0 was $900.

During the year, irrecoverable debts of $12,000 have been written off to administrative expenses.

After the year-end, but before the accounts had been completed, the entity discovered that a major customer had gone into liquidation and that their outstanding balance of $2,000 was unlikely to be paid.

Furthermore, as a result of the recent bad debt experience, the directors have decided to increase the irrecoverable debt provision at 31 December 20X0 to 10 per cent of outstanding trade receivables.

(6) **What is the correct balance for trade receivables, net of irrecoverable debt allowance, as at 31 December 20X0?**

A $3,600

B $5,400

C $14,400

D $16,200

(7) **What is the correct charge to the statement of profit or loss and other comprehensive income for irrecoverable debts and allowances for the year to 31 December 20X0?**

A $14,000

B $14,400

C $14,700

D $15,600

(8) **According to IAS 1, which of the following must be recognised in the statement of profit or loss?**

A Depreciation

B Equity dividends paid

C Revaluation gains

D Transfer from a revaluation reserve to retained earnings when a revalued asset is sold

(9) **According to IAS 1 which of the following will appear separately in an entity's statement of changes in equity?**

A Other income, dividends paid and proceeds from a share issue

B Other income, surplus arising on a revaluation and proceeds from a share issue

C Dividends paid, dividends received and proceeds from a share issue

D Dividends paid and proceeds from a share issue

(10) **Which of the following assets would be classified as current according to IAS 1 definition?**

Asset A which is expected to be sold within the next 12 months

Asset B which is not expected to be sold within the next 12 months but expected to be realised with the entity's normal operating cycle

Asset C which is held primarily for the purpose of being traded but for which there is currently no anticipated sale date

A Asset A only

B Asset A and Asset B

C Asset A and Asset C

D All of them

6 Summary diagram

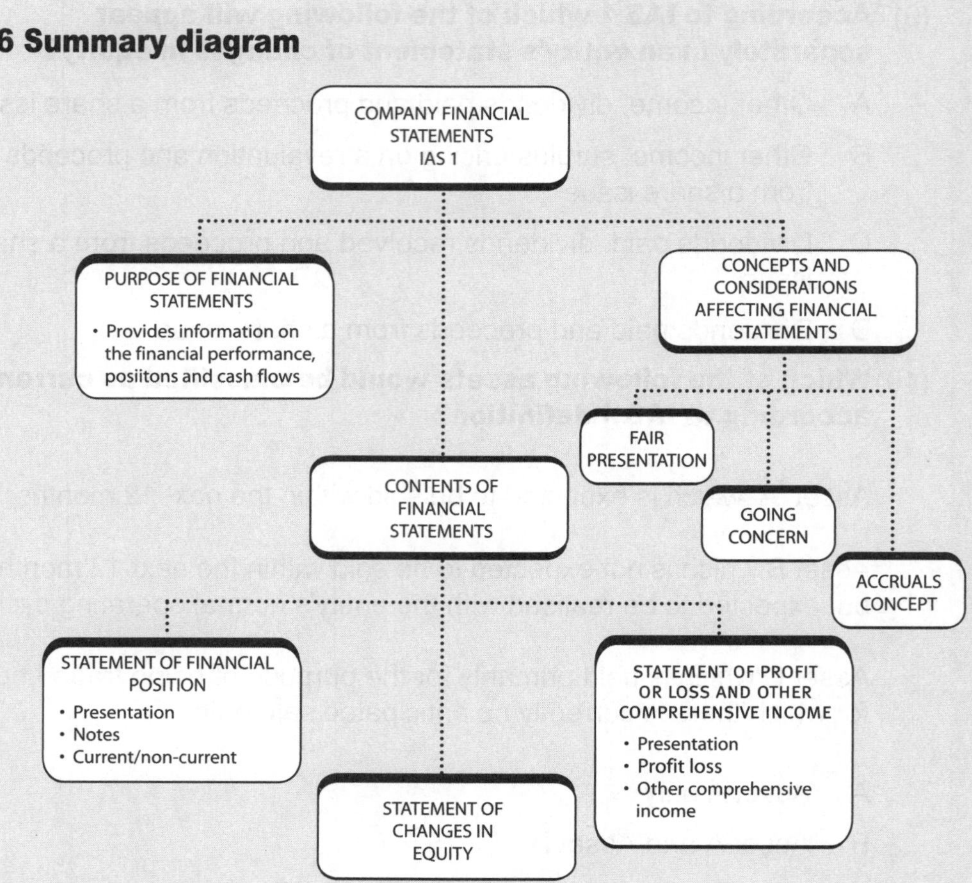

Test your understanding answers

Test your understanding 1 – SOCIE

Apples statement of changes in equity for the year ended 31 December 20X1

	Share capital	Share premium	Retained earnings	Total
	$	$	$	$
Balance at 1 January 20X1	100,000	50,000	200,000	350,000
Profit for the year	–	–	120,000	120,000
Issue of share capital (W1)	50,000	10,000		60,000
Dividends paid (W2)	–	–	(15,000)	(15,000)
Balance at 31 December 20X1	150,000	60,000	305,000	515.000

(W1) Share issue = 50,000 × $1 = $50,000 share capital and 50,000 × $0.20 = $10,000 share premium.

(W2) Dividend of $0.10 per share is based on 150,000 shares (100,000 b/wd plus 50,000 issued during the year)

Test your understanding 2 – P (part 1)

(a) Cost of sales

	$000
Opening inventory	164
Purchases	1,564
Less: Closing inventory	(150)
	1,578

(b) Profit from operations

	$000
Revenue	5,300
Cost of sales (part (a))	(1,578)
Distribution costs	(370)
Administrative expenses	(490)
	2,862

(c) Interest payable

	$000
Interest paid 1 October 20X0 (six months)	54
Accrual for 6 months to 31 March 20X1	54
	108

(d) Profit before tax

	$000
Profit from operations (part (b))	2,862
Interest payable (Part (c))	(108)
Income from investments	210
	2,964

(e) Total comprehensive income for the year

	$000
Profit before tax (part (d))	2,964
Income tax expense	(470)
	2,494

(f) Summary of retained earnings for the year

	$000
Retained earnings at 31 March 20X0	1,291
Total comprehensive income for the year	2,494
Dividends paid	(390)
	3,395

For reference:

P Statement of profit or loss and other comprehensive income for the year ended 31 March 20X1

	$000
Revenue	5,300
Cost of Sales	(1,578)
Gross profit	3,722
Distribution costs	(370)
Administrative expenses	(490)
Profit from operations	2,862
Income from investments	210
Finance cost	(108)
Profit before tax	2,964
Income tax expense	(470)
Profit for period	2,494
Other comprehensive income:	–
Total comprehensive income for the period	2,494

Test your understanding 3 - P (part 2)

(a) Current assets

	$000
Inventory	150
Trade and other receivables	418
Prepayments	25
Investments	2,700
Cash and cash equivalents	12
	3,305

(b) Retained earnings

	$000
Brought forward at 1 April 20X0	1,291
Profit after tax for the year	2,494
Dividends paid	(390)
Carried forward at 31 March 20X1	3,395

(c) Current liabilities

	$000
Trade payables	136
Income tax	470
Interest accrual (9% × $1,200 × 6/12)	54
	660

(d) **P Statement of changes in equity for the year ended 31 March 20X1**

	Share capital	Share premium	Retained earnings	Total
	$	$	$	$
Balance at 1 April 20X0	1,500	800	1,291	3,591
Total comprehensive income			2,494	2,494
Dividends			(390)	(390)
Balance at 31 March 20X1	1,500	800	3,395	5,695

Note: Dividends declared after the year end will not be adjusted for.

P Statement of financial position as at 31 March 20X1

	$000	$000
Non-current assets		
Property, plant and equipment		4,250
Current assets		
Inventories	150	
Trade and other receivables	418	
Prepayments	25	
Investments	2,700	
Cash and cash equivalents	12	
		3,305
Total assets		7,555
Equity and liabilities		
Capital and reserves		
Issued ordinary share capital	1,500	
Share premium	800	
Retained earnings	3,395	
		5,695
Non-current liabilities		
Long-term loans		1,200
Current liabilities		
Trade payables	136	
Income tax	470	
Interest accrual	54	
		660
Total equity and liabilities		7,555

Test your understanding 4 – Picklette (part 1)

Picklette Statement of profit or loss and other comprehensive income for the year ended 31 March 20X1

	$000
Revenue	1,300
Cost of Sales (W1)	(388)
Gross profit	912
Distribution costs (W1)	(246)
Administrative expenses (W1)	(176)
Profit from operations	490
Income from investments	–
Finance cost (W2)	(8)
Profit before tax	482
Income tax expense (W3)	(135)
Profit for the period	347
Other comprehensive income:	–
Total comprehensive income for the year	347

Workings

(W1)

	COS	**Distribution**	**Administration**
	$000	$000	$000
Purchases	470		
Opening inventory	150		
Distribution costs		240	
Administrative expenses			170
Closing inventory	(250)		
Dep'n – Buildings (5% × $100,000) (60:20:20)	3	1	1
Dep'n – Plant and machinery (20% × $125,000) (60:20:20)	15	5	5
	388	246	176

(W2) Loan interest expense (10% × $80,000) = $8,000 (P&L)

Amount paid per TB $5,000, therefore accrual required for $3,000

(W3) **Tax charge**

	$000
Estimated charge for the year	135

Test your understanding 5 - Picklette (part 2)

Picklette Statement of financial position as at 31 March 20X1

	$000	$000
Non-current assets		
Property, plant and equipment (W1)		182
Current assets		
Inventory	250	
Trade receivables	738	
Cash and cash equivalents	9	
		997
Total assets		1,179
Equity and liabilities		
Capital and reserves		
Share capital	200	
Retained earnings (W5)	611	
		811
Non-current liabilities		
10% Loan		80
Current liabilities		
Trade payables	60	
Accrued expenses (W3)	93	
Income tax	135	
		288
		1,179

(W1) **Property, plant and equipment**

	Land and buildings	Plant and machinery	Total
	$000	$000	$000
Cost			
At 1 April 20X0	210	125	335
At 31 March 20X1	210	125	335
Acc dep'n			
At 1 April 20X0	48	75	123
Charge for year (W2)	5	25	30
At 31 March 20X1	53	100	153
Carrying amount at 31 March 20X1	157	25	182
Carrying amount at 1 April 20X0	162	50	212

(W2) **Depreciation**

Buildings 5% × $100,000 = $5,000

Plant and machinery 20% × $125,000 = $25,000

(W3) **Accrued expenses**

	$000
As per TB	90
Interest accrual (W4)	3
As at 31 March 20X1	93

(W4) **Loan interest accrual**

Expense for the year (10% × $80,000) = $8,000 (P&L)

Amount paid per TB $5,000, therefore accrual required for $3,000.

(W5) **Retained earnings**

	$000
Retained earnings at 31 March 20X0	270
Dividends paid in the year	(6)
Profit after tax for the year	347
As at 31 March 20X1	611

Test your understanding 6 - Picklette (part 3)

Picklette Statement of changes in equity for the year ended 31 March 20X1

	Share capital	Retained earnings	Total
	$000	$000	$000
Balance at 1 April 20X0 (W1)	170	270	470
Share issue in year	30		
Total comprehensive income		347	347
Dividends paid in the year		(6)	(6)
Balance at 31 March 20X1	200	611	811

(W1) **Share capital at 1 April 20X0**

Share capital at 31 March 20X1 per TB = $200,000

Share issue in year per notes = $30,000

Therefore issued share capital at 1 April 20X0 = $200,000 - $30,000 = $170,000

Test your understanding 7 – Thistle

Thistle Statement of financial position as at 30 June 20X1

	$	$
Non-current assets		
Property, plant and equipment (W1)		1,459,220
Current assets		
Inventories (W3)	62,200	
Trade receivables	71,500	
Prepayments	970	
Cash and cash equivalents (W8)	129,360	
		264,030
Total assets		1,723,250
Equity and liabilities		
Capital and reserves		
Ordinary share capital	800,000	
Share premium	100,000	
Retained earnings	654,570	
		1,554,570
Non-current liabilities		
10% Loan		80,000
Current liabilities		
Trade payables	60,820	
Accruals	1,360	
Debenture interest owing (W4)	8,000	
Income tax	18,500	
		88,680
Total equity and liabilities		1,723,250

Thistle Statement of changes in equity for the year ended 30 June 20X1

	Share capital	Share premium	Retained earnings	Total
	$	$	$	$
Balance at 30 June 20X0	750,000	60,000	540,000	1,350,000
Total comprehensive income (W7)			114,570	114,570
Dividends (W2)			–	–
Issue of share capital (W2)	50,000	40,000	–	90,000
Balance at 30 June 20X1	800,000	100,000	654,570	1,554,570

Workings

(W1) **Property, plant and equipment**

	Land and buildings	Motor vehicles	Fixtures & fittings	Total
	$	$	$	$
Cost/Valuation				
At 1 July 20X0	1,400,000	67,500	19,800	1,487,300
Additions	100,000			100,000
Disposals		(24,000)		(24,000)
At 30 June 20X1	1,500,000	43,500	19,800	1,563,300

Accumulated depreciation:				
At 1 July 20X0	58,000	30,250	8,400	96,650
Charged during the year (W6)	14,000	5,450	1,980	21,430
Disposals		(14,000)		(14,000)
At 30 June 20X1	72,000	21,700	10,380	104,080
Carrying amount				
At 30 June 20X1	1,428,000	21,800	9,420	1,459,220
At 1 July 20X0	1,342,000	37,250	11,400	1,390,650

(W2) **Share capital**

50c ordinary shares	No.
Authorised shares	2,000,000
All issued shares are fully paid	
	No.
Number of issued shares at 1 July 20X0	1,500,000
Number Issued in the year	100,000
Number of issued shares at 30 June 20X1	1,600,000

Total proceeds = 100,000 × $0.90 = $90,000

Nominal value = 100,000 × $0.50 = $50,000 (share capital account)

Premium = 100,000 × $0.40 = $40,000 (share premium account)

An ordinary dividend of $70,000 (1,000,000 × 0.07) is declared but no adjustment as not done at year end.

(W3) **Inventory**

	$
Raw materials	32,500
Finished goods	29,700
	62,200

(W4) **Loan interest**

Interest due for the year $8,000 ($80,000 × 10%) payable 1 July 20X1

(W5) **Gain on disposal**

	$
Proceeds	12,000
Carrying value (24,000 – 14,000)	10,000
Profit on disposal	2,000

(W6) **Depreciation**

Building 2% × $700,000 (1,400,000 – land $800,000 + additions $100,000) = $14,000

Motor vehicles 20% × (cost $43,500 – depn ($30,250 – $14,000)) = 20% × $27,250 = $5,450

Fixtures and fittings 10% × $19,800 = $1,980

(W7) **Profit for year**

	$
Per TB	160,500
Gain on disposal (W5)	2,000
Depreciation(W6)	
– buildings	(14,000)
– motor vehicles	(5,450)
– fixtures & fittings	(1,980)
Income tax expense	(18,500)
Finance cost (W4)	(8,000)
Profit for the year	114,570

(W8) **Cash and cash equivalents**

	$
TB	217,360
Proceeds from sale of NCAs	12,000
Purchase of NCAs	(100,000)
Cash and cash equivalents	129,360

Test your understanding 8 – Practice questions

(1) B

(2) D

(3) C

(4) A

(5) C

(6) C – The irrecoverable debt must be written off against receivables before the allowance is calculated for the year, i.e. $18,000 – 2,000 = $16,000

The allowance for the year is calculated as 10% × $16,000 = $1,600

The balance on receivables to be shown on the SOFP will be $14,400 (16,000 – 1,600)

(7) C – The total for irrecoverable debts for the year will be $14,000 (12,000 + 2,000)

The allowance charged to the statement of profit or loss and other comprehensive income will be $700 (the movement 1,600 – 900)

(8) A – All other items will be shown in the SOCIE and not the statement of profit or loss. The revaluation gain (option C) will also be shown as other comprehensive income.

(9) D – Other income and dividends received form part of the statement of profit or loss

(10) D

chapter

12

IAS 7 Statement of Cash Flows

Chapter learning objectives

On completion of their studies students should be able to:

- Produce a statement of cash flows in a form suitable for publication.
- Identify the importance of the statement of cash flows.
- Identify the difference between the indirect and direct method of calculating cash generated from operations.

1 Session content

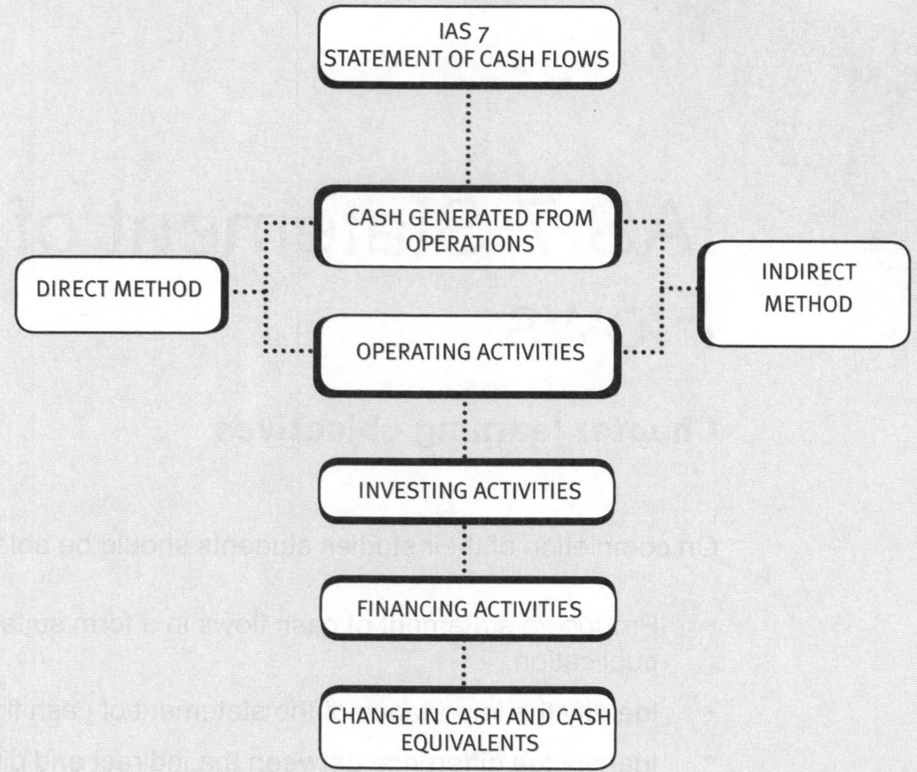

2 The importance of statements of cash flows

The statement of cash flows is an important part of the financial statements because:

- It helps users to assess liquidity and solvency – an adequate cash position is essential in the short term both to ensure the survival of the business and to enable debts and dividends to be paid.
- It helps users to assess financial adaptability – will the entity be able to take effective action to alter its cash flows in response to any unexpected events?
- It helps the users assess future cash flows – an adequate cash position in the longer term is essential to enable asset replacement, repayment of debt and to fund further expansion. Users will use current cash flow information to help them assess future cash flows.

- It helps to highlight where cash is being generated – the cash flow statement will clearly detail cash that is being generated from the core activities of the business and other non-operating activities.
- Cash flows are objective – a cash flow is a matter of fact whereas the calculation of profit is subjective.
- It can help to indicate problems early on.

3 Definitions In IAS 7

Cash

Cash 'comprises cash on hand and at bank including overdrafts and demand deposits'.

Cash equivalents

Cash equivalents are short-term, highly liquid investments that are readily convertible to known amounts of cash and which are subject to an insignificant risk of changes in value, e.g. short-dated treasury bill.

Operating activities

Operating activities are the principal revenue-producing activities of the enterprise and other activities that are not investing or financing activities.

Investing activities

Investing activities are the acquisition and disposal of long-term assets and other investments not included in cash equivalents.

Financing activities

Financing activities are activities that result in changes in the equity share capital and borrowings of the entity.

Proforma Statement of cash flows the year ended 31 December 20X9

	$	$
Cash flows from operating activities		
Profit before taxation	X	
Adjustments for:		
Depreciation/amortisation	X	
Provision increases /(decreases)	X/(X)	
(Profit)/loss on disposal	(X)/X	
Interest receivable/investment income	(X)	
Finance costs	X	
Operating profit before working capital changes	X	
(Increase)/decrease in inventories	(X)/X	
(Increase)/decrease in trade and other receivables	(X)/X	
Increase/(decrease) in trade and other payables	X/(X)	
Cash generated from operations	X	
Interest paid	(X)	
Tax paid	(X)	
Net cash from operating activities		X
Cash flows from investing activities		
Purchase of property, plant and equipment	(X)	
Purchase of intangibles	(X)	
Purchase of investments	(X)	
Proceeds from sale of property, plant and equipment	X	
Proceeds from sale of intangibles	X	
Proceeds from sale of investments	X	
Interest received	X	
Dividends received	X	
Net cash from investing activities		(X)
Cash flows from financing activities		
Proceeds from issue of ordinary shares	X	
Proceeds from issue of preference shares	X	
Proceeds from long-term borrowings	X	
Redemption of long-term borrowings	(X)	
Dividends paid	(X)	
Net cash from financing activities		(X)
Net increase/(decrease) in cash and cash equivalents		X/(X)
Cash and cash equivalents at beginning of period		X/(X)
Cash and cash equivalents at end of period		X/(X)

4 Cash generated from operations

The first main heading in the standard statement of cash flows proforma per IAS 7 is 'cash flows from operating activities. This can be broken down into 'cash generated from operations' (which is the focus of this section) and other cash flows from operating activities.

There are two ways the cash generated from operations can be calculated. The indirect method is the most likely to be examined in F1.

Indirect method

This method (shown in the above proforma), involves taking the profit before taxation from the statement of profit or loss, adjusting it for non-cash items and converting the income and expenses figure from the accruals basis to the cash basis, so that just the cash flows from operating activities remain.

Cash flows from operating activities	$
Profit before taxation	X
Adjustments for:	
Depreciation/amortisation/impairments	X
Provision increases/(decreases)	X/(X)
(Profit)/loss on disposal	(X)/X
Interest receivable/investment income	(X)
Finance costs	X
	—
Operating profit before working capital changes	X
(Increase)/decrease in inventories	(X)/X
(Increase)/decrease in trade and other receivables	(X)/X
Increase/(decrease) in trade and other payables	X/(X)
	—
Cash generated from operations	X

Adjustments using the indirect method

Depreciation/amortisation

Depreciation is not a cash flow.

- Capital expenditure purchases/disposals will be recorded under "investing activities" at the time of the cash outflow/inflow.
- Depreciation is the writing off of the capital expenditure over its useful life and simply an "accounting entry". It should be added back to profit because it was a non-cash expense deducted from the profit.

Profit/loss on disposal

When a non-current asset is disposed of:

- the cash inflow from the sale (the proceeds) is recorded under "investing activities"
- a profit/loss on disposal is an "accounting entry" calculated by comparing carrying value and proceeds which is recorded in the statement of profit or loss
- a loss on disposal should be added back because it is a non-cash expense deducted from the profit
- a profit on disposal should be deducted because it is a non-cash reduction to expenses added to the profit.

Provisions

Provisions are not a cash flow, they are an "accounting entry". They are required to ensure profits reflect the due amounts, rather than the amounts paid/received, hence applying the accruals concept. Therefore, an adjustment must be made for them when preparing the statement of cash flows.

When a provision is made:

- an increase should be added to profit because it is an expense from profit, which is not a cash item and
- a decrease should be deducted from profit because it is a reduction in an expense from profit, which is not a cash item.

Interest receivable/investment income

The amount from the statement of profit or loss should be deducted from the profit because this is not necessarily the amount that has been received (statement of profit or loss is prepared on the accruals basis). The actual cash amount received will appear under "investing activities".

Interest payable

The expense from the statement of profit or loss should be added to the profit because this is not necessarily the amount that has been paid. The actual cash amount will appear after cash generated from operations.

Change in receivables

- An increase in receivables is a reduction to cash (the more the customers owe, the less cash in the bank) and
- a decrease in receivable is an increase to cash.

Change in inventory

- An increase in inventory is a reduction to cash (the more inventory we buy, the less cash in the bank) and
- a decrease in inventory is an increase to cash.

Change in payables

- An increase in payables is an increase to cash (the more the suppliers are owed, the more cash we have in the bank) and
- a decrease in payables is a reduction to cash.

Direct method

This method involves simply adding cash inflows and deducting cash outflows in respect of operating activities.

	$
Cash receipts from customers	X
Cash receipts from other operational sources	X
Cash payments to suppliers	(X)
Cash payments to employees	(X)
Cash payments for expenses	(X)
	—
Cash generated from operations	X

Comparison of the methods

IAS 7 encourages, but does not require, the use of the direct method.

- Indirect method
  - The reconciliation highlights the fact that profit and cash are not equal.
  - Does not show significant elements of trading cash flows.
  - Low cost in preparing the information.

- Direct method
  - Discloses information not shown elsewhere in the financial statements.
  - Shows the cash flows from trading.
  - Gives the users more information in estimating future cash flows.

Illustration 1 – Indirect method

The following information is available for an entity Splatter for the year ended 30 September 20X1:

Statement of profit or loss

	$000
Revenue	444
Cost of sales	(269)
Gross profit	175
Distribution costs	(35)
Administrative expenses	(8)
Profit from operations	132
Finance costs	(18)
Profit before tax	114
Income tax expense	(42)
Profit for the year	72

The total expenses, i.e. cost of sales $269 + distribution costs $35 + administrative expenses $8, can be analysed as follows:

	$000
Wages	72
Auditors' remuneration	12
Depreciation	84
Cost of materials used	222
Profit on disposal of non-current assets	(60)
Rental income	(18)
	312

The following information is also available:

	30/09/X1	30/09/X0
	$000	$000
Inventories	42	24
Receivables	48	42
Payables	(30)	(18)

Required:

Produce the section of the statement of cash flows for cash generated from operations using the indirect method for the year ended 30 September 20X1 in compliance with IAS 7 Statement of Cash Flows.

Solution

Splatter Statement of cash flows for the year ended 30 September 20X1

	$000
Cash flows from operating activities	
Profit before tax	114
Depreciation	84
Profit on disposal of non-current assets	(60)
Finance costs	18
Operating profit before working capital changes	156
Increase in inventories (42 – 24)	(18)
Increase in trade receivables (48 – 42)	(6)
Increase in trade payables (30 – 18)	12
Cash generated from operations	144

Both inventory and receivable balances are increasing, hence a reduction in cash, i.e. the more money tied up in inventory or the more money owed by receivables the less cash we have available in the bank. Therefore, this is shown as a decrease in the statement.

Payables also increase but this means we have an increase in cash, i.e. the more money we owe suppliers, the longer we are keeping the cash in the bank.

Illustration 2 – Direct method

Required:

Using the information for Splatter in the previous illustration, produce the section of the statement of cash flows for cash generated from operations using the direct method for the year ended 30 September 20X1 in compliance with IAS 7 Statement of Cash Flows.

Solution

Splatter Statement of cash flows for the year ended 30 September 20X1

	$000
Cash flows from operating activities	
Cash receipts from customers (W1)	438
Rental income	18
Cash payments to suppliers (W2)	(228)
Cash payments to employees	(72)
Cash payments for expenses	(12)
Cash generated from operations	144

(W1)

Cash receipts from customers

	$000
Opening receivables	42
Sales revenue	444
Closing receivables	(48)
Cash received from customers	438

(W2)

Cash payments to suppliers

	$000
Opening inventories	24
Purchases (ß)	240
Closing	(42)
Cost of materials used	222

	$000
Opening payables	18
Purchases (above)	240
Closing payables	(30)
Payments to suppliers	228

Test your understanding 1 – Cash generated from operations

Yog's statement of profit or loss for the year ended 31 December 20X1 and statements of financial position as at 31 December 20X0 and 31 December 20X1 were as follows:

Statement of profit or loss for the year ended 31 December 20X1

	$000	$000
Sales		360
Raw materials consumed	35	
Staff costs	47	
Depreciation	59	
Loss on disposal	9	
		(150)
Profit from operations		210
Finance costs		(14)
Profit before tax		196
Income tax expense		(62)
Profit for the period		134

Statements of financial position as at

	31 Dec 20X1		31 Dec 20X0	
	$000	$000	$000	$000
Assets				
Non-current assets				
Cost		798		780
Depreciation		(159)		(112)
		639		668
Current assets				
Inventories	12		10	
Trade receivables	34		26	
Cash and cash equivalents	24		28	
		70		64
Total assets		709		732
Equity and liabilities				
Capital reserves				
Share capital			180	170
Share premium			18	12
Retained earnings			343	245
			541	427
Non-current liabilities				
Long-term loans			100	250
Current liabilities				
Trade payables		21	15	
Interest payable		7	5	
Income tax		40	35	
			68	55
Total equity and liabilities			709	732

During the year, the entity paid $45,000 for a new piece of equipment and a dividend was paid amounting to $36,000.

Required:

Calculate the cash generated from operations using the indirect method.

Test your understanding 2 – Direct method

Required:

Using the information for Yog in the previous TYU, produce the section of the statement of cash flows for cash generated from operations using the direct method for the year ended 31 December 20X1 in compliance with IAS 7 Statement of Cash Flows.

5 Other cash flows from operating activities

Cash outflows may include:

- interest paid and
- income tax paid.

The cash flow should be calculated using the following proforma:

Interest/Tax payable

Bank (ß)	X	Bal b/d (SOFP)	X
Bal c/d (SOFP)	X	Profit or loss	X
	X		X
		Bal b/d	X

Test your understanding 3 – Operating activities

Using the information in TYU 1 calculate the interest and tax paid by Yog.

6 Investing activities

Cash inflows may include:

- interest received
- dividends received and
- proceeds from the sale of non-current assets.

Cash outflows may include:

- purchase of non-current assets.

The cash flow for interest and dividends received should be calculated using the following proforma:

Interest/Dividends receivable

Bal b/d (SOFP)	X	Bank (ß)	X
Profit or loss	X	Bal c/d (SOFP)	X
	X		X
Bal b/d	X		

The cash flow for non-current assets should be calculated using the following proforma:

Non-current assets – Carrying amount

Bal b/d (SOFP)	X	Disposal (Carrying amount)	X
Additions (cash)	X	Depreciation for the year	X
Revaluation gain for the year	X	Bal c/d (SOFP)	X
	X		X
Bal b/d	X		

You may have to calculate the proceeds by working backwards from the profit or loss on disposal as follows:

Non-current assets – Disposal account

Cost	X	Accumulated depreciation	X
Profit on disposal (SPL)	X	Loss on disposal (SPL)	X
Bank (ß)	X		
	X		X

Further detail on the disposal of non-current assets can be found in Chapter 13.

Test your understanding 4 – Investing activities

Using the information in TYU 1 prepare the investing activities section of the statement of cash flow.

7 Financing activities

Cash inflows may include:

- proceeds from the issue of shares and
- proceeds from the issue of loans/debentures.

Cash outflows may include:

- repayments of loans/debentures and
- dividends paid.

The proceeds from share issues will be calculated by looking at the movement on the share capital and share premium accounts in the SOFP.

The proceeds/repayment of loans/debentures will be calculated by looking at the movement on the loan/debenture accounts in the SOFP.

The dividend payment can either be found in the SOCIE or by looking at the movement on the retained earnings account as follows:

Retained earnings

Dividend paid (ß)	X	Bal b/d (SOFP)	X
Bal c/d (SOFP)	X	Profit or loss for the year	X
	X		X
		Bal b/d	X

Test your understanding 5 – Financing activities

Using the information in TYU 1 produce the financing activities section of the statement of cash flows.

Test your understanding 6 – Statement of cash flows

Using all of you answers from TYU 1 – 4 produce the final statement of cash flows for Yog.

Illustration 3 – Statement of cash flows

Below are extracts from the financial statements of an entity Pincer:

Statement of profit or loss and other comprehensive income for the year ended 31 March 20X1

	$m
Sales revenue	1,162
Cost of sales	(866)
Gross profit	296
Distribution costs	(47)
Administrative expenses	(110)
Profit from operations	139
Interest receivable	79
Finance costs	(55)
Profit before tax	163
Income tax expense	(24)
Profit for the year	139
Other comprehensive income	
Gain on revaluation	251
Total comprehensive income for the year	390

Statements of financial position:

	31 March 20X1		31 March 20X0	
	$m	$m	$m	$m
Assets				
Non-current assets				
Property, plant and equipment	1,023		600	
Intangible assets	277		234	
Investments	69		68	
		1,369		902
Current assets				
Inventories	246		128	
Trade and other receivables	460		373	
Cash and cash equivalents	250		124	
		956		625
Total Assets		2,325		1,527
Equity and liabilities				
Capital and reserves				
Share capital	29		24	
Share premium	447		377	
Revaluation reserve	251		–	
Retained profit	116		26	
		843		427
Non-current liabilities				
Loan	755		555	
		755		555
Current liabilities				
Trade and other payables	244		311	
Overdrafts	437		207	
Taxation	46		27	
		727		545
Total equity and liabilities		2,325		1,527

Additional information:

- Profit from operations is after charging depreciation on the property, plant and equipment of $22 million and amortisation on the intangible assets of $7 million. The revaluation reserve relates wholly to property, plant and equipment.
- During the year ended 31 March 20X1, plant and machinery costing $1,464 million, which had a carrying amount of $424 million, was sold for $250 million.
- During the year ended 31 March 20X1 25 million 20c shares were issued at a premium of $2.80.
- Dividends paid during the year were $49 million.

Required:

Produce a statement of cash flows for Pincer for the year ended 31 March 20X1 in compliance with IAS 7 Statement of Cash Flows using the indirect method.

Solution

Pincer Statement of cash flows for the year ended 31 March 20X1

	$m	$m
Cash flows from operating activities		
Profit before tax	163	
Depreciation	22	
Amortisation	7	
Loss on disposal of non-current assets (250 – 424)	174	
Interest receivable	(79)	
Finance costs	55	
Operating profit before working capital changes	342	
Increase in inventories (246 – 128)	(118)	
Increase in trade receivables (460 – 373)	(87)	
Decrease in trade payables (244 – 311)	(67)	
Cash generated from operations	70	
Interest paid	(55)	
Income tax paid (W1)	(5)	
Net cash from operating activities		10

Cash flows from investing activities

Purchases of property, plant and equipment (W3)	(618)	
Purchase of intangibles (W2)	(50)	
Purchase of investments (69 – 68)	(1)	
Proceeds of property, plant and equipment	250	
Interest received	79	
Net cash from investing activities		(340)
Cash flow from financing activities		
Proceeds from issue of shares (W4)	75	
Proceeds from long-term borrowing (755 – 555)	200	
Dividends paid	(49)	
Net cash from financing activities		226
Net increase in cash and cash equivalents		(104)
Cash and cash equivalents at beginning of period (124 – 207)		(83)
Cash and cash equivalents at end of period (250 – 437)		(187)

Workings

(W1)

Tax

Bank (ß)	5	Bal b/d (current)	27
Bal c/d (current)	46	SPL	24
	51		51
		Bal b/d (current)	46

(W2)

Intangible non-current assets

Bal b/d	234	Amortisation	7
Bank (ß)	50	Bal c/d	277
	284		284
Bal b/d	277		

(W3)

Property, plant and equipment

Bal b/d	600	Dep'n	22
Reval'n	251	Disposal	424
Bank (ß)	618	Bal c/d	1,023
	1,469		1,469
Bal b/d	1,023		

(W4) 25 million × ($2.80 + 0.20) = $75 million

Test your understanding 7 – Practice question

Below are extracts from the financial statements of an entity Poochie:

Statement of profit or loss for the year ended 31 March 20X1

	$
Revenue	30,650
Cost of sales	(26,000)
Gross profit	4,650
Distribution costs	(900)
Administrative expenses	(500)
Profit from operations	3,250
Investment income	680
Finance costs	(400)
Profit before tax	3,530
Income tax expense	(300)
Profit for the period	3,230

Statements of financial position:

	31 March 20X1		31 March 20X0	
	$	$	$	$
Assets				
Non-current assets				
Property, plant and equipment	2,280		850	
Investments	2,500		2,500	
		4,780		3,350
Current assets				
Inventories	1,000		1,950	
Trade and other receivables	1,900		1,200	
Cash and cash equivalents	410		160	
		3,310		3,310
Total Assets		8,090		6,660
Equity and liabilities				
Capital and reserves				
Share capital	1,000		900	
Share premium	500		350	
Retained earnings	3,410		1,380	
		4,910		2,630
Non-current liabilities				
Long term borrowings	2,300		1,040	
		2,300		1,040
Current liabilities				
Trade and other payables	250		1,890	
Interest payable	230		100	
Taxation	400		1,000	
		880		2,990
Total equity and liabilities		8,090		6,660

Additional information:

- Profit from operations is after charging depreciation on the property, plant and equipment of $450.
- During the year ended 31 March 20X1, plant and machinery costing $80 and with accumulated depreciation of $60, was sold for $20.
- The receivables at the end of 20X1 includes $100 of interest receivable. There was no balance at the beginning of the year.
- Investment income of $680 is made up of $300 interest receivable and $380 dividends received.
- Dividends paid during the year were $1,200.

Required:

Note: The gap-fill statements have been included to make the question more challenging by requiring you to do things in a specified order as any part of a statement of cash flows could be examined in isolation.

(a) Complete the following gap-fill statements relating to the statement of cash flows of Poochie for the year ended 31 March 20X1 by inserting data as appropriate and by deleting words within brackets as required.

(1) The disposal of plant and machinery resulted in a (gain/loss) on disposal of $__________ that should be adjusted within (operating/investing/financing) activities, along with cash (paid/received) of $__________ to include within (operating/investing/financing) activities.

(2) The proceeds of the share issue were $__________ and this will be classified within (operating/investing/financing) activities.

(3) The movements in working capital within cash flows from operating activities can be summarised as follows:

(a) Inventories represent an (increase/decrease) in cash flows from operating activities of $__________.

(b) Trade receivables represent an (increase/decrease) in cash flows from operating activities of $__________.

(c) Trade payables represent an (increase/decrease) in cash flows from operating activities of $__________.

(4) During the year, there was cash paid of $__________ for the purchase of property, plant and equipment. This is classified as an (operating/investing/financing) activity.

(5) During the year, there was a net (increase/decrease) in cash and equivalents of $__________.

(6) During the year, there was tax paid of $__________ and this should be classified within (operating/investing/financing) activities.

(b) Using the information from part (a) plus any other workings that may be required, produce a statement of cash flows for Poochie for the year ended 31 March 20X1 in compliance with IAS 7 Statement of Cash Flows using the indirect method.

Test your understanding 8 – Practice question

Below are extracts from the financial statements of an entity Yam Yam:

Statement of profit or loss and other comprehensive income for the year ended 30 September 20X1

	$000
Revenue	2,900
Cost of sales	(1,734)
Gross profit	1,166
Distribution costs	(520)
Administrative expenses	(342)
Profit from operations	304
Investment income	5
Finance costs	(19)
Profit before tax	290
Income tax expense	(104)
Profit for the period	186

Other comprehensive income				
Gain on revaluation				50
				———
Total comprehensive income for the year				236

Statements of financial position

	30 September 20X1		30 September 20X0	
	$000	$000	$000	$000
Assets				
Non-current assets				
Property, plant and equipment	634		510	
	———		———	
		634		510
Current assets				
Inventories	420		460	
Trade receivables	390		320	
Interest receivable	4		9	
Investments	50		0	
Cash at bank	75		0	
Cash at hand	7		5	
	———		———	
		946		794
		———		———
Total Assets		1,580		1,304
		———		———
Equity and liabilities				
Capital and reserves				
Share capital $0.50 each	363		300	
Share premium	89		92	
Revaluation reserve	50		0	
Retained earnings	63		(70)	
	———		———	
		565		322
Non-current liabilities				
10% Loan notes	0		40	
5% Loan notes	329		349	
	———		———	
		329		389

Current liabilities				
Trade and other payables	550		400	
Bank overdraft	0		70	
Accruals	36		33	
Taxation	100		90	
		686		593
Total equity and liabilities		1,580		1,304

Additional information:

- On 1 October 20X0, Yam Yam issued 60,000 $0.50 shares at a premium of 100%. The proceeds were used to finance the purchase and cancellation of all of its 10% loan notes and some of its 5% loan notes, both at par. A bonus issue of one for ten shares held was made at 1 November 20X0; all shares in issue qualified for the bonus.
- The current asset investment was a 30 day government bond.
- Certain properties included certain properties that were revalued during the year.
- Plant and equipment disposed of during the year had a carrying amount of $75,000; cash received on disposal was $98,000.
- Depreciation charged for the year was $87,000.
- The accruals balance includes interest payable of $33,000 at 30 September 20X0 and $6,000 at 30 September 20X1.
- Interim dividends paid during the year were $53,000.

Required:

Note: The gap-fill statements have been included to make the question more challenging by requiring you to do things in a specified order as any part of a statement of cash flows could be examined in isolation.

(a) Complete the following gap-fill statements relating to the statement of cash flows of Yam Yam for the year ended 30 September 20X1 by inserting data as appropriate and by deleting words within brackets as required.

(1) The disposal of plant and machinery resulted in a (gain/loss) on disposal of $__________ that should be adjusted within (operating/investing/financing) activities, along with cash (paid/received) of $__________ to include within (operating/investing/financing) activities.

(2) The proceeds of the share issue were $__________ and this will be classified within (operating/investing/financing) activities.

(3) The movements in working capital within cash flows from operating activities can be summarised as follows:

(a) Inventories represent an (increase/decrease) in cash flows from operating activities of $__________.

(b) Trade receivables represent an (increase/decrease) in cash flows from operating activities of $__________.

(c) Trade payables represent an (increase/decrease) in cash flows from operating activities of $__________.

(4) During the year, there was cash paid of $__________ for the purchase of property, plant and equipment. This is classified as an (operating/investing/financing) activity.

(5) During the year, there was a net (increase/decrease) in cash and equivalents of $__________.

(6) During the year, there was tax paid of $__________ and this should be classified within (operating/investing/financing) activities.

(b) Using the information from part (a) plus any other workings that may be required, produce a statement of cash flows for Yam Yam for the year ended 30 September 20X1 in compliance with IAS 7 Statement of Cash Flows using the indirect method.

Test your understanding 9 – Practice questions

(1) Barlow uses the 'indirect method' for the purpose of calculating cash generated from operations in the statement of cash flows.

The following information is provided for the year ended 31 December 20X0:

	$
Profit before tax	5,600
Depreciation	956
Profit on sale of equipment	62
Increase in inventories	268
Increase in receivables	101
Increase in payables	322

What is the cash generated from operations?

A $6,571

B $6,541

C $6,447

D $5,803

(2) Evans had the following balances in its' statement of financial position as at 30 June 20X0 and 20X1:

	20X1	**20X0**
10% Loan	$130,000	$150,000
Share Capital	$120,000	$100,000
Share Premium	$45,000	$35,000

How much will appear in the statement of cash flows for the year ended 30 June 20X1 as the total for 'cash flows from financing activities'?

A $10,000 outflow

B $10,000 inflow

C $50,000 inflow

D $50,000 outflow

(3) At 1 January 20X0 Casey had property, plant and equipment with a carrying value of $250,000. In the year ended 31 December 20X0 the entity disposed of assets with a carrying amount of $45,000 for $50,000. The entity revalued a building from $75,000 to $100,000 and charged depreciation for the year of $20,000. At the end of the year, the carrying amount of property, plant and equipment was $270,000.

How much will be reported in the statement of cash flows for the year ended 31 December 20X0 as the total for 'cash flows from investing activities'?

A $10,000 outflow

B $10,000 inflow

C $35,000 outflow

D $50,000 inflow

The following information relates to Questions 4 and 5:

IAS 7 requires cash flows to be analysed under three headings – cash flows from operating activities, investing activities and financing activities. Several items that may appear in a cash flow statement are listed below:

(i) Cash paid for the purchase of non-current assets

(ii) Dividends received

(iii) Interest paid

(iv) Repayment of borrowings

(v) Tax paid

(4) **Which of the above items would appear under the heading 'cash flows from investing activities'?**

A i only

B i and ii

C i, ii, iii and iv

D ii, iii and iv

(5) **Which of the above items would appear under the heading 'cash flows from operating activities'?**

A i only

B iii and v

C iii, iv and v

D ii, iii and v

(6) **How much interest was paid in the year?**

	$000
Interest accrued b/fwd	600
Interest charged to the statement of profit or loss	700
Interest accrued c/fwd	500

A $600,000

B $700,000

C $800,000

D $1,300,000

(7) At 1 October 20X0, BK had the following balance:

Accrued interest payable $12,000 credit.

During the year ended 30 September 20X1, BK charged interest payable of $41,000 to its statement of profit or loss. The closing balance on accrued interest payable account at 30 September 20X1 was $15,000 credit.

How much interest paid should BK show on its statement of cash flows for the year ended 30 September 20X1?

A $38,000

B $41,000

C $44,000

D $53,000

(8) Accrued income tax payable, balance at 31 March 20X0 $1,120,000.

Accrued income tax payable, balance at 31 March 20X1 $1,140,000.

Taxation charge to the statement of profit or loss for the year to 31 March 20X1 $850,000.

How much should be included in the statement of cash flows for income tax paid in the year?

A $800,000

B $830,000

C $850,000

D $880,000

(9) During the year to 31st July Smartypants made a profit of $37,500 after accounting for depreciation of $2,500.

During the year non-current assets were purchased for $16,000, receivables increased by $2,000, inventories decreased by $3,600 and trade payables increased by $700.

What was the increase in cash and bank balances during the year?

A $21,300

B $21,700

C $24,900

D $26,300

(10) Which of the following lists consists of items that would be added to profit before taxation in the calculation of net cash from operating activities according to IAS 7?

A Decrease in trade receivables, increase in trade payables, profit on sale of non-current assets.

B Loss on sale of non-current assets, depreciation, increase in trade receivables.

C Decrease in inventories, depreciation, profit on sale of non-current assets.

D Decrease in trade receivables, increase in trade payables, loss on sale of non-current assets.

8 Summary diagram

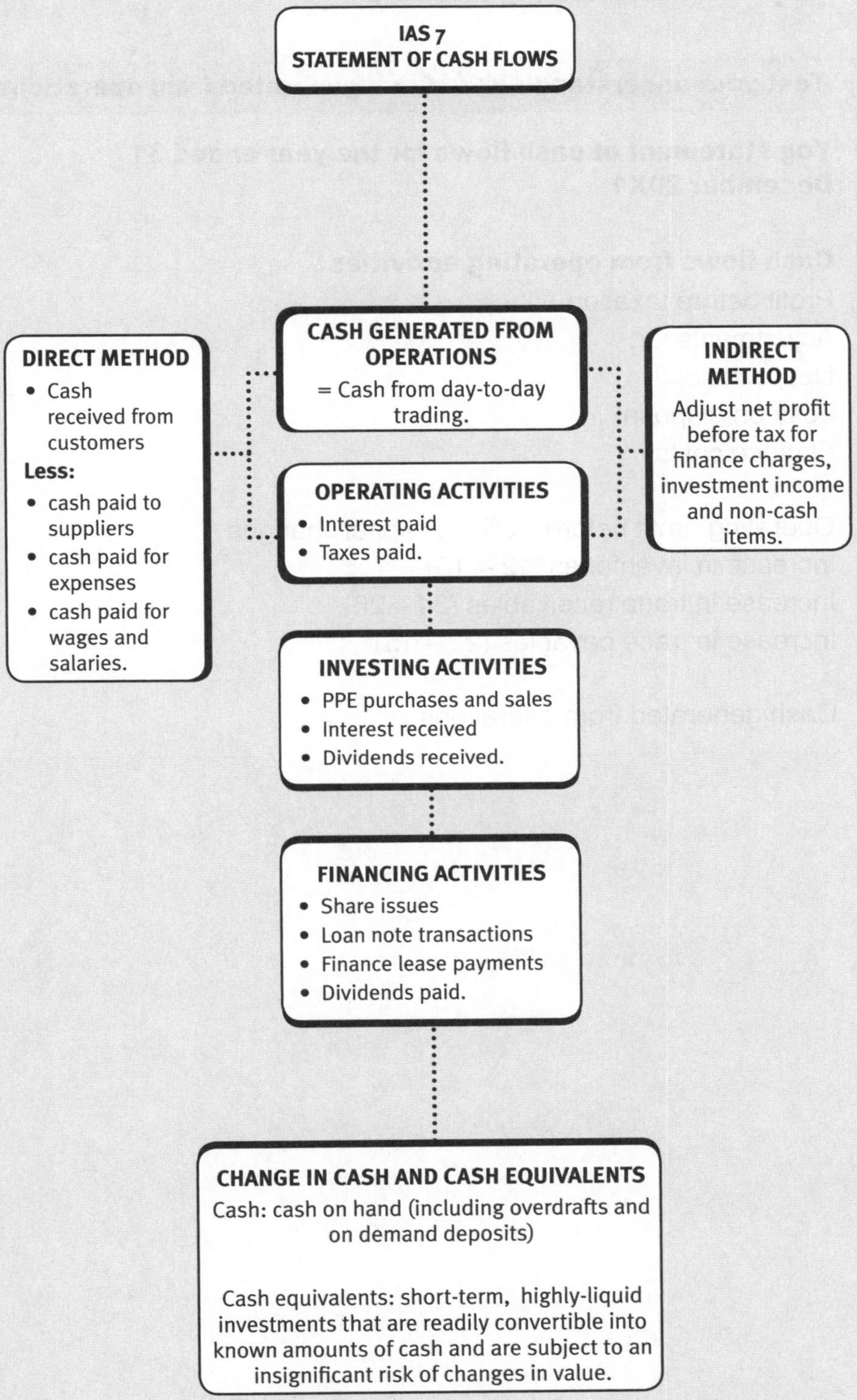

IAS 7
STATEMENT OF CASH FLOWS

DIRECT METHOD

- Cash received from customers

Less:

- cash paid to suppliers
- cash paid for expenses
- cash paid for wages and salaries.

CASH GENERATED FROM OPERATIONS

= Cash from day-to-day trading.

INDIRECT METHOD

Adjust net profit before tax for finance charges, investment income and non-cash items.

OPERATING ACTIVITIES

- Interest paid
- Taxes paid.

INVESTING ACTIVITIES

- PPE purchases and sales
- Interest received
- Dividends received.

FINANCING ACTIVITIES

- Share issues
- Loan note transactions
- Finance lease payments
- Dividends paid.

CHANGE IN CASH AND CASH EQUIVALENTS

Cash: cash on hand (including overdrafts and on demand deposits)

Cash equivalents: short-term, highly-liquid investments that are readily convertible into known amounts of cash and are subject to an insignificant risk of changes in value.

Test your understanding answers

Test your understanding 1 – Cash generated from operations

Yog statement of cash flows for the year ended 31 December 20X1

	$000
Cash flows from operating activities	
Profit before taxation	196
Adjustments for:	
Depreciation	59
Loss on disposal	9
Finance costs	14
	——
Operating profit before working capital changes	278
Increase in inventories (12 – 10)	(2)
Increase in trade receivables (34 – 26)	(8)
Increase in trade payables (21 – 15)	6
	——
Cash generated from operations	274

Test your understanding 2 – Direct method

Yog Statement of cash flows for the year ended 31 December 20X1

	$000
Cash flows from operating activities	
Cash receipts from customers (W1)	352
Cash payments to suppliers (W2)	(31)
Cash payments to employees	(47)
Cash generated from operations	274

(W1)

Cash receipts from customers

	$000
Opening receivables	26
Sales revenue	360
Closing receivables	(34)
Cash received from customers	352

(W2)

Cash payments to suppliers

	$000
Opening inventories	10
Purchases (ß)	37
Closing	(12)
Cost of materials used	35

	$000
Opening payables	15
Purchases (above)	37
Closing payables	(21)
Payments to suppliers	31

Test your understanding 3 – Operating activities

Interest paid (W1)	(12)
Income tax paid (W2)	(57)

Workings

(W1)

Interest payable

Bank (ß)	12	Bal b/d	5
Bal c/d	7	Profit or loss	14
	——		——
	19		19
	——		——
		Bal b/d	7

(W2)

Tax payable

Bank (ß)	57	Bal b/d	35
Bal c/d	40	Profit or loss	62
	——		——
	97		97
	——		——
		Bal b/d	40

Test your understanding 4 – Investing activities

Cash flows from investing activities

Purchase of non-current assets	(45)	
Proceeds from sale of non-current assets ($15 (W1) – loss on sale of $9 = $6)	6	
	——	
Net cash from investing activities		(39)

(W1)

Non-current assets – CV

Bal b/d	668	Disposal (ß)	15
		Depreciation for the year	59
Additions	45	Bal c/d	639
	——		——
	713		713
	——		——
Bal b/d	639		

Test your understanding 5 – Financing activities

Cash flows from financing activities

Proceeds from issues of ordinary shares (W1)	16	
Repayment of loans (100 – 250)	(150)	
Dividends paid	(36)	
	——	
Net cash from financing activities		(170)

(W1)

Share issue = (180 + 18) – (170 + 12) = $16

Test your understanding 6 – Statement of cash flows

Yog statement of cash flows for the year ended 31 December 20X1

	$000	$000
Cash flows from operating activities		
Profit before taxation	196	
Adjustments for:		
Depreciation	59	
Loss on disposal	9	
Finance costs	14	
Operating profit before working capital changes	278	
Increase in inventories (12 – 10)	(2)	
Increase in trade receivables (34 – 26)	(8)	
Increase in trade payables (21 – 15)	6	
Cash generated from operations (TYU 1)	274	
Interest paid (TYU 2)	(12)	
Income tax paid (TYU 2)	(57)	
Net cash from operating activities		205
Cash flows from investing activities		
Purchase of non-current assets	(45)	
Proceeds from sale of non-current assets (TYU 3)	6	
Net cash from investing activities		(39)
Cash flows from financing activities		
Proceeds from issues of ordinary shares (TYU 4)	16	
Repayment of loans (100 – 250)	(150)	
Dividends paid	(36)	
Net cash from financing activities		(170)
Net decrease in cash and cash equivalents		(4)
Cash and cash equivalents at beginning of period		28
Cash and cash equivalents at end of period		24

Test your understanding 7 – Practice question

(a) Gap-fill statements

(1) The disposal of plant and machinery resulted in a **gain** on disposal of $nil (W1) that should be adjusted within **operating** activities, along with cash **received** of $20 to include within **investing** activities.

(2) The proceeds of the share issue were $250 (W2) and this will be classified within **financing** activities.

(3) The movements in working capital within cash flows from operating activities can be summarised as follows:

(a) Inventories represent an **increase** in cash flows from operating activities of $950 (W3)

(b) Trade receivables represent a **decrease** in cash flows from operating activities of $600 (W4).

(c) Trade payables represent an **decrease** in cash flows from operating activities of $1,640 (W5).

(4) During the year, there was cash paid of $1,900 (W6) for the purchase of property, plant and equipment. This is classified as an **investing** activity.

(5) During the year, there was a net **increase** in cash and equivalents of $250 (W7).

(6) During the year, there was tax paid of $900 (W8) and this should be classified within **operating** activities.

(b)

Poochie Statement of cash flows for the year ended 31 March 20X1

	$	$
Cash flows from operating activities		
Profit before tax	3,530	
Depreciation	450	
Investment income	(680)	
Finance costs	400	
Operating profit before working capital changes	3,700	
Decrease in inventories (W3)	950	
Increase in trade receivables (W4)	(600)	
Decrease in trade payables (W5)	(1,640)	
Cash generated from operations	2,410	
Interest paid (W9)	(270)	
Income tax paid (W8)	(900)	
Net cash from operating activities		1,240
Cash flows from investing activities		
Purchase of property, plant and equipment (W6)	(1,900)	
Proceeds from sale of property, plant and equipment	20	
Interest received (W4)	200	
Dividends received	380	
Net cash from investing activities		(1,300)
Cash flow from financing activities		
Proceeds from issue of shares (W2)	250	
Proceeds from long-term borrowing (2,300 – 1,040)	1,260	
Dividends paid	(1,200)	
Net cash from financing activities		310
Net increase in cash and cash equivalents (W7)		250
Cash and cash equivalents at beginning of period		160
Cash and cash equivalents at end of period		410

(W1)

Gain or loss on machinery disposal

Cost	80	Accumulated depreciation	60
		Disposal proceeds	20
	80		80

(W2)

Remember that you need the total proceeds of the share issue - both share capital and share premium as follows:

Share capital increase: = ($1,000 - $900) = 100

Share premium increase: = ($500 - $350) = $150

Total proceeds = $250

(W3)

Decrease in inventory ($1,950 - $1,000) = 950 an increase in cashflows from operating activities

(W4)

Interest receivable

Bal b/d	0	Bank (ß)	200
Profit or loss	300	Bal c/d	100
	300		300
Bal b/d	100		

Receivable B/d = $1,200

Receivables C/d = $1,800 ($1,900 – $100 interest receivable)

Increase in trade receivables = $600 a decrease in cashflows from operating activities.

(W5)

Decrease in trade payables ($1,890 - $250) = $1,640 a decrease in cashflows from operating activities.

(W6)

Property, plant and equipment

Bal b/d	850	Dep'n	450
		Disposal (80 – 60)	20
Bank (ß)	1,900	Bal c/d	2,280
	2,750		2,750
Bal b/d	2,280		

(W7)

Net increase in cash and equivalents ($410 - $160) = $250.

(W8)

Tax

Bank (ß)	900	Bal b/d	1,000
Bal c/d	400	Profit or loss	300
	1,300		1,300
		Bal b/d	400

(W9)

Interest payable

Bank (ß)	270	Bal b/d	100
Bal c/d	230	Profit or loss	400
	500		500
		Bal b/d	230

Test your understanding 8 – Practice question

(a) Gap-fill statements

(1) The disposal of plant and machinery resulted in a **gain** on disposal of $23,000 (W1) that should be adjusted within **operating** activities, along with cash **received** of $98,000 to include within **investing** activities.

(2) The proceeds of the share issue were $60,000 (W2) and this will be classified within **financing** activities.

(3) The movements in working capital within cash flows from operating activities can be summarised as follows:

(a) Inventories represent an **increase** in cash flows from operating activities of $40,000 ($460,000 - $420,000).

(b) Trade receivables represent a **decrease** in cash flows from operating activities of $70,000 ($320,000 - $390,000).

(c) Trade payables represent an **increase** in cash flows from operating activities of $150,000 ($400,000 - $550,000).

(4) During the year, there was cash paid of $236,000 (W3) for the purchase of property, plant and equipment. This is classified as an **investing** activity.

(5) During the year, there was a net **increase** in cash and equivalents of $197,000 (W4).

(6) During the year, there was tax paid of $94,000 (W5) and this should be classified witihin **operating** activities.

(b) **Yam Yam Statement of cash flows for the year ended 30 September 20X1**

	$000	$000
Cash flows from operating activities		
Profit before tax	290	
Depreciation	87	
Profit on disposal of non-current asset (W1)	(23)	
Investment income	(5)	
Finance costs	19	
Operating profit before working capital changes	368	
Decrease in inventories (420 – 460)	40	
Increase in trade receivables (390 – 320)	(70)	
Increase in trade payables (550 – 400)	150	
Increase in sundry accruals (W8)	30	
Cash generated from operations	518	
Interest paid (W6)	(46)	
Income tax paid (W5)	(94)	
Net cash from operating activities		378
Cash flows from investing activities		
Purchase of property, plant and equipment (W3)	(236)	
Proceeds from sale of property, plant and equipment	98	
Interest received (W7)	10	
Net cash from investing activities		(128)
Cash flow from financing activities		
Proceeds from issue of shares (W2)	60	
Redemption of 10% loan notes (0 – 40)	(40)	
Redemption of 5% loan notes (329 – 349)	(20)	
Dividends paid	(53)	
Net cash from financing activities		(53)
Net increase in cash and cash equivalents (W4)		197
Cash and cash equivalents at beginning of period		(65)
Cash and cash equivalents at end of period		132

Workings

(W1)

Disposal of plant and equipment

Carrying amount	75,000	Disposal proceeds	98,000
Gain on disposal	23,000		
	——		——
	98,000		98,000
	——		——

(W2) **Share capital and share premium movements**

Share capital

		Bal b/d	300,000
		Cash proceeds (60,000 × 50c)	30,000
Bal c/d	363,000	Bonus issue	33,000
	——		——
	363,000		363,000
	——		——
		Bal b/d	363,000

Share premium

Bonus issue	33,000	Bal b/d	92,000
Bal c/d	89,000	Cash proceeds (60,000 × 50c)	30,000
	——		——
	122,000		122,000
	——		——
		Bal b/d	89,000

Total cash proceeds of share issue were 60,000 shares × $1 = $60,000 – note that the nominal vaue per share is 50c – therefore, the proceeds should be split between share capital and share premium.

The bonus issue was 1 for 10 – therefore there should be be a 10% increase in issued share capital which would be accounted for by an equivalent decrease in share premium account.

(W3)

Property, plant and equipment

Bal b/d	510,000	Dep'n	87,000
Revaluation	50,000	Disposal	75,000
Bank (ß)	236,000	Bal c/d	634,000
	796,000		796,000
Bal b/d	634,000		

(W4) **Increase in cash and cash equivalents**

	20X1 $000	20X0 $000	Increase $000
Short-term investments	50		
Cash at bank	75		
Cash in hand	7	5	
Overdraft		(70)	
	132	(65)	197

(W5)

Tax

Bank (ß)	94,000	Bal b/d	90,000
Bal c/d	100,000	Profit or loss	104,000
	194,000		194,000
		Bal b/d	100,000

(W6)

Interest payable

Bank (ß)	46,000	Bal b/d	33,000
Bal c/d	6,000	Profit or loss	19,000
	52,000		52,000
		Bal b/d	6,000

(W7)

Interest Receivable

Bal b/d	9,000	Bank (ß)	10,000
Profit or loss	5,000	Bal c/d	4,000
	14,000		14,000
Bal b/d	4,000		

(W8)

Accruals b/d (excluding interest) = $33,000 – $33,000 = 0

Accruals c/d (excluding interest) = $36,000 – $6,000 = $30,000

Increase in accruals = $30,000

Test your understanding 9 – Practice questions

(1) C

	$
Cash flows from operating activities	
Profit before tax	5,600
Adjustments for:	
Depreciation	956
(Profit)/loss on disposal	(62)
(Increase)/decrease in inventories	(268)
(Increase)/decrease in trade and other receivables	(101)
(Decrease)/increase in trade and other payables	322
Cash generated from operations	6,447

(2) B

Repayment of loans (150,000 – 130,000)	(20,000)
Issue of shares ((120,000 – 100,000) + (45,000 – 35,000))	30,000
Net inflow	10,000

(3) A

Property, plant and equipment

	$		$
Bal b/d	250,000	Disposals	45,000
Revaluation	25,000	Depreciation	20,000
Additions (ß)	60,000		
		Bal c/d	270,000
	335,000		335,000
Bal b/d	270,000		

Purchase of property, plant and equipment	(60,000)
Proceeds from sale of property, plant and equipment	50,000
Net outflow	(10,000)

(4) B

(5) B

(6) C

Interest payable

	$000		$000
Bank (ß)	800	Bal b/d (SOFP)	600
Bal c/d (SOFP)	500	Profit or loss	700
	1,300		1,300
		Bal b/d	500

(7) A

Interest payable

	$		$
Bank (ß)	38,000	Bal b/d (SOFP)	12,000
Bal c/d (SOFP)	15,000	Profit or loss	41,000
	53,300		53,000
		Bal b/d	15,000

(8) B

Tax payable

	$000		$000
Bank (ß)	830	Bal b/d (SOFP)	1,120
Bal c/d (SOFP)	1,140	Profit or loss	850
	1,970		1,970
		Bal b/d	1,140

(9) D

$37,500 + $2,500 – $16,000 – $2,000 + $3,600 + $700 = $26,300

(10) D

chapter

13

Non-current Assets

Chapter learning objectives

On completion of their studies students should be able to:

- Explain and apply the accounting rules contained in IASs dealing with:
  - tangible non-current assets
  - research and development expenditure
  - intangible non-current assets (other than goodwill on consolidation)
  - impairment of assets
  - borrowing costs

1 Session content

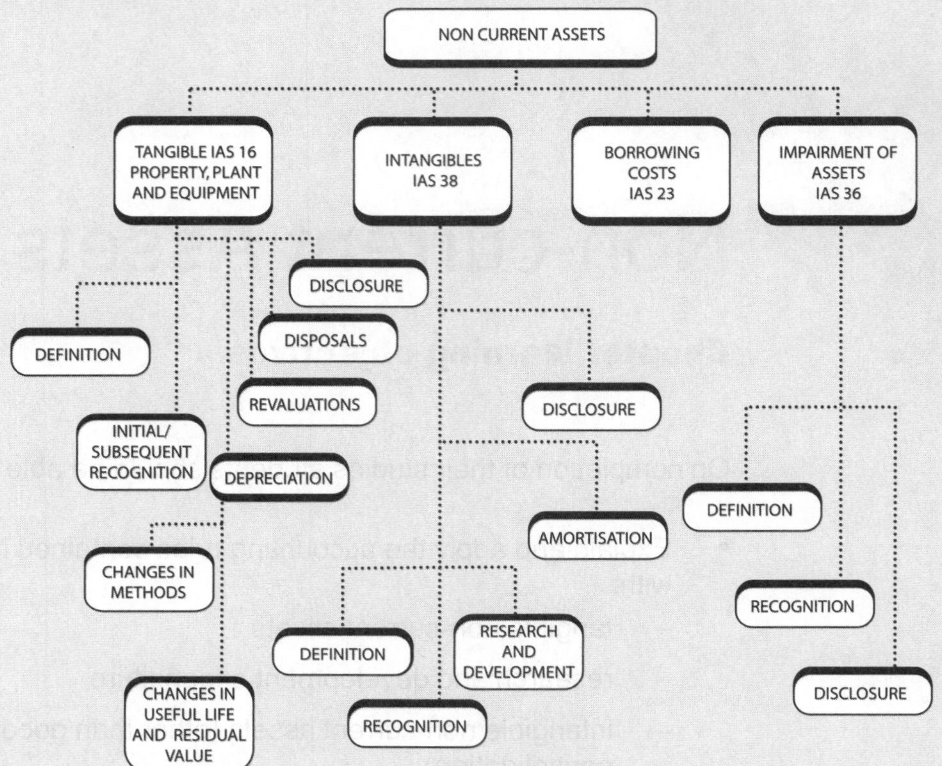

2 IAS 16 Property, Plant And Equipment

Definition

Property, plant and equipment are tangible assets that:

- are held by an entity for use in the production or supply of goods or services, for rental to others, or for administrative purposes and
- are expected to be used during more than one period.

You should know these definitions from your earlier studies. You need to ensure that you know all of the following definitions.

Carrying amount

The amount at which an asset is recognised, after deducting any accumulated depreciation and impairment losses. Also referred to as book value or carrying value.

Cost

The amount paid and the fair value of other consideration given to acquire an asset at the time of its acquisition or construction.

Depreciable amount

The cost or valuation of an asset less its residual value.

Depreciation

The systematic allocation of the depreciable amount of an asset over its useful life.

Fair value

The amount for which an asset can be exchanged between knowledgeable, willing parties in an arm's length transaction.

Impairment loss

The amount by which the carrying amount exceeds its recoverable amount.

Recoverable amount

The higher of an asset's net realisable value and its value in use.

Residual value

The residual value of an asset is the amount that the entity would currently obtain from disposal of the asset, after deducting the estimated costs of disposal, assuming that the asset was already at the point where it would be disposed of (using the age and condition that would be assumed to apply at the time of disposal).

Useful life

IAS 16 defines useful life as the period over which the asset is expected to be available for use by the entity or the volume of output expected from the asset.

Initial recognition

Property, plant and equipment should be recognised as an asset when:

- it is probable that future economic benefits will flow to the entity and
- the cost of the asset can be measured reliably.

The asset should initially be measured at its cost. This should include:

- its purchase price
- directly attributable costs to bring the asset to the location and condition necessary for it to be capable of operating for its intended use, i.e. site preparation, initial delivery costs, installation costs, testing costs, professional fees
- the initial estimate of the cost of dismantling and removing the item and restoring the site, where there is an obligation to incur such costs

The cost of a self-constructed asset is determined using the same principles.

Subsequent expenditure

Subsequent expenditure should be capitalised when:

- the expenditure improves the future economic benefits that the asset will generate
- it replaces a component of an asset and the carrying amount of the component replaced is derecognised, e.g. overhaul of a furnace or a roof (where both are separately identified as assets)
- it is the cost of a major inspection for faults and the carrying amount of the previous inspection is derecognised

The costs of day-to-day servicing should be recognised in the statement of profit or loss as incurred.

Illustration 1 – Initial measurement

Which one of the following should be accounted for as capital expenditure?

A The cost of painting a building

B Maintenance of a machine which keeps production at the same level

C The purchase of a car by a garage for resale

D Legal fees incurred on the purchase of a building

Solution

The answer is D because the legal fees are part of the initial cost of the asset, i.e. directly attributable costs to bring the asset to the location and condition necessary for it to be capable of operating for its intended use.

A and B are examples of revenue expenses, i.e. running costs and must be charged to the statement of profit or loss as an expense.

C would normally be an example of an asset to capitalise, however, as the business is a garage and the car is being bought for resale, it must be treated as a purchase expense (inventory) and not a non-current asset. The car is not a resource for running the business but an item purchased with the intention to sell.

Illustration 2 – Subsequent measurement

Which ONE of the following items would we recognise as subsequent expenditure on a non-current asset and capitalise as required by IAS 16 Property, Plant and Equipment?

A A furnace was purchased five years ago, when the furnace lining was separately identified in the accounting records. The furnace now requires re-lining at a cost of $200,000. When the furnace is re-lined it will enable the business to use the furnace for a further five years.

B An office building was badly damaged in a fire. The cost to restore the building to its original condition will be $250,000.

C A delivery vehicle has broken down and when inspected it was discovered a new engine would be required estimated at $5,000.

D A factory is closed for two weeks each year to enable the entity to undertake routine maintenance and repairs costing $75,000.

Solution

The answer is A because by re-lining the furnace we are adding something to the original asset by extending its useful life.

All other options are revenue expenses to be charged to the statement of profit or loss because they are simply repairs to the original asset.

Measurement after initial recognition

IAS 16 requires that entities either apply to cost model or the revaluation model

Cost Model	**Revaluation Model**
Carrying value = Cost	Carrying value = Fair Value
Less: Accumulated depreciation	Less: Accumulated depreciation
Less: Accumulated impairment losses	Less: Accumulated impairment losses

An entity may decide to use a combination of these two models for measuring assets but make sure each class of assets uses the same model, i.e. use the cost model for plant and machinery and the revaluation model for land and buildings.

Depreciation

Depreciation is the systematic allocation of the depreciable amount of an asset over its useful life.

Depreciable amount is the cost/valuation less residual value.

The depreciation charge should be recognised in the statement of profit or loss unless it is included in the carrying amount of an asset, e.g. depreciation on equipment used for development activities.

Land will not be depreciated since it has an unlimited life. Buildings, however, do have a limited life and so should be depreciated. Therefore, if we are given a total for land and buildings we must remember to remove the land element from the total **before** we calculate the depreciation on the building.

For example, total for land and buildings amounts to $100,000. This includes land at cost of $20,000. Buildings should be depreciated at 10% on a straight line basis. The depreciation would be calculated as ($100,000 – $20,000) × 10% = $8,000 a year.

Repair and maintenance does not negate the need to depreciate the asset.

If the residual value is greater than the carrying amount, the depreciation charge is zero.

How do we calculate depreciation?

Depreciation can be calculated using the straight line or the reducing balance method.

The straight line method is based on cost and will be calculated as a % of cost. Each year the depreciation charge will be the same. However, if the % is not given it can be calculated as:

$$\frac{\text{Cost – residual value}}{\text{useful economic life}}$$

Residual value is the amount the entity would expect to receive from disposal of the asset.

The reducing balance method is based on the carrying amount of the asset (CA). This is usually expressed as a %.

Once the depreciation is calculated the double entry will be:

Dr Depreciation expense (SPL)
Cr Accumulated depreciation (SOFP)

Changes in depreciation method

Depreciation methods should be reviewed periodically. If it is decided that there has been a change in the pattern of consumption of benefits, the depreciation method should be changed to reflect this, e.g. a change from the straight line method to the reducing balance method.

Any change in the depreciation method should be treated as a change in accounting estimate and so the new method should be applied in the current and future accounting periods (see IAS 8 later). Changes in depreciation methods do not represent a change in accounting policy and so depreciation charges of earlier periods should not be altered.

Illustration 3 – Changes in depreciation method

An asset was purchased two years ago for $100,000.

The directors chose to depreciate the asset using the reducing balance method and so used a rate of 20% per annum.

The directors have decided that a fairer presentation would be given if the depreciation method was changed to the straight line basis and will implement the new depreciation method in the year ended 30 June 20X1.

At this time the directors estimated that the useful life was eight years and that the residual value was $10,700.

Calculate the depreciation charge for the year ended 30 June 20X1 in respect of this asset.

Solution

The original depreciation was:

Year 1 = Cost $100,000 × 20% = $20,000

Year 2 = CA $80,000($100,000 – $20,000) × 20% = $16,000

The asset has been depreciated for 2 years when the change of depreciation method occurs and therefore CA would be:

Cost $100,000 – ($20,000 + $16,000) = $64,000

The CA at the date of the change is the carrying amount on the statement of financial position for the asset and must therefore be used to recalculate the new depreciation charge.

$$\frac{\text{CA – residual value}}{\text{Remaining useful economic life}} = \frac{\$64{,}000 - \$10{,}700}{8} = \$6{,}663 \text{ pa}$$

Test your understanding 1 – Methods

An asset was purchased two years ago for $150,000. The directors chose to depreciate the asset using the reducing balance method and so used a rate of 25% per annum. The directors have decided that a fairer presentation would be given if the depreciation method was changed to the straight line basis and will implement the new depreciation method in the year ended 30 June 20X1.At this time the directors estimated that the remaining useful life was eight years and that the residual value was $8,500.

Calculate the depreciation charge for the year ended 30 June 20X1 in respect of this asset.

Changes in useful life and residual value

On acquiring an asset, its useful life and residual value will be estimated. Subsequently, it may be appropriate to revise these estimates.

Again, any change in the useful life or residual value will result in adjustments to the depreciation charge for current and future periods but no changes should be made to past accounting periods, i.e. it is a change in accounting estimate, see IAS 8 later.

Illustration 4 – Changes in useful life

An asset was purchased three years ago for $50,000 at which time it was thought that the asset had a residual value of $5,000 and a useful economic life of ten years. The directors have decided that as a result of using the asset more than was originally planned the remaining useful economic life is only five years as at 1 July 20X0. Their estimate of residual value has remained unchanged. The asset is depreciated on the straight line basis.

Calculate the depreciation charge for the year ended 30 June 20X1 in respect of this asset.

Solution

The original depreciation was:

$$\frac{\text{Cost – residual value}}{\text{Useful economic life}} = \frac{\$50,000 - \$5,000}{10} = \$4,500 \text{ pa}$$

The asset has been depreciated for 3 years when the change of UEL life occurs and therefore CV would be:

Cost $50,000 – (3 × $4,500) = $36,500

The CV at the date of the change is the carrying value on the statement of financial position for the asset and must therefore be used to recalculate the new depreciation charge.

$$\frac{\text{CV – residual value}}{\text{Useful economic life}} = \frac{\$36,500 - \$5,000}{5} = \$6,300 \text{ pa}$$

Test your understanding 2 – Changes in useful life of an asset

An asset was purchased on 1 July 20X1 for $75,000 at which time it was thought that the asset had a residual value of $5,000 and a useful economic life of seven years. The directors have decided that as a result of not using the asset as much as was originally planned the remaining useful economic life is ten years as at 1 July 20X5. Their estimate of residual value has remained unchanged. The asset is depreciated on the straight line basis.

Calculate the depreciation charge for the year ended 30 June 20X6 in respect of this asset.

3 Revaluations

As discussed previously in the chapter, IAS 16 allows the treatment of assets to be shown at their revalued amount less accumulated depreciation and accumulated impairment losses.

The revalued amount of an asset is the asset's fair value at the date of revaluation.

IFRS 13 Fair value measurement, published in May 2011 and applicable for accounting periods commencing from 1 January 2013, sets out a single framework for measuring fair value.

IFRS 13 defines fair value as the price that would be received to sell an asset or transfer a liability in an orderly transaction between market participants at the measurement date.

Further detail on IFRS 13

IFRS 13 defines fair value as the price that would be received to sell an asset or paid to transfer a liability in an orderly transaction between market participants at the measurement date.

It requires an entity to determine the following when establishing fair values:

- the particular asset or liability that is subject to the measurement
- the principal (or most advantageous) market for the asset or liability
- the valuation technique(s) appropriate for the measurement

An entity is required to use a valuation technique appropriate in the circumstances and for which sufficient data is available to measure fair value, maximising the use of relevant observable inputs and minimising the use of unobservable inputs.

The three widely used valuation techniques specifically mentioned in IFRS 13 are:

- market approach – this approach uses prices and other relevant information generated by market transactions involving identical or comparable assets or liabilities.
- cost approach – this approach reflects the amounts that would be required currently to replace the service capacity of an asset.
- income approach – this approach converts future amounts (cash flows or income and expenses) to a single (discounted) amount, reflecting current market expectations about those future amounts.

The market approach would be considered the most appropriate approach for the majority of financial instruments.

If an asset is revalued, any accumulated depreciation at the date of the revaluation should be written off to the revaluation reserve.

Depreciation will then be calculated based on the revalued amount.

Revaluations must be made for the whole of the class of assets, i.e. if we revalue one building we must revalue the whole of the class of buildings at the same time.

The frequency of revaluations will depend upon the volatility of the fair values; the more volatile, the more frequent the revaluation.

Revaluations must be carried out by a professionally qualified valuer.

Steps to account for a revaluation:

(1) Restate asset cost to the revalued amount.

(2) Remove any existing accumulated depreciation.

(3) Transfer the increase in the cost account and the existing accumulated depreciation to the revaluation reserve.

(4) Recalculate current year's depreciation on the revalued amount if applicable.

Accounting entries:

Dr Asset Cost (revalued amount – original cost)

Dr Accumulated depreciation (depreciation up to the revaluation date) - at this point the balance of this account will be nil

Cr Revaluation Reserve (revalued amount – previous CV)

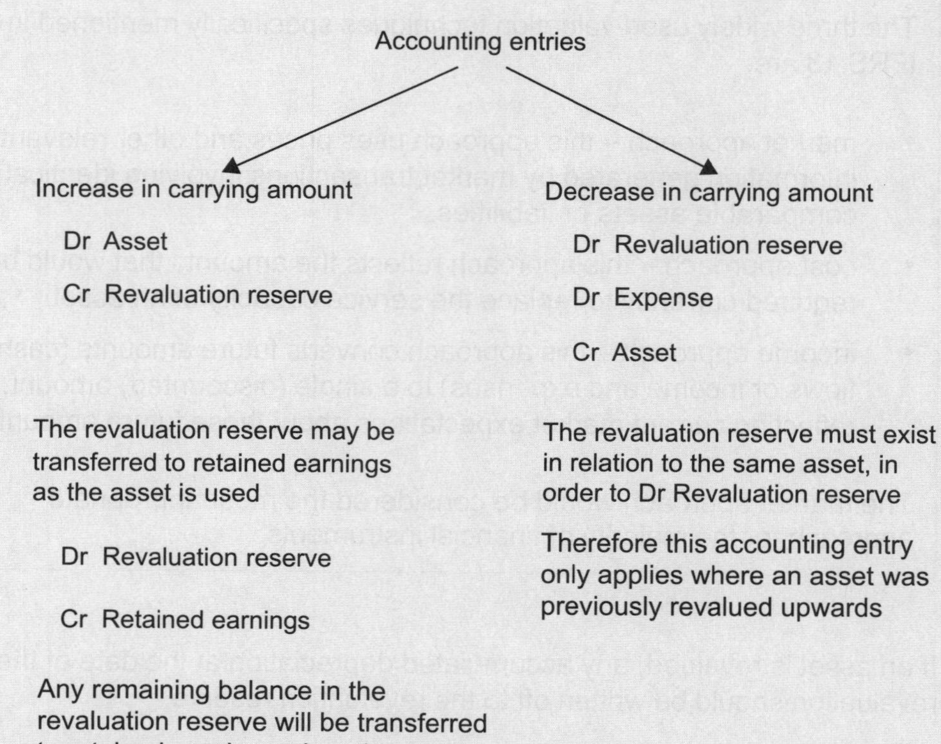
Accounting entries
Increase in carrying amount
Dr Asset
Cr Revaluation reserve
The revaluation reserve may be transferred to retained earnings as the asset is used
Dr Revaluation reserve
Cr Retained earnings
Any remaining balance in the revaluation reserve will be transferred to retained earnings when the asset is disposed
Decrease in carrying amount
Dr Revaluation reserve
Dr Expense
Cr Asset
The revaluation reserve must exist in relation to the same asset, in order to Dr Revaluation reserve
Therefore this accounting entry only applies where an asset was previously revalued upwards

Therefore, to conclude, if an asset increases in value we will increase the asset cost account (Dr) to the revalued amount and increase the revaluation reserve (Cr). This revaluation reserve will appear in the equity section of the statement of financial position.

An entity is allowed to gradually release this reserve into retained earnings over the life of the asset by reducing the revaluation reserve (Dr) and increasing the retained earnings (Cr): see expandable text below for more detail. This movement would be seen in the statement of changes in equity. However, from an assessment point of view you should not show this release of the reserve unless instructed to do so.

If an asset subsequently decreases in value we will reduce the cost account (Cr) to the revalued amount and decrease the revaluation reserve (Dr) **up to the maximum we have previously revalued for that particular asset**. Any excess amount must be charged to the statement of profit or loss as an expense for the year, i.e. an asset previously revalued upwards in year one by $10,000 has a decrease in revaluation in year two amounting to $15,000. We would reduce the cost by $15,000 (Cr), reduce the revaluation reserve by $10,000 (Dr) which is the maximum we have credited to that reserve in previous revaluations and the difference of $5,000 will be charged to the statement of profit or loss in an appropriate expense category.

Any revaluations we make during the year, upwards or downwards, must be shown on the face of the statement of profit or loss and other comprehensive income under the heading “other comprehensive income”.

The amount should reflect the movement made in the revaluation reserve during the year, i.e. the amount we have debited or credited to the reserve.

Therefore, using the above example we would show the $10,000 increase in year one in other comprehensive income, as a gain on revaluation, i.e. a positive figure.

In year two we would show the $10,000 decrease in other comprehensive income, as a loss on revaluation, i.e. a negative figure. Notice we **do not** show the $15,000 as a loss as we are only reflecting the movement that has taken place in the revaluation reserve.

Release of the revaluation reserve

In the text above we have seen how revaluation reserves are created when an asset is revalued upwards.

We can either create a revaluation reserve and leave it there until the revalued asset is sold or we are allowed to release the reserve into retained earnings gradually over the life of the asset if it is a depreciating asset.

This would be done by comparing the difference in the depreciation charge on the basis of the original asset value and on the basis of the revalued amount.

For example, an entity acquired an asset costing $100,000 on 1 January 20X5 with a useful life of ten years. The asset was revalued to $150,000 on 31 December 20X9. The useful life is unchanged.

At the revaluation date we must increase the asset value to $150,000 and remove any accumulated depreciation, i.e. $100,000/10 = $10,000 depreciation per year multiplied by 5 years, (remember we always depreciate as normal up to the revaluation date).

Debit	Accumulated depreciation ($10,000 × 5 years)	$50,000
Debit	Asset cost ($150,000 – $100,000)	$50,000
Credit	Revaluation reserve	$100,000

The revaluation reserve reflects the increase in the carrying amount of the asset, i.e. $100,000 – $50,000 = $50,000 increasing to $150,000.

The new depreciation charge will be based on the revalued amount of $150,000 over the remaining life of the asset of 5 years, i.e. $30,000 p.a. This is an increase in depreciation of $20,000, compared with the original depreciation amount of $10,000 p.a. This means each year we could release $20,000 from the revaluation reserve to retained earnings as follows:

Debit	Revaluation reserve	$20,000
Credit	Retained earnings	$20,000

By doing this we are recognising the revaluation reserve over the remaining life of the asset, i.e. $100,000/5 years = $20,000 p.a.

This would be shown as a movement in the SOCIE.

We should only do this in a question if we are instructed to do so.

Illustration 5 – Revaluations

Land was purchased at a cost of $30,000. It was subsequently revalued to:

Year 1	$40,000
Year 2	$33,000
Year 3	$24,000

Show how each of the gains or losses will be recorded within the revaluation reserve or the statement of profit or loss .

Solution

Year 1

The asset has increased in value from $30,000 to $40,000.

Dr Asset	$10,000
Cr Revaluation Reserve	$10,000

Year 2

The asset has decreased in value from $40,000 to $33,000. This decrease can be charged against the revaluation reserve because the reserve already has $10,000 in it from year 1 for that particular asset.

Dr Revaluation Reserve	$7,000
Cr Asset	$7,000

Year 3

The asset has decreased in value from $33,000 to $24,000. The decrease cannot all be charged against the revaluation reserve because there is only $3,000 left after year 2 for that particular asset. The reserve is reduced to nil and then the balance of the decrease is charged against profits in the statement of profit or loss.

Dr Revaluation Reserve	$3,000
Dr Statement of profit or loss	$6,000
Cr Asset	$9,000

e.g

Illustration 6 – Revaluations

Asset A cost $50,000 on 1 January 20X4. This asset has a useful life of 10 years and is revalued to $25,000 on 31 December 20X9.

Asset B cost $50,000 on 1 January 20X7. This asset has a useful life of 5 years and is revalued to $17,000 on 31 December 20X9.

Show how each of the gains or losses will be recorded within the revaluation reserve or the statement of profit or loss.

Solution

Asset A

On 31 December 20X9 Asset A has a carrying amount of $20,000 (cost $50,000 – depreciation $30,000 ($50,000/10 = $5,000 p.a. multiplied by 6 years).

The cost account will reduce from $50,000 to £25,000.

The accumulated depreciation of $30,000 will be removed from the books.

Overall the carrying amount of the asset has increased from $20,000 to $25,000. This increase of $5,000 will be credited to the revaluation reserve.

We must remember next year's depreciation will be based on the revalued amount of £25,000 over the remaining life of 4 years.

Cr Asset cost	$25,000
Dr Accumulated depreciation	$30,000
Cr Revaluation reserve	$5,000

Asset B

On 31 December 20X9 Asset B has a carrying amount of $20,000 (cost $50,000 – depreciation $30,000 ($50,000/5 = $10,000 p.a. multiplied by 3 years).

The cost account will reduce from $50,000 to £17,000.

The accumulated depreciation will be removed from the books, i.e. = $30,000.

Overall the carrying amount of the asset decreased in value from $20,000 to $17,000. The decrease of $3,000 is charged against profits in the SPL. This asset has not been revalued in the past and therefore does not have a revaluation reserve you can use. You cannot use the reserve from Asset A.

We must remember next year's depreciation will be based on the revalued amount of £17,000 over the remaining life of 2 years.

Dr Statement of profit or loss expense	$3,000
Dr Accumulated depreciation	$30,000
Cr Asset cost	$33,000

Note: The revaluation reserve relates to asset A. Therefore, only future downward valuations of asset A can be set against the revaluation reserve.

Test your understanding 3 – Revaluations

Building A was purchased on 01/01/X3 costing $50,000. It has a useful economic life of 50 years and no residual value.

Building B was purchased on 01/01/X3 costing $100,000. It has a useful economic life of 40 years and no residual value.

The entity has a policy to revalue its assets every four years and has done so as follows:

Building A

Valuation at 31/12/X6 $69,000

Valuation at 31/12/Y0 $84,000

Building B

Valuation at 31/12/X6 $108,000

Valuation at 31/12/Y0 $64,000

Show how the revaluations will be recorded, clearly showing the carrying amount of the assets at 31/12/Y1.

Further detail on revaluation decreases

We have already discussed revaluation decreases in the context that we can only reduce a revaluation reserve for any amounts we have previously revalued upwards on that particular asset.

For example, if an asset decreases in value we will reduce the cost account (Cr) to the revalued amount and decrease the revaluation reserve (Dr) up to the maximum we have previously revalued for that particular asset. Any excess amount must be charged to the statement of profit or loss as an expense for the year, i.e. an asset previously revalued upwards in year one by $10,000 has a decrease in revaluation in year two amounting to $15,000. We would reduce the cost by $15,000 (Cr), reduce the revaluation reserve by $10,000 (Dr) which is the maximum we have credited to that reserve in previous revaluations and the difference of $5,000 will be charged to the statement of profit or loss in an appropriate expense category.

However, let us consider what happens when the decrease in value occurs first, followed by a subsequent increase in value for the asset.

For example, If an asset decreases in value in year one by $10,000 we will reduce the cost account (Cr) to the revalued amount and charge the decrease immediately to the statement of profit or loss as an expense for the year, i.e. we would reduce the cost by $10,000 (Cr) and $10,000 will be charged to the statement of profit or loss in an appropriate expense category.

If the same asset was revalued upwards by $15,000 the following year we can reverse our previous entry to the statement of profit or loss and then show the excess from the revaluation in the revaluation reserve, i.e. increase the asset cost account (Dr) by $15,000, reverse the previous charge to the statement of profit or loss expense of $10,000 (Cr) and then show the difference of $5,000 in the revaluation reserve (Cr).

Retirement and disposals

An item of property, plant and equipment should be eliminated from the statement of financial position on disposal or when the asset is permanently withdrawn from use.

Gain/(loss) on disposal = Net disposal proceeds – Carrying amount

Gains or losses on disposal should be recorded in the statement of profit or loss in an appropriate expense category. If we have a loss on disposal this will increase the expense and a profit will reduce the expense.

We will look at retired assets in more detail in chapter 14 when we look at IFRS 5, specifically assets held for sale.

Disposals of revalued assets

When a previously revalued asset is disposed of the gain on disposal is measured as the difference between the carrying amount on the SOFP and the proceeds received.

However, if the asset has been revalued in the past, it will have an unrealised gain in the revaluation reserve that must now be removed.

The amount should be transferred from the revaluation reserve to retained earnings. This movement will be seen in the SOCIE and will not effect this year's profit.

Release of the revaluation reserve

When an asset is revalued the amount will be credited to the revaluation reserve.

An annual release of the reserve may be made (revaluation reserve to retained earnings) which represents the extra depreciation on the revalued amount compared to cost. A numerical example can be seen in earlier expandable text in this chapter.

Accounting entries:

Dr Revaluation reserve (depreciation on revaluation - depreciation on original cost)

Cr Retained earnings

This would mean the **unrealised gain** on revaluation would gradually be released into profits over the asset's life.

You would **not** be required to do this in this examination unless the examiner specifies.

Illustration 7 – Disposal of a revalued asset

An entity originally purchased a piece of land on 01/01/X7 for $100,000. On the 31/12/X8 the land was revalued to $150,000.

The land was sold for $180,000 on 31/12/Y1.

Calculate the profit or loss on disposal to be shown in the statement of profit or loss and any revaluation adjustments that need to be made.

Solution

When the land was revalued the entries would be made as follows:

This asset increases in value from $100,000 to $150,000. The increase is credited to the revaluation reserve.

Dr Asset	$50,000
Cr Revaluation reserve	$50,000

When the asset was sold the carrying amount was $150,000.

The gain on disposal to the statement of profit or loss would be $30,000 ($180,000 – $150,000)

This would be accounted for by:

Dr Bank	$180,000
Cr Land	$150,000
Cr Profit or loss	$30,000

The revaluation reserve for the land would now be released into profits as the gain is now realised.

Dr Revaluation reserve	$50,000
Cr Retained earnings	$50,000

This would be shown on the SOCIE.

Disclosure

IAS 16 requires the following disclosure requirements:

For each class of property, plant and equipment

- measurement bases, i.e. cost or valuation
- depreciation methods with useful life or depreciation rate
- gross carrying amount and accumulated depreciation at the beginning and end of the period
- reconciliation of additions, disposals, revaluations, impairments and depreciation
- when assets have been revalued:
  - basis of valuation
  - date of valuation
  - whether an independent valuer was used
  - carrying amount if no revaluation had taken place
  - revaluation surplus

Property, plant and equipment (PPE)

The property, plant and equipment note (IAS 16) shows the movements in the year for each category of asset.

	Land and buildings	Plant and equipment	Vehicles	Total
	$000	$000	$000	$000
Cost/Valuation				
At 1 January 20X0	X	X	X	X
Additions	X	X	X	X
Surplus/(deficit) on revaluations	X/(X)	–	–	–
Disposals	(X)	(X)	(X)	(X)
At 31 December 20X0	X	X	X	X
Accumulated Depreciation:				
At 1 January 20X0	X	X	X	X
Charged during the year	X	X	X	X
Revaluations	(X)	–	–	(X)
Disposals	(X)	(X)	(X)	(X)
At 31 December 20X0	X	X	X	X
Carrying amount				
At 1 January 20X0	X	X	X	X
At 31 December 20X0	X	X	X	X

Test your understanding 4 – PPE note

A building was purchased many years ago for $200,000. It has been depreciated at 2% per annum (50 year life)on the straight line basis and the carrying amount of the asset at 1 July 20X0 is $132,000. The directors have had the asset valued at $750,000 and would like to incorporate this valuation into the financial statements for the year ended 30 June 20X1.

Prepare a non-current asset note for the year ended 30 June 20X1 and calculate the revaluation surplus assuming that:

(a) **the valuation is as at 1 July 20X0;**

(b) **the valuation is as at 30 June 20X1.**

4 IAS 23 Borrowing Costs

Definition

Borrowing costs are interest and other costs incurred by an enterprise in connection with the borrowing of funds.

Treatment

Borrowing costs that are directly attributable to the acquisition or construction of a qualifying asset should be capitalised as part of the cost of that asset. All other borrowing costs should be recognised as an expense in the period in which they are incurred, i.e. finance cost.

Dr Asset (SOFP)

Cr Bank (SOFP)

A qualifying asset is defined as being an asset that necessarily takes a substantial period of time to get ready for its intended use.

Under this treatment, capitalisation of the borrowing costs will commence when expenditure on the asset and the borrowing costs are being incurred. Capitalisation must cease when substantially all the activities necessary to prepare the asset for use are complete.

Disclosure

IAS 23 requires the following disclosure requirements:

- The borrowing costs capitalised in the period.
- The capitalisation rate used.

IAS 23 states borrowing costs must be **capitalised** as part of the cost of the asset, provided the asset is a qualifying asset.

Illustration 8 – Borrowing costs

On 01/01/X0 Aseco began to construct a supermarket which has an estimated useful life of 40 years. They constructed a building at a cost of $25 million and fixtures and fittings at a cost of $9 million. In addition they had to pay legal costs amounting to $1 million. The construction of the supermarket was completed on 30/09/X0 and brought into use on 01/01/X1.

In order to complete this project Aseco had to borrow $20 million on 01/01/X0. The loan carried interest at 10%. It was repaid on 30/06/X1 after a successful six months of operation.

Calculate the total amount that can be capitalised as cost for property, plant and equipment in respect of this development for the year ending 31/12/X0.

Solution

The total amount that can be capitalised in property, plant and equipment at 31/12/X0 is:

	$
Building and lease	25,000,000
Fixtures and fittings	9,000,000
Legal costs	1,000,000
Interest capitalised ($20,000,000 × 10% × 9/12)	1,500,000
	36,500,000

Note: the interest can only be capitalised for 9 months from January to September when the asset is completed.

5 IAS 38 Intangible Assets

Definition

An intangible asset is an identifiable non-monetary asset without physical substance. An asset is identifiable if it is both:

- separable and
- arises from contractual or other legal rights.

Recognition

An intangible asset should be recognised only if:

- it is probable that the future economic benefits that are attributable to the asset will flow to the enterprise and
- the cost of the asset can be measured reliably.

An intangible asset should initially be measured at cost.

The cost should include the purchase price plus any directly attributable costs of preparing the asset for its intended use.

Intangible assets may be purchased or internally generated as the following illustration summarises:

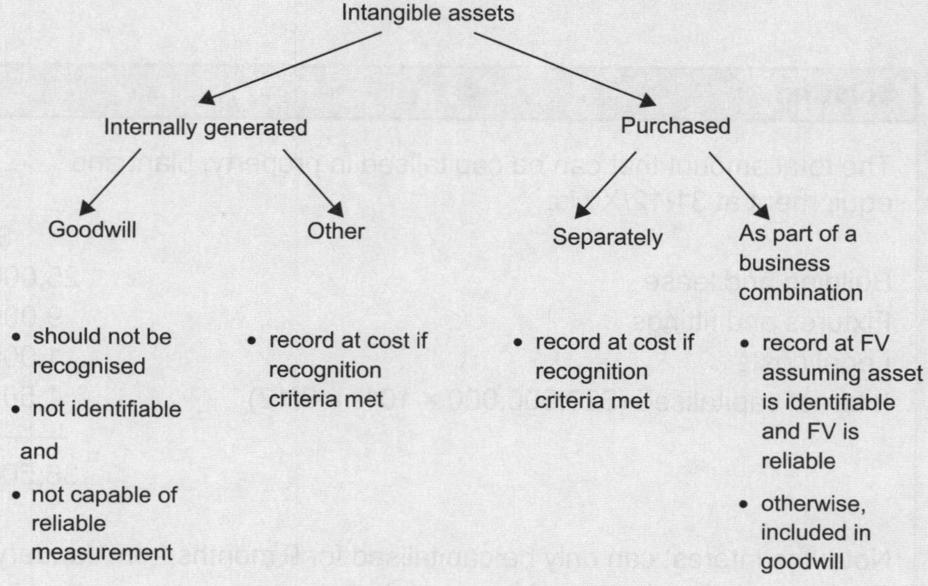

Purchased intangibles

Purchased intangibles should be recognised at cost, which could be cash paid at the date of purchase, or the fair value of any other consideration paid, such as shares issued or assets given in exchange. Examples of purchased intangibles include:

- brands
- patented technology
- licences
- franchise arrangements, and
- trademarks.

Items such as a licence or a patent may be for a specified period of time and, in that situation, it should be amortised over its expected useful life to the entity. The pattern of amortisation should reflect the pattern in which the future economic benefits from the asset are expected to be consumed. If the pattern of usage cannot be reliably estimated, the intangible should be amortised on a straight-line basis.

For other intangibles purchased, such as a brand, it may be less easy to determine an appropriate estimated useful life. In the event that the expected useful life of an intangible asset cannot be reliably determined, it should continue to be recognised at cost, but be subject to an annual impairment review.

Intangibles purchased as part of a business acquisition

If an intangible asset has been acquired as part of the acquisition of a business, and it can be reliably measured, it should be recognised as a separate asset, distinct from purchased goodwill. If an intangible asset acquired cannot be separately measured, it cannot be recognised and is effectively subsumed as part of goodwill on acquisition.

Further information - recognition and measurement

The cost of an intangible asset is measured in the same way as a tangible non-current asset. The cost of an intangible asset comprises:

- its purchase price, including import duties and non-refundable purchase taxes, after deducting trade discounts and rebates
- any directly attributable cost of preparing the asset for its intended use.

Examples of directly attributable costs are:

- costs of employee benefits arising directly from bringing the asset to its working condition
- professional fees.

Examples of costs that are not part of the cost of an intangible asset are:

- costs of introducing a new product or service (including costs of advertising and promotional activities)
- costs of conducting business in a new location or with a new class of customer (including costs of staff training)
- administration and other general overhead costs.

Such costs should be written off as expenses as and when they are incurred.

Previously, we considered the 'Conceptual Framework' and its definition of an asset: 'an asset is a resource controlled by the entity as a result of past events and from which future economic benefits are expected to flow to the entity'. To be recognised as an intangible asset, expenditure must give access to future economic benefits.

The management of the entity must consider the economic conditions that exist and are likely to exist over the useful life of the asset, and then assess the probability of future economic benefits. The assessment should be management's best estimate using all the evidence available, giving greater weight to external evidence. The asset should be measured initially at cost and amortised over its useful life.

Internally-generated intangibles

The general principle regarding recognition of internally generated intangibles is that their cost cannot normally be reliably measured, and therefore cannot be separately recognised as assets. However, there is an exception to this in the case of development costs which, provided that they meet specified criteria and can be reliabily measured, can be recognised in the financial statements.

A useful illustration of an internally generated brand could be a named product range created and promoted by an entity to distinguish its products from those of competitors. The named product range may even have a distinctive logo and have specific marketing activities undertaken to promote the sale of products from that range. However, it would not be possible to reliably measure the cost of creating that brand name which is sufficiently distinct from other expenditure incurred by the entity. Consequently, this internally generated brand would not meet the criteria to be recognised as an intangible asset on the statement of financial position.

The most common type of intangible you are likely to deal with in F1 will be research and development.

Research and development

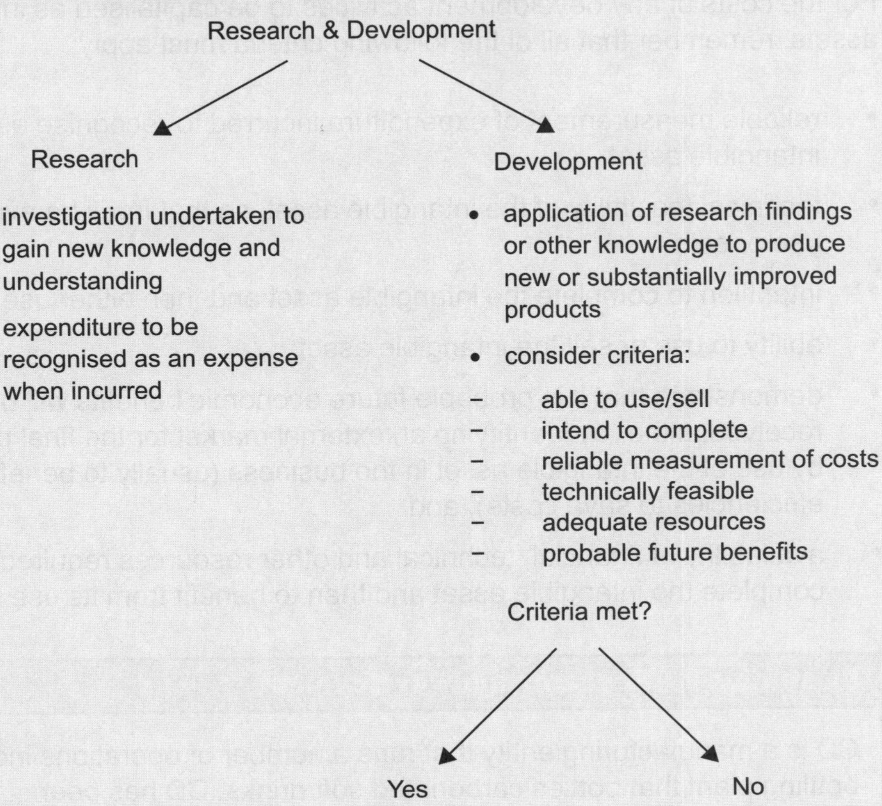
Research & Development
Research
Development
investigation undertaken to gain new knowledge and understanding
expenditure to be recognised as an expense when incurred
application of research findings or other knowledge to produce new or substantially improved products
consider criteria:
– able to use/sell
– intend to complete
– reliable measurement of costs
– technically feasible
– adequate resources
– probable future benefits
Criteria met?
Yes
No
capitalise as intangible asset
write off as expense

Research costs are investigations undertaken with the prospect of gaining new scientific or technical knowledge. These costs are written off as an expense as they are incurred.

Development costs are the application of the research findings to plan or design for the production of new or substantially improved processes, products or services prior to commercial production. In effect, the asset recognised is the knowledge and know-how gained from the development work, rather than the developed product itself. Examples of development activities include the following:

- design, construction and testing of prototypes and models
- design of tools, moulds and dies which involve new technology, and
- design, construction and testing of new or improved materials, devices, products or processes.

For the costs of any development activities to be capitalised as intangible assets, remember that all of the following criteria must apply:

- reliable measurement of expenditure incurred to recognise as an intangible asset
- technical feasibility of the intangible asset, so that it will be available for use or sale
- intentiion to complete the intangible asset and then either use it or sell it
- ability to use or sell the intangible asset
- demonstrate that it is probable future economic benefits will be received, either by identifying an external market for the final product or by use of the intangible asset in the business (usually to benefit from efficiencies to save costs), and
- availability of financial, technical and other resources required to complete the intangible asset and then to benefit from its use or sale.

Illustration 9 – Research and development

CD is a manufacturing entity that runs a number of operations including a bottling plant that bottles carbonated soft drinks. CD has been developing a new bottling process that will allow the bottles to be filled and sealed more efficiently.

The new process took a year to develop. At the start of development, CD estimated that the new process would increase output by 15% with no additional cost (other than the extra bottles and their contents). Development work commenced on 1 May 20X0 and was completed on 20 April 20X1. Testing at the end of the development confirmed CD's original estimates.

CD incurred expenditure of $180,000 on the above development.

CD plans to install the new process in its bottling plant and start operating the new process from 1 May 20X1.

The end of CD's reporting period is 30 April.

Required:

(a) Explain the requirements of IAS 38 Intangible Assets for the treatment of development costs.

(b) Explain how CD should treat its development costs in its financial statements for the year ended 30 April 20X1.

Solution

(a) Development expenditure can only be regarded as an intangible if it meets the criteria of IAS 38. If the criteria is not met the cost must be written off as an expense to the statement of profit or loss. The criteria the standard requires to be met in order to be able to capitalise the cost are as follows:

- the technical feasibility of completing the intangible asset so that it can be used or sold
- the intention to complete the asset to use it or sell it
- the ability to use or sell the asset
- that the asset will in fact generate probable future economic benefit – does a market exist for the asset if it is to be sold, or can the asset's usefulness be proven if the asset is to be used internally
- that it has the technical, financial and other resources to complete the project to make and use or sell the asset
- that it can measure the expenditure on the development of the asset reliably in order to incorporate the amount in the financial statements.

(b) All of the above criteria seem to have been met by CD's new process:

- it is technically feasible, it has been tested and is about to be implemented
- it has been completed and CD intends to use it
- the new process is estimated to increase output by 15% with no additional costs other than direct material costs
- the expenditure can be measured as the figures have been given.

CD will treat the $180,000 development cost as an intangible non-current asset in its statement of financial position at 30 April 20X1. Amortisation will start from 1 May 20X1 when the new process starts operation.

Amortisation

An intangible asset with a finite life should be amortised on a systematic basis over the best estimate of its useful life. Amortisation should begin when the asset is available for use and be charged to profit or loss.

Normally the pattern of amortisation should reflect the pattern in which the economic benefits of the asset are consumed by the entity. If this cannot be reliably estimated, then amortisation on a straight-line basis is acceptable.

Intangible assets are regarded as having an indefinite life if there is no foreseeable limit to the period over which the asset is expected to generate net cash inflows for the entity. An intangible asset with an indefinite life is not amortised but subject to an annual impairment review. Any impairment is charged to profit or loss.

Further information - amortisation

As with tangible assets, the most difficult decision for management is determining the useful life of the asset. The useful life of an intangible asset should take account of such things as:

- the expected usage of the asset
- possible obsolescence and expected actions by competitors
- the stability of the industry
- market demand for the products and services that the asset is generating.

The residual value of an intangible asset should be assumed to be zero unless there is a commitment from a third party to purchase the asset or the entity intends to sell the asset and a readily available active market exists.

The useful life and method of amortisation should be reviewed at least at each financial year-end. Changes to useful life or method of amortisation should be effective as soon as they are identified and should be accounted for as changes in accounting estimates (IAS 8), by adjusting the amortisation charge for the current and future periods.

Test your understanding 5 - Licence and brand

An entity purchased the following intangible assets during the year ended 31 March 20X5:

(a) a licence at a cost of $1 million on 1 April 20X4. The licence is due to expire after ten years and cannot be renewed.

(b) a brand at a cost of $2 million on 1 January 20X5. It was not possible to reliably estimate the useful life of the brand. During the year ended 31 March 20X6, the brand was subject to an impairment review and it was determined that it was impaired to the extent of $200,000

How should these costs be treated in the financial statements of the entity for the each of the years ended 31 March 20X5 and 20X6?

Assets acquired for research purposes

Research costs are treated as an expense in the statement of profit or loss, however, any non-current assets acquired for research purposes, e.g. machinery, will be capitalised like any other asset in NCA if it meets the definition of an asset, i.e.

Property, plant and equipment are tangible assets that:

- are held by an enterprise for use in the production or supply of goods or services, for rental to others, or for administrative purposes and
- are expected to be used during more than one period.

The research costs we expense to the statement of profit or loss are the day to day costs of research projects. Therefore, if the asset was to be used purely for research lasting less than one accounting period we would write it off as an expense immediately, like any other research cost.

Revaluations

Intangible assets may be revalued to their fair value. The fair value should be determined by reference to an active market.

An active market exists where all of the following conditions are met:

- items traded in the market are homogenous
- willing buyers and sellers can be found at any time
- prices are available to the public.

IAS 38 states it is 'uncommon' for an active market to exist for intangible assets. Therefore, intangible assets are invariably accounted for using the cost model.

Disclosure

IAS 38 requires the following disclosure requirements:

For each class of intangible assets:

- The useful lives or amortisation rates used.
- The amortisation methods used.
- The gross carrying amount and accumulated amortisation at the beginning and end of the period.
- The amount of amortisation charged for the period to the statement of profit or loss.
- A reconciliation between the beginning and end of the year balances, i.e. additions, disposals, changes due to impairments or revaluations, amortisation during the period.

The intangible note (IAS 38) shows the movements in the year for each category of asset.

	Development	**Patents**	**Trademarks**	**Total**
	$000	$000	$000	$000
Cost				
At 1 January 20X0	X	X	X	X
Additions	X	X	X	X
Disposals	(X)	(X)	(X)	(X)
At 31 December 20X0	X	X	X	X
Accumulated amortisation/impairment:				
At 1 January 20X0	X	X	X	X
Charged during the year	X	X	X	X
Disposals	(X)	(X)	(X)	(X)
At 31 December 20X0	X	X	X	X
Carrying amount				
At 1 January 20X0	X	X	X	X
At 31 December 20X0	X	X	X	X

Illustration 10- Development costs

An entity is developing a new production process. During the year ended 30 June 20X6, expenditure incurred was $2,000, of which $1,800 was incurred before 1 May 20X6 and $200 was incurred between 1 May 20X6 and 30 June 20X6. The entity is able to demonstrate that, at 1 May 20X6, the production process met the criteria for recognition as an intangible asset. The recoverable amount of the know-how embodied in the process was estimated to be $1,000.

How would this be accounted for in the financial statements for the year ended 30 June 20X6?

During the year ended 30 June 20X7, additional development expenditure was incurred amounting to $4,000. At 30 June 20X7, the recoverable amount of the know-how embodied in the process was estimated to be $3,800.

How would this be accounted for in the financial statements for the year ended 30 June 20X7?

Solution

30 June 20X6:

It is probable that the expected future benefits will exceed the development costs incurred and an asset of $200 can be recognised. The production process is recognised as an intangible asset at a cost of $200 (expenditure incurred since the date when the recognition criteria were met, i.e. 1 May 20X6). The $1,800 expenditure incurred up to 1 May 20X6 is recognised as an expense because the recognition criteria were not met until 1 May 20X6. This expenditure does not form part of the cost of the production process recognised in the statement of financial position.

30 June 20X7:

At 30 June 20X7, the cost of the production process was $4,200 ($200 expenditure recognised at 30 June 20X6 plus $4,000 expenditure during the year ended 30 June 20X7). If an impairment review is now performed, the carrying value of the know-how of $4,200 is compared with the recoverable amount of $3,800 and the entity recognises an impairment loss of $400 to adjust the carrying amount of the process before impairment loss ($4,200) to its recoverable amount ($3,800). Note that this impairment loss may be reversed in a subsequent reporting period if the requirements for the reversal of an impairment loss in IAS 36 are met (see later in this chapter).

Test your understanding 6 – R and D

An entity has incurred the following expenditure during the current year:

(a) $100,000 spent on the design of a new product – it is anticipated that this design will be taken forward over the next two year period to be developed and tested with a view to production in three years time.

(b) $500,000 spent on the testing of a new production system which has been designed internally and which will be in operation during the following accounting year. This new system should reduce the cost of production by 20%.

How should these costs be treated in the financial statements of the entity?

6 IAS 36 Impairment of Assets

An impairment loss is the amount by which the carrying amount of an asset exceeds its recoverable amount.

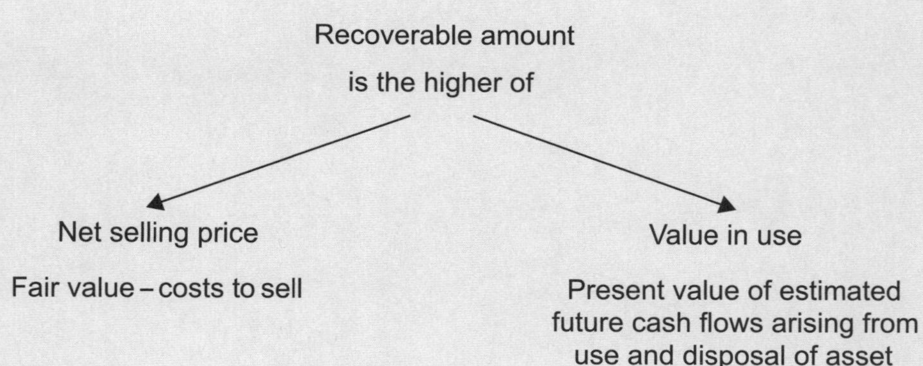

An entity should assess at each reporting date whether there is any indication that an asset may be impaired. If such indications exist, the recoverable amount should be estimated, i.e. an impairment review should be carried out. If no such indications exist, it is not necessary to carry out an impairment review.

The following situations may indicate that an asset has been impaired:

- decline in market value
- technological, legal or economic changes
- physical damage
- plans to dispose of asset.

Procedures to check for impairment

At the end of each reporting period an entity should assess whether there are internal or external indications that the value of any asset is impaired.

In assessing whether there is any indication that an asset may be impaired, an entity shall consider, as a minimum, the following indications:

External sources of information:

- During the period, an asset's market value has declined significantly more than would be expected as a result of the passage of time or normal use.
- Significant changes with an adverse effect on the entity have taken place during the period, or will take place in the near future, in the technological, market, economic or legal environment in which the entity operates or in the market to which an asset is dedicated.
- Market interest rates or other market rates of return on investments have increased during the period, and those increases are likely to affect the discount rate used in calculating an asset's value in use and decrease the asset's recoverable amount materially.
- The carrying amount of the net assets of the reporting entity is more than its market capitalisation.

Internal sources of information:

- Evidence is available of obsolescence or physical damage of an asset.
- Significant changes with an adverse effect on the entity have taken place during the period, or are expected to take place in the near future, in the extent to which, or manner in which, an asset is used or is expected to be used. These changes include the asset becoming idle, plans to discontinue or restructure the operation to which an asset belongs, and plans to dispose of an asset before the previously expected date.
- Evidence is available from internal reporting that indicates that the economic performance of an asset is, or will be, worse than expected.

Recognition and measurement of an impairment loss

When the recoverable amount of an asset is below its carrying amount, the difference is an impairment loss and must be recorded.

An impairment loss should be recorded as an expense in the statement of profit or loss, unless the asset has previously been revalued, in which case the impairment can be offset against the revaluation surplus.

Even if there are no indications of impairment, we must always test annually for impairment for goodwill acquired in a business combination (chapters 2 to 5) and intangible assets with indefinite useful lives.

Cash-generating units

If there is an indication of impairment of an asset the recoverable amount of the individual asset must be identified. If it is not possible to estimate the recoverable amount of the individual asset an entity must determine the recoverable amount of the cash-generating unit to which the asset belongs.

A cash-generating unit is the smallest identifiable group of assets that generates cash inflows that are largely independent of the cash inflows from other assets or groups of assets.

Illustration 11 – Impairment

The following information relates to three assets held by an entity:

	A	B	C
Carrying amount	200	200	200
Net Selling Price	220	125	140
Value in use	160	150	190

Calculate the impairment losses, if any, in respect of the three assets.

Solution

	A	B	C
Recoverable amount (higher of net selling price and value in use)	220	150	190
Carrying amount	200	200	200
Impairment	No	(50)	(10)

Test your understanding 7 – Impairment

The following information relates to three assets held by an entity:

	A	B	C
Carrying amount	200	200	200
Net Selling Price	250	175	160
Value in use	180	150	180

Calculate the impairment losses, if any, in respect of the three assets.

7 Reversal of impairments

Note that an impairment recognised in an earlier reporting period may subsequently be reversed, provided that the factor which led to the recognition of impairment loss has now reversed and is no longer applicable. If this is applicable, the revised carrying amount cannot exceed the amouint the asset would otherwise be stated at if there had been no impairment loss.

Disclosure

IAS 36 requires the following disclosure requirements:

For each class of property, plant and equipment:

- The amount of impairment losses recognised in the statement of profit or loss during the period and where it has been included, i.e. which expense category.
- The amount of reversals for impairment losses recognised in the statement of profit or loss during the period and where it has been included.
- The amount of impairment losses recognised directly in equity during the period.
- The amount of reversals of impairment losses recognised directly in equity during the period.

Test your understanding 8 – Practice questions

(1) Cowper has spent $20,000 researching new cleaning chemicals in the year ended 31 December 20X0. They have also spent $40,000 developing a new cleaning product which will not go into commercial production until next year. The development project meets the criteria laid down in IAS 38 Intangible Assets.

How should these costs be treated in the financial statements of Cowper for the year ended 31 December 20X0?

A $60,000 should be capitalised as an intangible asset on the SOFP.

B $40,000 should be capitalised as an intangible asset and should be amortised; $20,000 should be written off to the statement of profit or loss .

C $40,000 should be capitalised as an intangible asset and should not be amortised; $20,000 should be written off to the statement of profit or loss .

D $60,000 should be written off to the statement of profit or loss.

(2) An entity purchased a property 15 years ago at a cost of $100,000 and have been depreciating it at a rate of 2% per annum, on the straight line basis. The entity have had the property professionally revalued at $500,000.

What is the revaluation surplus that will be recorded in the financial statements in respect of this property?

A $400,000

B $500,000

C $530,000

D $430,000

(3) An entity owns two buildings, A and B, which are currently recorded in the books at carrying amounts of $170,000 and $330,000 respectively. Both buildings have recently been valued as follows:

Building A	$400,000
Building B	$250,000

The entity currently has a balance on the revaluation reserve of $50,000 which arose when building A was revalued several years ago. Building B has never been revalued in the past.

What double entry will need to be made to record the revaluations of buildings A and B?

A	Dr	Non-current assets	$150,000
	Dr	Statement of profit or loss	$80,000
	Cr	Revaluation reserve	$230,000
B	Dr	Non-current assets	$150,000
	Dr	Statement of profit or loss	$30,000
	Cr	Revaluation reserve	$180,000
C	Dr	Non-current assets	$150,000
	Cr	Revaluation reserve	$150,000
D	Dr	Non-current assets	$150,000
	Dr	Statement of profit or loss	$50,000
	Cr	Revaluation reserve	$200,000

(4) The following information relates to three assets held by an entity:

	Asset A	Asset B	Asset C
	$	$	$
Carrying amount	100	50	40
Value in use	80	60	35
Fair value less cost to sell	90	65	30

What is the total impairment loss?

A $15

B $30

C $Nil

D $1

(5) On 1 April 20X0 Slow and Steady showed non-current assets that had cost $312,000 and accumulated depreciation of $66,000. During the year ended 31 March 20X1, Slow and Steady disposed of non-current assets which had originally cost $28,000 and had a carrying amount of $11,200.

The entity's policy is to charge depreciation of 40% on the reducing balance basis, with no depreciation in the year of disposal of an asset.

What is the depreciation charge to the statement of profit or loss for the year ended 31 March 20X1?

A $113,600

B $98,400

C $93,920

D $87,200

(6) A building contractor decides to build an office building, to be occupied by his own staff. Tangible non-current assets are initially measured at cost.

Which of the following expenses incurred by the building contractor cannot be included as a part of the cost of the office building?

A Interest incurred on a specific loan taken out to pay for the construction of the new offices

B Direct building labour costs

C A proportion of the contractor's general administration costs

D Hire of plant and machinery for use on the office building site

(7) **The purpose of depreciation is to:**

A Allocate the cost less residual value on a systematic basis over the asset's useful economic life

B Write the asset down to its market value each period

C Charge profits for the use of the asset

D Recognise that assets lose value over time

(8) **Which of the following tangible non-current assets are NOT usually depreciated:**

A Machinery purchased through a finance lease

B Land

C Buildings with a life in excess of 30 years

D Vehicles

(9) Plant and machinery, costing $50,000, was purchased on 1 April 20X6. This was depreciated for 2 years at 20 per cent a year using the reducing balance method. On 1 April 20X8, the machinery (original cost $25,000) was sold for $12,000. Replacement machines were acquired on the same date for $34,000.

What was the carrying amount of plant and machinery at March 20X9?

(10) Roming purchased property costing $440,000 on 1 January 20X5. The property is being depreciated over 50 years on a straight-line basis. The property was revalued on 1 January 20X9 at $520,000. The useful life was also reviewed at that date and is estimated to be a further 40 years.

Prepare the accounting entries to record the revaluation and calculate the depreciation charge that will apply from 1 January 20X9.

8 Summary diagram

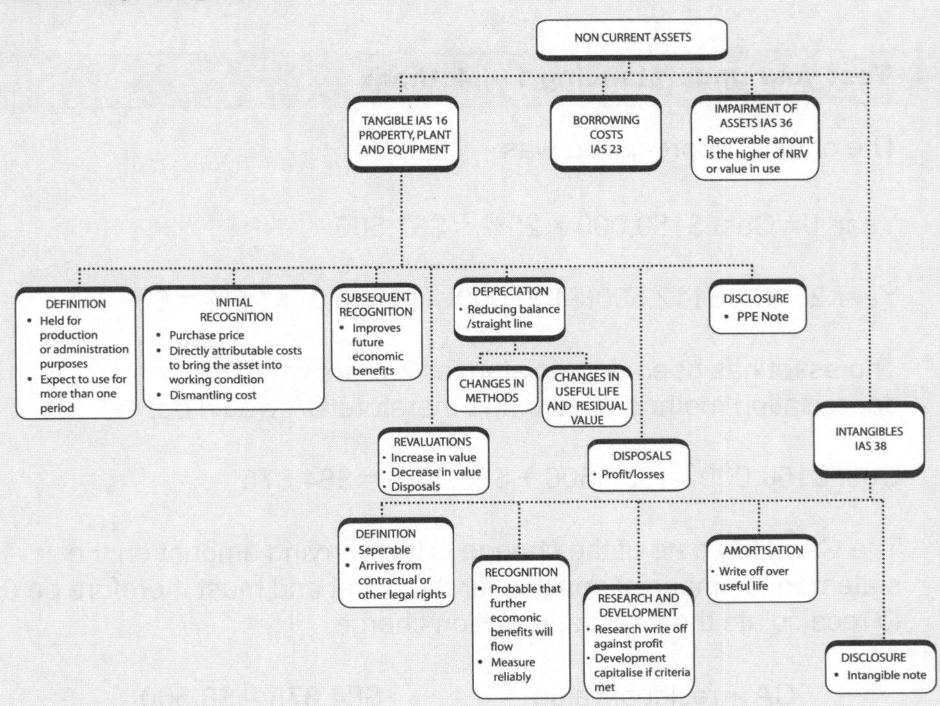

Test your understanding answers

Test your understanding 1 – Methods

The original depreciation was:

Year 1 = Cost $150,000 × 25% = $37,500

Year 2 = CA $112,500($150,000 – $37,500) × 25% = $28,125

The asset has been depreciated for 2 years when the change of depreciation method occurs and therefore CA would be:

Cost $150,000 – ($37,500 + $28,125) = $84,375

The CA at the date of the change is the carrying amount on the statement of financial position for the asset and must therefore be used to recalculate the new depreciation charge.

$$\frac{\text{CA – residual value}}{\text{Remaining useful economic life}} = \frac{\$84,375 – \$8,500}{8} = \$9,484 \text{ pa}$$

Test your understanding 2 – Changes in useful life of an asset

The original depreciation was:

$$\frac{\text{CA – residual value}}{\text{Remaining useful economic life}} = \frac{\$75,000 - \$5,000}{7} = \$10,000 \text{ pa}$$

The asset has been depreciated for 4 years when the change of depreciation method occurs and therefore CA would be:

Cost $75,000 – $40,000 = $35,000

The CA at the date of the change is the carrying amount on the statement of financial position for the asset and must therefore be used to recalculate the new depreciation charge.

$$\frac{\text{CA – residual value}}{\text{Remaining useful economic life}} = \frac{\$35,000 - \$5,000}{10} = \$3,000 \text{ pa}$$

Test your understanding 3 – Revaluations

Asset A

The asset initially cost increases by $19,000, ($50,000 to $69,000).

Depreciation is $10,000 pa ($50,000/50). Therefore accumulated depreciation at 31/12/X6 will be $4,000.

After 4 years (31/12/X6) the carrying amount will be $46,000 ($50,000 – $4,000).

The asset increases in value from $46,000 to $69,000. The increase of $23,000 is credited to the revaluation reserve.

Dr Asset cost	$19,000
Dr Accumulated depreciation	$4,000
Cr Revaluation Reserve	$23,000

The depreciation must now be recalculated on the revalued amount for the remaining life of 46 years.

Depreciation is $1,500 pa ($69,000/46)

After 4 years (31/12/Y0) the carrying amount will be $63,000 ($69,000 – $6,000)

The asset cost increases by $15,000, $69,000 to $84,000.

This assets carrying amount increases in value from $63,000 to $84,000. The increase of $21,000 is credited to the revaluation reserve.

Dr Asset cost	$15,000
Dr Accumulated depreciation	$6,000
Cr Revaluation Reserve	$21,000

The depreciation must now be recalculated on the revalued amount for the remaining life of 42 years.

Depreciation is $2,000 pa ($84,000/42)

The carrying amount at 31/12/Y1 will be:

$84,000 – $2,000 = $82,000

Asset B

The asset initially cost increases by $8,000, ($100,000 to $108,000).

Depreciation is $2,500 pa ($100,000/40). Therefore, accumulated depreciation at 31/12/X6 is $10,000.

After 4 years (31/12/X6) the CV will be $90,000 ($100,000 – $10,000)

This assets carrying value increases from $90,000 to $108,000. The increase of $18,000 is credited to the revaluation reserve.

Dr Asset cost	$8,000
Dr Accumulated depreciation	$10,000
Cr Revaluation Reserve	$18,000

The depreciation must now be recalculated on the revalued amount for the remaining life of 36 years.

Depreciation is $3,000 pa ($108,000/36)

After 4 years (31/12/Y0) the carrying amount will be $96,000 ($108,000 – $12,000)

The asset cost decreases by $44,000, ($108,000 to $64,000).

This assets carrying value decreases from $96,000 to $64,000. The decrease is charged to the revaluation reserve to reduce it to nil and the balance is charged against profits.

Dr Revaluation Reserve	$18,000
Dr Statement of profit or loss	$14,000
Dr Accumulated depreciation	$12,000
Cr Asset	$44,000

Note: The revaluation reserve for building A cannot be used for the reduction in value of building B.

The depreciation must now be recalculated on the revalued amount for the remaining life of 32 years.

Depreciation is $2,000 pa ($64,000/32)

The carrying amount at 31/12/Y1 will be:

$64,000 – $2,000 = $62,000

Under IAS 16 we need to revalue with sufficient regularity to ensure that carrying amount and fair value are not materially different. It is assumed that by revaluing every 4 years in the question meets this criteria.

Test your understanding 4 – PPE note

	(a)	(b)
Non-current asset note	$000	$000
Cost/Valuation		
At 1 July 20X0	200	200
Revaluation	550	550
At 30 June 20X1	750	750
Acc Dep'n		
At 1 July 20X0 (200-132)	68	68
Charge for year	23	4
Revaluation	(68)	(72)
At 30 June 20X1	23	0
Carrying amount		
At 1 July 20X0	132	132
At 30 June 20X1	727	750
Revaluation reserve	618	622
	(750 – 132)	(750 –128)

If the revaluation takes place at the beginning of the year, the current years depreciation charge should be based on the revalued amount. The depreciation charge was based on 2% of cost, i.e. $4,000 pa. If the carrying amount b/fwd is $132,000, it must mean we have already utilised the asset for 17 years ($4,000 × 17 = $68,000 depreciation to date). When the asset is revalued we must now depreciate the revalued amount over the remaining life of 33 years (50 – 17). This will result in the current year's depreciation charge of $22,727 ($750,000/33), rounded to $23,000.

If the revaluation takes place at the end of the year, the current year's depreciation should be based on the original amount, i.e. $200,000 × 2%. The total depreciation to date will then be removed from the books and transferred to the revaluation reserve, i.e. $68,000 + $4,000.

Test your understanding 5 - Licence and brand

The intangible assets should be accounted for as follows:

Statement of financial position extract	20X6	20X5
	$000	$000
Intangible assets:		
Licence	800	900
Brand	1,800	2,000
	2,600	2,900

Statement of profit or loss extract		
Amortisation of intangible asset	100	100
Impairment of intangible asset	200	

Note that the licence is amortised on a straight-line basis over its ten-year life. The carrying amount of the brand will not change from its original cost unless there was impairment in the year.

Test your understanding 6 – R and D

(a) These costs are research costs and must be written off to the statement of profit or loss for the period.

(b) These appear to be development costs that meet the capitalisation criteria, i.e. expect to complete, will produce economic benefits, etc. Therefore these costs should be capitalised as an intangible asset on the SOFP. Amortisation will not begin until production starts.

Test your understanding 7 – Impairment

	A	**B**	**C**
Recoverable amount	250	175	180
Carrying amount	200	200	200
Impairment	No	(25)	(20)

NB: Recoverable amount is the higher of the net selling price and value in use.

Test your understanding 8 – Practice questions

(1) C

(2) D

Current value	500,000
CV at date of revaluation (100,000 – (100,000 × 2% × 15yrs))	(70,000)
Revaluation gain	430,000

(3) A

	Building A	Building B
Current value	400,000	250,000
CV	(170,000)	(330,000)
Revaluation gain/loss	230,000	(80,000)

The gain on Building A will be credited to the revaluation reserve.

The loss on Building B will be debited to the statement of profit or loss expenses because we do not have a balance on the revaluation reserve in respect of building B to net the loss off against.

We make an overall Dr to fixed assets is \$230,000 – \$80,000 = \$150,000

(4) A

	Asset A	Asset B	Asset C
	\$	\$	\$
Carrying amount	100	50	40
Value in use	80	60	35
Fair value less cost to sell	90	65	30
Valued at higher of value in use/fair value	90	65	35
Impairment	10	Nil	5

Total Impairment = \$15

(5) C

Carrying amount at 1 April 20X0 ($312,000 – $66,000)	$246,000
Carrying amount of disposal	($11,200)
Carrying amount at 31 March 20X1	$234,800
Depreciation at 40%	$93,920

(6) C – Direct costs relating to the asset can be included such as labour costs, interest on loans to acquire the asset and hire costs. The administration cost is not a direct cost.

(7) A

(8) B

(9) The answer is $ 40,000

	$
Cost 1 April 20X6	50,000
20% depreciation	(10,000)
Carrying amount 31 March 20X7	40,000
20% depreciation	(8,000)
Carrying amount 31 March 20X8	32,000
Disposal book value ($25,000 × 80% × 80%)	(16,000)
(Cost $25,000 – depreciation for 2 years $9,000)	
Carrying amount after disposal	16,000
Purchase	34,000
	50,000
20% depreciation	(10,000)
Carrying amount at 31 March 20X9	40,000

(10) The annual charge for depreciation was $440,000/50 years 5 $8,800.

The asset had been used and depreciated for 4 years (2007 to 2010).

The carrying amount of the asset at the date of valuation was therefore $404,800 (cost of $440,000 – accumulated depreciation of $35,200).

The revaluation surplus is calculated as the valuation amount of $520,000 less the carrying amount of the asset of $404,800. The surplus is therefore $115,200.

The revaluation at 1 January 20X9 will be recorded as:

		$	$
Debit	Accumulated depreciation	35,200	
Debit	Cost ($520,000 – $440,000)	80,000	
Credit	Revaluation reserve		115,200

The depreciation charge for 20X9 and beyond will be based on the asset's valuation over the remaining useful life of the property. The useful life has also been revised to 40 years, so the depreciation will now be $13,000, being value of $520,000 over 40 years.

chapter

14

IFRS 5 Non-current Assets Held for Sale and Discontinued Operations

Chapter learning objectives

On completion of their studies students should be able to:

- Explain and apply the accounting rules contained in IFRS 5 dealing with reporting financial performance.
- Identify and correctly value an asset held for sale.
- Present discontinued operations correctly.

1 Session content

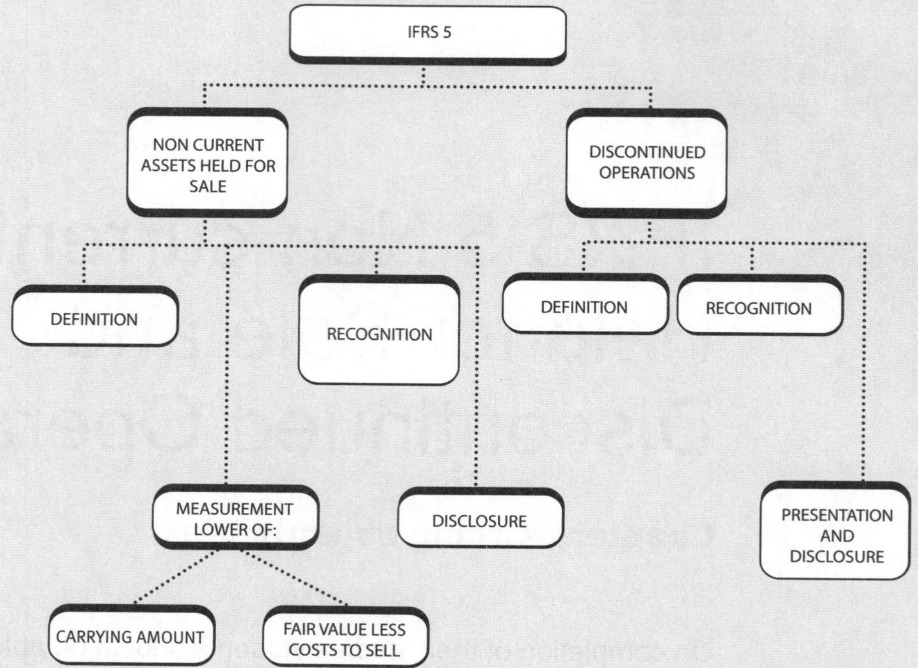

2 Introduction

The objective of IFRS 5 is to establish principles for reporting information about discontinued operations and non-current assets held for sale. IFRS 5 states any non-current assets held for sale should be presented separately on the statement of financial position and any results from discontinued operations presented separately on the statement of profit or loss. This is to ensure the users are able to better assess the future performance and cash flows of the entity.

3 Non-current assets held for sale

In chapter 13 we considered disposals of non-current assets.

The disposal of an asset means the asset has been sold and we saw how it was removed from our records and how we recorded the gain or loss on the sale.

At the date the financial statements are prepared we may not have disposed of the asset but it may no longer be used by the entity, e.g. an empty warehouse surplus to requirements.

An entity shall classify a non-current asset as held for sale if its carrying amount will be recovered principally through a sale transaction rather than through continuing use.

These assets will be treated as held for sale if all of the following criteria are met:

- available for immediate sale in its present condition
- the sale is highly probably
- a reasonable price has been set
- the sale is expected to complete within one year from the date of classification.

All criteria must be met if the non-current asset is to be held for sale.

For example, for the sale to be highly probable the management must be committed to selling the asset and they must have an active programme to locate a buyer. The asset must also be available to sell immediately in its present condition, i.e. no major repairs are requirement on a building before it could be put on the market to sell.

Measurement of non-current assets held for sale

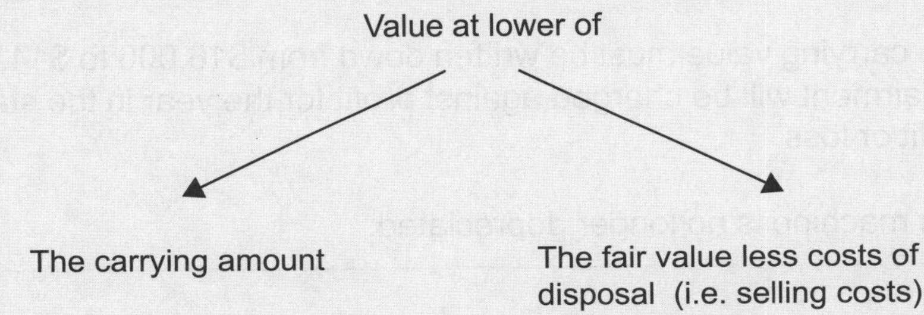

* Non-current assets 'held for sale' are not depreciated once they have been classified as such. However, such assets should be depreciated as normal until the classification date.

If the value of the asset held for sale is less than the carrying amount on the statement of financial position it should be written down and the impairment charged against profit.

Presentation and disclosure

- Separate disclosure of assets just below the current asset section.

Illustration 1 – Assets held for sale

On 1 January 20X8 an entity Mickey purchases a machine for $20,000. It has an expected useful life of 10 years and nil residual value. The entity uses the straight line method of depreciation.

On 31 December 20X9 the entity decides to sell the machine. Its current market value is $15,000 and the entity is confident they will find a buyer very quickly due the short supply in the market for this type of machinery. It will cost the entity $500 to dismantle the machine.

At what value should the machine be included in Mickey's statement of financial position at 31 December 20X9?

Solution

Current carrying value = 8/10 × $20,000 = $16,000 (we have had the machine for two years, hence charged two year's worth of depreciation against the asset).

Fair value less costs to sell = $15,000 – 500 = $14,500

The machine qualifies as an "asset held for sale" at 31 December 20X9 so should be valued at the lower of carrying value or fair value less costs to sell, i.e. $14,500.

The carrying value must be written down from $16,000 to $14,500. The impairment will be charged against profit for the year in the statement of profit or loss.

The machine is no longer depreciated.

The revaluation model

Any assets valued under the revaluation model that meet the criteria of an asset held for sale should first be revalued as normal and then separately written down to the fair value less costs to sell. For example an asset with a carrying amount of $10,000 met the criteria of an asset held for sale when the fair value of the asset was $12,000 and the costs to sell were $3,000. The asset would first be revalued by $2,000 by debiting the asset cost account and crediting the revaluation reserve and then written down to $9,000 by crediting the asset cost with $3,000 and debiting the SPL expense with $3,000. This results in the costs to sell being recognised as an immediate impairment cost to the SPL.

4 Discontinued operations

Definition

A discontinued operation is a component of an entity that either has been disposed of or is classified as held for sale, and:

- that represents a separate major line of business or geographical area of operations
- that is part of a single co-ordinated plan to dispose of a separate major line of business or geographical area of operations, or
- that is a subsidiary acquired exclusively with a view to resale.

Disclosure

Entities should disclose the following information in the financial statements:

Statement of profit or loss – there should be a single figure on the face of the statement for the total of:

- Profit after tax
- Gain or loss on disposal of assets
- Gain or loss arising from the adjustment in value from carrying value to fair value

Statement of profit or loss or note – the single figure should be analysed into:

- Revenues, expenses, profit/loss before tax and income tax expense of the discontinued operation
- The related tax expense
- Gain or loss arising from the adjustment in value from carrying value to fair value
- Gain or loss on disposal of assets

Statement of cash flows – there should be a disclosure of net cash flows for the discontinued operations for:

- Net cash flows from operating, investing and financing activities
- A description of the discontinued operation/ non-current asset
- A description of the facts and circumstances of the sale
- Expected manner and timing of the disposal (held for sale only)

Presentation

	$
Continued operations	
Revenue	X
Cost of Sales	(X)
Gross profit	X
Distribution costs	(X)
Administrative expenses	(X)
Profit from operations	X
Investment income	X
Finance cost	(X)
Profit before tax	X
Income tax expense	(X)
Profit for the period from continuing operations	X
Discontinued operations	
Profit for the period from discontinued operations (see note*)	X
Profit for the period	X

***Note:** Additional disclosure would be provided in the note to the accounts.

Presentation and disclosure

If presented in the statement of profit or loss it must be presented in a section identified as relating to discontinued operations, and be kept separate from continuing operations.

An entity shall disclose on the statement of cash flows or in the notes, net cash flows attributable to the operating, investing and financing activities of discontinued operations.

Comparative information for prior periods should be restated based on the classifications established in the current reporting period. For example, if the retail division is classified as a discontinued operation in 20X2 and its results are disclosed as such separately in the financial statements, then the comparative information for 20X1 should be restated (from continuing operations where it was included last year) and included as a direct comparison within discontinued operations.

Illustration 2 – Discontinued operations

Echo is an entity that operates with three divisions A, B and C. During the year ended 31 March 20X1 division B closed.

Extracts from the trial balance of Echo as at 31 March 20X1 are shown below.

	Dr	**Cr**
	$000	$000
Sales revenue divisions A & C		2,400
Sales revenue division B		650
Operating expenses divisions A & C	1,650	
Operating expenses divisions B	525	
Finance costs (all relating to continuing activities)	70	
Income tax	225	

The income tax charge for the year is made up of a charge of $200,000 on continuing activities and $25,000 for discontinued activities.

A loss of $50,000 was also incurred on the disposal of assets belonging to division B and $80,000 was spent on restructuring divisions A and C following the termination of division B.

Required:

Prepare the statement of profit or loss for the year ended 31 March 20X1 complying with IAS 1 (revised) Presentation of Financial Statements and IFRS 5 Discontinued Operations.

Solution

Statement of profit or loss for Echo for the year ended 31 March 20X1

	$000
Continued operations	
Revenue	2,400
Operating expenses	(1,650)
Profit from operations	750
Restructuring costs (see note*)	(80)
	670
Finance cost	(70)
Profit before tax	600
Income tax expense	(200)
Profit for the period from continuing operations	400
Discontinued operations	
Profit for the period from discontinued operations (see note**)	50
Profit for the period from total operations	450

Note* for restructuring costs

Restructuring costs have been treated as a material item due to their nature, i.e. unusual item not expected to occur on a regular basis and their size. This means they will be shown as a separate item on the statement of profit or loss, rather than be part of other operating expenses. They are not a regular operating expense of the business.

Note for discontinued operations**

Revenue	650
Operating expenses	(525)
Profit from operations	125
Loss on asset disposal	(50)
Tax expense	75
Profit for the period	(25)
	50

Extract from notes to the financial statements:

During the year ended 31 March 20X1, Echo closed down Division B, for which the results are separately disclosed. As a result of the discontinued operation, losses on the disposal of assets were incurred of $50,000.

As a consequence of the discontinuance of Division B, restructuring costs were incurred of $80,000 in order to rationalise the remaining divisions.

Test your understanding 1 – Discontinued operations

St Valentine produces cards and sells roses. However, half way through the year ended 31 March 20X1, the rose business was closed and the assets sold off, incurring losses on disposal of non-current assets of $76,000 and redundancy costs of $37,000. The directors reorganised the continuing business at a cost of $98,000.

Trading results are summarised as follows for the year:

	Cards	Roses
	$000	$000
Revenue	650	320
Cost of sales	320	150
Administrative expenses	120	110
Distribution costs	60	90

Other trading information (all relating to continuing activities) is as follows:

	Total
	$000
Finance costs	17
Tax expense	31

Required:

Draft the statement of profit or loss for the year ended 31 March 20X1 complying with IAS 1 (revised) Presentation of Financial Statements and IFRS 5 Discontinued Operations.

Test your understanding 2 – Discontinued operations

Dodgem is a diversified entity which has operated in four main areas for many years. Each of these activities has usually contributed approximately one-quarter of the entity's annual operating profit. During the year ended 31 December 20X0, the entity disposed of its glass-making division. The entity's chief accountant has prepared the following summary of revenues and expenses:

	Glass-making	Other divisions
	$000	$000
Turnover	150	820
Operating expenses	98	470
Losses on disposal of non-current assets	205	61

The entity also incurred finance costs of $37,000 during the year, all of which relates to continuing operations. The income tax charge for the year has been estimated at $24,000, made up of a $50,000 charge on the continuing activities and a $26,000 refund for discontinued operations. A dividend of $30,000 was paid during the year.

The entity made an issue of 100,000 $1 shares at a premium of 80c per share during the year. Equity at the beginning of the year was made up as follows:

	$000
Share capital	250
Share premium	150
Revaluation reserve	160
Retained earnings	670
	1,230

The balance on the revaluation reserve arose when the entity valued the land occupied by the properties used in its retail division. In view of recent developments, it has been decided that this reserve should be reduced to $90,000 to reflect the reduced value of the properties.

Required:

(a) Prepare an outline statement of profit or loss and other comprehensive income for the year ended 31 December 20X0 for Dodgem in a form suitable for publication, complying with the requirements of IFRS 5.

(b) Prepare a statement of changes in equity for Dodgem in accordance with the requirements of IAS 1.

Test your understanding 3 – Single entity accounts

The following shows an extract from Archy's nominal ledger at 30 April 20X1:

	$
Administrative expenses	950,000
Distribution costs	531,000
Purchases	2,875,000
Finance costs	9,000
Investment income	5,700
Revenue	5,350,000
Ordinary share capital $1	1,000,000
Receivables	55,700
Inventory at 1 May 20X0	1,670,000
Cash and cash equivalents	242,000
Land and buildings	
Cost at 1 May 20X0	900,000
Accumulated depreciation at 1 May 20X0	36,000
Plant and equipment	
Cost at 1 May 20X0	102,800
Accumulated depreciation at 1 May 20X0	36,400
Intangible asset – carrying value at 1 May 20X0	68,000
Retained earnings at 1 May 20X0	813,300
Bank loan (repayable on 1 June 20X9)	100,000
Payables	62,100

The following additional information is available:

(1) The tax charge for the year is estimated at $227,000.

(2) During the year a piece of plant costing $56,000 and accumulated depreciation of $21,000, met the criteria of IFRS 5 Non-current Assets Held for Sale and Discontinued Operations. The plant is available for sale at the price of $32,000 and costs of $1,000 will be incurred in order to complete the sale.

(3) Plant and machinery should be depreciated at 20% on cost and charged to cost of sales.

(4) The land and buildings were originally acquired on 1 May 20W7 for $900,000 of which $300,000 related to land. Depreciation is calculated on a straight line basis over a 50 year life and charged to administration expenses.

(5) At the beginning of the year Archy revalued their land and buildings to $1,400,000 of which $460,000 related to land. The remaining life remains unchanged. This has not been accounted for.

(6) Closing inventory was valued at $1,820,000 before any adjustments for damaged items. At the year-end inventory count it was discovered that one line of goods in the warehouse had been damaged. The count shows that 1,250 items were damaged. The inventory was recorded at cost of $150 per item, however, following the damage the items have a scrap value of $40 each.

(7) The intangible asset is a brand which was acquired for $68,000. The useful life of the brand is considered to be indefinite and therefore Archy carries out an annual impairment review to identify the recoverable amount. An expert has estimated the brand's fair value less costs to sell to be $60,000 and the financial controller has estimated the value in use to be $62,000.

Required:

Prepare a statement of profit or loss and other comprehensive income and statement of financial position for the year ended 30 April 20X1.

Test your understanding 4 – Practice questions

(1) **According to IFRS 5 Non-current Assets Held for Sale and Discontinued Operations which of the following relate to the criteria for an asset held for sale?**

(i) Available for immediate sale in its present condition

(ii) Sales is highly probable

(iii) The sale is expected to be completed within the next month

(iv) A reasonable price has been set

A All of the above

B i, ii and iii

C i, ii and iv

D ii, iii and iv

(2) **According to IFRS 5 Non-current Assets Held for Sale and Discontinued Operations which of the following amounts in respect of a discontinued operation must be included within the total shown on the face of the statement of profit or loss?**

(i) Revenues

(ii) Gross profit

(iii) Profit after tax

(iv) Operating profit

A All of the above

B iii only

C iii and iv

D iv only

(3) **According to IFRS 5 Non-current Assets Held for Sale and Discontinued Operations how should non-current assets held for sale be valued?**

A Lower of the carrying value or the fair value

B Lower of the carrying value or the fair value less costs of disposal

C Higher of the carrying value or the fair value

D Higher of the carrying value or the fair value less costs of disposal

(4) At the reporting date an asset is identified as an asset held for sale after meeting the criteria according to IFRS 5 Non-current Assets Held for Sale and Discontinued Operations . At the reporting date the carrying value of the asset was $150,000 (original cost $200,000). At the date of purchase, the asset had an estimated useful life of 10 years and an estimated residual value of $Nil. The entity has a policy to depreciate assets using the straight-line method.

What should the depreciation be for the year?

A $20,000

B $15,000

C None

D $25,000

(5) At the reporting date an asset is identified as an asset held for sale after meeting the criteria according to IFRS 5 Non-current Assets Held for Sale and Discontinued Operations.

Where should the asset appear on the statement of financial position?

A Part of the property, plant and equipment under non-current assets

B It is not shown on the statement of financial position

C Separately below non-current assets

D Separately below current assets

(6) During the financial year, Star carried out a reorganisation as follows:

- Division A, a UK division whose operations are being terminated and transferred to another UK division producing the same product.
- Division B, the sole operator in South America whose business is being sold externally to a third party.
- Activity F, which is part of Division Z, whose operations have been closed down. F's results have not been reported separately.

Which of the following should be classified as a discontinued operation according to IFRS 5 (Non-Current Assets Held for Sale and Discontinued Operations)?

A Division A only

B Division B only

C Division A and B only

D Division A and B and Activity F

(7) In order for an asset to be classified as held for sale under IFRS 5, certain conditions need to be met.

Which of these is not one of the conditions?

A Management has committed itself to scrap the asset.

B The asset is expected to be sold within 12 months following classification to held for sale.

C It is unlikely that the plan will be changed significantly.

D The sale is highly probable

(8) **Which of the following conditions must be satisfied in order for an operation to be treated as discontinued in accordance with IFRS 5 Non-current Assets Held for Sale and Discontinued Operations?**

(i) The operation represents a major line of business or geographical area of operation.

(ii) The operation can be clearly distinguished operationally and for financial reporting purposes.

(iii) The termination or sale must be completed within three months of the end of the reporting period.

(iv) The operation must have been disposed of by the year end.

A All of the above conditions

B (i) and (ii)

C (i) and (iii)

D (ii), (iii), and (iv)

(9) Kat has a year end of 31st December.

On the 1st January 20X9, it classified one of its freehold properties as held for sale. At that date the property had a carrying amount of $667,000 and had been accounted for according to the revaluation model. Its fair value was estimated at $825,000 and the costs to sell at $3,000.

In accordance with IFRS 5 (Non-current Assets Held for Sale and Discontinued Operations), what amounts should be recognised in the financial statements for the year to 31st December 20X9?

A Statement of profit or loss gain $155,000
Statement of profit or loss impairment loss $3,000
Revaluation gain nil

B Statement of profit or loss gain $158,000
Statement of profit or loss impairment loss nil
Revaluation gain nil

C Statement of profit or loss gain nil
Statement of profit or loss impairment loss nil
Revaluation gain $155,000

D Statement of profit or loss gain nil
Statement of profit or loss impairment loss $3,000
Revaluation gain $158,000

(10) Which of the following statements are true in relation to assets held for sale under IFRS 5 Assets Held for Sale And Discontinued Operations?

(i) Assets held for sale are always separately disclosed as discontinued rather than continuing activities within the statement of profit or loss.

(ii) An asset with a Carrying Value of £20,000 and a fair value less cost to sell of £18,000 would have suffered a £2,000 impairment.

A Both.

B (i) only

C (ii) only

D Neither

5 Summary diagram

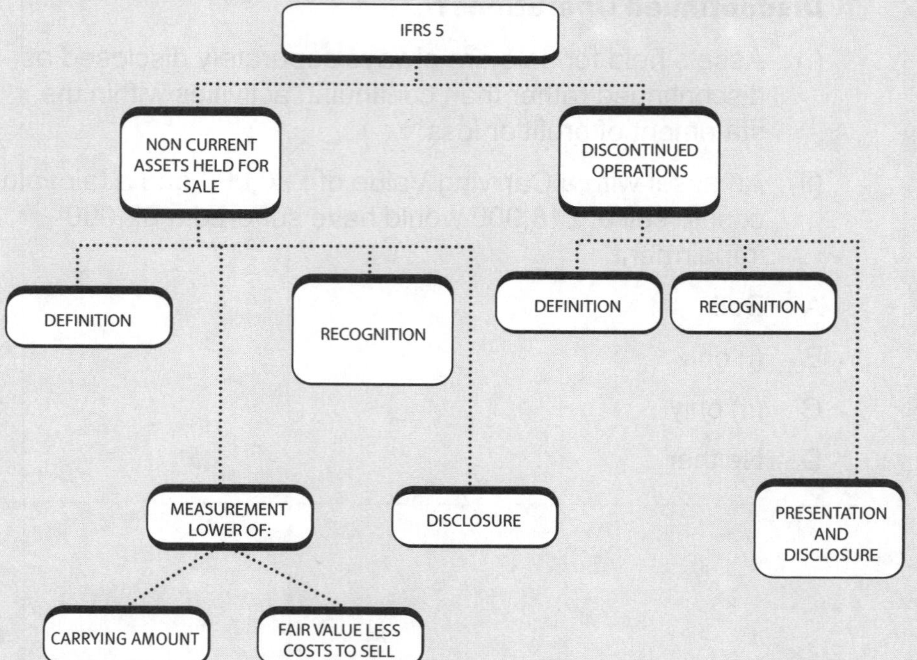

Test your understanding answers

Test your understanding 1 – Discontinued operations

Statement of profit or loss for St Valentine for the year ended 31 March 20X1

	$
Continued operations	
Revenue	650
Cost of Sales	(320)
Gross profit	330
Distribution costs	(60)
Administrative expenses	(120)
Profit from operations	150
Reorganisation costs	(98)
	52
Finance cost	(17)
Profit before tax	35
Income tax expense	(31)
Profit for the period from continuing operations	4
Discontinued operations	
Loss for the period from discontinued operations (see note*)	(143)
Loss for the period from total operations	(139)

Note for discontinued operations *

Revenue	320
Cost of Sales	(150)
Gross profit	170
Distribution costs	(90)
Administrative expenses	(110)
Loss from operations	(30)
Loss on disposal	(76)
Redundancy costs	(37)
	(143)

Test your understanding 2 – Discontinued operations

(a) **Statement of profit or loss and other comprehensive income for Dodgem for the year ended 31 December 20X0**

	$000
Continued operations	
Revenue	820
Operating expenses	(470)
Profit from operations	350
Loss on disposal of non-current asset	(61)
	289
Finance cost	(37)
Profit before tax	252
Income tax expense	(50)
Profit for the period from continuing operations	202

Discontinued operations

Loss for the period from discontinued operations (see note*)	(127)
Profit for the period from total operations	75
Other comprehensive income:	
Revaluation reduction	(70)
Total comprehensive income for the period	5

Note for discontinued operations

Revenue	150
Operating expenses	(98)
Operating profit	52
Loss on disposal of non-current assets	(205)
Income tax expense	26
	(127)

(c) **Dodgem Statement of Changes in Equity for the year ended 31 December 20X0**

	Share capital	Share premium	Revaluation reserve	Retained earnings	Total
	$000	$000	$000	$000	$000
Balance at 31 December 20W9	250	150	160	670	1,230
Revaluation adjustment			(70)		(70)
Profit for the period				75	75
Dividends paid				(30)	(30)
Issue of share capital	100	80			180
Balance at 31 December 20X0	350	230	90	715	1,385

Note: Share capital issue = 100,000 × $1 = $100,000 and share premium issue = 100,000 × 80c = $80,000

Test your understanding 3 – Single entity accounts

Archy statement of profit or loss and other comprehensive income for the year ended 30 April 20X1

	$
Revenue	5,350,000
Cost of Sales (W1)	(2,881,860)
Gross profit	2,468,140
Distribution costs	(531,000)
Administrative expenses (W1)	(970,000)
Profit from operations	967,140
Income from investments	5,700
Finance cost	(9,000)
Profit before tax	963,840
Income tax expense	(227,000)
Profit for year	736,840
Other comprehensive income:	
Revaluation gain (W4)	536,000
Total comprehensive income	1,272,840

Archy statement of financial position as at 30 April 20X1

	$	$
Non-current assets		
Property, plant and equipment (W4)		1402,040
Intangible (W3)		62,000
Current assets		
Inventories (W5)	1,682,500	
Trade receivables	55,700	
Cash and cash equivalents	242,000	
		1,980,200
Non-current asset held for sale (W2)		31,000
Total assets		3,475,240

Equity and liabilities

Capital and reserves

Share capital $1	1,000,000	
Revaluation reserve (W4)	536,000	
Retained earnings (W6)	1,550,140	
		3,086,140
Non-current liabilities		
Bank loan	100,000	
		100,000
Current liabilities		
Trade payables	62,100	
Income tax	227,000	
		289,100
		3,475,240

Workings

(W1)

Cost of sales	$
Purchases	2,875,000
Opening inventory	1,670,000
Closing inventory (W5)	(1,682,500)
Depreciation on plant	9,360
Impairment on asset held for sale (W2)	4,000
Impairment on intangible asset (W3)	6,000
	2,881,860

Administrative expenses	$
As per TB	950,000
Depreciation on building	20,000
	970,000

(W2)

Non-current asset held for sale -

Valued at the lower of:

Carrying value ($56,000 – $21,000) = $35,000 or

Net selling price ($32,000 – $1,000) = $31,000

Value at $31,000

Impairment charged to cost of sales ($35,000 – $31,000) = $4,000

The carrying value of this asset must be removed from the PPE total and shown as an individual line on the SOFP

(W3)

Intangible asset

Compare carrying value with the recoverable amount.

Recoverable amount is the higher of:

Net selling price $60,000

Value in use $62,000

Therefore, recoverable amount is $62,000

The carrying value is $68,000

Impairment charged to cost of sales ($68,000 – $62,000) = $6,000

(W4) **PPE**

	Property	**Plant & Equipment**	**Total**
	$	$	$
Cost/Valuation			
At 1 May 20X0	900,000	102,800	1,002,800
Additions	–	–	–
Disposals		–	–
Revaluation	500,000		500,000
Asset held for sale	–	(56,000)	(56,000)
At 30 April 20X1	1,400,000	46,800	1,446,800
Accumulated depreciation:			
At 1 May 20X0	36,000	36,400	72,400
Revaluation	(36,000)	–	(36,000)
Charged during the year *	20,000	9,360	29,360
Asset held for sale	–	(21,000)	(21,000)
At 30 April 20X1	20,000	24,760	44,760
Carrying value			
At 30 April 20X1	1,380,000	22,040	1,402,040
At 30 April 20X0	864,000	66,400	930,400

* The depreciation on the property on the TB represents 3 years ($900,000 – $300,000)/50 = $12,000 pa. The revaluation happens at the beginning of the year, hence, current year charge should be based on the revalued amount over the remaining life of 47 years = ($1,400,000 – $460,000)/47 = $20,000

The depreciation on the plant and equipment is calculated on the closing cost of $46,800 × 20% = $9,360

We do not depreciate assets held for sale.

(W5)

Inventory	$
Closing inventory at cost	1,820,000
Damaged stock at cost (1,250 × $150)	(187,500)
Damaged stock at NRV (1,250 × $40)	50,000
	1,682,500

Inventory is valued at the lower of cost or NRV

(W6)

Retained earnings	$
Balance at 1 May 20X0	813,300
Profit for the period	736,840
	1,550,140

Test your understanding 4 – Practice questions

(1) C

(2) B

(3) B

(4) A – The asset does not meet the criteria of an asset held for sale until the reporting date, hence depreciate the asset as normal for the year. No further depreciation will occur on this asset after the reporting date.

(5) D

(6) B

(7) A

(8) B

(9) D – The asset held for sale will be revalued to the fair value of $825,000 creating a gain of $158,000 to the revaluation reserve. The asset held for sale will then be reduced to the fair value less costs to sell value of $825,000 – $3,000, i.e. create an impairment cost of $3,000. There will not be a gain to the SPL until the asset is sold and the gain is realised.

(10) C – The asset held for sale will be valued at the fair value less costs to sell, i.e. $18,000. This will reduce the carrying value by $2,000 impairment. Item one is not correct as the asset held for sale appears on the SFP as a separate item and not on the SPL.

chapter

15

IAS 20 Government Grants and IAS 40 Investment Properties

Chapter learning objectives

On completion of their studies students should be able to:

- Apply the provisions of IAS 20 in relation to accounting for government grants.
- Identify and account for capital and revenue grants.
- Account for repayments of grants.
- Define investment properties.
- Discuss why the treatment of investment properties should differ from other properties.
- Apply the requirements of IAS 40 for investment properties.

1 Session Content

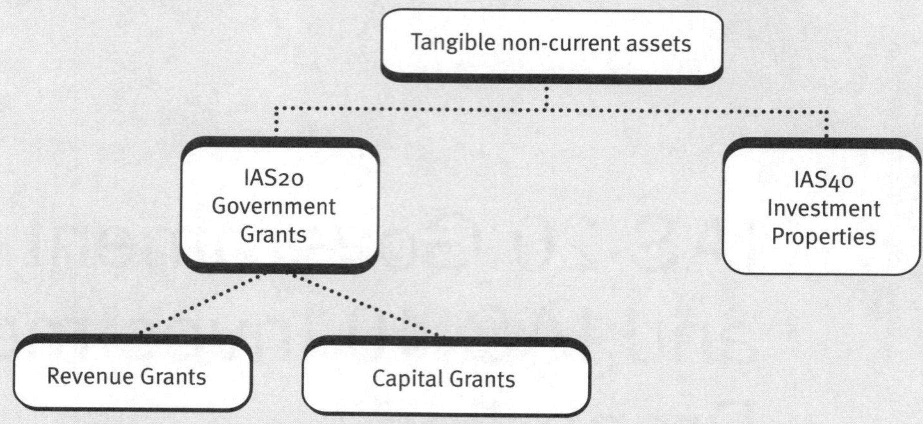

2 IAS 20 Accounting for government grants and disclosure of government assistance

Introduction

Governments often provide money or incentives to companies to export to or promote local employment.

Government grants could be:

- revenue grants, e.g. money towards wages
- capital grants, e.g. money towards purchase of non-current assets.

General principles

IAS 20 follows two general principles when determining the treatment of grants:

Prudence: grants should not be recognised until the conditions for receipt have been complied with and there is reasonable assurance the grant will be received.

Accruals: grants should be matched with the expenditure towards which they were intended to contribute.

IAS 20 definitions

Government refers to government, government agencies and similar bodies whether local, national or international.

Government assistance is action by government designed to provide an economic benefit specific to an entity or range of entities qualifying under certain criteria, e.g. the grant of a local operating licence.

Government grants are assistance by government in the form of transfers of resources to an entity in return for past or future compliance with certain conditions relating to the operating activities of the entity.

Grants related to assets are government grants whose primary condition is that an entity qualifying for them should purchase, construct or otherwise acquire long-term assets.

Grants related to income are government grants other than those related to assets – known as revenue grants.

Revenue grants

The recognition of the grant will depend upon the circumstances.

- If the grant is paid when evidence is produced that certain expenditure has been incurred, the grant should be matched with that expenditure.
- If the grant is paid on a different basis, e.g. achievement of a non-financial objective, such as the creation of a specified number of new jobs, the grant should be matched with the identifiable costs of achieving that objective.

A grant should only be recognised when there is reasonable assurance that:

- the entity will **comply** with conditions of the grant and
- the entity will **receive** the grant.

Presentation of revenue grants

IAS 20 allows such grants to either:

- be presented as a credit in the statement of profit or loss, or
- deducted from the related expense.

The grant should only be recognised in the statement of profit or loss as the conditions of the grant are being complied with. For example, if the grant has been received for wages to keep people employed for the next two years, the grant should be recognised in the statement of profit or loss over the two year period. The remainder of the grant will be held as deferred income until it is recognised in the statement of profit or loss.

Revenue grant presentation

Presentation as credit in the statement of profit or loss

Supporters of this method claim that it is inappropriate to net income and expense items, and that separation of the grant from the expense facilitates comparison with other expenses not affected by a grant.

Deduction from related expense

It is argued that with this method, the expenses might well not have been incurred by the entity if the grant had not been available, and presentation of the expense without offsetting the grant may therefore be misleading.

Capital grants

IAS 20 permits two treatments:

- Write off the grant against the cost of the non-current asset and depreciate the reduced cost.
- Treat the grant as a deferred credit and transfer a portion to other income each year, so offsetting the higher depreciation charge on the original cost.

Treatment of capital grants

Grants for purchases of non-current assets should be recognised over the expected useful lives of the related assets.

IAS 20 permits two treatments. Both treatments are equally acceptable and capable of giving a fair presentation.

Method 1

On initial recognition, deduct the grant from the cost of the non-current asset and depreciate the reduced cost.

Method 2

Recognise the grant initially as deferred income and transfer a portion to other income each year, so offsetting the higher depreciation charge based on the original cost.

Method 1 is obviously far simpler to operate. Method 2, however, has the advantage of ensuring that assets acquired at different times and in different locations are recorded on a uniform basis, regardless of changes in government policy.

In some countries, legislation requires that non-current assets should be stated by entities at purchase price and this is defined as actual price paid plus any additional expenses. Legal opinion on this matter is that entities subject to such legislation should not deduct grants from cost. In such countries Method 1 may only be adopted by unincorporated entities.

Illustration 1 – Capital grants

An entity opens a new factory and receives a government grant of $15,000 in respect of capital equipment costing $100,000. It depreciates all plant and machinery at 20% pa straight-line.

Show the statement of profit or loss and statement of financial position extracts in respect of the grant in the first year under both methods.

Solution

Method 1: Deduct from asset

Statement of profit or loss extract

	$
Depreciation (below)	(17,000)

Statement of financial position extract

	$
Non-current assets:	
Plant & machinery (100,000 – 15,000)	85,000
Accumulated depreciation (85,000 × 20%)	(17,000)
	68,000

Method 2: Treat grant as deferred income

Statement of profit or loss extract

	$
Depreciation (below)	(20,000)
Government grant credit (W1)	3,000

Statement of financial position extract

	$
Non-current assets:	
Plant & machinery	100,000
Accumulated depreciation (100,000 × 20%)	(20,000)
	80,000
Non-current liabilities	
Government grant (12,000 (W1) – 3,000 (current liability))	9,000
Current liabilities	
Government grant (15,000 × 20%)	3,000

(W1) **Government grant deferred income**

	$		$
Transfer to profit or loss (15,000 × 20%)	3,000	Grant cash received	15,000
Balance c/f	12,000		
	15,000		15,000

Test your understanding 1 – Capital grants

Timco opens a new factory and receives a government grant of $50,000 in respect of capital equipment costing $200,000. It depreciates all plant and machinery at 20% pa straight-line.

Required:

Record the double entries and show the statement of profit or loss and statement of financial position extracts in respect of the grant in the first year under both methods.

Repayment of grants

In some cases grants may need to be repaid if the conditions of the grant are breached. For example, the grant was given to produce 100 extra jobs in two years and this doesn't happen.

Revenue grants:

- Reduce deferred income, if any, and recognise the balance of the repayment immediately as an expense.

For example: An entity has a balance on the deferred income account of $10,000 relating to the balance of a grant given to them in order to produce 100 extra jobs. Due to a downturn in the economic climate the entity only managed to produce 50 extra jobs and the government asks for a repayment of $11,000. The following entries will be required:

Dr Deferred income	$10,000
Dr Statement of profit or loss	$1,000
Cr Bank	$11,000

Capital grants:

- Netting off method – increase the carrying value of the asset by the repayment amount and recognise any cumulative depreciation that should have been charged to the statement of profit or loss or
- Deferred income method – reduce deferred income and recognise any balance of repayment to the statement of profit or loss immediately as an expense.

Dr Deferred income/Non-current asset	X
Dr Statement of profit or loss	X
Cr Bank	X

Test your understanding 2 – Repayment of grants

On 1 January 20X1 an entity received a government grant of $120,000 conditional of employing 100 extra workforce over the next six years. At 31 December 20X4 changes in the economic climate suggested that this may not be possible and the government have asked for repayment of 70% of the grant.

Required:

Prepare the double entries required to record this repayment.

3 IAS 40 Investment Property

IAS 40 Definition

Investment property is land or a building held to earn rentals, or for capital appreciation or both, rather than for use in the entity or for sale by the entity in the ordinary course of business.

Owner-occupied property is excluded from the definition of investment property.

Accounting treatment

Investment properties should initially be measured at cost, which will include directly attributable expenditure such as professional fees and transaction costs.

IAS 40 then gives a choice between the following:

- a cost model
- a fair value model.

Once the model is chosen it should be used for all investment properties

Cost model

Under the cost model the asset should be accounted for in line with the cost model laid out in IAS 16. An entity that chooses the cost model must disclose the fair value of its investment property.

Fair value model

- the asset is revalued to fair value at the end of each year
- the gain or loss is shown directly in the statement of profit or loss
- no depreciation is charged on the asset.

Fair value is normally established by reference to current prices on an active market for properties in the same location and condition.

Test your understanding 3 – Investment properties

Celine, a manufacturing entity, purchases a property for $1 million on 1 January 20X1 for its investment potential. The land element of the cost is believed to be $400,000, and the buildings element is expected to have a useful life of 50 years. At 31 December 20X1, local property indices suggest that the fair value of the property has risen to $1.1 million.

Required:

Show how the property would be presented in the financial statements as at 31 December 20X1 if Celine adopts:

(a) the cost model

(b) the fair value model.

Test your understanding 4 – Practice questions

(1) A manufacturing entity receives a grant of $3million when it creates 50 jobs. $1.5m is payable when the figure is reached with the remaining $1.5m payable at the end of 4 years should the 50 jobs still be in existence. At the end of year one, 50 jobs have been created and there is reasonable assurance that the employment levels will be maintained when reached.

What is the deferred income balance at the end of the second year?

A nil

B $0.75million

C $1.5 million

D $2.25million

(2) On 1st January 20X1, Sky received £2m from the local government on the condition that they employ at least 100 staff each year for the next 4 years. On this date, it was virtually certain that Sky would meet these requirements. However, due to an economic downturn and reduced consumer demand, after one year, Sky no longer needed to employ anymore staff and the conditions of the grant required full repayment.

What should be recorded in the financial statements?

A Reduce deferred income balance by $1,500,000

B Reduce deferred income by $1,500,000 and recognise a loss in the financial statements of $500,000

C Reduce deferred income by $2,000,000

D Reduce deferred income by $2,000,000 and a gain in the financial statements of $500,000

(3) An entity purchased an investment property on 1 January 20X3 for a cost of $3.5m. The property had a UEL of 50 years, with no residual value and at 31 December 20X5 had a fair value of $4.2m. On 1 January 20X6 the property was sold for net proceeds of $4m.

Calculate the profit or loss on disposal under both the cost and FV model.

A Cost: $0.71m FV: ($0.20m)

B Cost: $0.2m FV $0.2m

C Cost $0.5m FV ($0.20m)

D Cost $0.71m FV: $0.05m

(4) **Which of the following properties would be classified as an investment property**:

A A stately home used for executive training but which is no longer required and is now being held for resale

B Purchased land for investment potential. Planning permission has not been obtained for building construction of any kind

C A new office building used by an insurance entity as its head office which was purchased specifically in the centre of a major city in order to exploit its capital gains potential

D A property held to lease under a finance lease

(5) An investment property was purchased by Amit on 1 January 20X9 for $200,000. By the year end the FV of the property had risen to $300,000, and it had a remaining useful economic life of 10 years. Amit measures its investment properties under the FV model.

What values would go through the statement of profit or loss in the year?

A Gain: $100,000 and Depreciation $30,000

B Gain: $0 and Depreciation of $30,000

C Gain: $100,000 and Depreciation of 0

D Gain: $100,000 and Depreciation of $30,000

4 Summary Diagram

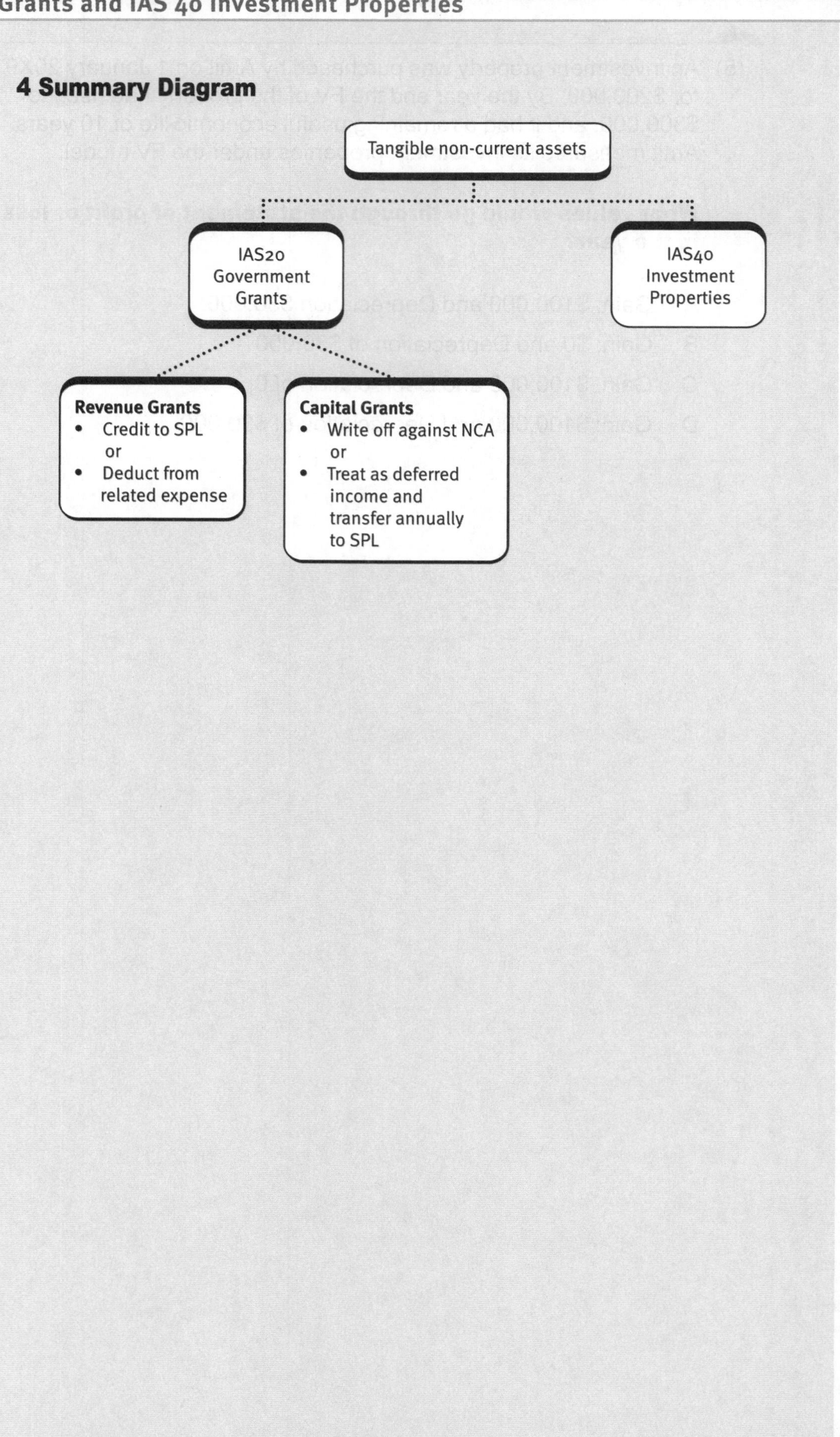

Test your understanding answers

Test your understanding 1 – Capital grants

Method 1: Deduct from asset

(1) Record the asset.

Dr Non-current asset	$200,000
Cr Bank	$200,000

(2) Record the grant.

Dr Bank	$50,000
Cr Non-current asset	$50,000

(3) Calculate the depreciation.

Depreciation expense ($200,000 – $50,000) × 20% = $30,000

Dr Depreciation expense	$30,000
Cr Accumulated depreciation	$30,000

Statement of profit or loss extract

	$
Depreciation expense	30,000

Statement of financial position extract

	$
Non-current assets:	
Plant & machinery (200,000 – 50,000)	150,000
Accumulated depreciation (150,000 × 20%)	(30,000
	120,000

Method 2: Treat grant as deferred income

(1) **Record the asset.**

Dr Non-current asset	$200,000
Cr Bank	$200,000

(2) Record the grant.

Dr Bank	$50,000
Cr Deferred income	$50,000

(3) Calculate the depreciation.

Depreciation expense $40,000 ($200,000 × 20%)

Dr Depreciation expense	$40,000
Cr Accumulated depreciation	$40,000

(4) **Release the grant.**

Grant $10,000 ($50,000 × 20%)

Dr Deferred income	$10,000
Cr Statement of profit or loss	$10,000

Statement of profit or loss extract

	$
Depreciation expense	(40,000)
Government grant credit (W1)	10,000

Statement of financial position extract

	$
Non-current assets:	
Plant & machinery	200,000
Accumulated depreciation (200,000 × 20%)	(40,000)
	160,000
Non-current liabilities	
Government grant (40,000 (W1) – 10,000 (current liability))	30,000
Current liabilities	
Government grant (50,000 × 20%)	10,000

(W1) **Government grant deferred income**

	$		$
Transfer to profit or loss (50,000 × 20%)	10,000	Bank	50,000
Balance c/f	40,000		
	50,000		50,000

Test your understanding 2 – Repayment of grants

This is an example of a revenue grant and therefore, the entity would have originally recorded:

Dr Bank	$120,000
Cr Deferred income	$120,000

Each year the entity would release 1/6 of the grant to the statement of profit or loss = $120,000/6 = $20,000 p.a

As at 31 December 20X4 (4 year's later) the entity would have released 4 × $20,000 = $80,000 to the statement of profit or loss and therefore have a balance on the deferred income account of $40,000.

The grant repayable is $120,000 × 70% = $84,000

The accounting entries will be:

Dr Deferred income	$40,000
Dr Statement of profit or loss (balance)	$44,000
Cr Bank	$84,000

Test your understanding 3 – Investment properties

(a) Cost model

Depreciation in the year is = $12,000 ($1,000,000 – land $400,000)/50

Therefore:

- in the statement of profit or loss, there will be a depreciation charge of $12,000
- in the statement of financial position, the property will be shown at a CV of $1,000,000 – $12,000 = $988,000.

(b) Fair value model

- In the statement of financial position, the property will be shown at its fair value of $1.1 million.
- In the statement of profit or loss, there will be a gain of $0.1 million representing the fair value adjustment.
- No depreciation is charged.

Test your understanding 4 – Practice questions

(1) C – $3,000,000 will be credited to the statement of profit or loss over the 4 year grant period at a rate of $750,000 pa. Therefore, at the end of year two $1,500,000 will have been released to the SPL and therefore a balance of $1,500,000 will remain in deferred income.

(2) B – When a revenue grant must be repaid we must remove the balance of deferred income account and charge the difference in the repayment to the SPL. $2,000,000 will be credited to the statement of profit or loss over the 4 year grant period at a rate of $500,000 pa. Therefore, at the end of year one $500,000 will have been released to the SPL and therefore a balance of $1,500,000 will remain in deferred income. This must be removed by debiting the account. The accounting entries to make the repayment will be debit deferred income $1,500,000, credit bank $2,000,000 and debit SPL $500,000.

(3) A – Under the cost model the property will be depreciated over 50 years for 3 years up to the date of disposal. Therefore, at the disposal date the carrying value would have been $3.5m – ($3.5/50 × 3 years) = $3.29m and the profit on disposal $0.71m ($4m – $3.29). Under the fair value model the property will not be depreciated hence the loss on disposal would be $0.2m (($4m – $4.2m).

(4) B

(5) C – Under the fair value model the property will not be depreciated hence the gain on valuation would be $100,000 ($300,000 – $200,000).

chapter

16

IAS 2, 8, 10, 34 and IFRS 8

Chapter learning objectives

On completion of their studies students should be able to:

- Explain and apply the accounting rules contained in IASs dealing with:
  - inventories
  - accounting policies, changes in estimates and errors
  - events after the reporting period
  - interim financial reporting
  - operating segments

1 Session content

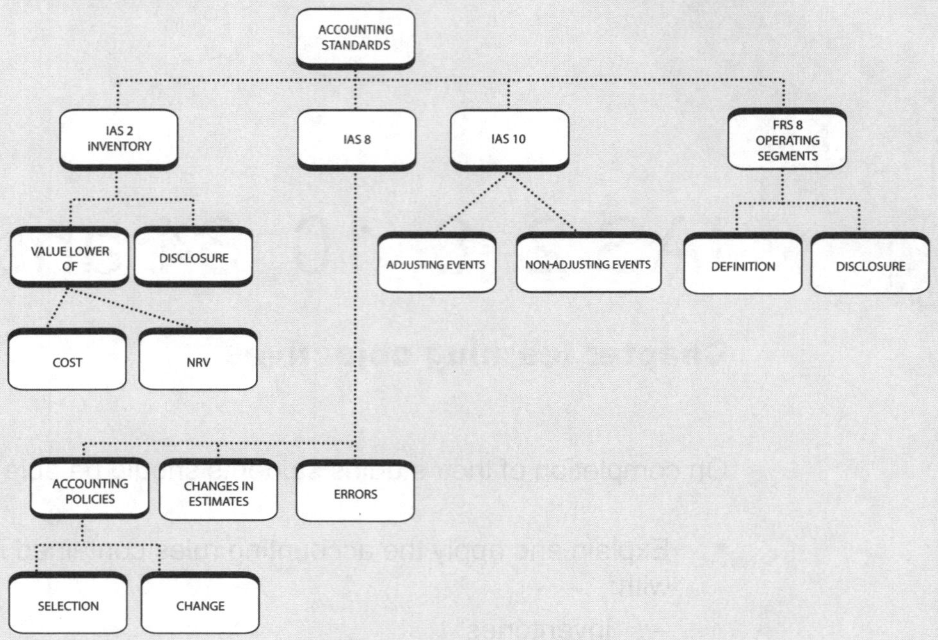

2 IAS 2 Inventories

Inventories are assets that are:

- held for sale
- in the process of production
- materials that will be used in the production process

Measurement of inventories

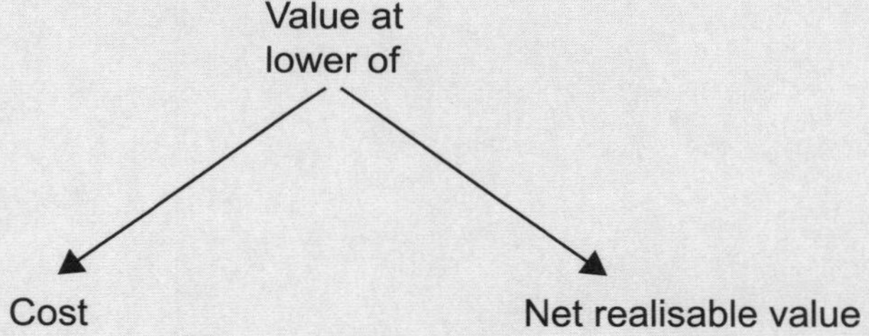

Cost of purchase, costs of conversion and costs to bring inventory to present location and condition.

Costs of conversion may include production overheads. These should be allocated based on normal production levels.

Estimated selling prices less costs to completion less costs to sell.

Costs not included in inventory

Examples of costs that should not be included in inventory are:

- abnormal amounts of wasted materials, labour, or other production costs;
- storage costs
- administration costs that do not contribute to bringing the inventories to their present location and condition
- selling and distribution costs

These costs should be treated as expenses against profit in the period that they arise.

Determining cost

Costs of purchase include the purchase price, import duties, handling costs and other costs directly connected with the acquisition of the goods.

Costs of conversion include costs directly related to the units being produced, e.g. direct labour costs, allocation of fixed and variable overhead costs incurred in production.

Variable production overheads are those indirect costs of production that vary directly with the volume produced, e.g. heat, light and power.

Fixed production overheads are those indirect costs of production that do not vary directly with the volume produced and remain constant regardless of the number of units produced, e.g. depreciation of machinery, factory administration costs.

Finance costs can be included if the requirements of IAS 23 Borrowing Costs are satisfied (see Chapter 13 for more detail on IAS 23).

Allocation of overheads

The allocation of fixed production overheads should be based on the normal capacity of the business. Any excess overheads due to inefficiencies or production problems should be treated as an expense in the period that they occur.

Illustration 1 – Calculation of the cost of inventory

The following costs relate to a unit of inventory:

Cost of raw materials	$1.00
Direct labour	$0.50

During the year $60,000 of fixed production overheads were incurred.

8,000 units were produced during the year which is lower than the normal level of 10,000 units. This was as a result of a fault with some machinery which resulted in 2,000 units having to be scrapped.

At the year-end, 700 units are in closing inventory.

Required:

What is the cost of closing inventory?

Solution

Production overheads should be allocated based on the normal level of production, i.e. 10,000 units.

$60,000/10,000 units = $6.00 per unit.

Cost per unit:

	$
Raw materials	1.00
Direct labour	0.50
Production overheads	6.00
Total cost per unit	7.50

Cost of 700 units in closing inventory = 700 × $7.50 = $5,250.

3 Calculation of costs

Inventory should be valued at cost – either the actual cost of an item (unit cost), or, if there are a large number of items in inventory which makes this impractical, a reasonable approximation to actual cost should be used. The most common approximations are:

(1) First in first out (FIFO). The closing inventory is assumed to consist of the latest purchases, i.e. oldest inventory is sold first. This means the closing inventory will be valued at the most recent purchase prices.

(2) Average cost. The weighted average cost is calculated by taking the total purchase price of all units purchased in the period divided by the total number of units purchased in the period. This can be calculated using periodic or a continuous method – see illustration 2 for more detail

Illustration 2 – Calculation of the cost of inventory

Calculation of the cost of inventory using FIFO and average cost

The following purchases and sales took place in Tyrone during the first four days of June:

Day 1 Opening inventory nil
Day 1 Purchase 200 units at $15 per unit
Day 2 Purchase 100 units at $18 per unit
Day 3 Sales of 250 units at $30 per unit
Day 4 Purchase 150 units at $20 per unit

Required:

Calculate the cost of inventory at the end of day 4 for Tyrone using:

(a) the FIFO method;

(b) the average cost method.

Solution

(a) **FIFO method**

Total purchases = 200 + 100 + 150 = 450 units

Sales = 250 units

Closing inventory = 450 – 250 = 200 units

FIFO method assumes the oldest inventory is sold first, therefore the 200 units remaining must be from the most recent purchases on day 4 (150 units) and the balance from the day 2 purchases (50 units).

Cost:

50 × $18 =	$900
150 × $20 =	$3,000
	$3,900

Total cost of closing inventory = $3,900

(b) **Average cost method**

Total purchases = 200 + 100 + 150 = 450 units

Total cost of purchases =

200 × $15 =	$3,000
100 × $18 =	$1,800
150 × $20 =	$3,000
	$7,800

Weighted average cost = $7,800/450 units = $17.33 per unit

Total cost of closing inventory = 200 units × $17.33 = $3,467

Note: An alternative approach could be to calculate the average cost after each transaction, i.e. after day 2 total purchases $4,800/total 300 units = cost of $16. After the sale has taken place this would leave 50 units in inventory valued at $16 per unit = $800. This would then be added to additional purchases to calculate future average costs. Therefore, on day 4, purchases of $3,000 would be added to $800 = $3,800/total units of 200 = cost of $19 per unit. This would result in a higher closing inventory value of $3,800.

Illustration 3 – Inventory valuation

Value the following items of inventory.

(a) Materials costing $12,000 bought for processing and assembly for a profitable special order. Since buying these items, the cost price has fallen to $10,000.

(b) Equipment constructed for a customer for an agreed price of $18,000. This has recently been completed at a cost of $16,800. It has now been discovered that, in order to meet certain regulations, further work with an extra cost of $4,200 will be required. The customer has accepted partial responsibility and agreed to meet half of the extra cost.

Solution

(a) Value at $12,000. $10,000 is irrelevant as this is the replacement cost. IAS 2 states value at lower of cost and NRV. The order is profitable and therefore NRV must be higher than cost.

(b) Value at NRV, i.e. $15,900 as below cost,

NRV = contract price of $18,000 – the entity's share of costs to complete $2,100 = $15,900.

Original cost = $16,800.

4 Disclosure

The main disclosure requirements of IAS 2 are:

- Accounting policy adopted, including the cost formula used.
- Total carrying amount, classified as follows:

	$
Raw materials	X
Work in progress	X
Finished goods	X
	X

This would be disclosed in a note to the financial statements. The total amount of closing inventory will be shown as a current asset on the statement of financial position and a reduction to the cost of sales in the statement of profit or loss.

- Amount of inventories carried at NRV.
- Amount of inventories recognised as an expense during the period.
- Details of circumstances that have led to the write-down of inventories to their NRV.

5 IAS 8 Accounting Policies, Changes in Accounting Estimates and Errors

IAS 8 governs the following topics:

- selection of accounting policies
- changes in accounting policies
- changes in accounting estimates
- correction of prior period errors

Accounting policies

Accounting policies are the principles, bases, conventions, rules and practices applied by an entity which specify how the effects of transactions and other events are reflected in the financial statements.

Accounting policies should be selected and applied so as to comply with the requirements of IFRSs.

If however, there are no specific policies for a particular transaction, the accounting policy should be developed so as to meet the following objectives:

- Relevant to the economic decision-making needs of users.
- Reliable, i.e.
  - report a faithful representation
  - report the economic substance of transactions in preference to legal form
  - neutral
  - prudent
  - complete
- Entities should consider IFRSs that deal with similar and related issues. They should also consider the definitions, recognition criteria and measurement concepts contained in the conceptual framework.

Changes in accounting policies

Selected policies should be applied consistently as far as possible.

Changes should only be made if:

- **required by an IFRS**
  e.g. New accounting standard

  For many years proposed dividends were treated as liabilities in the statement of financial position as adjusting events after the reporting date. IAS 10 now treats these as non-adjusting events and they are no longer liabilities but instead appear in the notes. In the year that the change was introduced, all entities had a "change in accounting policy".

- **the change improves the relevance and reliability of financial statements**
  e.g. Provision of more relevant and reliable information

  When an entity is using a manual accounting system for valuing year end inventory they often do this on a FIFO basis. However, when they invest in a computerised system they often switch to the weighted average cost method. This is because the software chosen, tailor made for their industry, is only capable of valuing inventory under the weighted average cost method, as this is the standard industry method. In this case a change in accounting policy is justified because it results in financial statements providing reliable and more relevant information, which is actually more comparable to other entities within the industry to which the entity belongs.

A change in accounting policy should be applied retrospectively, i.e. as if the new policy had always applied. Any resulting adjustment should be reported as an adjustment to the opening balance of retained earnings. Comparative information should be restated.

Changes in accounting policies

A change in accounting policy could occur because there has been a change in:

- recognition, e.g. an expense is now recognised as an asset
- presentation, e.g. depreciation is now classified as cost of sales rather than an administration expense
- measurement basis, e.g. stating assets should be valued as replacement cost rather than historical cost

Revaluations are **not** treated as a change in accounting policy but dealt within accordance with specific rules under IAS 16.

Illustration 4 – Change in accounting policy

During 20X1 Bowie changed its accounting policy with respect to the treatment of borrowing costs that are directly attributable to the construction of a hydro-electric power station, which is in the course of construction for use by Bowie.

In previous periods, Bowie had expensed such costs, in accordance with the allowed treatment in IAS 23 Borrowing Costs. IAS 23 now states Bowie must capitalise these costs.

Bowie had borrowing costs in 20X0 amounting to $2,600 and $5,200 in periods prior to 20X0.

Bowie's accounting records for 20X1 and 20X0 show:

	20X1	**20X0**
	$	$
Profit from operations	30,000	18,000
Finance cost	–	(2,600)
Profit before tax	30,000	15,400
Income tax	(9,000)	(4,620)
Profit for the period	21,000	10,780

In 20X0 opening retained earnings were $20,000 and closing retained earnings were $30,780. The income tax rate is 30%.

Required:

Show how the change in accounting policy will be recorded in the financial statements for the year ended 31 December 20X1. Comparatives should also be prepared.

Solution

Statement of profit or loss (extract)

	20X1	20X0
	$	$
Operating profit	30,000	18,000
Finance cost	–	–
PBT	30,000	18,000
Income tax	(9,000)	(5,400)
Profit for the period	21,000	12,600

Statement of changes in equity (extract)

	20X1	20X0
	$	$
Retained earnings b/d	30,780	20,000
Restatement due to change in accounting policy on interest costs (see note below)	5,460	3,640
	36,240	23,640
Profit for the period	21,000	12,600
Retained earnings c/d	57,240	36,240

Notes to financial statements (extract)

During 20X1 the entity changed its accounting policy for the treatment of interest costs. Previously the costs were written off as expenses as they were incurred but the costs are now capitalised where they relate to qualifying assets. The change in accounting policy has been accounted for retrospectively via a prior period adjustment. The new accounting policy is consistent with generally accepted accounting practice and increases the relevance and reliability of reported figures.

Explanatory note:

The adjustment in respect of costs capitalised prior to 20X0 is dealt with as a restatement to opening retained earnings in the 20X0 Statement of Changes in Equity. The $5,200 net of 30% tax is shown as an adjustment.

The adjustment of costs expensed during 20X0 is dealt with in the restated 20X0 comparative accounts.

The adjustment to 20X1 opening retained earnings comprises the overall effect of the 20X0 and prior adjustments, net of tax ($2,600 + $5,200) × 70%.

We must remember to consider whether the change in policy will effect profit for the year – if this is the case it will also effect the tax charge. Remember to read the question, as sometimes you will be told to ignore the tax effect.

Test your understanding 1 – Accounting policy

Wimbledon has always valued its inventories on the FIFO basis using a manual system. During 20X1 the entity purchased a computerised system and discovered that most industry equivalent entities use a weighted average cost method. The statements of profit or loss prior to the adjustments are:

	20X1	**20X0**
	$000	$000
Revenue	500	400
Cost of sales	(200)	(160)
Gross profit	300	240
Administrative expenses	(120)	(100)
Distribution costs	(50)	(30)
Profit from operations	130	110

The retained earnings balance as at the beginning of 20X0 was $600,000 and the closing retained earnings balance was $710,000.

The impact on inventory due to the change in policy was determined as:

Inventory as at 31 December 20W9: an increase of $20,000.
Inventory as at 31 December 20X0: an increase of $30,000.
Inventory as at 31 December 20X1: an increase of $40,000.

Required:

Show how the change in accounting policy will be recorded in the financial statements for the year 20X1. Comparatives should also be prepared. Assume that the adjustments have no effect on taxation charges.

Changes in accounting estimates

When preparing financial statements, inherent uncertainties result in estimates having to be made and subsequently, these estimates may need to be revised.

Distinguishing between changes in accounting policies and accounting estimates may be difficult. In these circumstances, the change is to be treated as a change in an accounting estimate.

Changes in accounting estimates should be accounted for prospectively. This means that the revised estimate should be included in the calculation of net profit or loss for the current period and future periods if appropriate.

Illustration 5 – Change in accounting estimate

An asset was purchased three years ago on 1 July 20X0 for $100,000 at which time it was thought that the asset had no residual value and a useful economic life of ten years. The directors have decided that as a result of using the asset more than was originally planned the remaining useful economic life is only five years as at 1 July 20X3. The asset is depreciated on the straight line basis.

Required:

Show how the change in accounting estimate will be recorded in the financial statements for the year ended 30 June 20X4.

Solution

The original depreciation was:

$$\frac{\text{Cost} - \text{residual value}}{\text{Useful economic life}} = \frac{\$100{,}000 - \text{Nil}}{10} = \$10{,}000 \text{ pa}$$

The asset has been depreciated for 3 years when the change of useful economic life occurs and therefore the carrying amount would be:

Cost $100,000 – (3 × $10,000) = $70,000

The carrying amount at the date of the change is the carrying amount on the statement of financial position for the asset and must therefore be used to recalculate the new depreciation charge.

$$\frac{\text{Carrying amount} - \text{residual value}}{\text{Useful economic life}} = \frac{\$70{,}000 - \text{Nil}}{5} = \$14{,}000\text{pa}$$

Statement of financial position(extract)

	20X4
	$
Cost	100,000
Accumulative depreciation	44,000
Carrying amount	56,000

Notes to financial statements (extract)

During 20X4 the entity changed its accounting estimate for economic useful life of an asset. Previously the asset had a useful economic life of ten years but due to the asset being used more than originally planned, the life has reduced to five years as at 1 July 20X3. This resulted in the annual depreciation charge increasing from $10,000 pa to $14,000 pa.

Explanatory note:

The adjustments are only required to future depreciation charges from the date of the change, i.e. 1 July 20X3. We do not need to change the depreciation already charged, so no adjustments will be made to retained earnings b/fwd and the comparatives will not be changed. Therefore, the SOFP reflects the historical depreciation of $30,000 charged upto the date of the change plus the new charge for the current year of $14,000.

Changes in accounting estimates

Examples of changes in accounting estimates are changes in:

- the useful lives of non-current assets
- the residual values of non-current assets
- the method of depreciating non-current assets
- warranties and provisions

Errors

Prior period errors are omissions from, and misstatements in, the entity's financial statements for one or more periods arising from a failure to use, or misuse of, reliable information that:

- was available when financial statements for these periods were authorised for issue; and
- could reasonably be expected to have been obtained and taken into account in the preparation and presentation of those financial statements.

Prior period errors should be corrected retrospectively. This means that, similarly to a change in accounting policy, any adjustment resulting from correction of the error should be reported as an adjustment to the opening balance of retained earnings. Comparative information should be restated.

Errors are therefore treated in the same way as accounting policy changes.

Fraud is effectively treated as an error.

Illustration 6 – Correction of prior period error

During 20X1 Beta discovered that certain products that had been sold during 20X0 were incorrectly included in inventory at 31 December 20X0 at $6,500.

Beta's accounting records show the following results for 20X1 and 20X0:

	20X1	20X0
	$	$
Revenue	104,000	73,500
Cost of sales	(86,500)	(53,500)
Profit before tax	17,500	20,000
Income tax expense	(5,250)	(6,000)
Profit for the period	12,250	14,000

In 20X0 opening retained earnings was $20,000 and closing retained earnings was $34,000. The income tax rate is 30%.

Required:

Show how the correction of the prior period error will be recorded in the financial statements for the year ended 31 December 20X1. Comparatives should also be prepared.

Solution

Statements of profit or loss (extract)

	20X1	20X0
	$	$
Revenue	104,000	73,500
Cost of sales	(80,000)	(60,000)
PBT	24,000	13,500
Income taxes	(7,200)	(4,050)
Profit for the period	16,800	9,450

Statement of changes in equity (extract)

	20X1	20X0
	$	$
Retained earnings b/d	34,000	20,000
Correction of error (see note below)	(4,550)	–
Retained earnings b/d	29,450	20,000
Profit for the period (as above)	16,800	9,450
Retained earnings c/d	46,250	29,450

Notes to financial statements (extract)

Some products that had been sold during 20X0 had been incorrectly included in inventory at the year end 31 December 20X0 amounting to $6,500. The financial statements for the year ending 31 December 20X0 have been restated to correct this error.

Explanatory note:

The correction is made as follows:

Dr cost of sales (closing inventory)	$6,500
Cr inventory	$6,500

This happens in the 20X0 accounts and has a knock-on effect on the opening inventory of 20X1.

The adjustment to 20X1 opening retained earnings is net of tax.

Test your understanding 2 – Error

During 20X1 Howie discovered that inventory had been stolen by an employee in the year to 31 December 20X0, resulting in the closing inventory balance being over-stated by $2,500.

Howie's accounting records show the following results for 20X1 and 20X0:

	20X1	20X0
	$	$
Revenue	52,100	48,300
Cost of sales	(33,500)	(30,200)
Profit before tax	18,600	18,100
Income tax expense	(4,600)	(4,300)
Profit for the year	14,000	13,800

In 20X0 opening retained earnings was $11,200 and closing retained earnings was $25,000. Assume the adjustment has no effect on the tax charge.

Required:

Show how the correction of the error will be recorded in the financial statements for the year ended 31 December 20X1. Comparatives should also be prepared.

6 IAS 10 Events after the Reporting Period

The purpose of IAS 10 is to define to what extent events that occur after the reporting period should be recognised in the financial statements.

It is a fundamental principle of accounting that regard must be had to all available information when preparing financial statements. This must include relevant events occurring after the reporting period, up to the date on which the financial statements are authorised for issue. The objective of IAS 10 is to:

- define the extent to which different types of events after the reporting period are to be reflected in financial statements
- define when an entity should adjust its financial statements for events after the reporting period;

- set out the disclosures that the entity should provide about the date the statement of financial position was authorised
- specify disclosures required about events arising after the end of the reporting period

IAS 10 defines an event after the end of the reporting period as 'events after the end of the reporting period are those events, favourable and unfavourable, that occur between the end of the reporting period and the date when the financial statements are authorised for issue.'

IAS 10 identifies two main types of events after the reporting period: adjusting events and non-adjusting events.

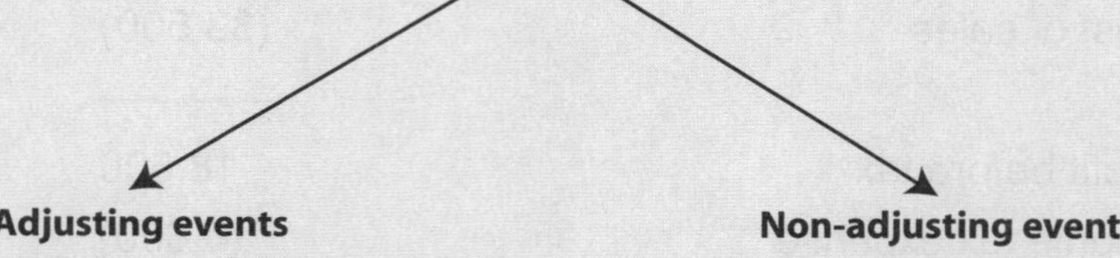

Adjusting events

'Those events which provide evidence of conditions that existed at the reporting date'

FS should be adjusted to reflect the adjusting event

Non-adjusting events

'Those that are indivative of conditions that arose after the reporting date'

FS should not be adjusted to reflect non-adjusting events

Non-adjusting events should be disclosed if they affect users' understanding of the FS

Dividends

A dividend will first be proposed by directors, then declared (confirmed) and then paid. Ordinary dividends should only be accounted for when declared, whereas preference dividends are always accrued (see chapter 11 for more detail on accounting entries).

Equity dividends declared after the reporting period should not be recognised as a liability at the reporting date but should be disclosed by note, provided they are declared before the financial statements are authorised for issue .

Going concern

If an event after the reporting date indicates that the entity is no longer a going concern, the financial statements for the current period should not be prepared on the going concern basis.

Disclosure

A material event after the end of the reporting period should be disclosed (by note) where it is a non-adjusting event of such importance that its non-disclosure would affect the ability of users of financial statements to reach a proper understanding of the financial position.

The note should disclose

- The nature of the event.
- An estimate of the financial effect, or a statement that it is not practicable to make such an estimate. The estimate should be made before taking account of taxation, with an explanation of the taxation implications where necessary for a proper understanding of the financial position.
- The date the directors approve financial statements. The date on which the financial statements are authorised for issue should be disclosed.

Examples of adjusting and non-adjusting events

The key is to look at whether the event gives evidence of conditions that existed at the reporting date. If this is so, and the financial statements have not yet been approved by the directors, then an adjustment will be required.

Examples of adjusting events would be:

- Evidence that inventory is incorrectly valued, i.e. NRV is less than cost.
- Evidence that a customer has gone into liquidation.
- Evidence of fraud or error.
- Completion of a court case entered into before the reporting date.
- Completion of an insurance claim relating to an event that occurred prior to the year-end.
- Determination after year end, of the sale or purchase price of assets sold or purchased before year end.

If the evidence shows conditions that have arisen since the reporting date, then no adjustment would be made.

Examples of non-adjusting events would be:

- Acquisition or disposal of a subsidiary after the year end.
- Announcements of a plan to discontinue an operation.
- Destruction of an asset by a fire or flood after the reporting date.
- Announcements of a plan to restructure.
- Share capital transactions after the reporting date.
- Changes in taxation or exchange rates after the reporting date.
- Strikes or other labour disputes

Illustration 7 – Events after the reporting period

Shortly after the reporting date, 31/12/X0, a major credit customer of an entity went into liquidation and it is expected that little or none of $12,000 debt will be recoverable. $10,000 of the debt relates to sales made before the year end.

In the 20X0 financial statements the whole of the debt has been written off but one of the directors has pointed out that, as the liquidation is an event after the reporting date, the debt should not have been written off but disclosure made by a note.

Advise whether the director is correct.

Solution

The liquidation of the customer is treated as an adjusting event. Only $10,000 debt existed at the reporting date.

Under IAS 10 only the existing debt should be written off in the 20X0 financial statements. The remaining $2,000 did not exist at the reporting date and should be written off in the 20X1 financial statements.

Test your understanding 3 – Events after the reporting period

Classify each of the following events, which all occurred after the reporting period ,as adjusting or non-adjusting.

	Adjusting event	Non-adjusting event
Insolvency of a major customer		
Decline in market value of investments		
Loss of non-current assets/inventory due to fire or flood		
Discovery of fraud/error showing that the FS were incorrect		
Announcement of plan to discontinue certain operations		
Evidence concerning the net realisable value of inventory being less than cost		
Resolution of a court case after the reporting date		

7 IAS 34 Interim Financial Reporting

IAS 34 sets out the principles that should be followed if an entity prepares an interim report and specifies the minimum content.

Interim financial reports are prepared for a period shorter than a full financial year. Entities may be required to prepare interim financial reports under local law or listing regulations.

You will not be required to prepare interim reports in your examination but should have an appreciation that this standard exists.

8 IFRS 8 Operating Segments

IFRS 8 requires an entity to disclose segment information to enable users of the financial statements to evaluate the nature and financial effect of business activities in which it engages and the economic environments in which it operates. Many entities produce a wide range of products and services, often in different countries. Further information on how the overall results of entities are made up from each of these operating segments will help the users of the financial statements.

The requirements of IFRS 8 must be applied by quoted entities. If non-quoted entities choose to report by segment they must comply with the requirements of IFRS 8.

Definitions

IFRS 8 defines an operating segment as a component of an entity:

(a) that engages in business activities from which it earns revenues and incurs expenses

(b) whose operating results are regularly reviewed by the entity's chief operating decision maker to make decisions about resources to be allocated to the segment and assess its performance

and

(c) for which discrete financial information is available

Identification of segments

A segment should be classified as a reportable segment if it contributes more than 10% of the total of any of the following:

- revenue (internal and external)
- profitable segments
- loss making segments
- assets

If, after allocating segments according to the 10% rule, the external revenue of reportable segments is less than 75% of the total revenue of the entity, additional segments will be classified as reportable segments even though they do not meet the 10% rule.

Disclosure

IFRS 8 requires the disclosure of the following:

- factors used to identify the entity's reportable segments, including the basis of segmentation (for example, whether operating segments are based on products or services or geographical areas)
- types of products and services from which each segment derives its revenue

For each reportable segment an entity should report:

- profit or loss
- revenues
- total assets
- total liabilities

Illustration 8 – Operating segments

Jimbo has five business segments which are currently reported in its financial statements. Jimbo is an international hotel group which reports to management on the basis of region. It does not currently report segmental information under IFRS 8 Operating Segments. The results of the regional segments for the year ended 31 May 20X9 are as follows:

	European	**Asia**	**Africa**	**Middle East**	**Others**	**Total**
	$m	**$m**	**$m**	**$m**	**$m**	**$m**
Revenue						
Internal	10	20	10	50	10	100
External	100	300	100	500	100	1100
Total	110	320	110	550	110	1200
Segmental profits	5	60	5	100	10	180
Segmental assets	150	800	50	1600	600	3200

Required:

Determine the entity's reportable operating segments using the information above.

Solution

The information can be analysed as follows:

	European	**Asia**	**African**	**Middle East**	**Others**	**Total**
	$m	**$m**	**$m**	**$m**	**$m**	**$m**
Revenue						
Internal	10	20	10	50	10	100
External	100	300	100	500	100	1100
Total	110	320	110	550	110	1200
% to total sales	**9.2%**	**26.7%**	**9.2%**	**45.7%**	**9.2%**	
Segmental profits	5	60	5	100	10	180
% to total profit	**2.8%**	**33.3%**	**2.8%**	**55.6%**	**5.5%**	
Segmental assets	150	800	50	1600	600	3200
% to total assets	**4.7%**	**25%**	**1.7%**	**50%**	**18.6%**	

Explanation:

The only segments that meet the 10% criteria are Asia and Middle East.

It is important to understand a segment does not have to be 10% of all of the criteria. To be recognised it can 10% of any of the criteria.

However, collectively external revenue is only 66.7% of the total revenue (Asia = 25% (300/1200) and Middle East = 41.7%(500/1200)).

Therefore, additional segments must also be reported to meet the 75% of revenue criteria, i.e. European segment as it is the next largest segment.

Test your understanding 4 – Practice questions

(1) Tracey's business sells three products – A, B and C. The following information was available at the year end:

	A	B	C
	$ per unit	$ per unit	$ per unit
Original cost	7	10	19
Estimated selling price	15	13	20
Selling and distribution costs	2	5	6
Units of inventory	20	25	15

The value of inventory at the year-end should be:

A $675

B $670

C $795

D $550

(2) Item XYZ has 150 items in inventory as at 31 March 20X1. The following alternative valuations have been found .

Which value should be used in the accounts at 31 March 20X1?

A Net realisable value $4,750

B Original cost $5,500

C Selling price $7,000

D Replacement cost $6,500

(3) **Which ONE of the following would be regarded as a change of accounting estimate according to IAS 8 Accounting Policies, Changes in Estimates and Errors?**

A An entity started capitalising borrowing costs for assets as required by IAS 23 Borrowing Costs. Borrowing costs had previously been charged to the statement of profit or loss.

B An entity started revaluing its properties, as allowed by IAS 16 Property, Plant and Equipment. Previously all property, plant and equipment had been carried at cost less accumulated depreciation.

C A material error in the inventory valuation methods caused closing inventory at 31 March 20X0 to be overstated by $900,000.

D An entity created a provision for irrecoverable debts of 2% of closing receivables but has decided that it should be increase to 5% to be more prudent .

(4) An entity has six segments A, B, C, D, E and F which account for 40%, 30%, 9%, 8%, 7% and 6% of total revenue respectively.

Which of the segments will be classified as reportable segments in accordance with IFRS 8 Operating Segments?

A All of them

B A, B, and D only

C A and B

D A, B and C

(5) Jackson's year end is 31 December 20X0. In February 20X1 a major customer went into liquidation and the directors' believe that they will not be able to recover the $450,000 owed to them.

How should this item be treated in the financial statements of Jackson for the year ended 31 December 20X0?

A The irrecoverable debt should be disclosed by note

B The financial statements are not affected

C The debt should be provided against

D The financial statements should be adjusted to write off the irrecoverable debt

(6) **Which of the following items are non-adjusting items per IAS 10 Events after the Reporting Period?**

(i) Changes in the rates of foreign exchange after the year-end.

(ii) Destruction of machinery by fire after the year-end.

(iii) Information regarding the value of inventory.

(iv) Plans for mergers and acquisitions.

(v) Insolvency of a customer who had a receivable balance at the year-end.

A (i), (ii) and (iv)

B (iii) and (v)

C (i), (iii) and (v)

D (ii), (iii) and (v)

(7) **Which of the following could be classified as an adjusting event occurring after the end of the reporting period:**

A A serious fire, occurring 1 month after the year-end, that damaged the sole production facility, causing production to cease for 3 months.

B One month after the year-end, a notification was received advising that a large receivables balance would not be paid as the customer was being wound up. No payments are expected from the customer.

C A large quantity of parts for a discontinued production line was discovered at the back of the warehouse during the year-end inventory count. The parts have no value except a nominal scrap value and need to be written off.

D The entity took delivery of a new machine from the USA in the last week of the financial year. It was discovered almost immediately afterwards that the entity supplying the machine had filed for bankruptcy and would not be able to honour the warranties and repair contract on the new machine. Because the machine was so advanced, it was unlikely that any local entity could provide maintenance cover.

(8) **Which of the following would require a retrospective adjustment under IAS 8?**

(i) A change in accounting policy on Non Current assets from historical cost to revaluations.

(ii) An entity decides to include depreciation within cost of sales where as previously it was included within administrative expenses.

(iii) A decision to change from weighted average to FIFO in valuing inventory.

(iv) A decision to change from reducing balance depreciation to straight line.

A (i) and (ii)

B (ii) and (iii)

C (iii) and (iv)

D (i) and (iv)

(9) **Which of the following situations would not require a prior year adjustment per IAS 8 Accounting Policies, Changes in Estimates and Errors?**

A A company overstated inventories by a material amount in last year's financial statements.

B A company has previously valued inventory using average cost. From now on it intends to use FIFO instead.

C A company has changed the way it calculates depreciation of plant, property and equipment from reducing balance method to straight line method.

D A new accounting standard has been issued that requires a company to change its accounting policy. The standard does not include specific transitional provisions applying to the change.

(10) **Which of the following would represent a change in accounting policy to be treated in accordance with IAS 8 Accounting policies, Changes in accounting estimates and errors?**

(i) A change in measurement of non-current assets from historical cost to fair value.

(ii) A change in measurement of depreciation from a 20 year life on a straight-line basis to a reducing balance basis using 20%.

(iii) A change of presentation where depreciation of an asset previously recognised in cost of sales is now to be recognised in administration expenses.

A All of the above

B (i) and (iii) only

C (i) only

D (iii) only

(11) The following material events took place after entity X's reporting date of 31/10/X1 but before the accounts were authorised:

– Ordinary dividends were approved by the shareholders in relation to the Financial Statements for the year ended 31/10/X1.

– The discovery of an error in relation to the year end inventory valuation.

Please state the correct accounting treatment:

A Dividends: Provide for dividend.
Error: Adjust accounts.

B Dividends: Disclose dividend.
Error: Adjust accounts.

C Dividends: Provide for dividend.
Error: Disclose error.

D Dividends: Disclose dividend.
Error: Disclose error.

(12) Bond Ltd has a 31st August year end and on 10th September the company received notification that one of their customers had gone into liquidation owing $30,000, $5,000 of which was from September sales.

Additionally on 10th October the company received $100,000 in insurance following a fire to their premises which occurred on 28th August.

What adjustments should take place to Bonds accounts under IAS 10 Events after the Reporting Period?

A Liquidation: $30,000.
Insurance: $Nil.

B Liquidation: $30,000.
Insurance: $100,000.

C Liquidation: $25,000.
Insurance: $Nil.

D Liquidation: $25,000.
Insurance: $100,000.

(13) **In accordance with IAS10 Events after the reporting period which of the following events, if any, should normally be classified as adjusting events?**

(i) The destruction by fire of a major non-current asset after the year-end.

(ii) The discovery of frauds which show that the financial statements were incorrect.

A (i) only

B (ii) only

C Both (i) and (ii)

D Neither

(14) An entities statement of profit or loss at 31 December 20X8 showed a profit before tax of $3,200,000. Early in 20X9, before the financial statements were authorised for issue, the following events took place.

A dividend was paid to ordinary shareholders of $2,600,000 which was proposed prior to the year-end.

A factory owned at the year end, with a carrying amount of $3,000,000, was severely damaged by a fire early in 20X9.

Inventory valued at a cost of $252,000 in the statement of financial position, was sold for $41,000 after the year-end due to smoke damage caused by the aforementioned fire.

A customer who owed $109,000 at the end of the reporting period went insolvent on 15 January owing a total of $117,000

In accordance with IAS 10 Events After the Reporting Period what is the correct profit for 20X8 after making the necessary adjustments for the above events?

A $491,000

B $2,880,000

C $3,091,000

D $3,200,000

(15) **Which of the following are non-adjusting items per IAS 10 Events after the Reporting Period?**

(i) Changes in the rates of foreign exchange

(ii) Destruction of machinery by fire

(iii) Information regarding the value of inventory at the year-end

(iv) Insolvency of a customer

A (i) and (ii)

B (i), (ii) and (iii)

C (ii) and (iv)

D (ii) only

9 Summary diagram

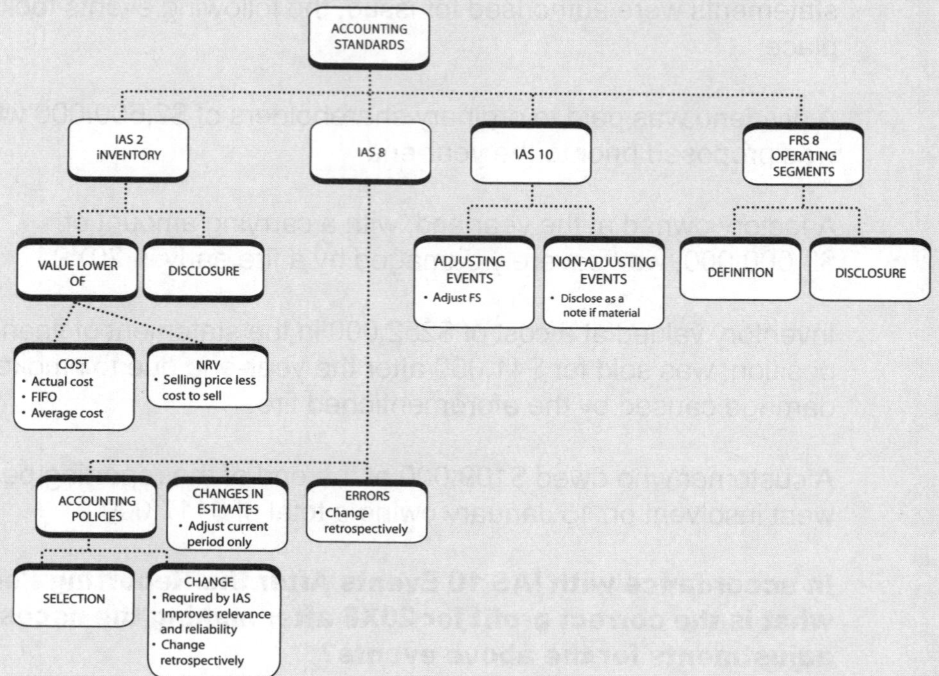
ACCOUNTING STANDARDS
IAS 2 INVENTORY
IAS 8
IAS 10
FRS 8 OPERATING SEGMENTS
VALUE LOWER OF
DISCLOSURE
ADJUSTING EVENTS
• Adjust FS
NON-ADJUSTING EVENTS
• Disclose as a note if material
DEFINITION
DISCLOSURE
COST
• Actual cost
• FIFO
• Average cost
NRV
• Selling price less cost to sell
ACCOUNTING POLICIES
CHANGES IN ESTIMATES
• Adjust current period only
ERRORS
• Change retrospectively
SELECTION
CHANGE
• Required by IAS
• Improves relevance and reliability
• Change retrospectively

Test your understanding answers

Test your understanding 1 – Accounting policy

Statements of profit or loss

	20X1	20X0
	$000	$000
Revenue	500	400
Cost of sales (W1)	(190)	(150)
Gross profit	310	250
Administration expenses	(120)	(100)
Distribution costs	(50)	(30)
Profit from operations	140	120

Statement of changes in equity (extract)

	20X1	20X0
	$000	$000
Retained earnings b/f	710	600
Restatement due to change in policy (note below) accounting policy	30	20
	740	620
Profit for the period	140	120
Retained earnings c/f	880	740

Notes to financial statements (extract)

During 20X1 the entity changed its accounting policy for the treatment of valuing inventory. Previously the inventory was valued using the FIFO method but due to the purchase of a new computer system is now valued using the weighted average cost method. The change in accounting policy has been accounted for retrospectively via a prior period adjustment. The new accounting policy is consistent with generally accepted accounting practice and increases the relevance and reliability of reported figures.

Explanatory note:

The adjustment in change in accounting policy prior to 20X0 is dealt with as a reserve movement in the 20X0 Statement of Changes in Equity.

The adjustment in change in accounting policy during 20X0 is dealt with in the 20X0 comparative accounts.

20X0 adjustment = prior to 20X0 = closing inventory increases by $20,000. This will decrease cost of sales and increase profit.

20X1 b/f = prior to 20X1 = opening inventory increases by $20,000 and closing inventory increases by $30,000 during 20X0. The net effect is profit will increase by $10,000 during 20X0. Therefore cumulatively the adjustment is now $20,000 (above) + $10,000 = $30,000

(W1) **Cost of sales adjustment**

	20X1	**20X0**
	$000	$000
Per original accounts	200	160
Opening inventory adjustment	30	20
Closing inventory adjustment	(40)	(30)
Per adjusted accounts	190	150

Test your understanding 2 – Error

Statements of profit or loss

	20X1	**20X0**
	$	$
Revenue	52,100	48,300
Cost of sales	(31,000)	(32,700)
Profit before tax	21,100	15,600
Income taxes	(4,600)	(4,300)
Profit for the period	16,500	11,300

Statement of changes in equity (extract)

	20X1	20X0
	$	$
Retained earnings b/d (as previously reported)	25,000	11,200
Correction of error (see note below)	(2,500)	–
Retained earnings b/d	22,500	11,200
Profit for the period (as above)	16,500	11,300
Retained earnings c/d	39,000	22,500

Notes to financial statements (extract)

Some products had been stolen during 20X0 and had been incorrectly included in inventory at the year end 31 December 20X0. The financial statements for the year ending 31 December 20X0 have been restated to correct this error.

Explanatory note:

The correction is made as follows:

Dr cost of sales (closing inventory)	$2,500
Cr inventory	$2,500

This happens in the 20X0 accounts and has a knock-on effect on the opening inventory of 20X1.

Test your understanding 3 – Events after the reporting period

Insolvency of a major customer	Adjusting event
Decline in market value of investments	Non-adjusting event
Loss of non-current assets/inventories due to fire/flood	Non-adjusting event
Discovery of fraud/error showing that the FS were incorrect	Adjusting event
Announcement of a plan to discontinue operations	Non-adjusting event
Evidence concerning the NRV of inventories	Adjusting event
Resolution of a court case	Adjusting event

Test your understanding 4 – Practice questions

(1) D

	A	**B**	**C**
Cost	7	10	19
NRV	13	8	14
Valuation	20 × 7 = 140	25 × 8 = 200	15 × 14 = 210

Total Valuation = 140 + 200 + 210 = 550

(2) A – IAS 2 states that inventory should be valued at the lower of cost or net realisable value.

(3) D

(4) D – Segments A and B only account for 70% of total revenues and therefore IFRS 8 would require C to be classified as a reportable segment even though it does not meet the 10% rule of revenue.

(5) D – This is an example of an adjusting event as per IAS 10.

(6) A

(7) B

(8) B – Option1 is outside the scope of IAS 8 and option 4 is an example of changes in estimates and not retrospective.

(9) C

(10) D – Option 1 is outside the scope of IAS 8 and option 2 is an example of an estimate.

(11) B – Dividends are only provided for when they are paid or declared at the reporting date, however, disclosure will be made if discovered prior to authorisation of the financial statements.

(12) D – The liquidation amounts can only be adjusted for the amount recoverable at the year-end, i.e. $25,000. The insurance money has not be received which relates to an event prior to the reporting date and must therefore be provided for at the year-end.

(13) B

(14) C – Profit of $3,200,000 must be adjusted for the adjusting event as per IAS 10, being insolvency of the customer $109,000 (amount owed at year-end). The fire and dividend are both treated as non-adjusting events.

(15) A

chapter

17

IAS 12 Income Taxes

Chapter learning objectives

On completion of their studies students should be able to:

- Explain and apply the accounting rules contained in IAS 12 for current taxation.
- Identify and account for under and over provisions.
- Prepare extracts to the financial statements for current taxation.

1 Session content

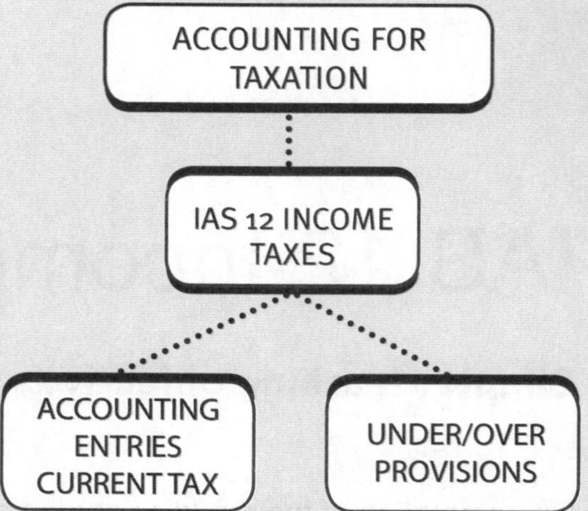

2 IAS 12 Income Taxes

IAS 12 covers the general principles of accounting for tax although tax systems may vary from country to country.

Tax consists of three elements:

- current tax expense
- over or under provisions in relation to the tax charges of the previous period
- deferred tax (outside of the scope of the F1 syllabus)

3 Current tax

Definitions

Current tax is the estimated amount of tax payable on the taxable profits of the entity for the period.

Taxable profits are the profits on which tax is payable, calculated in accordance with the rules of local tax authorities.

At the end of every accounting period, the entity will estimate the amount of tax payable in respect of the period. This estimate is normally recorded as a period end adjustment by making the following double entry:

Dr	Income tax expense (SPL)
Cr	Income tax liability (SOFP)

4 Under and over provisions

Definitions

In the following accounting period, the income tax will be paid. At this point, it will normally be discovered that the actual amount paid was over or under the estimate . Any over or under provision will then be recorded in this following accounting period as an adjustment to the income tax expense in the statement of profit or loss.

Illustration 1 – Under and over provisions

The following information is available for Happy :

	$
Income tax liability at 31 May 20X0	316,000
Income tax paid on 28 February 20X1	263,000
Income tax estimate for the year ended 31 May 20X1	383,500

Required:

Show the entries in the income tax account and the extracts from the financial statements for the year ended 31 May 20X1.

Solution

At 31 May 20X0 we had an opening liability for tax of $316,000. When we made the payment of $263,000, this resulted in an over-provision for 20X0 of $53,000 because we had provided for more tax than we needed to pay.

This credit balance would be shown on the trial balance before the adjustments were made for the current year's estimated taxation.

Tax

Bank	263,000	Bal b/d	316,000
Bal c/d	53,000		
	316,000		316,000
		Bal b/d	53,000

At 31 May 20X1 the current year tax is estimated at $383,500. This is the amount that **must** be shown on the current year statement of financial position as a liability. It is **not** the charge to the statement of profit or loss. The statement of profit or loss charge will be made up of this year's estimated tax liability but will have the credit for the over-provision made in the 20X0 financial statements.

Tax

		Bal b/d	53,000
Bal c/d	383,500	PL (ß)	330,500
	383,500		383,500
		Bal b/d	383,500

Statement of profit or loss for the year ended 31 May 20X1 (extract)

	$
Income tax expense (disclosure note)	330,500

Statement of financial position as at 31 May 20X1 (extract)

Current liabilities	
Income tax payable	383,500

Disclosure note

Income tax expense	
Current tax	383,500
Over-provision	(53,000)
	330,500

Test your understanding 1 – Under and over provisions

The following information is available for Sad:

	$
Income tax liability at 31 December 20X0	56,000
Income tax paid on 28 September 20X1	59,900
Income tax estimate for the year ended 31 December 20X1	70,000

Required:

Show the entries in the income tax account and the extracts from the financial statements for the year ended 31 December 20X1.

Summary

When we look at the trial balance after adjusting for tax paid in the year the following applies:

Debit balance = Under-provision in respect of the previous year

Credit balance = Over-provision in respect of the previous year

When we are preparing the financial statements:

Statement of profit or loss = current estimate + under-provision – over-provision

Statement of financial position current liability = current estimate

Test your understanding 2 – Accounting for tax

Aquarius's financial statements for the year ended 31 December 20X8 show a profit before tax of $145,000. Profit includes disallowable expenses of $5,000, disallowable accounting depreciation of $20,000 and tax depreciation has been calculated as $50,000.

For the year ended 31 December 20X9 the financial statements show a profit before tax of $170,000. Profit includes disallowable expenses of $8,000, disallowable accounting depreciation of $15,000 and tax depreciation has been calculated as $25,000.

Required:

Prepare relevant extracts from the financial statements for the year's ending 31 December 20X8 and 20X9 for the tax charge. You should assume the amounts paid for current tax are equal to the estimates made and tax is charged at a rate of 25% in both years.

Test your understanding 3 – Accounting for tax

Parker's financial statements show the following profit before tax figures for the entity's first three years of trading:

Y.E. 30.6.20X8	$450,000
Y.E. 30.6.20X9	$550,000
Y.E. 30.6.20Y0	$300,000

Income tax which has been calculated based on taxable profits is as follows:

Y.E. 30.6.20X8	$96,000
Y.E. 30.6.20X9	$108,000
Y.E. 30.6.20Y0	$59,000

Payments of tax were made nine months following each year-end as follows:

Y.E. 30.6.20X8	$90,000
Y.E. 30.6.20X9	$118,000
Y.E. 30.6.20Y0	$55,000

Required:

Prepare the relevant extracts from the financial statements for each of the three years in respect of income tax.

Test your understanding 4 – Single entity accounts

The following trial balance relates to Molly at 31 December 20X1:

	Dr	Cr
	$	$
Revenue		50,000
Purchases	20,000	
Distribution costs	10,400	
Administrative expenses	15,550	
Loan interest paid	400	
Non-current assets carrying amount	35,000	
Income tax		500
Interim dividend paid	1,600	
Trade receivables and payables	10,450	29,000
Inventory as at 1 January 20X1	8,000	
Cash and cash equivalents	8,100	
Ordinary shares $0.50		8,000
Share premium		3,000
10% Loan notes		8,000
Retained earnings at 1 January 20X1		11,000
	109,500	109,500

The following is to be taken into account:

(1) Land that cost $5,000 is to be revalued to $11,000.

(2) A final ordinary dividend of 10c per share is declared before the year-end.

(3) The balance on the income tax account represents an over-provision of tax for the previous year.

(4) The income tax for the current year is estimated at $3,000.

(5) Closing inventory is valued at $16,000 at cost for the year. Included in this amount is inventory that cost $8,000 but during the inventory count it was identified that these goods had become damaged and as result the selling price was reduced. The goods are now believed to have a selling price of $4,500 and will incur rectification costs of $500.

(6) The loan was taken out many years ago by Molly.

Required:

Prepare a statement of profit or loss and other comprehensive income, statement of financial position and statement of changes in equity for the year-ended 31 December 20X1.

Test your understanding 5 – Practice questions

(1) The following information has been extracted from the accounting records of Clara:

Estimated income tax for the year ended 30 September 20X0	$75,000
Income tax paid in 20X1 for the year ended 30 September 20X0	$80,000
Estimated income tax for the year ended 30 September 20X1	$83,000

What figures will be shown in the statement of profit or loss for the year ended 30 September 20X1 and the statement of financial position as at that date in respect of income tax?

	SPL	SOFP
A	$83,000	$83,000
B	$88,000	$83,000
C	$83,000	$88,000
D	$88,000	$88,000

(2) Tamsin's accounting records show the following:

Income tax payable for the year	$60,000
Over provision in relation to the previous year	$4,500

What is the income tax expense that will be shown in the Statement of profit or loss for the year?

A $60,000

B $64,500

C $55,500

D $4,500

(3) WS prepares its financial statements to 30 June. The following profits were recorded from 20X1 to 20X3:

20X1 $100,000
20X2 $120,000
20X3 $110,000

The entity provides for tax at a rate of 30% and incorporates this figure in the year-end accounts. The actual amounts of tax paid in respect of 20X1 and 20X2 were $28,900 and $37,200.

Required:

Prepare extracts from the statement of profit or loss and statement of financial position of WS for each of the 3 years, showing the tax charge and tax liability. You should assume there are no adjustments to be made to accounting profits for this entity and hence accounting profits equate to taxable profits.

(4) Entity X has a credit balance of $3,000 sitting on its Tax account after paying last years tax liability. The estimated charge for the current year is $150,000.

What will be the correct figures to be included as the tax expense in the statement of profit or loss and statement of financial position current liability in the statement of financial position?

A SPL $147,000 and SOFP $150,000

B SPL $153,000 and SOFP $150,000

C SPL $150,000 and SOFP $147,000

D SPL $153,000 and SOFP $147,000

(5) Entity Z has a debit balance of $2,000 on their trial balance having settled last years' tax charge.

The correct treatment is to:

A Add $2,000 to the tax liability to be included in statement of financial position

B Deduct $2,000 from the tax liability to be included in statement of financial position

C Add $2,000 to the tax charge in the current years statement of profit or loss

D Deduct $2,000 from the tax charge in the current years statement of profit or loss

5 Summary diagram

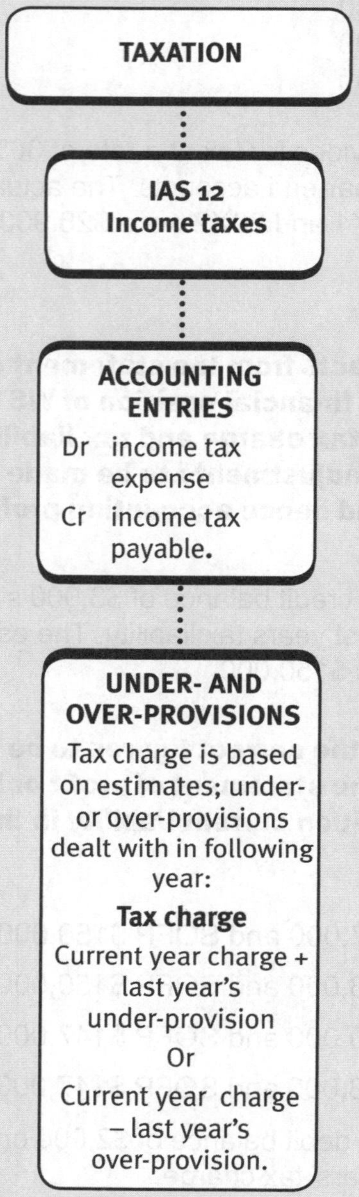

TAXATION

IAS 12 Income taxes

ACCOUNTING ENTRIES

Dr income tax expense

Cr income tax payable.

UNDER- AND OVER-PROVISIONS

Tax charge is based on estimates; under- or over-provisions dealt with in following year:

Tax charge

Current year charge + last year's under-provision

Or

Current year charge – last year's over-provision.

Test your understanding answers

Test your understanding 1 – Under and over provisions

At 31 December 20X0 we had an opening liability for tax of $56,000. When we made the payment of $59,900, this resulted in an under-provision for 20X0 of $3,900 because we had provided for less tax than we needed to pay.

This debit balance would be shown on the trial balance before the adjustments were made for the current years taxation.

Tax

Bank	59,900	Bal b/d	56,000
		Bal c/d	3,900
	59,900		56,000
Bal b/d	3,900		

At 31 December 20X1 the current year tax is estimated at $70,000. This is the amount that **must** be shown on the current year statement of financial position as a liability. It is **not** the charge to the statement of profit or loss. The statement of profit or loss charge will be made up of this years estimated tax liability but will have to be increased for the under-provision made in 20X0 financial statements.

Tax

Bal b/d	3,900		
Bal c/d	70,000	PL (ß)	73,900
	73,900		73,900
		Bal b/d	70,000

Statement of profit or loss for the year ended 31 December 20X1 (extract)

	$
Income tax expense (disclosure note)	73,900

Statement of financial position as at 31 December 20X1 (extract)

Current liabilities	
Income tax payable	70,000

Disclosure note

Income tax expense	
Current tax	70,000
Under-provision	3,900
	73,900

Test your understanding 2 – Accounting for tax

Statement of profit or loss (extract)

	20X8	20X9
	$	$
Profit before tax	145,000	170,000
Income tax expense	(30,000)	(42,000)
Profit for the year	120,000	128,000

Statement of financial position (extract)

	20X8	20X9
	$	$
Current liabilities:		
Income tax payable	30,000	42,000

Current tax liability: YE 31/12/X8

Dr Income tax expense (SPL)	30,000
Cr Current tax liability (SOFP)	30,000

Current tax liability: YE 31/12/X9

Dr Income tax expense (SPL)	42,000
Cr Current tax liability (SOFP)	42,000

Calculation of current tax:

	$	$
Accounting profit	145,000	170,000
Add back: disallowable expenses	5,000	8,000
Add back: disallowable depreciation	20,000	15,000
Deduct: tax depreciation	(50,000)	(25,000)
Taxable profit	120,000	168,000
Tax at 25%	**30,000**	**42,000**

Test your understanding 3 – Accounting for tax

Statement of profit or loss (extract)

	20X8	20X9	20Y0
	$	$	$
Profit before taxation	450,000	550,000	300,000
Income tax expense (W1)	(96,000)	(102,000)	(69,000)
Profit for the period	354,000	448,000	231,000

Statements of financial position (extract)

	20X8	20X9	20Y0
	$	$	$
Current liabilities			
Income tax payable	96,000	108,000	59,000

(W1) **Income tax expense**

	20X8	20X9	20Y0
	$	$	$
Current tax estimate	96,000	108,000	59,000
(Over)/under provision (W2)	0	(6,000)	10,000
	96,000	102,000	69,000

(W2) **Under/over provisions**

	20X8	20X9	20Y0
	$	$	$
Current tax estimate	96,000	108,000	59,000
Amount paid 9 months later	90,000	118,000	55,000
Under/(over) provision	(6,000)	10,000	(4,000)

Remember these under/(over) provisions will not have an effect on the current year accounts but the following year accounts due to the timing of payments.

Test your understanding 4 – Single entity accounts

Molly Statement of profit or loss and other comprehensive income for the year ended 31 December 20X1

	$
Revenue	50,000
Cost of Sales (W1)	(16,000)
Gross profit	34,000
Distribution costs	(10,400)
Administrative expenses	(15,550)
Profit from operations	8,050
Income from investments	–
Finance cost (W2)	(800)
Profit before tax	7,250
Income tax expense (W3)	(2,500)
Profit for year	4,750
Other comprehensive income:	
Revaluation gain (W4)	6,000
Total comprehensive income	10,750

Molly statement of financial position as at 31 December 20X1

	$	$
Non-current assets		
Property, plant and equipment (W4)		41,000
Current assets		
Inventories (W5)	12,000	
Trade receivables	10,450	
Cash and cash equivalents	8,100	
		30,550
Total assets		71,550

Equity and liabilities		
Capital and reserves		
Share capital $0.50	8,000	
Share premium	3,000	
Revaluation reserve	6,000	
Retained earnings	12,550	
		29,550
Non-current liabilities		
10% Loan	8,000	
		8,000
Current liabilities		
Trade payables	29,000	
Loan interest payable (W2)	400	
Dividends proposed (W6)	1,600	
Income tax	3,000	
		34,000
		71,550

Molly statement of changes in equity for the year ended 31 December 20X1

	Share capital	**Share premium**	**Reval'tion reserve**	**Retained earnings**	**Total**
	$	$	$	$	$
Balance at 1 January 20X1	8,000	3,000	–	11,000	22,000
Total comprehensive income			6,000	4,750	10,750
Dividends paid				(1,600)	(1,600)
Dividends declared (W6)				(1,600)	(1,600)
Balance at 31 December 20X1	8,000	3,000	6,000	12,550	29,550

Workings

(W1)

Cost of sales	$
Purchases	20,000
Opening inventory	8,000
Closing inventory (W5)	(12,000)
	16,000

(W2)

Loan interest

Due (10% × $8,000) = $800 (SPL)

Amount paid (TB) $400, therefore accrual required for $400

(W3)

Income tax expense	$
TB over-provision	(500)
Current year estimate	3,000
	2,500

(W4)

PPE	$
TB carrying value	35,000
Increase in valuation of land ($5,000 to $11,000)	6,000
	41,000

(W5)

Inventory	$
Closing inventory at cost	16,000
Damaged inventory at cost	(8,000)
Damaged inventory at NRV ($4,500 – $500)	4,000
	12,000

Inventory is valued at the lower of cost or NRV

(W6)

Dividends

0.10 × 16,000 shares ($8,000/0.50) = $1,600 declared before year-end, therefore provide.

Test your understanding 5 – Practice questions

(1) B

Statement of profit or loss (extract)

	$
Current tax y.e. 30.9.X1	83,000
Under-provision for y.e. 30.9.X0 (80,000 – 75,000)	5,000
	88,000

Statement of financial position (extract)

Income tax payable	83,000

(2) C

Statement of profit or loss (extract)

	$
Current tax	60,000
Over-provision	(4,500)
	55,500

(3) **Statement of profit or loss (extract)**

	20X1	20X2	20X3
	$	$	$
Profit before taxation	100,000	120,000	110,000
Income tax expense (W1)	(30,000)	(34,900)	(34,200)
Profit for the period	70,000	85,100	75,800

Statements of financial position (extract)

	20X1	20X2	20X3
	$	$	
Current liabilities			
Income tax payable (profits × 30%)	30,000	36,000	33,000

(W1) **Income tax expense**

	20X1	20X2	20X3
	$	$	$
Current tax estimate	30,000	36,000	33,000
Under/(over) provision (W2)	0	(1,100)	1,200
	30,000	34,900	34,200

(W2) **Under/over provisions**

	20X1	20X2	20X3
	$	$	$
Current tax estimate	30,000	36,000	33,000
Amount paid	28,900	37,200	?
Under/(over) provision	(1,100)	1,200	?

Remember these under/(over) provisions will not have an effect on the current year accounts but the following year accounts due to the timing of payments.

(4) A – The tax expense to the SPL should represent this year's estimate of $150,000 plus or minus any under or over-provisions from the previous year. Therefore, the SPL tax expense = $150,000 – $3,000 = $147,000. The liability on the SOFP should always represent the this year's estimate, i.e. the amount we expect to pay of $150,000.

(5) C – A debit balance on the trial balance represents an under-provision from the previous year's tax expense and must be added to this year's tax expense in the SPL.

chapter

18

IAS 21 – The Effects of Changes in Foreign Exchange Rates

Chapter learning objectives

On completion of their studies students should be able to:

- Explain foreign currency translation principles, including the principles of functional and presentation currencies.
- Account for initial transactions involving foreign currency.
- Account for settled and unsettled transactions at the reporting date for both monetary and non-monetary items.

1 Session content

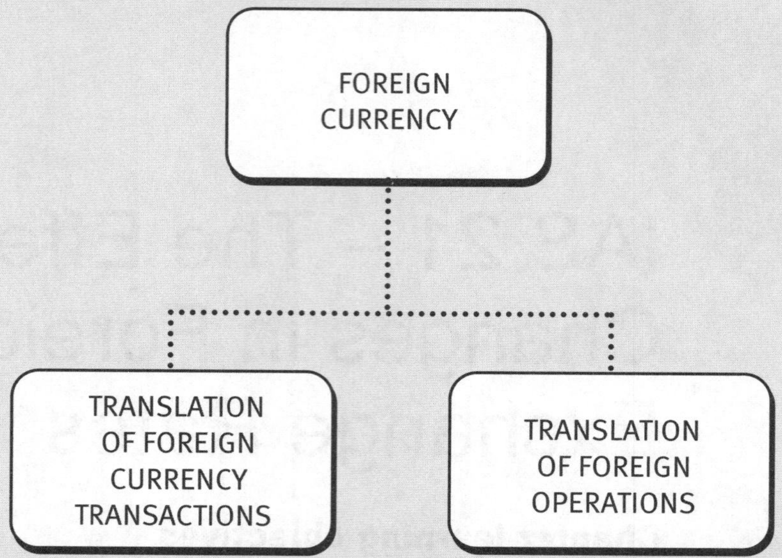

2 IAS 21 The effects of changes in exchange rates

IAS 21 deals with:

- the definition of functional and presentation currencies
- accounting for individual transactions in a foreign currency
- translating the financial statements of a foreign operation (this topic is beyond the scope of the F1 syllabus and will be studied at F2.)

3 Functional and presentation currencies

The **functional currency** is the currency of the primary economic environment in which the entity operates. In most cases this will be the local currency.

An entity should consider the following when determining its functional currency:

- The currency that mainly influences sales prices for goods and services.
- The currency of the country whose competitive forces and regulations mainly determine the sales prices of goods and services.
- The currency that mainly influences labour, material and other costs of providing goods and services.

The following factors may also be considered:

- The currency in which funding from issuing debt and equity is generated.
- The currency in which receipts from operating activities are usually retained.

The entity maintains its day-to-day financial records in its functional currency.

The **presentation currency** is the currency in which the entity presents its financial statements. This can be different from the functional currency, particularly if the entity in question is a foreign owned subsidiary. It may have to present its financial statements in the currency of its parent, even though that is different to its own functional currency. This will be covered in greater depth at F2.

4 Translation of foreign currency transactions

Where an entity enters into a transaction denominated in a currency other than its functional currency, that transaction must be translated into the functional currency before it is recorded.

Examples of foreign currency transactions

Whenever a business enters into a contract where the consideration is expressed in a foreign currency, it is necessary to translate that foreign currency amount into the functional currency for inclusion in its own accounts. Examples include:

- imports of raw materials
- exports of finished goods
- importation of foreign manufactured non-current assets
- investments in foreign securities
- raising an overseas loan

Initial recognition

- The transaction will initially be recorded by applying the spot exchange rate, i.e. the exchange rate at the date of the transaction.

Subsequent measurement – settled transactions

When cash settlement occurs, for example payment by a receivable, the settled amount should be translated using the spot exchange rate on the settlement date.

If this amount differs from that recorded when the transaction occurred, there will be an exchange difference which is taken to the statement of profit or loss in the period in which it arises.

Illustration 1 – Settled transactions

An entity based in the US sells goods to the UK for £200,000 on 28 February 20X3 when the exchange rate was $/£0.55 (that is $1 = £0.55).

The customer pays in April 20X3 when the rate was $/£0.60 (that is $1 = £0.60).

Required:

How does the US entity account for the transaction in its financial statements for the year ended 31 July 20X3?

Solution

On the sale on 28 February 20X3:

Translate the sale at the spot rate prevailing on the transaction date.

£200,000/0.55 = $363,636

		$
Dr	Receivables	363,636
Cr	Sales	363,636

When the cash is received on 28 April 20X3:

$ value of cash received = £200,000/0.60 = $333,333

Loss on transaction = $363,636 – $333,333 = $30,303

		$
Dr	Bank	333,333
Cr	Receivables	363,636
Dr	P/L (loss)	30,303

Test your understanding 1 – Settled transactions

Butler, whose functional currency is the $, has a year end of 31 December. On 27 November 20X6 Butler buys goods from a Swedish supplier for SwK 324,000.

On 19 December 20X6 Butler pays the Swedish supplier in full.

Exchange rates are as follows:

27 November 20X6 $/SwK 11.15 (that is $1 = SwK 11.15)

19 December 20X6 $/SwK 10.93 (that is $1 = SwK 10.93)

Required:

Show the accounting entries for these transactions for the year ended 31 December 20X6.

Subsequent measurement – unsettled transactions

The treatment of any foreign currency assets or liabilities remaining in the statement of financial position at the year end will depend on whether they are classified as monetary or non-monetary.

Monetary items	**Non-monetary items**
Currency held and assets or liabilities to be received or paid in a foreign currency.	Other items in the statement of financial position.
E.g. cash, receivables, payables, loans	E.g. non-current assets, inventory, investments
Treatment: Retranslate using the closing rate (year end exchange rate)	**Treatment:** Do not translate i.e. leave at historic rate

Any exchange difference arising on the retranslation of monetary items must be taken to the statement of profit or loss in the period in which it arises.

Illustration 2 – Unsettled transactions

A US entity sells apples to an entity based in Moldovia where the currency is the Moldovian pound (Mol). The apples were sold on 1 October 20X1 for Mol 200,000 and were paid for in February 20X2.

The rate on 1 October 20X1 is US$/Mol 1.55 (that is $1 = Mol 1.55).

The rate on 31 December 20X1 (the reporting date) is US$/Mol 1.34 (that is $1 = Mol 1.34).

The rate on 4 February 20X2 is US$/1.41 (that is $1 = Mol 1.41).

Required:

How does the US entity account for the transaction in its financial statements for the years ended 31 December 20X1 and 31 December 20X2?

Solution

On the sale on 1 October 20X1:

Translate the sale at the spot rate prevailing on the transaction date.

Mol 200,000/1.55 = $129,032

		$
Dr	Receivables	129,032
Cr	Sales	129,032

At the reporting date 31 December 20X1:

The receivables balance is a monetary item and so must be retranslated using the closing rate.

Mol 200,000/1.34 = $149,254

Gain = $149,254 – $129,032 = $20,222

		$
Dr	Receivables	20,222
Cr	P/L (gain)	20,222

At settlement on 4 February 20X2:

The cash received of Mol 200,000 is translated at Mol 200,000/1.41 = $141,844.

Mol 200,000/1.34 = $149,254

Loss = $149,254 – $141,844 = $7,410

		$
Dr	Bank	141,844
Cr	Receivables	149,254
Dr	P/L (loss)	7,410

Test your understanding 2 – Unsettled transactions

On 15 March 20X1 an entity, whose functional currency is the $, purchases a non-current asset on one month's credit for KR20,000.

Exchange rates

15 March 20X1	$/KR5 (that is $1 = KR5)
31 March 20X1	$/KR4 (that is $1 = KR4)

Required:

(a) Explain and illustrate how the transaction is recorded and dealt with given a financial year end of 31 March 20X1.

The following transactions were undertaken by Jeyes, whose functional currency is the $, in the accounting year ended 31 December 20X1.

Date	**Narrative**	**Amount KR**
1 January 20X1	Purchase of a non-current asset on credit	100,000
31 March 20X1	Payment for the non-current asset	100,000
	Purchases on credit	50,000
30 June 20X1	Sales on credit	95,000
30 September 20X1	Payment for purchases	50,000
30 November 20X1	Long-term loan taken out	200,000

Exchange rates	$/KR
1 January 20X1	2.0
31 March 20X1	2.3
30 June 20X1	2.1
30 September 20X1	2.0
30 November 20X1	1.8
31 December 20X1	1.9

Required:

(b) Prepare journal entries to record the above transactions for the year ended 31 December 20X1.

Foreign exchange and the cash flow statement

When an entity has foreign currency transactions during the year resulting in exchange rate gains or losses we must consider the effect this will have on the cash flow statement.

An exchange rate gain or loss will be adjust the opening balances as follows:

	Gain	Loss
Receivables	Increase	Decrease
Payables	Decrease	Increase

A gain on receivables means the opening balance is too low due to foreign exchange and a loss means the opening balance is too high.

A gain on payables means the opening balance is too high due to foreign exchange and a loss means the opening balance is too low.

For example:

Extracts from the statements of financial position at the beginning and end of the year are as follows:

	Closing	Opening
	$000	$000
Inventory	150	240
Receivables	275	200
Payables	180	90

At the year-end the following exchange differences were recorded upon re-translation of monetary items:

	$000	
Receivables	35	Gain
Payables	18	Loss

Calculate the adjustments required in respect of movements in working capital that should be shown in the operating activities section of the statement of cash flows.

Solution

Statement of cash flow (extract)

Cash flows from operating activities	$000
Decrease in inventory (150 – 240)	90
Increase in receivables (275 – (200 + 35))	(40)
Increase in payables (180 – (90 +18))	72

Test your understanding 3 – Practice questions

Data for questions (1) to (4)

An entity based in the US sells goods to the UK for £200,000 on 28 March 20X3 when the exchange rate was $/£0.65.

The customer pays in April 20X3 when the rate was $/£0.70.

The exchange rate at the year ended 30 June 20X3 was $/£0.75.

(1) **Prepare the journal entries to record the sale of the goods by the US entity.**

(2) **Calculate the amount debited to the US entity bank account at the date of payment.**

(3) **Calculate the gain or loss recorded in the US entity's statement of profit or loss for the year ended 30 June 20X3, and show the journal entries to record the loss.**

(4) **Calculate the amount recorded in the receivables account by the US entity at the year ended 30 June 20X3 assuming the amount was unsettled on that date.**

(5) An entity based in the US purchases goods from the UK for £200,000 on 28 March 20X3 when the exchange rate was £0.65: $1.

The exchange rate at the year ended 30 June 20X3 was £0.75:£1.

Calculate the amount recorded in the inventory account by the US entity at the year ended 30 June 20X3 assuming the amount was unsettled and the inventory unsold.

(6) A German entity buys a non-current asset from a US entity for $100,000 when the exchange rate was $/EUR 0.85. At the year end the German entity has not paid its US $ payable. The exchange rate at the year end is $/EUR 0.92.

Prepare the journal entries to record the initial acquisition of the non-current asset and any journal entries required at the year end.

5 Summary Diagram

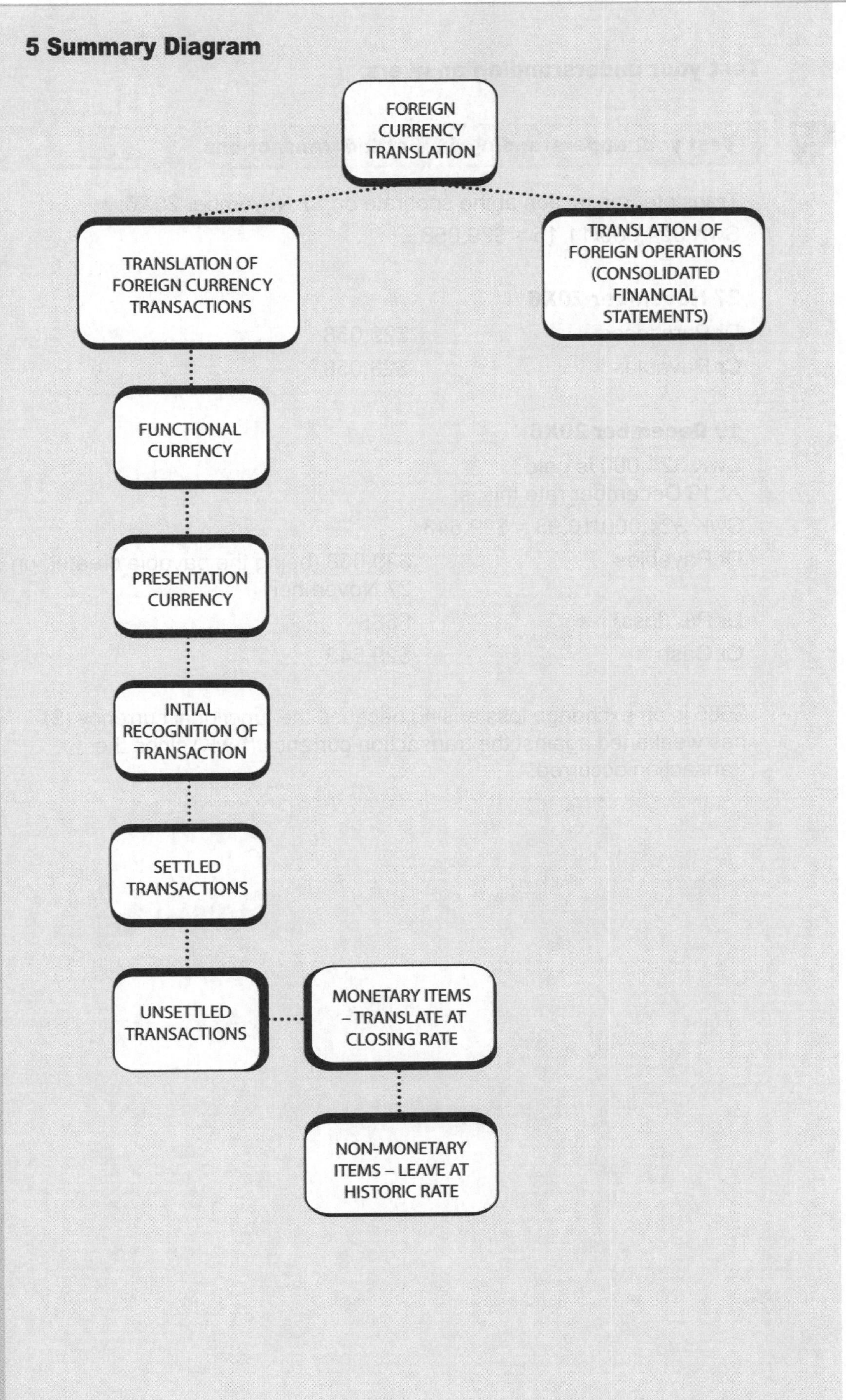

Test your understanding answers

Test your understanding 1 – Settled transactions

Translate transaction at the spot rate on 27 November 20X6:
SwK 324,000/11.15 = $29,058

27 November 20X6

Dr Purchases	$29,058
Cr Payables	$29,058

19 December 20X6

SwK 324,000 is paid.
At 19 December rate this is:
SwK 324,000/10.93 = $29,643

Dr Payables	$29,058 (being the payable created on 27 November)
Dr P/L (loss)	$585
Cr Cash	$29,643

$585 is an exchange loss arising because the functional currency ($) has weakened against the transaction currency (SwK) since the transaction occurred.

Test your understanding 2 – Unsettled transactions

Part (a)

On 15 March the purchase is recorded using the exchange rate on that date.

Dr Non-current asset	(KR20,000/5)	$4,000
Cr Payable		$4,000

- At the year end the non-current asset, being a non-monetary item, is not retranslated but remains measured at $4,000.
- The payable remains outstanding at the year-end. This is a monetary item and must be retranslated using the closing rate: KR20,000/4 = $5,000
- The payable must be increased by $1,000, giving rise to an exchange loss:

Dr P/L (exchange loss)	$1,000
Cr Payable	$1,000

Part (b)

1 Jan 20X1	KR100,000/2.0	= $50,000	Dr Non-current assets	$50,000
			Cr Payable	$50,000
31 Mar 20X1	KR100,000/2.3	= $43,478	Dr Payable	$50,000
			Cr Cash	$43,478
			Cr P/L (gain)	$6,522
	KR 50,000/2.3	= $21,739	Dr Purchases	$21,739
			Cr Payables	$21,739
30 Jun 20X1	KR 95,000/2.1	= $45,238	Dr Receivables	$45,238
			Cr Sales revenue	$45,238
30 Sept 20X1	KR50,000/2.0	= $25,000	Dr Payables	$21,739
			Dr P/L (loss)	$3,261
			Cr Cash	$25,000
30 Nov 20X1	KR200,000/1.8	= $111,111	Dr Cash	$111,111
			Cr Loan	$111,111

31 Dec 20X1	KR95,000/1.9	= $50,000	Dr Receivables Cr P/L (gain)	$4,762 $4,762
	KR200,000/1.9	= $105,263	Dr Loan Cr P/L (gain)	$5,848 $5,848

Test your understanding 3 – Practice questions

(1) **On the sale:**

Translate the sale at the spot rate prevailing on the transaction date.

£200,000/0.65 = $307,692

	$
Dr Receivables	307,692
Cr Sales	307,692

(2) **When the cash is received:**

Dollar value of cash received at the date of receipt = £200,000/0.70 = $285,714

(3) **Loss on transaction = $307,692 – $285,714 = $21,978**

The journal entries would be as follows:

Dr Bank	285,714
Cr Receivables	307,692
Dr P/L (loss)	21,978

(4) **The monetary transaction must retranslated at the reporting date rate of exchange:**

Dollar value of the reporting date = £200,000/0.75 = $266,667

This results in a reduction in the receivables account of $41,025

For tutorial purposes the journal entry would be as follows:

Loss on transaction = $307,692 – $266,667= $41,025

Cr Receivables	41,025
Dr P/L (loss)	41,025

(5) **At the reporting date:**

No adjustment will be made at year end to the inventory account because the transaction is a non-monetary item.

For tutorial purposes the journal entry would be as follows:

On the sale:

Translate the sale at the spot rate prevailing on the transaction date.

£200,000/0.65 = $307,693

This amount would remain unchanged at the reporting date

	$
Dr Purchases (within inventory)	307,693
Cr Payables	307,693

The payables account would then be restated at year end .

Dollar value of the reporting date = £200,000/0.75 = $266,667

Gain on transaction = 307,692 – 266,667= 41,025

Cr P/L (gain)	41,025
Dr Payables	41,025

(6) **At acquisition:**

$100,000 × 0.85 = EUR 85,000

	$
Dr Non-current asset	85,000
Cr Payables	85,000

The monetary transaction must retranslated at the reporting date rate of exchange:

EUR value of the reporting date = 100,000 × 0.92 = EUR 92,000

This results in an increase in the payables account of EUR 7,000

Loss on transaction = EUR 92,000 – EUR 85,000 = EURO 7,000

Cr Payables	7,000
Dr P/L (loss)	7,000

chapter

19

IAS 19 – Employee benefits

Chapter learning objectives

On completion of their studies students should be able to:

- Explain pension schemes and the treatment of actuarial deficits and surpluses.
- Identify types of pension plans, i.e. defined contribution plans and defined benefit plans.
- Apply the provisions of IAS 19 to account for different types of pension plans.

1 Session content

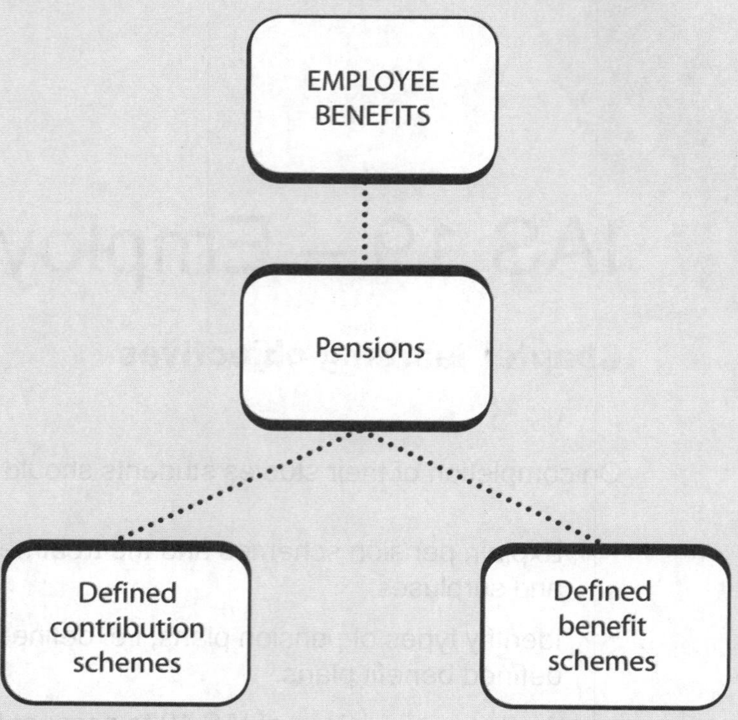

2 Types of pension plan

Introduction

A pension plan (sometimes called a post-employment benefit scheme) consists of a pool of assets and a liability for pensions owed to employees. Pension plan assets normally consist of investments, cash and (sometimes) properties. The return earned on the assets is used to pay pensions.

There are two main types of pension plan:

- defined contribution plans
- defined benefit plans

Defined contribution plans

The pension payable on retirement depends on the contributions paid into the plan by the employee and the employer.

- The employer's contribution is usually a fixed percentage of the employee's salary. The employer has no further obligation after this amount is paid.
- Therefore, the annual cost to the employer is reasonably predictable.
- Defined contribution plans present few accounting problems.

Defined benefit plans

The pension payable on retirement normally depends on either the final salary or the average salary of the employee during their career.

- The employer undertakes to finance a pension income of a certain amount, e.g.

  2/3 × final salary × (years of service/40 years)

- The employer has an ongoing obligation to make sufficient contributions to the plan to fund the pensions.
- An actuary calculates the amount that must be paid into the plan each year in order to provide the promised pension. The calculation is based on various estimates and assumptions including:
  – life expectancy
  – expected length of service to retirement/employee turnover
  – investment returns
  – wage inflation.
- Therefore, the cost of providing pensions is not certain and varies from year to year.

The actual contribution paid in a period does not usually represent the true cost to the employer of providing pensions in that period. The financial statements must reflect the true cost of providing pensions.

3 Accounting for pension plans (IAS 19)

Defined contribution plans

The expense of providing pensions in the period is normally the same as the amount of contributions paid.

- The entity should charge the agreed pension contribution to profit or loss as an employment expense in each period.
- An asset (prepayment) or liability (accrual) for pensions only arises if the cash paid does not equal the amount of contributions due.
- IAS 19 requires disclosure of the amount recognised as an expense in the period.

Illustration 1 – Defined contribution

An entity makes contributions to the pension fund of employees at a rate of 5% of gross salary. The contributions made are $10,000 per month for convenience with the balance being contributed in the first month of the following accounting year. The wages and salaries for 20X6 are $2.7m.

Required:

Calculate the pension expense for 20X6 and the accrual/prepayment at the end of the year.

Solution

The charge to the statement of profit or loss should be:

$2.7m × 5% = $135,000

The statement of financial position will therefore show an accrual of $15,000, being the difference between the $135,000 and the $120,000 paid in the year.

Test your understanding 1 – Defined contribution

J operates a defined contribution scheme on which it pays 6% of employees gross salaries per annum. At the end of last year, J had accrued $10,000 for pension contributions due. Gross salaries for the current year amounted to $650,000 and J had paid contributions totalling $35,000 into the pension fund during the year.

Required:

What amounts will be recorded in the financial statements in respect of the pension plan for the current year?

Defined benefit plans: the basic principle

An entity will set up a defined benefit pension plan on behalf of its employees. Both employees and the employer (the entity), will pay into the plan. It is important to note that the pension plan is separate from the entity.

The entity recognises the net defined benefit liability (or asset) in the statement of financial position.

- If the pension plan liability exceeds its assets, there is a deficit (the usual situation) and a liability is reported in the statement of financial position of the entity.
- If the pension plan assets exceeds its liability, there is a surplus and an asset is reported in the statement of financial position of the entity.

Measuring the pension plan liability and assets

In practice, the actuary measures the plan assets and liabilities using a number of estimates and assumptions on an annual basis.

- The plan liability is measured at the present value (PV) of the defined benefit obligation. Discounting is necessary because the liability will be settled many years in the future and therefore the effect of the time value of money is material.
- Plan assets are measured at fair value (FV) at the reporting date. This is normally market value.

Recognising the amounts in the financial statements

Defined benefit pension plan

Statement of comprehensive income
- Within profit or loss:
  - Service cost component
  - Net interest component
- Within other comprehensive income
  - Remeasurement component

Statement of financial position
- PV of plan liability
- FV of plan assets

Explanation of the terms used.

- **Service cost component** includes current and past service costs, together with any gains or losses on curtailments or settlements.
  - **Current service cost** is the increase in the actuarial liability (present value of the defined benefit obligation) resulting from employee service in the current period.
  - **Past service cost** is the increase in the present value of the liability (defined benefit obligation) resulting from a plan amendment or curtailment.
  - **Curtailment and settlement gains/losses** arise when significant reductions are made to the number of employees covered by the plan or the benefits promised to them.
- **Net interest component** is determined by multiplying the net defined benefit liability (or asset) at the start of the period by the discount rate. It can be viewed as comprising interest income on the plan assets and the unwinding of the discount, creating an interest cost, on the plan liability.
- **Remeasurement component** principally comprises actuarial gains and losses and also includes any return on plan assets not already recognised in the net interest component. The remeasurement component is recognised in other comprehensive income for the year. It cannot be reclassified to profit or loss in future periods.
  - **Actuarial gains and losses** result from increases or decreases in the pension asset or liability that occur either because the actuarial assumptions have changed or because of differences between the previous actuarial assumptions and what has actually happened (experience adjustments).

Effect on statement of comprehensive income for the period

The changes in the defined benefit asset/liability in the period are treated as follows:

Current and past service costs	Dr SPL (employment costs) Cr Pension liability
Interest cost (on liability)	Dr SPL (finance cost) Cr Pension liability
Interest income (on asset)	Dr Pension asset Cr SPL (net off against finance cost)
Curtailments and settlements (if any)	Dr or Cr SPL Cr or Dr Pension liability

Remeasurement component gain/loss	Dr or Cr Other comprehensive income (via reserves) Cr or Dr Pension asset / liability

Other entries affecting the pension plan assets and liabilities

There are additional changes in the defined benefit plan asset/liability in the period affecting only the statement of financial position:

Contributions (from the employer)	Dr Pension asset Cr Bank
Benefits paid	Dr Pension liability Cr Pension asset

Illustration 2 – Defined benefit

T has a defined benefit pension plan and makes up financial statements to 31 March each year. The net pension liability (i.e. obligation less plan assets) at 31 March 20X3, was $40 million ($35 million at 31 March 20X2). The following additional information is relevant for the year ended 31 March 20X3:

- The discount rate relevant to the net liability at the start of the year was 10%.
- The current service cost was $45 million.
- At the end of the year the entity granted additional benefits to existing pensioners that have a present value of $10 million. These were not allowed for in the original actuarial assumptions.
- The entity paid pension contributions of $40 million.

Required:

Calculate the re-measurement component gains/losses arising in the year ended 31 March 20X3.

Prepare extracts from the statement of profit or loss and other comprehensive income for the year ended 31 March 20X3 and the statement of financial position at 31 March 20X3 showing how the defined benefit scheme would be presented.

Solution

	$m
Net liability brought forward	(35)
Net interest cost (10% × 35)	(3.5)
Current service cost	(45)
Additional benefits granted (past service costs)	(10)
Pension contributions paid	40
Actuarial gain (bal fig)	13.5
Net liability carried forward	(40)

You were given the net pension liability at the start and end of the year and needed to use the double entries listed above to calculate the balancing figure for the actuarial gain. This is the gap between what the actuary expected at the start of the year and what actually happened by the end of the year.

If benefits paid had been provided in the question no adjustment is required because the entries reduce pension assets and reduce pension liabilities, thereby having no effect on the net pension liability.

Statement of financial position (extract) at 31 March 20X3

	$m
Net pension liability	40

Statement of profit or loss and other comprehensive income (extracts) for the year ended 31 March 20X3

	$m
Statement of profit or loss	
Service cost component (45 + 10)	(55)
Net interest component	(3.5)
Net effect on profit	(58.5)
Items that will not be reclassified to profit or loss:	
Remeasurement component – gain	13.5
Net effect on total comprehensive income	(45)

Test your understanding 2 – Defined benefit

Alpha operates a defined benefit pension scheme.

As at 1 January 20X6, Alpha's statement of financial position showed pension plan assets measured at a fair value of $1,400,000 and pension plan liabilities measured at a present value of $1,350,000.

The current service cost for the year was estimated at $130,000 and the discount rate used was 8%.

Alpha paid contributions totalling $120,000 into the scheme during the year and benefits were paid to scheme members totalling $110,000.

As at 31 December 20X6, the pension plan assets have been valued at $1,565,000 and the pension plan liabilities at $1,630,000.

Required:

Calculate the re-measurement component gains/losses arising on the pension plan assets and liability on in the year ended 31 December 20X6.

Prepare extracts from the statement of profit or loss and other comprehensive income for the year ended 31 December 20X6 and the statement of financial position at 31 December 20X6 showing how the defined benefit scheme would be presented.

Test your understanding 3 – Defined benefit

The following data relates to a defined benefit scheme for the year ended 31 December 20X4.

	$000
Discount rate	10% per annum
Pension liabilities at start of year	1,030
Pension asset at start of year	1,010
Current service costs	140
Past service costs	35
Curtailment costs	15
Benefits paid out	105
Contributions paid in	110
Pension liability at year end	1,280
Pension asset at year end	1,240

Required:

Prepare extracts from the statement of profit or loss and other comprehensive income for the year ended 31 December 20X4 and the statement of financial position at 31 December 20X4 showing how the defined benefit scheme would be presented.

Test your understanding 4 – Defined benefit

EAU operates a defined benefit pension plan for its employees. At 1 January 20X0 the fair value of the pension plan assets was $2,600,000 and the present value of the plan liabilities was $2,900,000.

The actuary estimates that the current and past service costs for the year ended 31 December 20X0 is $450,000 and $90,000 respectively. The past service cost is caused by an increase in pension benefits. The plan liabilities reflected at the start of the year and 31 December 20X0 correctly reflect the impact of this increase.

The relevant discount rate for the year ended 31 December 20X0 was estimated at 5%.

The pension plan paid $240,000 to retired members in the year to 31 December 20X0. EAU paid $730,000 in contributions to the pension plan and this included $90,000 in respect of past service costs.

At 31 December 20X0 the fair value of the pension plan assets is $3,400,000 and the present value of the plan liabilities is $3,500,000.

Required:

Calculate the amounts that will be included in other comprehensive income for the year ended 31 December 20X0 (round all figures to the nearest $000).

Test your understanding 5 – Practice questions

(1) An entity makes contributions to the pension fund of employees at a rate of 5% of gross salary. The contributions made are $20,000 per month for convenience with the balance being contributed in the first month of the following accounting year. The wages and salaries for 20X3 are $4m.

Calculate the pension expense for 20X3 and clearly state whether it is an accrual or prepayment at the end of the year.

(2) Travis has a defined benefit pension plan and makes up financial statements to 31 March each year. The net pension liability (i.e. obligation less plan assets) at 31 March 20X3, was $80 million ($70 million at 31 March 20X2). The following additional information is relevant for the year ended 31 March 20X3:

- The discount rate relevant to the net liability at the start of the year was 10%.
- The current service cost was $90 million.
- At the end of the year the entity granted additional benefits to existing pensioners that have a present value of $20 million. These were not allowed for in the original actuarial assumptions.
- The entity paid pension contributions of $80 million.

What amount would be shown on the statement of financial position for the year ended 31 March 20X3?

(3) **Using the information from question 2 what amount would show on the statement of profit or loss as net interest? Clearly state whether the net interest is an income or cost.**

(4) **Using the information from question 2 what is the total effect of the pension scheme on profit?**

(5) **Using the information from questions 2 to 4 calculate the remeasurement gain or loss that would be measured in other comprehensive income.**

4 Summary Diagram

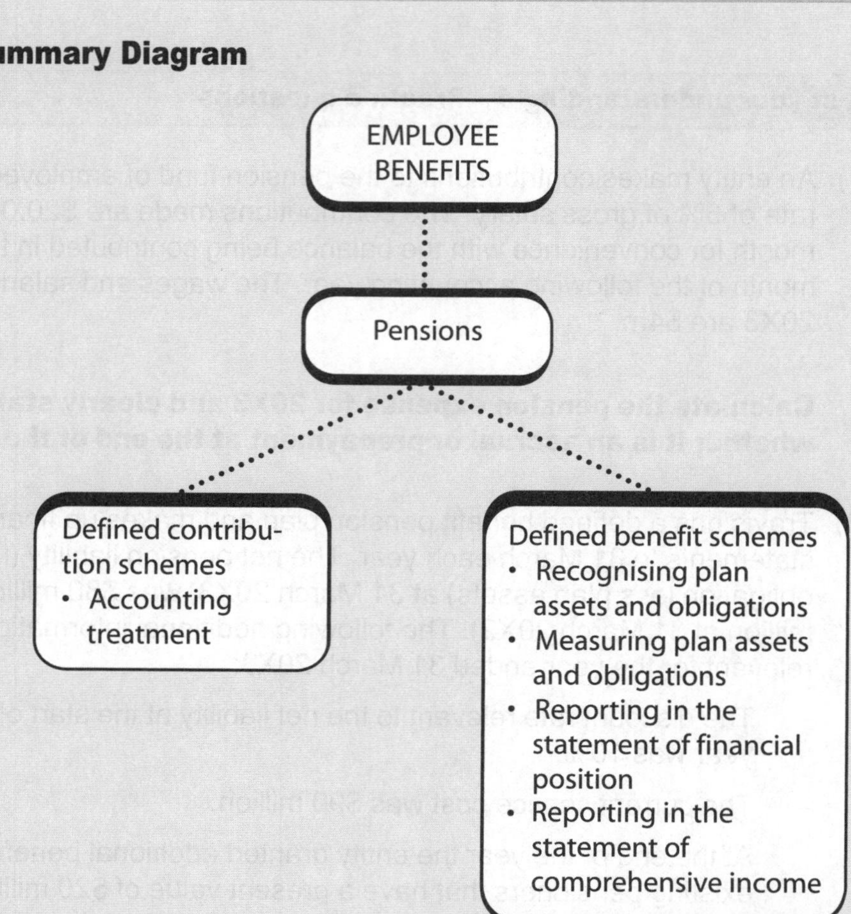
EMPLOYEE BENEFITS
Pensions
Defined contribution schemes
• Accounting treatment
Defined benefit schemes
• Recognising plan assets and obligations
• Measuring plan assets and obligations
• Reporting in the statement of financial position
• Reporting in the statement of comprehensive income

Test your understanding answers

Test your understanding 1 – Defined contribution

Statement of financial position

Current liabilities

Accrued pension contributions (10,000 + 39,000 – 35,000)	$14,000

Statement of profit or loss

Pension contributions (6% × 650,000)	$39,000

Test your understanding 2 – Defined benefit

	Assets	Liabilities	Net
	$000	$000	$000
Brought forward at 1 January 20X6	1,400	1,350	50
Current service cost	–	130	(130)
Interest income/cost (8% of opening balance)	112	108	4
Contributions	120	–	120
Benefits	(110)	(110)	–
	1,522	1,478	44
Remeasurement component gain/loss – balance	Gain 43	Loss 152	Loss (109)
Carried forward at 31 December 20X6	1,565	1,630	(65)

Statement of financial position (extract) at 31 December 20X6

	$000
Net pension liability (1,630 – 1,565)	65

Statement of profit or loss and other comprehensive income (extracts) for the year ended 31 March 20X3

	$000
Statement of profit or loss	
Service cost component	(130)
Net interest component	4
Net effect on profit	(126)
Other comprehensive income	
Items that will not be reclassified to profit or loss:	
Net remeasurement component	(109)
Net effect on total comprehensive income	(235)

Test your understanding 3 – Defined benefit

Statement of financial position (extract) as at 31 December 20X4

	$000
Net pension liability (1,280 – 1,240)	40

Statement of profit or loss (extracts) for the year ended 31 December 20X4

	$000
Service cost component (140 + 35 + 15)	(190)
Net interest component	(2)
Net expense recognised in the SPL	(192)

Other comprehensive income for the year ended 31 December 20X4

Items that will not be reclassified to profit or loss:

Net remeasurement component (W1)	62
Net impact on total comprehensive income for the year	(130)

Workings

(W1) **Remeasurement component**	**Assets**	**Liabilities**	**Net**
	$000	$000	$000
Opening net assets	1,010	1,030	(20)
Benefits paid out	(105)	(105)	–
Contributions paid in	110	–	110
Interest at 10% (on opening balances)	101	103	(2)
Current service cost	–	140	(140)
Past service cost	–	35	(35)
Curtailment cost	–	15	(15)
	1,116	1,218	(102)
Remeasurement component gain/ loss (balance)	Gain 124	Loss 62	Gain 62
Closing net assets	1,240	1,280	(40)

Test your understanding 4 – Defined benefit

Other comprehensive income

Items that will not be reclassified to profit or loss:	$000
Re-measurement component net gain (W1)	25

Workings

(W1) **Remeasurement component**	**Assets**	**Liabilities**	**Net**
	$000	$000	$000
Opening net assets	2,600	2,900	(300)
Current service cost	–	450	(450)
Past service cost	–	90	(90)
Interest at 5% (on opening balances)	130	145	(15)
Benefits paid out	(240)	(240)	–
Contributions paid in	730	–	730
	3,220	3,345	(125)
Remeasurement component gain/ loss (balance)	Gain 180	Loss 155	Gain 25
Closing net assets	3,400	3,500	(100)

Test your understanding 5 – Practice questions

(1) The charge to the statement of profit or loss should be:

$4m × 5% = $200,000

The statement of financial position will therefore show a prepayment of $40,000, being the difference between the $200,000 and the $240,000 paid in the year.

(2) **Statement of financial position (extract) at 31 March 20X3**

	$m
Net pension liability (closing balance)	80

(3) Net interest cost (10% × 70) = 7

The interest is calculated by multiplying the interest rate against the liability at the beginning of the year.

(4) The statement of profit or loss and other comprehensive income:

	$m
Statement of profit or loss	
Service cost component (90 + 20)	(110)
Net interest component (question 3)	(7)
Net effect on profit	(117)

(5) The remeasurement gain is $27m

	$m
Net liability brought forward	(70)
Net interest cost (10% × 70)	(7)
Current service cost	(90)
Additional benefits granted (past service costs)	(20)
Pension contributions paid	80
Actuarial gain (bal fig)	27
Net liability carried forward	(80)

chapter

20

Short-term finance and investments

Chapter learning objectives

On completion of their studies students should be able to:

- Describe sources of short-term funding.
- Describe alternatives for investment of short-term cash surpluses.
- Identify appropriate methods of finance for trading internationally.
- Illustrate numerically the financial impact of short-term funding and investment methods.

1 Session content

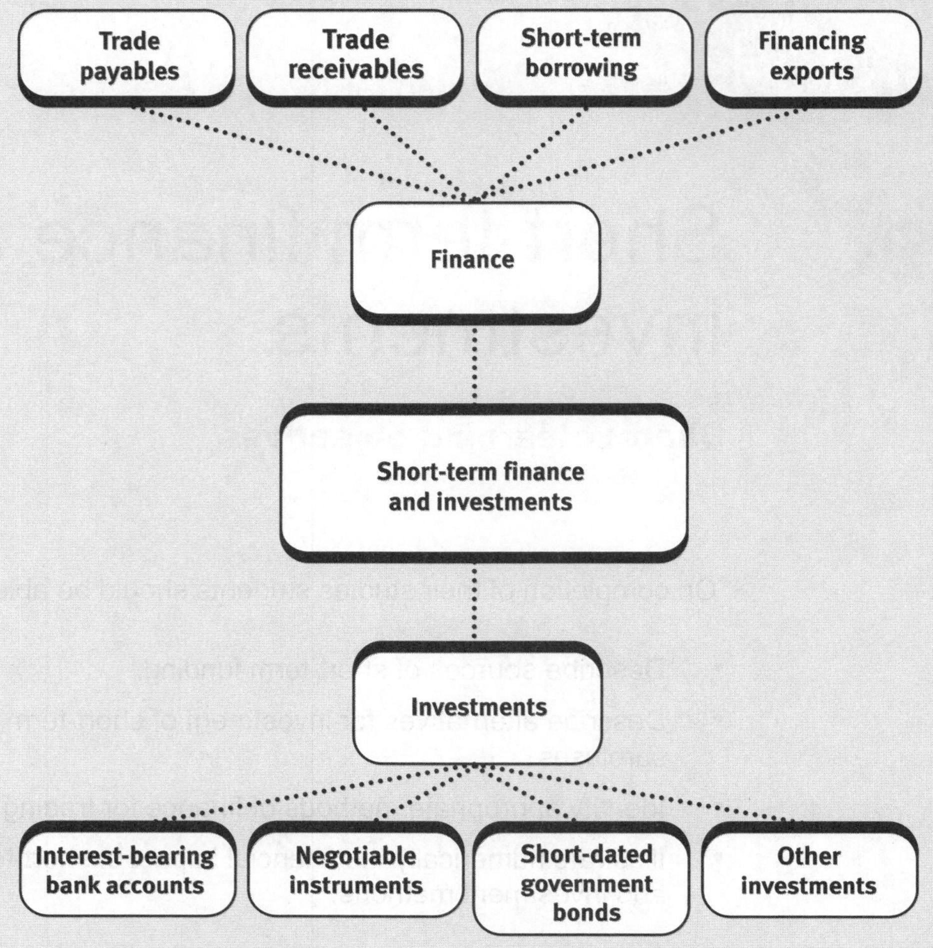

2 Short-term finance

Current liabilities should not be allowed to increase to a level where the cash position and liquidity of the company are at risk. This requires careful management of short-term finance.

The main sources of short-term funding are:

- trade payables
- factoring or invoice discounting of trade receivables
- bank overdrafts and short-term loans
- financing exports

Trade payables

Payables may be used as a source of short-term finance by delaying payment to suppliers.

By paying on credit the entity is able to 'fund' its inventory of material through its suppliers. To maximize this benefit, the entity should aim to pay as late as possible without damaging its trading relationship with its suppliers.

If a cash discount is offered, the entity must weigh the saving from the discount against the additional cost of borrowing the funds needed to finance the early payment. The entity must also be aware of whether the funds are available to take up the discount.

Benefits of paying suppliers late	Potential problems when paying suppliers late
• alleviates cash flow difficulties	• loss of any settlement discount
• cash can earn a return whilst still in the paying entity's account	• could obtain a poor credit rating
	• supplier may stop further supplies
	• supplier may increase future selling prices to compensate
	• could face legal action from the supplier

Trade payables as a source of short-term funds

Suppliers are a source of short-term finance because they provide goods (inventory) on credit. In some cases, suppliers might not be paid until after the goods they have supplied have been re-sold. This occurs, for example, in supermarkets. A supermarket might re-sell the goods provided by a supplier many days before the supplier is eventually paid.

It is a well-established business practice that trade credit should be agreed, which means that suppliers finance the business of their customers to some extent.

The amount of trade credit varies from one industry to another, and can also vary with changes in economic conditions. However, if normal credit terms are 30 days, and a company purchases, say, $1,200,000 of goods on credit each year, it is normally financed by $100,000 of trade credit on average.

A huge attraction of trade credit is that it has no interest cost. Unlike banks, trade suppliers do not charge interest on debts unless payment occurs after the due date, in which case suppliers might charge interest.

Trade receivables

Receivables may be used as a source of short-term finance by:

- Factoring
- Invoice discounting

Factoring

This is outsourcing of the credit control department to a third party. The debts of the entity are effectively sold to a factor (normally owned by a bank). The factor takes on the responsibility to collect the debt for a fee. The factor offers three services:

(1) **Debt collection** – The credit control function.

(2) **Financing** – Funds may be advanced to the company prior to the debt being collected.

(3) **Credit insurance** – The factor may take the responsibility for irrecoverable debt. For this to be the case the factor would dictate to whom the entity was able to offer credit. This is called 'without recourse' factoring.

The factor is often more successful at enforcing credit terms, leading to a lower level of debts outstanding. Factoring is therefore not only a source of short-term finance but also an external means of controlling or reducing the level of receivables.

Invoice discounting

This is a service also provided by a factoring entity. Selected invoices are used as security against which the entity may borrow funds. This is a temporary source of finance, repayable when the debt is cleared. The key advantage of invoice discounting is that it is a confidential service and the customer need not know about it.

One use for invoice discounting is as a key financing tool for new businesses such as management buyouts (MBOs). The creditworthiness of their customers is probably higher than their own and is utilised to borrow funds.

Short-term borrowing

Short-term cash requirements can also be funded by borrowing from the bank. There are two main sources of bank lending:

- bank overdraft
- bank loans

Bank overdrafts are mainly provided by the clearing banks and are an important source of finance for an entity.

Advantages	**Disadvantages**
• Flexibility • Only pay for what is used, so generally cheaper	• Repayable on demand • May require security • Variable finance costs

Bank loans are a contractual agreement for a specific sum, loaned for a fixed period, at an agreed rate of interest. They are less flexible and more expensive than overdrafts but provide greater security.

Short term borrowing

Finance costs on bank loans and overdrafts are normally variable, i.e. they alter in line with base rates. Fixed rate loans are available, but are less popular with firms (and providers of finance).

Bank overdrafts

A common source of short-term financing for many businesses is a bank overdraft. These are mainly provided by the clearing banks and represent permission by the bank to draw funds even though the firm has insufficient funds deposited in the account to meet the expected withdrawal amount.

An overdraft limit will be placed on this facility, but provided the limit is not exceeded, the firm is free to make as much or as little use of the overdraft as it desires. The bank charges interest on amounts outstanding at any one time, and the bank may also require repayment of an overdraft at any time.

The advantages of overdrafts are the following.

- Flexibility – they can be used as required.
- Cheapness – interest is only payable on the finance actually used, usually at 2–5% above base rate (and all loan interest is a tax deductible expense).

The disadvantages of overdrafts are as follows.

- Overdrafts are legally repayable on demand. Normally, however, the bank will give customers assurances that they can rely on the facility for a certain time period, say six months.
- Security is usually required by way of fixed or floating charges on assets or sometimes, in private entities and partnerships, by personal guarantees from owners.
- Interest costs vary with bank base rates. This makes it harder to forecast and exposes the business to future increases in interest rates.

Overall, bank overdrafts are one of the most important sources of short-term finance for industry.

Bank loans

A bank loan represents a formal agreement between the bank and the borrower, that the bank will lend a specific sum for a specific period (one to seven years being the most common). Interest must be paid on the whole of this sum for the duration of the loan.

This source is, therefore, liable to be more expensive than the overdraft and is less flexible but, on the other hand, there is no danger that the source will be withdrawn before the expiry of the loan period. Interest rates and requirements for security will be similar to overdraft lending.

Comparison of bank loans and overdrafts

Consider a company that requires a maximum of $600 over the next four months. However, it is only halfway through month four that it actually requires the full amount.

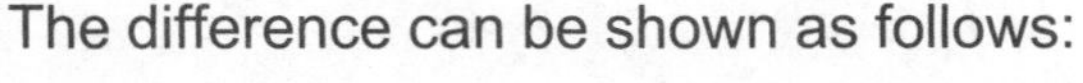

The difference can be shown as follows:

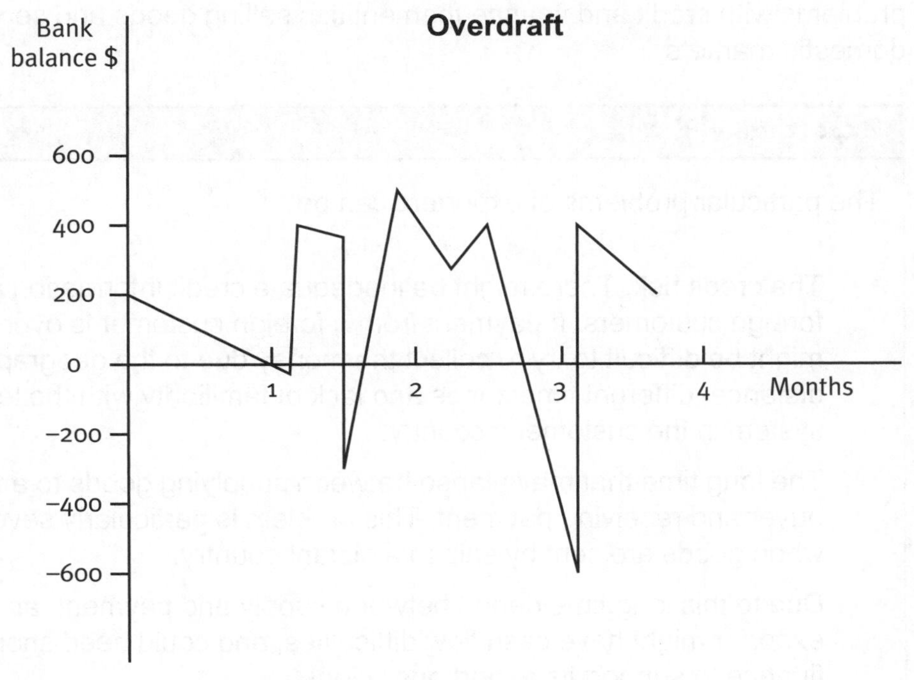

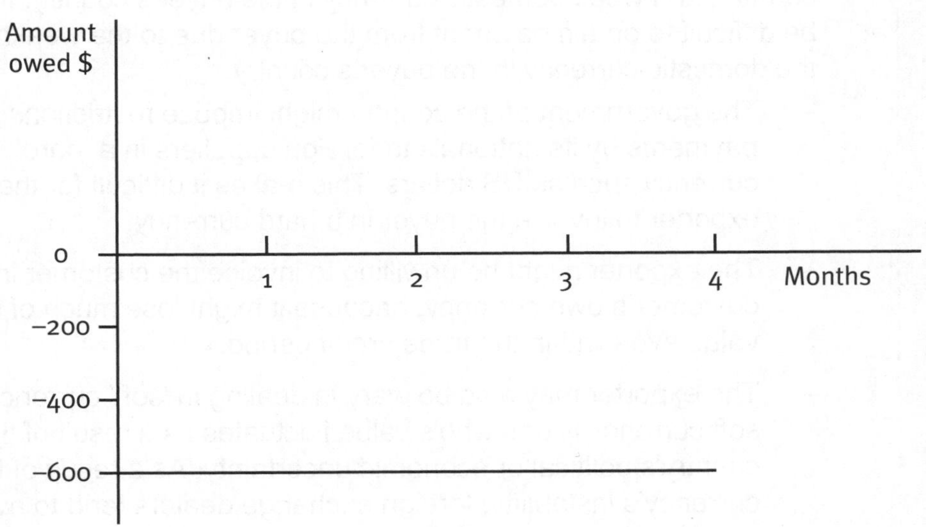

If an overdraft is used, the company will pay interest on the maximum amount part way through month 4. For the remainder of the period it will pay interest on an overdraft of substantially less than that, or it will pay no interest at all as it has a positive bank balance. If it borrows $600 by way of a bank loan at the beginning of the four months, it must pay interest for four months on the amount borrowed, despite the fact that it rarely requires the full sum.

3 Financing exports

Entities exporting goods to other countries often have much greater problems with credit and finance than entities selling goods and services to domestic markets.

Export risks

The particular problems of exporters can be:

- The credit risk. There might be inadequate credit information about foreign customers. If payment from a foreign customer is overdue, it might be difficult to try to collect the money due to the geographical distance, different time zones and lack of familiarity with the legal system in the customer's country.
- The long time that may elapse between supplying goods to a foreign buyer and receiving payment. This problem is particularly severe when goods are sent by ship to a distant country.
- Due to this long time period between supply and payment, an exporter might have cash flow difficulties, and could need short-term finance to support its export operations.
- There may be foreign exchange control restrictions in the buyer's country, and weak domestic currency in the buyer's country. It might be difficult to obtain payment from the buyer due to the weakness of the domestic currency in the buyer's country.
  - The government of the country might impose restrictions on payments by its nationals to foreign suppliers in a 'hard' currency such as US dollars. This makes it difficult for the exporter to invoice the buyer in a hard currency.
  - The exporter might be unwilling to invoice the customer in the customer's own currency, because it might lose much of its value even within the trade credit period.
  - The exporter may also be wary in dealing in 'soft' currencies. A soft currency is one who's value fluctuates as a result of the country's political or economic uncertainty. As a result of this currency's instability, foreign exchange dealers tend to avoid it as it is difficult to predict and 'price'. It may therefore be difficult for the exporter to sell this currency and convert it back to their own domestic currency.

Several methods are available for dealing with the problems of financing exports and controlling the credit risk. These include:

- documentary credits
- bills of exchange
- export factoring
- forfaiting

Financial instruments

Documentary credits (irrevocable letters of credit)

A letter of credit is a document, issued by a bank on behalf of a customer, authorising a person to draw money to a specified amount from its branches or correspondents, usually in another country, when the conditions set out in the document have been met.

Business transactions between businesses in some countries are carried out on normal commercial terms. For example, trading between entities in the European Union is carried out mainly on normal credit terms, although a foreign currency might be involved for either the buyer or seller.

Trading between other countries, however, is more complex, particularly when it will take a considerable time to ship the goods from the exporter's country to the importer. The exporter might want payment as soon as possible, but the importer needs to be satisfied before paying, that the exporter has complied with the terms of the sale agreement.

The problem of guaranteeing payment can be overcome by using an irrevocable letter of credit, also called an irrevocable documentary credit. A letter of credit is an undertaking given by its issuer that payment will be guaranteed for the exporter, provided that the exporter complies with certain specific requirements within a specified time limit.

The specific requirements relate mainly to the provision of satisfactory documentation for the exports, such as valid shipping documents and insurance documents, and valid import or export licences. The exporter must provide these as evidence that goods of the proper quantity and description are being shipped in the agreed manner, and are properly insured. This gives comfort to the buyer that the goods will be delivered as ordered.

The letter of credit is provided not by the importer, but by a bank on behalf of the importer. It might be issued by a bank in the importer's country, and confirmed by another bank in the exporter's country. A confirmed irrevocable letter of credit therefore provides payment guarantees to the exporter from two banks, thereby minimising the credit risk. Once issued, the irrevocable letter of credit cannot be revoked and cancelled. However, it ceases to apply if the exporter fails to comply with any of the specified terms and conditions.

An irrevocable letter of credit is arranged as follows:

- The importer asks a bank in its country to provide an irrevocable letter of credit for an import transaction. The exporter might require the letter of credit also to be confirmed by another bank in its own country.
- The letter of credit is issued, and a copy is given to the exporter.
- The cost of the letter of credit is usually paid by the importer.
- The exporter complies with the requirements of the letter of credit, and provides the specified documentation to a bank that will check to make sure that all the documentation is in order. This bank could be either the bank that issued the letter of credit or the confirming bank.
- If the documents are in order, the exporter will be paid under the terms of the letter of credit. In many cases, this involves a bill of exchange (see below).

The guarantee provided by the issuing bank in its letter of credit relates to compliance by the exporter with requirements relating to the documentation. The bank does not get involved in the details of the trading transaction itself.

- Even if the goods are shipped correctly, the bank will not guarantee payment if the documentation fails to meet the specifications in the letter of credit.
- If there is a dispute between the exporter and the importer about the actual shipment, the bank will honour its guarantee provided that the documentation was provided correctly and as specified in the letter of credit.

A bill of exchange

A bill of exchange is a negotiable instrument, drawn by one party on another, for example, by a supplier of goods on a customer, who by accepting (signing) the bill, acknowledges the debt, which may be payable immediately (a sight draft) or at some future date (a time draft). The holder of the bill can thereafter use an accepted time draft to pay a debt to a third party, or can discount it to raise cash.

A bill of exchange is a method of arranging a payment. There are three parties to a bill of exchange:

- the drawer, who is the person who issues the bill
- the drawee, who is the person to whom the bill is addressed, and
- the payee, who is the person to whom payment should be made.

The drawer and the payee are often the same person. A bill of exchange might be a sight bill, which is payable immediately, but bills used for export finance are term bills, which are payable at a specified future date.

Payment by means of a bill of exchange is arranged as follows:

- The drawer issues a bill of exchange (or 'draws the bill on the drawee'). It might help to think of the bill at this stage as a 'You Owe Me'. It specifies that a sum of money must be paid by the drawee to the payee on a specified date.
- The drawee acknowledges the obligation to make the payment by signing the bill. The drawee is said to 'accept' the bill by signing it. In effect, an accepted bill is no longer a 'You Owe Me' from the drawer, but an 'I promise to pay' by the drawee.
- The accepted bill is returned to the drawer, who might hold it until maturity.
- When the bill reaches its maturity (the payment date specified), the drawer presents the bill for payment through the banking system.

A significant characteristic of bills of exchange is that:

- the drawee is given a period of credit before having to pay a term bill, but
- the drawer or payee can obtain payment earlier than the bill's maturity date, by means of discounting the bill.

When a bill is discounted, it is sold in the financial markets at a discount to face value. The size of the discount reflects the rate of interest that the buyer of the bill requires from holding the bill to maturity.

Export factoring

Export factoring is similar to ordinary factoring, with the exception that the factoring organisation agrees to factor the client's trade receivables for exports. The factor's services include administration of the receivables ledger and collecting payment, and providing factor finance.

In view of the problems that can arise with collecting payments from customers in other countries, the expertise of an export factor can be very helpful, particularly for small and medium-sized businesses with little experience in collecting foreign payments.

Forfaiting

Forfaiting can be a source of medium-term trade finance. It is particularly suitable for the financing of export transactions for which, due to the nature of the goods involved or the size of the transactions, payments are made over a period of several years. It has been used fairly widely in Europe, particularly in Switzerland and Germany where forfaiting originated.

An importer might want to buy capital goods, such as machinery or equipment, but needs finance for the purchase. The capital goods will be used to earn profits in future years, and the importer might want to use these future profits to provide the cash to pay for the goods.

In order to set up a forfaiting arrangement, the importer must be prepared to:

- pay some of the purchase price on delivery, and
- make the remaining payments at regular intervals over a period of several years.

In a forfaiting arrangement:

- The importer issues a number of promissory notes with payment dates at regular intervals. A promissory note is a promise to make a specified payment, and by issuing a series of promissory notes the importer is promising to make a series of payments at future dates, over a period of several years. (Instead of using promissory notes, the importer might be required to accept a series of term bills of exchange drawn on it by the exporter.)
- The importer must then find a bank that is prepared to guarantee the promissory notes. Guaranteeing a promissory note is called avalising the note. The avalised notes can be sold, like bank bills of exchange, at 'fine' rates of discount.
- The exporter's bank finds another bank that is willing to act as forfeiter. Some banks specialise in this type of finance. Forfaiting involves buying the avalised promissory notes at a discount to face value (or buying bills of exchange at a discount). The rate of discount at which the forfaiting bank buys the notes is specified as a fixed rate in the forfaiting agreement.
- The exporter therefore receives immediate payment from the forfaiting bank for the notes that it has purchased.
- The forfaiting bank holds onto the notes, and at the appropriate payment dates presents them to the importer for payment.

The forfaiter buys the promissory notes without recourse to the exporter. The exporter has therefore obtained payment for the goods, without any risk of having to return the money if the importer fails to meet its payment obligations.

The forfaiter therefore accepts the risk of non-payment by the importer (failing to honour the promissory notes or bills of exchange).

The key features of forfaiting are therefore that:

- The importer obtains medium-term finance for much of the purchase cost of the goods.
- The exporter receives immediate payment.
- The credit risk is accepted by the forfaiting bank, although this risk is reduced by the avalisation of the promissory notes by the avalising bank.

Forfaiting has been defined in CIMA's Official Terminology as follows: 'Forfaiting is the purchase of financial instruments such as bills of exchange … on a non-recourse basis by a forfaiter, who deducts interest (in the form of a discount) at an agreed rate for the period covered by the notes. The forfaiter assumes the responsibility for collecting the debts from the importer (buyer) who initially accepted the financial instrument drawn by the seller of the goods. Traditionally, forfaiting is fixed rate medium-term (one-to-five year) finance.'

4 Short-term investments

A business might have surplus cash for a period of time. Surplus cash is usually temporary and available for several weeks or months. Eventually it will be used to pay suppliers or settle other liabilities, invest in new non-current assets or pay a dividend.

Money in an operational bank account earns no income, because banks do not pay interest to businesses for cash in their day-to-day accounts. If a business wishes to maximise its profits, it should consider using the cash to earn some return in the time when it is temporarily surplus to requirements.

Cash surpluses can be invested in a range of short-term interest-earning investments such as:

- Interest-bearing bank accounts
- Negotiable instruments
- Short-dated government bonds
- Other short-term investments

Investment criteria

When a business has surplus cash to invest temporarily, it has to decide which investments to select from the different choices available. There are several criteria that should be considered when making these choices:

- maturity
- return
- risk
- liquidity
- diversification

More details

Maturity

A short-term investment might involve investing an amount of money for a specific period of time, and receiving interest and the payment of a principal amount at a specified future date (the 'maturity' of the investment). If the investment is cashed in or sold before maturity, there could be a risk of some loss of market value or some loss of interest.

The maturity of a short-term investment should ideally be no longer than the duration of the cash surplus. If the cash is needed before the investment reaches maturity, the investment will have to be 'cashed in' early, with some risk of loss of capital value or interest.

Return

With short-term investments, return is the interest yield on the investment. Some investments offer a higher yield than others. If the investment is 'redeemable' (i.e. where a capital amount will be repaid to the investor) then the capital repayment will also form part of the return.

Risk

Some investments are more risky than others. Risk refers to the possibility that the investment might fall in value, or that there might be some doubt about the eventual payment of interest or repayment of investment principal. As a general rule, higher-risk investments have to offer a higher return in order to attract investors.

For example, suppose that two banks offer high-interest savings accounts to businesses, for which there is a minimum notice period of two weeks for withdrawal of funds. Bank A might be a major bank with a 'triple-A' credit rating, and Bank B might be a regional bank in a developing country. To attract investors, Bank B would have to offer a higher interest rate on its savings accounts than Bank A, because the perceived risk for investors in an investment in Bank B would be higher.

Investing in equities is high risk. The value of equities depends on the profitability and future prospects of the company, and share prices also rise or fall more generally in line with broader movements in the stock market. Since share prices can fall by a large amount in a short period of time, equities are generally regarded as an unsuitable form of short-term investment.

Short-term investments should usually be preferred to longer-dated investments, because the risk of a fall in market value is less. Prudent entities should also avoid high-risk investments such as equities, and should look for short-term investments that will keep the value of the investment secure.

Liquidity

Liquidity refers to the ease with which an investment can be 'cashed in' quickly, without any significant loss of value or interest. All short-term investments are less liquid than cash in an operational bank account, but some are more liquid than others. For example, many savings accounts or deposit accounts are reasonably liquid, and a depositor can often withdraw cash immediately losing only several days' interest.

In contrast, works of art such as paintings might be a profitable long-term investment, but they are very illiquid as short-term investments. Paintings cannot be sold quickly without a significant risk of having to sell at below true market value.

Diversification

There is a general rule that investors should not 'put all their eggs in one basket'. They should perhaps diversify by investing in a range of different investments. In this way, if some investments perform badly, the investor is not exposed to significant losses, because the other investments in the portfolio should perform better.
However, diversification is less essential for investing short-term cash surpluses than for investing long-term in equities and bonds.

Interest-bearing accounts

These can fall into two categories:

- bank deposit accounts
- money market deposits

Deposit accounts

- Some deposit accounts are 'instant access' accounts, which allow the investor to withdraw the money without notice and without loss of interest. The interest rate is usually low on these accounts, and they are used when the investor wants to earn some interest on surplus cash, but places great importance on instant liquidity.
- Some deposit accounts or savings accounts allow the investor to withdraw funds without notice, but the investor will suffer some loss of interest. For example, a deposit account might require a notice of withdrawal of at least seven days, but the investor might be permitted to withdraw the funds without notice with a penalty of seven days' lost interest.
- In some cases, an investor might be unable to withdraw funds from the account without giving a minimum notice period.

Money market deposits

Money market deposits are amounts of money deposited through a bank in the money markets. These are the financial markets for short-term borrowing and lending. The money markets are used largely by banks and other financial institutions, for depositing and lending funds. Banks can deposit short-term funds with other banks, or borrow short-term from other banks in the inter-bank market.

Interest yields in the inter-bank market are often reasonably attractive, and it is now quite common for entities with large temporary cash surpluses to arrange with their bank to have the money deposited in the money markets (inter-bank market) or at money market interest rates.

Money invested in a money market deposit cannot be withdrawn until the deposit matures. It is therefore important that money should not be invested for a period longer than the investor's expected cash surplus. Money market deposits can be for very short periods of time, as little as one day, or for as long as several months (and even up to one year). However, very short-term deposits should be large amounts of money, so that the interest earned justifies the effort of making the deposits.

Effective annual interest yield

Interest on bank deposits accumulates on the principal sum invested. Interest is added at specified regular intervals, such as every month, every three months, every six months or annually. The frequency of adding interest affects the actual interest yield on the investment.

Test your understanding 1 – Returns

An entity has $1,000,000 to invest for 12 months.

The choices available are:

- a deposit account offering interest at 10% per year, with interest calculated quarterly
- a deposit account offering interest at 10.25% per year, with interest added annually.

Required:

Calculate which deposit provides the best return.

Interest earned

You might be required to calculate the amount of interest earned on a deposit or savings account within a particular period of time. If you are given the effective annual yield (or if you are given an 'annual yield' with no further information), the interest calculation is simply:

$$\text{Interest} = \text{Amount deposited} \times \text{annualised interest rate} \times \frac{\text{Number of days' interest earned}}{\text{Annual day count}}$$

The annual day count is the number of days in the year, for interest calculation purposes. This might seem unusual, since a year has either 365 or 366 days. However, in the financial markets, there are special conventions for the number of days in a year. Whereas interest on sterling is calculated on the assumption of a 365-day year, interest on the US dollar in the money markets is calculated on the assumption of 360 days in the year.

Negotiable instruments

Negotiable instruments are financial instruments that may be obtained as investments. A key feature of negotiable instruments is that title passes when the instrument is handed from one person to another. They are 'bearer instruments', and ownership does not have to be recorded in a register of owners. This means that a negotiable instrument can easily be sold by one person to another or one entity to another.

Examples of negotiable instruments are:

- bank notes
- bearer bonds
- Certificates of Deposit
- Bills of Exchange
- Treasury bills

The most important negotiable instruments as short-term investments are Certificates of Deposit and Treasury bills, and possibly also bills of exchange (particularly bank bills of high quality banks).

More details

Certificate of Deposit

A Certificate of Deposit or CD is a negotiable instrument that provides evidence of a short-term deposit with a bank for a fixed term and earning a specified amount of interest. The maturity of the deposit is usually 90 days or less, but can be longer. The amount deposited is at least US$100,000 (or its equivalent in other currencies), but usually larger.

The holder of the CD at maturity has the right to take the deposit with interest. The CD holder presents the CD at maturity to a recognised bank, which will then present the instrument to the bank holding the deposit, and arrange for the withdrawal of the deposit with interest.

Until maturity, the money is 'locked up' with the bank, and cannot be withdrawn.

When an organisation has a temporary cash surplus, it might arrange with its bank to place the money in a fixed term deposit account, and for the bank to issue a CD. The CD will state the identity of the bank, the amount deposited, the maturity date of the deposit and the interest that will accumulate.

- The organisation can hold the CD until maturity and then claim the money.
- Alternatively, if it needs cash before the deposit matures, it can sell the CD. There is an active secondary market in Certificates of Deposit, and a company can arrange for its bank to sell a CD on its behalf.

Another company with a short-term cash surplus could either arrange its own Certificate of Deposit or purchase an existing CD in the secondary market.

Investment yield on CDs

Since Certificates of Deposit are negotiable instruments, they are more attractive investments than money market deposits from the point of view of liquidity. A CD holder can sell the CD to obtain funds quickly, whereas a money market deposit cannot be withdrawn until maturity. Yields on CDs are therefore slightly lower than interest yields on money market deposits.

Bills of exchange

Bills of exchange have been described earlier in the chapter, in the context of export finance, although they have a broader use and are not restricted to export finance arrangements.

The significance of bills of exchange as a short-term investment is that they are negotiable instruments. There is an active money market for bills of exchange (which is called the discount market) and investors can buy bills. The market is particularly active in bills of exchange that are payable by top-quality banks: in the UK these are sometimes called 'eligible bank bills'.

The buyer of a bill of exchange obtains the right to receive payment by the issuer of the bill when it matures. A bill of exchange is usually an undertaking to pay a fixed sum of money at maturity, with no interest. An investor in a bill will therefore buy the bill at a discount to face value (and hence the right to receive the payment). Bills of exchange are therefore examples of discount paper.

Although it is possible to buy bills of exchange that have been accepted (and so are payable) by trading entities, investors place more value in bank bills. These are bills of exchange that have been accepted by a bank, and are payable by the bank. If the bank has a high credit status, the risk of investing in its bills is very low.

Yields on bills vary according to the credit risk associated with the bill, and an investor will be prepared to pay more for a top-quality bank bill than for a trade bill with much higher credit risk.

Treasury bills

Treasury bills are negotiable instruments issued by the government, with a maturity of less than one year. In practice, most Treasury bills have a maturity of three months (91 days). Treasury bills are used by a government to finance short-term cash requirements, and in countries such as the US and the UK, Treasury bills are issued at regular intervals when investors are invited to apply to buy bills in the new issue.

Since Treasury bills are debts of the government, they have a high credit quality, risk is low, and yields for investors are therefore also lower than for many other short-term investments. Treasury bills issued by a government and denominated in the domestic currency should be risk-free. For example, US Treasury bills are risk-free investments, because there is no doubt that the US government will redeem the debt at maturity.

Treasury bills are redeemable at face value. For example, the US government will redeem a 91-day $1,000 Treasury bill for $1,000 91 days after its issue. Since the bills are redeemable at par, investors pay less than face value to buy them. Like bills of exchange, Treasury bills are examples of discount paper.

Although yields on Treasury bills are relatively low, they can be attractive short-term investments because of their risk-free nature and their liquidity. There is a large and active secondary market in Treasury bills, such as US Treasury bills in the US and UK government Treasury bills in the UK.

Calculations

The amount of discount on a bill can be calculated as follows:

$D = R \times F \times T/Y$

where:

D = the amount of the discount

R = the rate of discount or discount yield, expressed as a proportion (for example, 6% = 0.06)

F = the face value of the bill: this will be paid to the bill holder at maturity

T = time, measured as the number of days in the interest period

Y = the days in a standard year (applying the appropriate 'day count convention' for the number of days in a year)

The issue price of a discount interest instrument such as a Treasury bill or bill of exchange is its face value less the discount:

Price = F – D

The discount explained

Whereas some investments such as bank deposit accounts and money market deposits earn interest on a capital sum invested, other instruments are issued at a discount to face value, and investors earn their return from the difference between the discount price on purchase and the par redemption value at maturity. The mathematics of discount paper returns are slightly different from the calculation of interest-yielding investments.

When a financial instrument is quoted on a discount interest basis, it is redeemed at maturity at its face value, and issued at a discount to face value. For example, a 91-day Treasury bill for $1,000 might be issued at $998.25 and redeemed at $1,000. The difference between the issue price and the redemption value is the discount which represents the return that the investor will make by holding the bill until maturity. The size of this return can be measured as a discount interest rate.

Test your understanding 2 – Treasury bills

A US Treasury bill with a face value of $1,000 is issued at a 5% discount yield for 91 days.

Calculate its issue price?

(There are 360 days in a year for interest purposes.)

Short-dated government bonds

Entities can invest temporary surplus cash in government bonds. If they do:

- they will receive interest on the due payment dates
- they can liquidate their investment at any time by selling the bonds in the secondary market
- if the bonds are short-dated when purchased, they can hold the bonds to maturity and have them redeemed at par.

However, there is some price risk with bonds, particularly longer-dated bonds. If interest rates change in the market, the market value of bonds will rise or fall. Bond prices rise when interest rates fall, but prices fall when interest rates go up. The movement in price is greater for longer-dated bonds.

Government bonds

Treasury bills are government debt instruments with a maturity of less than one year when they are issued. Government bonds are longer-dated government debt instruments, with a maturity of several years, sometimes 20 years or longer, when they are issued.

Government bonds are issued by governments in order to borrow long-term, and they can be purchased by any investors, including private individuals and entities. Investors can buy government bonds when they are first issued. Alternatively, they can be purchased in the secondary market at any time up to maturity of the bonds. There is a very large and active secondary market for the bonds of some governments, such as:

- the 'Treasuries' market in the US for US government Treasury bonds and notes (a note is similar to a bond, but with a shorter maturity on issue), and
- the 'gilts' market in the UK. 'Gilts' is short for gilt-edged securities, which is a term used to describe Treasury Stock and other bonds issued by the UK government.

An attractive feature of government bonds issued by a national government, is that in many countries they can be considered to be almost risk-free when they are issued in the domestic bond market and denominated in the domestic currency. For example, UK gilt-edged securities denominated in sterling are risk-free, in the sense that there is no credit risk. It is absolutely certain that the UK government will pay the due interest on time and will redeem the bonds at maturity. It should be noted that this might not apply in all countries and the international financial crisis in 2009/2010 threw up many examples of countries who were unable to meet their payments.

Investors with a temporary cash surplus, wishing to invest in government bonds should ideally invest in short-dated bonds. These are bonds with only a short time remaining to maturity. However, they can invest instead in longer-dated bonds, which can be sold easily in the secondary market when cash is needed.

Characteristics

Government bonds and corporate bonds (bonds issued by entities) have many features in common

- **Face value.** Bonds have a face value or nominal value.
- **Coupon.** Interest is payable on bonds at regular intervals, such as every six months or every year. Interest is usually a fixed rate, although some bonds (floating rate notes or FRNs) pay a variable rate of interest. For example, if bonds have an 8% 'coupon' on which interest is payable every six months, interest will be paid at the rate of 4% (8%/2) on the face value of the bonds every six months.
- **Redemption date and redemption value.** Bonds are redeemable at maturity (unless they are 'perpetual bonds' or unless they are 'convertible' into another financial instrument). Bonds are usually redeemable at their face value ('at par').
- **Market value.** Bonds are not necessarily issued at par, although they are usually issued at close to their par value. Their market value will vary over time, between their issue and their redemption. However, if they are redeemable at par, their value will move towards par value as the redemption date approaches. For comparative purposes, the market prices of bonds are quoted relative to their par value of $100. For example, if bonds are priced at $102.50, this means that their current market price is $102.50 for every $100 face value of the bonds.

Calculations

The yield on a bond investment is usually measured as a **redemption yield**. The redemption yield can be calculated as the discounted annual rate of return (internal rate of return) at which the present value of the future interest payments and the redemption value of the bond at maturity are equal to the current market value of the bond.

More details

Although interest on bonds is shown as a coupon rate, the actual investment yield earned by investors in bonds is a different percentage. There are two reasons for this:

- The market value of a bond is not the same as its face value. For example, suppose that a bond with a 4% coupon has a market value of $95.00. The coupon is 4%, but the interest yield is 4.21% (4/95.00).
- The market price of a bond is not the same as its eventual redemption value, which is usually at par, and the yield for the investor should also take into account the gain or the loss for the investor from holding the bond to maturity. For example, if a bond has a market price of $95.00 and is redeemable in four years at $100.00, the investor will gain $5.00 on the investment of $95.00 by holding the bond for four more years.

The yield on a bond investment is usually measured as the yield to maturity. This is the yield that will be obtained from an investment in the bond at a price P, and holding the bond until maturity. The yield to maturity is a combination of:

- the interest yield on the bond (the coupon as a percentage of the market price),
- plus an annualised return to maturity from the capital gain on redemption of the bond at par,
100 – P, where P is less than 100, or
- minus an annualised negative return from the capital loss at redemption, P – 100, where P is higher than 100.

The yield to maturity can be calculated as the discounted annual rate of return (internal rate of return) at which the present value of the future interest payments and the redemption value of the bond at maturity are equal to the current market value of the bond.

Investors are interested in the yield to maturity from a bond, not the coupon yield.

Test your understanding 3 – Government bonds

A bond with a coupon rate of 7% is redeemable in eight years' time for $100. Its current purchase price is $82 ex-interest (this is a term used to explain that interest has just been paid and that the next interest payment will not be due for another year).

Calculate the percentage yield to maturity?

Other short-term investments

This chapter has described the short-term investments that are most commonly purchased or used by entities. There are other short-term investments such as:

- corporate bonds, and
- commercial paper (CP).

These are more likely to be purchased by investment institutions rather than by entities with a short-term cash surplus.

More details

Corporate bonds

Corporate bonds are bonds issued by an entity. They are long-term investments, and so unsuitable for investing a short-term cash surplus, and they can also be a high risk investment. Bond prices fluctuate with movements in the general level of interest rates, and corporate bond values are also affected by the perceived credit risk of the entity issuing the bonds.

Commercial paper (CP)

Commercial paper consists of short-dated negotiable debt instruments issued by an entity, and sold by a bank managing the entity's commercial paper programme. In practice, although CP is negotiable, it is generally purchased by large investment institutions and held to maturity. It is not normally regarded as a suitable type of short-term investment of cash surpluses by a trading entity.

Test your understanding 4 – Practice questions

(1) **Identify which of the following investments offers the highest effective annual interest yield:**

- A A deposit account paying interest at 5%, interest payable monthly
- B A deposit account paying interest at 5.25%, interest payable quarterly
- C A deposit account paying interest at 5.4%, interest payable every six months
- D A deposit account paying interest at 5.5%, interest payable annually

(2) On 1 April 20X4 an entity placed $5 million on deposit at an interest rate of 6.25%. The deposit has a maturity date of 30 June 20X4 (91 days later).

Calculate the amount of cash that the entity will receive on maturity of the deposit.

(There are 360 days in a year for interest purposes.)

(3) **Which of the following would not normally be used to deal with the credit risk associated with exporting:**

- A Documentary credits
- B Forfaiting
- C Bills of exchange
- D Treasury bills

(4) A Treasury bill with a face value of $100 is issued at a 8% discount yield for 30 days.

Calculate its issue price.

(There are 360 days in a year for interest purposes.)

(5) **Which of the following factors would not normally be considered when choosing between different sources of investment:**

A Risk

B Liquidity

C Currency

D Maturity

Summary Diagram

Trade payables
- Benefits
- Problems

Trade receivables
- Factors
- Invoice discounting

Short-term borrowing
- Overdrafts
- Loans

Financing exports
- Documentary credits
- Bills of exchange
- Export factoring

Finance

Short-term finance and investments

Investments

Interest-bearing bank accounts
- Bank deposit accounts
- Money market deposits

Negotiable instruments
- Bank notes
- Bearer bonds
- Certificates of deposit
- Bills of exchange
- Treasury bills

Short-dated government bonds

Other investments
- Corporate bonds
- Commercial paper

Test your understanding answers

Test your understanding 1 – Returns

It might seem that the better investment is the deposit account offering 10.25%, but this is not the case.

When interest is quoted at 10% per year, payable quarterly, this means that the interest rate is 10%/4 = 2.5% each quarter. Interest is paid on the initial deposit plus the interest accumulated in previous quarters. In other words, interest is earned on the interest. The actual effective annual yield on an investment at 10% with interest paid quarterly is:

$[(1 + 2.5\%)^4 - 1] \times 100\%$

$= [(1.025)^4 - 1] \times 100\%$

$= [1.1038 - 1] \times 100\%$

$= 10.38\%$.

This is a higher effective annual yield than a deposit paying 10.25% annually.

Test your understanding 2 – Treasury bills

$D = R \times F \times T/Y$

where:

R = 5%
F = $1000
T = 91
Y = 360

$D = 0.05 \times 1000 \times 91/360 = \$12.64$

Price = F – D

= $1,000 – $12.64

= $987.36

Test your understanding 3 – Government bonds

To answer, this question you will need to use the annuity factors and discount rates from the tables.

We need to assume two discount rates between which the required percentage is likely to fall. The yield to maturity will obviously be greater than 7% as the bond was purchased for less than its par value, so we will use rates of 10% and 12%:

t = 8; r = 10

PV = PV of interest + PV of redemption return – Initial investment

= (7 × 5.335) + (100 × 0.467) – 82.00 = 37.345 + 46.7 – 82.00 = $2.045

t = 8; r = 12

= (7 × 4.968) + (100 × 0.404) – 82.00 = 34.776 + 40.4 – 82.00 = $–6.824

By interpolation:

10% + (((2.045)/(2.045 – (–6.824)) × 2) =

10% + (2.045/8.869 × 2) =

10% + 0.461 = **10.46%**

Test your understanding 4 – Practice questions

(1) The correct answer is D.

A

Interest at 5% per year, payable monthly means interest at 5%/12 = 0.4167% each month.

The effective annual yield is $[(1.004167)^{12} – 1] \times 100\% = 5.12\%$.

B

Interest at 5.25% per year, interest payable three-monthly means interest at 5.25%/4 = 1.3125% every three months.

The effective annual yield is $[(1.013125)^{4} – 1] \times 100\% = 5.35\%$.

C

Interest at 5.4% per year, interest payable six-monthly means interest at 5.4%/2 = 2.7% every six months.

The effective annual yield is $[(1.027)^{2} – 1] \times 100\% = 5.47\%$.

D

The effective annual yield on the deposit account paying interest annually is 5.5%.

(2) The interest on the deposit will be \$5 million × 6.25% × 91/360 = \$78,993.
At maturity the deposit will be \$5 million + \$78,993 = \$5,078,993.

(3) The correct answer is D.

Treasury bills are used as a source of investment rather than a way for reducing export risks.

(4) D = R × F × T/Y

where:

R = 8%
F = \$100
T = 30
Y = 360

D= 0.08 × 100 × 30/360 = \$0.67

$$P = F - D$$
$$= \$100 - \$0.67$$
$$= \$99.33$$

(5) The correct answer is C.

Currency may influence areas such as risk and liquidity of the investment, but the currency itself would largely be irrelevant as long as the investment was within acceptable risk limits and sufficiently liquid.

chapter

21

Working capital management

Chapter learning objectives

On completion of their studies students should be able to:

- Calculate and interpret working capital ratios.
- Discuss policies for the overall management of the total level of investment in working capital.
- Evaluate the impact and risks of overtrading.
- Discuss approaches to the financing of the investment in working capital.

1 Session Content

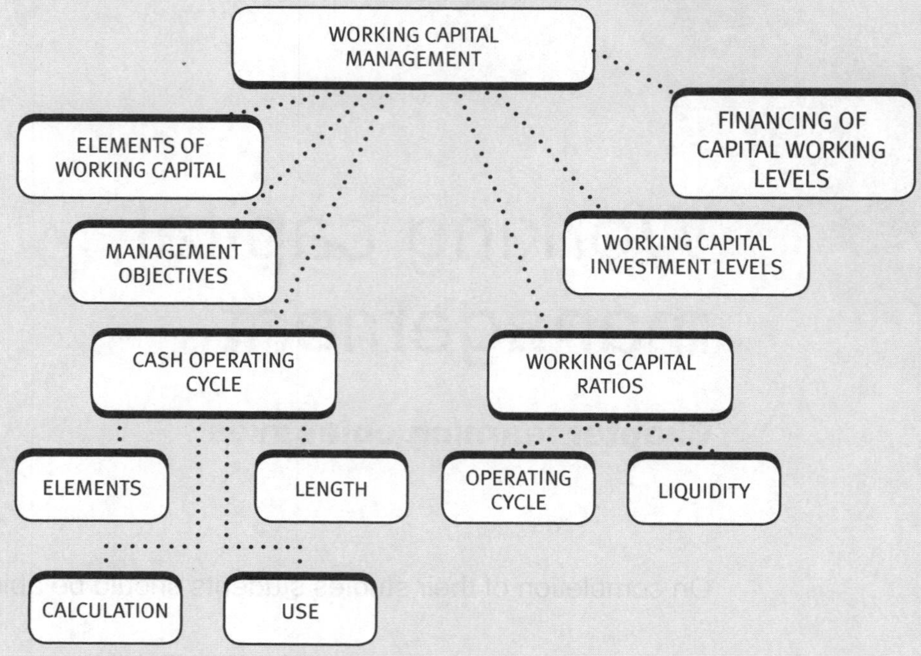

2 The elements of working capital

Working capital is the capital available for conducting the day-to-day operations of an organisation. This is normally the excess of current assets over current liabilities.

Working capital management is the management of all aspects of both current assets and current liabilities, to minimise the risk of insolvency while maximising the return on assets.

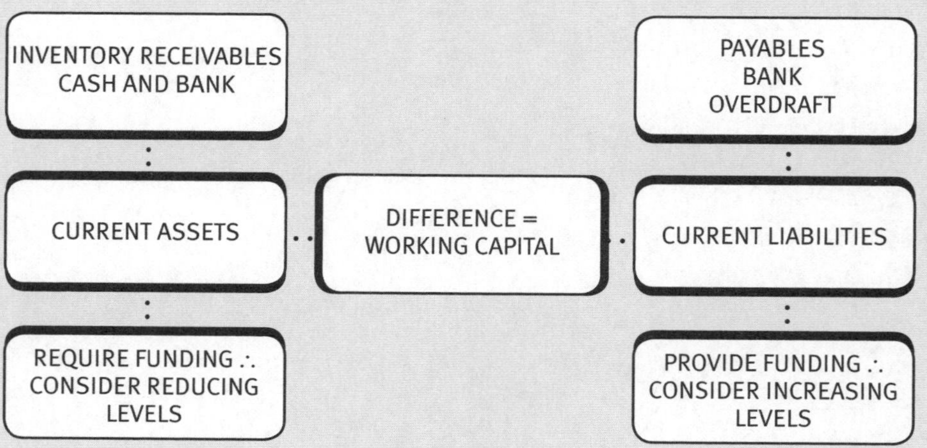

Investing in working capital has a cost, which can be expressed either as:

- the cost of funding it, or
- the opportunity cost of lost investment opportunities because cash is tied up and unavailable for other uses.

3 The objectives of working capital management

The main objective of working capital management is to get the balance of current assets and current liabilities right.

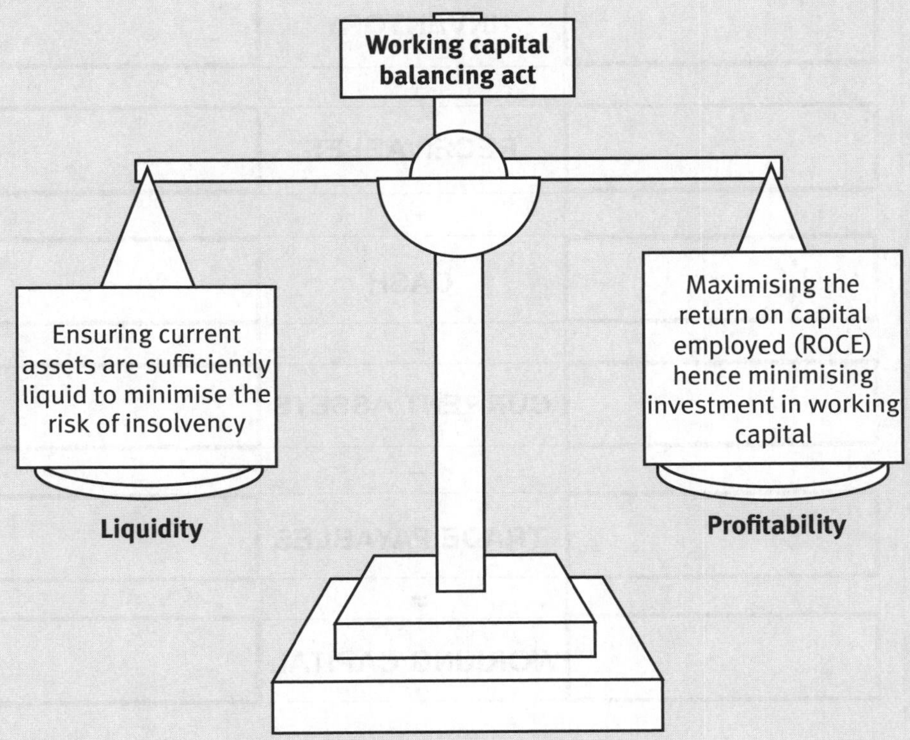

This can also be seen as the trade-off between cash flow versus profits.

Current assets are a major item on the statement of financial position and are especially significant to smaller firms. Mismanagement of working capital is therefore a common cause of business failure, e.g.

- inability to meet bills as they fall due
- demands on cash during periods of growth being too great (overtrading)
- overstocking

The trade-off between liquidity and profitability and its role in determining a business' overall investment in working capital is fundamental to your understanding of working capital management for the examination.

Test your understanding 1 – Liquidity v profitability

Fill in the blanks in the table to identify the advantages of having more or less working capital.

Advantages of keeping it high ↑		Advantages of keeping it low ↓
	INVENTORY	
	+	
	RECEIVABLES	
	+	
	CASH	
	=	
	CURRENT ASSETS	
	–	
	TRADE PAYABLES	
	=	
	WORKING CAPITAL	

Profitability v liquidity

The decision regarding the level of overall investment in working capital is a cost/benefit trade-off – **liquidity versus profitability**, or **cash flow versus profits**.

Cash flow versus profit

It is worth while stressing the difference between cash flow and profits. Cash flow is as important as profit. Unprofitable entities can survive if they have liquidity. Profitable entities can fail if they run out of cash to pay their liabilities (wages, amounts due to suppliers, overdraft interest, etc.).

Some examples of transactions that have this 'trade-off' effect on cash flows and on profits are as follows:

(a) Purchase of non-current assets for cash. The cash will be paid in full to the supplier when the asset is delivered, however profits will be charged with the cost of the asset gradually over the life of the asset in the form of depreciation.

(b) Sale of goods on credit. Profits will be credited in full once the sale has been confirmed, however the cash may not be received for some considerable period afterwards.

(c) With some payments such as tax, there may be a significant timing difference between the impact on reported profit and the cash flow.

Clearly, cash balances and cash flows need to be monitored just as closely as trading profits. The need for adequate cash flow information is vital to enable management to fulfil this responsibility.

Profitability versus liquidity

Liquidity in the context of working capital management means having enough cash (or ready access to cash) to meet all payment obligations when these fall due. The main sources of liquidity are usually:

- cash in the bank
- short-term investments that can be cashed in easily and quickly
- cash inflows from normal trading operations (cash sales and payments by receivables for credit sales)
- an overdraft facility or other ready source of extra borrowing.

The basis of the trade off is where an entity is able to improve its profitability but at the expense of tying up cash. For example,

- receiving a bulk purchase discount (improved profitability) for buying more inventory than is currently required (reduced liquidity), or
- offering credit to customers (attracts more customers so improves profitability but reduces liquidity).

Sometimes, the opposite situation can be seen where an entity can improve its liquidity position but at the expense of profitability. For example, offering an early settlement discount to customers.

4 The working capital cycle

The elements of the working capital cycle

The working capital cycle is the length of time between the entity 's outlay on raw materials, wages and other expenditures and the inflow of cash from the sale of goods.

The faster a firm can 'push' items around the cycle the lower its investment in working capital will be.

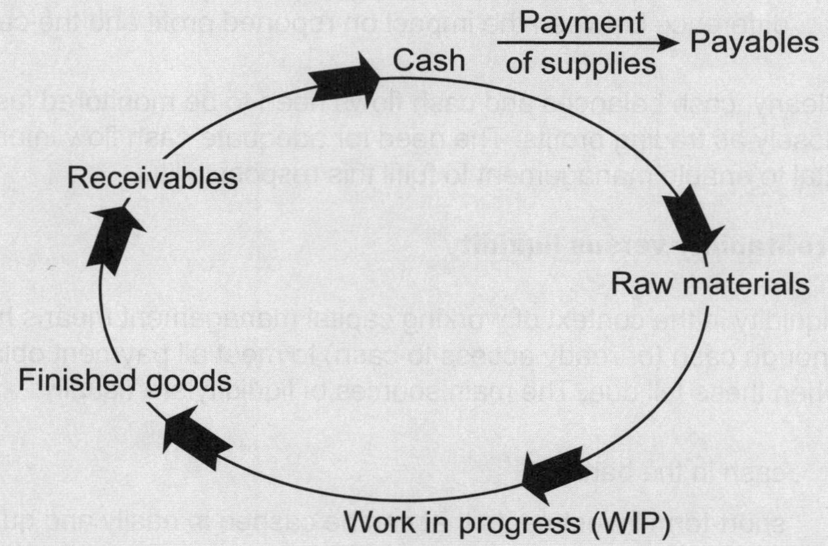

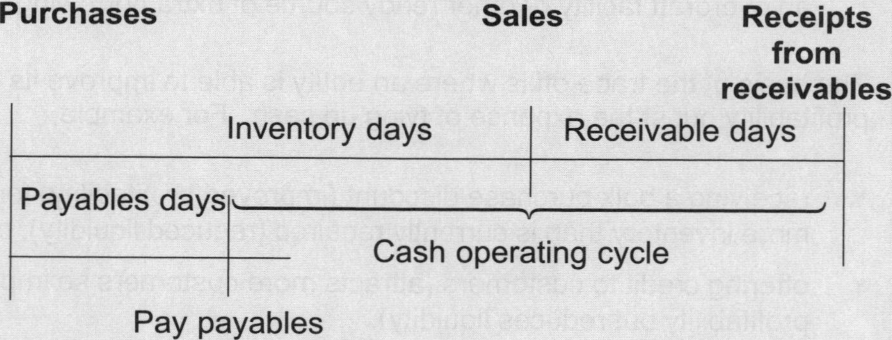

The working capital cycle

The working capital cycle reflects a firm's investment in working capital as it moves through the production process towards sales. The investment in working capital gradually increases, first being only in raw materials, but then in labour and overheads as production progresses. This investment must be maintained throughout the production process, the holding period for finished goods and up to the final collection of cash from trade receivables.

(**Note:** The net investment can be reduced by taking trade credit from suppliers.)

Factors affecting the length of the operating cycle

The length of the cycle depends on:

- liquidity versus profitability decisions
- management efficiency
- industry norms, e.g. retail versus construction.

The optimum level of working capital is the amount that results in no idle cash or unused inventory, but does not put a strain on liquid resources.

The length of the cycle

The length of the cycle depends on how the balancing act between liquidity and profitability is resolved, the efficiency of management and the nature of the industry.

Trying to shorten the cash cycle may have detrimental effects elsewhere, with the organisation lacking the cash to meet its commitments and losing sales, since customers will generally prefer to buy from suppliers who are prepared to extend trade credit, and who have items available when required.

Additionally, any assessment of the acceptability or otherwise of the length of the cycle must take into account the nature of the business involved.

A supermarket chain will tend to have a very low or negative cycle as they have very few, if any, credit customers, they have a high inventory turnover and they can negotiate quite long credit periods with their suppliers.

A construction entity will have a long cycle as their projects tend to be long-term, often extending over more than a year, and whilst progress payments may be made by the customer (if there is one), the bulk of the cash will be received towards the end of the project.

The amount of cash required to fund the working capital cycle will increase as either:

- the cycle gets longer
- the level of activity/sales increases.

This can be summed up as follows:

Activity/sales	Length of cycle	Funds needed increase proportionate to:
Stays constant =	Increases ↑	Days in cycle
Increase ↑	Stays constant =	Sales

Where level of activity (sales) is constant and the number of days of the working capital cycle increase, the amount of funds required for working capital will increase in approximate proportion to the number of days.

Where the cycle remains constant but activity (sales) increase, the funds required for working capital will increase in approximate proportion to sales.

By monitoring the working capital cycle, the manager gains a macro view of the relative efficiency of the working capital utilisation. Further more it may be a key target to reduce the operating cycle to improve the efficiency of the business.

5 The investment in working capital

All entities require working capital, but there is no standard fixed requirement.

The actual amount required will depend on many factors, such as :

- the industry within which the firm operates - in some industries, customers expect long payment periods (impacting receivables) whereas in other industries cash payments are the norm (low receivables)
- the type of products sold – a business selling perishable products will have to keep a lower level of inventory

- whether products are manufactured or bought in – a manufacturing company will have high levels of raw material and work in progress inventory as well as finished goods
- the level of sales – if sales are high, it is likely that receivables will be high too
- inventory management, receivables collection and payables payment policies – these impact on the length of the operating cycle
- the efficiency with which working capital is managed.

For example, a retail company will usually have very low receivables (because most sales are for cash) but high levels of inventories. In contrast, an IT support company will tend to have high levels of receivables (long credit terms offered to attract customers) and high levels of work in progress (inventories). Even comparing businesses in the same business sector can reveal different levels of working capital caused by different working capital management policies (aggressive, moderate and conservative policies are covered below), and one firm being more efficient at collecting debts than another.

It is essential that an appropriate amount of working capital is budgeted for to meet anticipated future needs.

In conditions of uncertainty, entities must hold some minimal level of cash and inventories based on expected revenue, plus an additional safety buffer.

More detail on aggressive, moderate and conservative policies

A company could pursue a more aggressive approach towards the management of working capital or a more conservative (relaxed) approach.

Benefits of a more aggressive approach:

(1) Lower levels of current assets therefore lower financing costs.

(2) The lower financing costs should result in better profitability.

(3) Quicker cash turnover may allow more reinvestment and hence allow the business to expand more quickly.

Benefits of a more conservative approach:

(1) Lower liquidity risk i.e. less risk of the company running out of cash or going into liquidation.

(2) Greater ability to meet a sudden surge in sales demand.

(3) More relaxed credit policy for receivables may improve sales.

Note:

Generally the more conservative the approach, the lower the risk, but the higher the cost in terms of money tied up in working capital.

Working capital investment levels

The level of working capital required is affected by the following factors

(1) The nature of the business, e.g. manufacturing entities need more inventory than service entities.

(2) Uncertainty in supplier deliveries. Uncertainty would mean that extra inventory needs to be carried in order to cover fluctuations.

(3) The overall level of activity of the business. As output increases, receivables, inventory, etc. all tend to increase.

(4) The entity's credit policy. The tighter the entity's policy, the lower the level of receivables.

(5) The length of the working capital cycle. The longer it takes to convert material into finished goods into cash, the greater the investment in working capital

(6) The credit policy of suppliers. The less credit the entity is allowed to take, the lower the level of payables and the higher the net investment in working capital.

Test your understanding 2 – Working capital investment levels

XY has the following expectations for the forthcoming period.

	$m
Sales revenue	10
Cost of sales	(6)
Non-production costs	(2)
Net profit	2

The following working capital ratios are expected to apply.

Finished goods inventory days	30 days
Receivables days	60 days
Payables days	40 days

Required:

Calculate the working capital requirement.

6 The financing of the working capital level

The traditional approach to working capital funding

Traditionally current assets were seen as fluctuating, originally with a seasonal pattern. Current assets would then be financed out of short-term credit, which could be paid off when not required, whilst non-current assets would be financed by long-term funds (debt or equity).

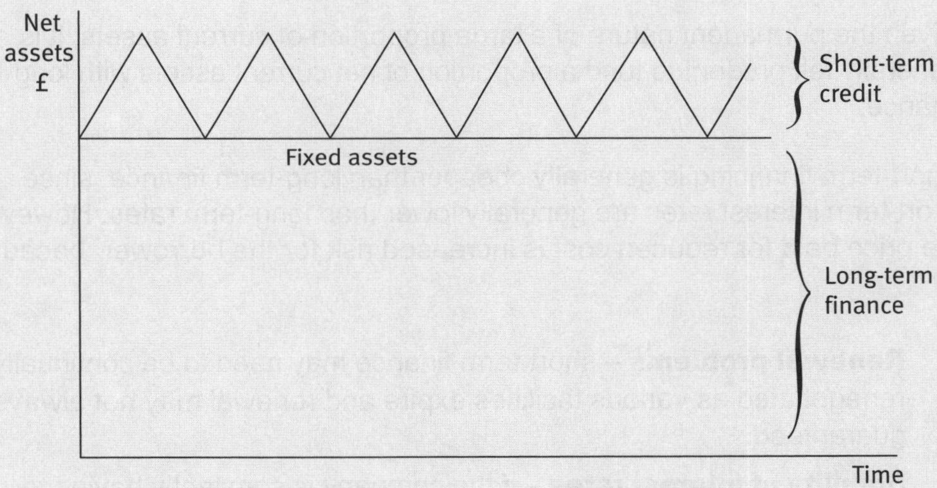

This analysis is rather simplistic. In most businesses a proportion of the current assets are fixed over time, being thus expressed as 'permanent'.

For example, certain base levels of inventory are always carried, or a certain level of trade credit is always extended. If growth were added to this situation a more realistic business picture would be as follows:

Working capital requirements with growth

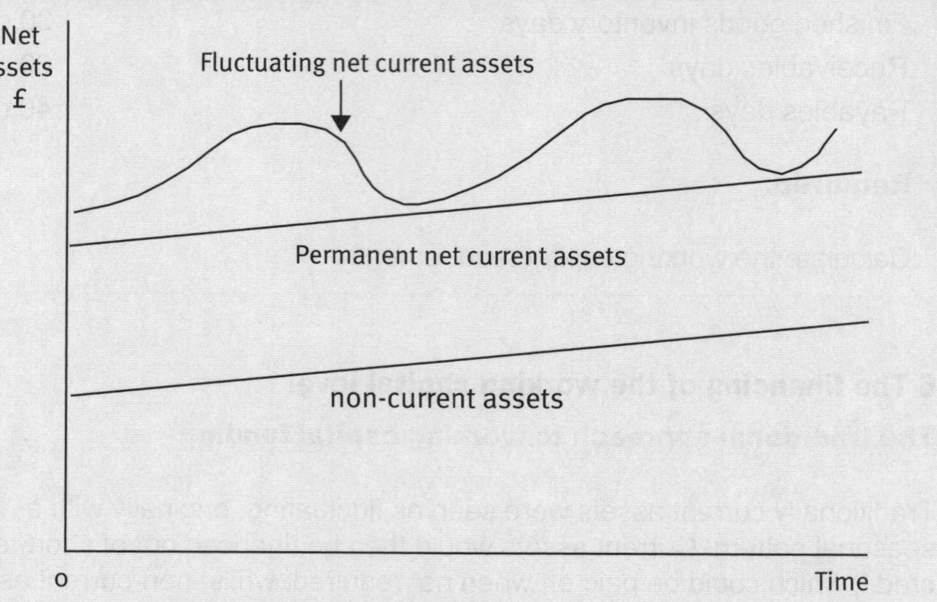

The modern approach to working capital funding

Given the permanent nature of a large proportion of current assets, it is generally felt prudent to fund a proportion of net current assets with long-term finance.

Short-term financing is generally cheaper than long-term finance, since short-term interest rates are generally lower than long-term rates. However, the price paid for reduced cost is increased risk for the borrower, because of:

- **Renewal problems** – short-term finance may need to be continually renegotiated as various facilities expire and renewal may not always be guaranteed.
- **Stability of interest rates** – if the company is constantly having to renew its funding arrangements it will be at the mercy of fluctuations in short-term interest rates.

Aggressive, moderate and conservative financing policies

The financing of working capital depends upon how current- and non-current asset funding is divided between long-term and short-term sources of funding.

The choice is a matter for managerial judgement, and depends to an extent on the cost v risk trade-off described above.

Three possible policies exist, as follows:

An **aggressive policy** for financing working capital uses short-term financing to fund all the fluctuating current assets as well as some of the permanent part of the current assets. This policy carries the greatest risk of illiquidity, as well as the greatest returns.

Aggressive financing policy

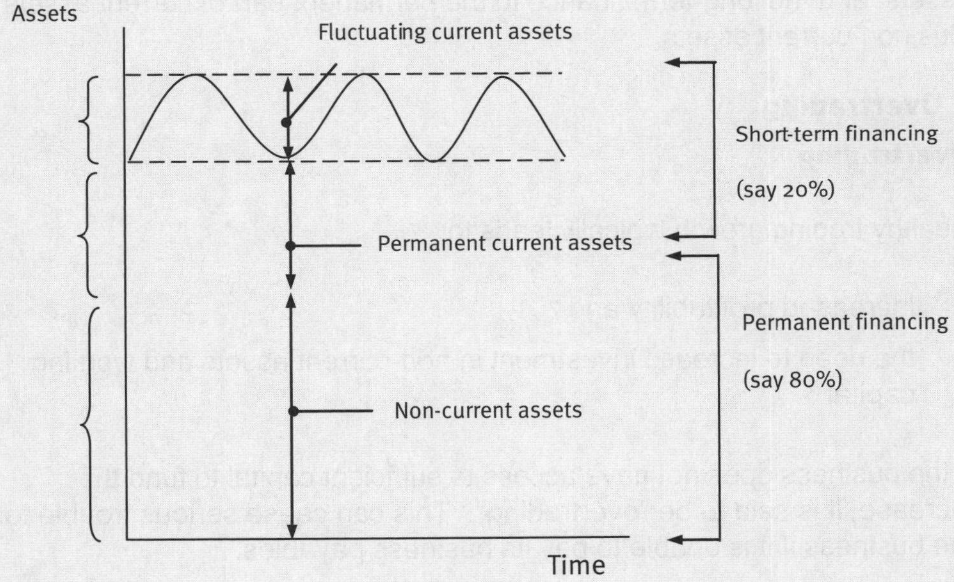

A **conservative policy** is where all of the permanent assets – both non-current assets and the permanent part of the current assets (i.e. the core level of investment in inventory and receivables, etc.) – are financed by long-term funding, as well as part of the fluctuating current assets. Short-term financing is used only for part of the fluctuating current assets.

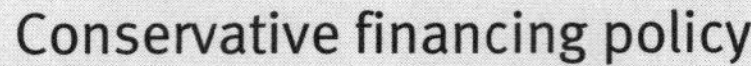

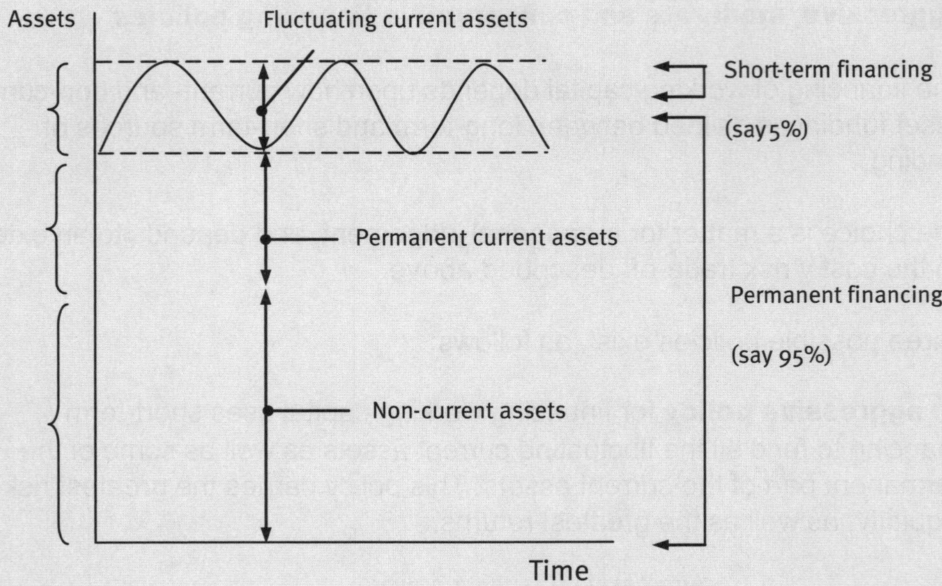

A **moderate policy** matches the short-term finance to the fluctuating current assets, and the long-term finance to the permanent part of current assets plus non-current assets.

7 Overtrading

Overtrading

Healthy trading growth typically leads to:

- increased profitability and
- the need to increase investment in non-current assets and working capital.

If the business does not have access to sufficient capital to fund the increase, it is said to be "overtrading". This can cause serious trouble for the business if it is unable to pay its business payables.

Test your understanding 3 – Overtrading

Over-trading is best described by which of the following statements?

A It occurs when an entity tries to grow too rapidly, backed by too small a capital base

B It occurs when an entity tries to operate its equipment too far above its designed capacity

C It occurs when sales grow rapidly, fuelled by extending longer credit periods

D It occurs when an entity uses short-term finance in preference to long-term finance

Typical indicators of overtrading

- A rapid increase in turnover
- A rapid increase in the volume of current assets
- Most of the increase in assets being financed by credit
- A dramatic drop in the liquidity ratios (see next section)

Solutions to overtrading

Overtrading can be a very serious risk, especially if there is a possibility that the bank will withdraw its overdraft facility. Potential solutions to the problem include:

- raising more long-term capital, in the form of new shares or loans
- slowing down growth to reduce the increases in working capital requirements until sufficient cash has been built up to finance it
- improving working capital management, so that there is a reduction in the inventory holding period or a reduction in the average time for customers to pay

8 Working capital ratios

The periods used to determine the working capital cycle are calculated by using a series of working capital ratios.

The ratios for the individual components (inventory, receivables and payables) are normally expressed as the number of days/weeks/months of the relevant statement of profit or loss figure they represent.

Calculation of the working capital cycle

For a manufacturing business, the working capital cycle is calculated as:

Raw materials holding period	x
Less: payables' payment period	(x)
WIP holding period	x
Finished goods holding period	x
Receivables' collection period	x
	x

For a wholesale or retail business, there will be no raw materials or WIP holding periods, and the cycle simplifies to:

Inventory holding period	x
Less: payables' payment period	(x)
Receivables' collection period	x
	x

The cycle may be measured in days, weeks or months and it is advisable, when answering a question, to use the measure used in the question (although typically it will be days).

Test your understanding 4 – Working capital cycle

An entity has provided the following information.

Receivables collection period	56 days
Raw material inventory holding period	21 days
Production period (WIP)	14 days
Suppliers' payment period	42 days
Finished goods holding period	28 days

Calculate the length of the working capital cycle

Illustration 1 – Working capital ratios

XYZ has the following figures from its most recent accounts.

	$m
Average trade receivables	4
Average trade payables	2
Average raw material inventory	1
Average WIP inventory	1.3
Average finished goods inventory	2
Sales (80% on credit)	30
Materials usage	20
Materials purchases (all on credit)	18
Production cost	23
Cost of sales	25

Required:

Use this information to answer the illustrations below, to calculate the relevant working capital ratios. Round your answers to the nearest day.

Raw material inventory holding period

This is the length of time raw materials are held between purchase and being used in production.

Calculated as:

$$= \frac{\text{Average raw material inventory held}}{\text{Material usage}} \times 365$$

$$= \frac{(\text{Opening inventory} + \text{closing inventory}) \div 2}{\text{Material usage}} \times 365$$

NB. Where usage cannot be calculated, purchases gives a good approximation.

Illustration 2 – Raw material holding period

Using the information from illustration 1 calculate the raw materials holding period. Round your answer to the nearest day.

Solution

$$\frac{\$1m}{\$20m} \times 365 = 18 \text{ days}$$

WIP holding period

This is the length of time goods spend in production.

Calculated as:

$$= \frac{\text{Average WIP}}{\text{Production cost}} \times 365$$

NB. Where production cost cannot be calculated, cost of goods sold gives a good approximation.

Illustration 3 – WIP holding period

Using the information from illustration 1 calculate the WIP holding period. Round your answer to the nearest day.

Solution

$$\frac{\$1.3m}{\$23m} \times 365 = 21 \text{ days}$$

Finished goods inventory holding period

This is the length of time finished goods are held between purchase/completion and sale.

Calculated as:

$$= \frac{\text{Average finished goods inventory held}}{\text{Cost of goods sold}} \times 365$$

For all inventory period ratios, a low ratio is usually seen as a sign of good working capital management. It is very expensive to hold inventory and thus minimum inventory holding usually points to good practice.

Illustration 4 – Finished goods inventory holding period

Using the information from illustration 1, calculate the finished goods inventory holding period. Round your answer to the nearest day.

Solution

$$\frac{\$2m}{\$25m} \times 365 = 29 \text{ days}$$

Inventory turnover

For each ratio, the corresponding turnover ratio can be calculated as

$$\text{Inventory turnover (no of times)} = \frac{\text{Cost of goods sold}}{\text{Average inventory held}}$$

Generally this is less useful.

Using finished goods information from illustration 1:

$$\text{Inventory turnover} = \frac{\$25\text{m}}{\$2\text{m}} = 12.5 \text{ times}$$

Thus finished goods inventory turns round/is turned into sales 12.5 times in the year.

Interpreting inventory periods

If inventory days are relatively high, this may indicate that inventory is too high and there is additional finance tied up in inventory which could perhaps be used more effectively elsewhere. If cash is paid out when the inventories are purchased, but the cash does not come back in until the inventory is sold to a customer, then this temporary negative cash flow will have to be financed by the company. Moreover, if the inventory is sold on credit terms and the customer does not pay for, say 1 month, then the delay in getting the cash back in is even longer.

If the inventory is too low, this may show an overzealous application of the 'just in time' concept and consequential risks of running out of inventory. It may also indicate a company meeting a cash flow crisis by running down inventory levels.

Inventory days needs to be compared to other companies and compared to previous years in the same company. Increasing inventory days may be investigated further by separately analysing raw materials (RM), work in progress (WIP) and finished goods (FG) to cost of goods sold. An increase in RM days may indicate mismanagement in the buying department; an increase in WIP may indicate production delays. If FG days increase, this may be a sign of decline in demand for the product and an increase in obsolete items.

Inventory levels are very much a balancing act between the risk of stock-outs and the cost associated with high levels of inventory.

Trade receivables days

This is the length of time credit is extended to customers.

Calculated as:

$$= \frac{\text{Average receivables}}{\text{Credit sales}} \times 365$$

Generally shorter credit periods are seen as financially prudent but the length will also depend upon the nature of the business.

Illustration 5 – Receivable days

Using the information from illustration 1 calculate the trade receivable days. Round your answer to the nearest day.

Solution

$$\frac{\$4\text{m}}{\$30\text{m} \times 80\%} \times 365 \quad = 61 \text{ days}$$

Interpreting trade receivables collection periods

Businesses which sell goods on credit terms specify a credit period. Failure to send out invoices on time or to follow up late payers will have an adverse effect on the cash flow of the business. The receivables collection period measures the average period of credit allowed to customers.

In general, the shorter the collection period the better because receivables are effectively 'borrowing' from the entity. Remember, however, that the level of receivables reflects not only the ability of the credit controllers but also the sales and marketing strategy adopted, and the nature of the business. Any change in the level of receivables must therefore be assessed in the light of the level of sales.

Trade payables days

This is the average period of credit extended by suppliers.

Calculated as:

$$= \frac{\text{Average payables}}{\text{Credit purchases}} \times 365$$

Illustration 6 – Payable days

Using the information from illustration 1 calculate the trade payable days. Round your answer to the nearest day.

Solution

$$\frac{\$2m}{\$18m} \times 365 = 41 \text{ days}$$

Complications in calculations

There are differences in the way that the ratio might be calculated:

- Total purchases for the year should be used where possible. If the figure for purchases is not available, the cost of sales in the year should be used instead.
- The figure for purchases excludes any sales tax recoverable, whereas the carrying amount for payables includes sales tax. To make a like-for-like comparison, it might be appropriate to add recoverable sales tax back into purchases, or remove the sales tax element from trade payables. However, this is not usually done.
- Where available, the average trade payables during the year should be used, normally calculated as the average of the trade payables at the beginning and the end of the year. However, if you wish to compare the average payment period in the most recent year and the previous year, and you only have figures for the two years, it will be necessary to use the end-of-year trade payables rather than an average value for the year. The same issue will arise when making receivables calculations.

Interpreting trade payable collection periods

The result of this ratio can also be compared with the receivables days. An entity does not normally want to offer its customers more time to pay than it gets from its own suppliers, otherwise this could affect cash flow. Generally, the longer the payables payment period, the better, as the entity holds on to its cash for longer, but care must be taken not to upset suppliers by delaying payment, which could result in the loss of discounts and reliability.

Generally, increasing payables days suggests advantage is being taken of available credit but there are risks

- losing supplier goodwill
- losing prompt payment discounts
- suppliers increasing the price to compensate.

It is important to recognise when using these ratios that it is the trend of ratios that is important, not the individual values. Payment periods are longer in some types of entity than in others.

The working capital cycle

The ratios can then be brought together to produce the working capital cycle.

	Days
Raw material inventory days	18
Trade payables days	(41)
WIP period	21
Finished goods inventory days	29
Receivables days	61
Length of working capital cycle	88

The working capital cycle tells us it takes the entity 88 days between paying out for material purchases and eventually receiving cash back from customers.

As always this must then be compared with prior periods or industry average for meaningful analysis.

Test your understanding 5 – Raw material holding period

Statement of profit or loss account extract	$	$
Revenue		350,000
Cost of sales		264,400
Gross profit		85,600

Statement of financial position extract	$	$
Current assets		
Inventory		
Raw materials	25,000	
Work in progress	33,500	
Finished goods	46,500	105,000
Trade receivables		35,200
		140,200
Current liabilities		
Trade payables		55,200

Required:

Calculate the raw materials holding period. Round your answer to the nearest day.

Test your understanding 6 – WIP holding period

Using the information from TYU 5 calculate the WIP holding period. Round your answer to the nearest day.

Test your understanding 7 – Finished goods inventory holding

Using the information from TYU 5 calculate the finished goods inventory holding period and list possible reasons why this may change over time. Round your answer to the nearest day.

Test your understanding 8 – Receivable days

Using the information from TYU 5 calculate the receivable days collection period and list possible reasons why this may change over time. Round your answer to the nearest day.

Test your understanding 9 – Payable days

Using the information from TYU 5 calculate the payable days and list possible reasons why this may change over a period of time. Round your answer to the nearest day.

Test your understanding 10 – Working capital cycle

Using the information from TYU's 5 to 9 calculate the working capital cycle.

Two key measures, the current ratio and the quick ratio, are used to assess short-term liquidity. Generally a higher ratio indicates better liquidity.

Current ratio

This measures how much of the total current assets are financed by current liabilities.

$$\text{Current ratio} = \frac{\text{Current assets}}{\text{Current liabilities}}$$

A measure of 2:1 means that current liabilities can be paid twice over out of existing current assets.

Quick (acid test) ratio

The quick or acid test ratio

- measures how well current liabilities are covered by liquid assets
- is particularly useful where inventory holding periods are long.

$$\text{Quick ratio (acid test)} = \frac{\text{Current assets} - \text{Inventory}}{\text{Current liabilities}}$$

A measure of 1:1 means that the entity is able to meet existing liabilities if they all fall due at once.

Typical targets

These liquidity ratios are a guide to the risk of cash flow problems and insolvency. If an entity suddenly finds that it is unable to renew its short-term liabilities (for instance if the bank suspends its overdraft facilities), there will be a danger of insolvency unless the entity is able to turn enough of its current assets into cash quickly.

In general, high current and quick ratios are considered 'good' in that they mean that an organisation has the resources to meet its commitments as they fall due. However, it may indicate that working capital is not being used efficiently, for example, and that there is too much idle cash that should be invested to earn a return.

What constitutes a 'safe' ratio varies widely between different types of business, because businesses in different industries have differing operating cash flow patterns. It is more useful to look at changes in the ratios over time, or for an entity to compare its ratios with the ratios of other entities in the same industry.

When the current ratio is less than 1.0 (1:1), this means that the business has more current liabilities than it has current assets. This could be an indication of liquidity problems. However, entities in certain industries can operate successfully with low current ratios, without any liquidity problems. For example, a supermarket has no receivables because all its sales are for cash, and its inventory holding period is often much shorter than the time it takes to pay its suppliers. As a result, unless the supermarket holds on to its spare cash, its current liabilities will usually be larger than its current assets. A supermarket is likely to have both a low current ratio and a very low quick ratio.

Note on overdrafts

Some entities use an overdraft as part of their long-term finance, in which case the current and quick ratios may appear worryingly low. In such questions, you could suggest that the firm reschedule the overdraft as a loan. Not only would this be cheaper but it would also improve liquidity ratios.

Additional points for calculating ratios

The ratios may be needed to provide analysis of an entity's performance or simply to calculate the length of the working capital cycle.

There are a few simple points to remember which will be of great use in the examination.

- Where the period is required in days, the multiple in the ratios is 365, for months the multiple is 12, or 52 for weeks.
- If you are required to compare ratios between two statements of financial position, it is acceptable to base each holding period on closing figures on the statement of financial position each year, rather than an average, in order to see whether the ratio has increased or decreased.
- For each ratio calculated above, the corresponding turnover ratio can be calculated by inverting the ratio given and removing the multiple.
- When using the ratios to appraise performance, it is essential to compare the figure with others in the industry or identify the trend over a number of periods.
- Ratios have their limitations and care must be taken because:
  - the statement of financial position values at a particular time may not be typical
  - balances used for a seasonal business may not represent average levels, e.g. a fireworks manufacturer
  - ratios can be subject to window dressing/manipulation
  - ratios concern the past (historic) not the future
  - figures may be distorted by inflation and/or rapid growth.

Shortening the working capital cycle

A number of steps can be taken to shorten the working capital cycle:

- Reduce raw materials inventory holding. This may be done by reviewing slow-moving lines, reorder levels and reorder quantities. Inventory control models may be considered, if not already in use. More efficient links with suppliers could also help. Reducing inventory may involve loss of discounts for bulk purchases, loss of cost savings from price rises, or could lead to production delays due to inventory shortages.
- Obtain more finance from suppliers by delaying payments, preferably through negotiation. This could result in a deterioration in commercial relationships or even loss of reliable sources of supply. Discounts may be lost by this policy.

- Reduce work in progress by improving production techniques and efficiency (with the human and practical problems of achieving such change).
- Reduce finished goods inventory perhaps by reorganising the production schedule and distribution methods. This may affect the efficiency with which customer demand can be satisfied and result ultimately in a reduction of sales.
- Reduce credit given to customers by invoicing and following up outstanding amounts more quickly, or possibly offering discount incentives. The main disadvantages would be the potential loss of customers as a result of chasing too hard and a loss of revenue as a result of discounts.
- Debt factoring, generating immediate cash flow by the sale of receivables to a third party on immediate cash terms. The main disadvantages would be that this may be costly to the entity to pay a factor.

The working capital cycle is the time span between incurring production costs and receiving cash returns. It says nothing in itself about the amount of working capital that will be needed over this period.

Illustration 7 - Extended example

You have been provided with the following information for an entity:

Summarised statements of profit or loss and other comprehensive income for the year ended 30 June

	20X7		20X6	
	$000	$000	$000	$000
Revenue		209		196
Opening inventory	37		29	
Purchases	162		159	
	199		188	
Closing inventory	42		37	
		157		151
Gross profit		52		45
Finance costs	4		4	
Depreciation	9		9	
Sundry expenses	14		11	
		27		24
Operating profit		25		21
Taxation		10		10
Profit for the year		15		11
Other comprehensive income:				
Item that will not be reclassified to profit or loss in future accounting periods:				
Property, plant and equipment - revaluation surplus		10		-
Total comprehensive income for the year		25		11

Summarised statements of financial position at 30 June

	20X7		20X6	
	$000	$000	$000	$000
Non-current assets (carrying value)		130		139
Current assets:				
Inventory	42		37	
Receivables	29		23	
Cash and cash equivalents	3		5	
		74		65
Total assets		204		204
Equity and liabilities				
Ordinary share capital (50 cent shares)		35		35
Share premium		17		17
Revaluation reserve		10		–
Retained earnings (22 b/fwd +15)	37		27	
Less: dividend paid in year	6		5	
		31		22
		93		74
Non-current liabilities				
5% loan notes		65		65
Current liabilities				
Trade payables	36		55	
Taxation	10		10	
		46		65
Total equity and liabilities		204		204

Required:

(a) Calculate the liquidity ratios in 20X6 and 20X7

(b) Calculate the length of the working capital cycle in 20X6 and 20X7

(c) Evaluate whether working capital is being managed effectively

Solution

(a) **Liquidity ratios**

The current ratio

20X7		20X6	
$\frac{74}{46}$	= 1.6	$\frac{65}{65}$	= 1.0

The quick (or acid test) ratio

20X7		20X6	
$\frac{32}{46}$	= 0.7	$\frac{28}{65}$	= 0.4

Working capital cycle

To better understand the liquidity ratios you should review each individual component of working capital as follows:

The inventory holding period (based upon average inventory)

20X7		20X6	
$\frac{(1/2\,(37 + 42))}{157}$	× 365 days = 92 days	$\frac{(1/2\,(29 + 37))}{151}$	× 365 days = 80 days

The receivables collection period

Average daily sales:

20X7		20X6	
$\frac{\$209,000}{365}$	= $573	$\frac{\$196,000}{365}$	= $537
$\frac{\$29,000}{\$573}$	= 50.6 days	$\frac{\$23,000}{\$537}$	= 42.8 days

Alternatively:

$$\frac{\$29{,}000}{\$209{,}000} \times 365 \text{ days} = 50.6 \text{ days} \qquad \frac{\$23{,}000}{\$196{,}000} \times 365 \text{ days} = 42.8 \text{ days}$$

The payables payment period

Average daily purchases:

20X7	20X6
$\frac{\$162{,}000}{365} = \$444$	$\frac{\$159{,}000}{365} = \$436$
$\frac{\$36{,}000}{\$444} = 81.1$ days	$\frac{\$55{,}000}{\$436} = 126.1$ days

Alternatively:

$$\frac{\$36{,}000}{\$162{,}000} \times 365 \text{ days} = 81.1 \text{ days} \qquad \frac{\$55{,}000}{\$159{,}000} \times 365 \text{ days} = 126.2 \text{ days}$$

Length of the working capital cycle:

	20X7	**20X6**
	days	days
Inventory holding period	92	80
Plus:		
Receivables' collection period	51	43
Less:		
Payables' payment period	(81)	(126)
Total	62	(3)

Commentary

Assessment of liquidity ratios

Both of these ratios show an improvement from 20X6. The extent of the change between the two years seems surprising and would require further investigation. It would also be useful to know how these ratios compare with those of a similar business, since typical liquidity ratios for supermarkets, say, are quite different from those for heavy engineering businesses.

In 20X7 current liabilities were well covered by current assets. Liabilities payable within the next tewlve months are 70% covered by cash and receivables (a liquid asset, close to cash).

Assessment of the working capital cycle

Inventory

The inventory holding period has lengthened. In general, the shorter the inventory holding period the better. It is very expensive to hold inventory and thus minimum inventory holding usually points to good management.

The current ratio calculation now seems less optimistic, considering the holding period for inventory of 92 days. Inventory that takes nearly four months to sell is not very liquid! It would be better to focus attention on the acid test ratio.

Receivables

Compared with 20X6, the receivables collection period has worsened in 20X7. It would be important to establish the company policy on credit allowed. If the average credit allowed to customers was, say, 30 days, then something is clearly wrong. Further investigation might reveal delays in sending out invoices or failure to 'screen' new customers.

This situation suggests yet a further review of the liquidity ratios. The acid test ratio ignores inventory but still assumes receivables are liquid. If debt collection is a problem then receivables too are illiquid and the company could struggle to pay its current liabilities were they all to fall due in a short space of time.

Payables

The payables' payment period has reduced substantially from last year. It is, however, in absolute terms still a high figure. Often, suppliers request payment within 30 days. The company is taking nearly three months. Trade creditors are thus financing much of the working capital requirements of the business, which is beneficial to the company.

A high level of creditor days may be good in that it means that all available credit is being taken, but there are three potential disadvantages of taking extended credit:

(1) future supplies may be endangered.

(2) availability of cash discounts is lost.

(3) suppliers may quote a higher price for the goods knowing the company takes extended credit

Additionally when viewed alongside the previous ratios calculated, this might suggest a cash flow problem causing suppliers to be left unpaid.

Overall

Our example shows that, in 20X7, there is approximately a 62-day gap between paying cash to suppliers for goods, and receiving the cash back from customers. However, in 20X6, there was the somewhat unusual situation where cash was received from the customers, on average, more than 3 days before the payment to suppliers was needed.

Test your understanding 11 – Practice questions

(1) **Calculate the length of the working capital cycle from the following information:**

Raw materials holding period	10 days
Receivables collection period	60 days
Average time to pay suppliers	45 days
Finished goods inventory holding period	20 days
Production period (WIP)	5 days

(2) An entity has a quick (or acid test) ratio of 0.80:1 and has a positive cash balance. **State whether the quick ratio would increase or decrease in each of the following situations.**

(Take each situation individually, not together.)

(a) It receives payment of an amount owed by a trade customer.

(b) It sells an item of inventory at a loss

(c) It pays an invoice from a trade supplier.

(3) Marlboro estimates the following figures for the coming year.

Sales – all on credit	$3,600,000
Average receivables	$306,000
Gross profit margin *	25% on sales
Finished goods	$200,000
Work in progress	$350,000
Raw materials (balance held)	$150,000
Trade payables	$130,000

Inventory levels are constant.

* Raw materials are 80% of cost of sales – all on credit.

Required:

Calculate the raw materials holding period. Round your answer to the nearest day.

(4) **Using the information from question 3, calculate the WIP holding period.** Round your answer to the nearest day.

(5) **Using the information from question 3, calculate the finished goods inventory holding period.** Round your answer to the nearest day.

(6) **Using the information from question 3, calculate the receivable days.** Round your answer to the nearest day.

(7) **Using the information from question 3, calculate the payable days.** Round your answer to the nearest day.

(8) **Using the information from questions 3 to 7, calculate the working capital cycle**.

(9) **Identify which of the following transactions will result in an increase in working capital:**

A Writing off a debt as uncollectable

B Paying the invoice of a trade supplier

C Selling goods on credit at a profit

D Buying inventory for cash

9 Summary Diagram

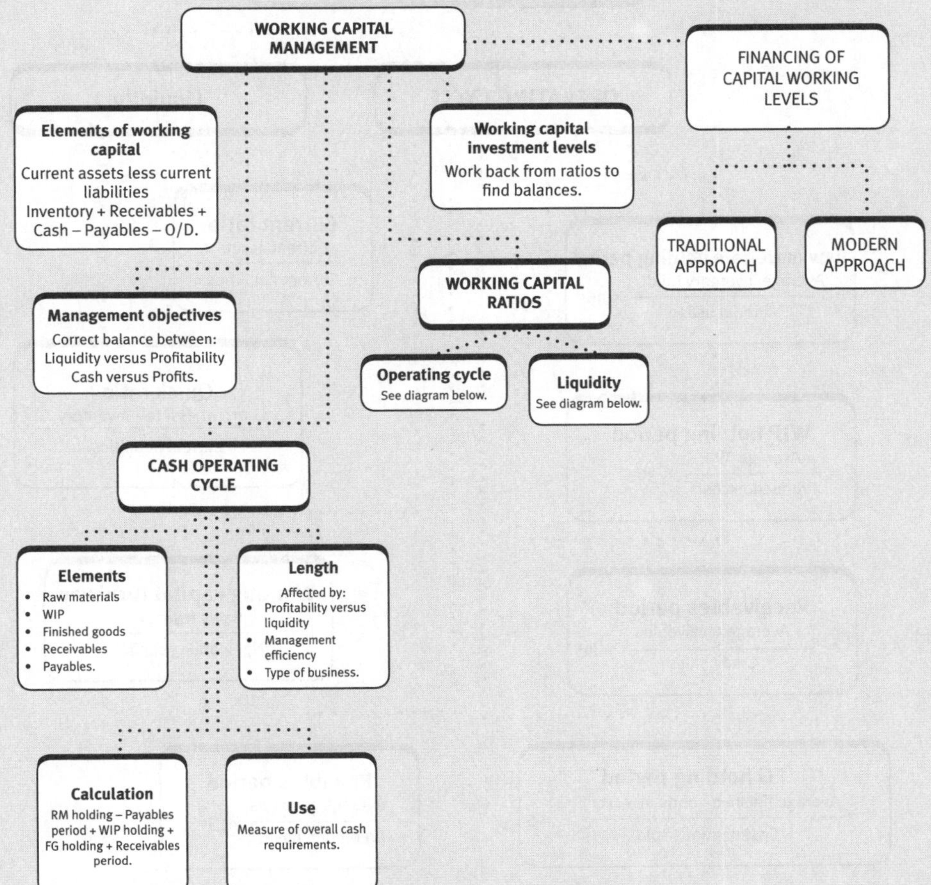
WORKING CAPITAL MANAGEMENT
FINANCING OF CAPITAL WORKING LEVELS
Elements of working capital
Current assets less current liabilities
Inventory + Receivables + Cash – Payables – O/D.
Working capital investment levels
Work back from ratios to find balances.
TRADITIONAL APPROACH
MODERN APPROACH
WORKING CAPITAL RATIOS
Management objectives
Correct balance between:
Liquidity versus Profitability
Cash versus Profits.
Operating cycle
See diagram below.
Liquidity
See diagram below.
CASH OPERATING CYCLE
Elements
Raw materials
WIP
Finished goods
Receivables
Payables.
Length
Affected by:
Profitability versus liquidity
Management efficiency
Type of business.
Calculation
RM holding – Payables period + WIP holding + FG holding + Receivables period.
Use
Measure of overall cash requirements.

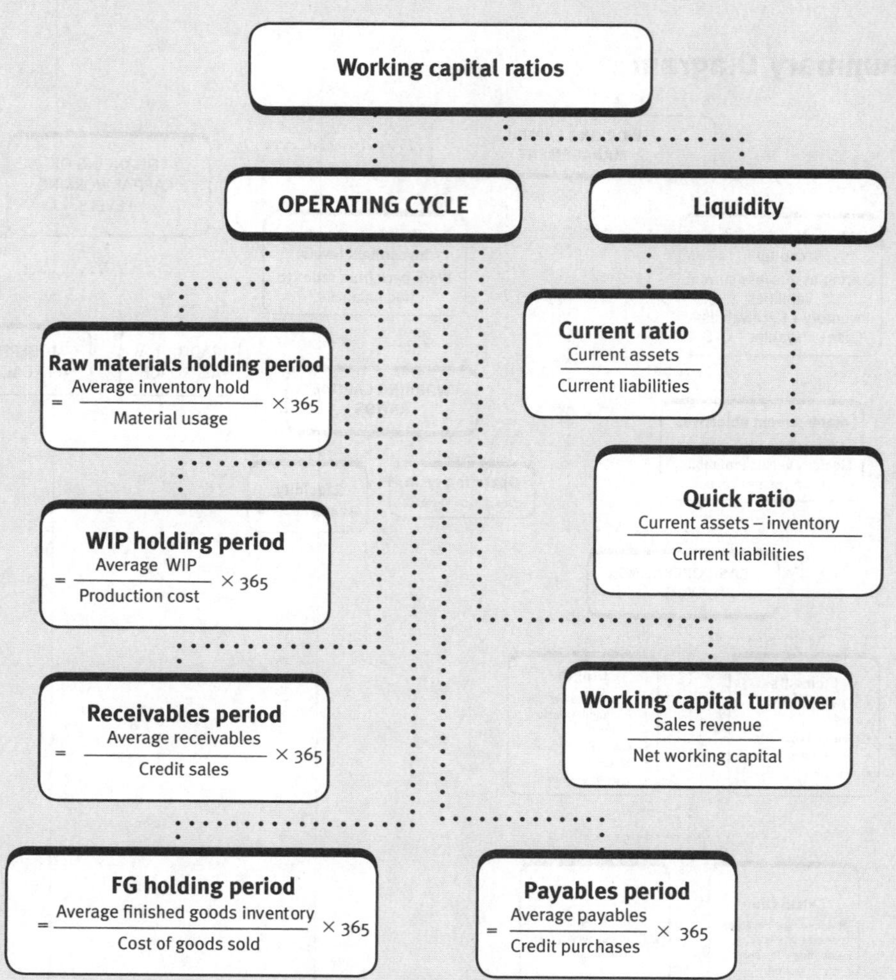
Working capital ratios
OPERATING CYCLE
Liquidity
Raw materials holding period
= Average inventory hold / Material usage × 365
WIP holding period
= Average WIP / Production cost × 365
Receivables period
= Average receivables / Credit sales × 365
FG holding period
= Average finished goods inventory / Cost of goods sold × 365
Payables period
= Average payables / Credit purchases × 365
Current ratio
Current assets / Current liabilities
Quick ratio
Current assets – inventory / Current liabilities
Working capital turnover
Sales revenue / Net working capital

Test your understanding answers

Test your understanding 1 – Liquidity v profitability

Advantages of keeping it high ⇧		⇩ Advantages of keeping it low
Few stockouts Bulk purchase discounts Reduced ordering costs	**INVENTORY**	Less cash tied up in inventory Lower storage costs
	+	
Customers like credit – ∴ profitable as attracts more sales	**RECEIVABLES**	Less cash tied up Less chance of irrecoverable debts Reduced costs of credit control
	+	
Able to pay bills on time Take advantage of unexpected opportunities Avoid high borrowing costs	**CASH**	Can invest surplus to earn high returns Less vulnerable to takeover
	=	
	CURRENT ASSETS	
	–	
Preserves own cash – cheap source of finance	**TRADE PAYABLES**	Lose prompt payment discounts Loss of credit status Less favourable supplier treatment
	=	
	WORKING CAPITAL	

Test your understanding 2 – Working capital investment levels

We need to use the ratios to calculate statement of financial position values in order to construct the projected working capital position.

				$m
Inventory	=	30 ÷ 365	× $6m	= 0.49
Receivables	=	60 ÷ 365	× $10m	1.64
Trade payables	=	40 ÷ 365	× $6m	= (0.66)
Working capital required				1.47

Test your understanding 3 – Overtrading

A

Test your understanding 4 – Working capital cycle

	Days
Raw materials inventory holding period	21
Less: suppliers' payment period	(42)
WIP holding period	14
Finished goods holding period	28
Receivables' collection period	56
Operating cycle (days)	77

Test your understanding 5 – Raw material holding period

$$\frac{25{,}000}{264{,}400} \times 365 = 35 \text{ days}$$

Test your understanding 6 – WIP holding period

$$\frac{33{,}500}{264{,}400} \times 365 = 46 \text{ days}$$

Test your understanding 7 – Finished goods inventory holding

$$\frac{46{,}500}{264{,}400} \times 365 = 64 \text{ days}$$

Remember that this is an average figure and that it is likely to include some items of inventory which are fast-moving and other items which are held in inventory for longer periods. For example, in a supermarket, all dairy produce all is sold within, say, 1-2 days whereas some canned goods may remain on the shelves for, 7-10 days.

Reasons why this may increase over time include:

- some items of inventory may be damaged or obsolete
- poor inventory management to purchase or produce items not required
- some items of inventory may not be what customers demand e.g. fashion clothing
- some itmes of inventory may not be the latest technology e.g. mobile phones and laptops
- deliberate stock-building to meet expected seasonal demand e.g. chocolatiers producing Easter eggs
- deliberate stock-building in advance of a marketing initiative to boost sales
- making purchases in bulk to take advantage of trade discount terms

Reasons why this may fall over time include:

- improvement in inventory management to ensure that goods purchased or produced can be sold
- 'stock-out' situations when there are no goods available to sell to customers
- a change in the sales mix, so that proportionately more sales are made to customers with shorter credit periods

Test your understanding 8 – Receivable days

$$\frac{35,200}{350,000} \times 365 = 37 \text{ days}$$

Remember that this is an average figure and that it is likely to include some receivables which are, say, only a few days old and others which may be considerably older, perhaps several months.

Reasons why this may increase over time include:

- delay in the issue of sales invoices following delivery of goods as customers usually regard the credit period starting from the date of receiving the invoice
- extended credit terms have been granted to customers
- poor credit acceptance procedures, resulting in credit being granted to customers with a high risk of default
- poor credit control procedures, resulting in customers not being followed up when payment has not been received when due
- a change in the sales mix, so that, perhaps, there are more export sales, which may have longer agreed credit periods

Reasons why this may fall over time include:

- improvement in credit acceptance and control procedures when it was previously poor
- credit customers taking advantage of discounts allowed for early settlement
- a change in the sales mix, so that proportionately more sales are made to customers with shorter credit periods

Test your understanding 9 – Payable days

$$\frac{55{,}200}{264{,}400} \times 365 = 76 \text{ days}$$

Remember that this is an average figure and that it is likely to include some payables which are, say, only a few days old and others which may be considerably older, perhaps several months.

Reasons why this may increase over time include:

- cash flow problems creating difficulty to make payments to suppliers when falling due
- extended credit terms have been granted by suppliers
- poor credit control procedures by suppliers resulting in a business being able to delay or withhold payment
- a change of suppliers, perhaps from foreign suppliers, which may include negotiation of extended credit periods

Reasons why this may fall over time include:

- improvement in credit acceptance and control procedures by suppliers when it was previously poor
- making early payment to take advantage of discounts allowed for early settlement
- a change of suppliers who have been able to impose shorter credit periods, perhaps in exchange for guarantees regarding the cost of goods supplied, reliability of supply or quality assurance of goods provided

Test your understanding 10 – Working capital cycle

The answer is 106 days.

See summary below:

		Days
Inventory days		
Raw materials	$\frac{25,000}{264,400} \times 365 =$	35
Work-in-progress	$\frac{33,500}{264,400} \times 365 =$	46
Finished goods	$\frac{46,500}{264,400} \times 365 =$	64
Receivable days	$\frac{35,200}{350,000} \times 365 =$	37
Less Payable days	$\frac{55,200}{264,400} \times 365 =$	(76)
Total		106

Test your understanding 11 – Practice questions

(1)

	Days
Raw materials holding period	10
Production period (WIP)	5
Finished goods inventory holding period	20
Receivables collection period	60
	95
Average time to pay suppliers	(45)
Working capital cycle	50

(2)

(a) There is no change in the quick ratio. There is no change in current assets excluding inventory, and no change in current liabilities. The effect of the transaction is to reduce receivables and increase cash by the same amount.

(b) The quick ratio will rise higher than 0.80:1. The sale of the inventory, even at a loss, will result in an increase in either receivables or cash. Inventory is not included in the calculation of the quick ratio; therefore the reduction in inventory is irrelevant. Since current assets, excluding inventory increase and current liabilities are unchanged, the quick ratio must increase.

(c) The quick ratio will fall. There will be an equal decrease in cash and trade payables.

It may be easier to understand by making up some numbers. Say the current assets (without inventories) were $80,000 and current liabilities were $100,000 to begin with. If a $30,000 supplier invoice was paid, then the new balances would be $50,000 of current assets and $70,000 of current liabilities. The quick ratio would have lowered to ($50,000/$70,000) 0.714:1.

(3) **Statement of profit or loss**

	$	$
Turnover		3,600,000
Cost of sales		
Materials – 80% (given)	2,160,000	
Other (balancing figure)	540,000	
		2,700,000
Gross profit – 25% (given)		900,000

Raw materials holding period

$$\frac{\$150{,}000}{\$2{,}160{,}000} \times 365 = 25 \text{ days}$$

(4) **WIP holding days**

$$\frac{\$350{,}000}{\$2{,}700{,}000} \times 365 = 47 \text{ days}$$

(5) **Finished goods holding period**

$$\frac{\$200{,}000}{\$2{,}700{,}000} \times 365 = 27 \text{ days}$$

(6) **Receivables collection period**

$$\frac{\$306{,}000}{\$3{,}600{,}000} \times 365 = 31 \text{ days}$$

(7) **Trade payables days**

$$\frac{\$130{,}000}{\$2{,}160{,}000} \times 365 = 22 \text{ days}$$

(8) **The working capital cycle is 108 days**

Raw materials holding period

$$\frac{\$150,000}{\$2,160,000} \times 365 = 25 \text{ days}$$

Trade payables days

$$\frac{\$130,000}{\$2,160,000} \times 365 = (22) \text{ days}$$

WIP holding days

$$\frac{\$350,000}{\$2,700,000} \times 365 = 47 \text{ days}$$

Finished goods holding period

$$\frac{\$200,000}{\$2,700,000} \times 365 = 27 \text{ days}$$

Receivables collection period

$$\frac{\$306,000}{\$3,600,000} \times 365 = 31 \text{ days}$$

108 days

(9) The correct answer is C

Items B and D result in no change in working capital. Item B results in an equal reduction in both cash and trade payables. Item D results in an increase in inventory but an equal decrease in cash. Writing off a receivable (item A) reduces working capital, because there is a reduction in receivables but no reduction in current liabilities. Selling goods on credit reduces inventory but increases receivables by a larger amount (= the gross profit on the sale); therefore total working capital increases by the amount of the gross profit.

chapter

22

Working capital management – accounts receivable and payable

Chapter learning objectives

On completion of their studies students should be able to:

- Discuss policies for the management of trade receivable and trade payable balances.
- Evaluate the impact of different trade receivable and payable policies.

1 Session content

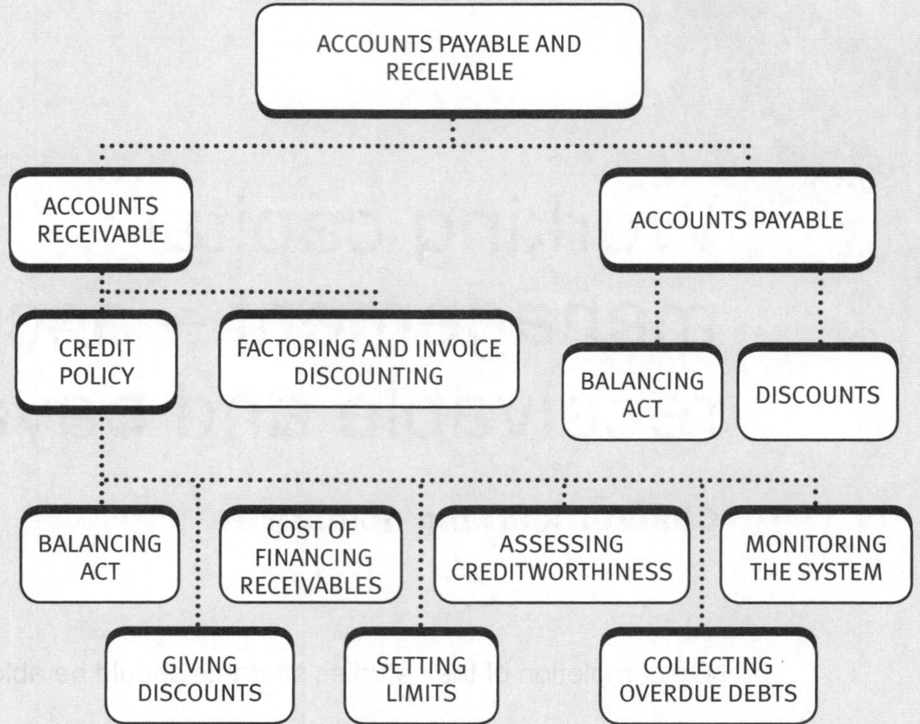

2 Accounts receivable – establishing a credit policy

The balancing act

Management must establish a credit policy. The optimum level of trade credit extended represents a balance between two factors

- profit improvement from sales obtained by allowing credit
- the cost of credit allowed.

Why have a credit policy?

A firm must establish a policy for credit terms given to its customers. Ideally the firm would want to obtain cash with each order delivered, but that is impossible unless substantial settlement (or cash) discounts are offered as an inducement. It must be recognised that credit terms are part of the firm's marketing policy. If the trade or industry has adopted a common practice, then it is probably wise to keep in step with it.

A lenient credit policy may well attract additional customers, but at a disproportionate increase in cost.

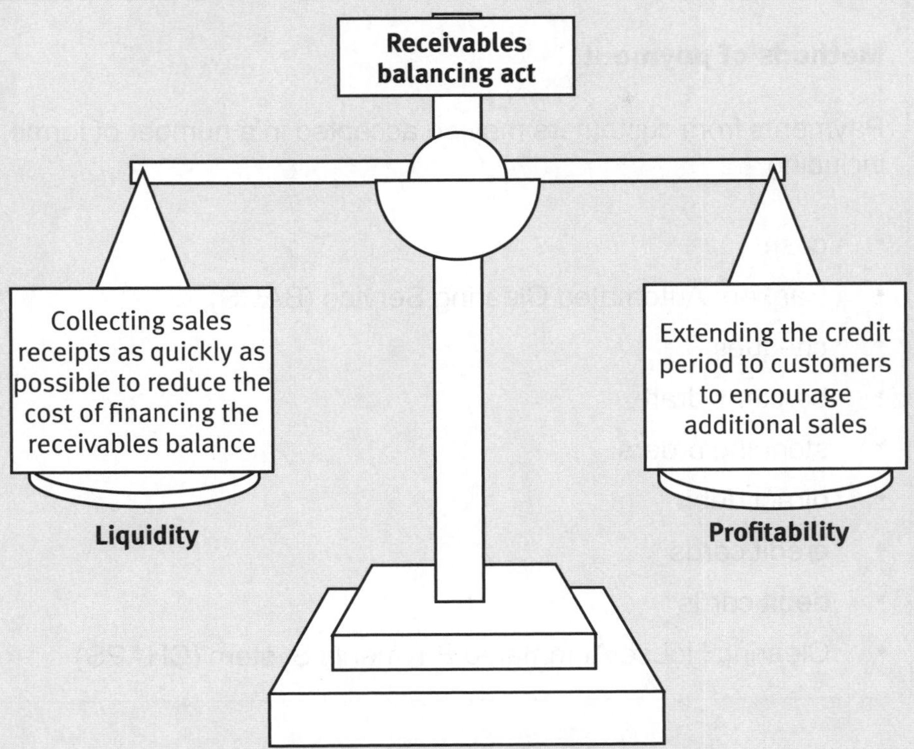

Remember this trade-off is a key factor in determining the entity's working capital investment.

Different payment terms

The payment terms will need to consider the period of credit to be granted and how the payment will be made. The terms agreed will need to specify the price, the date of delivery, the payment date or dates, and any discounts to be allowed for early settlement.

Examples of payment terms may be

- Payment within a specified period. For example, customers must pay within 30 days.
- Payment within a specified period with discount. For example, a 2 per cent discount would be given to customers who pay within 10 days, and others would be required to pay within 30 days.
- Weekly credit. This would require all supplies in a week to be paid by a specified day in the following week.
- Related to delivery of goods. For example, cash on delivery (COD).

Methods of payment

Payments from customers may be accepted in a number of forms, including

- cash
- Bankers Automated Clearing Service (BACS)
- cheques
- banker's draft
- standing orders
- direct debit
- credit cards
- debit cards
- Clearing House Automated Payments System (CHAPS)

For accounts receivable, the entity's credit policy will be influenced by

- demand for products
- competitors' terms
- risk of irrecoverable debts
- financing costs
- costs of credit control

Receivables management has four key aspects:

(1) Assessing creditworthiness of customers.

(2) Setting credit limits.

(3) Invoicing promptly and collecting overdue debts.

(4) Monitoring the credit system.

This is a useful structure to adopt for examination questions that ask about the management of receivables.

3 Assessing creditworthiness

A firm should assess the creditworthiness of

- all new customers immediately, before offering credit terms
- existing customers periodically

Information may come from

- bank references
- trade references
- visit to the customer's premises
- competitors
- published information
- credit reference agencies
- legal sources of credit information
- entity's own sales records
- credit scoring
- credit rating (large corporate customers only)

Assessing creditworthiness

To minimise the risk of irrecoverable debts occurring, an entity should investigate the credit worthiness of all new customers (credit risk), and should review that of existing customers from time to time, especially if they request that their credit limit should be raised. Information about a customer's credit rating can be obtained from a variety of sources.

These include

- Bank references – A customer's permission must be sought. These tend to be fairly standardised in the UK, and so are not perhaps as helpful as they could be.
- Trade references – Suppliers already giving credit to the customer can give useful information about how good the customer is at paying bills on time. There is a danger that the customer will only nominate those suppliers that are being paid on time.
- Visit to the customer's premises – A sales representative might visit the business premises of the customer. A visit will provide information about the actual 'physical' operations and assets of the customer, and might provide some reassurance that the customer's business has substance.

- Competitors – in some industries such as insurance, competitors share information on customers, including creditworthiness.
- Published information – The customer's own annual accounts and reports will give some idea of the general financial position of the entity and its liquidity.
- Credit reference agencies – Agencies such as Dunn & Bradstreet publish general financial details of many entities, together with a credit rating. They will also produce a special report on an entity if requested. The information is provided for a fee.
- Legal sources of credit information – Instead of using a credit reference agency, an entity might check available legal records itself to find out whether the customer has a history of insolvency or non-payment. For example, in the UK information can be obtained from the Register of County Court Judgements and from the Individual Insolvency Register.
- Entity's own sales records – For an existing customer, the sales ledgers will show how prompt a payer the entity is, although they cannot show the ability of the customer to pay.
- Credit scoring – Indicators such as family circumstances, home ownership, occupation and age can be used to predict likely creditworthiness. This is useful when extending credit to the public where little other information is available. A variety of software packages is available which can assist with credit scoring.
- Large corporate customers only: credit rating – Very large entities might have a credit rating from one of the major credit rating agencies, Moody's and Standard & Poors. A supplier might use an entity's credit rating to decide how much credit to allow, without having to carry out a detailed credit check itself.

4 Setting credit limits

When setting credit limits there are two limits that need to be set

- the amount of credit available and
- the length of time allowed before payment is due.

Both of these limits might be adjusted in accordance to the risk profile of the customer.

Managing existing customers

The 'risk' associated with a customer's credit status should be based on

- the customer's payment record and history of prompt or late payments, and
- any new information that is obtained about the customer, for example from its most recent annual financial statements or recent press reports.

The level of credit available and the length of settlement period offered to a customer (if across-the-board standard terms are not used) should then be based on the assessment of this risk.

Example

An entity might group its existing customers into six categories, as follows:

Customer categories

	Financially strong	Financially stable	Financially weak
Prompt payer	Category A	Category B	Category C
Late payer	Category D	Category E	Category F

The amount of credit offered to the customer (and possibly also the length of the payment terms) would vary according to the category of the customer. If a customer moves from one category to a stronger category, a higher credit limit (or longer settlement period) would be allowed if required.

If the customer's credit status does not improve, a request for more credit from the customer should be refused.

The ledger account should be monitored to take account of orders in the pipeline as well as invoiced sales, before further credit is given.

5 Invoicing and collecting overdue debts

A credit period only begins once an invoice is received so prompt invoicing is essential. If debts go overdue, the risk of default increases, therefore a system of follow-up procedures is required

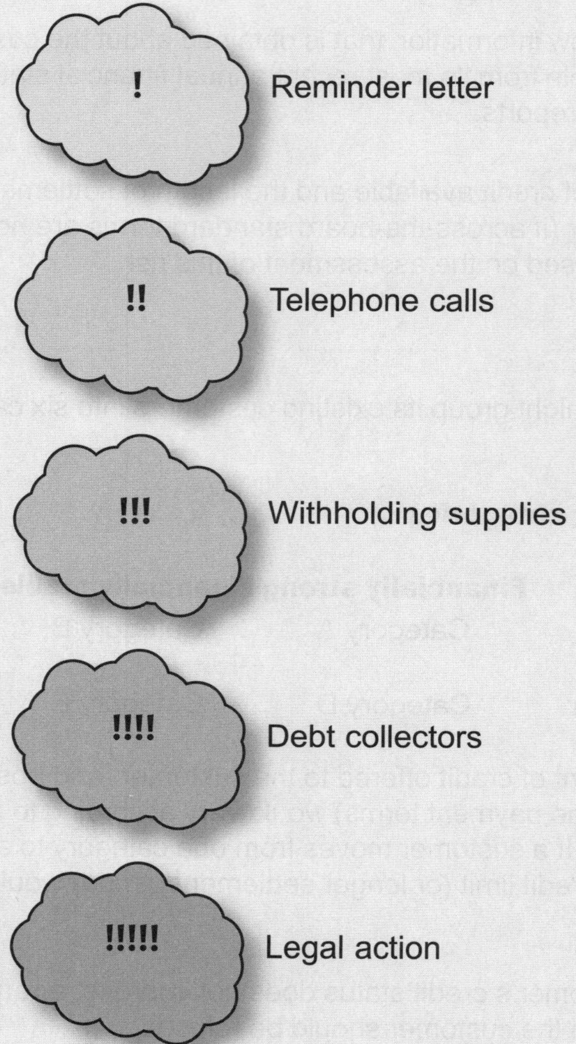

Invoicing and collecting overdue debts

The longer a debt is allowed to run, the higher the probability of eventual default. A system of follow-up procedures is required, bearing in mind the risk of offending a valued customer to such an extent that their business is lost.

Techniques for 'chasing' overdue debts include the following

- Reminder letters – these are often regarded as being a relatively poor way of obtaining payment, as many customers simply ignore them. Sending reminders by email have proven to be more productive than using the postal system as it is harder for customers to claim that they have not received them.
- Telephone calls – these can be an efficient way of speeding up payment and identifying problems at an early stage.
- Withholding supplies – putting customers on the 'stop list' for further orders or spare parts can encourage rapid settlement of debts.
- Debt collection agencies and trade associations - these offer debt collection services on a fixed fee basis or on 'no collection no charge' terms. The quality of service provided varies considerably and care should be taken in selecting an agent.
- Legal action – this is often seen as a last resort. A solicitor's letter often prompts payment and many cases do not go to court. Court action is usually not cost effective but it can discourage other customers from delaying payment.

Motivating debt collection staff (credit control staff) using collection targets

If employees in the payments collection team are to operate effectively, they need to be convinced of the value of their work and their contribution to the objectives of the organisation. One way of improving performance and increasing staff motivation might be to set collection targets. A collection target is a target for the amount of payments to collect for trade receivables within a given period of time. Targets can be set for

- individual members of the collection team, and
- the credit control team as a whole.

Targets for collection will not be a motivator, however, unless performance is assessed and individuals are rewarded (with a bonus) on the basis of meeting or exceeding targets.

Illustration on collection targets

Consider the following example of an entity aiming to set a collection target

At the end of March, the trade receivables of M were as follows:

		$
From March sales	(100% of sales in the month)	1,200,000
From February sales	(70% of sales in the month)	700,000
From January sales	(30% of sales in the month)	270,000
		2,170,000

This represents an average of 60 days' sales outstanding, made up as follows

		Days
From March sales	(100% × 31 days)	31
From February sales	(70% × 28 days)	20
From January sales	(30% × 31 days)	9
		60

The entity wants to reduce its average days sales outstanding from 60 days to 50 days by the end of April. Sales in April are expected to be $1,100,000, all on credit. It intends to do this by aiming to collect payments of the oldest outstanding receivables.

Required

Calculate the collection target that should be set for staff.

Solution

- If no money is collected at all during April, the days sales outstanding would increase from 60 days to 90 days (= 60 days + 30 days in April).
- If days sales outstanding is reduced to 50 days, representing the most recent sales, these will be the sales in April and 20 days of sales in March.
- To reach the target of 50 days by collecting the oldest unpaid receivables, the entity must collect 40 days of sales, representing

	Days	$
From March sales *	11	425,806
From February sales	20	700,000
From January sales	9	270,000
		1,395,806

* March amount calculated as (11/31 x $1,200,000)

The collection target for April should therefore be $1,395,806, probably rounded up to $1,400,000.

Note in this example, the collection target focuses on the trade receivables that have been unpaid for the longest time. A different policy could be followed, such as chasing the customers who are most likely to pay early, or chasing customers who are overdue with their payment by only one or two weeks.

6 Monitoring the system

The position of receivables should be regularly reviewed as part of managing overall working capital and corrective action taken when needed. Methods include:

- age analysis
- ratios
- statistical data.

Monitoring the system

Management will require regular information to take corrective action and to measure the impact of giving credit on working capital investment. Typical management reports on the credit system will include the following points.

- Age analysis of outstanding debts.

  As an aid to effective credit control, an age analysis of outstanding debts may be produced. This is simply a list of the customers who currently owe money, showing the total amount owed and the period of time for which the money has been owed. The actual form of the age analysis report can vary widely, but a typical example is shown below for a sole trader called Robins.

Account number	Name	Balance	Up to 30 days	31–60 days	61–90 days	Over 90 days
B002	Brennan	294.35	220.15	65.40	8.80	0.00
G007	Goodridge	949.50	853.00	0.00	96.50	0.00
T005	Taylor	371.26	340.66	30.60	0.00	0.00
T010	Thorpe	1,438.93	0.00	0.00	567.98	870.95
T011	Tinnion	423.48	312.71	110.77	0.00	0.00
Totals		3,477.52	1,726.52	206.77	673.28	870.95
Percentage		100%	50%	6%	19%	25%

To prepare the analysis, either use a computer programme or manually analyse each customer, account. For each customer, every invoice is allocated to the month it was issued. Then when payment is received, the invoice is cancelled from the analysis, leaving the total of unpaid invoices for each month. Difficulties analysing the balance can occur if the customer pays lump sum on account, rather than specific invoices. Care must be taken to allocate all adjustments other than cash, such as credit notes, discounts given, etc.

The age analysis of trade receivables can be used to help decide what action should be taken about debts that have been outstanding for longer than the specified credit period. It can be seen from the table above that 41% of Robin's outstanding trade receivable balance is due by Thorpe. It may be that Thorpe is experiencing financial difficulties. There may already have been some correspondence between the two entities about the outstanding debts.

As well as providing information about individual customer balances, the age analysis of trade receivables provides additional information about the efficiency of cash collection. The table above shows that over 50 per cent of debts have been outstanding for more than 30 days. If the normal credit period is 30 days, there may be a suggestion of weaknesses in credit control. It may also be useful to show the credit limit for each customer on the report, to identify those customers who are close to, or have exceeded, their credit limit.

The age analysis can also provide information to assist in setting and monitoring collection targets for the credit control section. A collection target could be expressed as a percentage of credit sales collected within a specified period or it could be expressed in terms of the average number of trade receivable days outstanding. When trying to achieve a collection target ,the age analysis can be very useful in identifying large balances that have been outstanding for long periods. These can be targeted for action to encourage payment.

- Ratios, compared with the previous period or target, to indicate trends in credit levels and the incidence of overdue and irrecoverable debts.
- Statistical data to identify causes of default and the incidence of irrecoverable debts among different classes of customer and types of trade.

Test your understanding 1 – Credit limits

Explain the factors that might be considered when revising a credit limit for an existing customer, and list the tools that a credit controller can use to help in making a credit limit decision.

7 Accounts receivable – calculations

Costs of financing receivables

Key working:

Finance cost = Receivable balance × Interest (overdraft) rate

↓

$$\text{Receivable balance} = \text{Sales} \times \frac{\text{Receivable days}}{365}$$

Test your understanding 2 – Cost of financing receivables

Paisley has sales of $20 million for the previous year. Receivables at the year end were $4 million, and the cost of financing receivables is covered by an overdraft at the interest rate of 12% pa.

Required

(a) Calculate the receivables days for Paisley

(b) Calculate the annual cost of financing receivables.

Early settlement discounts

Cash discounts are given to encourage early payment by customers. The cost of the discount is balanced against the savings the entity receives from having less capital tied up due to a lower receivables balance and a shorter average collection period. Discounts may also reduce the number of irrecoverable debts.

The calculation of the annual cost can be expressed as a formula:

$$\text{Annual cost of discount} = \left[1 + \frac{\text{discount}}{\text{amount left to pay}}\right]^{\text{no.of periods}} - 1$$

$$\text{where no. of periods} = \frac{365 / 52 / 12}{\text{no. of days / weeks / months earlier the money is received.}}$$

Notice that the annual cost calculation is always based on the amount left to pay, i.e. the amount net of discount.

If the cost of offering the discount exceeds the rate of overdraft interest, then the discount should not be offered.

Test your understanding 3 – Early settlement discounts

Paisley has sales of $20 million for the previous year, receivables at the year end of $4 million and the cost of financing receivables is covered by an overdraft at the interest rate of 12% pa. It is now considering offering a cash discount of 2% for payment of debts within 10 days.

Calculate whether the annualised cost of offering the discount and state whether you would advise the discount to be offered.

Evaluating a change in credit policy

In an examination, you may be required to evaluate whether a proposed change in credit policy is financially justified. The illustration below illustrates the approach required to carry out this evaluation.

Evaluating a change in credit policy

An example is given below.

The table below gives information extracted from the annual accounts of Supergeordie.

	$
Raw materials	180,000
Work in progress	93,360
Finished goods	142,875
Purchases	720,000
Cost of goods sold	1,098,360
Sales	1,188,000
Trade receivables	297,000
Trade payables	126,000

The sales director of Supergeordie estimates that if the period of credit allowed to customers was reduced from its current level to 60 days, this would result in a 25 per cent reduction in sales but would probably eliminate about $30,000 per annum bad debts. It would be necessary to spend an additional $20,000 per annum on credit control. The entity at present relies heavily on overdraft finance costing 9 per cent per annum.

You are required to make calculations showing the effect of these changes, and to advise whether they would be financially justified. Assume that purchases and inventory holdings would be reduced proportionally to the reduction in sales value.

Solution

The first stage is to identify the reduction in the level of working capital investment as a result of the change in policy. Inventory and trade payables are assumed to fall by 25 per cent in line with sales, but the new level of trade receivables will need to be calculated using the trade receivable collection formula.

Reduction in working capital

	Existing level		New level	Change
	$		$	$
Raw materials	180,000	× 75% =	135,000	45,000
Work in progress	93,360	× 75% =	70,020	23,340
Finished goods	142,875	× 75% =	107,156	35,719
Trade receivables	297,000	(W1)	146,466	150,534
Trade payables	(126,000)	× 75% =	(94,500)	(31,500)
Total	587,235		364,142	223,093

Working

(W1)

$$\text{Receivable collection period} = \frac{\text{trade receivables}}{\text{sales}} \times 365$$

$$60 = \frac{\text{trade receivables}}{1{,}188{,}000 \times 75\%} \times 365$$

$$\text{Trade receivables} = \frac{891{,}000 \times 60}{365}$$

$$= \$146{,}466$$

The second stage is to consider the annual costs and benefits of changing the credit policy. A key element here is to recognise the saving in finance costs as a result of the reduction in the level of working capital investment recognised above.

Annual costs and benefits

		$
Saving in finance costs (223,093 × 9%)	=	20,078
Reduction in gross profit (1,188,000 – 1,098,360)	= 89,640 × 25% =	(22,410)
Reduction in bad debts	=	30,000
Credit control costs	=	(20,000)
Net saving per annum before tax		7,668

The change in credit policy appears to be justified financially, but it should be remembered that there are a number of assumptions built in that could invalidate the calculations.

8 Accounts receivable – factoring

Factoring is the 'sale of debts to a third party (the factor) at a discount in return for prompt cash' (CIMA Official Terminology).

The debts of the entity are effectively sold to a factor (normally owned by a bank). The factor takes on the responsibility of collecting the debt for a fee. The entity can choose one or both of the following services offered by the factor

(1) debt collection and administration – recourse or non-recourse

(2) credit insurance

These are of particular value to

- smaller firms
- fast growing firms

Make sure you can discuss the various services offered and remember that non-recourse factoring is more expensive as the factor bears the costs of any irrecoverable debts.

More details

Debt collection and administration – the factor takes over the whole of the entity's sales ledger, issuing invoices and collecting debts.

Credit insurance – the factor agrees to insure the irrecoverable debts of the client. The factor would then determine to whom the entity was able to offer credit.

Some entities realise that, although it is necessary to extend trade credit to customers for competitive reasons, they need payment earlier than agreed in order to assist their own cash flow. Factors exist to help such entities.

Factoring is primarily designed to allow entities to accelerate cash flow, providing finance against outstanding trade receivables. This improves cash flow and liquidity. The factor will advance up to 80% of the value of a debt to the entity. The remainder (minus finance costs) being paid when the debts are collected. The factor becomes a source of finance. Finance costs are usually 1.5% to 3% above bank base rate and interest is charged on a daily basis.

Factoring is most suitable for

- small and medium-sized firms which often cannot afford sophisticated credit and sales accounting systems, and
- firms that are expanding rapidly. These often have a substantial and growing investment in receivables, which can be turned into cash by factoring the debts. Factoring debts can be a more flexible source of financing working capital than an overdraft or bank loan.

Factoring can be arranged on either a 'without recourse' basis or a 'with recourse' basis.

- When factoring is without recourse or 'non-recourse', the factor provides protection for the client against irrecoverable debts. The factor has no 'comeback' or recourse to the client if a customer defaults. When a customer of the client fails to pay a debt, the factor bears the loss and the client receives the money from the debt.
- When the service is with recourse ('recourse factoring'), the client must bear the loss from any irrecoverable debt, and so has to reimburse the factor for any money it has already received for the debt.

Credit protection is provided only when the service is non-recourse and this is obviously more costly.

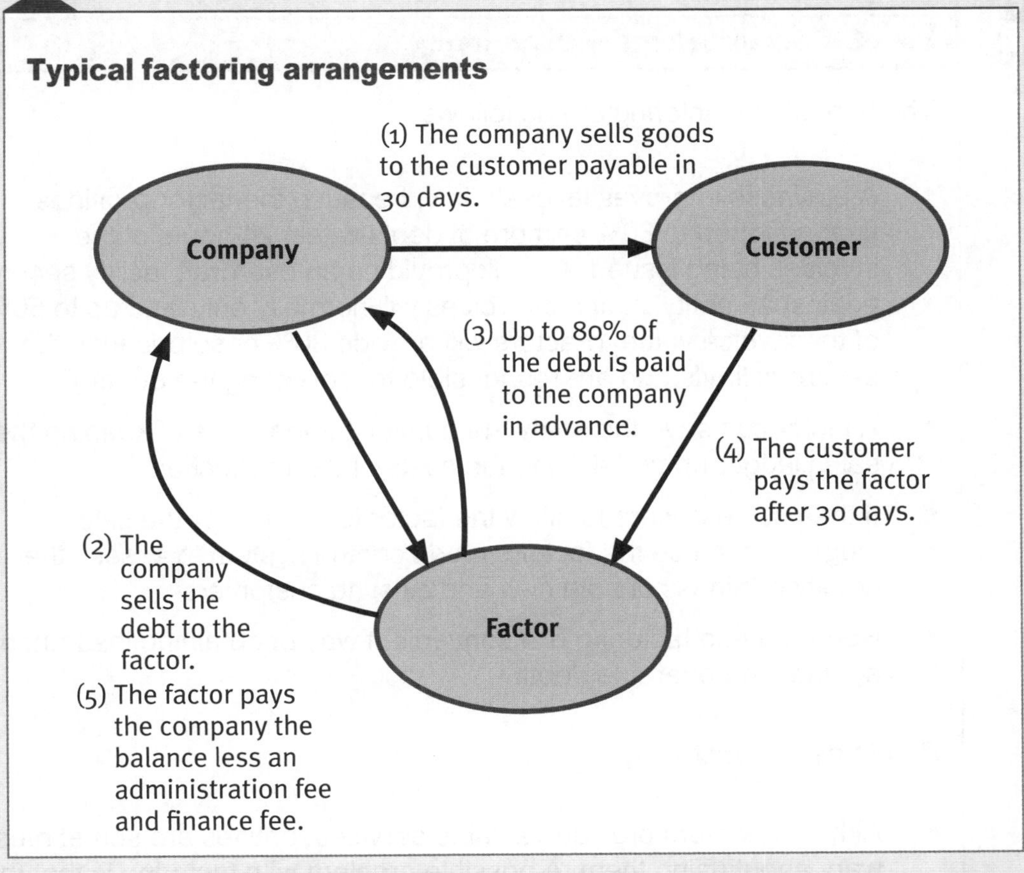
Typical factoring arrangements
(1) The company sells goods to the customer payable in 30 days.
Company
Customer
(3) Up to 80% of the debt is paid to the company in advance.
(4) The customer pays the factor after 30 days.
(2) The company sells the debt to the factor.
Factor
(5) The factor pays the company the balance less an administration fee and finance fee.

Advantages	**Disadvantages**
(1) Saving in administration costs. (2) Reduction in the need for management control. (3) Particularly useful for small and fast growing businesses where the credit control department may not be able to keep pace with volume growth.	(1) Likely to be more costly than an efficiently run internal credit control department. (2) Factoring has a bad reputation associated with failing companies; using a factor may suggest your company has money worries. (3) Customers may not wish to deal with a factor. (4) Once you start factoring it is difficult to revert easily to an internal credit control system. (5) The company may give up the opportunity to decide to whom credit may be given (non-recourse factoring).

Benefits and problems with factoring

The benefits of factoring are as follows.

- A business improves its cash flow, because the factor provides finance for up to 80% or more of debts within 24 hours of the invoices being issued. A bank providing an overdraft facility secured against an entity's unpaid invoices will normally only lend up to 50% of the invoice value. (Factors will provide 80% or so because they set credit limits and are responsible for collecting the debts.)
- A factor can save the entity the administration costs of keeping the sales ledger up to date and the costs of debt collection.
- If the business were to allow the factor to administer the sales ledger, it can use the factor's credit control system to assess the creditworthiness of both new and existing customers.
- Non-recourse factoring is a convenient way of obtaining insurance against irrecoverable debts.

Problems with factoring

- Although factors provide valuable services, entities are sometimes wary about using them. A possible problem with factoring is that the intervention of the factor between the factor's client and the debtor entity could endanger trading relationships and damage goodwill. Customers might prefer to deal with the business, not a factor.
- When a non-recourse factoring service is used, the client loses control over decisions about granting credit to its customers.
- For this reason, some clients prefer to retain the risk of irrecoverable debts, and opt for a 'with recourse' factoring service. With this type of service, the client and not the factor decides whether extreme action (legal action) should be taken against a non-payer.
- On top of this, when suppliers and customers of the client find out that the client is using a factor to collect debts, it may arouse fears that the entity is beset by cash flow problems, raising fears about its viability. If so, its suppliers may impose more stringent payment terms, thus negating the benefits provided by the factor.

Test your understanding 4 – Factoring arrangements

Edden is a medium-sized entity producing a range of engineering products, which it sells to wholesale distributors. Recently, its sales have begun to rise rapidly due to economic recovery. However, it is concerned about its liquidity position and is looking at ways of improving cash flow.

Its sales are $16 million pa, and average receivables are $3.3 million (representing about 75 days of sales).

One way of speeding up collection from receivables is to use a factor. It has considered an agreement from an interested factoring entity.

The factor will pay 80% of the book value of invoices immediately, with finance costs charged on the advance at 10% pa.

The factor will charge 1% of sales as their fee for managing the sales ledger and there will be administrative savings of $100,000. It will be a non-recourse agreement – which means that the factor will bear the responsibility for any irrecoverable debts.

The entity is currently paying 8% interest on its overdraft.

Required

Calculate the relative costs of using the factor and state whether it would be beneficial to the entity to use this facility.

9 Accounts receivable – invoice discounting

Invoice discounting is a method of raising finance against the security of receivables without using the sales ledger administration services of a factor.

While specialist invoice discounting firms exist, this is a service also provided by a factoring entity. Selected invoices are used as security against which the entity may borrow funds. This is a temporary source of finance, repayable when the debt is cleared. The key advantage of invoice discounting is that it is a confidential service, and the customer need not know about it.

In some ways it is similar to the financing part of the factoring service without control of credit passing to the factor.

Ensure you can explain the difference between factoring and invoice discounting, and the situations where one may be more appropriate than the other.

Invoice discounting

Typical arrangement

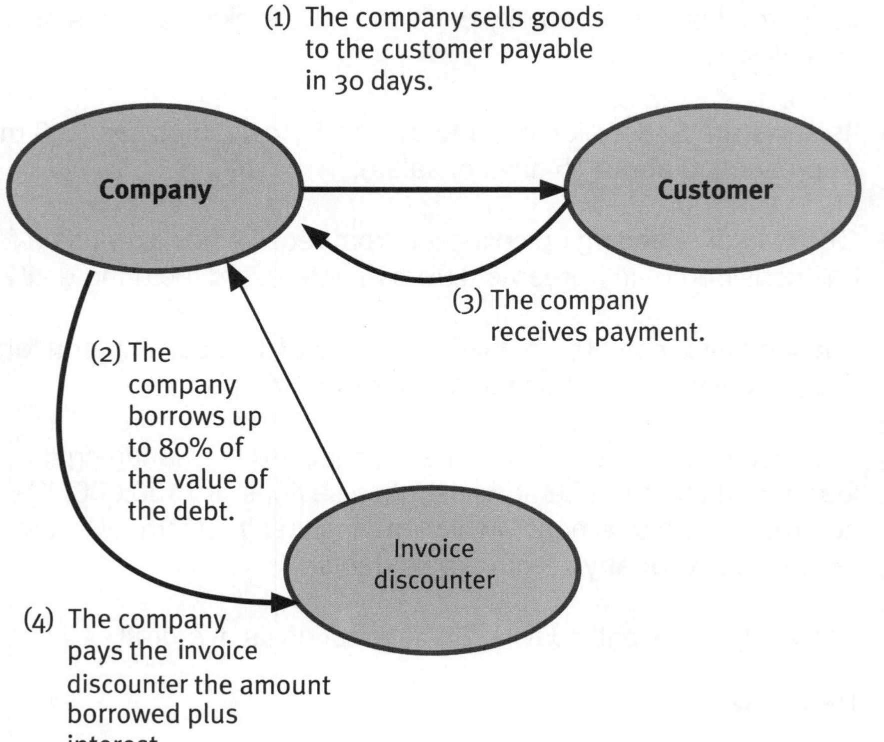
(1) The company sells goods to the customer payable in 30 days.
Company
Customer
(3) The company receives payment.
(2) The company borrows up to 80% of the value of the debt.
Invoice discounter
(4) The company pays the invoice discounter the amount borrowed plus interest.

Invoice discounting is a method of raising finance against the security of receivables without using the sales ledger administration services of a factor. With invoice discounting, the business retains control over its sales ledger, and confidentiality in its dealings with customers. Firms of factors will also provide invoice discounting to clients.

The method works as follows:

- The business sends out invoices, statements and reminders in the normal way, and collects the debts. With 'confidential invoice discounting', its customers are unaware that the business is using invoice discounting.
- The invoice discounter provides cash to the business for a proportion of the value of the invoice, as soon as it receives a copy of the invoice and agrees to discount it. The discounter will advance cash up to 80% of face value.
- When the business eventually collects the payment from its customer, the money must be paid into a bank account controlled by the invoice discounter. The invoice discounter then pays the business the remainder of the invoice, less interest and administration charges.

Invoice discounting can help a business that is trying to improve its cash flows, but does not want a factor to administer its sales ledger and collect its debts. It is therefore equivalent to the financing service provided by a factor.

Administration charges for this service are around 0.5–1% of a client's turnover. It is more risky than factoring since the client retains control over its credit policy. Consequently, such facilities are usually confined to established entities with high sales revenue, and the business must be profitable. Finance costs are usually in the range 3–4% above base rate, although larger entities and those which arrange credit insurance may receive better terms.

The invoice discounter will check the sales ledger of the client regularly, perhaps every three months, to check that its debt collection procedures are adequate.

Illustration of the invoice discounting process

At the beginning of August, Basildon sells goods for a total value of $300,000 to regular customers but decides that it requires payment earlier than the agreed 30-day credit period for these invoices.

A discounter agrees to finance 80% of their face value, i.e. $240,000, at an interest cost of 9% pa.

The invoices were due for payment in early September, but were subsequently settled in mid-September, exactly 45 days after the initial transactions. The invoice discounter's service charge is 1% of invoice value. A special account is set up with a bank, into which all payments are made.

The sequence of cash flows is:

August	Basildon receives cash advance of $240,000.	
Mid-September	Customers pay $300,000.	
	Invoice discounter receives the full $300,000 paid into the special bank account.	
	Basildon receives the balance payable, less charges, i.e.	
	Service fee = 1% × $300,000 =	$3,000
	Finance cost = 9% × $240,000 × 45/365 =	$2,663
	Total charges	$5,663
	Basildon receives:	
	Balance of payment from customer	$60,000
	Less charges	$5,663
		$54,337
Summary $300,000 invoiced	Total receipts by Basildon: $240,000 + $54,337	$294,337
	Invoice discounter's fee and interest charges	$5,663

10 Accounts payable – managing trade credit

Trade credit is the simplest and most important source of short-term finance for many entities.

Again it is a balancing act between liquidity and profitability.

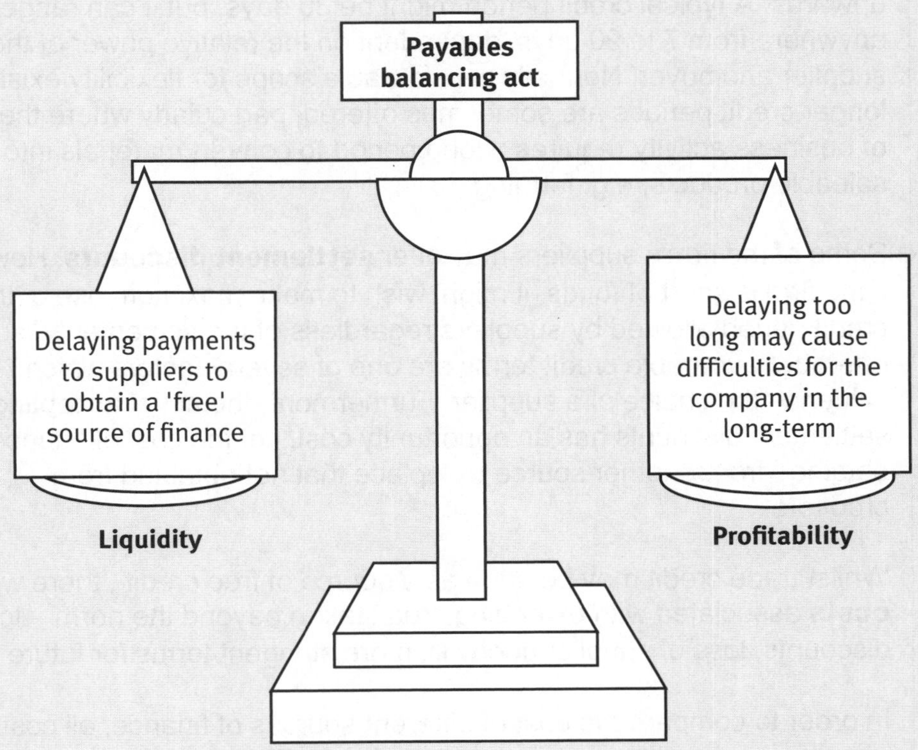

By delaying payment to suppliers, entities face possible problems

- supplier may refuse to supply in future
- supplier may only supply on a cash basis
- there may be loss of reputation
- supplier may increase price in future

Trade credit is normally seen as a 'free' source of finance. Whilst this is normally true, it may be that the supplier offers a discount for early payment. In this case, delaying payment is no longer free, since the cost will be the lost discount.

In the examination, you need to be able to calculate the cost of this discount foregone.

Trade payables

Using **trade credit** a firm is able to obtain goods (or services) from a supplier without immediate payment, the supplier accepting that the firm will pay at a later date.

Trade credit periods vary from industry to industry and each industry will have what is a generally accepted norm which would be from seven days upwards. A typical credit period might be 30 days, but it can range anywhere from 7 to 90 days, dependent on the relative power of the supplier and buyer. Normally considerable scope for flexibility exists and longer credit periods are sometimes offered, particularly where the type of business activity requires a long period to convert materials into saleable products, e.g. farming.

Some of the firm's suppliers may offer **settlement discounts**. However, if the firm is short of funds, it might wish to make maximum use of the credit period allowed by suppliers regardless of the settlement discounts offered. Favourable credit terms are one of several factors which influence the choice of a supplier. Furthermore, the act of accepting settlement discounts has an opportunity cost, i.e. the cost of finance obtained from another source to replace that not obtained from creditors.

Whilst trade credit may be seen as a source of free credit , there will be **costs** associated with extending credit taken beyond the norm – lost discounts, loss of supplier goodwill, more stringent terms for future sales.

In order to compare the cost of different sources of finance, all costs are usually converted to a rate per annum basis. The cost of extended trade credit is usually measured by loss of discount, but the calculation of its cost is complicated by such variables as the number of alternative sources of supply, and the general economic conditions.

Certain assumptions have to be made concerning (a) the maximum delay in payment which can be achieved before the supply of goods is withdrawn by the supplier, and (b) the availability of alternative sources of supply.

Also, it is a mistake to reduce working capital by holding on to creditors' money for a longer period than is allowed as, in the long-term, this will affect the **supplier's willingness to supply** goods and raw materials, and cause further embarrassment to the firm.

Test your understanding 5 – Discounts for early payment

One supplier has offered a discount to Box of 2% on an invoice for $7,500, if payment is made within one month, rather than the three months normally taken to pay. If Box's overdraft rate is 10% pa, calculate if it is financially worthwhile for them to accept the discount and pay early?

Age analysis of payables

The value of an age analysis of trade payables is probably less obvious than the value of an age analysis of trade receivables. However, management needs to be aware of

- the total amount payable to suppliers
- when the money will be payable
- the amounts payable to each individual supplier, and how close this is to the credit limit available from the supplier
- whether the entity is failing to pay its trade suppliers on time

Test your understanding 6 – Practice questions

(1) **Which of the following will not influence an entity's overall credit policy.**

A Demand for products

B Costs of credit control

C Volume of purchases

D Risk of irrecoverable debts

(2) An entity expects credit sales of $110,000 in July, rising by $10,000 each month for the next two months. Outstanding trade receivables at the beginning of July were $165,000, representing all of June sales and 22 days of May sales. Sales in June were $95,000.

The entity wishes to reduce the average days sales outstanding to 45 days by the end of July and 40 days by the end of August.

On the assumption that the target should be to collect first the receivables that have been unpaid for the longest time, calculate the collection targets for

(a) July, and

(b) August.

(3) **List five methods of carrying out a credit check on a potential new customer, before deciding whether to give credit and if so, what the credit limit should be.**

(4) An entity is considering a change in its credit policy. It has estimated that if credit terms are extended from 30 days to 60 days, total annual sales will increase by 10% from the current level of $12 million. It has been estimated that as a consequence of the change in credit terms and the higher sales volume, irrecoverable debts would increase from 2% to 3% of sales. The entity 's cost of capital is 8%.

The increase in sales would not affect annual fixed costs. The contribution to sales ratio is 40%.

Required

Calculate the effect of the change in credit policy on the annual profit before taxation. Assume a 360-day year of 30 days each month.

(5) An entity is offering a cash discount of 2.5% to receivables if they agree to pay debts within one month. The usual credit period taken is three months.

Calculate the effective annualised cost of offering the discount and should it be offered, if the bank would loan to the entity at 18% pa?

(6) **Calculate the equivalent annual cost of the following credit terms: 1.75% discount for payment within three weeks. Alternatively, full payment must be made within eight weeks of the invoice date.**

Assume there are 50 weeks in a year.

(7) Marton produces a range of specialised components, supplying a wide range of customers, all on credit terms. 20% of revenue is sold to one firm. Having used generous credit policies to encourage past growth, Marton Co now has to finance a substantial overdraft and is concerned about its liquidity.

Marton borrows from its bank at 13% pa interest. No further sales growth in volume or value terms is planned for the next year.

In order to speed up collection from customers, Marton is considering two alternative policies:

Option one

Factoring on a non-recourse basis with the factor administering and collecting payment from Marton Co's customers. This is expected to generate administrative savings of $200,000 pa and to lower the average receivable collection period by 15 days. The factor will make a service charge of 1% of Marton Co's revenue and also provide credit insurance facilities for an annual premium of $80,000.

Option two

Offering discounts to customers who settle their accounts early. The amount of the discount will depend on speed of payment as follows.

Payment within 10 days of despatch of invoices 3%

Payment within 20 days of despatch of invoices 1.5%

It is estimated that customers representing 20% and 30% of Marton Co's sales respectively will take up these offers, the remainder continuing to take their present credit period.

Extracts from Marton's most recent accounts are given below.

	($000)
Sales (all on credit)	20,000
Cost of sales	(17,000)
Operating profit	3,000
Current assets	
Inventory	2,500
Receivables	4,500
Cash	Nil

Calculate the costs and benefits of the entity using option one.

(8) **Using the information from question 7 calculate the costs and benefits of the entity using option two.**

(9) **Using the information from questions 7 and 8 identify the most financially advantageous policy.**

(10) Fredrico has sales of $40 million for the previous year, receivables at the year end were $6 million, and the cost of financing receivables is covered by an overdraft at the interest rate of 10% pa.

Required:

(a) Calculate the receivables days for Paisley

(b) Calculate the annual cost of financing receivables.

11 Summary Diagram

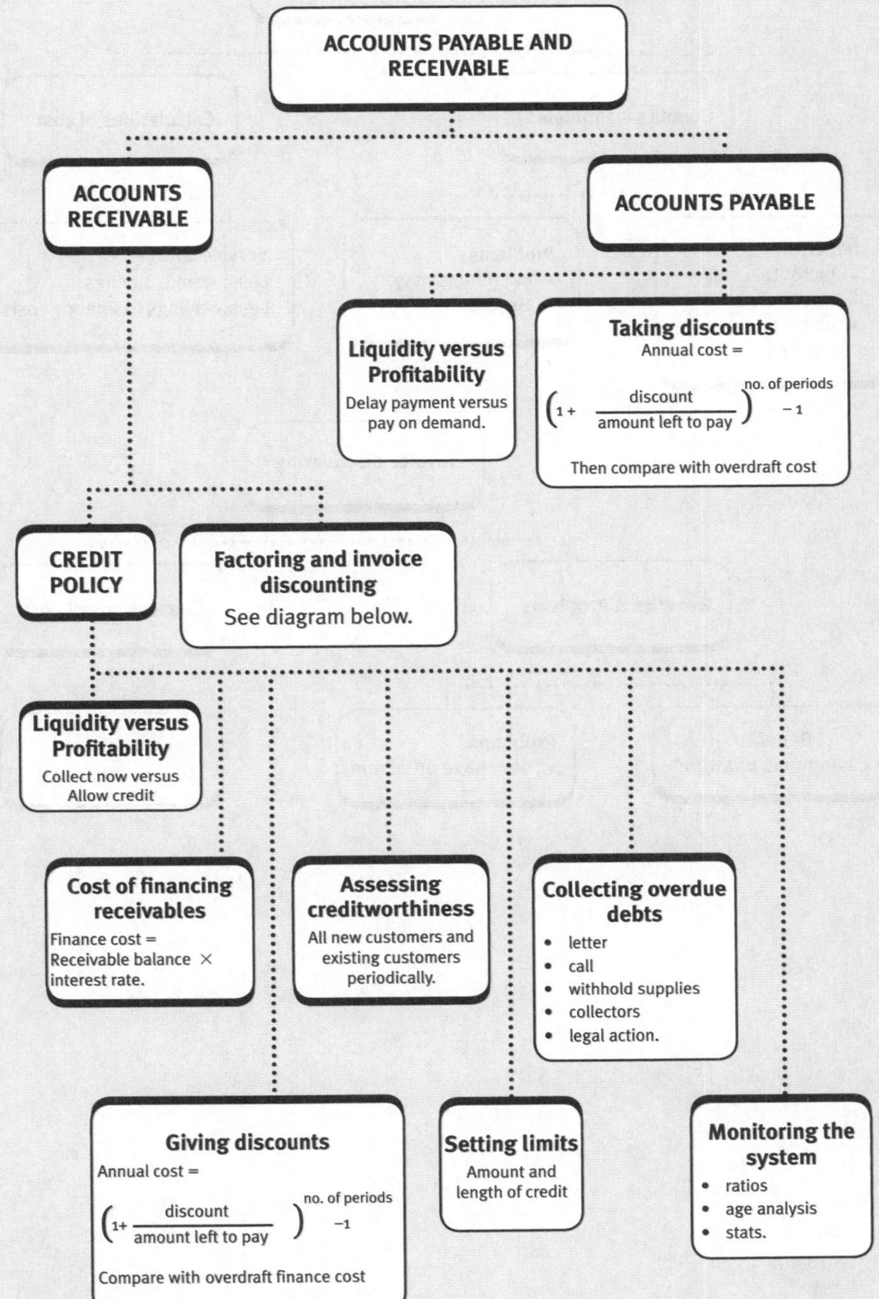
ACCOUNTS PAYABLE AND RECEIVABLE
ACCOUNTS RECEIVABLE
ACCOUNTS PAYABLE
Liquidity versus Profitability
Delay payment versus pay on demand.
Taking discounts
Annual cost =
$\left(1+\frac{\text{discount}}{\text{amount left to pay}}\right)^{\text{no. of periods}}-1$
Then compare with overdraft cost
CREDIT POLICY
Factoring and invoice discounting
See diagram below.
Liquidity versus Profitability
Collect now versus Allow credit
Cost of financing receivables
Finance cost = Receivable balance × interest rate.
Assessing creditworthiness
All new customers and existing customers periodically.
Collecting overdue debts
• letter
• call
• withhold supplies
• collectors
• legal action.
Giving discounts
Annual cost =
$\left(1+\frac{\text{discount}}{\text{amount left to pay}}\right)^{\text{no. of periods}}-1$
Compare with overdraft finance cost
Setting limits
Amount and length of credit
Monitoring the system
• ratios
• age analysis
• stats.

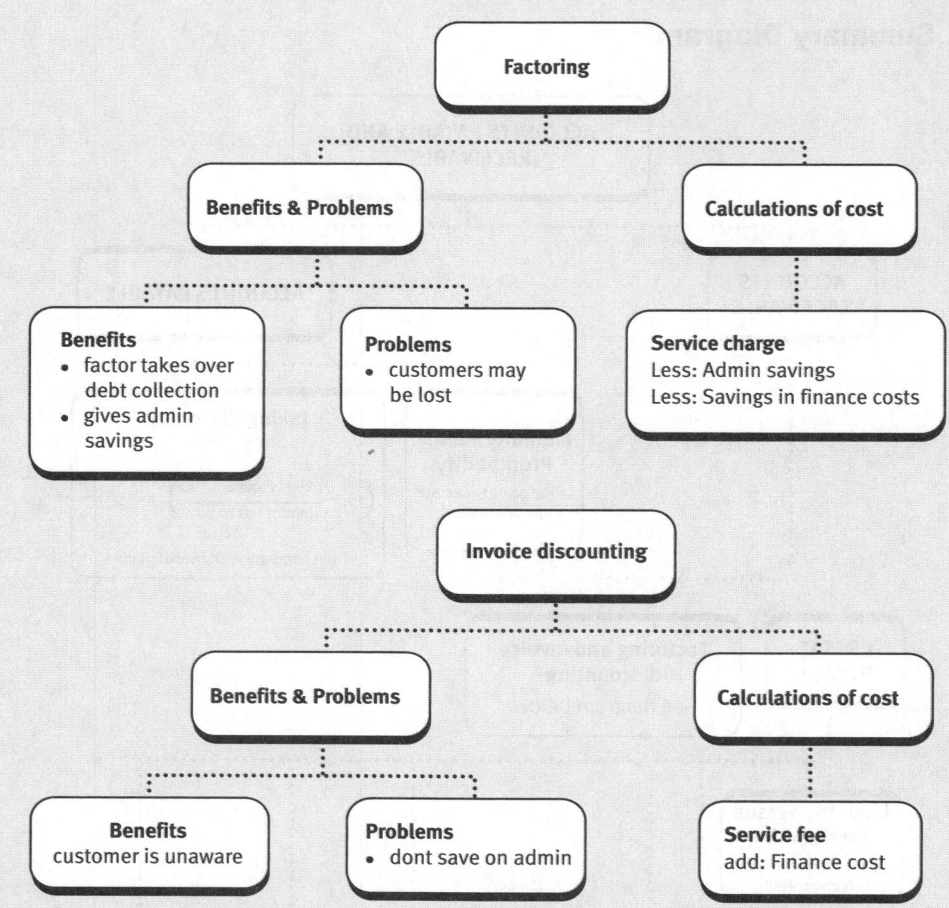
Factoring
Benefits & Problems
Calculations of cost
Benefits
• factor takes over debt collection
• gives admin savings
Problems
• customers may be lost
Service charge
Less: Admin savings
Less: Savings in finance costs
Invoice discounting
Benefits & Problems
Calculations of cost
Benefits
customer is unaware
Problems
• dont save on admin
Service fee
add: Finance cost

Test your understanding answers

Test your understanding 1 – Credit limits

There are a number of factors which a credit controller might consider, such as:

- the customers past payment history. If a customer has usually paid on time in the past then a higher credit limit might be approved.
- any new public information about the customer. For example, if recent press reports suggest that the customer might be in financial difficulty then it may be unwise to raise a customers credit limit.
- a change in the customers credit rating. For large customers especially, credit ratings are easily obtained and any change to a rating should have an impact on the amount of credit offered to the customer.

In making the decision the credit controller will be able to use a variety of tools, such as:

- past customer history
- an aged receivables report
- credit reference agencies
- ratio analysis

Test your understanding 2 – Cost of financing receivables

(a) Receivables days = \$4m ÷ \$20m × 365 = 73 days

(b) Annual cost of financing receivables = \$4m × 12% = \$480,000.

Test your understanding 3 – Early settlement discounts

Discount as a percentage of amount left to pay = 2 ÷ 98 = 2.04%

Receivables days are currently 73 ($4m/$20m × 365), so:

Saving is 63 days (dropping from 73 days to 10) and there are 365 ÷ 63 = 5.794 periods in a year

Annualised cost of discount % is

$(1 + 0.0204)^{5.794} - 1 = 0.1241 = 12.41\%$.

The overdraft rate is 12%.

It would be marginally cheaper to borrow the money from the bank rather than offer the discount.

Test your understanding 4 – Factoring arrangements

	Costs of factoring	Savings
	$	$
Sales ledger administration 1% × $16m	160,000	
Administration cost savings		100,000
Cost of factor finance 10% × 80% × $3.3m *	264,000	
Overdraft finance costs 8% × 80% × $3.3m saved		211,200
Total	424,000	311,200
Net cost of factoring	112,800	

The firm will have to balance this cost against the security offered by improved cash flows and greater liquidity.

* 80% of the average receivable balance is outstanding at any one time.

Test your understanding 5 – Discounts for early payment

Discount saves 2% of $7,500 = $150

Financed by overdraft for extra two months in order to pay early:

Cost = $10\% \times \frac{2}{12} \times \$7,500 = (\$125)$

Net saving = $25

It is worth accepting the discount.

Alternatively:

Discount as a percentage of amount to be paid= $\frac{150}{7,350} = 2.04\%$

Saving is 2 months and there are $\frac{12}{2}$ = 6 periods in a year

Annualised cost of not taking the discount (and therefore borrowing from the supplier) is: $(1+0.0204)^6 - 1 = 0.1288 = 12.88\%$

The overdraft rate is 10%.

It would be cheaper to borrow the money from the bank to pay early and accept the discount.

Test your understanding 6 – Practice questions

(1) The correct answer is C.

The credit worthiness of customers does not influence the entity's credit policy but will be considered when dealing with receivables management, i.e. deciding whether to give a customer credit or not.

(2) **Target receivables**

End of July	**Days**		**$**
July sales	31		110,000
June sales (balance)	14	(14/30 × $95,000)	44,333
	45		154,333

End of August	**Days**		**$**
August sales	31		120,000
July sales (balance)	9	(9/31 × $110,000)	31,935
	40		151,935

Target collections

	July $	**August** $
Receivables at the beginning of the month	165,000	154,533
Sales in the month	110,000	120,000
	275,000	274,333
Receivables at the end of the month	(154,333)	(151,935)
Target collections in the month	120,667	122,398

(3) Choose 5 from the following list:

- bank references
- trade references
- visit to the customer's premises
- competitors
- published information
- credit reference agencies
- legal sources of credit information
- entity sales records
- credit scoring
- credit rating (large corporate customers only).

(4) The two options can be analysed as follows:

	Without the new credit policy	With the new credit policy
Annual sales	$12,000,000	$13,200,000
Average trade receivables	$1,000,000 ($12m × 30/360)	$2,200,000 ($13.2m × 60/360)
Increase in trade receivables		$1,200,000
Irrecoverable debts	$240,000 (= 2%)	$396,000 (= 3%)
Increase in Irrecoverable debts		$156,000
Increase in annual sales		$1,200,000

	$	$
Increase in annual contribution (40%)		480,000
Increase in Irrecoverable debts	156,000	
Increase in interest cost of receivables (8% × $1,200,000)	96,000	
		(252,000)
Net increase in profit before tax		228,000

(5) Discount as a percentage of amount to be paid = 2.5/97.5 = 2.56%

Saving is 2 months and there are 12/2 = 6 periods in a year.

Annualised cost of discount % is

$(1+0.0256)^6 - 1 = 0.1638 = 16.38\%$.

The loan rate is 18%.

It would therefore be worthwhile offering the discount.

(6) The answer is 19.5%

Step 1

Work out the discount available and the amount due if the discount were taken.

Discount available on a $100 invoice = 1.75% × $100 = $1.75.

Amount due after discount = $100 × $1.75 = $98.25

Step 2

The effective interest cost of not taking the discount is:

1.75 ÷ 98.25 = 0.0178 (rounded to 0.018)

for an 8 – 3 = five-week period.

Step 3

Calculate the equivalent annual rate. There are ten five-week periods in a year.

The equivalent interest annual rate is $(1 + 0.018)^{10} - 1 = 0.195$ or 19.5%.

(7) The relative costs and benefits are as follows:

Option 1 – Factoring

Reduction in receivables days	= 15 days		
Reduction in receivables	= 15 ÷ 365 × $20m	=	$821,916
Effect on profit before tax:			
Finance cost saving	= (13% × $821,916)	=	$106,849
Administrative savings		=	$200,000
Service charge	= (1% × $20m)	=	($200,000)
Insurance premium		=	($80,000)
Net profit benefit		=	$26,849

(8) The relative costs and benefits are as follows

Option 2 – The discount

With year-end receivables at $4.5 million, the receivables collection period was: $4.5m ÷ $20m × 365 = 82 days.

The scheme of discounts would change this as follows:

10 days for 20% of customers

20 days for 30% of customers

82 days for 50% of customers

Average receivables days become:

(20% × 10) + (30% × 20) + (50% × 82) = 49 days

Hence, average receivables would reduce from the present $4.5 million to

49 × $20m ÷ 365 = $2,684,932

Finance cost saving = 13% × ($4,500,000 – $2,684,932) = $235,959

The cost of the discount:

(3% × 20% × $20m) + (1.5% × 30% × $20m) = ($210,000)

The net benefit to profit before tax : $25,959

(9) The figures imply that **factoring is marginally the more attractive**, but this result relies on the predicted proportions of customers actually taking up the discount and paying on time. It also neglects the possibility that some customers will insist on taking the discount without bringing forward their payments. Marton would have to consider a suitable response to this problem.

Conversely, the assessment of the value of using the factor depends on the factor lowering Marton's receivables days. If the factor retains these benefits for itself, rather than passing them on to Marton, this will raise the cost of the factoring option. The two parties should clearly specify their mutual requirements from the factoring arrangement on a contractual basis.

(10) The answer is

(a) Receivables days = \$6m ÷ \$40m × 365 = 55 days

(b) Cost of financing receivables = \$6m × 10% = \$600,000.

chapter

23

Working capital management – inventory control

Chapter learning objectives

On completion of their studies students should be able to:

- Discuss the objectives and costs of inventory management.
- Evaluate the impacts of alternative policies for inventory management.
- Calculate EOQ.

1 Session content

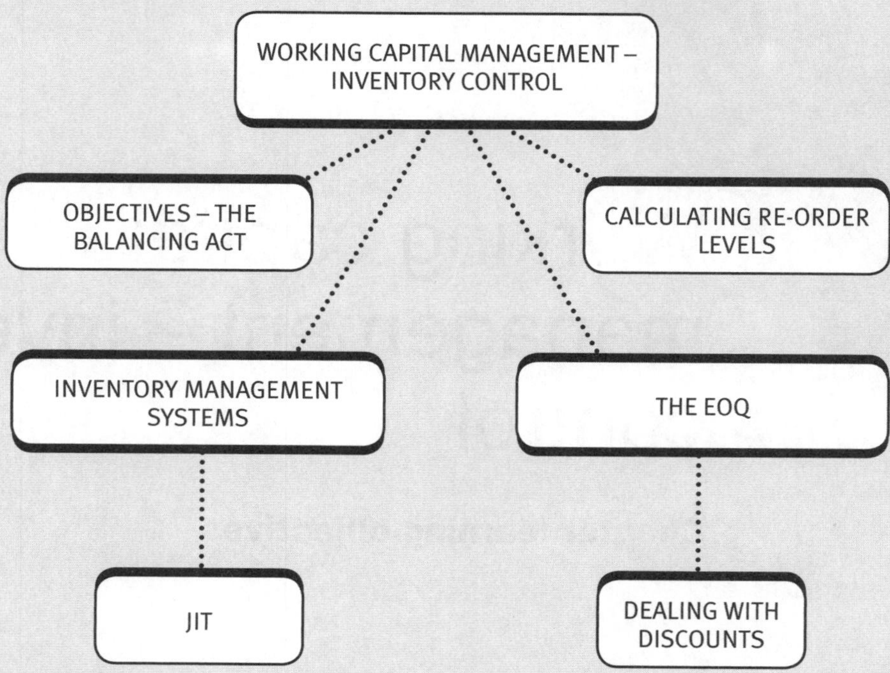

2 The objectives of inventory management

Inventory is a major investment for many entities. Manufacturing entities can potentially be carrying inventory equivalent to between 3 and 6 months worth of sales depending on where they source their inventory from and the relative power of suppliers. It is therefore essential to reduce the levels of inventory held to the necessary minimum.

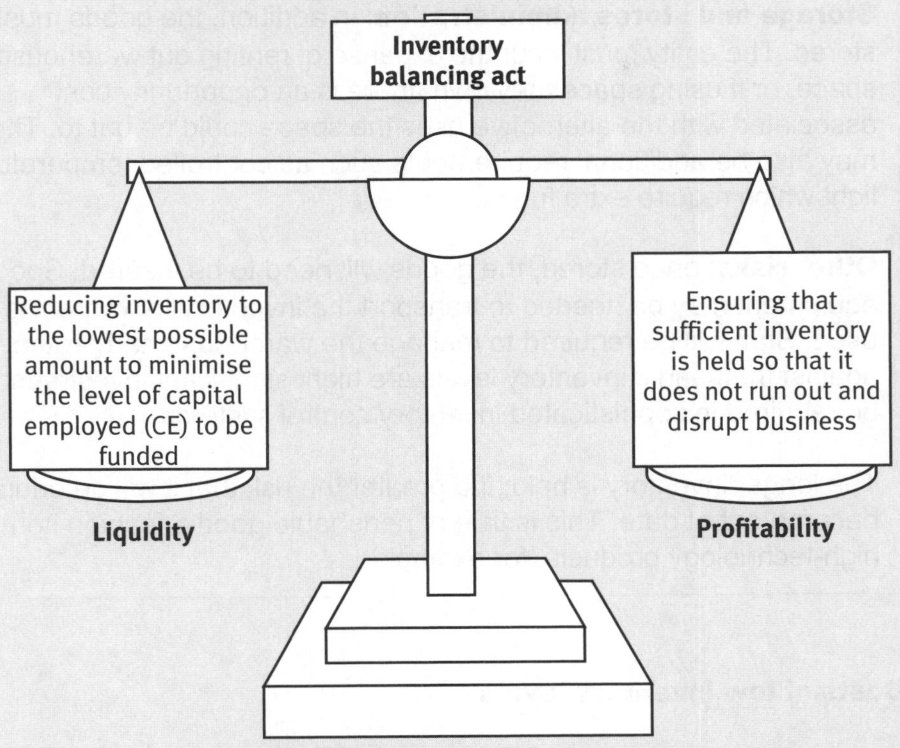
Inventory balancing act
Reducing inventory to the lowest possible amount to minimise the level of capital employed (CE) to be funded
Ensuring that sufficient inventory is held so that it does not run out and disrupt business
Liquidity
Profitability

Costs of high inventory levels

Keeping inventory levels high is expensive owing to:

- the foregone interest that is lost from tying up capital in inventory
- holding costs:
  - storage
  - stores administration
  - risk of theft/damage/obsolescence

Costs of high inventory levels

Carrying inventory involves a major working capital investment and therefore levels need to be very tightly controlled. The cost is not just that of purchasing the goods, but also storing, insuring, and managing them once they are in inventory.

Interest costs: once goods are purchased, capital is tied up in them and until sold on (in their current state or converted into a finished product), the capital earns no return. This lost return is an opportunity cost of holding the inventory.

Storage and stores administration: in addition, the goods must be stored. The entity must incur the expense of renting out warehouse space, or if using space they own, there is an opportunity cost associated with the alternative uses the space could be put to. There may also be additional requirements such as controlled temperature or light which require extra funds.

Other risks: once stored, the goods will need to be insured. Specialist equipment may be needed to transport the inventory to where it is to be used. Staff will be required to manage the warehouse and protect against theft and if inventory levels are high, significant investment may be required in sophisticated inventory control systems.

The longer inventory is held, the greater the risk that it will deteriorate or become out of date. This is true of perishable goods, fashion items and high-technology products, for example.

Costs of low inventory levels

If inventory levels are kept too low, the business faces alternative problems:

- stockouts:
  - lost contribution
  - production stoppages
  - emergency orders
- high re-order/setup costs
- lost quantity discounts

Costs of low inventory levels

Stockout: if a business runs out of a particular product used in manufacturing it may cause interruptions to the production process – causing idle time, stockpiling of work-in-progress (WIP) or possibly missed orders. Alternatively, running out of finished goods or inventory can result in dissatisfied customers and perhaps future lost orders if custom is switched to alternative suppliers. If a stockout looms, the business may attempt to avoid it by acquiring the goods needed at short notice. This may involve using a more expensive or poorer quality supplier.

Re-order/setup costs: each time inventory runs out, new supplies must be acquired. If the goods are bought in, the costs that arise are associated with administration – completion of a purchase requisition, authorisation of the order, placing the order with the supplier, taking and checking the delivery and final settlement of the invoice. If the goods are to be manufactured, the costs of setting up the machinery will be incurred each time a new batch is produced.

Lost quantity discounts: purchasing items in bulk will often attract a discount from the supplier. If only small amounts are bought at one time in order to keep inventory levels low, the quantity discounts will not be available.

The challenge

The objective of good inventory management is therefore to determine:

- the optimum re-order level – how many items should be left in inventory when the next order is placed, and
- the optimum re-order quantity – how many items should be ordered when the order is placed

In practice, this means striking a balance between holding costs on the one hand and stockout and re-order costs on the other.

The balancing act between liquidity and profitability, which might also be considered to be a trade-off between holding costs and stockout/re-order costs, is key to any discussion on inventory management.

Terminology

Other key terms associated with inventory management include:

- lead time – the lag between when an order is placed and the item is delivered
- buffer inventory – the basic level of inventory kept for emergencies. A buffer is required because both demand and lead time will fluctuate and predictions can only be based on best estimates.

Ensure you can distinguish between the various terms used: re-order level, re-order quantity, lead time and buffer inventory.

3 Economic order quantity (EOQ)

For businesses that do not use just in time (JIT) inventory management systems (discussed in more detail below), there is an optimum order quantity for inventory items, known as the EOQ.

The challenge

The aim of the EOQ model is to minimise the total cost of holding and ordering inventory.

EOQ explanation

To minimise the total cost of holding and ordering inventory, it is necessary to balance the relevant costs. These are:

- the variable costs of holding the inventory
- the fixed costs of placing the order

Holding costs

The model assumes that it costs a certain amount to hold a unit of inventory for a year (referred to as C_H in the formula). Therefore, as the average level of inventory increases, so too will the total annual holding costs incurred.

Because of the assumption that demand per period is known and is constant (see below), conclusions can be drawn over the average inventory level in relationship to the order quantity.

When new batches or items of inventory are purchased or made at periodic intervals, the inventory levels are assumed to exhibit the following pattern over time.

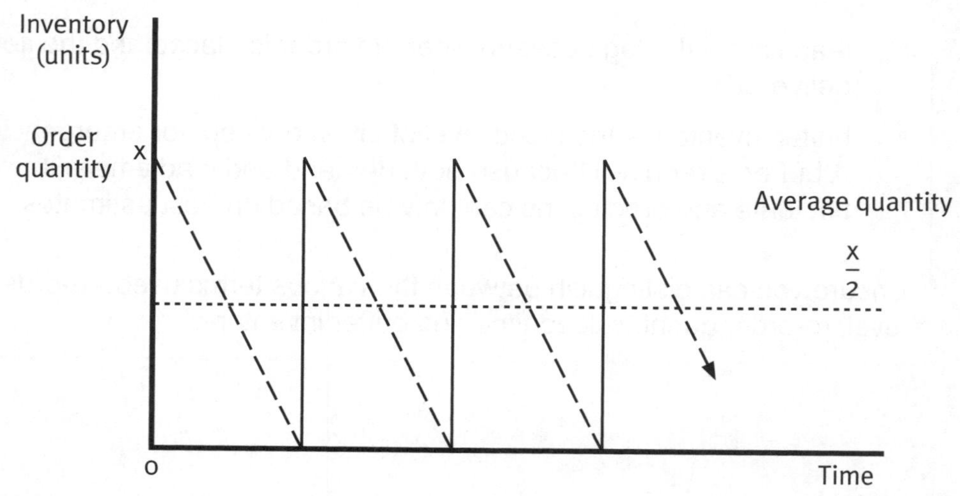

If x is the quantity ordered, the annual holding cost would be calculated as:

Holding cost per unit × Average inventory:

$$C_H \times \frac{x}{2}$$

We therefore see an upward sloping, linear relationship between the re-order quantity and total annual holding costs.

Ordering costs

The model assumes that a fixed cost is incurred every time an order is placed (referred to as C_O in the formula). Therefore, as the order quantity increases, there is a fall in the number of orders required, which reduces the total ordering cost.

If D is the annual expected sales demand, the annual order cost is calculated as:

Order cost per order × no. of orders per annum.

$$C_O \times \frac{D}{x}$$

However, the fixed nature of the cost results in a downward sloping, curved relationship.

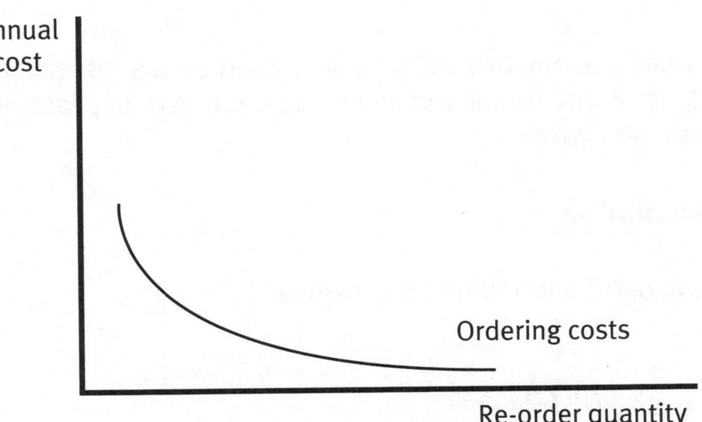

Total costs

Because we are trying to balance these two costs (one which increases as re-order quantity increases and one which falls), total costs will always be minimised at the point where the total holding costs equals the total ordering costs. This point will be the economic order quantity (when the re-order quantity chosen minimises the total cost of holding and ordering).

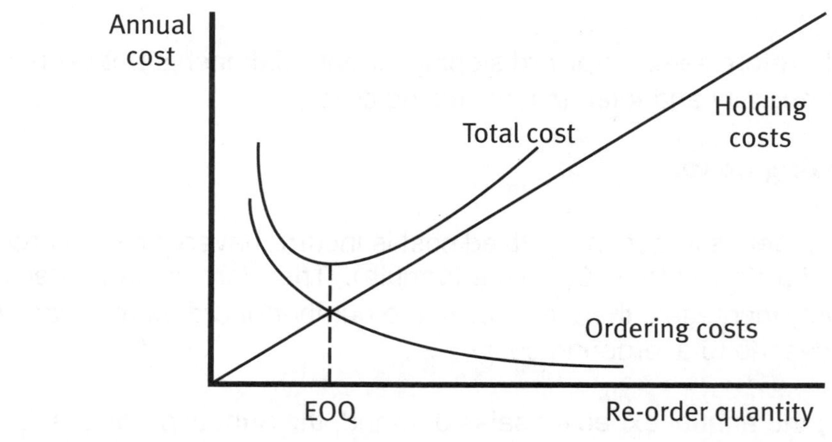

Assumptions

The following assumptions are made:

- demand and lead time are constant and known
- purchase price is constant
- no buffer inventory held as it is assumed that it is not needed since demand and lead times are known with certainty

These assumptions are critical and should be discussed when considering the validity of the model and its conclusions, e.g. in practice, demand and/or lead time may vary.

The calculation

The EOQ can be found using a formula:

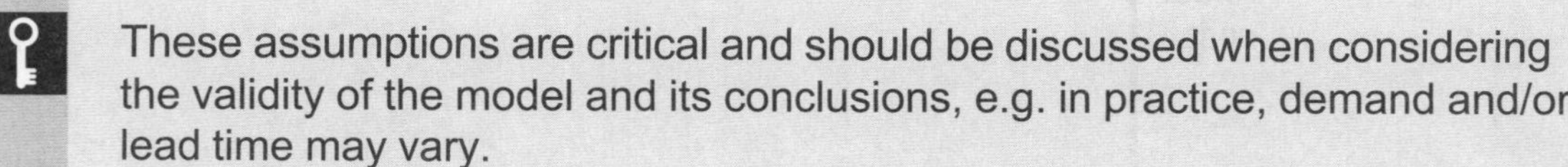

$$EOQ = \sqrt{\frac{2C_O D}{C_H}}$$

where:

C_O = cost per order

D = annual demand

C_H = cost of holding one unit for one year.

Test your understanding 1 – EOQ

An entity requires 1,000 units of material X per month. The cost per order is $30 regardless of the size of the order. The annual holding costs are $2.88 per unit.

Required:

Investigate the total cost of buying the material in quantities of 400, 500, or 600 units at one time. Identify the cheapest option.

Apply the EOQ formula to prove your answer is correct.

Dealing with quantity discounts

Discounts may be offered for ordering in large quantities. If the EOQ is smaller than the order size needed for a discount, should the order size be increased above the EOQ?

To work out the answer you should carry out the following steps:

Step 1: Calculate EOQ, ignoring discounts.

Step 2: If the EOQ is below the quantity qualifying for a discount, calculate the total annual inventory cost arising from using the EOQ.

Step 3: Recalculate total annual inventory costs using the order size required to just obtain each discount.

Step 4: Compare the cost of Steps 2 and 3 with the saving from the discount, and select the minimum cost alternative.

Step 5: Repeat for all discount levels.

Test your understanding 2 – EOQ and discounts

Wolvo is a retailer of barrels. The entity has an annual demand of 30,000 barrels. The barrels cost $12 each. Supplies can be obtained immediately, with ordering and transport costs amounting to $200 per order. The annual cost of holding one barrel in stock is estimated to be $1.20 per barrel.

A 2% discount is available on orders of at least 5,000 barrels and a 2.5% discount is available if the order quantity is 7,500 barrels or above.

Required:

Calculate the EOQ ignoring the discount and calculate if it would change once the discount is taken into account.

Criticisms of EOQ

The EOQ model can be criticised in several ways:

- It is based on simplifying assumptions, such as constant and predictable material usage rates.
- It will not indicate the optimal purchase quantity when there are price discounts for buying in larger quantities.
- It ignores the problem of managing stock-outs.
- It is inconsistent with the philosophy of just-in-time management and total quality management.

4 Inventory control systems

Three main systems are used to monitor and control inventory levels:

(1) reorder level system (whereby inventory is ordered at a particular, set order level)

(2) periodic review system (whereby inventory is checked and ordered at set periods in time)

(3) mixed systems, incorporating elements of both of the above.

Control systems explained

Reorder level system

With this system, whenever the current inventory level falls below a pre-set 'reorder level' (ROL), a replenishment (replacement) order is made. Since there is normally a gap (lead time) between the placing of an order and receipt of supplies this has to be allowed for. Buffer inventory is usually held as insurance against variations in demand and lead time.

This system used to be known as the 'two-bin' system. Inventory is kept in two bins, one with an amount equal to the ROL quantity, and the rest in the other. Inventory is drawn from the latter until it runs out, whence a replenishment order is triggered.

A reorder level system is simple enough to implement if the variables (such as average usage, supplier lead time, etc.) are known with certainty. In practice, this is rarely the case.

Periodic review system

This is also referred to as a 'constant cycle' system. Inventory levels are reviewed after a fixed interval, for example, on the first of the month. Replenishment orders are issued where necessary, to top up inventory levels to pre-set target levels. This means that order sizes are variable.

Mixed systems

In practice, mixtures of both systems are sometimes used, depending on the nature of the problem, the amount of computerisation and so on.

Calculating the re-order level (ROL)

Known demand and lead time

Having decided how much inventory to re-order, the next problem is when to re-order. The firm needs to identify a level of inventory which can be reached before an order needs to be placed.

The **ROL** is the quantity of inventory on hand when an order is placed.

When demand and lead time are known with certainty the ROL may be calculated exactly, i.e. ROL = demand in the lead time.

Test your understanding 3 – ROL

Using the data for Wolvo, assume that the entity adopts the EOQ as its order quantity and that it now takes two weeks for an order to be delivered.

Calculate how frequently the entity will place an order? Calculate how much inventory it will have on hand when the order is placed?

ROL with variable demand or variable lead time

When there is uncertainty over demand or lead time are known then the **ROL will be calculated as maximum demand x maximum lead time**. This will lead to the creation of **buffer stock**.

Buffer stock

Buffer stock is a quantity of inventory that should not usually be needed, but that might be needed if actual demand during the supply lead time exceeds the average demand or if lead times are longer than expected. Buffer stock has a cost. The annual cost of holding buffer stock is the amount of the buffer stock multiplied by the annual holding cost for one unit of the inventory item.

Calculating buffer stock:

	Units
Reorder level* (Maximum demand per day, in units x maximum re-order lead time)	X
Average usage (Average demand per day, in units x average re-order lead time)	Y
Buffer Stock	X – Y

* note that this is the ROL when demand or lead time are uncertain.

Where there is uncertainty, an optimum level of buffer stock (or inventory) must be found.

This depends on:

- variability of demand
- cost of holding inventory
- cost of stockouts

You will not be required to perform this calculation in the examination.

Inventory warning levels

Two warning levels might also be used, to indicate when the quantity of an item in inventory is either:

- higher than should be expected, or
- below the buffer stock level.

If the quantity of inventory goes above the maximum level or below the minimum level, the inventory manager should monitor the position carefully, and where appropriate take control measures.

The **maximum inventory level** should be:

- Reorder level
- Plus reorder quantity
- Minus [Minimum demand per day/week, in units] × [Minimum re-order lead time].

The maximum inventory level will occur when a new order has just been delivered by the supplier, the order has been delivered within the minimum lead time, and demand has been at a minimum during the lead time.

The **minimum inventory level** should be the buffer stock level:

- Reorder level
- Minus [Average demand per day/week, in units] × [Average re-order lead time].

Test your understanding 4 – Practice questions

(1) **Identify which of the following is not a required assumption for the basic EOQ model?**

A The lead time is zero

B There are no stock-outs

C The demand is known and constant

D The purchase price is constant regardless of order quantity

(2) Monthly demand for a product is 10,000 units. The purchase cost is \$10/unit. Holding costs comprise the cost of finance of 15% per annum plus warehouse storage costs of \$2/unit per annum. The supplier charges \$200 per order for delivery.

Calculate the EOQ.

(3) Doris uses component V22 in its construction process. The entity has a demand of 45,000 components pa. They cost \$4.50 each. There is no lead time between order and delivery, and ordering costs amount to \$100 per order. The annual cost of holding one component in inventory is estimated to be \$0.65.

A 0.5% discount is available on orders of at least 3,000 components and a 0.75% discount is available if the order quantity is 6,000 components or above.

Calculate the EOQ.

(4) **Using the information from question 3 calculate the total annual costs for the entity.**

(5) **Using the information from questions 3 and 4 calculate the cost of ordering 6,000 units and identify any savings that could be made.**

(6) Using the data in question 3 and ignoring discounts, assume that the entity adopts the EOQ as its order quantity and that it now takes three weeks for an order to be delivered.

Calculate how frequently will the entity place an order.

(7) **Using the data in question 6 calculate how much inventory it will have on hand when the order is placed.**

(8) An entity has estimated that for the coming season weekly demand for components will be 80 units. Suppliers take three weeks on average to deliver goods once they have been ordered and a buffer inventory of 35 units is held.

If the inventory levels are reviewed every six weeks, calculate how many units will be ordered at a review where the count shows 250 units in inventory.

(9) **Which ONE of the following would not normally be considered a cost of holding inventory?**

A Inventory obsolescence

B Insurance cost of inventory

C Interest cost of cash invested in inventory

D Loss of sales from a stock-out.

(10) An entity uses the economic order quantity model (EOQ model). Demand for the entity's product is 36,000 units each year and is evenly distributed each day. The cost of placing an order is $10 and the cost of holding a unit of inventory for a year is $2.

How many orders should the entity make in a year?

A 60

B 120

C 300

D 600

5 Summary Diagram

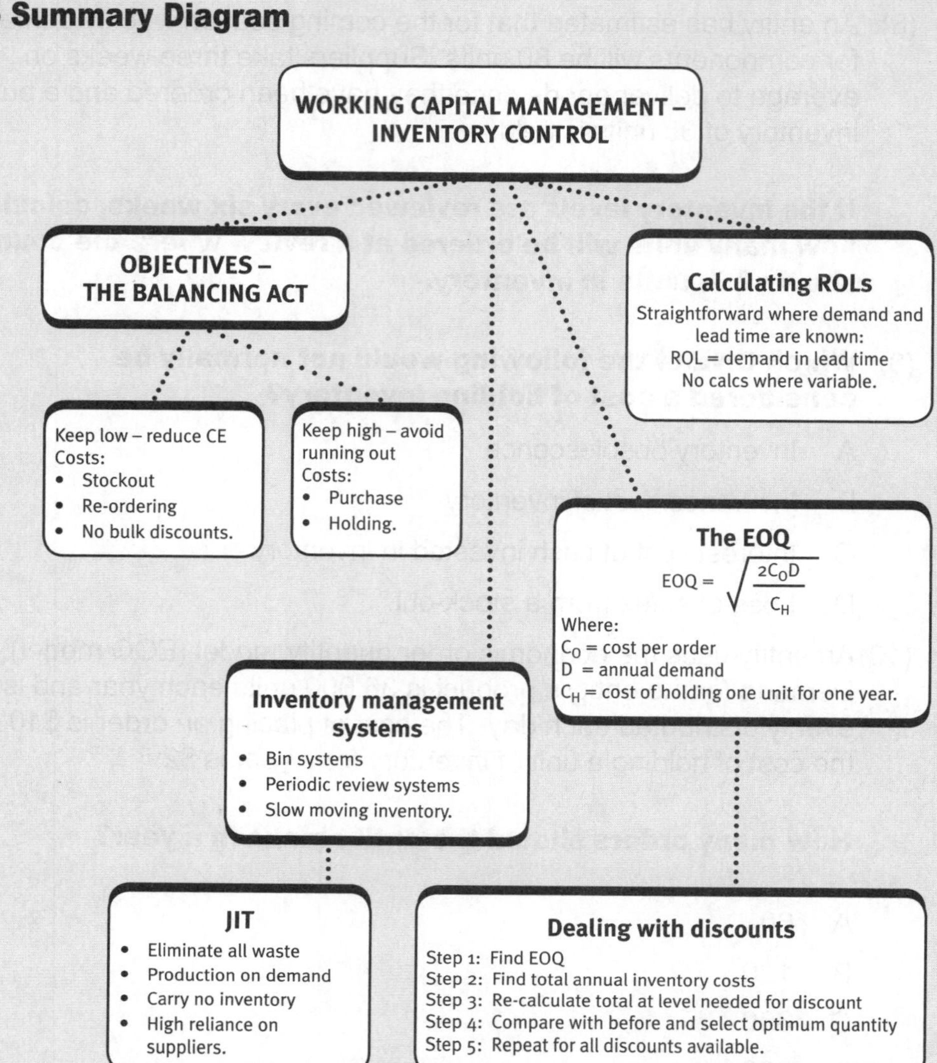

WORKING CAPITAL MANAGEMENT – INVENTORY CONTROL
OBJECTIVES – THE BALANCING ACT
Keep low – reduce CE
Costs:
• Stockout
• Re-ordering
• No bulk discounts.
Keep high – avoid running out
Costs:
• Purchase
• Holding.
Calculating ROLs
Straightforward where demand and lead time are known:
ROL = demand in lead time
No calcs where variable.
The EOQ
$EOQ = \sqrt{\frac{2C_OD}{C_H}}$
Where:
C_O = cost per order
D = annual demand
C_H = cost of holding one unit for one year.
Inventory management systems
• Bin systems
• Periodic review systems
• Slow moving inventory.
JIT
• Eliminate all waste
• Production on demand
• Carry no inventory
• High reliance on suppliers.
Dealing with discounts
Step 1: Find EOQ
Step 2: Find total annual inventory costs
Step 3: Re-calculate total at level needed for discount
Step 4: Compare with before and select optimum quantity
Step 5: Repeat for all discounts available.

Test your understanding answers

Test your understanding 1 – EOQ

	Order quantity		
	400 units	**500 units**	**600 units**
Average inventory	200	250	300
No. of orders per annum	30	24	20
	$	$	$
Holding cost – average inventory × $2.88	576	720	864

	Order quantity		
	400 units	500 units	600 units
Ordering cost – no. of orders × $30	900	720	600
Total cost	1,476	1,440	1,464

Therefore the best option is to order 500 units each time.

Note that this is the point at which total cost is minimised and the holding costs and order costs are equal.

Solution using the formula:

$$\text{EOQ} = \sqrt{\frac{2C_OD}{C_H}}$$

$C_O = 30$

$D = 1,000 \times 12 = 12,000$

$C_H = 2.88$

$$\text{EOQ} = \sqrt{\frac{\text{EOQ} = 2 \times 30 \times 12,000}{2.88}} = 500$$

Test your understanding 2 – EOQ and discounts

Step 1 Calculate EOQ, ignoring discounts.

$$EOQ = \sqrt{\frac{2C_OD}{C_H}}$$

C_O = $200

D = 30,000 units

C_H = $1.20

$$EOQ = \sqrt{\frac{2 \times 200 \times 30,000}{1.2}} = 3,162$$

Step 2 As this is below the level for discounts, calculate total annual inventory costs.

Total annual costs for the entity will comprise holding costs plus re-ordering costs.

= (Average inventory × C_H) + (Number of re-orders pa × C_O)

$$= \frac{3,162}{2} \times \$1.20 + \frac{30,000}{3,162} \times \$200$$

= $1,897.20 + $1,897.53

= $3,794.73

= $3,795

Step 3 Recalculate total annual inventory costs using the order size required to just obtain the discount.

At order quantity 5,000, total costs are as follows.

= (Average inventory × C_H) + (Number of re-orders pa × C_O)

$$= \frac{5{,}000}{2} \times \$1.20 + \frac{30{,}000}{5{,}000} \times \$200$$

= $3,000 + $1,200

= $4,200

	$
Extra costs of ordering in batches of 5,000 (4,200 – 3,795)	(405)
Saving on discount 2% × $12 × 30,000	7,200
Step 4 Net saving	6,795

Hence batches of 5,000 are worthwhile.

Step 3 (again)

At order quality 7,500, total costs are as follows:

= (Average inventory × C_H) + (Number of re-orders pa × C_O)

$$= \frac{7{,}500}{2} \times \$1.20 + \frac{30{,}000}{7{,}500} \times \$200$$

= $4,500 + $800

= $5,300

Extra costs of ordering in batches of 7,500 (5,300 – 4,200)	(1,100)
Saving on extra discount (2.5% – 2%) × $12 × 30,000)	1,800
Step 4 Net saving (again)	700

So a further cost saving can be made on orders of 7,500 units.

Note: If Step 1 produces an EOQ at which a discount would have been available, and the holding cost would be reduced by taking the discount, i.e. where C_H is based on the purchase price × the cost of finance, the EOQ must be recalculated using the new C_H before the above steps are followed.

Alternative approach

An alternative approach is to compare the total costs at each level and choose the lowest total cost as the best order level. The total cost will be made up of the total purchasing costs, the holding costs and the order costs as follows:

Order size	**3,162**	**5,000**	**7,500**
	$	$	$
Total purchase costs (30,000 barrels x $12 each)	360,000	360,000	360,000
Discount	nil	(7,200)	(9,000)
Holding and order costs	3,795	4,200	5,300
	363,795	357,000	356,300

(Note that many of the same calculations would be needed in order to complete this table)

This confirms that the best order size would be 7,500 units.

Test your understanding 3 – ROL

- Annual demand is 30,000. The original EOQ is 3,162. The entity will therefore place an order once every

  3,162 ÷ 30,000 × 365 days = 38 days

- The entity must be sure that there is sufficient inventory on hand when it places an order to last the two weeks' lead time. It must therefore place an order when there is two weeks' worth of demand in inventory:

  i.e. ROL is 2 ÷ 52 × 30,000 = 1,154 units

Test your understanding 4 – Practice questions

(1) The correct answer is A.

The EOQ model assumes a known and constant order lead time. The lead time does not have to be zero.

(2) The EOQ is 3,703 units

$$EOQ = \sqrt{\frac{2C_oD}{C_H}}$$

$C_O = 200$

$D = 10{,}000 \times 12 = 120{,}000$

$C_H = (10 \times 0.15) + 2 = 3.5$

$$EOQ = \sqrt{\frac{2 \times 200 \times 120{,}000}{3.5}} = 3{,}703$$

(3) **EOQ =3721 units**

$$EOQ = \sqrt{\frac{2C_OD}{C_H}}$$

$C_O = 100$

$D = 45{,}000$

$C_H = 0.65$

$$EOQ = \sqrt{\frac{2 \times 100 \times 45{,}000}{0.65}} =$$ 3,721, which would qualify for a 0.5% discount

(4) Total annual costs for the entity will comprise holding costs plus re-ordering costs.

= (Average inventory × C_H) + (Number of re-orders pa × C_O)

$$= \left(\frac{3{,}721}{2} \times \$0.65\right) + \left(\frac{45{,}000}{3{,}721} \times \$100\right)$$

= $2,419

(5) At order quantity 6,000, total costs are as follows.

(6,000 × \$0.65/2) + (45,000 × \$100 ÷ 6,000) = \$2,700

A saving can be made on orders of 6,000 units as follows:

	\$
Extra costs of ordering in batches of 6,000 (2,700 – 2,419)	(281)
Less: Saving on extra discount (0.75% – 0.5%) × \$4.5 × 45,000	506.25
Net cost saving	225.25

(6) Annual demand is 45,000. The original EOQ is 3,721. The entity will therefore place an order once every

3,721 ÷ 45,000 × 365 days = 30 days

(7) The entity must be sure that there is sufficient inventory on hand when it places its order to last the three weeks lead time. It must therefore place an order when there is three weeks work of demand in inventory, i.e. 3/52 × 45,000 = 2,596 units.

(8) Demand per week is 80 units. The next review will be in six weeks by which time 80 × 6 = 480 units will have been used.

An order would then be placed and during the lead time – three weeks – another 80 × 3 = 240 units will be used.

The business therefore needs to have 480 + 240 = 720 units in inventory to ensure a stockout is avoided. Since buffer inventory of 35 units is required, the total number needed is 755 units.

Since the current inventory level is 250 units, an order must be placed for 755 – 250 = 505 units.

(9) D

(10) A

$$EOQ = \sqrt{\frac{2C_oD}{C_H}}$$

$C_O = 10$

$D = 36,000$

$C_H = 2$

$$EOQ = \sqrt{\frac{EOQ = 2 \times 30 \times 12,00}{2.88}} = 500$$

Therefore, EOQ = 600

If demand = 36,000 units per year and we order in quantities of 600 we will need to place 60 orders per year (36,000/600).

chapter

24

Working capital management – cash control

Chapter learning objectives

On completion of their studies students should be able to:

- Prepare and analyse short-term cash flow forecasts.
- Identify measures to improve a cash forecast situation.
- Identify principles of short-term investment of cash surpluses.
- Compare and contrast the use and limitations of cash management models and identify when each model is most appropriate.

1 Session content

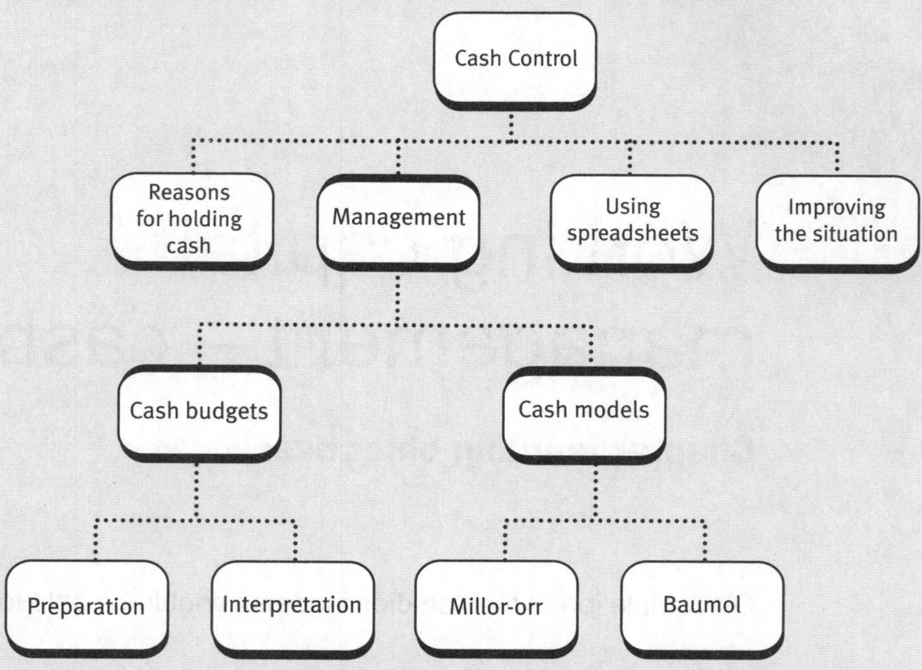

2 Reasons for holding cash

Although cash needs to be invested to earn returns, businesses need to keep a certain amount readily available. The reasons include:

- transactions motive
- precautionary motive
- investment/speculative motive

Failure to carry sufficient cash levels can lead to:

- loss of settlement discounts
- loss of supplier goodwill
- poor industrial relations
- potential liquidation

Reasons for holding cash

Cash is required for a number of reasons:

Transactions motive – cash required to meet day-to-day expenses, e.g. payroll, payment of suppliers, etc.

Precautionary motive – cash held to give a cushion against unplanned expenditure (the cash equivalent of buffer inventory).

Investment/speculative motive – cash kept available to take advantage of market investment opportunities.

The cost of running out of cash depends on the firm's particular circumstances but may include not being able to pay debts as they fall due which can have serious operational repercussions:

- settlement discounts for early payment are unavailable
- trade suppliers refuse to offer further credit, charge higher prices or downgrade the priority with which orders are processed
- if wages are not paid on time, industrial action may well result, damaging production in the short-term and relationships and motivation in the medium-term
- the court may be petitioned to wind up the entity if it consistently fails to pay bills as they fall due.

3 Efficient cash management

The amount of cash available to an entity at any given time is largely dependent on the efficiency with which cash flows are managed. The key principles of cash management are:

- collect debts as quickly as possible
- pay suppliers as late as possible
- bank cash takings promptly

Once again the firm faces a balancing act:

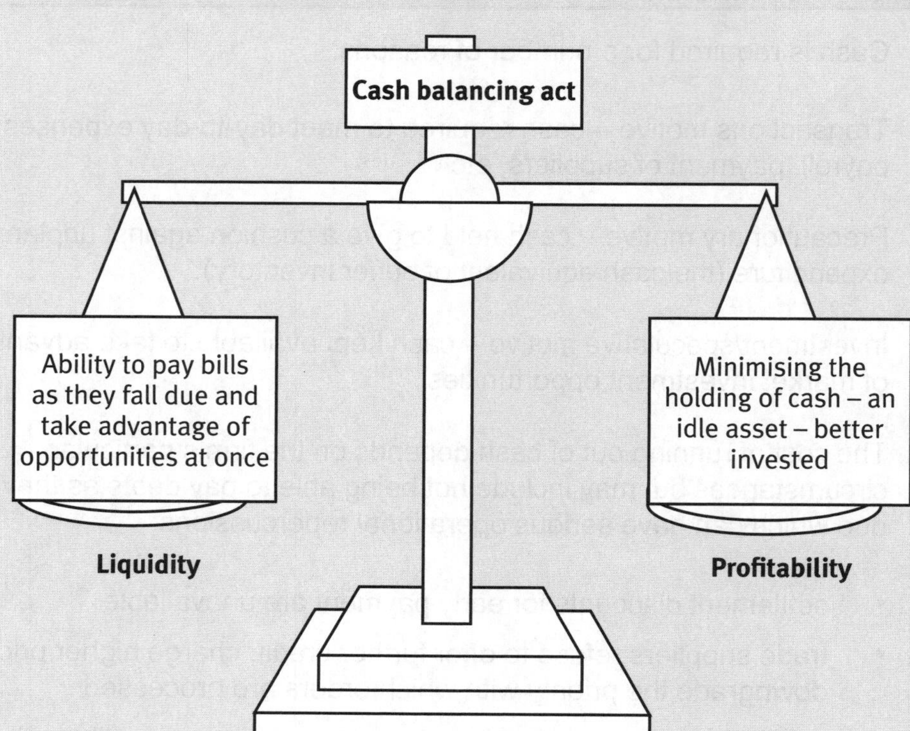

Remember to consider the motives for holding cash and the liquidity/profitability trade-off in a question that asks for a discussion of cash management.

There are three areas associated with managing cash:

- the cash budget and cash flow forecast
- the Miller-Orr Model
- the Baumol Model

4 Cash budgets and cash flow forecasts

A **cash forecast** is an estimate of cash receipts and payments for a future period under existing conditions.

A **cash budget** is a commitment to a plan for cash receipts and payments for a future period after taking any action necessary to bring the forecast into line with the overall business plan.

Cash budgets are used to:

- assess and integrate operating budgets
- plan for cash shortages and surpluses
- compare with actual spending.

There are two different techniques that can be used to create a cash budget:

- a receipts and payments forecast
- a statement of financial position forecast

Receipts and payments forecast

This is a forecast of cash receipts and payments based on predictions of sales and cost of sales and the timings of the cash flows relating to these items.

Preparing forecasts from planned receipts and payments

Every type of cash inflow and receipt, along with their timings, must be forecast. Note that cash receipts and payments differ from sales and cost of sales in the statement of profit or loss because:

- not all cash receipts or payments affect the statement of profit or loss, e.g. the issue of new shares or the purchase of a non-current asset
- some statement of profit or loss items are derived from accounting conventions and are not cash flows, e.g. depreciation or the profit/loss on the sale of a non-current asset
- the timing of cash receipts and payments does not coincide with the statement of profit or loss accounting period, e.g. a sale is recognised in the statement of profit or loss when the invoice is raised, yet the cash payment from the receivable may not be received until the following period or later.
- irrecoverable debts will never be received in cash and doubtful debts may not be received. When you are forecasting the cash receipts from debtors you must remember to adjust for these items.

Approach to preparing a cash forecast:

Step 1 – Prepare a proforma

There is no definitive format that should be used for a cash budget. However, whichever format you decide to use, it should include the following:

(i) A clear distinction between the cash receipts and cash payments for each control period. Your budget should not consist of a jumble of cash flows. It should be logically arranged with a subtotal for receipts and a subtotal for payments.

(ii) A figure for the net cash flow for each period. It could be argued that this is not an essential feature of a cash budget. However, you will find it easier to prepare and analyse a cash budget if you include the net cash flow. Also, managers find in practice that a figure for the net cash flow helps to draw attention to the cash flow implications of their actions during the period.

(iii) The closing cash balance for each control period. The closing balance for each period will be the opening balance for the following period.

The following is a typical format:

Month:	1	2	3	4
	$	$	$	$
Receipts (few lines)				
Sub total				
Payments (Many lines)				
Sub total				
Net cash flow				
Opening balance				
Closing balance				

Step 2 – Fill in the simple figures

Some payments need only a small amount of work to identify the correct figure and timing and can be entered straight into the proforma. These would usually include:

- wages and salaries
- fixed overhead expenses
- dividend payments
- purchase of non-current assets.

Step 3 – Work out the more complex figures

The information on sales and purchases can be more time consuming to deal with, e.g.:

- timings for both sales and purchases must be found from credit periods
- variable overheads may require information about production levels
- purchases may require calculations based on production schedules and inventory balances.

Test your understanding 1 – Forecast cash receipts

The forecast sales for an entity are as follows:

	January	February	March	April
	$	$	$	$
Sales	6,000	8,000	4,000	5,000

All sales are on credit and receivables tend to pay in the following pattern:

	%
In month of sale	10
In month after sale	40
Two months after sale	45

The entity expects the rate of irrecoverable debts to be 5%.

Calculate the forecast cash receipts from receivables in April.

Test your understanding 2 – Forecast cash payments

A manufacturing business makes and sells widgets. Each widget requires two units of raw materials, which cost $3 each. Production and sales quantities of widgets each month are as follows:

Month	Sales and production units
December (actual)	50,000
January (budget)	55,000
February (budget)	60,000
March (budget)	65,000

In the past, the business has maintained its inventories of raw materials at 100,000 units. However, it plans to increase raw material inventories to 110,000 units at the end of January and 120,000 units at the end of February. The business takes one month's credit from its suppliers.

Calculate the forecast payments to suppliers for January, February and March for raw material purchases.

It is important to note you will **not** have to prepare a full cash flow forecast in your examination but may be asked to prepare any part of it. You should therefore practice the following TYU to ensure you can do this.

Test your understanding 3 – Full cash flow forecast

The following budgeted statement of profit or loss has been prepared for Quest entity for the four months January to April:

	January $000	February $000	March $000	April $000
Sales	60.0	50.0	70.0	60.0
Cost of production	50.0	55.0	32.5	50.0
(Increase)/decrease in inventory	(5.0)	(17.5)	20.0	(5.0)
Cost of sales	45.0	37.5	52.5	45.0
Gross profit	15.0	12.5	17.5	15.0
Administration and selling overhead	(8.0)	(7.5)	(8.5)	(8.0)
Profit before interest	7.0	5.0	9.0	7.0

The working papers provide the following additional information:

- 40% of the production cost relates to direct materials. Materials are bought in the month prior to the month in which they are used. 50% of purchases are paid for in the month of purchase. The remainder are paid for one month later.
- 30% of the production cost relates to direct labour which is paid for when it is used.
- The remainder of the production cost is production overhead. $5,000 per month is a fixed cost which includes $3,000 depreciation. Fixed production overhead costs are paid monthly in arrears. The remaining overhead is variable. The variable production overhead is paid 40% in the month of usage and the balance one month later.
- The administration and selling costs are paid quarterly in advance on 1 January, 1 April, 1 July and 1 October. The amount payable is $15,000 per quarter.
- Trade payables on 1 January Year 5 are expected to be:
  - Direct materials: $10,000
  - Production overheads: $11,000
- All sales are on credit. 20% of receivables are expected to be paid in the month of sale and 80% in the following month. Unpaid trade receivables at the beginning of January were $44,000.
- The entity intends to purchase capital equipment costing $30,000 in February which will be payable in March.
- The bank balance on 1 January Year 5 is expected to be $5,000 overdrawn.

Required:

Prepare a cash budget for each of the months January to March Year 5 for Quest and comment upon the results obtained.

Preparing a cash budget from a statement of financial position

This is a forecast derived from predictions of future statement of financial positions. Predictions are made of all items except cash, which is then derived as a balancing figure.

Illustration

Used to predict the cash balance at the end of a given period, this method will typically require forecasts of:

- changes to non-current assets (acquisitions and disposals)
- future inventory levels
- future receivables levels
- future payables levels
- changes to share capital and other long-term funding (e.g. bank loans)
- changes to retained profits.

Example

CBA is a manufacturing entity in the furniture trade. Its sales have risen sharply over the past six months as a result of an improvement in the economy and a strong housing market. The entity is now showing signs of 'overtrading' and the financial manager, Ms Smith, is concerned about its liquidity. The entity is 1 month from its year-end. Estimated figures for the full 12 months of the current year and forecasts for next year, on present cash management policies, are shown below.

	Next year	**Current year**
	$000	$000
Statement of profit or loss		
Turnover	5,200	4,200
Less:		
Cost of sales (Note 1)	3,224	2,520
Operating expenses	650	500
Operating profit	1,326	1,180
Interest paid	54	48
Tax payable	305	283
Profit after tax	967	849
Dividends declared	387	339

Current assets and liabilities at year end:		
Inventory/work in progress	625	350
Trade receivables	750	520
Cash	0	25
Trade payables	(464)	(320)
Other payables (incl. dividends)	(692)	(622)
Overdraft	(11)	0
Total equity and liabilities	208	(47)

Note 1:

Cost of sales includes depreciation of	225	175

Ms Smith is considering methods of improving the cash position. A number of actions are being discussed:

Trade receivables

Offer a 2 per cent discount to customers who pay within 10 days of despatch of invoices. It is estimated that 50 per cent of customers will take advantage of the new discount scheme. The other 50 per cent will continue to take the average credit period for next year.

Trade payables and inventory

Reduce the number of suppliers currently being used and negotiate better terms with respect to flexibility of delivery and lower purchase prices. The aim for next year will be to reduce the end-of-year forecast cost of sales (excluding depreciation) by 5 per cent and inventory/work in progress levels by 10 per cent. However, the number of days' credit taken by the entity will have to fall to 30 days to help persuade suppliers to improve their prices.

Other information

- All sales are on credit. Official terms of sale at present require payment within 30 days. Interest is not charged on late payments.
- All purchases are made on credit.
- Operating expenses for next year will be $650,000 under either the existing or proposed policies.
- Tax and interest payments are paid in the year in which they arise.
- Dividends are paid in the year after they are declared.
- Capital expenditure of $550,000 is planned for next year.

Required:

(a) Provide a cash flow forecast for next year, assuming:

(i) the entity does not change its policies and

(ii) the entity's proposals for managing trade receivables, trade payables and inventory are implemented.

In both cases, assume a full twelve-month period, i.e. the changes will be effective from day 1 of next year.

(b) As assistant to Ms Smith, write a short report to her evaluating the proposed actions. Include comments on the factors, financial and non-financial, that the entity should take into account before implementing the new policies.

Solution

(a)

All figures in $000s

	No change	**With change**
Profit from operations	1,326	1,424
+ depreciation	225	225
+/– change in trade receivables	–230	72
+/– change in trade payables	144	–86
Operating profit	1,465	1,635
Interest paid	–54	–48
Tax paid	–305	–283
Dividends declared	–339	–339
Investing activities		
Non-current assets	–550	–550
Inventory	–275	–212
Net cash flow	–36	206
Opening balance	25	25
Closing balance	–11	231

Changes implemented

(1) **Profit from operations**

Turnover	5200
Less discounts	–52
Cost of sales	–3,074
(3,224 – 225) × 95% + 225)	
Operating expenses (unchanged)	–650
Profit	1,424

(2) **Change in current assets**

Decrease in trade receivables

= 520 – [(2,600/365 × 53*) + (2,600/365 × 10*)] = 72

Decrease in trade payables

= [320 – (2,849**/365 × 30)] = 86

Change in inventory

= 350 – (625 × 90%) = 212

* Forecast receivables = 750/5,200 × 365 = 53, reduces to 10 days for 50% of turnover

** Forecast payables = 3,224 – 225 = 2,999, these reduce by 5% to 2,849.

(b) **Report**

To: Ms Smith

From: Assistant

Subject: Proposed working capital policy changes

The answer should be set out in report format and include the following key points:

- Comment that cash flow is improved by almost a quarter of a million pounds if the proposed changes are made.
- Problems appear to have arisen because trade receivables and inventory control have not been adequate for increased levels of turnover.

- Liquidity: current ratio was 0.95:1 (all current assets to trade and other payables), will be around 1.2:1 under both options. Perversely, ratio looks to improve even if the entity takes no action and causes an overdraft. This is because of high receivables and inventory levels. Moral: high current assets do not mean high cash. Cash ratio perhaps a better measure.
- Receivables' days last year was 45, forecast to rise to 53 on current policies despite 'official' terms being 30. Entity could perhaps look to improve its credit control before offering discounts.
- Trade payables' days were 46, forecast to rise to 52. Are discounts being ignored? Are relationships with suppliers being threatened?*
- Dramatic increase in inventory levels forecast: 50 days last year, 71 days forecast this year. If change implemented, inventory will still be 67 days.*
- Operating profit percentage forecast to fall to 25.5% from 28.1% if no changes made. Percentage will fall to 27.4% if changes implemented; a fall probably acceptable if cash flow improved and overdraft interest saved.
- Non-financial factors include relationships with customers and suppliers.
- Other financial factors, is increase in turnover sustainable?

*Using cost of sales figures including depreciation.

Interpretation of a cash budget

Examples of factors to consider when interpreting a cash budget include:

- Is the balance at the end of the period acceptable/matching expectations?
- Does the cash balance become a deficit at any time in the period?
- Is there sufficient finance (e.g. an overdraft) to cover any cash deficits? Should new sources of finance be sought in advance?
- What are the key causes of cash deficits?
- Can/should discretionary expenditure (such as asset purchases) be made in another period in order to stabilise the pattern of cash flows?
- Is there a plan for dealing with cash surpluses (such as reinvesting them elsewhere)?
- When is the best time to make discretionary expenditure?

Illustration

If we were to examine the cash budget in TYU 3, the following issues might be brought to management's attention:

This cash budget forewarns the management of the business that their plans will lead to a cash deficit of $16,650 at the end of March. They can also see that it will be a short-term deficit and can take appropriate action.

They may decide to delay the purchase of the capital equipment for one month in order to allow the cash position to move to a positive one before the investment is made. Alternatively, an extension of the overdraft facilities may be arranged for the appropriate period.

If it is decided that overdraft facilities are to be arranged, it is important that due account is taken of the timing of the receipts and payments within each month.

For example, all of the payments in January may be made at the beginning of the month but receipts may not be expected until nearer the end of the month. The cash deficit could then be considerably greater than it appears from looking only at the month-end balance.

If the worst possible situation arose, the overdrawn balance during January could become as large as $5,000 (Opening balance) minus $66,000 (January payments) = $71,000 before the receipts begin to arise. If management had used the month-end balances as a guide to the overdraft requirement during the period then they would not have arranged a large enough overdraft facility with the bank. It is important, therefore, that they look in detail at the information revealed by the cash budget, and not simply at the closing cash balances.

5 Using spreadsheets in cash forecasting

Many businesses prepare cash budgets and cash forecasts using a computer and spreadsheet software such as Excel®.

Spreadsheets are useful for cash forecasting for several important reasons:

- They **save time** in preparing forecasts. When the basic 'model' has been constructed, it is a relatively simple task to insert figures into the model, and leave it to the model to produce the completed forecast. The model, once established, can then be used whenever a new forecast is required.

- They are extremely useful for **sensitivity analysis**. When there is uncertainty in the forecast, the assumptions for the forecast can be changed and an alternative forecast produced. This allows management to consider a range of different possible outcomes, without needing much time or effort.
- Cash flow forecasts **can be consolidated**. For example, if the same spreadsheet model is used to prepare cash forecasts for each division or region in the entity, a spreadsheet model can also automatically produce a consolidated cash flow forecast for the entity as a whole.

More details - Sensitivity analysis

Sensitivity analysis

When budgets are prepared, there are a very large number of assumptions and estimates, for example the estimated sales each month, the estimates of costs, assumptions about when receivables will pay and when suppliers will be paid, and so on. Any of these estimates and assumptions could turn out to be inaccurate.

One of the enormous benefits of using spreadsheets to prepare a cash budget is that it is very easy to carry out sensitivity analysis.

Sensitivity analysis involves asking 'What if...?' questions, and finding out by how much the expected results will change if some of the forecasts or assumptions are altered.

For example, what if sales are 10% less than predicted, or what if capital expenditure is double the amount forecast? Depending on what the results of the analysis show, management might decide to take action to reduce the potential risks.

The results of sensitivity analysis work could then be incorporated into the forecast to ensure that there are adequate cash resources within the business. For example, if sales revenue was to fall by 10%, what would be the maximum overdraft required during the forecast period? A float or margin of error could then be added to this requirement to determine the additional overdraft facility requested from the bank. The float could be determined by use of cash management models developed by Baumol and Miller-Orr.

The results of the sensitivity analysis may also lead on to consideration of other factors when a deficit has been forecast, such as policies to shorten the operating cycle, which should improve net cash flows during the forecast period.

Further consideration is given to how a forecast deficit may be managed, or consequent decisions that may need to be taken, are considered elsewhere in this chapter.

More details - Consolidation of forecasts

Consolidation

As well as being of assistance in preparing cash flow forecasts for individual business units, a computerised spreadsheet package may also be used to consolidate individual forecasts into one overall forecast for the organisation as a whole.

Individual forecasts may be prepared by:

- the various group entities
- individual operating units, e.g. branches of a retail store
- individual cost centres, e.g. stores, purchasing, production, service centres
- individual budget holders, e.g. marketing.

If all the individual forecasts are prepared using the same spreadsheet software, it will be possible for these to be uploaded to a central computer, programmed to produce a consolidated forecast.

6 Measures to improve a cash forecast situation

Upon completion of a cash flow forecast, it should be reviewed to ensure that it properly reflects the underlying assumptions and circumstances used to prepare the forecast. This may include, for example, use of sensitivity analysis to establish how sensitive key data is to changes to underlying estimates or assumptions.

The forecast should then be evaluated to determine how the entity can use the information to manage and control its business activities. This could, for example, identify that cash resources are expected to increase during the forecast period, or that they may decrease, whilst still being adequate to meet expected needs and plans. It could also be that a shortfall has been forecast, in which case corrective action will be required to manage the shortfall, perhaps by raising additional finance or by amending plans manage the business within the expected available cash resources.

Additional context

An initial cash forecast might predict an unsatisfactory cash flow situation. The forecast might indicate that the entity will have a cash deficit that cannot be met by existing short-term borrowing arrangements, such as a bank overdraft facility.

When this situation occurs, action will need to be taken to manage future cash flows in order to improve the forecast position. The nature of this management action will depend upon the answers to the following questions:

- Does the forecast indicate a continuing trend of an increasing surplus or an increasing cash deficit, or do net monthly balances move between surplus and deficit on a seasonal basis?
- What size of cash surpluses are forecast (if any) and for how long will they be available?
- Are the forecast cash deficits within the current overdraft facility?
- Which cash flows are to some extent discretionary, either in size or timing?

Cash deficits can arise from:

- Basic trading factors underlying the business, such as falling sales or increasing costs. To correct these, normal business measures need to be taken. Sales may be improved by increased marketing activity or revised pricing policies. Cost cutting exercises may also be necessary.
- Short-term deficiencies in the working capital cycle, such as an exceptionally long average holding period for inventory or a long average time to pay by credit customers.

Possible decisions that could be taken to deal with forecast short-term cash deficits include:

- increasing prices charged for goods and services sold to customers, although this will be subject to commercial constraints, such as responses from competitors
- arranging additional short-term borrowing
- negotiating a higher overdraft limit with the bank
- the sale of short-term investments, if the entity has any
- using different forms of financing to reduce cash flows in the short term, such as leasing instead of buying outright

- entering into a sale and leaseback arrangement to receive a cash lump sum, even though there will be subsequent lease payments
- changing the amount of discretionary cash flows, deferring expenditures or bringing forward revenues. For example:
  - reducing the dividend to shareholders
  - postponing or deferring non-essential capital expenditure
  - bringing forward the planned disposal of non-current assets
  - reducing inventory levels, perhaps incorporating 'just-in-time' techniques (although this will take time to implement), or implementing more rigorous inventory control procedures. (The management of inventories is dealt with in chapter 23)
  - shortening the operating cycle by reducing the time taken to collect receivables, perhaps by offering a discount or using a factor or invoice discounting. (The management of trade receivables is dealt with more fully in chapter 22.)
  - shortening the operating cycle by delaying payment to payables. (The management of trade payables is dealt with in chapter 22.)
  - application of a cash management model (e.g. Baumol or Miller-Orr) to ensure that there is adequate float or available cash resources to accommodate any differences between forecast and actual cash flows

Dealing with surpluses

If the forecast shows cash surpluses, these will be dealt with according to their size and duration. Management should consider a policy for how surplus cash should be invested or used so as to achieve a return on the money, but without investing in items where the risk of a fall in value is considered too high. The interest or other return earned can be used to improve the overall cash position. Care must be taken to ensure these investments can be realised as needed, to fund forecast deficits.

Where long-term cash surpluses are forecast, management might consider other possible uses of the surpluses. For example, the following issues may need to be considered:

- How long, and to what extent, is the forecast position likely to persist?
- How is the surplus to be used or invested?
- Can some loan obligations be settled early, perhaps on advantageous terms?
- Can amounts due to trade payables be paid early to take advantage of settlement discounts available?

- Can capital expenditure plans be brought forward to make use of any surplus?
- Can dividend payments be made or increased?

Investing cash surpluses is dealt with in much more detail in chapter 20.

7 Cash models

The Miller-Orr Model

Merton Miller and Daniel Orr developed a model for setting the target cash balance which incorporates uncertainty in the cash inflows and outflows. They assumed that the distribution of daily net cash flows is approximately normal. Each day, the net cash flow could be the expected value or some higher or lower value drawn from a normal distribution. Thus the daily net cash flow follows a trendless random walk.

The diagram shows how the model works over time. The model sets higher and lower control limits, H and L, respectively, and a target cash balance, Z. When the cash balance reaches H, then H – Z pounds are transferred from cash to marketable securities, that is the firm buys H – Z pounds of securities. Similarly when the cash balance hits L, then Z – L pounds are transferred from marketable securities to cash.

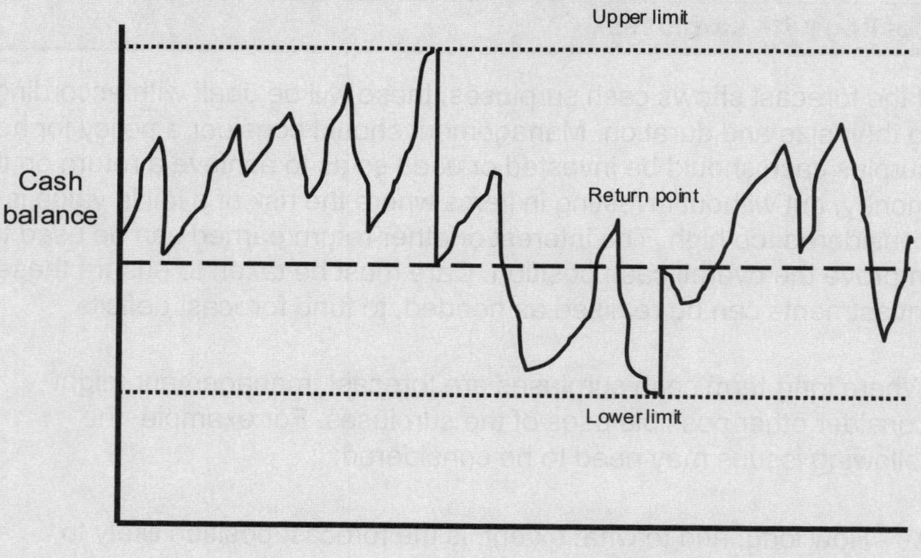

The lower limit, L is set by management depending upon how much risk of a cash shortfall the firm is willing to accept, and this, in turn, depends both on access to borrowings and on the consequences of a cash shortfall.

Key workings for Miller-Orr model

(1) Lower limit – must be given by the question

(2) Upper limit = lower limit + spread

(3) Return point = lower limit +1/3 × spread

Formula will be given to you if required in the assessment.

$$\text{Spread} = 3\left[\frac{\frac{3}{4} \times \text{transaction cost} \times \text{variance of cash flows}}{\text{Interest rate}}\right]^{1/3}$$

Test your understanding 4 – Millor-Orr Model

An entity is wishing to control its cash balance more efficiently and has given you the following information:

- Management has decided on a minimum current account balance of $1,500 [this gives us the lower limit and will be related to whether management is aggressive or conservative].
- The entity's cash flow has a **daily** standard deviation of $300 [and so the daily **variance** is $90,000].
- There is a $5 transaction charge every time money is switched between deposit account and current account or vice versa.
- The **annual** deposit account interest rate is 12% [this corresponds to 0.033% per day].

Required:

Calculate the spread, upper limit, return point and how much must be transferred from the accounts when the upper and lower limits are reached.

The Baumol Model

William Baumol first noted that cash balances are in many respects similar to inventories, and that the EOQ inventory model can be used to establish the target cash balance. Baumol's model assumes that the firm uses cash at a steady predictable rate and that the firm's cash inflows also occur at a steady predictable rate.

$$Q = \sqrt{\frac{2Co.D}{Ch}}$$

Where

Co = The brokerage cost of making a securities trade or borrowing

D = The total amount of net new cash needed for transactions over the entire period, or the excess cash available to invest in short-term securities

Ch = Opportunity cost of holding cash (equals the rate of return generated by marketable securities or the cost of borrowing in order to hold cash)

Test your understanding 5 – Baumol Model

An entity generates $10,000 per month excess cash which it intends to invest in short-term securities. The interest rate it can expect to earn on its investment is 5% per annum. The transaction costs associated with each separate investment of funds is constant at $50.

Required:

(a) What is the optimum amount of cash to be invested in each transaction?

(b) How many transactions will arise each year?

(c) What is the cost of making those transactions per annum?

Test your understanding 6 – Practice questions

(1) A business has estimated that 10% of its sales will be cash sales, and the remainder credit sales. It is also estimated that 50% of credit customers will pay in the month following sale, 30% two months after sale and 15% three months after sale and irrecoverable debts will be 5% of credit sales.

Total sales figures are as follows:

Month	$
October	80,000
November	60,000
December	40,000
January	50,000
February	60,000
March	90,000

Required:

Prepare a month-by-month budget of cash receipts from sales for the months January to March.

(2) Winters expects 75% of sales to be collected in the month of sale, 20% in the month following and 5% to be irrecoverable debts. At 31 December 20X4, $50,000 of December's sales are still outstanding receivables.

Identify receipts in January from sales in December:

A 10,000

B 20,000

C 37,500

D 40,000

(3) An entity sells a range of services, all on credit. Customers on average pay as follows:

	%
In month after sale	30
Two months after sale	65

The organisation expects an irrecoverable debt rate of 5%.

At 1 January Year 2, opening trade receivables were $322,200, before deducting any allowance for doubtful debts. Sales in December Year 1 were $213,000.

Required:

Calculate the receipts from the opening trade receivables in January Year 2 and in February Year 2

(4) You are given the following budgeted information about an entity:

	January	**February**	**March**
Opening inventory in units	100	150	120
Closing inventory in units	150	120	180
Sales in units	400	450	420

The cost of materials is $2 per unit. 40% of purchases are paid for immediately in cash. 60% of purchases are on credit and are paid two months after the purchase.

Required:

Calculate the budgeted payments in March for purchases of materials.

(5) **Identify which of the following is unsuitable as a cash flow to be deferred to avoid a temporary cash shortage:**

A Replacement of office furniture

B Investment in a short-term cash deposit

C Investment in a long-term strategic expansion

D Dividend payment (deferral agreed by the shareholders)

(6) **Examine the validity of the following statements with respect to the Miller-Orr cash management model.**

Statement 1	The greater the variability in cash flows, the greater is the spread between the upper and lower cash balance limits.
Statement 2	The return point is the lower limit plus one third of the spread.

	Statement 1	Statement 2
A	True	False
B	True	True
C	False	False
D	False	True

(7) An entity uses the Baumol cash management model and generates $20,000 per month excess cash which it intends to invest in short-term securities. The interest rate it can expect to earn on its investment is 5% per annum. The transaction costs associated with each separate investment of funds is constant at $30. **What is the optimum amount of cash to be invested in each transaction?**

(8) **Using the information from TYU 7 calculate to the nearest figure how many transactions will arise each year.**

(9) **Using the information from TYUs 7 and 8 calculate the cost of making those transactions per annum.**

(10) An entity uses the Millor-Orr model to control its cash balance more efficiently and has given you the following information:

- Management has decided on a minimum current account balance of $2,500 [this gives us the lower limit and will be related to whether management is aggressive or conservative].
- The entity's cash flow has a **daily variance** of $300,000.
- There is a $30 transaction charge every time money is switched between deposit account and current account or vice versa.
- The **annual** deposit account interest rate is 0.025% per day.

Calculate the spread, return point and upper limit.

8 Summary Diagram

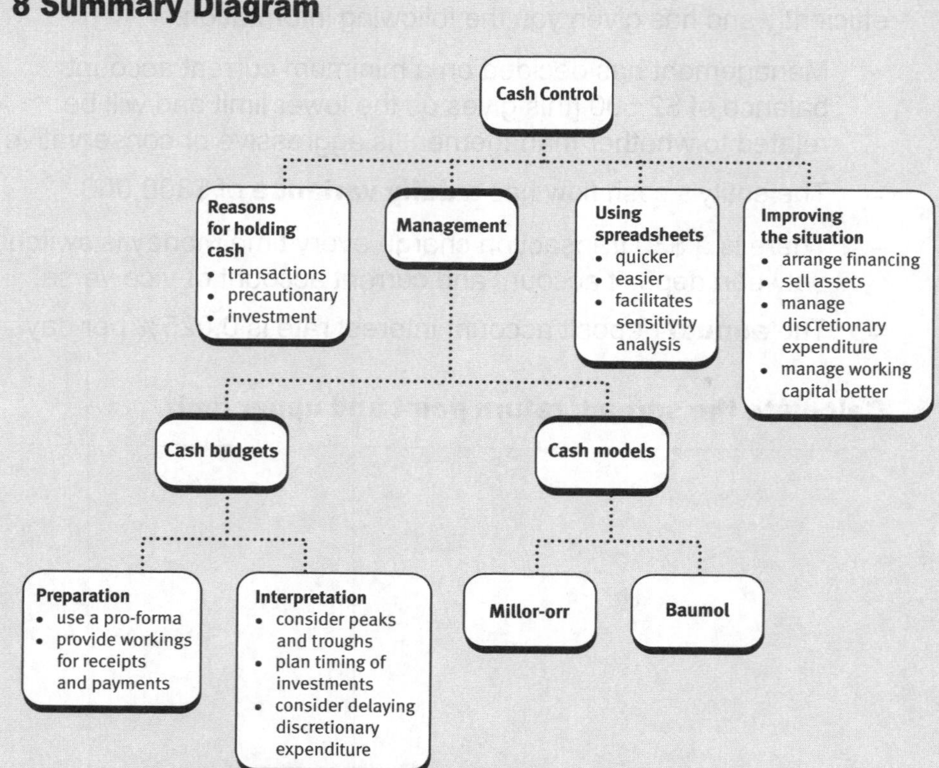

Test your understanding answers

Test your understanding 1 – Forecast cash receipts

Cash from:		$
April sales:	10% × $5,000	500
March sales:	40% × $4,000	1,600
February sales:	45% × $8,000	3,600
		5,700

Test your understanding 2 – Forecast cash payments

When inventories of raw materials are increased, the quantities purchased will exceed the quantities consumed in the period.

Figures for December are shown because December purchases will be paid for in January, which is in the budget period.

Quantity of raw material purchased in units:

		Material (@ 2 units per widget)			
	Units of widgets produced	**December**	**January**	**February**	**March**
	Units	Units	Units	Units	Units
December	50,000	100,000			
January	55,000		110,000		
February	60,000			120,000	
March	65,000				130,000
Increase in inventories		–	10,000	10,000	–
Total purchase quantities		100,000	120,000	130,000	130,000
At $3 per unit		300,000	360,000	390,000	390,000

Having established the purchases each month, we can go on to budget the amount of cash payments to suppliers each month. Here, the business will take one month's credit.

	January	February	March
	$	$	$
Payment to suppliers	300,000	360,000	390,000

At the end of March, there will be payables of $390,000 for raw materials purchased, which will be paid in April.

Test your understanding 3 – Full cash flow forecast

We can take each item of cash flow in turn, and use workings tables to calculate what the monthly cash flows are.

(W1) **Cash from sales**

	Total sales $	Cash receipts January $	Cash receipts February $	Cash Receipts March $
Opening receivables		44,000	–	–
January	60,000	12,000	48,000	–
February	50,000	–	10,000	40,000
March	70,000	–	–	14,000
		56,000	58,000	54,000

(W2) **Payments for materials purchases**

Material purchases are made in the month prior to the month in which they are used, so the starting point for working out materials purchases and payments for the purchases is the production costs in each month.

	January	February	March	April
	$	$	$	$
Total cost of production	50,000	55,000	32,500	50,000
Material cost of production (40%)	20,000	22,000	13,000	20,000
Purchases in the month	22,000	13,000	20,000	unknown

Payments are made 50% in the month of purchase and 50% in the following month. The trade payables at 1 January will all be paid in January, since these represent 50% of material purchases in December.

	Purchases	January	February	March
	$	$	$	$
Opening payables for materials		10,000		
January	22,000	11,000	11,000	–
February	13,000	–	6,500	6,500
March	20,000	–	–	10,000
Total payments		21,000	17,500	16,500

(W3) **Payments for overheads**

In this example, we have to separate fixed and variable overheads. Total overhead costs are 30% of production costs (100% – 40% direct materials – 30% direct labour).

	January	February	March
	$	$	$
Total cost of production	50,000	55,000	32,500
Overhead cost of production (30%)	15,000	16,500	9,750
Fixed costs	(5,000)	(5,000)	(5,000)
Variable overhead costs	10,000	11,500	4,750

Of the monthly fixed overhead costs of $5,000, $3,000 is depreciation which is not a cash expenditure. Monthly fixed cost cash expenditure is therefore $2,000.

The opening balance of unpaid overhead costs at the beginning of January must consist of $2,000 fixed overheads and $9,000 (the balance) variable overheads. All these costs should be paid for in January. Variable overheads are paid 40% in the month of expenditure and 60% the following month.

Fixed overheads	**Cost** $	**January** $	**February** $	**March** $
Opening payables for fixed overheads		2,000		
January	2,000	–	2,000	–
February	2,000	–	–	2,000
March	2,000	–	–	–
Total payments		2,000	2,000	2,000

Variable overheads	**Cost** $	**January** $	**February** $	**March** $
Opening payables for variable overheads		9,000		
January	10,000	4,000	6,000	–
February	11,500	–	4,600	6,900
March	4,750	–	–	1,900
Total payments		13,000	10,600	8,800

The other items of cash flow are straightforward, although it is important to notice that the payments for administration and selling overheads are paid quarterly, and the cash payment ($15,000) is not the same as the total overhead cost for the quarter. Presumably there are depreciation charges within the total costs given.

Payments for direct labour are 30% of direct labour costs (= 30% of production costs) in the month.

The cash budget can be prepared as follows:

	January	February	March
	$	$	$
Receipts			
From sales	56,000	58,000	54,000
Payments			
Capital expenditure	–	–	30,000
For direct materials	21,000	17,500	16,500
For direct labour (30% x prod'n cost)	15,000	16,500	9,750
For fixed production overheads	2,000	2,000	2,000
For variable production overheads	13,000	10,600	8,800
For admin/selling overhead	15,000	–	–
Total outflow	66,000	46,600	67,050
Net cash flow for month	(10,000)	11,400	(13,050)
Opening balance	(5,000)	(15,000)	(3,600)
Closing balance	(15,000)	(3,600)	(16,650)

Comments:

The entity will be overdrawn throughout the three-month period, therefore it is essential that it should have access to borrowings to cover the shortfall. The bank might already have agreed an overdraft facility, but this should be at least $16,650 and ideally higher, to allow for the possibility that the actual cash flows will be even worse than budgeted.

However, note that if any of the elements of the forecast are inaccurate, the cash requirement would change. For example, 10% of receivables were regarded as irrecoverable, then cash receipts would ultimately fall by $11,000 and the closing cash position would be a deficit of up to ($16,550 + $11,000) $27,550, depending upon when the non-collection was taken into account.

Sensitivity analysis on the figures in the forecast (see later in the chapter) could be performed to evaluate the impact of variations between forecasts made using different assumptions. The entity may also want to consider adding a float to the cash requirement to accommodate any subseuent differences arising between the forecast and actual cash flows. This may be quantified by use of cash requirement models as developed by Miller-Orr and Baumol.

Also, for the purposes of preparing the forecast, receipts and payments have been identified on a monthly basis. If, for example, expenses were paid at the start of the month and cash received at the end of the month, this would also exacerbate any deficit during each month.

What can be done to reduce the cash requirement?

(1) Defer the capital expendure planned for March, which will eliminate the forecast deficit completely, although that expenditure will still need to be financed at some future date.

(2) If possible, spread the admin/selling overhead on a monthly, rather than quarterly, basis. This will reduce the cash outflows in January and February, although the total outflow will not change.

(3) Increasing the selling price of goods, and trying to collect in a greater proportion of cash from receivables earlier tnan currently forecast (perhaps by offering early settlement discounts) would help to improve the situation.

Test your understanding 4 – Millor-Orr Model

$$\text{Spread} = 3\left[\frac{\tfrac{3}{4} \times \text{transaction cost} \times \text{variance of cash flows}}{\text{Interest rate}}\right]^{1/3}$$

$$3\left[\frac{\tfrac{3}{4} \times 5 \times 90{,}000}{0.00033}\right]^{1/3} = 3{,}023$$

Remember this is the spread, to find the upper limit we have to add the minimum current account of balance of $1,500. **This gives an upper limit of $4,523.**

Thus once the current account balance falls to $1,500 additional funds should be transferred to it. On the other hand once cash balances exceed $6,298 funds should be transferred out of the current account to the interest bearing deposit account. This raises the question of how much should be transferred on these occasions. In other words what is the **return point?** This is given below as:

Return point = lower limit + 1/3 of the spread

= $2,508

This means that when the cash balance falls to $1,500 we should transfer $1,008 from the deposit account to raise the balance to its return point of $2,508. Similarly when the current account balance reaches $4,523 we would have to transfer $2,015 to the deposit account to take the current account balance back down to its return point of $2,508.

Test your understanding 5 – Baumol Model

(a) $Q = \sqrt{\frac{2 \times \$50 \times \$120{,}000}{0.05}} = \$15{,}492$ per transaction

(b) Number of transactions p.a. = $120,000/$15,492 per trans.
= 7.75 transactions p.a.

(c) Cost of transactions = 7.75 transactions × $50
= $387.5

Test your understanding 6 – Practice questions

(1) The cash budget is as follows:

Sales month	**Total sales** $	**Cash receipts January** $	**Cash receipts February** $	**Cash receipts March** $
October	80,000	10,800	–	–
November	60,000	16,200	8,100	–
December	40,000	18,000	10,800	5,400
January	50,000	5,000	22,500	13,500
February	60,000	–	6,000	27,000
March	90,000	–	–	9,000
Total Receipts		50,000	47,400	54,900

(2) The correct answer is D.

$50,000 represents 25% of December sales (100% – 75%).

Total sales in December were therefore $5,000/25% = $200,000.

Expected amount to be received in January = 20% × $200,000 = $40,000.

(3) The trade receivables at the beginning of January Year 2 represent 100% of sales in December Year 1 and the unpaid receivables for sales in November Year 1. They can be analysed as follows:

	$
Total trade receivables	322,200
Consisting of:	
100% of sales for December Year 1	(213,000)
Unpaid amounts for sales in November Year 1	109,200

The unpaid amounts from November Year 1 represent 70% of total sales in that month, because 30% pay in the month following sale (December Year 1).

It therefore follows that total sales in November Year 1 were $109,200/70% = $156,000.

Sales month	Total sales		Cash receipts January		Cash receipts February
	$		$		$
November	156,000	65%	101,400	–	–
December	213,000	30%	63,900	65%	138,450
			165,300		138,450

(4) The budget will be as follows:

Purchases	January units	February units	March units
Sales quantity	400	450	420
Less: opening inventory	(100)	(150)	(120)
Add: closing inventory	150	120	180
Production in units = units purchased	450	420	480
Cost of purchase @ $2 per unit	$900	$840	$960

Payments in March		$
For January purchases	(60% of $900)	540
For March purchases	(40% of $960)	384
Total payments for materials		924

(5) The correct answer is B.

A short-term deposit is a cash equivalent. Deferring the transfer of cash to a short-term deposit will not deal with the problem of a temporary cash shortage, because it will usually be possible to withdraw the cash from deposit on demand, for the loss of some or all of the interest.

(6) B

(7) The optimal amount to transfer is $16,970

$$Q = \sqrt{\frac{2 \times \$30 \times \$240,000}{0.05}} = \$16,970 \text{ per transaction}$$

(8) The number of transaction are 15
$240,000/16,970 = 14.14, rounded to 15 transactions

(9) The cost = 15 transactions × $30 each = $450

(10) The spread = $9,000
The upper limit = $5,500
The return point = $11,500

The spread of $9,000 can be calculated as follows:

$$3\left[\frac{\frac{3}{4} \times 30 \times 300,000}{0.00025}\right]^{1/3}$$

To find the upper limit we have to add the minimum current account of balance of $2,500. **This gives an upper limit of $2,500 + $9,000 = $11,500.**

Thus once the current account balance falls to $2,500 additional funds should be transferred to it. On the other hand once cash balances exceed $11,500 funds should be transferred out of the current account to the interest bearing deposit account. This raises the question of how much should be transferred on these occasions. In other words what is the return point? **This is calculated as return point = lower limit + 1/3 of the spread, i.e. $2,500 + $9,000/3 = $5,500.**

This means that when the cash balance falls to $2,500 we should transfer $3,000 from the deposit account to raise the balance to its return point of $5,500. Similarly when the current account balance reaches $11,500 we would have to transfer $6,000 to the deposit account to take the current account balance back down to its return point of $5,500.

Index

Index

E

F

G

H

I

Index

Index

S

T

U

V

W